INTRODUCTION
TO
COMPUTER
THEORY

INTRODUCTION TO COMPUTER THEORY

SECOND EDITION

Daniel I. A. Cohen
Hunter College
City University of New York

John Wiley & Sons, Inc.
New York   Chichester   Brisbane   Toronto   Singapore   Weinheim

ACQUISITIONS EDITOR   Regina Brooks
MARKETING MANAGER   Jay Kirsch
SENIOR PRODUCTION EDITOR   Tony VenGraitis
DESIGN SUPERVISOR   Anne Marie Renzi
MANUFACTURING MANAGER   Mark Cirillo
ILLUSTRATION COORDINATOR   Rosa Bryant
PRODUCTION MANAGEMENT   J. Carey Publishing Service

This book was set in 10/12 Times Roman by Digitype and
printed and bound by Hamilton Printing. The cover was printed by Lehigh Press.

PREFACE
TO THE FIRST EDITION

It has become clear that some abstract Computer Theory should be included in the education of undergraduate Computer Science majors.

Leaving aside the obvious worth of knowledge for its own sake, the terminology, notations, and techniques of Computer Theory are necessary in the teaching of courses on computer design, Artificial Intelligence, the analysis of algorithms, and so forth. Of all the programming skills undergraduate students learn, two of the most important are the abilities to recognize and manipulate context-free grammars and to understand the power of the recursive interaction of parts of a procedure. Very little can be accomplished if each advanced course has to begin at the level of defining rules of production and derivations. Every interesting career a student of Computer Science might pursue will make significant use of some aspects of the subject matter of this book.

Yet we find today, that the subjects of Automata Theory, Formal Languages, and Turing machines are almost exclusively relegated to the very advanced student. Only textbooks demanding intense mathematical sophistication discuss these topics. Undergraduate Computer Science majors are unlikely to develop the familiarity with set theory, logic, and the facility with abstract manipulation early enough in their college careers to digest the material in the existing excellent but difficult texts.

Bringing the level of sophistication to the exact point where it meets the expected preparation of the intended student population is the responsibility of every carefully prepared textbook. Of all the branches of Mathematics, Computer Science is one of the newest and most independent. Rigorous mathematical proofs of the most profound theorems in this subject can be constructed without the aid of Calculus, Number Theory, Algebra, or Topology. Some degree of understanding of the notion of proof is, of course, required, but the techniques employed are so idiosyncratic to this subject that it is preferable to introduce them to the student from first principles. Characteristic methods, such as making accurate conclusions from diagrams, analyzing graphs, or searching trees, are not tools with which a typical mathematics major is familiar. Hardly any students come prepared for the convoluted surprise of the Halting Problem. These then are the goals of this textbook: (1) to introduce a student of Computer Science to the need for and the working of mathematical proof; (2) to develop facility with the concepts, notations, and techniques of the theories of Automata, Formal Languages, and Turing machines; and (3) to provide historical perspective on the creation of the computer with a profound understanding of some of its capabilities and limitations.

Basically, this book is written for students with no presumed background of any kind. Every mathematical concept used is introduced from scratch. Extensive examples and illustrations spell out everything in detail to avoid any possibility of confusion. The bright student is encouraged to read at whatever pace or depth seems appropriate.

For their excellent care with this project I thank the staff at John Wiley & Sons: Richard J. Bonacci, acquisitions editor, and Lorraine F. Mellon, Eugene Patti, Elaine Rauschal, and Ruth Greif of the editorial and production staffs. Of the technical people who reviewed the manuscript I thank Martin Kaliski, Adrian Tang, Martin Davis, and especially H. P. Edmundson, whose comments were invaluable and Martin J. Smith whose splendid special support was dispositive. Rarely has an author had an assistant as enthusiastic, dedicated, knowledgeable and meticulous as I was so fortunate to find in Mara Chibnik. Every aspect of this project from the classnotes to the page proofs benefited immeasurably from her scrutiny. Very little that is within these covers—except for the few mistakes inserted by mischievous Martians—does not bare the mark of her relentless precision and impeccable taste. Every large project is the result of the toil of the craftsmen and the sacrifice and forebearance of those they were forced to neglect. Rubies are beneath their worth.

Daniel I. A. Cohen

PREFACE
TO THE SECOND EDITION

In the first edition I intentionally omitted some topics because their discussion and/or proof involved mathematics that I felt was hopelessly beyond the scope of my intended audience. Students have not gotten more mathematically sophisticated but I have figured out how to demystify some of these themes in a much simpler way *with no loss of rigor*. Along the way various proofs that used to be cumbersome have been somewhat streamlined, and some embarrassing errors have been unearthed and demolished.

Undergraduate Computer Science majors generally do not speak the language of mathematical symbolism fluently, nor is it important at their level that they do more than try. The value of mathematical iconography is that it enables professionals to perform their research and communicate their results more efficiently. The symbolism is not a profound discovery in and of itself. It is at best a means, not an end. To those to whom it is opaque, it is a hindrance to understanding. When this happens it is mathematically dysfunctional and a pedagogical anathema. Anyone who believes that $\{j : 1 \leq j \leq n\}$ is somehow more rigorous than $\{1, 2, \ldots . n\}$ is misguided. He has forgotten how the typography "$1 \leq j \leq n$" was defined to him in the first place. All mathematical symbolism can be reduced to human language because it is through iterations of human language substitutes that it was defined initially. Instead of introducing "mathematics" in an alienating form that only has to be expounded anyway, I prefer to skip the pretentious detour and provide the explanation itself directly. Computer science has needlessly carried an inferiority complex among the branches of mathematics, causing a defensive embedding into mainstream symbolism to lend it an aura of legitimacy. Yet it has been, as Hilbert himself predicted, one of the principal departments of mathematical discovery in the last century.

Still no pretense is made to encyclopedic completeness. This textbook is an introduction to computer theory and contains the minimum collegiate requirements of theory for computer science majors. No, I have not added a chapter on NP-completeness, primitive and partial recursion, program verification, artificial intelligence, nor Renaissance architecture. These are all topics worthy of being included in some course but to squeeze them in here would necessarily displace some of the more pertinent and fundamental aspects of theory, and would thereby disadvantage the student.

High on my list of cheap tricks is the inclusion of material in textbooks that is never meant to be covered in the intended course in the first place. I have heard members of textbook selection committees who say, "Let's adopt X's elementary calculus text because he has a chapter on general relativity while our current textbook contains only calculus." Salesmanship should not be the business of textbook authors—educating students should. Making students pay for 300 extra pages of material that is not intended to be covered in the course harms them in financial, muscular, and psychological ways.

Ideally a textbook should begin at the level of understanding of the students taking the course. It should include all the material they have contracted to learn presented in a fashion maximally suited for them to absorb. When it has completed the syllabus it should stop. Allowances may be made for instructor discretion in choosing material that is basic to the course and in the selection of which topics warrant special emphasis. However, there are some fanatics who have the grandiose notion that to be a great teacher is to stuff more material into a course than their students can learn. I view this as sheer and simple breach of contract. Let these zealots adopt a graduate textbook and let their students protest accordingly. There is no comparison between the error of covering too little and covering too much. To attempt to cover too much is to rob the students of the chance to learn and to undermine their self-confidence.

This book is unabashedly easy to read. It is intentionally slow-paced and repetitive. Let the bright student blitz through it, but let the slower student find comfort and elucidation. The nuances in this material are unlike anything (mathematical or otherwise) seen before in a course or textbook. A leisurely stroll through these charming gems can be enjoyable, stimulating, and rewarding. My duty to computer science students is to protect them against their own fear of mathematics, to demonstrate to them that a proof is no more or less than an understanding of why the theorem is true, and to allow them to savor the intellectual richness of the theoretical foundations of what is ultimately the most important invention since antiquity.

Is this book ideal? That would be unlikely, wouldn't it? But it is designed with good scientific intentions and sincere concern for those interested in learning.

It gives me pleasure to thank Chanah Brenenson who served as the technical editor and tireless critic to this edition. May she live long and prosper.

DIAC

CONTENTS

PART II   PUSHDOWN AUTOMATA THEORY

PART III   TURING THEORY

PART I

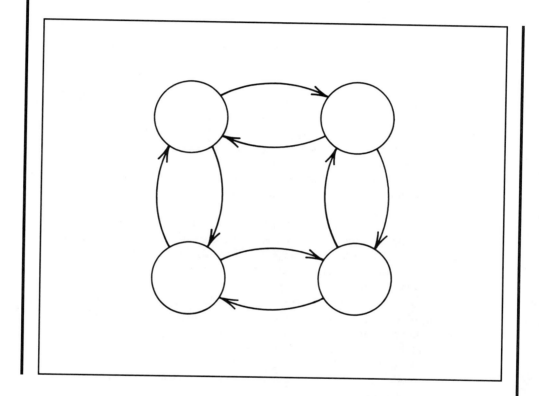

Automata
Theory

CHAPTER 1

Background

The twentieth century has been filled with the most incredible shocks and surprises: the theory of relativity, the rise and fall of communism, psychoanalysis, nuclear war, television, moon walks, genetic engineering, and so on. As astounding as any of these is the advent of the computer and its development from a mere calculating device into what seems like a "thinking machine."

The birth of the computer was not wholly independent of the other events of this century. Its inception was certainly impelled if not provoked by war and its development was facilitated by the evolution of psycho-linguistics, and it has interacted symbiotically with all the aforementioned upheavals. The history of the computer is a fascinating story; however, it is not the subject of this course. We are concerned instead with the **theory of computers,** which means that we shall form several mathematical models that will describe with varying degrees of accuracy parts of computers, types of computers, and similar machines. The concept of a "mathematical model" is itself a very modern construct. It is, in the broadest sense, a game that describes some important real-world behavior. Unlike games that are simulations and used for practice or simply for fun, mathematical models abstract, simplify, and codify to the point that the subtle observations and conclusions that can be made about the game relate back in a meaningful way to the physical world, shedding light on that which was not obvious before. We may assert that chess is a mathematical model for war, but it is a very poor model because wars are not really won by the simple assassination of the leader of the opposing country.

The adjective "mathematical" in this phrase does not necessarily mean that classical mathematical tools such as Euclidean geometry or calculus will be employed. Indeed, these areas are completely absent from the present volume. What *is* mathematical about the models we shall be creating and analyzing is that the only conclusions that we shall be allowed to draw are claims that can be supported by pure deductive reasoning; in other words, we are obliged to *prove* the truth about whatever we discover. Most professions, even the sciences, are composed of an accumulation of wisdom in the form of general principles and rules that usually work well in practice, such as "on such and such a wood we recommend this undercoat," or "these symptoms typically respond to a course of medication X." This is completely opposite from the type of thing we are going to be doing. While most of the world is (correctly) preoccupied by the question of how best to do something, we shall be completely absorbed with the question of whether certain tasks can be done at all. Our main conclusions will be of the form, "this can be done" or "this can never be done." When we reach conclusions of the second type, we shall mean not just that techniques for performing these tasks are unknown at the present time, but that such techniques will never exist in the future no matter how many clever people spend millennia attempting to discover them.

The nature of our discussion will be the frontiers of capability in an absolute and time-less sense. This is the excitement of mathematics. The fact that the mathematical models that we create serve a practical purpose through their application to computer science, both in the development of structures and techniques necessary and useful to computer programming and in the engineering of computer architecture, means that we are privileged to be playing a game that is both fun and important to civilization at the same time.

The term computer is practically never encountered in this book—we do not even de-fine the term until the final pages. The way we shall be studying about computers is to build mathematical models, which we shall call machines, and then to study their limitations by analyzing the types of inputs on which they operate successfully. The collection of these successful inputs we shall call the **language** of the machine, by analogy to humans who can understand instructions given to them in one language but not another. Every time we intro-duce a new machine we will learn its language, and every time we develop a new language we shall try to find a machine that corresponds to it. This interplay between languages and machines will be our way of investigating problems and their potential solution by auto-matic procedures, often called algorithms, which we shall describe in a little more detail shortly.

The history of the subject of computer theory is interesting. It was formed by fortunate coincidences, involving several seemingly unrelated branches of intellectual endeavor. A small series of contemporaneous discoveries, by very dissimilar people, separately moti-vated, flowed together to become our subject. Until we have established more of a founda-tion, we can only describe in general terms the different schools of thought that have melded into this field.

The most fundamental component of computer theory is the theory of mathematical logic. As the twentieth century started, mathematics was facing a dilemma. Georg Cantor had recently invented the theory of sets (unions, intersections, inclusion, cardinality, etc.). But at the same time he had discovered some very uncomfortable paradoxes—he created things that looked like contradictions in what seemed to be rigorously proven mathematical theorems. Some of his unusual findings could be tolerated (such as the idea that infinity comes in different sizes), but some could not (such as the notion that some set is bigger than the universal set). This left a cloud over mathematics that needed to be resolved.

To some the obvious solution was to ignore the existence of set theory. Some others thought that set theory had a disease that needed to be cured, but they were not quite sure where the trouble was. The naive notion of a general "set" seemed quite reasonable and in-nocent. When Cantor provided sets with a mathematical notation, they should have become mathematical objects capable of having theorems about them proven. All the theorems that dealt with finite sets appeared to be unchallengeable, yet there were definite problems with the acceptability of infinite sets. In other branches of mathematics the leap from the finite to the infinite can be made without violating intuitive notions. Calculus is full of infinite sums that act much the way finite sums do; for example, if we have an infinite sum of infinitesi-mals that add up to 3, when we double each term, the total will be 6. The Euclidean notion that the whole is the sum of its parts seems to carry over to infinite sets as well; for example, when the even integers are united with the odd integers, the result is the set of all integers. Yet, there was definitely an unsettling problem in that some of Cantor's "theorems" gave contradictory results.

In the year 1900, David Hilbert, as the greatest living mathematician, was invited to ad-dress an international congress to predict what problems would be important in the century to come. Either due to his influence alone, or as a result of his keen analysis, or as a tribute to his gift for prophecy, for the most part he was completely correct. The 23 areas he indicated in that speech have turned out to be the major thrust of mathematics for the twentieth century. Although the invention of the computer itself was not one of his predictions, several of his topics turn out to be of seminal importance to computer science.

First of all, he wanted the confusion in set theory resolved. He wanted a precise axiomatic system built for set theory that would parallel the one that Euclid had laid down for geometry. In Euclid's classic texts, each true proposition is provided with a rigorous proof in which every line is either an axiom or follows from the axioms and previously proven theorems by a specified small set of rules of inference. Hilbert thought that such an axiom system and set of rules of inference could be developed to avoid the paradoxes Cantor (and others) had found in set theory.

Second, Hilbert was not merely satisfied that every provable result should be true; he also presumed that every true result was provable. And even more significant, he wanted a methodology that would show mathematicians how to find this proof. He had in his mind a specific model of what he wanted.

In the nineteenth century, mathematicians had completely resolved the question of solving systems of linear equations. Given any algebraic problem having a specified number of linear equations, in a specified set of unknowns, with specified coefficients, a system had been developed (called linear algebra) that would guarantee one could decide weather the equations had any simultaneous solution at all, and find the solutions if they did exist.

This would have been an even more satisfactory situation than existed in Euclidean geometry at the time. If we are presented with a correct Euclidean proposition relating line segments and angles in a certain diagram, we have no guidance as to how to proceed to produce a mathematically rigorous proof of its truth. We have to be creative—we may make false starts, we may get completely lost, frustrated, or angry. We may never find the proof, even if many simple, short proofs exist. Linear algebra guarantees that none of this will ever happen with equations. As long as we are tireless and precise in following the rules, we must prevail, no matter how little imagination we ourselves possess. Notice how well this describes the nature of a computer. Today, we might rephrase Hilbert's request as a demand for a set of computer programs to solve mathematical problems. When we input the problem, the machine generates the proof.

It was not easy for mathematicians to figure out how to follow Hilbert's plan. Mathematicians are usually in the business of creating the proofs themselves, not the proof-generating techniques. What had to be invented was a whole field of mathematics that dealt with algorithms or procedures or programs (we use these words interchangeably). From this we see that even before the first computer was ever built, some people were asking the question of what programs can be written. It was necessary to codify the universal language in which algorithms could be stated. Addition and circumscribing circles were certainly allowable steps in an algorithm, but such activities as guessing and trying infinitely many possibilities at once were definitely prohibited. The language of algorithms that Hilbert required evolved in a natural way into the language of computer programs.

The road to studying algorithms was not a smooth one. The first bump occurred in 1931 when Kurt Gödel proved that there was no algorithm to provide proofs for all the true statements in mathematics. In fact, what he proved was even worse. He showed that either there were some true statements in mathematics that had no proofs, in which case there were certainly no algorithms that could provide these proofs, or else there were some false statements that did have proofs of their correctness, in which case the algorithm would be disastrous.

Mathematicians then had to retreat to the question of what statements do have proofs and how can we generate these proofs? The people who worked on this problem, Alonzo

Church, Stephen Kleene, Emil Post, Andrei Andreevich Markov, John von Neumann, and Alan Turing, worked mostly independently and came up with an extraordinarily simple set of building blocks that seemed to be the atoms from which all mathematical algorithms can be comprised. They each fashioned various (but similar) versions of a universal model for all algorithms—what, from our perspective, we would call a universal algorithm machine. Turing then went one step farther. He proved that there were mathematically definable fundamental questions about the machine itself that the machine could not answer.

On the one hand, this theorem completely destroyed all hope of ever achieving any part of Hilbert's program of mechanizing mathematics, or even of deciding which classes of problems had mechanical answers. On the other hand, Turing's theoretical model for an algorithm machine employing a very simple set of mathematical structures held out the possibility that a physical model of Turing's idea could actually be constructed. If some human could figure out an algorithm to solve a particular class of mathematical problem, then the machine could be told to follow the steps in the program and execute this exact sequence of instructions on any inserted set of data (tirelessly and with complete precision).

The electronic discoveries that were needed for the implementation of such a device included vacuum tubes, which just coincidentally had been developed recently for engineering purposes completely unrelated to the possibility of building a calculating machine. This was another fortuitous phenomenon of this period of history. All that was required was the impetus for someone with a vast source of money to be motivated to invest in this highly speculative project. It is practically sacrilegious to maintain that World War II had a serendipitous impact on civilization no matter how unintentional, yet it was exactly in this way that the first computer was born—sponsored by the Allied military to break the German secret code, with Turing himself taking part in the construction of the machine.

What started out as a mathematical theorem about mathematical theorems—an abstraction about an abstraction—became the single most practically applied invention since the wheel and axle. Not only was this an ironic twist of fate, but it all happened within the remarkable span of 10 years. It was as incredible as if a mathematical proof of the existence of intelligent creatures in outer space were to provoke them to land immediately on Earth.

Independently of all the work being done in mathematical logic, other fields of science and social science were beginning to develop mathematical models to describe and analyze difficult problems of their own. As we have noted before, there is a natural correspondence between the study of models of computation and the study of linguistics in an abstract and mathematical sense. It is also natural to assume that the study of thinking and learning—branches of psychology and neurology—play an important part in understanding and facilitating computer theory. What is again of singular novelty is the historical fact that, rather than turning their attention to mathematical models to computerize their own applications, their initial development of mathematical models for aspects of their own science directly aided the evolution of the computer itself. It seems that half the intellectual forces in the world were leading to the invention of the computer, while the other half were producing applications that were desperate for its arrival.

Two neurophysiologists, Warren McCulloch and Walter Pitts, constructed a mathematical model for the way in which sensory receptor organs in animals behave. The model they constructed for a "neural net" was a theoretical machine of the same nature as the one Turing invented, but with certain limitations.

Modern linguists, some influenced by the prevalent trends in mathematical logic and some by the emerging theories of developmental psychology, had been investigating a very similar subject: What is language in general? How could primitive humans have developed language? How do people understand it? How do they learn it as children? What ideas can be expressed, and in what ways? How do people construct sentences from the ideas in their minds?

Noam Chomsky created the subject of mathematical models for the description of languages to answer these questions. His theory grew to the point where it began to shed light on the study of computer languages. The languages humans invented to communicate with one another and the languages necessary for humans to communicate with machines shared many basic properties. Although we do not know exactly how humans understand language, we do know how machines digest what they are told. Thus, the formulations of mathematical logic became useful to linguistics, a previously nonmathematical subject. Metaphorically, we could say that the computer then took on linguistic abilities. It became a word processor, a translator, and an interpreter of simple grammar, as well as a compiler of computer languages. The software invented to interpret programming languages was applied to human languages as well. One point that will be made clear in our studies is why computer languages are easy for a computer to understand, whereas human languages are very difficult.

Because of the many influences on its development, the subject of this book goes by various names. It includes three major fundamental areas: the **theory of automata,** the **theory of formal languages,** and the **theory of Turing machines.** This book is divided into three parts corresponding to these topics.

Our subject is sometimes called **computation theory** rather than computer theory, because the items that are central to it are the types of tasks (algorithms or programs) that can be performed, not the mechanical nature of the physical computer itself. However, the name "computation" is misleading, since it popularly connotes arithmetical operations which comprise only a fraction of what computers can do. The term computation is inaccurate when describing word processing, sorting, and searching and awkward in discussions of program verification. Just as the term "number theory" is not limited to a description of calligraphic displays of number systems but focuses on the question of which equations can be solved in integers, and the term "graph theory" does not include bar graphs, pie charts, and histograms, so too "computer theory" need not be limited to a description of physical machines but can focus on the question of which tasks are possible for which machines.

We shall study different types of theoretical machines that are mathematical models for actual physical processes. By considering the possible inputs on which these machines can work, we can analyze their various strengths and weaknesses. We then arrive at what we may believe to be the most powerful machine possible. When we do, we shall be surprised to find tasks that even it cannot perform. This will be our ultimate result, that no matter what machine we build, there will always be questions that are simple to state that it cannot answer. Along the way, we shall begin to understand the concept of **computability,** which is the foundation of further research in this field. This is our goal. Computer theory extends further to such topics as complexity and verification, but these are beyond our intended scope. Even for the topics we do cover—automata, languages, Turing machines—much more is known than we present here. As intriguing and engaging as the field has proven so far, with any luck the most fascinating theorems are yet to be discovered.

CHAPTER 2

Languages

⚜ LANGUAGES IN THE ABSTRACT

In English we distinguish the three different entities: letters, words, and sentences. There is a certain parallelism between the fact that groups of letters make up words and the fact that groups of words make up sentences. Not all collections of letters form a valid word, and not all collections of words form a valid sentence. The analogy can be continued. Certain groups of sentences make up coherent paragraphs, certain groups of paragraphs make up coherent stories, and so on. What is more important to note is that, to a large degree, humans agree on which sequences are valid and which are not. How do they do that?

This situation also exists with computer languages. Certain character strings are recognizable words (DO, IF, END . . .). Certain strings of words are recognizable commands. Certain sets of commands become a program (with or without data) that can be compiled, which means translated into machine commands.

To construct a general theory that unifies all these examples, it is necessary for us to adopt a definition of a "language structure," that is, a structure in which the decision of whether a given string of units constitutes a valid larger unit is not a matter of guesswork, but is based on explicitly stated rules. For our purposes at this time, it is more important that there be rules for recognizing whether an input is a valid communication than rules for deciphering exactly what the communication means. It is important that the program compiles whether or not it does what the programmer intended. If it compiles, it was a valid example of a statement or communication in the language and the machine is responsible for executing the specified sequence of instructions. What we are looking for are ways of determining whether the input is a valid communication. Just as with any set, it is important for a language to be able to tell who is in and who is out.

It is very hard to state all the rules for the language "spoken English," since many seemingly incoherent strings of words are actually understandable utterances. This is due to slang, idiom, dialect, and our ability to interpret poetic metaphor and to correct unintentional grammatical errors in the sentences we hear. However, as a first step to defining a general theory of abstract languages, it is right for us to insist on precise rules, especially since computers are not quite as forgiving about imperfect input commands as listeners are about informal speech.

When we call our study the **theory of formal languages,** the word "formal" refers to the fact that all the rules for the language are explicitly stated in terms of what strings of symbols can occur. No liberties are tolerated, and no reference to any "deeper understanding" is required. Language will be considered solely as symbols on paper and not as expressions of ideas in the minds of humans. In this basic model, language is not communication among intellects, but a game of symbols with formal rules. The term "formal" used here emphasizes that it is the *form* of the string of symbols we are interested in, not the *meaning*.

We begin with only one finite set of fundamental units out of which we build structures. We shall call this the **alphabet.** A certain specified set of strings of characters from the alphabet will be called the **language.** Those strings that are permissible in the language we call **words.** The symbols in the alphabet do not have to be Latin letters, and the sole universal requirement for a possible string is that it contains only finitely many symbols. The question of what it means to "specify" a set of strings is, in reality, the major issue of this book.

We shall wish to allow a string to have no letters. This we call the **empty string** or **null string,** and we shall denote it by the symbol Λ. No matter what "alphabet" we are considering, the null string is always Λ and for all languages the null word, if it is a word in the language, is also Λ. Two words are considered the same if all their letters are the same and in the same order, so there is only one possible word of no letters. For clarity, we usually do not allow the symbol Λ to be part of the alphabet for any language.

There is a subtle but important difference between the word that has no letters, Λ, and the language that has no words. We shall denote the language that has no words by the standard symbol for the null set, ϕ. It is not true that Λ is a word in the language ϕ since this language has no words at all. If a certain language L does not contain the word Λ and we wish to add it to L, we use the "union of sets" operation denoted by "+" to form $L + \{\Lambda\}$. This language is not the same as L. On the other hand, $L + \phi$ *is* the same as L since no new words have been added.

The fact that ϕ is a language even though it has no words will turn out to be an important distinction. If we have a method for producing a language and in a certain instance the method produces nothing, we can say either that the method failed miserably, or that it successfully produced the language ϕ. We shall face just such a situation later.

The most familiar example of a language for us is English. The alphabet is the usual set of letters plus the apostrophe and hyphen. Let us denote the whole alphabet by the Greek letter capital sigma:

$$\Sigma = \{a \quad b \quad c \quad d \quad e \quad \ldots \quad z \quad ' \quad -\}$$

It is customary to use this symbol to denote whichever collection of letters form the alphabet for the words in the language L. This is not because the Greek word for "alphabet" starts with the letter sigma—the Greek word for alphabet is *alphabetor* and starts with an A. However, this subject started as a branch of mathematics well before computers and desktop publishing, and when researchers were looking for a symbol less ambiguous than A to denote alphabet, they employed the special characters already found in mathematical printing: Σ and Γ as well as ϕ and Λ for other purposes. This has become a time-honored tradition. To some it makes computer theory seem more mathematical and to some this is an advantage. Our investigations will be completely mathematical with as little resort to irrelevant symbolic complexity as possible.

Sometimes, we shall list a set of elements separated by spaces and sometimes by commas. If we wished to be supermeticulous, we would also include in Σ the uppercase letters and the seldom used diacritical marks.

We can now specify which strings of these letters are valid words in our language by listing them all, as is done in a dictionary. It is a long list, but a finite list, and it makes a perfectly good definition of the language. If we call this language ENGLISH-WORDS, we may write

ENGLISH-WORDS = {all the words in a standard dictionary}

In the preceding line, we have intentionally mixed mathematical notation (the equal sign and the braces denoting a set) and a prose phrase. This results in perfectly understandable communication; we take this liberty throughout. All of our investigations will be agglomerates of informal discussion and precise symbolism. Mathematical symbolism is of value only when it is somehow better than seeing the same thought expressed in human language, for example, when it is more understandable, or more concise in cases where space is a problem, or when it points out similarities between items whose resemblance is otherwise obscure, and so on. The belief that mathematical symbolism is more rigorous and therefore more accurate than English prose is quite ridiculous since every mathematical symbol was defined in English in the first place and every mathematical formula can be translated into English if need be. There are two problems with pure mathematical symbolism: It alienates some who for want of familiarity could otherwise understand the concepts being expressed, and it often gives one a false sense of precision—many, many false proofs have been published in mathematics journals because their notation was so opaque that it confused the editors. Since the goal in a textbook is not to minimize the space required to explain concepts but to maximize the chance of understanding, we shall find little use for complex symbolism.

Only a language with finitely many words can be defined by an all-inclusive list called a dictionary. If we tried to define a language of infinitely many words by an infinite list, we would arrive at the problem of the impossibility of searching this list (even if it is arranged in alphabetical order) to determine whether a given word is in the language or not. But even though there are tricks to overcome the searching problem (as we shall soon see), we do not allow the possibility of defining a language by an infinite dictionary. How could we be handed an infinite dictionary? It would have to be described to us in some manner, but then the description and not the dictionary would be the language definition.

Returning to the language of ENGLISH-WORDS, we note that this is not what we usually mean by "English." To know all the words in a finite language like English does not imply the ability to create a viable sentence.

Of course, the language ENGLISH-WORDS, as we have specified it, does not have any grammar. If we wish to make a formal definition of the language of the sentences in English, we must begin by saying that this time our basic *alphabet* is the entries in the dictionary. Let us call this alphabet Γ, the capital gamma:

Γ = {the entries in a standard dictionary, plus a blank space, plus the usual punctuation marks}

In order to specify which strings of elements from Γ produce valid words in the language ENGLISH-SENTENCES, we must rely on the grammatical rules of English. This is because we could never produce a complete list of all possible words in this language; that would have to be a list of all valid English sentences. Theoretically, there are infinitely many different words in the language ENGLISH-SENTENCES. For example,

I ate one apple.
I ate two apples.
I ate three apples.

. . . .

The trick of defining the language ENGLISH-SENTENCES by listing all the rules of English grammar allows us to give a finite description of an infinite language.

If we go by the rules of grammar only, many strings of alphabet letters seem to be valid words; for example, "I ate three Tuesdays." In a *formal* language we must allow this string. It is *grammatically* correct; only its *meaning* reveals that it is ridiculous. Meaning is something we do not refer to in formal languages. As we make clear in Part II of this book, we are primarily interested in syntax alone, not semantics or diction. We shall be like the bad teacher who is interested only in the correct spelling, not the ideas in a homework composition.

In general, the abstract languages we treat will be defined in one of two ways. Either they will be presented as an alphabet and the exhaustive list of all valid words, or else they will be presented as an alphabet and a set of rules defining the acceptable words. The set of rules defining English is a **grammar** in a very precise sense. We shall take a much more liberal view about what kinds of "sets of rules" define languages.

Earlier we mentioned that we could define a language by presenting the alphabet and then *specifying* which strings are words. The word "specify" is trickier than we may at first suppose. Consider this example of the language called MY-PET. The alphabet for this language is

$$\{a \quad c \quad d \quad g \quad o \quad t\}$$

There is only one word in this language, and for our own perverse reasons we wish to *specify* it by this sentence:

If the Earth and the Moon ever collide, then

$$\text{MY-PET} = \{cat\}$$

but, if the Earth and the Moon never collide, then

$$\text{MY-PET} = \{dog\}$$

One or the other of these two events will occur, but at this point in the history of the universe, it is impossible to be certain whether the word *dog* is or is not in the language MY-PET.

This sentence is therefore not an adequate specification of the language MY-PET because it is not useful. To be an acceptable specification of a language, a set of rules must enable us to decide, in a finite amount of time, whether a given string of alphabet letters is or is not a word in the language. Notice also that we never made it a requirement that all the letters in the alphabet need to appear in the words selected for the language. English itself used to have a letter called "eth" that has thankfully disappeared. We could add it back to the alphabet of letters and leave the language ENGLISH-WORDS unchanged.

⚜ INTRODUCTION TO DEFINING LANGUAGES

The set of language-defining rules can be of two kinds. They can either tell us how to test a string of alphabet letters that we might be presented with, to see if it is a valid word, or they can tell us how to construct all the words in the language by some clear procedures. We investigate this distinction further in the next chapter.

Let us consider some simple examples of languages. If we start with an alphabet having only one letter, the letter x,

$$\Sigma = \{x\}$$

we can define a language by saying that any nonempty string of alphabet characters is a word:

$$L_1 = \{x \quad xx \quad xxx \quad xxxx \ldots\}$$

We could write this in an alternate form:

$$L_1 = \{x^n \quad \text{for} \quad n = 1 \quad 2 \quad 3 \ldots\}$$

where we have identified letter juxtaposition with algebraic multiplication. We shall see that this is sometimes a messy business.

Because of the way we have defined it, this language does not include the null string. We could have defined it so as to include Λ, but we did not.

In this language, as in any other, we can define the operation of **concatenation,** in which two strings are written down side by side to form a new longer string. In this example, when we concatenate the word xxx with the word xx, we obtain the word $xxxxx$. The words in this language are clearly analogous to the positive integers, and the operation of concatenation is analogous to addition:

$$x^n \text{ concatenated with } x^m \text{ is the word } x^{n+m}$$

It will often be convenient for us to designate the words in a given language by new symbols, that is, other than the ones in the alphabet. For example, we could say that the word xxx is called a and that the word xx is b. Then to denote the word formed by concatenating a and b, we write the letters side by side:

$$ab = xxxxx$$

It is not always true that when two words are concatenated they produce another word in the language. For example, if the language is

$$
\begin{aligned}
L_2 &= \{x \quad xxx \quad xxxxx \quad xxxxxxx \ldots\} \\
&= \{x^{odd}\} \\
&= \{x^{2n+1} \quad \text{for} \quad n = 0 \quad 1 \quad 2 \quad 3 \ldots\}
\end{aligned}
$$

then $a = xxx$ and $b = xxxxx$ are both words in L_2, but their concatenation $ab = xxxxxxxx$ is not in L_2. Notice that the alphabet for L_2 is the same as the alphabet for L_1. Notice also the liberty we took with the middle definition.

In these simple examples, when we concatenate a with b, we get the same word as when we concatenate b with a. We can depict this by writing

$$ab = ba$$

But this relationship does not hold for all languages. In English when we concatenate "house" and "boat," we get "houseboat," which is indeed a word but distinct from "boathouse," which is a different thing—not because they have different meanings, but because they are different words. "Merry-go-round" and "carousel" mean the same thing, but they are different words.

EXAMPLE

Consider another language. Let us begin with the alphabet:

$$\Sigma = \{0 \quad 1 \quad 2 \quad 3 \quad 4 \quad 5 \quad 6 \quad 7 \quad 8 \quad 9\}$$

and define the set of words:

$$L_3 = \{\text{any finite string of alphabet letters that does not start with the letter zero}\}$$

This language L_3 then looks like the set of all positive integers written in base 10:

$$L_3 = \{1 \quad 2 \quad 3 \quad 4 \quad 5 \quad 6 \quad 7 \quad 8 \quad 9 \quad 10 \quad 11 \quad 12 \ldots\}$$

We say "looks like" instead of "is" because L_3 is only a formal collection of strings of symbols. The integers have other mathematical properties. If we wanted to define the language L_3 so that it includes the string (word) 0, we could say:

$L_3 = \{$any finite string of alphabet letters that, if it starts with a 0, has no more letters after the first$\}$ ■

The box, ■, that ends the line above is an **end marker.** When we present an example of a point in the text, we shall introduce it with the heading:

EXAMPLE

and finish it with an end marker ■. This will allow us to keep the general discussion separate from the specific examples. We shall use the same end marker to denote the end of a definition or a proof.

DEFINITION

_____
_____
_____ ■

PROOF

_____
_____
_____ ■

The old-fashioned end marker denoting that a proof is finished is Q.E.D. This box serves the same purpose.

DEFINITION

We define the function **length** of a string to be the number of letters in the string. We write this function using the word "length." For example, if $a = xxxx$ in the language L_1, then

$$\text{length}(a) = 4$$

If $c = 428$ in the language L_3, then

$$\text{length}(c) = 3$$

Or we could write directly that in L_1

$$\text{length}(xxxx) = 4$$

and in L_3

$$\text{length}(428) = 3$$

In any language that includes the empty string Λ, we have

$$\text{length}(\Lambda) = 0$$

For any word w in any language, if length$(w) = 0$, then $w = \Lambda$. ■

We can now present yet another definition of L_3.

$L_3 = \{$any finite string of alphabet letters that, if it has length more than 1, does not start with a $0\}$

This is not necessarily a better definition of L_3, but it does illustrate that there are often different ways of specifying the same language.

There is some inherent ambiguity in the phrase "any finite string," since it is not clear whether we intend to include the null string (Λ, the string of no letters). To avoid this ambiguity, we shall always be more careful. The language L_3 does not include Λ, since we intended that that language should look like the integers, and there is no such thing as an integer with no digits. On the other hand, we may wish to define a language like L_1 but that does contain Λ:

$$L_4 = \{\Lambda \quad x \quad xx \quad xxx \quad xxxx . . .\}$$
$$= \{x^n \quad \text{for} \quad n = 0 \quad 1 \quad 2 \quad 3 . . .\}$$

Here we have said that $x^0 = \Lambda$, not $x^0 = 1$ as in algebra. In this way, x^n is always the string of n x's. This may seem like belaboring a trivial point, but the significance of being careful about this distinction will emerge over and over again.

In L_3 it is very important not to confuse 0, which is a string of length 1, with Λ. Remember, even when Λ is a word in the language, it is not a letter in the alphabet.

DEFINITION

Let us introduce the function **reverse**. If a is a word in some language L, then reverse(a) is the same string of letters spelled backward, called the reverse of a, even if this backward string is not a word in L. ∎

EXAMPLE

$$\text{reverse}(xxx) = xxx$$
$$\text{reverse}(xxxxx) = xxxxx$$
$$\text{reverse}(145) = 541$$

But let us also note that in L_3

$$\text{reverse}(140) = 041$$

which is not a word in L_3. ∎

DEFINITION

Let us define a new language called **PALINDROME** over the alphabet

$$\Sigma = \{a \quad b\}$$

PALINDROME = $\{\Lambda$, and all strings x such that reverse(x) = $x\}$ ∎

If we begin listing the elements in PALINDROME, we find

PALINDROME = $\{\Lambda \quad a \quad b \quad aa \quad bb \quad aaa \quad aba \quad bab \quad bbb \quad aaaa \quad abba . . .\}$

The language PALINDROME has interesting properties that we shall examine later.

Sometimes, when we concatenate two words in PALINDROME, we obtain another word in PALINDROME such as when *abba* is concatenated with *abbaabba*. More often, the concatenation is not itself a word in PALINDROME, as when *aa* is concatenated with *aba*. Discovering when this does happen is left as a problem at the end of this chapter.

⚜ KLEENE CLOSURE

DEFINITION

Given an alphabet Σ, we wish to define a language in which any string of letters from Σ is a word, even the null string. This language we shall call the **closure** of the alphabet. It is denoted by writing a star (an asterisk) after the name of the alphabet as a superscript:

$$\Sigma*$$

This notation is sometimes known as the **Kleene star** after the logician who was one of the founders of this subject.   ∎

EXAMPLE

If $\Sigma = \{x\}$, then

$$\Sigma* = L_4 = \{\Lambda \quad x \quad xx \quad xxx \ldots\}$$ ∎

EXAMPLE

If $\Sigma = \{0 \quad 1\}$, then

$$\Sigma* = \{\Lambda \quad 0 \quad 1 \quad 00 \quad 01 \quad 10 \quad 11 \quad 000 \quad 001 \ldots\}$$ ∎

EXAMPLE

If $\Sigma = \{a \quad b \quad c\}$, then

$$\Sigma* = \{\Lambda \quad a \quad b \quad c \quad aa \quad ab \quad ac \quad ba \quad bb \quad bc \quad ca \quad cb \quad cc \quad aaa \ldots\}$$ ∎

We can think of the Kleene star as an **operation** that makes an infinite language of strings of letters out of an alphabet. When we say "infinite language," we mean infinitely many words, each of *finite* length.

Notice that when we wrote out the first several words in the language, we put them in size order (words of shortest length first) and then listed all the words of the same length alphabetically. We shall usually follow this method of sequencing a language. This ordering is called **lexicographic** order. In a dictionary, the word *aardvark* comes before *cat*; in lexicographic ordering it is the other way. Whereas both orderings are useful for the problem of searching for a given word, in the list for infinite sets lexicographic ordering has some distinct advantages. In the language just above, there are infinitely many words that start with the letter a and they all come alphabetically before the letter b. When listed in the usual alphabetical order, the first five words of this language are Λ- a- aa- aaa- $aaaa$ and the three-dot ellipsis ". . ." would not inform us of the real nature of the language.

We shall now generalize the use of the star operator to sets of words, not just sets of alphabet letters.

DEFINITION

If S is a set of words, then by $S*$ we mean the set of all finite strings formed by concatenating words from S, where any word may be used as often as we like, and where the null string is also included.   ∎

Let us not make the mistake of confusing the two languages

ENGLISH-WORDS*   and   ENGLISH-SENTENCES

The first language contains the word *butterbutterbutterhat,* whereas the second does not. This is because words in ENGLISH-WORDS* are the concatenate of arbitrarily many words from ENGLISH-WORDS, while words in ENGLISH-SENTENCES are restricted to juxtaposing only words from ENGLISH-WORDS in an order that complies with the rules of grammar.

EXAMPLE

If $S = \{aa \quad b\}$, then

$S^* = \{\Lambda$ plus any word composed of factors of aa and $b\}$
$\quad = \{\Lambda$ plus all strings of a's and b's in which the a's occur in even clumps$\}$
$\quad = \{\Lambda \quad b \quad aa \quad bb \quad aab \quad baa \quad bbb \quad aaaa \quad aabb \quad baab \quad bbaa \quad bbbb$
$\quad\quad aaaab \quad aabaa \quad aabbb \quad baaaa \quad baabb \quad bbaab \quad bbbaa \quad bbbbb \ldots\}$

The string *aabaaab* is not in S^* since it has a clump of a's of length 3. The phrase "clump of a's" has not been precisely defined, but we know what it means anyway. ◼

EXAMPLE

Let $S = \{a \quad ab\}$. Then

$S^* = \{\Lambda$ plus any word composed of factors of a and $ab\}$
$\quad = \{\Lambda$ plus all strings of a's and b's except those that start with b and those that contain a double $b\}$
$\quad = \{\Lambda \quad a \quad aa \quad ab \quad aaa \quad aab \quad aba \quad aaaa \quad aaab \quad aaba \quad abaa \quad abab \quad aaaaa$
$\quad\quad aaaab \quad aaaba \quad aabaa \quad aabab \quad abaaa \quad abaab \quad ababa \ldots\}$

By the phrase "double b," we mean the substring bb. For each word in S^* every b must have an a immediately to its left. The substring bb is impossible, as is starting with a b. Any string without the substring bb that begins with an a can be factored into terms of (ab) and (a).

The middle definition of this language is not an obvious consequence of the definition of *, but it can be deduced in this case. ◼

To prove that a certain word is in the closure language S^*, we must show how it can be written as a concatenate of words from the base set S.

In the last example, to show that *abaab* is in S^*, we can factor it as follows:

$$(ab)(a)(ab)$$

These three factors are all in the set S; therefore, their concatenation is in S^*. This is the only way to factor this string into factors of (a) and (ab). When this happens, we say that the factoring is **unique.**

Sometimes, the factoring is not unique. For example, consider $S = \{xx \quad xxx\}$. Then

$S^* = \{\Lambda$ and all strings of more than one $x\}$
$\quad = \{x^n \quad$ for $\quad n = 0 \quad 2 \quad 3 \quad 4 \quad 5 \ldots\}$
$\quad = \{\Lambda \quad xx \quad xxx \quad xxxx \quad xxxxx \quad xxxxxx \ldots\}$

Notice that the word x is not in the language S^*. The string *xxxxxx* is in this closure for any of these three reasons. It is

$$(xx)(xx)(xxx) \quad\quad \text{or} \quad\quad (xx)(xxx)(xx) \quad\quad \text{or} \quad\quad (xxx)(xx)(xx)$$

Also, x^6 is either $x^2x^2x^2$ or else x^3x^3.

It is important to note here that the parentheses, ( ), are not letters in the alphabet, but are used for the sole purpose of demarcating the ends of factors. So, we can write $xxxxx = (xx)(xxx)$. In cases where parentheses *are* letters of the alphabet,

$$\Sigma = \{x\ (\ )\}$$

$$\text{length}(xxxxx) = 5$$

$$\text{but length}((xx)(xxx)) = 9$$

Let us suppose that we wanted to prove mathematically that this set S^* contains all x^n for $n \neq 1$. Suppose that somebody did not believe this and needed convincing. We could proceed as follows.

First, we consider the possibility that there were some powers of x that we could not produce by concatenating factors of (xx) and (xxx).

Obviously, since we can produce x^4, x^5, x^6, the examples of strings that we cannot produce must be large. Let us ask the question, "What is the smallest power of x (larger than 1) that we cannot form out of factors of xx and xxx?" Let us suppose that we start making a list of how to construct the various powers of x. On this list we write down how to form x^2, x^3, x^4, x^5, and so on. Let us say that we work our way successfully up to x^{373}, but then we cannot figure out how to form x^{374}. We become stuck, so a friend comes over to us and says, "Let me see your list. How did you form the word x^{372}? Why don't you just concatenate another factor of xx in front of this and then you will have the word x^{374} that you wanted." Our friend is right, and this story shows that while writing this list out, we can never really become stuck. This discussion can easily be generalized into a mathematical proof of the fact that S^* contains all powers of x greater than 1.

We have just established a mathematical fact by a method of proof that we have rarely seen in other courses. It is a proof based on showing that something exists (the factoring) because we can describe how to create it (by adding xx to a previous case). What we have described can be formalized into an algorithm for producing all the powers of x from the factors xx and xxx. The method is to begin with xx and xxx and, when we want to produce x^n, we take the sequence of concatenations that we have already found will produce x^{n-2}, and we concatenate xx onto that.

The method of proving that something exists by showing how to create it is called **proof by constructive algorithm.** This is the most important tool in our whole study. Most of the theorems in this book will be proven by the method of constructive algorithm. It is, in general, a very satisfying and useful method of proof, that is, provided that anybody is interested in the objects we are constructing. We may have a difficult time selling powers of x broken into factors of xx and xxx.

Let us observe that if the alphabet has no letters, then its closure is the language with the null string as its only word, because Λ is always a word in a Kleene closure. Symbolically, we write

If $\Sigma = \emptyset$ (the empty set),
then $\Sigma^* = \{\Lambda\}$

This is not the same as

If $S = \{\Lambda\}$,
then $S^* = \{\Lambda\}$

which is also true but for a different reason, that is, $\Lambda\Lambda = \Lambda$.

The Kleene closure always produces an infinite language unless the underlying set was one of the two examples above. Unless we insist on calling Kleene closure a very forgiving

NOTE *important*

rule of grammar (anything goes), we have introduced a new method for defining languages that works only for infinite languages.

The Kleene closure of two sets can end up being the same language even if the two sets that we started with were not.

EXAMPLE

Consider the two languages

$$S = \{a \quad b \quad ab\} \quad \text{and} \quad T = \{a \quad b \quad bb\}$$

Then both S^* and T^* are languages of all strings of a's and b's since any string of a's and b's can be factored into syllables of either (a) or (b), both of which are in S and T. ∎

If for some reason we wish to modify the concept of closure to refer to only the concatenation of some (not zero) strings from a set S, we use the notation $^+$ instead of $*$. For example,

$$\text{If } \Sigma = \{x\}, \quad \text{then } \Sigma^+ = \{x \quad xx \quad xxx \ldots\}$$

which is the language L_1 that we discussed before.

If S is a set of strings not including Λ, then S^+ is the language S^* without the word Λ. Likewise, if T is a set of letters, then T^+ means the same as T^*, except that it can never mean Λ. If S is a language that does contain Λ, then $S^+ = S^*$.

This "plus operation" is sometimes called positive closure.

If $S = \{xx \quad xxx\}$, then S^+ is the same as S^* except for the word Λ, which is not in S^+. This is not to say that S^+ cannot, in general, contain the word Λ. It can, but only on the condition that S contains the word Λ initially. In this case, Λ is in S^+, since it is the concatenation of some (actually one) word from S (Λ itself). Anyone who does not think that the null string is confusing has missed something. It is already a problem, and it gets worse later.

EXAMPLE

If S is the set of three words

$$S = \{w_1 \quad w_2 \quad w_3\}$$

then

$$S^+ = \{w_1 \quad w_2 \quad w_3 \quad w_1w_1 \quad w_1w_2 \quad w_1w_3 \quad w_2w_1 \quad w_2w_2 \quad w_2w_3$$
$$w_3w_1 \quad w_3w_2 \quad w_3w_3 \quad w_1w_1w_1 \quad w_1w_1w_2 \ldots\}$$

no matter what the words w_1, w_2, and w_3 are.

If $w_1 = aa$, $w_2 = bbb$, $w_3 = \Lambda$, then $S^+ = \{aa \quad bbb \quad \Lambda \quad aaaa \quad aabbb \ldots\}$

The words in the set S are listed above in the order corresponding to their w-sequencing, not in the usual lexicographic or size-alphabetical order. ∎

What happens if we apply the closure operator twice? We start with a set of words S and look at its closure S^*. Now suppose we start with the set S^* and try to form *its* closure, which we denote as

$$(S^*)^* \quad \text{or} \quad S^{**}$$

If S is not the trivial empty set or the set consisting solely of Λ, then S^* is infinite, so we are taking the closure of an infinite set. This should present no problem since every string in the closure of a set is a combination of only finitely many words from the set. Even if the set S has infinitely many words, we use only finitely many at a time. This is the same as with ordinary arithmetic expressions, which can be made up of only finitely many numbers at a time even though there are infinitely many numbers to choose from.

From now on we shall let the closure operator apply to infinite sets as well as finite sets.

THEOREM 1

For any set S of strings we have $S^* = S^{**}$.

CONVINCING REMARKS

First, let us illustrate what this theorem means. Say, for example, that $S = \{a \quad b\}$. Then S^* is clearly all strings of the two letters a and b of any finite length whatsoever. Now what would it mean to take strings from S^* and concatenate them? Let us say we concatenated $(aaba)$ and $(baaa)$ and $(aaba)$. The end result $(aababaaaaaba)$ is no more than a concatenation of the letters a and b, just as with all elements of S^*.

$$aababaaaaaba$$
$$= (aaba)(baaa)(aaba)$$
$$= [(a)(a)(b)(a)]\,[(b)(a)(a)(a)]\,[(a)(a)(b)(a)]$$
$$= (a)(a)(b)(a)(b)(a)(a)(a)(a)(a)(b)(a)$$

Let us consider one more illustration. If $S = \{aa \quad bbb\}$, then S^* is the set of all strings where the a's occur in even clumps and the b's in groups of $3, 6, 9 \ldots$. Some words in S^* are

$$aabbbaaaa \quad bbb \quad bbbaa$$

If we concatenate these three elements of S^*, we get one big word in S^{**}, which is again in S^*.

$$aabbbaaaabbbbbbaa$$
$$= [(aa)(bbb)(aa)(aa)]\,[(bbb)]\,[(bbb)(aa)]$$

This theorem expresses a trivial but subtle point. It is analogous to saying that if people are made up of molecules and molecules are made up of atoms, then people are made up of atoms.

PROOF

Every word in S^{**} is made up of factors from S^*. Every factor from S^* is made up of factors from S. Therefore, every word in S^{**} is made up of factors from S. Therefore, every word in S^{**} is also a word in S^*. We can write this as

$$S^{**} \subset S^*$$

using the symbol "$\subset$" from set theory, which means "is contained in or equal to."

Now, in general, it is true that for any set A we know that $A \subset A^*$, since in A^* we can choose as a word any one factor from A. So if we consider A to be our set S^*, we have

$$S^* \subset S^{**}$$

Together, these two inclusions prove that

$$S^* = S^{**} \qquad \blacksquare$$

⚜ PROBLEMS

1. Consider the language $S*$, where $S = \{a \quad b\}$.
How many words does this language have of length 2? of length 3? of length n?

2. Consider the language $S*$, where $S = \{aa \quad b\}$.
How many words does this language have of length 4? of length 5? of length 6? What can be said in general?

3. Consider the language $S*$, where $S = \{ab \quad ba\}$. Write out all the words in $S*$ that have seven or fewer letters. Can any word in this language contain the substrings aaa or bbb? What is the smallest word that is *not* in this language?

4. Consider the language $S*$, where $S = \{a \quad ab \quad ba\}$. Is the string $(abbba)$ a word in this language? Write out all the words in this language with six or fewer letters. What is another way in which to describe the words in this language? Be careful, this is not simply the language of all words without bbb.

5. Consider the language $S*$, where $S = \{aa \quad aba \quad baa\}$. Show that the words $aabaa$, $baaabaaa$, and $baaaaababaaaa$ are all in this language. Can any word in this language be interpreted as a string of elements from S in two different ways? Can any word in this language have an odd total number of a's?

6. Consider the language $S*$, where $S = \{xx \quad xxx\}$. In how many ways can x^{19} be written as the product of words in S? This means: How many different factorizations are there of x^{19} into xx and xxx?

7. Consider the language PALINDROME over the alphabet $\{a \quad b\}$.
   (i) Prove that if x is in PALINDROME, then so is x^n for any n.
   (ii) Prove that if y^3 is in PALINDROME, then so is y.
   (iii) Prove that if z^n is in PALINDROME for some n (greater than 0), then z itself is also.
   (iv) Prove that PALINDROME has as many words of length 4 as it does of length 3.
   (v) Prove that PALINDROME has as many words of length $2n$ as it has of length $2n - 1$. How many words is that?

8. Show that if the concatenation of two words (neither Λ) in PALINDROME is also a word in PALINDROME, then both words are powers of some other·word; that is, if x and y and xy are all in PALINDROME, then there is a word z such that $x = z^n$ and $y = z^m$ for some integers n and m (maybe n or $m = 1$).

9. (i) Let $S = \{ab \quad bb\}$ and let $T = \{ab \quad bb \quad bbbb\}$. Show that $S* = T*$.
   (ii) Let $S = \{ab \quad bb\}$ and let $T = \{ab \quad bb \quad bbb\}$. Show that $S* \neq T*$, but that $S* \subset T*$.
   (iii) What principle does this illustrate?

10. How does the situation in Problem 9 change if we replace the operator * with the operator $^+$ as defined in this chapter? Note the language S^+ means the same as $S*$, but does not allow the "concatenation of no words" of S.

11. Prove that for all sets S,
   (i) $(S^+)* = (S*)*$
   (ii) $(S^+)^+ = S^+$
   (iii) Is $(S*)^+ = (S^+)*$ for all sets S?

12. Let $S = \{a \quad bb \quad bab \quad abaab\}$. Is *abbabaabab* in $S*$? Is *abaabbabbaabb*? Does any word in $S*$ have an odd total number of b's?

13. Suppose that for some language L we can always concatenate two words in L and get another word in L if and only if the words are *not* the same. That is, for any words w_1 and w_2 in L where $w_1 \neq w_2$, the word $w_1 w_2$ is in L but the word $w_1 w_1$ is not in L. Prove that this cannot happen.

14. Let us define

$$(S**)* = S***$$

Is this set bigger than $S*$? Is it bigger than S?

15. Let w be a string of letters and let the language T be defined as adding w to the language S. Suppose further that $T* = S*$.

  (i) Is it necessarily true that $w \in S$?
  (ii) Is it necessarily true that $w \in S*$?

16. Give an example of a set S such that the language $S*$ has more six-letter words than seven-letter words. Give an example of an $S*$ that has more six-letter words than eight-letter words. Does there exist an $S*$ such that it has more six-letter words than twelve-letter words?

17.   (i) Consider the language $S*$, where $S = \{aa \quad ab \quad ba \quad bb\}$. Give another description of this language.
  (ii) Give an example of a set S such that $S*$ *only* contains all possible strings of a's and b's that have length divisible by 3.
  (iii) Let S be all strings of a's and b's with odd length. What is $S*$?

18.   (i) If $S = \{a \quad b\}$ and $T* = S*$, prove that T must contain S.
  (ii) Find another pair of sets S and T such that if $T* = S*$, then $S \subset T$.

19. One student suggested the following algorithm to test a string of a's and b's to see if it is a word in $S*$, where $S = \{aa \quad ba \quad aba \quad abaab\}$. Step 1, cross off the longest set of characters from the front of the string that is a word in S. Step 2, repeat step 1 until it is no longer possible. If what remains is the string Λ, the original string was a word in $S*$. If what remains is not Λ (this means some letters are left, but we cannot find a word in S at the beginning), the original string was not a word in $S*$. Find a string that disproves this algorithm.

20. A language L_1 is smaller than another language L_2 if $L_1 \subset L_2$ and $L_1 \neq L_2$. Let T be any language closed under concatenation; that is, if $t_1 \in T$ and $t_2 \in T$, then $t_1 t_2$ is also an element of T. Show that if T contains S but $T \neq S*$, then $S*$ is smaller than T. We can summarize this by saying that $S*$ is the smallest closed language containing S.

CHAPTER 3

Recursive
Definitions

⚜ A NEW METHOD FOR DEFINING LANGUAGES

One of the mathematical tools that we shall find extremely useful in our study, but which is largely unfamiliar in other branches of mathematics, is a method of defining sets called **recursive definition**. A recursive definition is characteristically a three-step process. First, we specify some basic objects in the set. Second, we give rules for constructing more objects in the set from the ones we already know. Third, we declare that no objects except those constructed in this way are allowed in the set.

Let us take an example. Suppose that we are trying to define the set of positive even integers for someone who knows about arithmetic, but has never heard of the even numbers. One standard way of defining this set is

EVEN is the set of all positive whole numbers divisible by 2.

Another way we might try is this:

EVEN is the set of all $2n$ where $n = 1$ 2   3   4 . . . .

The third method we present is sneaky, by recursive definition:

The set EVEN is defined by these three rules:

Rule 1   2 is in EVEN.

Rule 2   If x is in EVEN, then so is $x + 2$.

Rule 3   The *only* elements in the set EVEN are those that can be produced from the two rules above.

The last rule above is completely redundant. We state it this once only for pedagogical reasons, but it is tacitly presumed in all recursive definitions.

There is a reason that the third definition is less popular than the others: It is much harder to use in most practical applications.

For example, suppose that we wanted to prove that 14 is in the set EVEN. To show this using the first definition, we divide 14 by 2 and find that there is no remainder. Therefore, it is in EVEN. To prove that 14 is in EVEN by the second definition, we have to somehow come up with the number 7 and then, since $14 = (2)(7)$, we know that it is in EVEN. To prove that 14 is in EVEN using the recursive definition is a lengthier process. We could proceed as below:

By Rule 1, we know that 2 is in EVEN.

Then by Rule 2, we know that $2 + 2 = 4$ is also in EVEN.

Again by Rule 2, we know that since 4 has just been shown to be in EVEN, $4 + 2 = 6$ is also in EVEN.

The fact that 6 is in EVEN means that when we apply Rule 2, we deduce that $6 + 2 = 8$ is in EVEN, too.

Now applying Rule 2 to 8, we derive that $8 + 2 = 10$ is another member of EVEN.

Once more applying Rule 2, this time to 10, we infer that $10 + 2 = 12$ is in EVEN.

And, at last, by applying Rule 2, yet again, to the number 12, we conclude that $12 + 2 = 14$ is, indeed, in EVEN.

Pretty horrible. This, however, is not the only recursive definition of the set EVEN. We might use:

The set EVEN is defined by these two rules:

Rule 1   2 is in EVEN.

Rule 2   If x and y are both in EVEN, then so is

$$x + y$$

It should be understood that we can apply Rule 2 also to the case where x and y stand for the same number.

We can now prove that 14 is in EVEN in fewer steps:

By Rule 1   2 is in EVEN.

By Rule 2 $x = 2, y = 2 \rightarrow 4$ is in EVEN.

By Rule 2 $x = 2, y = 4 \rightarrow 6$ is in EVEN.

By Rule 2 $x = 4, y = 4 \rightarrow 8$ is in EVEN.

By Rule 2 $x = 6, y = 8 \rightarrow 14$ is in EVEN.

This is a better recursive definition of the set EVEN because it produces shorter proofs that elements are in EVEN. The set EVEN, as we have seen, has some very fine definitions that are not recursive. In later chapters, we shall be interested in certain sets that have no better definition than the recursive one.

Before leaving this example, let us note that although the second recursive definition is still harder to use (in proving that given numbers are even) than the two nonrecursive definitions, it does have some advantages. For instance, suppose we want to prove that the sum of two numbers in EVEN is also a number in EVEN. This is a trivial conclusion from the second recursive definition, but to prove this from the first definition is decidedly harder. Whether or not we want a recursive definition depends on two things: one, how easy the other possible definitions are to understand; and two, what types of theorems we may wish to prove about the set.

EXAMPLE

The following is a recursive definition of the positive integers:

Rule 1   1 is in INTEGERS.

Rule 2   If x is in INTEGERS, then so is $x + 1$.

If we wanted the set INTEGERS to be defined to include both the positive and negative integers, we might use the following recursive definition:

Rule 1   1 is in INTEGERS.

Rule 2   If both x and y are in INTEGERS, then so are $x + y$ and $x - y$.

Since $1 - 1 = 0$ and, for all positive x, $0 - x = -x$, we see that the negative integers and zero are all included in this definition.   ∎

EXAMPLE

If we wanted a recursive definition for all the positive real numbers, we could try a definition of the form:

Rule 1 x is in POSITIVE.

Rule 2   If x and y are in POSITIVE, then so are $x + y$ and xy.

But the problem is that there is no smallest positive real number x on which to build the rest of the set. We could try:

Rule 1   If x is in INTEGERS, "." is a decimal point, and y is any finite string of digits, even one that starts with some zeros, then $x.y$ is in POSITIVE.

This definition for POSITIVE has two problems. One, it does not generate all real numbers (e.g., π is not included because of its infinite length). Two, the definition is not *recursive* since we did not use known elements of POSITIVE to create new elements of POSITIVE; we used an element of INTEGERS and a string of digits instead. We could try:

Rule 1   1 is in POSITIVE.

Rule 2   If x and y are in POSITIVE, then so are $x + y$, $x*y$, and x/y.

This does define some set, but it is not the set of positive real numbers (see Problem 17 at the end of this chapter).   ∎

Let us consider the way polynomials are usually defined:

A polynomial is a finite sum of terms, each of which is of the form a real number times a power of x (that may be $x^0 = 1$).

Now let us consider a recursive definition that is designed for people who know algebraic notation, but do not know what a polynomial is:

The set POLYNOMIAL is defined by these three rules:

Rule 1   Any number is in POLYNOMIAL.

Rule 2   The variable x is in POLYNOMIAL.

Rule 3   If p and q are in POLYNOMIAL, then so are $p + q$, $p - q$, (p), and pq.

The symbol pq, which looks like a concatenation of alphabet letters, in algebraic notation refers to multiplication.

Some sequence of applications of these rules can show that $3x^2 + 7x - 9$ is in POLYNOMIAL:

By Rule 1   3 is in POLYNOMIAL.

By Rule 2 x is in POLYNOMIAL.

By Rule 3 $(3)(x)$ is in POLYNOMIAL; call it $3x$.

By Rule 3 $(3x)(x)$ is in POLYNOMIAL; call it $3x^2$.

By Rule 1   7 is in POLYNOMIAL.

By Rule 3 $(7)(x)$ is in POLYNOMIAL.

By Rule 3 $3x^2 + 7x$ is in POLYNOMIAL.

By Rule 1 -9 is in POLYNOMIAL.

By Rule 3 $3x^2 + 7x + (-9) = 3x^2 + 7x - 9$ is in POLYNOMIAL.

In fact, there are several other sequences that could also produce this result.

There are some advantages to this definition as well as the evident disadvantages. On the plus side, it is immediately obvious that the sum and product of polynomials are both themselves polynomials. This is a little more complicated to see if we had to provide a proof based on the classical definition.

Suppose for a moment that we were studying calculus and we had just proven that the derivative of the sum of two functions is the sum of the derivatives and that the derivative of the product fg is $f'g + fg'$. As soon as we prove that the derivative of a number is 0 and that the derivative of x is 1, we have automatically shown that we can differentiate all polynomials. This becomes a theorem that can be proven directly from the recursive definition. It is true that we do not then *know* that the derivative of x^n is nx^{n-1}, but we do know that it can be calculated for every n.

In this way, we can prove that it is possible to differentiate all polynomials without giving the best algorithm to do it. Since the topic of this book is computer theory, we are very interested in proving that certain tasks are possible for a computer to do even if we do not know the best algorithms by which to do them. It is for this reason that recursive definitions are important to us.

Before proceeding to more serious matters, let us note that recursive definitions are not completely alien to us in the real world. What is the best definition of the set of people who are descended from Henry VIII? Is it not:

Rule 1   The children of Henry VIII are all elements of DESCENDANTS.

Rule 2   If x is an element of DESCENDANTS, then so are x's children.

Given a soldier, policeman, and mailman, it is sometimes not evident whether they are properly termed members of the federal executive branch of government or some other type of public servant. This definition clears up the matter:

Rule 1   The President is in EXECUTIVE-BRANCH-OF-GOVERNMENT.

Rule 2   If x is in EXECUTIVE-BRANCH-OF-GOVERNMENT and y works for x, then y is in EXECUTIVE-BRANCH-OF-GOVERNMENT.

Also, in mathematics we often see the following definition of factorial:

Rule 1 $0! = 1$.

Rule 2 $n! = n \cdot (n - 1)!$.

The reason that these definitions are called "recursive" is that one of the rules used to define the set mentions the set itself. We define EVEN in terms of previously known elements of EVEN, POLYNOMIAL in terms of previously known elements of POLYNOMIAL. We define $(n + 1)!$ in terms of the value of $n!$. In computer languages, when we allow a procedure to call itself, we refer to the program as recursive. These definitions have the same self-referential sense.

EXAMPLE

Observe how natural the following definitions are:

Rule 1 x is in L_1.

Rule 2   If w is any word in L_1, then xw is also in L_1.

$$L_1 = x^+ = \{x \quad xx \quad xxx \ldots\}$$

or

Rule 1 Λ is in L_4.

Rule 2   If w is any word in L_4, then xw is also in L_4.

$$L_4 = x^* = \{\Lambda \quad x \quad xx \quad xxx \ldots\}$$

or

Rule 1 x is in L_2.

Rule 2   If w is any word in L_2, then xxw is also in L_2.

$$L_2 = \{x^{\text{odd}}\} = \{x \quad xxx \quad xxxxx \ldots\}$$

or

Rule 1 1 2 3 4 5 6 7 8 9 are in INTEGERS.

Rule 2   If w is any word in INTEGERS, then $w0$ $w1$ $w2$ $w3$ $w4$
$w5$ $w6$ $w7$ $w8$ $w9$ are also words in INTEGERS.   ∎

The definition of Kleene closure might have benefited from a recursive definition:

Rule 1   If S is a language, then all the words of S are in S^*.

Rule 2 Λ is in S^*.

Rule 3   If x and y are in S^*, then so is their concatenation xy.

⚜ AN IMPORTANT LANGUAGE: ARITHMETIC EXPRESSIONS

Suppose we ask ourselves what constitutes a valid arithmetic expression that can be typed on one line, in a form digestible by computers. The alphabet for this language is

$$\Sigma = \{0 \quad 1 \quad 2 \quad 3 \quad 4 \quad 5 \quad 6 \quad 7 \quad 8 \quad 9 \quad + \quad - \quad * \quad / \quad (\quad)\}$$

Obviously, the following strings are not good:

$$(3 + 5) + 6) \qquad 2(/8 + 9) \qquad (3 + (4 -)8) \qquad 2) - (4$$

The first contains unbalanced parentheses; the second contains the forbidden substring (/ . The third contains the forbidden substring −) . The fourth has a close parenthesis before the corresponding open parenthesis. Are there more rules? The subsequences // and */ are also forbidden. Are there still more? The most natural way of defining a valid arithmetic expression, AE, is by using a recursive definition rather than a long list of forbidden substrings and parentheses requirements. The definition can be written as:

Rule 1   Any number (positive, negative, or zero) is in AE.

Rule 2   If x is in AE, then so are

(i) (x)

(ii) $-x$ (provided x does not already start with a minus sign)

Rule 3   If x and y are in AE, then so are:

    (i) $x + y$ (if the first symbol in y is not $+$ or $-$)
    (ii) $x - y$ (if the first symbol in y is not $+$ or $-$)
    (iii) $x*y$
    (iv) x/y
    (v) $x**y$ (our notation for exponentiation)

We have called this the "most natural" definition because, even though we may never have articulated this point, it truly is the method we use for recognizing arithmetic expressions in real life. If we are presented with

$$(2 + 4) * (7 * (9 - 3)/4)/4 * (2 + 8) - 1$$

and asked to determine whether it is a valid arithmetic expression, we do not really scan over the string looking for forbidden substrings or count the parentheses. We imagine it in our mind broken down into its components. $(2 + 4)$ that is OK, $(9 - 3)$ that is OK, $7 * (9 - 3)/4$ that is OK, and so on. We may never have seen a definition of "arithmetic expressions" before, but this is what we have always intuitively meant by the phrase.

This definition gives us the possibility of writing $2 + 3 + 4$, which is not ambiguous. But it also gives us $8/4/2$, which is. It could mean $8/(4/2) = 4$ or $(8/4)/2 = 1$. Also, $3 + 4 * 5$ is ambiguous. So, we usually adopt conventions of operator hierarchy and left-to-right execution. By applying Rule 2, we could always put in enough parentheses to avoid any confusion if we so desired. We return to this point in Part II, but for now this definition adequately defines the language of all valid strings of symbols for arithmetic expressions. Remember, the ambiguity in the string $8/4/2$ is a problem of *meaning*. There is no doubt that the string is a word in AE, only doubt about what it means.

This definition determines the set AE in a manner useful for proving many theorems about arithmetic expressions.

THEOREM 2

An arithmetic expression cannot contain the character $.

PROOF

This character is not part of any number, so it cannot be introduced into an AE by Rule 1. If the character string x does not contain the character $, then neither do the strings (x) and $-(x)$, so it cannot be introduced into an AE by Rule 2. If neither x nor y contains the character $, then neither do any of the expressions defined by Rule 3. Therefore, the character $ can never get into an AE.   ∎

THEOREM 3

No AE can begin or end with the symbol /.

PROOF

No number begins or ends with this symbol, so it cannot occur by Rule 1. Any AE formed by Rule 2 must begin and end with parentheses or begin with a minus sign, so the / cannot be introduced by Rule 2. If x does not already begin with a / and y does not end with a /, then any AE formed by any clause in Rule 3 will not begin or end with a /. Therefore, these rules will never introduce an expression beginning or ending with a /. ∎

These proofs are like the story of the three chefs making a stew. One can add only meat to the pot. One can add only carrots to the pot. One can add only potatoes to the pot. Even without knowing exactly in what order the chefs visit the pot or how often, we still can conclude that the pot cannot end up with an alarm clock in it. If no rule contributes a $, then one never gets put in even though if x had a $, then $x + y$ would also.

The symbol "/" has many names. In computer science, it is usually called a "slash"; other names are "oblique stroke," "solidus," and "virgule." It also has another theorem.

THEOREM 4

No AE can contain the substring //.

PROOF

For variation, we shall prove this result by contradiction, even though a direct argument similar to those above could easily be given.

Let us suppose that there were some AEs that contained the substring //. Let a shortest of these be a string called w. This means that w is a valid AE that contains the substring //, but there is no shorter word in AE that contains this substring. There may be more strings of the same length as w that contain //, but it does not matter which of these we begin with and choose to call w.

Now we know that w, like all words in AE, is formed by some sequence of applications of Rules 1, 2, and 3. Our first question is: Which was the last rule used in the production of w? This is easy to answer. We shall show that it must have been Rule 3(iv). If it were Rule 3(iii), for instance, then the // must either be found in the x or y part. But x and y are presumed to be in AE, so this would mean that there is some shorter word in AE than w that contains the substring //, which contradicts the assumption that w is the shortest. Similarly, we can eliminate all the other possibilities. Therefore, the last rule used to produce w must have been 3(iv).

Now, since the // cannot have been contributed to w from the x part alone or from the y part alone (or else x or y are shorter words in AE with a double slash), it must have been included by finding an x part that ended in a / or a y part that began with a /. But since both x and y are AEs, our previous theorem says that neither case can happen. Therefore, even Rule 3(iv) cannot introduce the substring //.

Therefore, there is no possibility left for the last rule from which w can be constructed. Therefore, w cannot be in the set AE. Therefore, there is no shortest AE that contains the substring //. Therefore, nothing in the set AE can have the substring //. ∎

This method of argument should sound familiar. It is similar to the proof that $\{xx \quad xxx\}$* contains all x^n, for $n \neq 1$.

The long-winded but careful proof of the last theorem is given to illustrate that recursive definitions can be conveniently employed in rigorous mathematical proofs. Admittedly, this was a trivial example of the application of this method. Most people would be just as convinced by the following "proof":

How could an arithmetic expression contain the substring //? What would it mean? Huh? What are you, crazy or something?

We should bear in mind that we are only on the threshold of investigating a very complex and profound subject and that in this early chapter we wish to introduce a feel for the techniques and viewpoints that will be relied on heavily later, under far less obvious circumstances. We will use our learner's permit to spend a few hours driving around an empty parking lot before venturing onto the highway.

Another common use for recursive definitions is to determine what expressions are valid in symbolic logic. We shall be interested in one particular branch of symbolic logic called sentential calculus or propositional calculus. The version we shall define here uses only negation $\neg$ and implication $\rightarrow$ along with the phrase variables, although conjunction and disjunction could easily be added to the system. The valid expressions in this language are traditionally called WFFs for **well-formed formulas.**

As with AE, parentheses are letters in the alphabet:

$$\Sigma = \{\neg \quad \rightarrow \quad (\quad) \quad a \quad b \quad c \quad d \ldots\}$$

There are other symbols sometimes used for negation, such as $\vdash$, $-$, and $\sim$.

The rules for forming WFFs are:

Rule 1   Any single Latin letter is a WFF,

$$a \quad b \quad c \quad d \ldots$$

Rule 2   If p is a WFF, then so are (p) and $\neg p$.

Rule 3   If p and q are WFFs, then so is $p \rightarrow q$.

Some sequences of applications of these rules enable us to show that

$$p \rightarrow ((p \rightarrow p) \rightarrow q)$$

is a WFF. Without too much difficulty, we can also show that

$$p \rightarrow \qquad \rightarrow p \qquad (p \rightarrow \quad p) \qquad p) \rightarrow p($$

are all not WFFs.

As a final note in this section, we should be wary that we have sometimes used recursive definitions to define *membership in a set,* as in the phrase "x is in POLYNOMIAL" or "x is in EVEN," and sometimes to define a *property,* as in the phrase "x is a WFF" or "x is even." This should not present any problem.

⚜ PROBLEMS

1. Write another recursive definition for the language L_1 of Chapter 2.

2. Using the second recursive definition of the set EVEN, how many different ways can we prove that 14 is in EVEN?

3. Using the second recursive definition of EVEN, what is the smallest number of steps required to prove that 100 is EVEN? Describe a good method for showing that $2n$ is in EVEN.

4. Show that the following is another recursive definition of the set EVEN:

   Rule 1   2 and 4 are in EVEN.

   Rule 2   If x is in EVEN, then so is $x + 4$.

5. Show that there are infinitely many different recursive definitions for the set EVEN.

6. Using any recursive definition of the set EVEN, show that all the numbers in it end in the digits 0, 2, 4, 6, or 8.

7. The set POLYNOMIAL defined in this chapter contains only the polynomials in the one variable x. Write a recursive definition for the set of all polynomials in the two variables x and y.

8. Define the set of valid algebraic expressions ALEX as follows:

Rule 1   All polynomials are in ALEX.

Rule 2   If $f(x)$ and $g(x)$ are in ALEX, then so are:

    (i) $(f(x))$
    (ii) $-(f(x))$
    (iii) $f(x) + g(x)$
    (iv) $f(x) - g(x)$
    (v) $f(x)g(x)$
    (vi) $f(x)/g(x)$
    (vii) $f(x)^{g(x)}$
    (viii) $f(g(x))$

(a) Show that $(x + 2)^{3x}$ is in ALEX.
(b) Show that elementary calculus contains enough rules to prove the theorem that all algebraic expressions can be differentiated.
(c) Is Rule 2 (viii) really necessary?

9. Using the fact that $3x^2 + 7x - 9 = (((((3)x) + 7)x) - 9)$, show how to produce this polynomial from the rules for POLYNOMIAL using multiplication only twice. What is the smallest number of steps needed for producing $x^8 + x^4$? What is the smallest number of steps needed for producing $7x^7 + 5x^5 + 3x^3 + x$?

10. Show that if n is less than 31, then x^n can be shown to be in POLYNOMIAL in fewer than eight steps.

11. In this chapter, we mentioned several substrings of length 2 that cannot occur in arithmetic expressions, such as (/, +), //, and */. What is the complete list of substrings of length 2 that cannot occur?

12. Are there any substrings of length 3 that cannot occur that do not contain forbidden substrings of length 2? (This means that /// is already known to be illegal because it contains the forbidden substring //.) What is the longest forbidden substring that does not contain a shorter forbidden substring?

13. The rules given earlier for the set AE allow for the peculiar expressions

$$((((9))))) \qquad \text{and} \qquad -(-(-(-(9))))$$

It is not really harmful to allow these in AE, but is there some modified definition of AE that eliminates this problem?

14. (i) Write out the full recursive definition for the propositional calculus that contains the symbols $\vee$ and $\wedge$ as well as $\neg$ and $\rightarrow$.
(ii) What are all the forbidden substrings of length 2 in this language?

15. (i) When asked to give a recursive definition for the language PALINDROME over the alphabet $\Sigma = \{a \quad b\}$, a student wrote:

Rule 1   *a* and *b* are in PALINDROME.

Rule 2   If *x* is in PALINDROME, then so are *axa* and *bxb*.

Unfortunately, all the words in the language defined above have an odd length and so it is not all of PALINDROME. Fix this problem.

(ii) Give a recursive definition for the language EVENPALINDROME of all palindromes of even length.

16. (i) Give a recursive definition for the set ODD = {1   3   5   7. . .}.
(ii) Give a recursive definition for the set of strings of digits 0, 1, 2, 3, . . . 9 that cannot start with the digit 0.

17. In this chapter, we attempted to define the positive numbers by the following rules:

Rule 1   1 is in *L*.

Rule 2   If *x* and *y* are in *L*, then so are $x + y$, $x*y$, and x/y.

The language *L* defined in this way is a famous mathematical set. What is it? Prove it.

18. Give two recursive definitions for the set

$$\text{POWERS-OF-TWO} = \{1 \quad 2 \quad 4 \quad 8 \quad 16. . .\}$$

Use one of them to prove that the product of two POWERS-OF-TWO is also a POWER-OF-TWO.

19. Give recursive definitions for the following languages over the alphabet {*a*   *b*}:

(i) The language EVENSTRING of all words of even length.
(ii) The language ODDSTRING of all words of odd length.
(iii) The language AA of all words containing the substring *aa*.
(iv) The language NOTAA of all words not containing the substring *aa*.

20. (i) Consider the following recursive definition of 3-PERMUTATION:

Rule 1   123 is a 3-PERMUTATION.

Rule 2   If *xyz* is a 3-PERMUTATION, then so are *zyx* and *yzx*.

Show that there are six different 3-PERMUTATIONs.
(ii) Consider the following recursive definition of 4-PERMUTATION:

Rule 1   1234 is a 4-PERMUTATION.

Rule 2   If *xyzw* is a 4-PERMUTATION, then so are *wzyx* and *yzwx*.

How many 4-PERMUTATIONs are there (by this definition)?

CHAPTER 4

Regular
Expressions

⚜ DEFINING LANGUAGES BY ANOTHER NEW METHOD

We wish now to be very careful about the phrases we use to define languages. We defined L_1 in Chapter 2 by the symbols:

$$L_1 = \{x^n \quad \text{for} \quad n = 1 \quad 2 \quad 3 \ldots\}$$

and we presumed that we all understood exactly which values n could take. We might even have defined the language L_2 by the symbols:

$$L_2 = \{x^n \quad \text{for} \quad n = 1 \quad 3 \quad 5 \quad 7 \ldots\}$$

and again we could presume that we all agree on what words are in this language.

We might define a language by the symbols:

$$L_5 = \{x^n \quad \text{for} \quad n = 1 \quad 4 \quad 9 \quad 16 \ldots\}$$

but now the symbols are becoming more of an IQ test than a clear definition.

What words are in the language

$$L_6 = \{x^n \quad \text{for} \quad n = 3 \quad 4 \quad 8 \quad 22 \ldots\} ?$$

Perhaps these are the ages of the sisters of Louis XIV when he assumed the throne of France. More precision and less guesswork are required, especially where computers are concerned. In this chapter, we shall develop some new language-defining symbolism that will be much more precise than the ellipsis.

Let us reconsider the language L_4 of Chapter 2:

$$L_4 = \{\Lambda \quad x \quad xx \quad xxx \quad xxxx \ldots\}$$

In that chapter, we presented one method for indicating this set as the closure of a smaller set.

$$\text{Let } S = \{x\}. \text{ Then } L_4 = S*.$$

As shorthand for this, we could have written

$$L_4 = \{x\}*$$

We now introduce the use of the Kleene star applied not to a set, but directly to the letter x and written as a superscript as if it were an exponent:

$$\mathbf{x}^*$$

The simple expression $\mathbf{x}^*$ will be used to indicate some sequence of x's (maybe none at all). This x is intentionally written in boldface type to distinguish it from an alphabet character.

$$\mathbf{x}^* = \Lambda \quad \text{or} \quad x \quad \text{or} \quad x^2 \quad \text{or} \quad x^3 \quad \text{or} \quad x^4 \ldots$$
$$= x^n \quad \text{for some } n = 0 \quad 1 \quad 2 \quad 3 \quad 4 \ldots$$

We can think of the star as an unknown power or undetermined power. That is, $\mathbf{x}^*$ stands for a string of x's, but we do not specify how many. It stands for any string of x's in the language L_4.

The star operator applied to a letter is analogous to the star operator applied to a set. It represents an arbitrary concatenation of copies of that letter (maybe none at all). This notation can be used to help us define languages by writing

$$L_4 = \text{language}(\mathbf{x}^*)$$

Since $\mathbf{x}^*$ is any string of x's, L_4 is then the set of all possible strings of x's of any length (including Λ).

We should not confuse $\mathbf{x}^*$, which is a language-defining symbol, with L_4, which is the name we have given to a certain language. This is why we use the word "language" in the equation. We shall soon give a name to the world in which this symbol $\mathbf{x}^*$ lives, but not quite yet. Suppose that we wished to describe the language L over the alphabet $\Sigma = \{a \quad b\}$, where

$$L = \{a \quad ab \quad abb \quad abbb \quad abbbb \ldots\}$$

We could summarize this language by the English phrase "all words of the form one a followed by some number of b's (maybe no b's at all)."

Using our star notation and boldface letters, we may write

$$L = \text{language}(\mathbf{a} \quad \mathbf{b}^*)$$

or without the space

$$L = \text{language}(\mathbf{ab}^*)$$

The meaning is clear: This is a language in which the words are the concatenation of an initial a with some or no b's (i.e., $\mathbf{b}^*$).

Whether we put a space inside $\mathbf{ab}^*$ or not is only for the clarity of reading; it does not change the set of strings this represents. No string can contain a blank unless a blank is a character in the alphabet Σ. If we want blanks to be in the alphabet, we normally introduce some special symbol to stand for them, as blanks themselves are invisible to the naked eye. The reason for putting a blank between $\mathbf{a}$ and $\mathbf{b}^*$ in the product above is to emphasize the point that the star operator is applied to the $\mathbf{b}$ only. We have now used a boldface letter without a star as well as with a star.

We can apply the Kleene star to the whole string ab if we want, as follows:

$$(\mathbf{ab})^* \quad = \quad \Lambda \quad \text{or} \quad ab \quad \text{or} \quad abab \quad \text{or} \quad ababab \ldots$$

Parentheses are not letters in the alphabet of this language, so they can be used to indicate factoring without accidentally changing the words. Since the star represents some kind of exponentiation, we use it as powers are used in algebra, where by universal understanding the expression xy^2 means $x(y^2)$, not $(xy)^2$.

If we want to define the language L_1 this way, we may write

$$L_1 = \text{language}(\mathbf{xx}^*)$$

This means that we start each word of L_1 by writing down an x and then we follow it with some string of x's (which may be no more x's at all). Or we may use the $^+$ notation from Chapter 2 and write

$$L_1 = \text{language}(\mathbf{x}^+)$$

meaning all words of the form x to some positive power (i.e., not $x^0 = \Lambda$). The $^+$ notation is a convenience, but is not essential since we can say the same thing with *'s alone.

EXAMPLE

The language L_1 can be defined by any of the expressions below:

$$\mathbf{xx}^* \quad \mathbf{x}^+ \quad \mathbf{xx}^*\mathbf{x}^* \quad \mathbf{x}^*\mathbf{xx}^* \quad \mathbf{x}^+\mathbf{x}^* \quad \mathbf{x}^*\mathbf{x}^+ \quad \mathbf{x}^*\mathbf{x}^*\mathbf{x}^*\mathbf{xx}^*$$

Remember, $\mathbf{x}^*$ can always be Λ. ■

EXAMPLE

The language defined by the expression

$$\mathbf{ab}^*\mathbf{a}$$

is the set of all strings of a's and b's that have at least two letters, that begin and end with a's, and that have nothing but b's inside (if anything at all).

$$\text{Language}(\mathbf{ab}^*\mathbf{a}) = \{aa \quad aba \quad abba \quad abbba \quad abbbba \ldots\}$$

It would be a subtle mistake to say only that this language is the set of all words that begin and end with an a and have only b's in between, because this description may also apply to the word a, depending on how it is interpreted. Our symbolism eliminates this ambiguity. ■

EXAMPLE

The language of the expression

$$\mathbf{a}^*\mathbf{b}^*$$

contains all the strings of a's and b's in which all the a's (if any) come before all the b's (if any).

$$\text{Language}(\mathbf{a}^*\mathbf{b}^*) = \{\Lambda \quad a \quad b \quad aa \quad ab \quad bb \quad aaa \quad aab \quad abb \quad bbb \quad aaaa \ldots\}$$

Notice that ba and aba are not in this language. Notice also that there need not be the same number of a's and b's. ■

Here we should again be very careful to observe that

$$\mathbf{a}^*\mathbf{b}^* \neq (\mathbf{ab})^*$$

since the language defined by the expression on the right contains the word $abab$, whereas the language defined by the expression on the left does not. This cautions us against thinking of the * as a normal algebraic exponent.

The language defined by the expression **a*b*a*** contains the word *baa* since it starts with zero *a*'s followed by one *b* followed by two *a*'s.

EXAMPLE

The following expressions both define the language $L_2 = \{x^{odd}\}$:

$$\mathbf{x(xx)^*} \qquad \text{or} \qquad \mathbf{(xx)^*x}$$

but the expression

$$\mathbf{x^*xx^*}$$

does not since it includes the word $(xx)\,x\,(x)$.   ∎

We now introduce another use for the plus sign. By the expression **x + y** where *x* and *y* are strings of characters from an alphabet, we mean "either *x* or *y*." This means that **x + y** offers a choice, much the same way that **x*** does. Care should be taken so as not to confuse this with $^+$ as an exponent.

EXAMPLE

Consider the language *T* defined over the alphabet $\Sigma = \{a \quad b \quad c\}$:

$$T = \{a \quad c \quad ab \quad cb \quad abb \quad cbb \quad abbb \quad cbbb \quad abbbb \quad cbbbb \ . \ . \ .\}$$

All the words in *T* begin with an *a* or a *c* and then are followed by some number of *b*'s. Symbolically, we may write this as

$$T = \text{language}((\mathbf{a + c})\mathbf{b^*})$$
$$= \text{language(either } a \text{ or } c \text{ then some } b\text{'s)}$$

We should, of course, have said "some or no *b*'s." We often drop the zero option because it is tiresome. We let the word "some" always mean "some or no," and when we mean "some positive number of," we say that.

We say that the expression **(a + c)b*** defines a language in the following sense. For each * or +, used as a superscript, we must select some number of factors for which it stands. For each other +, we must decide whether to choose the right-side expression or the left-side expression. For every set of choices, we have generated a particular string. The set of all strings that can be produced by this method is the language of the expression. In the example

$$(\mathbf{a + c})\mathbf{b^*}$$

we must choose either *a* or *c* for the first letter and then we choose how many *b*'s the **b*** stands for. Each set of choices is a word. If from **(a + c)** we choose *c* and we choose **b*** to mean *bbb*, we have the word *cbbb*.   ∎

EXAMPLE

Now let us consider a finite language *L* that contains all the strings of *a*'s and *b*'s of length three exactly:

$$L = \{aaa \quad aab \quad aba \quad abb \quad baa \quad bab \quad bba \quad bbb\}$$

The first letter of each word in L is either an a or a b. The second letter of each word in L is either an a or a b. The third letter of each word in L is either an a or a b. So, we may write

$$L = \text{language}((\mathbf{a} + \mathbf{b})(\mathbf{a} + \mathbf{b})(\mathbf{a} + \mathbf{b}))$$

or for short,

$$L = \text{language}((\mathbf{a} + \mathbf{b})^3) \qquad \blacksquare$$

If we want to define the set of all seven-letter strings of a's and b's, we could write $(\mathbf{a} + \mathbf{b})^7$. In general, if we want to refer to the set of all possible strings of a's and b's of any length whatsoever, we could write

$$(\mathbf{a} + \mathbf{b})*$$

This is the set of *all possible strings* of letters from the alphabet $\Sigma = \{a \quad b\}$ including the null string. This is a very important expression and we shall use it often.

Again, this expression represents a language. If we choose that * stands for 5, then

$$(\mathbf{a} + \mathbf{b})*$$

gives

$$(\mathbf{a} + \mathbf{b})^5 = (\mathbf{a} + \mathbf{b})(\mathbf{a} + \mathbf{b})(\mathbf{a} + \mathbf{b})(\mathbf{a} + \mathbf{b})(\mathbf{a} + \mathbf{b})$$

We now have to make five more choices: either a or b for the first letter, either a or b for the second letter, and so on.

This is a very powerful notation. We can describe all words that begin with the letter a simply as

$$\mathbf{a}(\mathbf{a} + \mathbf{b})*$$

that is, first an a, then anything (as many choices as we want of either letter a or b).

All words that begin with an a and end with a b can be defined by the expression

$$\mathbf{a}(\mathbf{a} + \mathbf{b})*\mathbf{b} = a(\text{arbitrary string})b$$

⚜ FORMAL DEFINITION OF REGULAR EXPRESSIONS

After all the introduction we have endured of the slow evolution of these language-defining expressions, it is time for us to identify them with their proper name and give them a mathematical definition. As is no surprise to those who have read the title of this chapter, these are called **regular expressions.** Similarly, the corresponding languages that they define are referred to as **regular languages.** We shall soon see that this language-defining tool is of limited capacity in that there are many interesting languages that cannot be defined by regular expressions, which is why this volume has more than 100 pages. A regular language is one that can be defined by a regular expression even though it may also have many other fine definitions. A regular expression, on the other hand, must take a very rigorous form as defined below recursively.

DEFINITION

The symbols that appear in regular expressions are the letters of the alphabet Σ, the symbol for the null string Λ, parentheses, the star operator, and the plus sign.

The set of **regular expressions** is defined by the following rules:

Rule 1   Every letter of Σ can be made into a regular expression by writing it in bold-face; Λ itself is a regular expression.

Rule 2   If $\mathbf{r}_1$ and $\mathbf{r}_2$ are regular expressions, then so are:

(i) $(\mathbf{r}_1)$
(ii) $\mathbf{r}_1\mathbf{r}_2$
(iii) $\mathbf{r}_1 + \mathbf{r}_2$
(iv) $\mathbf{r}_1{}^*$

Rule 3   Nothing else is a regular expression.   ■

We could have included the plus sign as a superscript in $\mathbf{r}_1{}^+$ as part of the definition, but since we know that $\mathbf{r}_1{}^+ = \mathbf{r}_1\mathbf{r}_1{}^*$, this would add nothing valuable.

This is a language of language-definers. It is analogous to a book that lists all the books in print. Every word in such a book is a book-definer. The same confusion occurs in everyday speech. The string "French" is both a word (an adjective) and a language-defining name (a noun). However difficult computer theory may seem, common English usage is much harder.

Because of Rule 1, we may have trouble in distinguishing when we write an a whether we mean a, the letter in Σ; a, the word in Σ^*; $\{a\}$, the one-word language; or $\mathbf{a}$, the regular expression for that language. Context and typography will guide us.

As with the recursive definition of arithmetic expressions, we have included the use of parentheses as an option, not a requirement. Let us emphasize again the implicit parentheses in $\mathbf{r}_1{}^*$. If $\mathbf{r}_1 = \mathbf{aa} + \mathbf{b}$, then the expression $\mathbf{r}_1{}^*$ technically refers to the expression

$$\mathbf{r}_1{}^* = \mathbf{aa} + \mathbf{b}^*$$

which is the formal concatenation of the symbols for $\mathbf{r}_1$ with the symbol *, but what we generally mean when we write $\mathbf{r}_1{}^*$ is actually $(\mathbf{r}_1)^*$:

$$\mathbf{r}_1{}^* = (\mathbf{r}_1)^* = (\mathbf{aa} + \mathbf{b})^*$$

which is different. Both are regular expressions and both can be generated from the rules, but their languages are quite different. Care should always be taken to produce the expression we actually want, but this much care is too much to ask of mortals, and when we write $\mathbf{r}_1{}^*$ in the rest of the book, we really mean $(\mathbf{r}_1)^*$.

The definition we have given for regular expressions contains one subtle but important omission: the language $\boldsymbol\phi$. This language is not the same as the one represented by the regular expression Λ, or by any other regular expression that comes from our definition. We already have a symbol for the word with no letters and a symbol for the language with no words. Do we really need to invent yet another symbol for the regular expression that defines the language with no words? Would it simply be the regular expression with no characters, analogous to the word lambda (Λ) in the language of regular expressions? To the purely logical Vulcan mind, that would be the only answer, but since we have already employed the boldface lambda (Λ) to mean the regular expression defining the word lambda, we take the liberty of using the boldface phi ($\boldsymbol\phi$) to be the regular expression for the null language. We have already wasted enough thought on the various degrees of nothingness to qualify as medieval ecclesiastics; the desire for more precision would require psycho-active medication. For any $\mathbf{r}$, we have

$$\mathbf{r} + \boldsymbol\phi = \mathbf{r}$$

and

$$\boldsymbol\phi\mathbf{r} = \boldsymbol\phi$$

but what is far less clear is exactly what ϕ* should mean. We shall avoid this philosophical crisis by never using this symbolism and avoiding those who do.

EXAMPLE

Let us consider the language defined by the expression

$$(a + b)* \ a \ (a + b)*$$

At the beginning, we have $(a + b)*$, which stands for anything, that is, any string of a's and b's, then comes an a, then another anything. All told, the language is the set of all words over the alphabet $\Sigma = \{a \quad b\}$ that have an a in them somewhere. The only words left out are those that have only b's and the word Λ.

For example, the word *abbaab* can be considered to be derived from this expression by three different sets of choices:

$$(\Lambda)a(bbaab) \quad \text{or} \quad (abb)a(ab) \quad \text{or} \quad (abba)a(b)$$

If the only words left out of the language defined by the expression above are the words without a's (Λ and strings of b's), then these omitted words are exactly the language defined by the expression **b***. If we combine these two, we should produce the language of all strings. In other words, since

$$\text{all strings} = (\text{all strings with an } a) + (\text{all strings without an } a)$$

it should make sense to write

$$(a + b)* = (a + b)*a(a + b)* + b*$$

Here, we have added two language-defining expressions to produce an expression that defines the *union* of the two languages defined by the individual expressions. We have done this with languages as sets before, but now we are doing it with these emerging language-defining expressions.

We should note that this use of the plus sign is consistent with the principle that in these expressions plus means choice. When we add sets to form a union, we are saying first choose the left set or the right set and then find a word in that set. In the expression above, first choose $(a + b)*a(a + b)*$ or **b*** and then make further choices for the pluses and stars and finally arrive at a word that is included in the total language defined by the expression. In this way, we see that the use of plus for union is actually a natural equivalence of the use of plus for choice.

Notice that this use of the plus sign is far from the normal meaning of addition in the algebraic sense, as we can see from

$$a* = a* + a*$$
$$a* = a* + a* + a*$$
$$a* = a* + aaa$$

For plus as union or plus as choice, these all make sense; for plus as algebra, they lead to presumptions of subtractions that are misguided. ∎

EXAMPLE

The language of all words that have at least two *a*'s can be described by the expression

$$(\mathbf{a} + \mathbf{b})^*\mathbf{a}(\mathbf{a} + \mathbf{b})^*\mathbf{a}(\mathbf{a} + \mathbf{b})^*$$

= (some beginning)(the first important *a*)(some middle)(the second important *a*)(some end)

where the arbitrary parts can have as many *a*'s (or *b*'s) as they want.   ■

EXAMPLE

Another expression that denotes all the words with at least two *a*'s is

$$\mathbf{b}^*\mathbf{ab}^*\mathbf{a}(\mathbf{a} + \mathbf{b})^*$$

We scan through some jungle of *b*'s (or no *b*'s) until we find the first *a*, then more *b*'s (or no *b*'s), then the second *a*, then we finish up with anything. In this set are *abbbabb* and *aaaaa*.
    We can write

$$(\mathbf{a} + \mathbf{b})^*\mathbf{a}(\mathbf{a} + \mathbf{b})^*\mathbf{a}(\mathbf{a} + \mathbf{b})^* = \mathbf{b}^*\mathbf{ab}^*\mathbf{a}(\mathbf{a} + \mathbf{b})^*$$

where by the equal sign we do not mean that these *expressions* are equal algebraically in the same way as

$$x + x = 2x$$

but that they are equal because they describe the same item, as with

16th President = Abraham Lincoln

We could write

language$((\mathbf{a} + \mathbf{b})^*\mathbf{a}(\mathbf{a} + \mathbf{b})^*\mathbf{a}(\mathbf{a} + \mathbf{b})^*)$
= language$(\mathbf{b}^*\mathbf{ab}^*\mathbf{a}(\mathbf{a} + \mathbf{b})^*)$
= all words with at least two *a*'s

To be careful about this point, we say that two expressions are **equivalent** if they describe the same language.
    The expressions below also describe the language of words with at least two *a*'s:

$$(\mathbf{a} + \mathbf{b})^*\mathbf{ab}^*\mathbf{ab}^*$$
$$\uparrow \quad \uparrow$$
next-to- last *a*
last *a*

and

$$\mathbf{b}^*\mathbf{a}(\mathbf{a} + \mathbf{b})^*\mathbf{ab}^*$$
$$\uparrow \qquad\qquad \uparrow$$
first *a*   last *a*   ■

EXAMPLE

If we wanted all the words with *exactly* two *a*'s, we could use the expression

$$\mathbf{b}^*\mathbf{ab}^*\mathbf{ab}^*$$

which describes such words as *aab, baba,* and *bbbabbbab*. To make the word *aab*, we let the first and second **b*** become **Λ** and the last becomes *b*. ∎

EXAMPLE

The language of all words that have at least one *a* and at least one *b* is somewhat trickier. If we write

$$(a + b)^*a(a + b)^*b(a + b)^*$$
$$= \text{(arbitrary) } a\text{(arbitrary) } b\text{(arbitrary)}$$

we are then requiring that an *a* precede a *b* in the word. Such words as *ba* and *bbaaaa* are not included in this set. Since, however, we know that either the *a* comes before the *b* or the *b* comes before the *a*, we could define this set by the expression

$$(a + b)^*a(a + b)^*b(a + b)^* + (a + b)^*b(a + b)^*a(a + b)^*$$

Here, we are still using the plus sign in the general sense of disjunction (or). We are taking the union of two sets, but it is more correct to think of this + as offering alternatives in forming words.

There is a simpler expression that defines the same language. If we are confident that the only words that are omitted by the first term

$$(a + b)^*a(a + b)^*b(a + b)^*$$

are the words of the form some *b*'s followed by some *a*'s, then it would be sufficient to add these specific exceptions into the set. These exceptions are all defined by the regular expression

$$bb^*aa^*$$

The language of all words over the alphabet $\Sigma = \{a \quad b\}$ that contain both an *a* and a *b* is therefore also defined by the expression

$$(a + b)^*a(a + b)^*b(a + b)^* + bb^*aa^*$$

Notice that it is necessary to write **bb*aa*** because **b*a*** will admit words we do not want, such as *aaa*.

We have shown that

$$(a + b)^*a(a + b)^*b(a + b)^* + (a + b)^*b(a + b)^*a(a + b)^* = (a + b)^*a(a + b)^*b(a + b)^* + bb^*aa^*$$

∎

EXAMPLE

The only words that do not contain both an *a* and a *b* in them somewhere are the words of all *a*'s, all *b*'s, or **Λ**. When these are included, we get everything. Therefore, the regular expression

$$(a + b)^*a(a + b)^*b(a + b)^* + bb^*aa^* + a^* + b^*$$

defines all possible strings of *a*'s and *b*'s. The word **Λ** is included in both **a*** and **b***.

We can then write

$$(a + b)^* = (a + b)^*a(a + b)^*b(a + b)^* + bb^*aa^* + a^* + b^*$$

which is not a very obvious equivalence at all. ∎

We must not misinterpret the fact that every regular expression defines some language to mean that the associated language has a simple English description, such as in the preceding examples. It may very well be that the regular expression itself is the simplest description of the particular language. For example,

$$(\Lambda + \mathbf{ba}^*)(\mathbf{ab}^*\mathbf{a} + \mathbf{ba}^*)^*\mathbf{b}(\mathbf{a}^* + \mathbf{b}^*\mathbf{a})\mathbf{bab}^*$$

probably has no cute concise alternate characterization. And even if it does reduce to something simple, there is no way of knowing this. That is, there is no algorithm to discover hidden **meaning.**

EXAMPLE

All temptation to treat these language-defining expressions as if they were algebraic polynomials should be dispelled by these equivalences:

$$(\mathbf{a} + \mathbf{b})^* = (\mathbf{a} + \mathbf{b})^* + (\mathbf{a} + \mathbf{b})^*$$
$$(\mathbf{a} + \mathbf{b})^* = (\mathbf{a} + \mathbf{b})^* + \mathbf{a}^*$$
$$(\mathbf{a} + \mathbf{b})^* = (\mathbf{a} + \mathbf{b})^*(\mathbf{a} + \mathbf{b})^*$$
$$(\mathbf{a} + \mathbf{b})^* = \mathbf{a}(\mathbf{a} + \mathbf{b})^* + \mathbf{b}(\mathbf{a} + \mathbf{b})^* + \Lambda$$
$$(\mathbf{a} + \mathbf{b})^* = (\mathbf{a} + \mathbf{b})^*\mathbf{ab}(\mathbf{a} + \mathbf{b})^* + \mathbf{b}^*\mathbf{a}^*$$

The last of these equivalences requires some explanation. It means that all the words that do not contain the substring *ab* (which are accounted for in the first term) are all *a*'s, all *b*'s, Λ, or some *b*'s followed by some *a*'s. All four missing types are covered by $\mathbf{b}^*\mathbf{a}^*$.   ■

Usually, when we employ the star operator, we are defining an infinite language. We can represent a finite language by using the plus sign (union sign) alone. If the language L over the alphabet $\Sigma = \{a \quad b\}$ contains only the finite list of words

$$L = \{abba \quad baaa \quad bbbb\}$$

then we can represent L by the symbolic expression

$$L = \text{language}(\mathbf{abba} + \mathbf{baaa} + \mathbf{bbbb})$$

Every word in L is some choice of options of this expression.

If L is a finite language that includes the null word Λ, then the expression that defines L must also employ the symbol Λ.

For example, if

$$L = \{\Lambda \quad a \quad aa \quad bbb\}$$

then the symbolic expression for L must be

$$L = \text{language}(\Lambda + \mathbf{a} + \mathbf{aa} + \mathbf{bbb})$$

The symbol Λ is a very useful addition to our system of language-defining symbolic expressions.

EXAMPLE

Let V be the language of all strings of a's and b's in which either the strings are all b's or else there is an a followed by some b's. Let V also contain the word Λ:

$$V = \{\Lambda \quad a \quad b \quad ab \quad bb \quad abb \quad bbb \quad abbb \quad bbbb \ . \ . \ .\}$$

We can define V by the expression

$$\mathbf{b}^* + \mathbf{ab}^*$$

where the word Λ is included in the term $\mathbf{b}^*$. Alternatively, we could define V by the expression

$$(\Lambda + \mathbf{a})\mathbf{b}^*$$

This would mean that in front of the string of some b's, we have the option of either adding an a or nothing. Since we could always write $\mathbf{b}^* = \Lambda \mathbf{b}^*$, we have what appears to be some sort of distributive law at work:

$$\Lambda \mathbf{b}^* + \mathbf{ab}^* = (\Lambda + \mathbf{a})\mathbf{b}^*$$

We have factored out the $\mathbf{b}^*$ just as in algebra. It is because of this analogy to algebra that we have denoted our disjunction by the plus sign instead of the union sign $\cup$ or the symbolic logic sign $\vee$. Sometimes, we like it to look algebraic; sometimes, we do not. ∎

We have a hybrid system: The $*$ is somewhat like an exponent and the $+$ is somewhat like addition. But the analogies to algebra should be approached very suspiciously, since addition in algebra never means choice and algebraic multiplication has properties different from concatenation (even though we sometimes conventionally refer to it as a product):

$$ab = ba \qquad \text{in algebra, they are the same numerical product}$$
$$ab \neq ba \qquad \text{in formal languages, they are different words}$$

Let us reconsider the language

$$T = \{a \quad c \quad ab \quad cb \quad abb \quad cbb \ . \ . \ .\}$$

T can be defined as above by

$$(\mathbf{a} + \mathbf{c})\mathbf{b}^*$$

but it can also be defined by

$$\mathbf{ab}^* + \mathbf{cb}^*$$

This is another example of the distributive law.

However, the distributive law must be used with extreme caution. Sometimes, it is difficult to determine whether if the law is applicable. Expressions may be distributed but operators cannot. Certainly, the star alone cannot always be distributed without changing the meaning of the expression. For example, as we have noted earlier, $(\mathbf{ab})^* \neq \mathbf{a}^*\mathbf{b}^*$. The language associated with $(\mathbf{ab})^*$ is words with alternating a's and b's, whereas the language associated with $\mathbf{a}^*\mathbf{b}^*$ is only strings where all the a's (if any) precede all the b's (also if any).

To make the identification between the regular expressions and their associated languages more explicit, we need to define the operation of multiplication of sets of words, a concept we have used informally already.

DEFINITION

If S and T are sets of strings of letters (whether they are finite or infinite sets), we define the **product set** of strings of letters to be.

$ST = \{$all combinations of a string from S concatenated with a string from T in that order$\}$

∎

EXAMPLE

If

$$S = \{a \quad aa \quad aaa\}, \qquad T = \{bb \quad bbb\}$$

then

$$ST = \{abb \quad abbb \quad aabb \quad aabbb \quad aaabb \quad aaabbb\}$$

Note that these words are not in proper lexicographic order. ■

EXAMPLE

If

$$S = \{a \quad bb \quad bab\}, \qquad T = \{a \quad ab\}$$

then

$$ST = \{aa \quad aab \quad bba \quad bbab \quad baba \quad babab\}$$ ■

EXAMPLE

If

$$P = \{a \quad bb \quad bab\}, \qquad Q = \{\Lambda \quad bbbb\}$$

then

$$PQ = \{a \quad bb \quad bab \quad abbbb \quad bbbbbb \quad babbbbb\}$$ ■

EXAMPLE

If L is any language, then

$$L\,\Lambda = \Lambda\,L = L$$ ■

EXAMPLE

If

$$M = \{\Lambda \quad x \quad xx\}, \qquad N = \{\Lambda \quad y \quad yy \quad yyy \quad yyyy \ . \ . \ .\}$$

then

$$MN = \{\Lambda \quad y \quad yy \quad yyy \quad yyyy \ . \ . \ .$$
$$x \quad xy \quad xyy \quad xyyy \quad xyyyy \ . \ . \ .$$
$$xx \quad xxy \quad xxyy \quad xxyyy \quad xxyyyy \ . \ . \ .\}$$ ■

Using regular expressions, we can write these five examples as

$$(\mathbf{a} + \mathbf{aa} + \mathbf{aaa})(\mathbf{bb} + \mathbf{bbb}) = \mathbf{abb} + \mathbf{abbb} + \mathbf{aabb} + \mathbf{aabbb} + \mathbf{aaabb} + \mathbf{aaabbb}$$
$$(\mathbf{a} + \mathbf{bb} + \mathbf{bab})(\mathbf{a} + \mathbf{ab}) = \mathbf{aa} + \mathbf{aab} + \mathbf{bba} + \mathbf{bbab} + \mathbf{baba} + \mathbf{babab}$$

$$(a + bb + bab)(\Lambda + bbbb) = a + bb + bab + ab^4 + b^6 + bab^5$$
$$r\Lambda = \Lambda r = r$$
$$(\Lambda + x + xx)(y^*) = y^* + xy^* + xxy^*$$

EXAMPLE

If FRENCH and GERMAN are their usual languages, then the product FRENCHGERMAN is the language of all strings that start with a FRENCH word and finish with a GERMAN word. Some words in this language are ennuiverboten and souffléGesundheit. ∎

It might not be clear why we cannot just leave the rules for associating a language with a regular expression on the informal level, with the informal instruction "make choices for + and *." The reason is that the informal phrase "make choices" is much harder to explain precisely than the formal mathematical presentation below.

⚜ LANGUAGES ASSOCIATED WITH REGULAR EXPRESSIONS

We are now ready to give the rules for associating a language with every regular expression. As we might suspect, the method for doing this is given recursively.

DEFINITION

The following rules define the **language associated** with any regular expression:

Rule 1   The language associated with the regular expression that is just a single letter is that one-letter word alone and the language associated with Λ is just $\{\Lambda\}$, a one-word language.

Rule 2   If r_1 is a regular expression associated with the language L_1 and r_2 is a regular expression associated with the language L_2, then:

    (i)   The regular expression $(r_1)(r_2)$ is associated with the product $L_1 L_2$ that is the language L_1 times L_2:

$$\text{language}(r_1 r_2) = L_1 L_2$$

    (ii)   The regular expression $r_1 + r_2$ is associated with the language formed by the union of the sets L_1 and L_2:

$$\text{language}(r_1 + r_2) = L_1 + L_2$$

    (iii)   The language associated with the regular expression $(r_1)^*$ is L_1^*, the Kleene closure of the set L_1 as a set of words:

$$\text{language}(r_1^*) = L_1^*$$ ∎

Once again, this collection of rules *proves* recursively that there is some language associated with every regular expression. As we build up a regular expression from the rules, we simultaneously are building up the corresponding language.

The rules seem to show us how we can interpret the regular expression as a language, but they do not really tell us how to *understand* the language. By this we mean that if we apply the rules above to the regular expression

$$(a + b)^*a(a + b)^*b(a + b)^* + bb^*aa^*$$

we can develop a description of some language, but can we understand that this is the language of all strings that have both an *a* and a *b* in them? This is a question of meaning.

This correspondence between regular expressions and languages leaves open two other questions. We have already seen examples where completely different regular expressions end up describing the same language. Is there some way of telling when this happens? By "way" we mean, of course, an algorithm. We shall present an algorithmic procedure in Chapter 11 to determine whether or not two regular expressions define the same language.

Another fundamental question is this: We have seen that every regular expression is associated with some language; is it also true that every language can be described by a regular expression? In our next theorem, we show that every *finite* language can be defined by a regular expression. The situation for languages with infinitely many words is different. We shall prove in Chapter 10 that there are some languages that cannot be defined by any regular expression.

As to the first and perhaps most important question, the question of *understanding* regular expressions, we have not a clue. Before we can construct an algorithm for obtaining understanding, we must have some good definition of what it means *to understand*. We may be centuries away from being able to do that, if it can be done at all.

⚜ FINITE LANGUAGES ARE REGULAR

THEOREM 5

If *L* is a finite language (a language with only finitely many words), then *L* can be defined by a regular expression. In other words, all finite languages are regular.

PROOF

To make one regular expression that defines the language *L*, turn all the words in *L* into boldface type and insert plus signs between them. Voilà.

For example, the regular expression that defines the language

$$L = \{baa \quad abbba \quad bababa\}$$

is

baa + abbba + bababa

If

$$L = \{aa \quad ab \quad ba \quad bb\}$$

the algorithm described above gives the regular expression

aa + ab + ba + bb

Another regular expression that defines this language is

(a + b)(a + b)

so the regular expression need not be unique, but so what. We need only show that at least *one* regular expression exists.

The reason this trick only works for finite languages is that an infinite language would become a regular expression that is infinitely long, which is forbidden. ∎

EXAMPLE

Let

$$L = (\Lambda \quad x \quad xx \quad xxx \quad xxxx \quad xxxxx)$$

The regular expression we get from the theorem is

$$\Lambda + x + xx + xxx + xxxx + xxxxx$$

A more elegant regular expression for this language is

$$(\Lambda + x)^5$$

Of course, the 5 is, strictly speaking, not a legal symbol for a regular expression although we all understand it means

$$(\Lambda + x)(\Lambda + x)(\Lambda + x)(\Lambda + x)(\Lambda + x)$$

∎

⚜ HOW HARD IT IS TO UNDERSTAND A REGULAR EXPRESSION

Let us examine some regular expressions and see if we are lucky enough to understand something about the languages they represent.

EXAMPLE

Consider the expression

$$(a + b)^*(aa + bb)(a + b)^*$$

This is the set of strings of *a*'s and *b*'s that at some point contain a double letter. We can think of it as

$$(\text{arbitrary})(\text{double letter})(\text{arbitrary})$$

Let us now ask, "What strings do not contain a double letter?" Some examples are Λ *a* *b* *ab* *ba* *aba* *bab* *abab* *baba* . . . . The expression (**ab**)* covers all of these except those that begin with *b* or end in *a*. Adding these choices gives us the regular expression

$$(\Lambda + b)(ab)^*(\Lambda + a)$$

Combining these two gives

$$(a + b)^*(aa + bb)(a + b)^* + (\Lambda + b)(ab)^*(\Lambda + a)$$

Who among us is so boldfaced as to claim that seeing the expression above they could tell immediately that it defines all strings? ∎

EXAMPLE

Consider the regular expression below:

$$E = \ \textbf{(a + b)}\textbf{*} \ \textbf{a} \ \textbf{(a + b)}\textbf{*} \quad \textbf{(a + } \Lambda\textbf{)} \quad \textbf{(a + b)}\textbf{*} \ \textbf{a} \ \textbf{(a + b)}\textbf{*}$$
$$= \text{(arbitrary)} \ a \ \text{(arbitrary)} \ (a \text{ or nothing)} \ \text{(arbitrary)} \ a \ \text{(arbitrary)}$$

One obvious fact is that all the words in the language of E must have at least two a's in them. Let us break up the middle plus sign into its two cases: Either the middle factor contributes an a or else it contributes a Λ. Therefore,

$$E = \textbf{(a + b)*a(a + b)*a(a + b)*a(a + b)*}$$
$$+ \ \textbf{(a + b)*a(a + b)*} \Lambda \textbf{(a + b)*a(a + b)*}$$

This is a more detailed use of the distributive law. The first term above clearly represents all words that have at least three a's in them. Before we analyze the second term, let us make the observation that

$$\textbf{(a + b)*} \Lambda \textbf{(a + b)*}$$

which occurs in the middle of the second term, is only another way of saying "any string whatsoever" and could be replaced with the more direct expression

$$\textbf{(a + b)*}$$

This would reduce the second term of the expression to

$$\textbf{(a + b)*a(a + b)*a(a + b)*}$$

which we have already seen is a regular expression representing all words that have at least two a's in them.

Therefore, the language associated with E is the union of all strings that have three or more a's with all strings that have two or more a's. But since all strings with three or more a's are themselves already strings with two or more a's, this whole language is just the second set alone.

The language associated with E is no different from the language associated with

$$\textbf{(a + b)*a(a + b)*a(a + b)*}$$

which we have examined before with three of its avatars. ■

It is possible by repeated application of the rules for forming regular expressions to produce an expression in which the star operator is applied to a subexpression that already has a star in it.

Some examples are

$$\textbf{(a + b*)*} \quad \textbf{(aa + ab*)*} \quad \textbf{((a + bbba*) + ba*b)*}$$

In the first of these expressions, the internal * adds nothing to the language

$$\textbf{(a + b*)*} = \textbf{(a + b)*}$$

since all possible strings of a's and b's are described by both expressions.

Also, in accordance with Theorem 1 on p. 18,

$$\textbf{(a*)*} = \textbf{a*}$$

However,

$$(aa + ab*)* \neq (aa + ab)*$$

since the language for the expression on the left includes the word *abbabb*, whereas the language on the right does not. (The language defined by the regular expression on the right cannot contain any word with a double *b*.)

If one had not just seen this explained, would it be obvious?

EXAMPLE

Consider the regular expression

$$(a*b*)*$$

The language defined by this expression is all strings that can be made up of factors of the form **a*b***, but since both the single letter *a* and the single letter *b* are words of the form **a*b***, this language contains all strings of *a*'s and *b*'s. It cannot contain more than everything, so

$$(a*b*)* = (a + b)*$$ ∎

The equation above casts a major doubt on the possibility of finding a set of algebraic rules to reduce one regular expression to another equivalent one. Yet, it is still unknown whether this can be done.

EXAMPLE

Consider the language defined by the regular expression

$$b*(abb*)*(\Lambda + a)$$

This is the language of all words *without* a double *a*. The typical word here starts with some *b*'s. Then come repeated factors of the form **abb*** (an *a* followed by at least one *b*). Then we finish up with a final *a* or we leave the last *b*'s as they are. This is another starred expression with a star inside. ∎

If we are simply interested in being devilish and creating a mess, we can do so recursively. Let us start with the observation that all strings either have a double *a* or isolated *a*'s as in the example above:

$$(a + b)* = (a + b)*aa(a + b)* + b*(abb*)*(\Lambda + a)$$

Now, let us use **(a*b*)*** instead of the first **(a + b)***:

$$(a + b)* = (a*b*)*aa(a + b)* + b*(abb*)*(\Lambda + a)$$

Now, once we note that the entire right-hand side is equivalent to **(a + b)***, we can use it (the whole expression) to substitute for the subexpression **(a + b)*** on the right. This gives

$$(a + b)* = (a*b*)*aa[(a*b*)*aa(a + b)* + b*(abb*)*(\Lambda + a)] + b*(abb*)*(\Lambda + a)$$

There is still a substring **(a + b)*** on the right-hand side and we can again recursively replace it by the whole expression above. And so on, ad nauseam. The sole application of creating needlessly complicated expressions equivalent to much simpler ones is to make the instructor's job in grading homework exponentially more difficult.

⚜ INTRODUCING EVEN-EVEN

One very interesting example, which we consider now in great detail and carry with us throughout the book, is

$$E = [\mathbf{aa} + \mathbf{bb} + (\mathbf{ab} + \mathbf{ba})(\mathbf{aa} + \mathbf{bb})^*(\mathbf{ab} + \mathbf{ba})]^*$$

This regular expression represents the collection of all words that are made up of "syllables" of three types:

$$\text{type}_1 = \mathbf{aa}$$
$$\text{type}_2 = \mathbf{bb}$$
$$\text{type}_3 = (\mathbf{ab} + \mathbf{ba})(\mathbf{aa} + \mathbf{bb})^*(\mathbf{ab} + \mathbf{ba})$$
$$E = [\text{type}_1 + \text{type}_2 + \text{type}_3]^*$$

Suppose that we are scanning along a word in the language of E from left to right, reading the letters two at a time. First, we come to a double a (type$_1$), then to a double b (type$_2$), then to another double a (type$_1$ again). Then perhaps we come upon a pair of letters that are not the same. Say, for instance, that the next two letters are ba. This must begin a substring of type$_3$. It starts with an undoubled pair (either ab or ba), then it has a section of doubled letters (many repetitions of either aa or bb), and then it finally ends with another undoubled pair (either ab or ba again). One property of this section of the word is that it has an even number of a's and an even number of b's, counting the two undoubles and all the doubles. After this section of type$_3$, we could proceed with more sections of type$_1$ or type$_2$ until we encountered another undoubled pair, starting another type$_3$ section. We know that another undoubled pair will be coming up to balance off the initial one. The total effect is that every word of the language of E contains an even number of a's and an even number of b's.

If this were all we wanted to conclude, we could have done so more quickly. All words in the language of E are made up of these three types of substrings and, since each of these three has an even number of a's and an even number of b's, the whole word must, too. However, a stronger statement is also true. *All* strings with an even number of a's and an even number of b's belong to the language of E. The proof of this parallels our argument above.

Consider a word w with even a's and even b's. If the first two letters are the same, we have a type$_1$ or type$_2$ syllable. Scan over the doubled letter pairs until we come to an unmatched pair such as ab or ba. Continue scanning by skipping over the double a's and double b's that get in the way until we find the *balancing unmatched* pair (either ab or ba) to even off the count of a's and b's. If the word ends before we find such a pair, the a's and b's are not even. Once we have found the balancing unmatched pair, we have completed a syllable of type$_3$. By "balancing," we do not mean it has to be the same unmatched pair: ab can be balanced by either ab or ba. Consider them bookends or open and close parentheses; whenever we see one, we must later find another. Therefore, E represents the language of all strings with even a's and even b's.

Let us consider this as a computer algorithm. We are about to feed in a long string of a's and b's, and we want to determine whether this string has the property that the number of a's is even and the number of b's is even. One method is to keep two binary flags, the a flag and the b flag. Every time an a is read, the a flag is reversed (0 to 1, or 1 to 0); every time a b is read, the b flag is reversed. We start both flags at 0 and check to be sure they are both 0 at the end. This method will work.

But there is another method that also works which uses only one flag—the method that corresponds to the discussion above. Let us have only one flag called the type$_3$ flag. We read the letters in two at a time. If they are the same, then we do not touch the type$_3$ flag, since we have a factor of type$_1$ or type$_2$. If, however, the two letters read do not match, we throw the type$_3$ flag. If the flag starts at 0, then whenever it is 1, we are in the middle of a type$_3$ factor;

whenever it is 0, we are not. If it is 0 at the end, then the input string contains an even number of a's and an even number of b's.

For example, if the input is

$$(aa)(ab)(bb)(ba)(ab)(bb)(bb)(bb)(ab)(ab)(bb)(ba)(aa)$$

the flag is reversed six times and ends at 0.

We will refer to this language again later, so we give it the name EVEN-EVEN.

$$\text{EVEN-EVEN} = \{\Lambda \quad aa \quad bb \quad aaaa \quad aabb \quad abab \quad abba \quad baab \quad baba$$
$$bbaa \quad bbbb \quad aaaaaa \quad aaaabb \quad aaabab \ldots\}$$

Notice that there do not have to be the same number of a's and b's, just an even quantity of each.

⚜ PROBLEMS

1. Let $\mathbf{r}_1$, $\mathbf{r}_2$, and $\mathbf{r}_3$ be three regular expressions. Show that the language associated with $(\mathbf{r}_1 + \mathbf{r}_2)\mathbf{r}_3$ is the same as the language associated with $\mathbf{r}_1\mathbf{r}_3 + \mathbf{r}_2\mathbf{r}_3$. Show that $\mathbf{r}_1(\mathbf{r}_2 + \mathbf{r}_3)$ is equivalent to $\mathbf{r}_1\mathbf{r}_2 + \mathbf{r}_1\mathbf{r}_3$. This will be the same as proving a "distributive law" for regular expressions.

For Problems 2 through 11, construct a regular expression defining each of the following languages over the alphabet $\Sigma = \{a \quad b\}$:

2. All words in which a appears tripled, if at all. This means that every clump of a's contains 3 or 6 or 9 or 12 . . . a's.

3. All words that contain at least one of the strings $s_1, s_2, s_3,$ or s_4.

4. All words that contain exactly two b's or exactly three b's, not more.

5. (i) All strings that end in a double letter.
(ii) All strings that do not end in a double letter.

6. All strings that have exactly one double letter in them.

7. All strings in which the letter b is *never* tripled. This means that no word contains the substring bbb.

8. All words in which a is tripled or b is tripled, but not both. This means each word contains the substring aaa or the substring bbb but not both.

9. (i) All words that do not have the substring ab.
(ii) All words that do not have both the substrings bba and abb.

10. All strings in which the *total* number of a's is divisible by 3 no matter how they are distributed, such as $aabaabbaba$.

11. (i) All strings in which any b's that occur are found in clumps of an odd number at a time, such as $abaabbbab$.
(ii) All strings that have an even number of a's and an odd number of b's.
(iii) All strings that have an odd number of a's and an odd number of b's.

12. (i) Let us reconsider the regular expression

$$(\mathbf{a} + \mathbf{b})*\mathbf{a}(\mathbf{a} + \mathbf{b})*\mathbf{b}(\mathbf{a} + \mathbf{b})*$$

Show that this is equivalent to

$$(a + b)*ab(a + b)*$$

in the sense that they define the same language.
(ii) Show that

$$(a + b)*ab(a + b)* + b*a* = (a + b)*$$

(iii) Show that

$$(a + b)*ab[(a + b)*ab(a + b)* + b*a*] + b*a* = (a + b)*$$

(iv) Is (iii) the last variation of this theme or are there more beasts left in this cave?

13. We have defined the product of two sets of strings in general. If we apply this to the case where both factors are the same set, $S = T$, we obtain squares, S^2. Similarly, we can define $S^3, S^4, \ldots$. Show that it makes some sense to write:
    (i) $S^* = \Lambda + S + S^1 + S^2 + S^3 + S^4 + \cdots$
    (ii) $S^+ = S + S^1 + S^2 + S^3 + S^4 + \cdots$

14. If the only difference between L and L^* is the word Λ, is the only difference between L^2 and L^* the word Λ?

For Problems 15 through 17, show that the following pairs of regular expressions define the same language over the alphabet $\Sigma = \{a \quad b\}$:

15. (i) **(ab)*a** and **a(ba)***
    (ii) **(a* + b)*** and **(a + b)***
    (iii) **(a* + b*)*** and **(a + b)***

16. (i) **Λ*** and **Λ**
    (ii) **(a*b)*a*** and **a*(ba*)***
    (iii) **(a*bbb)*a*** and **a*(bbba*)***

17. (i) **((a + bb)*aa)*** and **Λ + (a + bb)*aa**
    (ii) **(aa)*(Λ + a)** and **a***
    (iii) **a(aa)*(Λ + a)b + b** and **a*b**
    (iv) **a(ba + a)*b** and **aa*b(aa*b)***
    (v) **Λ + a(a + b)* + (a + b)*aa(a + b)*** and **((b*a)*ab*)***

18. Describe (in English phrases) the languages associated with the following regular expressions:
    (i) **(a + b)*a(Λ + bbbb)**
    (ii) **(a(a + bb)*)***
    (iii) **(a(aa)*b(bb)*)***
    (iv) **(b(bb)*)*(a(aa)*b(bb)*)***
    (v) **(b(bb)*)*(a(aa)*b(bb)*)*(a(aa)*)***
    (vi) **((a + b)a)***

19. (D. N. Arden) Let R, S, and T be three languages and assume that Λ is not in S. Prove the following statements:
    (i) From the premise that $R = SR + T$, we can conclude that $R = S^*T$.
    (ii) From the premise that $R = S^*T$, we can conclude that $R = SR + T$.

20. (i) Explain why we can take any pair of equivalent regular expressions and replace the letter a in both with any regular expression **R** and the letter b with any regular ex-

pression **S** and the resulting regular expressions will have the same language. For example, 16(ii), which says

$$(a*b)*a* = a*(ba*)*$$

becomes the identity

$$(R*S)*R* = R*(SR*)*$$

which is true for all regular expressions **R** and **S**. In particular, **R** = **a** + **bb**, **S** = **ba*** results in the complicated identity

$$((a + bb)*(ba*))*(a + bb)* = (a + bb)*((ba*)(a + bb)*)*$$

(ii) What identity would result from using

$$R = (ba*)* \qquad S = (\Lambda + b)$$

CHAPTER 5

Finite Automata

⚜ YET ANOTHER METHOD FOR DEFINING LANGUAGES

Several games that children play fit the following description. Pieces are set up on a playing board. Dice are thrown (or a wheel is spun), and a number is generated at random. Depending on the number, the pieces on the board must be rearranged in a fashion completely specified by the rules. The child has no options about changing the board. Everything is determined by the dice. Usually, it is then some other child's turn to throw the dice and make his or her move, but this hardly matters, because no skill or choice is involved. We could eliminate the opponent and have the one child move first the white pieces and then the black. Whether or not the white pieces win the game is dependent entirely on what sequence of numbers is generated by the dice, not on who moves them.

Let us look at all possible positions of the pieces on the board and call them **states.** The game changes from one state to another in a fashion determined by the input of a certain number. For each possible number, there is one and only one resulting state. We should allow for the possibility that after a number is entered, the game is still in the same state as it was before. (For example, if a player who is in "jail" needs to roll doubles in order to get out, any other roll leaves the board in the same state.) After a certain number of rolls, the board arrives at a state that means a victory for one of the players and the game is over. We call this a **final state.** There might be many possible final states that result in victory for this player. In computer theory, these are also called **halting states, terminal states,** or **accepting states.**

Beginning with the initial state (which we presume to be unique), some input sequences of numbers lead to victory for the first child and some do not.

Let us put this game back on the shelf and take another example. A child has a simple computer (input device, processing unit, memory, output device) and wishes to calculate the sum of 3 plus 4. The child writes a program, which is a sequence of instructions that are fed into the machine one at a time. Each instruction is executed as soon as it is read, and then the next instruction is read. If all goes well, the machine outputs the number 7 and terminates execution. We can consider this process to be similar to the board-game. Here the board is the computer and the different arrangements of pieces on the board correspond to the different arrangements of 0's and 1's in the cells of memory. Two machines are in the same state if their output pages look the same and their memories look the same cell by cell.

The computer is also **deterministic,** by which we mean that, on reading one particular input instruction, the machine converts itself from the state it was in to some particular other state (or remains in the same state if given a NO-OP), where the resultant state is completely determined by the prior state and the input instruction. Nothing else. No choice is involved. No knowledge is required of the state the machine was in six instructions ago. Some sequences of input instructions may lead to success (printing the 7) and some may not. Success is entirely determined by the sequence of inputs. Either the program will work or it will not.

As in the case of the board-game, in this model we have one initial state and the possibility of several successful final states. Printing the 7 is what is important; what is left in memory does not matter.

One small difference between these two situations is that in the child's game the number of pieces of input is determined by whether either player has yet reached a final state, whereas with the computer the number of pieces of input is a matter of choice made before run time. Still, the input string is the sole determinant as to whether the game child or the computer child wins his or her victory.

In the first example, we can consider the set of all possible dice rolls to be the letters of an alphabet. We can then define a certain language as the set of strings of those letters that lead to success, that is, lead to a final victory state. Similarly, in the second example we can consider the set of all computer instructions as the letters of an alphabet. We can then define a language to be the set of all words over this alphabet that lead to success. This is the language whose *words* are all *programs* that print a 7.

The most general model, of which both of these examples are instances, is called a **finite automaton**—"finite" because the number of possible states and number of letters in the alphabet are both finite, and "automaton" because the change of states is totally governed by the input. The determination of what state is next is automatic (involuntary and mechanical), not willful, just as the motion of the hands of a clock is automatic, while the motion of the hands of a human is presumably the result of desire and thought. We present the precise definition below. *Automaton* comes to us from the Greek, so its correct plural is *automata*.

DEFINITION

A **finite automaton** is a collection of three things:

1. A finite set of states, one of which is designated as the initial state, called the **start state,** and some (maybe none) of which are designated as **final states.**
2. An **alphabet** Σ of possible input letters.
3. A finite set of **transitions** that tell for each state and for each letter of the input alphabet which state to go to next. ■

The definition above is incomplete in the sense that it describes what a finite automaton *is* but not how it *works*. It works by being presented with an input string of letters that it reads letter by letter starting at the leftmost letter. Beginning at the start state, the letters determine a sequence of states. The sequence ends when the last input letter has been read.

Instead of writing out the whole phrase "finite automaton," it is customary to refer to one by its initials, FA. Computer theory is rife with acronyms, so we have many in this book. The term FA is read by naming its letters, so we say "an FA" even though it stands for "a finite automaton" and we say "two FAs" even though it stands for "two finite automata."

Some people prefer to call the object we have just defined a **finite acceptor** because its sole job is to **accept** certain input strings and reject others. It does not do anything like print output or play music. Even so, we shall stick to the terminology "finite automaton." When we build some in Chapter 8 that do do something, we give them special names, such as "finite automata with output."

Let us begin by considering in detail one particular example.

Suppose that the input alphabet has only the two letters a and b. Throughout this chapter, we use only this alphabet (except for a couple of problems at the end). Let us also assume that there are only three states, x, y, and z. Let the following be the rules of transition:

Rule 1   From state x and input a, go to state y.

Rule 2   From state x and input b, go to state z.

Rule 3   From state y and input a, go to state x.

Rule 4   From state y and input b, go to state z.

Rule 5   From state z and any input, stay at state z.

Let us also designate state x as the starting state and state z as the only final state.

We now have a perfectly defined finite automaton, because it fulfills all three requirements demanded above: states, alphabet, transitions.

Let us examine what happens to various input strings when presented to this FA. Let us start with the string aaa. We begin, as always, in state x. The first letter of the string is an a, and it tells us to go to state y (by Rule 1). The next input (instruction) is also an a, and this tells us by Rule 3 to go back to state x. The third input is another a, and by Rule 1 again we go to state y. There are no more input letters in the input string, so our trip has ended. We did not finish up in the final state (state z), so we have an unsuccessful termination of our run.

The string aaa is not in the language of all strings that leave this FA in state z. The set of all strings that do leave us in a final state is called **the language defined by the finite automaton**. The input string aaa is not in the language defined by this FA. Using other terminology, we may say that the string aaa is **not accepted** by this finite automaton because it does not lead to a final state. We use this expression often. We may also say, "aaa is **rejected** by this FA." The set of all strings accepted is the **language associated** with the FA. We say, "this FA **accepts** the language L," or "L is the **language accepted** by this FA." When we wish to be anthropomorphic, we say that L is the **language of** the FA. If language L_1 is contained in language L_2 and a certain FA accepts L_2 (all the words in L_2 are accepted and all the inputs accepted are words in L_2), then this FA also must accept all the words in language L_1 (because they are also words in L_2). However, we do not say, "L_1 is accepted by this FA" because that would mean that all the words the FA accepts are in L_1. This is solely a matter of standard usage.

At the moment, the only job an FA does is define the language it accepts, which is a fine reason for calling it an acceptor, or better still a **language-recognizer.** This last term is good because the FA merely recognizes whether the input string is in its language much the same way we might recognize when we hear someone speak Russian without necessarily understanding what it means.

Let us examine a different input string for this same FA. Let the input be $abba$. As always, we start in state x. Rule 1 tells us that the first input letter, a, takes us to state y. Once we are in state y, we read the second input letter, which is a b. Rule 4 now tells us to move to state z. The third input letter is a b, and because we are in state z, Rule 5 tells us to stay there. The fourth input letter is an a, and again Rule 5 says stay put. Therefore, after we have followed the instruction of each input letter, we end up in state z. State z is designated a final state, so we have won this game. The input string $abba$ has taken us successfully to the final state. The string $abba$ is therefore a word in the language associated with this FA. The word $abba$ is accepted by this FA.

It is not hard for us to predict which strings will be accepted by this FA. If an input string is made up of only the letter a repeated some number of times, then the action of the FA will be to jump back and forth between state x and state y. No such word can ever be accepted. To get into state z, it is necessary for the string to have the letter b in it. As soon as a b is encountered in the input string, the FA jumps immediately to state z no matter what state it was in before. Once in state z, it is impossible to leave. When the input string runs out, the FA will still be in state z, leading to acceptance of the string.

The FA above will accept all strings that have the letter b in them and no other strings. Therefore, the language associated with (or accepted by) this FA is the one defined by the regular expression

$$(a + b)*b(a + b)*$$

The list of transition rules can grow very long. It is much simpler to summarize them in a table format. Each row of the table is the name of one of the states in the FA, and each column of the table is a letter of the input alphabet. The entries inside the table are the new states that the FA moves into—the transition states. The **transition table** for the FA we have described is

	a	b
Start x	y	z
y	x	z
Final z	z	z

We have also indicated along the left side which states are start and final states. This table has all the information necessary to define an FA.

Instead of the lengthy description of the meaning of motion between states caused by input letters, FAs could simply and equivalently have been defined as static transition tables. Any table of the form

	a	b
x	•	•
y	•	•
z	•	•

in which the dots are filled with the letters x, y, and z in any fashion, and which specifies the start state and the final states, will be an FA. Similarly, every three-state FA corresponds to such a table.

Even though it is no more than a table of symbols, we consider an FA to be a **machine,** that is, we understand that this FA has dynamic capabilities. It moves. It processes input. Something *goes* from state to state as the input is read in and executed. We may imagine that the state we are in at any given time is lit up and the others are dark. An FA running on an input string then looks like a pinball machine in operation.

We may make the definition of FAs even more mathematically abstract (with no greater precision and decreased understanding) by replacing the transition table with a total function whose input is a pair of state and alphabet letter and whose output is a single state. This function is called the transition function, usually denoted δ (lowercase Greek delta) (for reasons lost to computer historians). The abstract definition of an FA is then:

1. A finite set of states $Q = \{q_0 \quad q_1 \quad q_2 \ldots\}$ of which q_0 is the start state.

2. A subset of Q called the final states.

3. An alphabet $\Sigma = \{x_1 \quad x_2 \quad x_3 \ldots\}$.

4. A transition function δ associating each pair of state and letter with a state:

$$\delta(q_i, x_j) = x_k$$

We shall never refer to this transition function again in this volume.

From the table format, it is hard to see the moving parts. There is a pictorial representation of an FA that gives us more of a feel for the motion. We begin by representing each state by a small circle drawn on a sheet of paper. From each state, we draw arrows showing to which other states the different letters of the input alphabet will lead us. We **label** these arrows with the corresponding alphabet letters.

If a certain letter makes a state go back to itself, we indicate this by an arrow that returns to the same circle — this arrow is called a **loop.** We can indicate the start state by labeling it with the word "start" or by a minus sign, and the final states by labeling them with the word "final" or plus signs. Notice that some states are neither − nor +. The machine we have already defined by the transition list and the transition table can be depicted by the **transition diagram**

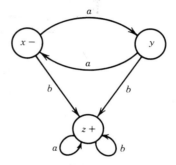

Sometimes, a start state is indicated by an arrow and a final state by drawing a box or another circle around its circle. The minus and plus signs, when employed, are drawn inside or outside the state circles. This machine can also be depicted as

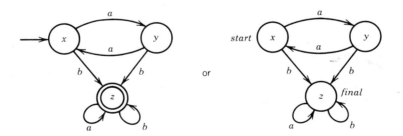

Every input string can be interpreted as traversing a path beginning at the start state and moving among the states (perhaps visiting the same state many times) and finally settling in some particular rest state. If it is a final state, then the path has ended in success. The letters of the input string dictate the directions of travel. They are the directions and the fuel needed for motion. When we are out of letters, we must stop.

Let us look at this machine again and at the paths generated by the input strings *aaaabba* and *bbaabbbb.*

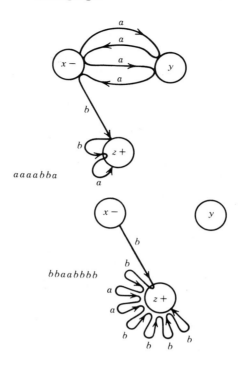

aaaabba

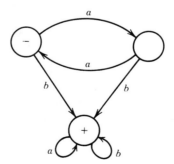

bbaabbbb

When we depict an FA as circles and arrows, we say that we have drawn a **directed graph.** Graph theory is an exciting subject in its own right, but for our purposes there is no real need to understand directed graphs in any deeper sense than as a collection of circles and arrows. We borrow from graph theory the name **directed edge,** or simply **edge,** for the arrow between states. An edge comes from one state and leads to another (or the same, if it is a loop). Every state has as many **outgoing edges** as there are letters in the alphabet. It is possible for a state to have no **incoming edges** or to have many.

There are machines for which it is not necessary to give the states specific names. For example, the FA we have been dealing with so far can be represented simply as

Even though we do not have names for the states, we can still determine whether a particular input string is accepted by this machine. We start at the minus sign and proceed along the indicated edges until we are out of input letters. If we are then at a plus sign, we accept the word; if not, we reject it as not being part of the language of the machine.

Let us consider some more simple examples of FAs.

EXAMPLE

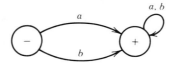

In the picture above, we have drawn one edge from the state on the right back into itself and given this loop the two labels a and b, separated by a comma, meaning that this is the path traveled if either letter is read. (We save ourselves from drawing a second loop edge.) We could have used the same convention to eliminate the need for two edges running from the minus state to the plus state. We could have replaced these with one edge with the label a, b, but we did not. At first glance, it looks as if this machine accepts everything. The first letter of the input takes us to the right-hand state and, once there, we are trapped forever. When the input string runs out, there we are in the correct final state. This description, however, omits the possibility that the input is the null string Λ. If the input string is the null string, we are left in the left-hand state, and we never get to the final state. There is a small problem about understanding how it is possible for Λ ever to be an input string to an FA, because a string, by definition, is executed (run) by reading its letters one at a time. By convention, we shall say that Λ starts in the start state and then ends right there on all FAs.

The language accepted by this machine is the set of all strings except Λ. This has the regular expression definitions

$$\mathbf{(a + b)(a + b)}\ast = \mathbf{(a + b)}^{+} \qquad\qquad \blacksquare$$

EXAMPLE

One of the many FAs that accepts all words is

Here, the sign $\pm$ means that the same state is both a start and a final state. Because there is only one state and no matter what happens we must stay there, the language for this machine is

$$\mathbf{(a + b)}\ast \qquad\qquad \blacksquare$$

Similarly, there are FAs that accept no language. These are of two types: FAs that have no final states, such as

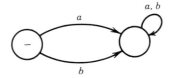

and FAs in which the circles that represent the final states cannot be reached from the start state. This may be either because the picture is in two separate components as with

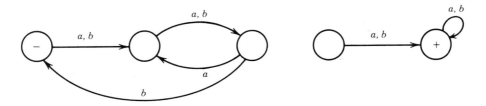

(in this case, we say that the graph is **disconnected**), or for a reason such as that shown below:

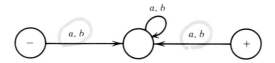

We consider these examples again in Chapter 11.

⚜ FAs AND THEIR LANGUAGES

It is possible to look at the world of FAs in two ways. We could start with the machine and try to analyze it to see what language it accepts, or we could start with a desired language in our mind and try to construct an FA that would act as a language-recognizer or language-definer. Needless to say, in real life we seldom discover an FA falling out of a cereal box or etched onto a mummy's sarcophagus; it is usually our desire to construct an FA from scratch for the precise purpose of acting as a language-recognizer for a specific language for which we were looking for a practical algorithmic definition.

When a language is defined by a regular expression, it is easy to produce some arbitrary words that are in the language by making a set of choices for the meaning of the pluses and stars, but it is harder to recognize whether a given string of letters is or is not in the language defined by the expression. The situation with an FA is just the opposite. If we are given a specific string, we can decide by an algorithmic procedure whether or not it is in the language defined by the machine—just run it and see if the path it determines ends in a final state. On the other hand, given a language defined by an FA, it is not so easy to write down a bunch of words that we know in advance the machine will accept.

Therefore, we must practice studying FA from two different angles: Given a language, can we build a machine for it, and given a machine, can we deduce its language?

EXAMPLE

Let us build a machine that accepts the language of all words over the alphabet {a   b} with an even number of letters. We can start our considerations with a human algorithm for identifying all these words. One method is to run our finger across the string from left to right and count the number of letters as we go. When we reach the end of the string, we examine the total and we know right away whether the string is in the language or not. This may be the way a mathematician would approach the problem, but it is not how a computer scientist would solve it. Because we are not interested in what the exact length of the string is, this number represents extraneous information gathered at the cost of needlessly many calculations. A good programmer would employ instead what is called a Boolean flag; let us call it *E* for even. If the number of letters read so far is indeed even, then *E* should have the value TRUE. If the number of letters read is not even, then *E* should have the value FALSE. Initially, we set *E* equal to TRUE, and every time we read a letter, we reverse the value of *E* until we have exhausted the input string. When the input letters have run out, we check the value of *E*. If it is TRUE, then the input string is in the language; if false, it is not.

The program looks something like this:

> set E = TRUE
> while not out of data do
>   read an input letter
>   E becomes not(E)
> if E = TRUE, accept the input string
>   else reject the string

Because the computer employs only one storage location in the processing of this program and that location can contain only one of two different values, the finite automaton for this language should require only two states:

State 1   *E* is TRUE; this is the start state and the accept or final state.

State 2   *E* is FALSE.

Every time an input letter is read, whether it is an *a* or a *b*, the state of the FA changes. This machine is pictured below:

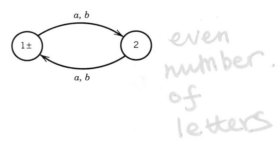

even number. of letters

EXAMPLE

Suppose we want to build a finite automaton that accepts all the words in the language

$$a(a + b)*$$

that is, all the strings that begin with the letter *a*. We start at state *x* and, if the first letter read is a *b*, we go to a dead-end state *y*. (A "dead-end state" is an informal way of describing a state that no string can leave once it has entered.) If the first letter is an *a*, we go to the dead-end state *z*, where *z* is a final state. The machine looks like this:

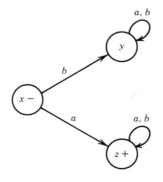

The same language may be accepted by a four-state machine, as below:

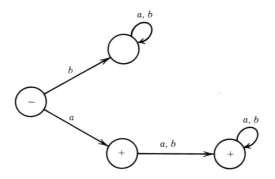

Only the word *a* ends in the first + state. All other words starting with an *a* reach and finish in the second + state where they are accepted.

This idea can be carried further to a five-state FA as below:

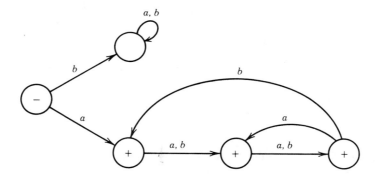

The examples above are FAs that have more than one final state. From them, we can see that there is not a unique machine for a given language. We may then ask the question, "Is there always at least one FA that accepts each possible language? More precisely, if *L* is some language, is there necessarily a machine of this type that accepts exactly the inputs in *L*, while forsaking all others?" We shall see shortly that this question is related to the question, "Can all languages be represented by regular expressions?" We shall prove, in Chapter 7, that every language that can be accepted by an FA can be defined by a regular expression and, conversely, every language that can be defined by a regular expression can be accepted by some FA. However, we shall see that there are languages that are neither definable by a regular expression nor accepted by an FA. Remember, for a language to be *the* language accepted by an FA means not only that all the words in the language run to final states, but also that *no strings not in the language do*.

Let us consider some more examples of FAs.

EXAMPLE

Let us contemplate the possibility of building an FA that accepts all words containing a triple letter, either *aaa* or *bbb*, and only those words.

The machine must have a start state. From the start state, it must have a path of three edges, with no loop, to accept the word *aaa*. Therefore, we begin our machine with

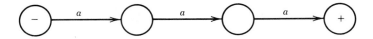

For similar reasons, we can deduce that there must be a path for *bbb*, that has no loop, and uses entirely different states. If the *b*-path shared any of the same states as the *a*-path, we could mix *a*'s and *b*'s and mistakenly get to + anyway. We need only two additional states because the paths could share the same final state without a problem, as below:

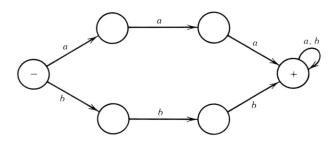

If we are moving anywhere along the *a*-path and we read a *b* before the third *a*, we jump to the *b*-path in progress and vice versa. The whole FA then looks like this:

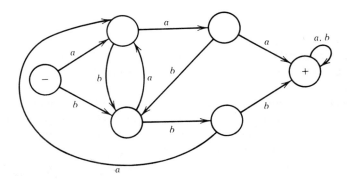

We can understand the language and functioning of this FA because we have seen how it was built. If we had started with the final picture and tried to interpret its meaning, we would be sailing uncharted waters.   ■

EXAMPLE

Consider the FA pictured below:

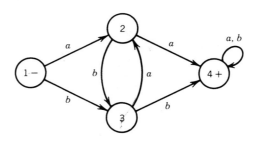

Before we begin to examine what language this machine accepts, let us trace the paths associated with some specific input strings. Let us input the string *ababa*. We begin at the start state 1. The first letter is an *a*, so it takes us to state 2. From there the next letter, *b*, takes us to state 3. The next letter, *a*, then takes us back to state 2. The fourth letter is a *b* and that takes us to state 3 again. The last letter is an *a* that returns us to state 2 where we end. State 2 is not a final state (no +), so this word is not accepted.

Let us trace the word *babbb*. As always, we start in state 1. The first letter, *b*, takes us to state 3. An *a* then takes us to state 2. The third letter, *b*, takes us back to state 3. Now another *b* takes us to state 4. Once in state 4, we cannot get out no matter what the rest of the string is. Once in state 4, we must stay in state 4, and because that is the final state, the string is accepted.

There are two ways to get to state 4 in this FA. One is from state 2, and the other is from state 3. The only way to get to state 2 is by reading the input letter *a* (while in either state 1 or state 3). So when we are in state 2, we know we have just read an *a*. If we read another *a* immediately, we go straight to state 4. It is a similar situation with state 3. To get to state 3, we need to read a *b*. Once in state 3, if we read another *b* immediately, we go to state 4; otherwise, we go to state 2.

Whenever we encounter the substring *aa* in an input string, the first *a* must take us to state 4 or 2. Either way, the next *a* takes us to state 4. The situation with *bb* is analogous. If we are in any of the four states 1, 2, 3, or 4 and we read two *a*'s, we end up in state 4. If we are in any state and read two *b*'s, we end up in state 4. State 4, once entered, cannot be left. To end in state 4, we must read a double letter.

In summary, the words accepted by this machine are exactly those strings that have a double letter in them. This language, as we have seen, can also be defined by the regular expression

$$(a + b)^*(aa + bb)(a + b)^*$$

The four states in this machine can be characterized by the purposes they serve:

State 1   Start here but do not get too comfortable; you are going to leave immediately.

State 2   We have just read an *a* that was not preceded by an *a* and we are looking for a second *a* as the next input.

State 3   We have just read a *b* that was not preceded by a *b* and we are looking for a second *b* as the next input.

State 4   We have already discovered the existence of a double letter in the input string and we are going to wait out the rest of the input sequence and then announce acceptance when it is all over.

In this characterization, if we read a b while in state 2, we go to state 3, hoping for another b, whereas if we read an a in state 3, we go to state 2, hoping for a baby a.   ■

EXAMPLE

Let us consider the FA pictured below:

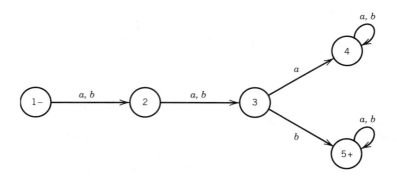

This machine will accept all words with b as the third letter and reject all other words. States 1 and 2 are only waiting states eating up the first two letters of input. Then comes the decision at state 3. A word that has fewer than three letters cannot qualify, and its path ends in one of the first three states, none of which is designated +. Once we get to state 3, only the low road leads to acceptance.

Some regular expressions that define this language are

$$(\mathbf{aab} + \mathbf{abb} + \mathbf{bab} + \mathbf{bbb})(\mathbf{a} + \mathbf{b})^*$$

and

$$(\mathbf{a} + \mathbf{b})(\mathbf{a} + \mathbf{b})(\mathbf{b})(\mathbf{a} + \mathbf{b})^* = (\mathbf{a} + \mathbf{b})^2 \mathbf{b}(\mathbf{a} + \mathbf{b})^*$$

Notice that this last formula is not, strictly speaking, a regular expression, because it uses the symbol 2, which is not included in the kit.   ■

EXAMPLE

Let us consider a very specialized FA, one that accepts only the word *baa*:

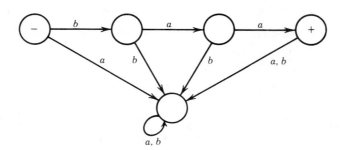

Starting at the start state, anything but the sequence *baa* will drop down into the collecting bucket at the bottom, never to be seen again. Even the word *baabb* will fail. It will reach the final state marked with a +, but then the next letter will <u>suicide</u> over the edge.

The language accepted by this FA is 自毀 .

$$L = \{baa\}$$ ∎

EXAMPLE

The FA below accepts exactly the two strings *baa* and *ab*:

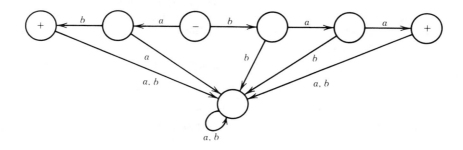

<u>Big machine, small language.</u> ∎

EXAMPLE

Let us take a trickier example. Consider the FA shown below:

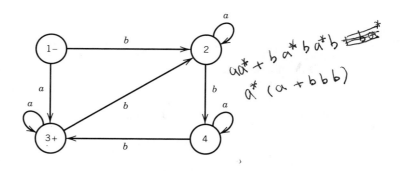

What is the language accepted by this machine? We start at state 1, and if we are reading a word starting with an *a*, we go straight to the final state 3. We can stay at state 3 as long as we continue to read only *a*'s. Therefore, all words of the form

aa*

are accepted by this machine. What if we began with some *a*'s that take us to state 3 but then we read a *b*? This then transports us to state 2. To get back to the final state, we must proceed to state 4 and then to state 3. These trips require two more *b*'s to be read as input. Notice that in states 2, 3, and 4 all *a*'s that are read are ignored. Only *b*'s cause a change of state.

Recapitulating what we know: If an input string begins with an *a* and then has some *b*'s, it must have 3 *b*'s to return us to state 3, or 6 *b*'s to make the trip (state 2, state 4, state 3) twice, or 9 *b*'s, or 12 *b*'s and so on. In other words, an input string starting with an *a* and having a total number of *b*'s divisible by 3 will be accepted. If it starts with an *a* and has a total number of *b*'s not divisible by 3, then the input is rejected because its path through the machine ends at state 2 or 4.

What happens to an input string that begins with a *b*? It finds itself in state 2 and needs two more *b*'s to get to state 3 (these *b*'s can be separated by any number of *a*'s). Once in state 3, it needs no more *b*'s, or three more *b*'s, or six more *b*'s, and so on.

All in all, an input string, whether beginning with an *a* or a *b*, must have a total number of *b*'s divisible by 3 to be accepted. It is also clear that any string meeting this requirement will reach the final state.

The language accepted by this machine can be defined by the regular expression

$$a*(a*ba*ba*ba*)*(a + a*ba*ba*ba*)$$

The only purpose for the last factor is to guarantee that Λ is not a possibility because it is not accepted by the machine. If we did not mind Λ being included in the language, we could have used this simpler FA:

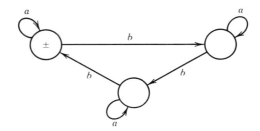

The regular expression

$$(a + ba*ba*b)^+$$

also defines the original (non-Λ) language, whereas the regular expression

$$(a*ba*ba*ba*)*$$

defines the language of the second machine.   ■

EXAMPLE

The following FA accepts only the word Λ:

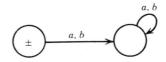

Notice that the left state is both a start and a final state. All words other than Λ go to the right state and stay there. ■

EXAMPLE

Consider the following FA:

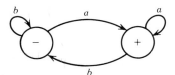

No matter which state we are in, when we read an *a*, we go to the right-hand state, and when we read a *b*, we go to the left-hand state. Any input string that ends in the + state must end in the letter *a*, and any string ending in *a* must end in +. Therefore, the language accepted by this machine is

$$(a + b)*a$$ ■

EXAMPLE

The language in the example above does not include Λ. If we add Λ, we get the language of all words that do not end in *b*. This is accepted by the FA below:

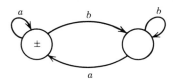

■

EXAMPLE

Consider the following FA:

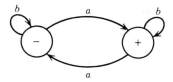

The only letter that causes motion between the states is *a*; *b*'s leave the machine in the same state. We start at −. If we read a first *a*, we go to +. A second *a* takes us back. A third *a* takes us to + again. We end at + after the first, third, fifth, seventh, . . . *a*. The language accepted by this machine is all words with an odd number of *a*'s, which could also be defined by the regular expression

$$b*ab*(ab*ab*)*$$ ■

EXAMPLE

Consider the following FA:

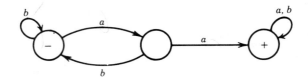

This machine will accept the language of all words with a double a in them somewhere. We stay in the start state until we read our first a. This moves us to the middle state. If the very next letter is another a, we move to the $+$ state, where we must stay and eventually be accepted. If the next letter is a b, however, we go back to $-$ to wait for the next a.

We can identify the purposes that these states serve in the machine as follows:

Start state   The previous input letter (if there was one) was not an a.

Middle state   We have just read an a that was not preceded by an a.

Final state   We have already encountered a double a and we are going to sit here until the input is exhausted.

Clearly, if we are in the start state and we read an a, we go to the middle state, but if we read a b, we stay in the start state. When in the middle state, an a sends us to nirvana, where ultimate acceptance awaits us, whereas a b sends us back to start, hoping for the first a of a double letter.

The language accepted by this machine can also be defined by the regular expression

$$(a + b)*aa(a + b)*$$ ■

EXAMPLE

The following FA accepts all words that have *different* first and last letters. If the word begins with an a, to be accepted it must end with a b and vice versa.

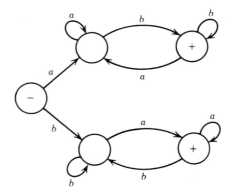

If we start with an a, we take the high road and jump back and forth between the two top states ending on the right (at $+$) only if the last letter read is a b. If the first letter read is a b, we go south. Here, we get to the $+$ on the bottom only when we read a as the last letter.

This can be better understood by examining the path through the FA of the input string *aabbaabb*, as shown below:

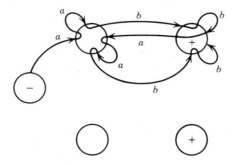

It will be useful for us to consider this FA as having a primitive memory device. For the top two states, no matter how much bouncing we do between them, remember that the first letter read from the input string was an *a* (otherwise, we would never have gotten up here to begin with). For the bottom two states, remember that the first input letter was a *b*.

Lower non + state   The input started with a *b* and the last letter we have read from the input string is also a *b*.

Lower + state   The input started with a *b* and the last letter read so far is an *a*.   ■

EVEN-EVEN REVISITED

EXAMPLE

As the next example of an FA in this chapter, let us consider the picture below:

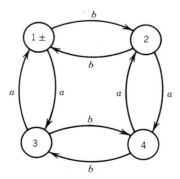

To process a string of letters, we start at state 1, which is in the upper left of the picture. Every time we encounter a letter *a* in the input string, we take an *a* train. There are four edges labeled *a*. All the edges marked *a* go either from one of the upper two states (states 1 and 2) to one of the lower two states (states 3 and 4), or else from one of the lower two states to one of the upper two states. If we are north and we read an *a*, we go south. If we are south and we read an *a*, we go north. The letter *a* reverses our up/down status.

What happens to a word that gets accepted and ends up back in state 1? Without knowing anything else about the string, we can say that it must have had an even number of *a*'s in it. Every *a* that took us south was balanced by some *a* that took us back north. We crossed the Mason–Dixon line an even number of times, one for each *a*. So, every word in the language of this FA has an even number of *a*'s in it. Also, we can say that every input string with an even number of *a*'s will finish its path in the north (state 1 or 2).

There is more that we can say about the words that are accepted by this machine. There are four edges labeled *b*. Every edge labeled *b* either takes us from one of the two states on the left of the picture (states 1 and 3) to one of the two states on the right (states 2 and 4), or else takes us from one of the two states on the right to one of the two states on the left. Every *b* we encounter in the input is an east/west reverser. If the word starts out in state 1, which is on the left, and ends up back in state 1 (on the left), it must have crossed the Mississippi an even number of times. Therefore, all the words in the language accepted by this FA have an even number of *b*'s as well as an even number of *a*'s. We can also say that every input string with an even number of *b*'s will leave us in the west (state 1 or 3).

These are the only two conditions on the language. All words with an even number of *a*'s and an even number of *b*'s must return to state 1. All words that return to state 1 are in EVEN-EVEN. All words that end in state 2 have crossed the Mason–Dixon line an even number of times but have crossed the Mississippi an odd number of times; therefore, they have an even number of *a*'s and an odd number of *b*'s. All the words that end in state 3 have an even number of *b*'s but an odd number of *a*'s. All words that end in state 4 have an odd number of *a*'s and an odd number of *b*'s. So again, we see that all the EVEN-EVEN words must end in state 1 and be accepted.

One regular expression for the language EVEN-EVEN was discussed in detail in the previous chapter.   ∎

Notice how much easier it is to understand the FA than the regular expression. Both methods of defining languages have advantages, depending on the desired application. But in a theory course we rarely consider applications except in the following example.

EXAMPLE

We are programmers hired to write a word processor. As part of this major program, we must build a subroutine that scans any given input string of English letters and spaces and locates the first occurrence of the substring *cat* whether it is a word standing alone or part of a longer word such as *abdicate*.

We envision the need for four states:

State 1   We have not just read a *c*; this is the start state.

State 2   The last letter read was a *c*.

State 3   The last letter read was an *a* that came after a *c*.

State 4   We have just encountered the substring *cat* and control of this program must transfer somewhere else.

If we are in state 1 and read anything but a *c*, we stay there. In state 1 if we read a *c*, we go unconditionally to state 2.

If we are in state 2 and we read an *a*, we go to state 3. If we read another *c*, we stay in state 2 because this other *c* may be the beginning of the substring *cat*. If we read anything else, we go back to state 1.

If we are in state 3 and we read a *t*, then we go to state 4. If we read any other letter except *c*, we have to go back to state 1 and start all over again, but if we read a *c*, then we go to state 2 because this could be the start of something interesting.

The machine looks like this:

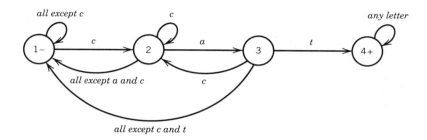

The input *Boccaccio* will go through the sequence of states 1-1-1-2-2-3-2-2-1-1 and the input will not be accepted.

The input *desiccate* will go through the states: 1-1-1-1-1-2-3-4-4 and terminate (which in this example is some form of acceptance) before reading the final *e*. ∎

⚜ PROBLEMS

1. Write out the transition tables for the FAs on pp. 56, 58 (both), 63, 64, and 69 that were defined by pictures.

2. Build an FA that accepts only the language of all words with *b* as the second letter. Show both the picture and the transition table for this machine and find a regular expression for the language.

3. Build an FA that accepts only the words *baa*, *ab*, and *abb* and no other strings longer or shorter.

4. (i) Build an FA with three states that accepts all strings.
   (ii) Show that given any FA with three states and three +'s, it accepts all input strings.
   (iii) If an FA has three states and only one +, must it reject some inputs?

5. (i) Build an FA that accepts only those words that have more than four letters.
   (ii) Build an FA that accepts only those words that have fewer than four letters.
   (iii) Build an FA that accepts only those words with *exactly* four letters.

6. Build an FA that accepts only those words that do *not* end with *ba*.

7. Build an FA that accepts only those words that begin or end with a double letter.

8. Build an FA that accepts only those words that have an even number of substrings *ab*.

9. (i) Recall from Chapter 4 the language of all words over the alphabet {*a* *b*} that have both the letter *a* and the letter *b* in them, but not necessarily in that order. Build an FA that accepts this language.

(ii) Build an FA that accepts the language of all words with only a's or only b's in them. Give a regular expression for this language.

10. Consider all the possible FAs over the alphabet $\{a \quad b\}$ that have exactly two states. An FA must have a designated start state, but there are four possible ways to place the $+$'s:

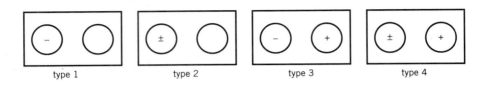

(from left to right) type 1   type 2   type 3   type 4

Each FA needs four edges (two from each state), each of which can lead to either of the states. There are $2^4 = 16$ ways to arrange the labeled edges for each of the four types of FAs. Therefore, in total there are 64 different FAs of two states. However, they do not represent 64 nonequivalent FAs because they are not all associated with different languages. All type 1 FAs do not accept any words at all, whereas all FAs of type 4 accept all strings of a's and b's.

(i) Draw the remaining FAs of type 2.
(ii) Draw the remaining FAs of type 3.
(iii) Recalculate the total number of two-state machines using the transition table definition.

11. Show that there are exactly 5832 different finite automata with three states x, y, z over the alphabet $\{a \quad b\}$, where x is always the start state.

12. Suppose a particular FA, called FIN, has the property that it had only one final state that was not the start state. During the night, vandals come and switch the $+$ sign with the $-$ sign and reverse the direction of all the edges.

(i) Show that the picture that results might not actually be an FA at all by giving an example.
(ii) Suppose, however, that in a particular case what resulted was, in fact, a perfectly good FA. Let us call it NIF. Give an example of one such machine.
(iii) What is the relationship between the language accepted by FIN and the language accepted by NIF as described in part (ii)? Why?
(iv) One of the vandals told me that if in FIN the plus state and the minus state were the same state, then the language accepted by the machine could contain only palindromic words. Defeat this vandal by example.

13. We define a removable state as a state such that if we erase the state itself and the edges that come out of it, what results is a perfectly good-looking FA.

(i) Give an example of an FA that contains a removable state.
(ii) Show that if we erase a removable state the language defined by the reduced FA is exactly the same as the language defined by the old FA.

14. (i) Build an FA that accepts the language of all strings of a's and b's such that the next-to-last letter is an a.
(ii) Build an FA that accepts the language of all strings of length 4 or more such that the next-to-last letter is equal to the second letter of the input string.

15. Build a machine that accepts all strings that have an even length that is not divisible by 6.

16. Build an FA such that when the labels *a* and *b* are swapped the new machine is different from the old one but equivalent (the language defined by these machines is the same).

17. Describe in English the languages accepted by the following FAs:

(i)

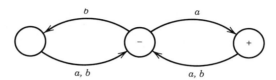

(ii)

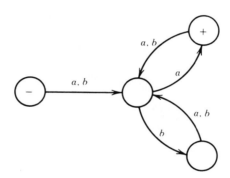

(iii)

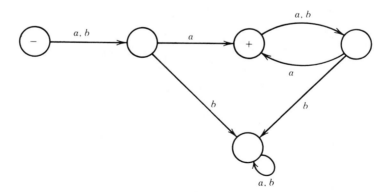

(iv) Write regular expressions for the languages accepted by these three machines.

18. The following is an FA over the alphabet $\Sigma = \{a \quad b \quad c\}$. Prove that it accepts all strings that have an odd number of occurrences of the substring *abc*.

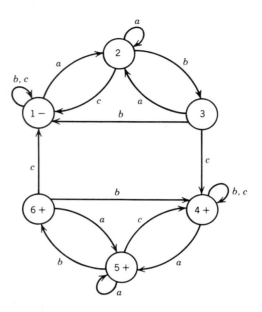

19. Consider the following FA:

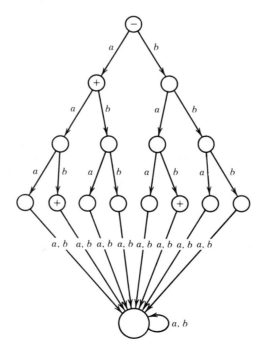

   (i) Show that any input string with more than three letters is not accepted by this FA.
  (ii) Show that the only words accepted are *a*, *aab*, and *bab*.
 (iii) Show that by changing the location of + signs alone, we can make this FA accept the language {*bb* *aba* *bba*}.
 (iv) Show that any language in which the words have fewer than four letters can be accepted by a machine that looks like this one with the + signs in different places.
  (v) Prove that if *L* is a finite language, then there is some FA that accepts *L* extending the binary-tree part of this machine several more layers if necessary.

20. Let us consider the possibility of an infinite automaton that starts with this infinite binary tree:

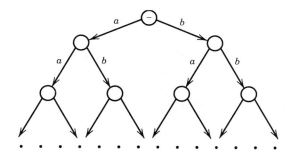

Let *L* be any infinite language of strings of *a*'s and *b*'s whatsoever. Show that by the judicious placement of +'s, we can turn the picture above into an infinite automaton to accept the language *L*. Show that for any given finite string, we can determine from this machine, in a finite time, whether it is a word in *L*. Discuss why this machine would not be a satisfactory language-definer for *L*.

CHAPTER 6

Transition Graphs

⚜ RELAXING THE RESTRICTION ON INPUTS

We saw in the last chapter that we could build an FA that accepts only the word *baa*. The example we gave required five states primarily because an FA can read only one letter from the input string at a time. Suppose we designed a more powerful machine that could read either one or two letters of the input string at a time and could change its state based on this input information. We might design a machine like the one below:

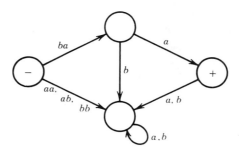

Because when we say "build a machine," all we have to do is scribble on paper—we do not have to solder, weld, and screw—we could easily change the rules of what constitutes a machine and allow such pictures as the one above. The objects we deal with in this book are only mathematical models. In general, practically anything can be a mathematical model so long as it is a well-defined set of rules for playing with some abstract constructs, but the obvious question remains: a mathematical model of what?

The FAs defined in the previous chapter started out on a dubious note when they were analogized to being mathematical models of children's games. However, we did later produce some reasons for thinking that they were of use to computer science because they represent, in a meaningful way, states in certain programmable algorithms. The mathematical models that we shall introduce in this chapter will differ in a significant way. We cannot as of yet explain the direct application of these entities to the normal experience of a programming student. That does not mean that their importance must be accepted on blind faith—merely patience. They will be of utmost practical value for us in the all-important next chapter. Beyond that service, the underlying special features that distinguish them from FAs will introduce us to a theme that will recur often in our study of computer theory. As for the moment, we are proposing to investigate a variation of FAs. There are still states and edges that consume input letters, but we have abandoned the requirement that the edges eat just one letter at a time. As we shall see soon, this is accompanied by several other coordinated adjustments.

If we are interested in a machine that accepts only the word *baa*, why stop at assuming that the machine can read just two letters at a time? A machine that accepts this word and that can read up to three letters at a time from the input string could be built with even fewer states:

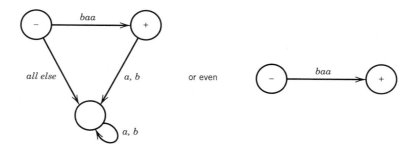

If we interpret the picture on the right as an FA-like machine, we see that not only does *baa* alone get to the final state, but all other input strings end up actually nowhere. If we start in the minus state and the first letter of the input is an *a*, we have no direction as to what to do. The picture on the left at least tells us that when the input fails to be of the desired form, we must go to the garbage collection state and read through the rest of the input string in the full knowledge that we can never leave there.

The picture on the right gives us another problem with the input *baabb*. The first three letters take us to the accept state, but then something undetermined (presumably bad) happens when we read any more of the input letters. According to the rules of FAs, one cannot stop reading input letters until the input string completely runs out. The picture on the right does not tell us where to go for most of the situations we may have to face while reading inputs. By convention, we shall assume that there is associated with the picture, but not drawn, some trash-can state that we must go to when we fail to be able to make any of the allowable indicated legal edge crossings in the picture. Once in this state, we must abandon all hope of ever leaving and getting to acceptance. Many of the FAs in the previous chapter had such inescapable nonacceptance black holes that had to be drawn in detail. We now consider the two pictures above to be equivalent for all practical purposes. They are only distinguishable in trivial ways, such as by having a different number of states, but they accept the exact same language.

Rather than an imaginary hell-state as we have described just now, it is more standard to introduce a new term to describe what happens when an input is running on a machine and gets into a state from which it cannot escape though it has not yet been fully read.

DEFINITION

When an input string that has not been completely read reaches a state (final or otherwise) that it cannot leave because there is no outgoing edge that it may follow, we say that the input (or the machine) **crashes** at that state. Execution then terminates and the input must be rejected.   ■

Let us make note of the fact that on an FA it is not possible for any input to crash because there is always an outgoing *a*-edge and an outgoing *b*-edge from each state. As long as there remain letters unread, progress is possible.

There are now two different ways that an input can be rejected: It could peacefully trace a path ending a nonfinal state, or it could crash while being processed. These two different ways of being unsuccessful are the experience of all programmers.

If we hypothesize that a machine can read one or two letters at a time, then one can be built using only two states that can recognize all words that contain a double letter:

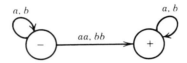

If we are going to bend the rules to allow for a machine like the last one, we must realize that we have changed something more fundamental than just the way the edges are labeled or the number of letters read at a time. This last machine makes us exercise some *choice* in its running. We must *decide* how many letters to read from the input string each time we go back for more. This decision is quite important.

Let us say, for example, that the input string is *baa*. It is easy to see how this string can be accepted by this machine. We first read the letter *b*, which leaves us back at the start state by taking the loop on the left. Then we decide to read both letters *aa* at once, which allows us to take the highway to the final state where we end. However, if after reading the single character *b*, we then decided to read the single character *a*, we would loop back and be stuck at the start state again. When the third letter is read, we would still be at the starting post. We could not then accept this string. There are two different paths that the input *baa* can take through this machine. This is totally different from the situation we had before, especially because one path leads to acceptance and one to rejection.

Another bad thing that might have happened is that we could have started processing the string *baa* by reading the first two letters at once. Because *ba* is not a double letter, we could not move to the final state. In fact, when we read *ba*, no edge tells us where to go, because *ba* is not the label of any edge leaving the start state. The processing of this string breaks down at this point and the machine crashes. So, there is the inherent possibility of reading variable amounts of letters from the input at each state. Therefore, the input string can follow a variety of paths through the machine, differing not only in their edge-length but also in their final disposition. Some paths may lead to acceptance the usual way and some to rejection two ways: either by ending in a nonfinal state or by causing the whole machine to crash. What shall we say? Is this input string part of the language of this machine or not? It cannot be made to depend on the cleverness or whim of the machine operator and the number of letters he or she feels like inputting at each state — it must be an absolute yes or no, or else the language is not *well defined* in the sense that we have been using.

The result of these considerations is that if we are going to change the definition of our abstract machine to allow for more than one letter to be read at a time, we must also change the definition of acceptance. We shall say that a string is accepted by a machine if there is *some* way it could be processed so as to arrive at a final state. There may also be ways in which this string does not get to a final state, but we ignore all failures.

We are about to create machines in which any edge in the picture can be labeled by any string of alphabet letters, but first we must consider some additional consequences. We could now encounter the following problem:

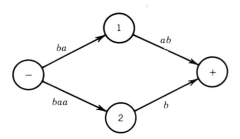

On this machine, we can accept the word *baab* in two different ways. First, we could take *ba* from the start state to state 1 and then *ab* would take us to the final state. Or else we could read the three letters *baa* and go to state 2 from which the final letter, *b*, would take us to the final state.

Previously, when we were dealing only with FAs, we had a unique path through the machine for every input string. Now some strings have no paths at all, while some have several.

We now have observed many of the difficulties inherent in expanding our definition of "machine" to allow word-labeled edges (or, equivalently, to reading more than one letter of input at a time). We shall leave the definition of the finite automaton alone and call these new machines **transition graphs** because they are more easily understood when defined directly as graphs than as tables later turned into pictures.

DEFINITION

A **transition graph,** abbreviated **TG,** is a collection of three things:

1. A finite set of states, at least one of which is designated as the start state ($-$) and some (maybe none) of which are designated as final states ($+$).
2. An alphabet Σ of possible input letters from which input strings are formed.
3. A finite set of transitions (edge labels) that show how to go from some states to some others, based on reading specified substrings of input letters (possibly even the null string Λ). ∎

When we give a pictorial representation of a transition graph, clause 3 in the definition means that every edge is labeled by some string or strings of letters, not necessarily only one letter. We are also not requiring that there be any specific number of edges emanating from any state. Some states may have no edge coming out of them at all, and some may have thousands (e.g., edges labeled *a, aa, aaa, aaaa, . . .*).

Transition graphs were invented by John Myhill in 1957 for reasons revealed in the next chapter.

A **successful path** through a transition graph is a series of edges forming a path beginning at some start state (there may be several) and ending at a final state. If we concatenate in order the string of letters that label each edge in the path, we produce a word that is accepted by this machine.

For example, consider the following TG:

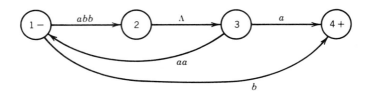

The path from state 1 to state 2 to state 3 back to state 1 then to state 4 corresponds to the string $(abb)(\Lambda)(aa)(b)$. This is one way of factoring the word *abbaab*, which, we now see, is accepted by this machine. Some other words accepted are *abba*, *abbaaabba*, and *b*.

When an edge is labeled with the string Λ, it means that we can take the ride it offers free (without consuming any letters from the input string). Remember that we do not *have* to follow that edge, but we can if we want to.

If we are presented with a particular string of *a*'s and *b*'s to run on a given TG, we must decide how to break the word into substrings that might correspond to the labels of edges in a path. If we run the input string *abbab* on the machine above, we see that from state 1, where we must start, we can proceed along the outgoing edge labeled *abb* or the one labeled *b*. This word then moves along the edge from state 1 to state 2. The input letters *abb* are read and consumed. What is left of the input string is *ab*, and we are now in state 2. From state 2, we must move to state 3 along the Λ-edge. At state 3, we cannot read *aa*, so we must read only *a* and go to state 4. Here, we have a *b* left in the input string but no edge to follow, so despite our best efforts we still must crash and reject the input string *abbab*.

Because we have allowed some edges to be traversed for free, it is logical to allow for the possibility of more than one start state. The reason we say that these two points are related is that we could always introduce more start states if we wanted to, simply by connecting them to the original start state by edges labeled Λ. This point is illustrated by the following example. There is no real difference between the TG

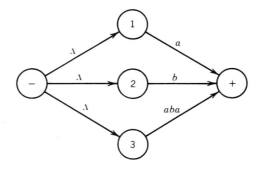

and the TG

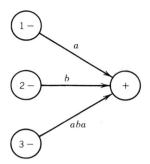

in the sense that all the strings accepted by the first are accepted by the second and vice versa. There are differences between the two machines such as the total number of states they have, but as *language-acceptors* they are equivalent.

It is extremely important for us to notice that every FA is also a TG. This means that any picture that represents an FA can be interpreted as a picture of a TG. Of course, not every TG satisfies the definition of an FA.

⚜ LOOKING AT TGs

Let us consider some more examples of TGs.

The picture above represents a TG that accepts nothing, not even the null string **Λ**. To be able to accept anything, it must have a final state.

The machine

accepts only the string **Λ**. Any other string cannot have a successful path to the final state through labels of edges because there are no edges (and hence no labels).

Any TG in which some start state is also a final state will always accept the string **Λ**; this is also true of FAs. There are some other TGs that accept the word **Λ**. For example,

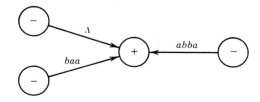

This machine accepts only the words **Λ**, *baa*, and *abba*. Anything read while in the + state will cause a crash, because the + state has no outgoing edges.

EXAMPLE

The following TGs also only accept **Λ**:

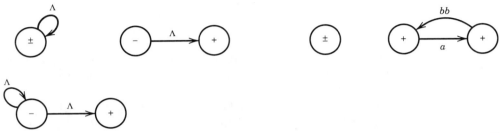

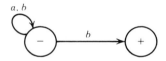

■

EXAMPLE

Consider the following TG:

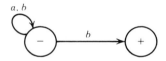

We can read all the input letters one at a time and stay in the left-side state. When we read a *b* in the − state, there are two possible edges we can follow. If the very last letter is a *b*, we can use it to go to the + state. This *b* must be the very last letter, because once in the right-side state, if we try to read another letter, we crash.

Notice that it is also possible to start with a word that does end with a *b*, but to follow an unsuccessful path that does not lead to acceptance. We could either make the mistake of following the nonloop *b*-edge too soon (on a nonfinal *b*), in which case we crash on the next letter, or else we might make the mistake of looping back to − when we read the last *b*, in which case we reject without crashing. But still, all words that end in *b* *can* be accepted by some path, and that is all that is required.

The language accepted by this TG is all words ending in *b*. One regular expression for this language is **(a + b)*b** and an FA that accepts the same language is

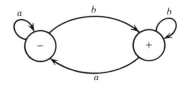

■

EXAMPLE

The following TG:

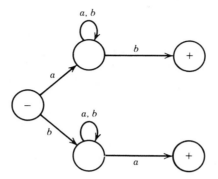

accepts the language of all words that begin and end with different letters. This follows as a logical extension of the reasoning for the previous example. ∎

EXAMPLE

The following TG:

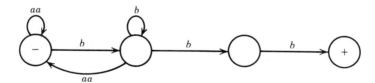

accepts the language of all words in which the *a*'s occur only in even clumps and that end in three or more *b*'s. There is never an edge that reads a single *a* and it takes *bbb* at the end to get to +. ∎

EXAMPLE

Consider the following TG:

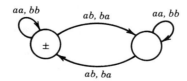

In this TG, every edge is labeled with a pair of letters. This means that for the string to be accepted, it must have an even number of letters that are read and processed in groups of two's.

Let us call the left state the balanced state and the right state the unbalanced state. If the first pair of letters that we read from the input string is a double (*aa* or *bb*), then the machine stays in the balanced state. In the balanced state, the machine has read an even number of *a*'s and an even number of *b*'s. However, when a pair of unmatched letters is read (either *ab* or *ba*), the machine flips over to the unbalanced state, which signifies that it has read an odd number of *a*'s and an odd number of *b*'s. We do not return to the balanced state until another "corresponding" unmatched pair is read (not necessarily the same unmatched pair but any unequal pair). The discovery of two unequal pairs makes the total number of *a*'s and the total number of *b*'s read from the input string even again. This TG is an example of a machine that accepts exactly the familiar language EVEN-EVEN of all words with an even number of *a*'s and an even number of *b*'s.

Of the three examples of definitions or descriptions of this language we have reviewed (the regular expression, the FA, and the TG), this last is the most understandable.   ■

There is a practical problem with TGs. There are occasionally so many possible ways of grouping the letters of the input string that we must examine many possibilities before we know whether a given string is accepted or rejected.

EXAMPLE

Consider this TG:

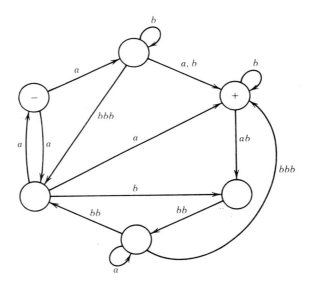

Is the word *abbbabbbabba* accepted by this machine? (Yes, in three ways.)   ■

When we allow Λ-edges, we may have an infinite number of ways of grouping the letters of an input string. For example, the input string *ab* may be factored as

$$
\begin{array}{cccccc}
(a) & (b) \\
(a) & (\Lambda) & (b) \\
(a) & (\Lambda) & (\Lambda) & (b) \\
(a) & (\Lambda) & (\Lambda) & (\Lambda) & (b)
\end{array}
$$

· · ·

Instead of presenting a definite algorithm right now for determining whether a particular string is accepted by a particular TG, we shall wait until Chapter 11 when the task will be easier. There are, of course, difficult algorithms for performing this task that are within our abilities to analyze at this moment. One such algorithm is outlined in Problem 20 on page 91.

The existence of Λ-edges also allows for a new and completely unsettling set of possibilities — it allows infinite things to happen in seemingly finite situations.

Consider the following TG:

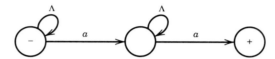

Obviously, the only word accepted by this machine is the single word *aa*, but it can be accepted by infinitely many different paths. It is even possible to conceive that this machine accepts the word *aa* through paths of infinite length by looping infinitely many times before moving to the next state. But by our understanding, "paths" of necessity mean only "finite paths." Λ-loop-edges can make life difficult, and just as obviously their utility is nil. If we take any TG with Λ-loops and trim away these loops, the resultant picture is still a TG and accepts the same set of input strings. Why did we ever allow Λ-loops in the first place? One answer is so that we leave our definition as simple and universal-sounding as possible ("any edges, anywhere, with any labels") and another is that Λ-loops are not the only way of getting an infinite path out of a finite input string. Behold the Λ-circuit:

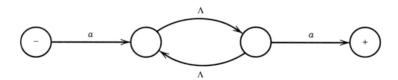

It is obvious how to eliminate this particular Λ-circuit, but with the machine

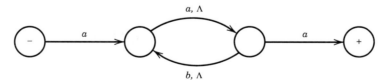

if any Λ option is erased, the resultant language is changed.

Yet, another reason for not adding extra clauses to the definition of the TG to avoid this problem is that Λ-edges, as we shall see in Chapter 7, are *never* necessary at all, in the sense that any language that can be accepted by a TG with Λ-edges can be accepted by some different TG without Λ-edges.

⚜ GENERALIZED TRANSITION GRAPHS

The ultimate step liberating state-to-state transitions is to allow the input to progress from one place to another by contributing a substring restricted to being a word in a predetermined language. For example,

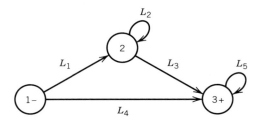

We can travel from start to state 2 by reading any (of course finite) word from the (possibly infinite) set of choices L_1 and, similarly, between all other states.

For the moment, we will not be so arbitrary as to allow just any language to be used as labels, not only those languages defined by regular expressions.

This gives us a new concept of a transition graph.

DEFINITION

A **generalized transition graph (GTG)** is a collection of three things:

1. A finite set of states, of which at least one is a start state and some (maybe none) are final states.

2. An alphabet Σ of input letters.

3. Directed edges connecting some pairs of states, each labeled with a regular expression.

∎

EXAMPLE

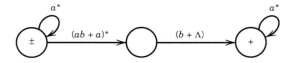

This machine accepts all strings without a double b. Notice that the word b takes a Λ-edge from start to middle.   ∎

In a very real sense, there is no difference between the Kleene star closure for regular expressions and a loop in our previous transition graphs, or FAs for that matter. Compare

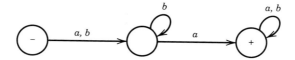

and

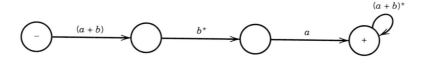

In the first picture, we may loop in the middle state as many times as we want or go straight to the third state. To not loop corresponds to taking the **Λ** choice from the **b*** in the second example.

⚜ NONDETERMINISM

Generalized transition graphs force us to face a deep but subtle and disturbing fact that sneaked past us quietly with TGs. Just as the * and the + in a regular expression represent a potential multiplicity of choices, so does the possible multiplicity of paths to be selected from a TG. In the GTG, the choices are both static and dynamic. We often have a range of choices of edges, each labeled with an infinite language of alternatives. The number of ways of going from state 1 to state 4 might be infinite.

A blatant example of the inherent need for choice is offered in the fragment of the TG shown below:

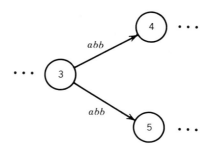

If we tried to forbid people from writing this directly, they could still sneak it into their TGs in other ways:

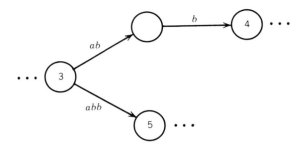

Even if we restrict labels to strings of only one letter or Λ, we may indirectly permit these two equivalent situations:

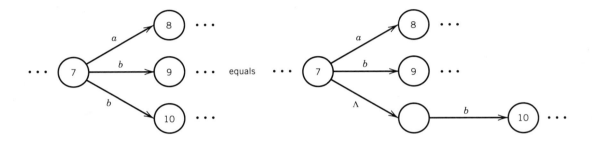

We have already seen that in a TG a particular string of input letters may trace through the machine on different paths, depending on our choice of grouping. For instance, *abb* can go from state 3 to 4 or 5 in the middle of the three preceding examples, depending on whether we read the letters two and one or all three at once. The ultimate path through the machine is not determined by the input alone. Therefore, we say this machine is **nondeterministic.** Human choice becomes a factor in selecting the path; the machine does not make all its own determinations.

⚜ PROBLEMS

1. For each of the five FAs pictured in Problems 17, 19, and 20 in Chapter 5, build a transition graph that accepts the same language but has fewer states.

2. For each of the next 10 words, decide which of the six machines on the next page accept the given word.

    (i) Λ
    (ii) *a*
   (iii) *b*
   (iv) *aa*
    (v) *ab*
   (vi) *aba*
  (vii) *abba*
 (viii) *bab*
   (ix) *baab*
    (x) *abbb*

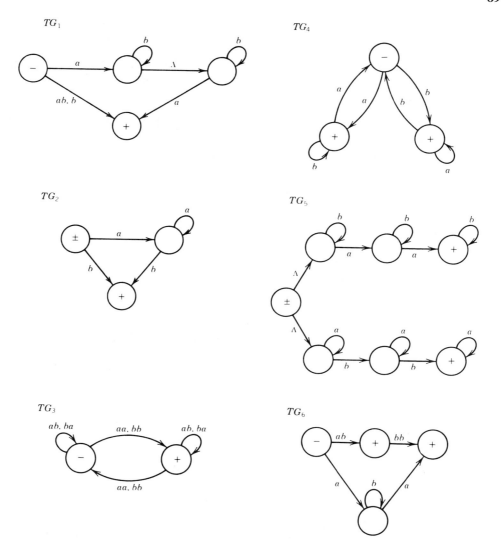

3. Show that any language that can be accepted by a TG can be accepted by a TG with an even number of states.

4. How many different TGs are there over the alphabet {a b} that have two states?

5. Prove that for every TG there is another TG that accepts the same language but has only one + state.

6. Build a TG that accepts the language L_1 of all words that begin and end with the same double letter, either of the form $aa \ldots aa$ or $bb \ldots bb$. *Note: aaa and bbb are not words in this language.*

7. If OURSPONSOR is a language that is accepted by a TG called Henry, prove that there is a TG that accepts the language of all strings of a's and b's that end in a word from OURSPONSOR.

8. (i) Suppose that L is a finite language whose words are w_1, w_2, w_3, . . . , w_{83}. Prove that there is a TG that accepts exactly the language L.

(ii) Of all TGs that accept exactly the language L, what is the one with the fewest number of states?

9. Given a TG, called TG_1, that accepts the language L_1 and a TG, called TG_2, that accepts the language L_2, show how to build a new TG (called TG_3) that accepts exactly the language $L_1 + L_2$.

10. Given TG_1 and TG_2 as described in Problem 9, show how to build TG_4 that accepts exactly the language $L_1 L_2$.

11. Given a TG for some arbitrary language L, what language would it accept if every $+$ state were to be connected back to every $-$ state by Λ-edges? For example, by this method,

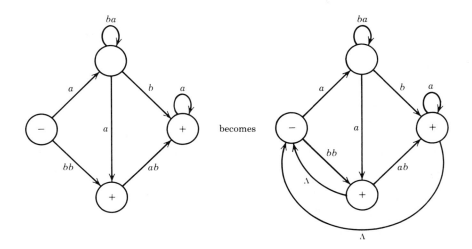

Hint: Why is the answer not always L^*?

12. (i) Let the language L be accepted by the transition graph T and let L not contain the word Λ. Show how to build a new TG that accepts exactly all the words in L and the word Λ.

(ii) Given TG_1 that accepts the language L_1, show how to build a TG that accepts the language L^*. (*Hint:* Use Problems 11 and 12(i) and sound authoritative.)

13. Using the results of Problems 8, 9, 10, and 12 in an organized fashion, prove that if L is any language that can be defined by a regular expression, then there is a TG that accepts exactly the language L^*.

14. Verify that there are indeed three and only three ways for the TG on p. 84 to accept the word *abbbabbbabba*.

15. An FA with four states was sitting unguarded one night when vandals came and stole an edge labeled a. What resulted was a TG that accepted exactly the language $\mathbf{b}^*$. In the morning the FA was repaired, but the next night vandals stole an edge labeled b and what resulted was a TG that accepted $\mathbf{a}^*$. The FA was again repaired, but this time the vandals stole two edges, one labeled a and one labeled b, and the resultant TG accepted the language $\mathbf{a}^* + \mathbf{b}^*$. What was the original FA?

16. Let the language L be accepted by the transition graph T and let L not contain the word *ba*. We want to build a new TG that accepts exactly L and the word *ba*.

   (i) One suggestion is to draw an edge from $-$ to $+$ and label it *ba*. Show that this does not always work.

   (ii) Another suggestion is to draw a new $+$ state and draw an edge from any $-$ state to it labeled *ba*. Show that this does not always work.

   (iii) What does work?

17. Let L be any language. Let us define the **transpose** of L to be the language of exactly those words that are the words in L spelled backward. If $w \in L$, then reverse(w) $\in L$. For example, if

$$L = \{a \quad abb \quad bbaab \quad bbbaa\}$$

then

$$\text{transpose}(L) = \{a \quad bba \quad baabb \quad aabbb\}$$

   (i) Prove that if there is an FA that accepts L, then there is a TG that accepts the transpose of L.

   (ii) Prove that if there is a TG that accepts L, then there is a TG that accepts the transpose of L.

   Note: It is true, but much harder to prove, that if an FA accepts L, then some FA accepts the transpose of L. However, after Chapter 7 this will be trivial to prove.

   (iii) Prove that transpose$(L_1 L_2)$ = transpose(L_2)·transpose(L_1).

18. Transition graph T accepts language L. Show that if L has a word of odd length, then T has an edge with a label with an odd number of letters.

19. A student walks into a classroom and sees on the blackboard a diagram of a TG with two states that accepts only the word Λ. The student reverses the direction of exactly one edge, leaving all other edges and all labels and all $+$'s and $-$'s the same. But now the new TG accepts the language a*. What was the original machine?

20. Let us now consider an algorithm for determining whether a specific TG that has no Λ-edges accepts a given word:

   Step 1   Number each edge in the TG in any order with the integers 1, 2, 3, . . ., x, where x is the number of edges in the TG.

   Step 2   Observe that if the word has y letters and is accepted at all by this machine, it can be accepted by tracing a path of not more than y edges.

   Step 3   List all strings of y or fewer integers, each of which $\leq x$. This is a finite list.

   Step 4   Check each string on the list in step 3 by concatenating the labels of the edges involved to see whether they make a path from a $-$ to a $+$ corresponding to the given word.

   Step 5   If there is a string in step 4 that works, the word is accepted. If none work, the word is not in the language of the machine.

   (i) Prove that this algorithm does the job.

   (ii) Why is it necessary to assume that the TG has no Λ-edges.

CHAPTER 7

Kleene's Theorem

⚜ UNIFICATION

In the last three chapters, we introduced three separate ways of defining a language: generation by regular expression, acceptance by finite automaton, and acceptance by transition graph. In this chapter, we will present a theorem proved by Kleene in 1956, which (in our version) says that if a language can be defined by any one of these three ways, then it can also be defined by the other two. One way of stating this is to say that all three of these *methods* of defining languages are *equivalent*.

THEOREM 6

Any language that can be defined by

    regular expression, or

    finite automaton, or

    transition graph

can be defined by all three methods.

This theorem is the most important and fundamental result in the theory of finite automata. We are going to take extreme care with its proof. In the process, we shall introduce four algorithms that have the practical value of enabling us actually to construct the corresponding machines and expressions. More than that, the importance of this chapter lies in its value as an illustration of thorough theoretical thinking in this field.

The logic of this proof is a bit involved. If we were trying to prove the mathematical theorem that the set of all ZAPS (whatever they are) is the same as the set of all ZEPS, we could break the proof into two parts. In Part 1, we would show that all ZAPS are also ZEPS. In Part 2, we would show that all ZEPS are also ZAPS. Together, this would demonstrate the equivalence of the two sets.

Here, we have a more ambitious theorem. We wish to show that the set of ZAPS, the set of ZEPS, and the set of ZIPS are all the same. To do this, we need three parts. In Part 1, we shall show that all ZAPS are ZEPS. In Part 2, we shall show that all ZEPS are ZIPS. Finally, in Part 3, we shall show that all ZIPS are ZAPS. Taken together, these three parts will establish the equivalence of the three sets:

$$[\text{ZAPS} \subset \text{ZEPS} \subset \text{ZIPS} \subset \text{ZAPS}] \equiv [\text{ZAPS} = \text{ZEPS} = \text{ZIPS}]$$

PROOF

The three sections of our proof will be:

Part 1   Every language that can be defined by a finite automaton can also be defined by a transition graph.

Part 2   Every language that can be defined by a transition graph can also be defined by a regular expression.

Part 3   Every language that can be defined by a regular expression can also be defined by a finite automaton.

When we have proven these three parts, we have finished our theorem.

Proof of Part 1

This is the easiest part. Every finite automaton *is* itself already a transition graph. Therefore, any language that has been defined by a finite automaton has already been defined by a transition graph. Done.

⚜ TURNING TGs INTO REGULAR EXPRESSIONS

Proof of Part 2

The proof of this part will be by constructive algorithm. This means that we present a procedure that starts out with a transition graph and ends up with a regular expression that defines the same language. To be acceptable as a method of proof, any algorithm must satisfy two criteria. It must work for every conceivable TG, and it must guarantee to finish its job in a finite time (a finite number of steps). For the purposes of theorem-proving alone, it does not have to be a good algorithm (quick, least storage used, etc.). It just has to work in every case.

Let us start by considering an abstract transition graph T. T may have many start states. We first want to simplify T so that it has only one start state that has no incoming edges. We do this by introducing a new state that we label with a minus sign and that we connect to all the previous start states by edges labeled with Λ. Then we drop the minus signs from the previous start states. Now all inputs must begin at the new unique start state. From there, they can proceed free of charge to any of the old start states. If the word w used to be accepted by starting at previous start state 3 and proceeding through the machine to a final state, it can now be accepted by starting at the new unique start state and progressing to the old start state 3 along the edge labeled Λ. This trip does not use up any of the input letters. The word then picks up its old path and becomes accepted. This process is illustrated below on a fragment of a TG that has three start states: 1, 3, and 5:

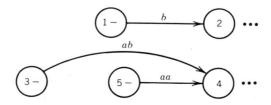

This becomes

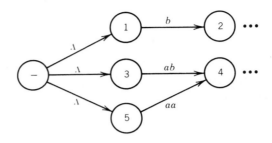

The ellipses in the pictures above indicate other sections of the TG that are irrelevant because they contain no start states.

Another simplification we can make in T is that it can be modified to have a unique un-exitable final state without changing the language it accepts. If T had no final states to begin with, then it accepts no strings at all and has no language and we need produce no regular expression other than the null, or empty, expression ϕ (see p. 36). If T has several final states, let us un-final them and instead introduce a new unique final state labeled with a plus sign. We draw new edges from all the former final states to the new one, dropping the old plus signs, and labeling each new edge with the null string Λ. When an input string runs out of letters and it is in an old final state, it can now take a free Λ-edge ride to the new unique final state. This process is depicted below:

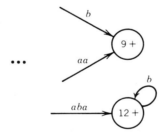

becomes

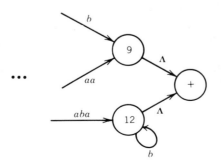

The new final state has no outgoing edges.

We shall require that the unique final state be a different state from the unique start state. If an old state used to have ±, then both signs are removed from it to newly created states.

It should be clear that the addition of these two new states does not affect the language that T accepts. Any word accepted by the old T is also accepted by the new T, and any word rejected by the old T is also rejected by the new T. Furthermore, the machine now has the following shape:

where there are no other − or + states. If the TG was already in this shape, this step could have been skipped but, even then, executing it could not have hurt either.

We are now going to build piece by piece the regular expression that defines the same language as T. To do so, we will change T into a GTG.

Let us suppose that T has some state (called state x) inside it (not the − or + state) that has more than one loop circling back to itself:

where r_1, r_2, and r_3 are all regular expressions or simple strings. In this case, we can replace the three loops by one loop labeled with a regular expression:

The meaning here is that from state x we can read any one string from the input that fits the regular expression $r_1 + r_2 + r_3$ and return to the same state.

Similarly, suppose two states are connected by more than one edge going in the same direction:

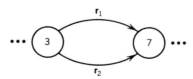

where the labels r_1 and r_2 are each regular expressions or simple strings. We can replace this with a single edge that is labeled with a regular expression:

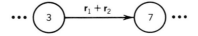

We can now define the **bypass and state elimination operation.** In some cases, if we have three states in a row connected by edges labeled with regular expressions (or simple strings), we can eliminate the middleman and go directly from one outer state to the other by a new edge labeled with a regular expression that is the concatenation of the two previous labels.

For example, if we have

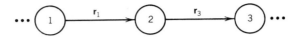

we can replace this with

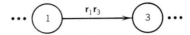

We say "replace" because we no longer need to keep the old edges from state 1 to state 2 and state 2 to state 3 unless they are used in paths other than the ones from state 1 to state 3. The elimination of edges and states is our goal.

We can do this trick only as long as state 2 does not have a loop going back to itself. If state 2 *does* have a loop, we must use this model:

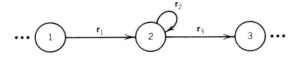

becomes

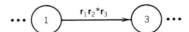

We have had to introduce the * because once we are at state 2, we can loop the loop-edge as many times as we want, or no times at all, before proceeding to state 3. Any string that fits the description $r_1r_2{}^*r_3$ corresponds to a path from state 1 to state 3 in either picture.

If state 1 is connected to state 2 and state 2 is connected to more than one other state (say, to states 3, 4, and 5), then when we eliminate the edge from state 1 to state 2, we have to add edges that show how to go from state 1 to states 3, 4, and 5. We do this as in the following pictures:

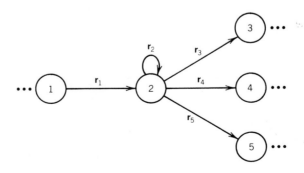

becomes

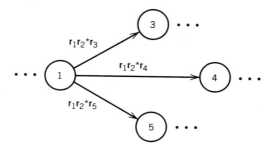

We see that in this way we can eliminate the edge from state 1 to state 2, bypassing state 2 altogether.

In fact, every state that leads into state 2 can be made to bypass state 2. If state 9 leads into state 2, we can eliminate the edge from state 9 to state 2 by adding edges from state 9 to states 3, 4, and 5 directly. We can repeat this process until nothing leads into state 2. When this happens, we can eliminate state 2 entirely, because it then cannot be in a path that accepts a word. We drop the whole state, and the edges leading from it, from the picture for T.

What have we done to transition graph T? Without changing the set of words that it accepts, we have eliminated one of its states.

We can repeat this process again and again until we have eliminated all the states from T except for the unique start state and the unique final state. (We shall illustrate this presently.)

What we come down to is a picture that looks like this:

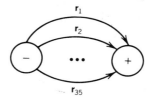

with each edge labeled by a regular expression. We can then combine this once more to produce

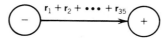

The resultant regular expression is then the regular expression that defines the same language T did originally.

For example, if we have

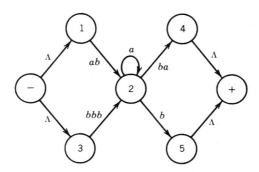

we can bypass state 2 by introducing a path from state 1 to state 4 labeled **aba*ba**, a path from state 1 to state 5 labeled **aba*b**, a path from state 3 to state 4 labeled **bbba*ba**, and a path from state 3 to state 5 labeled **bbba*b**. We can then erase the edges from state 1 to state 2 and from state 3 to state 2. Without these edges, state 2 becomes unreachable. The edges from state 2 to states 4 and 5 are then unless because they cannot be part of any path from − to +. Dropping this state and these edges will not affect whether any word is accepted by this TG.

The machine that results from this operation is

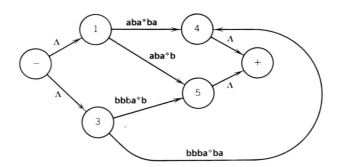

If there had previously been any edges from state 1 to state 5, we leave these alone.

If we wish to eliminate a given state, say, state 2, we must first list all the edges going into that state from other states (say, from states 7 and 9) and also make a list of all the states that could be reached from state 2 by an edge (say, states 11, 4, and 5). If state 2 were to disappear, it would interrupt all the paths input strings could have taken that pass through it on their way to +. We do not wish to destroy any possible paths input strings might take because that could change the language by killing some input string's only path to acceptance, which would eliminate it from the language of the machine. It is too hard for us to check whether all the accepted input strings have some alternate paths to acceptance that do not go through state 2, so we make a careful point of replacing all destroyed routes with equivalent detours.

It is our requirement to be sure that whatever change we make in the machine, all the strings that could have previously been accepted can still be accepted by the modified machine. In order to safely eliminate state 2 without disturbing any routes from − to +, we must install bypass roads going from each incoming state to every outgoing state and be sure that the labels of the bypass road correspond to the trips obliterated.

In this hypothetical example, we must replace routes from state 7 to states 11, 4, and 5 and from state 9 to states 11, 4, and 5. When we draw these new edges, we must label them with the appropriate tolls that are the charges of going into state 2, around state 2, and from state 2. If the machine segment we are analyzing started by looking like:

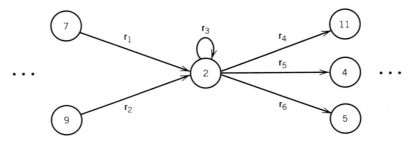

it must become

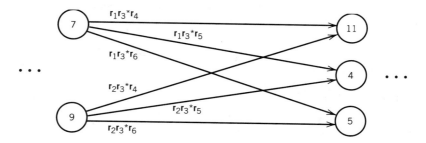

Before we claim to have finished describing this algorithm, there are some special cases that we must examine more carefully. In the picture

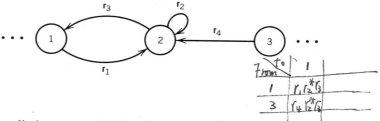

we might want to eliminate state 2. This is an illustration of the possibility that one of the source states to the prospective bypassed state is also a destination state from that state.

This case is really not different from the general situation described above. We still need to replace all the paths through the machine that previously went through state 2. The incoming states are 1 and 3 and the outgoing state is only 1. Therefore, we must add edges connecting state 3 to state 1 and state 1 to state 1. The edge we shall add to connect state 1 to itself is a loop that summarizes and replaces the trip from 1 to 2 to 1. The machine then becomes

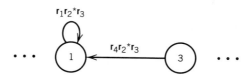

Originally, it was possible to take a path from state 3 to state 2 to state 1 to state 2 and back to state 1 again at the cost of $r_4r_2{}^*r_3r_1r_2{}^*r_3$. This path is still represented in the reduced machine. It is reflected in the 3-1 edge $r_4r_2{}^*r_3$ followed by the loop at state 1, $r_1r_2{}^*r_3$. Therefore, no real problem arises even when the sets of incoming states and the set of outgoing states have some overlap.

Even the complicated

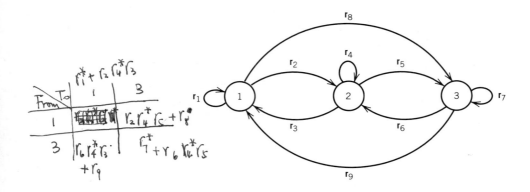

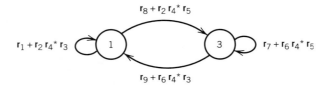

is algorithmically reduced to this equivalent form:

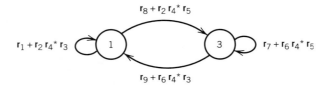

The path 1-2-1-1-2-3-1-2-2-2-3-2-3 in the original picture could be thought of as a looping twice at 1, followed by a trip to 3, followed by a trip to 1, then back to 3 and a loop at 3. All these edges traveled are still represented in the modified machine.

Whenever we remove an edge or a state, we must be sure that we have not destroyed any paths through T that may previously have existed or create new paths that did not exist before.

We now have a well-described method of producing regular expressions equivalent to given transition graphs. All words accepted by T are paths through the picture of T. If we change the picture but preserve all paths and their labels, we must keep the language unchanged.

This algorithm terminates in a finite number of steps, because T has only finitely many states to being with, and one state is eliminated with each iteration of the bypass procedure. The other important observation is that the method works on all transition graphs. Therefore, this algorithm provides a satisfactory proof that there is a regular expression for each transition graph.

Before detailing the steps of this procedure, let us illustrate the algorithm on a particular example.

EXAMPLE   (Inside the proof)

The TG we shall consider is the one below, which accepts all words that begin and end with double letters (having at least length 4). This is by no means the only TG that accepts this language:

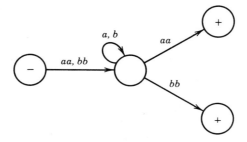

As it stands, this machine has only one start state with no incoming edges, but it has two final states, so we must introduce a new unique final state following the method prescribed by the algorithm:

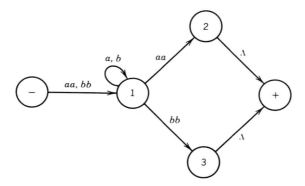

The next modification we perform is to note that the edge from the start state to state 1 is a double edge—we can travel over it by an *aa* or a *bb*. We replace this by the regular expression **aa + bb**. We also note that there is a double loop at state 1. We can loop back to state 1 on a single *a* or on a single *b*. The algorithm says we are supposed to replace this double loop by a single loop labeled with the regular expression **a + b**. The picture of the machine has now become

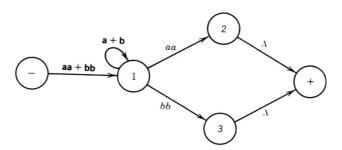

The algorithm does not actually tell us which state of the TG we must bypass next. The order of elimination is left up to our own discretion. The algorithm (when we formally state

it) implies that it really does not matter. As long as we continue to eliminate states, we shall be simplifying the machine down to a single regular expression representation.

Let us choose state 2 for elimination. The only path we are now concerned with is

The algorithm says we can replace this with one edge from state 1 to state + that bears the label that is the concatenation of the regular expressions on the two parts of the path. In this case, *aa* is concatenated with Λ, which is only *aa* again. Once we have eliminated the edge from state 1, we can eliminate state 2 entirely. The machine now looks like this:

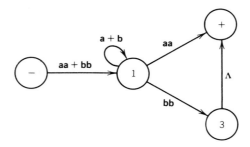

It seems reasonable now for us to choose to eliminate state 3 next. But the algorithm does not require us to be reasonable, and because this is an illustrative example and we have already seen something like this path, we shall choose a different section of *T* to modify.

The technique described above does not require us to choose the order of eliminating states in a logical, efficient, intelligent, or aesthetic manner. All these considerations are completely inappropriate to the consideration of what is an algorithm. An algorithm must be so clearly stated that it works successfully no matter how little forethought, experience, cleverness, or artistic sensibility the applier of the procedure possesses. The algorithm must be able to be completely and successfully executed by a dimwit, a half-wit, or even a no-wit such as a computer. To execute an algorithm, all we are allowed to presume on the part of the executing agent is tireless diligence and immaculate precision.

If we could presume that gifted insight on the part of the executor was routinely available, the algorithm would be much simpler:

Step 1   Look at the machine, figure out its language, and write down an equivalent regular expression.

Unfortunately, people are not as reliably creative as they are reliable drones, and the whole purpose of an algorithm is so that we can get some jobs done on a daily basis without waiting for DaVinci to be in the suitable mood. All the requisite cleverness must be incorporated into the algorithm itself by the creator of the algorithm.

If we want the algorithm to be efficient, we must design one that will force the drone to turn out efficient products. If we want the output to be aesthetic, we must build that in, too. Computer science courses that are concerned with how good an algorithm is are fundamentally different from this course. We are primarily concerned with whether an algorithm to accomplish a certain task exists or not—we are never in search of the "best" one by any standards of what it means to be best. That said, we shall, however, occasionally present more than one algorithm for accomplishing a certain task, but the reason for this will always be that each of the algorithms we develop can be generalized to other tasks in different ways.

As such, they are each the seed of different classes of procedures and each deserves individual attention.

Let us continue with the example of the TG we are in the process of reducing to a regular expression. Let us stubbornly insist on bypassing state 1 before eliminating state 3.

Only one edge comes into state 1 and that is from state −. There is a loop at state 1 with the label (**a** + **b**). State 1 has edges coming out of it that lead to state 3 and state +.

The algorithm explains that we can eliminate state 1 and replace these edges with an edge from state − to state 3 labeled (**aa** + **bb**)(**a** + **b**)*(**bb**) and an edge from state − to state + labeled (**aa** + **bb**)(**a** + **b**)*(**aa**).

After we eliminate state 1, the machine looks like this:

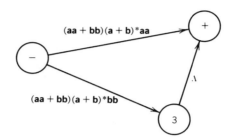

It is obvious that we must now eliminate state 3, because that is the only bypassable state left. When we concatenate the regular expression from state − to state 3 with the regular expression from state 3 to state +, we are left with the machine

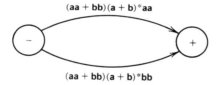

Now by the last rule of the algorithm, this machine defines the same language as the regular expression

$$(aa + bb)(a + b)*(aa) + (aa + bb)(a + b)*(bb)$$

It is entirely conceivable that if we eliminated the states in a different order, we could end up with a different-looking regular expression. But by the logic of the elimination process, these expressions would all have to represent the same language.

If we had to make up a regular expression for the language of all strings that begin and end with double letters, we would probably have written

$$(aa + bb)(a + b)*(aa + bb)$$

which is equivalent to the regular expression that the algorithm produced because the algebraic distributive law applies to regular expressions. ∎

Without going through lengthy descriptions, let us watch the algorithm work on one more example. Let us start with the TG that accepts strings with an even number of *a*'s and an even number of *b*'s, the language EVEN-EVEN. (We keep harping on these strings not because they are so terribly important, but because it is the hardest example we thoroughly understand to date, and rather than introduce new hard examples, we keep it as an old conquest.)

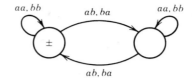

becomes first

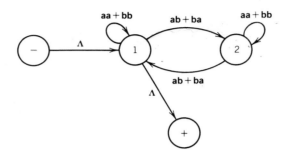

When we eliminate state 2, the path from 1 to 2 to 1 becomes a loop at state 1:

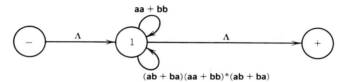

which becomes

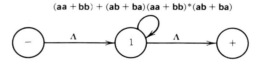

which becomes

$$[(aa + bb) + (ab + ba)(aa + bb)*(ab + ba)]*$$

which reduces to the regular expression

$$[(\textbf{aa} + \textbf{bb}) + (\textbf{ab} + \textbf{ba})(\textbf{aa} + \textbf{bb})*(\textbf{ab} + \textbf{ba})]*$$

which is exactly the regular expression we used to define this language before. Anyone who was wondering how we could have thought up that complicated regular expression we presented in Chapter 4 can see now that it came from the obvious TG for this language by way of our algorithm.

We still have one part of Kleene's theorem yet to prove. We must show that for each regular expression we can build a finite automaton that accepts the same language.

We have so far tacitly maintained that we can consider the state being bypassed without regard to any extra complications in the rest of the TG. Is this really so? It is often hard to tell whether we have accounted for all the exceptional situations that might arise. Remember, it is not a complete algorithm if it breaks down in any case no matter how remote or freakish an occurrence. How can we tell when we have covered all possibilities? Who knows? There is no algorithm to tell whether the algorithm we have proposed has omitted an important case — but here is a surprise — this very statement about the limitations of analyzing algorithms by other algorithms will be proven later on in this book.

Let us consider a complicated, most general-looking case and see whether our simple rules work on it without the introduction of any new difficulties. Consider the TG fragment below:

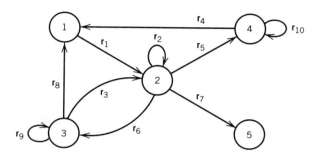

Our state targeted for bypass is state 2. Proceeding in an orderly fashion, we list all the states connected to state 2 by incoming and outgoing edges. The incoming edges are from states 1 and 3, the outgoing are to states 3, 4, and 5. Because each previously possible path must still exist, we need to introduce six new edges (including the loop at 3):

From	To	Labeled
1	3	$r_1 r_2{}^* r_6$
1	4	$r_1 r_2{}^* r_5$
1	5	$r_1 r_2{}^* r_7$
3	3	$r_3 r_2{}^* r_6$
3	4	$r_3 r_2{}^* r_5$
3	5	$r_3 r_2{}^* r_7$

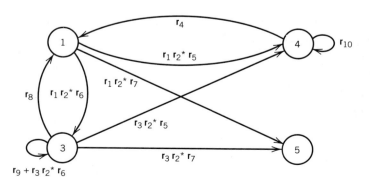

Because there is already a loop at state 3, we can add this regular expression to the existing one and the resultant picture is this:

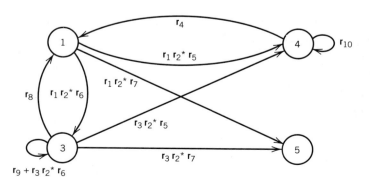

State 2 has disappeared but all paths that used to travel through it remain possible and, equally important, no new paths are possible in this new TG that were not possible for the same cost of input letters in the original TG.

For example, the old trip through states 1-2-4-4-1-2-3-3-2-5 can still be made. It now, however, travels through the state sequence 1-4-4-1-3-3-5 whose concatenation of regular expressions is exactly the same as before.

ALGORITHM

Now that we already have a fairly good idea of what the state-elimination algorithm is all about, we are ready to present a semiformal statement of the general rules defining the constructive algorithm that proves that all TGs can be turned into regular expressions that define the exact same language:

Step 1   Create a unique, unenterable minus state and a unique, unleaveable plus state.

Step 2   One by one, in any order, bypass and eliminate all the non − or + states in the TG. A state is bypassed by connecting each incoming edge with each outgoing edge. The label of each resultant edge is the concatenation of the label on the incoming edge with the label on the loop edge if there is one and the label on the outgoing edge.

Step 3   When two states are joined by more than one edge going in the same direction, unify them by adding their labels.

Step 4   Finally, when all that is left is one edge from − to +, the label on that edge is a regular expression that generates the same language as was recognized by the original machine.   ∎

We have waffled about calling this representation a "semiformal" description of the procedure. The addition of phrases (or symbols) that say things like "for all states q_x that enter state q_y by a single directed edge (q_x, q_y) labeled $\mathbf{r(x, y)}$, and for all states q_z such that (q_y, q_z) is a single directed edge labeled $\mathbf{r(y, z)}$, create the directed edge (q_x, q_z) and label it $[\mathbf{r(x, y)} \mathbf{r(y, y)}*\mathbf{r(y, z)}]$, where $\mathbf{r(y, y)}$ is the regular expression labeling the possible loop at state q_y, while deleting the state q_y and all its associated edges," and so on, would please some people more, but would not help anyone go from a state of not understanding the algorithm to a state of understanding it.

There is one logical possibility that we have not accounted for in the description of the algorithm given above; that is, when we finish step 3, there may be no path left at all that connects − to +. In this case, we say that the original machine accepted no words, which means that it accepted only the null language φ whose regular expression has no symbols. We shall consider the logical consequences of this possibility in a later chapter; at the moment, all it means is that completing the algorithm guarantees producing a regular expression for all machines that accept a language and no expression for those that do not.

EXAMPLE

Consider the TG

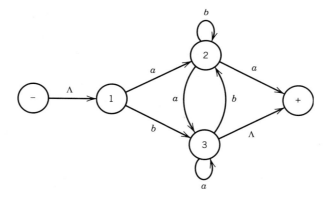

Eliminating the states in the order 1, 2, 3 gives this procession of TGs:

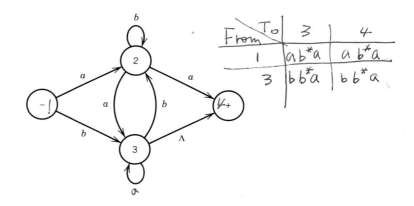

then

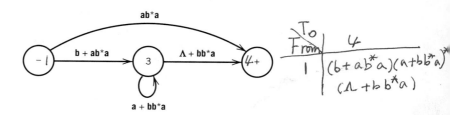

then

$$ab^*a + [b + ab^*a][a + bb^*a]^*[\Lambda + bb^*a]$$

Eliminating the states in the order 3, 2, 1 gives this procession of TGs:

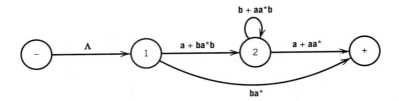

then

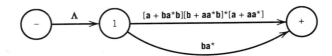

then

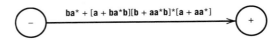

If we had not seen how they were derived, we might have no clue as to whether these two regular expressions define the same language.   ∎

⚜ CONVERTING REGULAR EXPRESSIONS INTO FAs

Proof of Part 3

The proof of this part will be by recursive definition and constructive algorithm at the same time. This is the hardest part of our whole theorem, so we shall go very slowly.

We know that every regular expression can be built up from the letters of the alphabet Σ and Λ by repeated application of certain rules: addition, concatenation, and closure. We shall see that as we are building up a regular expression, we could at the same time be building up an FA that accepts the same language.

We present our algorithm recursively.

Rule 1   There is an FA that accepts any particular letter of the alphabet. There is an FA that accepts only the word Λ.

Proof of Rule 1

If x is in Σ, then the FA

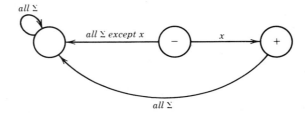

accepts only the word x.

One FA that accepts only Λ is

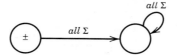

It would be easier to design these machines as TGs, but it is important to keep them as FAs.

Rule 2   If there is an FA called FA_1 that accepts the language defined by the regular expression $\mathbf{r}_1$ and there is an FA called FA_2 that accepts the language defined by the regular expression $\mathbf{r}_2$, then there is an FA that we shall call FA_3 that accepts the language defined by the regular expression $(\mathbf{r}_1 + \mathbf{r}_2)$.

Proof of Rule 2

We are going to prove Rule 2 by showing how to *construct* the new machine in the most reasonable way from the two old machines. We shall prove FA_3 exists by showing how to construct it.

Before we state the general principles, let us demonstrate them in a specific example. Suppose we have the machine FA_1 pictured below, which accepts the language of all words over the alphabet $\Sigma = \{a \quad b\}$ that have a double a somewhere in them

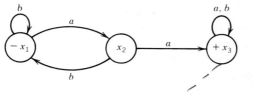

	a	b
$-x_1$	x_2	x_1
x_2	x_3	x_1
$+x_3$	x_3	x_3

and the familiar machine FA_2, which accepts all words that have both an even number of total a's and an even number of total b's (EVEN-EVEN)

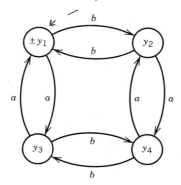

	a	b
$\pm y_1$	y_3	y_2
y_2	y_4	y_1
y_3	y_1	y_4
y_4	y_2	y_3

We shall show how to design a machine that accepts both sets. That is, we shall build a machine that accepts all words that either have an *aa* or are in EVEN-EVEN and rejects all strings with neither characteristic.

The language the new machine accepts will be the *union* of these two languages. We shall call the states in this new machine z_1, z_2, z_3, and so on, for as many as we need. We shall define this machine by its transition table.

Our guiding principle is this: The new machine will simultaneously keep track of where the input would be if it were running on FA_1 alone and where the input would be if it were running on FA_2 alone.

First of all, we need a start state. This state must combine x_1, the start state for FA_1, and y_1, the start state for FA_2. We call it z_1. If the string were running on FA_1, it would start in x_1 and if on FA_2 in y_1. z_1 combine x_1 and y_1

All z-states in the FA_3 machine carry with them a double meaning—they keep track of which x state the string would be in and which y state the string would be in. It is not as if we are uncertain about which machine the input string is running on—it is running on both FA_1 and FA_2, and we are keeping track of both games simultaneously.

What new states can occur if the input letter a is read? If the string were being run on the first machine, it would put the machine into state x_2. If the string were running on the second machine, it would put the machine into state y_3. Therefore, on our new machine an a puts us into state z_2, which means either x_2 or y_3, in the same way that z_1 means either x_1 or y_1. Because y_1 is a final state for FA_2, z_1 is also a final state in the sense that any word whose path ends there on the z-machine would be accepted by FA_2.

$$\pm z_1 = x_1 \quad \text{or} \quad y_1$$
$$z_2 = x_2 \quad \text{or} \quad y_3$$

On the machine FA_3, we are following both the path the input would make on FA_1 and the input's path on FA_2 at the same time. By keeping track of both paths, we know when the input string ends, whether or not it has reached a final state on either machine.

Let us not consider this "x or y" disjunction as a matter of uncertainty. We know for a fact that the same input is running on both machines; we might equivalently say "x and y." We may not know whether a certain person weighed 100 or 200 lb to start with, but we are certain that after gaining 20 lb, then losing 5, and then gaining 1, his total weight is now exactly either 116 or 216 lb. So, even if we do not know in which initial state the string started, we can still be certain that given a known sequence of transformations, it is now definitely in either one of two possible conditions.

If we are in state z_1 and we read the letter b, then being in x_1 on FA_1 and reading a b, we return to x_1, whereas being in y_1 on FA_2 and reading a b send us to y_2.

$$z_3 = x_1 \quad \text{or} \quad y_2$$

The beginning of our transition table for FA_3 is

	a	b
$\pm z_1$	z_2 $\{x_2, y_3\}$	z_3 $\{x_1, y_2\}$

Suppose that somehow we have gotten into state z_2 and then we read an a. If we were in FA_1, we would now go to state x_3, which is a final state. If we were in FA_2, we would now go back to y_1, which is also a final state. We will call this condition z_4, meaning either x_3 or y_1. Because this string could now be accepted on one of these two machines, z_4 is a final state for FA_3. As it turns out, in this example the word is accepted by both machines at once, but this is not necessary. Acceptance by either machine FA_1 or FA_2 is enough for acceptance by FA_3. Membership in either language is enough to guarantee membership in the union.

If we are in state z_2 and we happen to read a b, then in FA_1 we are back to x_1, whereas in FA_2 we are in y_4. Call this new condition $z_5 = $ state x_1 or y_4.

$$+z_4 = x_3 \quad \text{or} \quad y_1$$
$$z_5 = x_1 \quad \text{or} \quad y_4$$

At this point, our transition table looks like this:

	a	b
$\pm z_1$	z_2	z_3
z_2	z_4	z_5

What happens if we start from state z_3 and read an a? If we were in FA_1, we are now in x_2; if in FA_2, we are now in y_4. This is a new state in the sense that we have not encountered this combination of x and y before; call it state z_6.

$$z_6 = x_2 \quad \text{or} \quad y_4$$

What if we are in z_3 and we read a b? In FA_1 we stay in x_1, whereas in FA_2 we return to y_1. This means that if we are in z_3 and we read a b, we return to state z_1. This is the first time that we have not had to create a new state. If we never got any use out of the old states, the machine would grow ad infinitum.

Our transition table now looks like this:

	a	b
$\pm z_1$	z_2	z_3
z_2	z_4	z_5
z_3	z_6	z_1

What if we are in z_4 and we read an a? If we are tracing FA_1, the input remains in x_3, whereas if we are tracing the input on FA_2, it goes to y_3. This is a new state; call it z_7. If we are in z_4 and we read a b, the FA_1 part stays at x_3, whereas the FA_2 part goes to y_2. This is also a new state; call it z_8.

$$+z_7 = x_3 \quad \text{or} \quad y_3$$
$$+z_8 = x_3 \quad \text{or} \quad y_2$$

Both of these are final states because a string ending here on the z-machine will be accepted by FA_1, because x_3 is a final state for FA_1.

If we are in z_5 and we read an a, we go to x_2 or y_2, which we shall call z_9.
If we are in z_5 and we read a b, we go to x_1 or y_3, which we shall call z_{10}.

$$z_9 = x_2 \quad \text{or} \quad y_2$$
$$z_{10} = x_1 \quad \text{or} \quad y_3$$

If we are in z_6 and we read an a, we go to x_3 or y_2, which is our old z_8.
If we are in z_6 and we read a b, we go to x_1 or y_3, which is z_{10} again.
If we are in z_7 and we read an a, we go to x_3 or y_1, which is z_4 again.
If we are in z_7 and we read a b, we go to x_3 or y_4, which is a new state, z_{11}.

$$+z_{11} = x_3 \quad \text{or} \quad y_4$$

If we are in z_8 and we read an a, we go to x_3 or $y_4 = z_{11}$.
If we are in z_8 and we read a b, we go to x_3 or $y_1 = z_4$.
If we are in z_9 and we read an a, we go to x_3 or $y_4 = z_{11}$.
If we are in z_9 and we read a b, we go to x_1 or $y_1 = z_1$.
If we are in z_{10} and we read an a, we go to x_2 or y_1, which is our last new state, z_{12}.

$$+z_{12} = x_2 \quad \text{or} \quad y_1$$

If we are in z_{10} and we read a b, we go to x_1 or $y_4 = z_5$.

If we are in z_{11} and we read an a, we go to x_3 or $y_2 = z_8$.

If we are in z_{11} and we read a b, we go to x_3 or $y_3 = z_7$.

If we are in z_{12} and we read an a, we go to x_3 or $y_3 = z_7$.

If we are in z_{12} and we read a b, we go to x_1 or $y_2 = z_3$.

Our machine is now complete. The full transition table is

	a	b
$\pm z_1$	z_2	z_3
z_2	z_4	z_5
z_3	z_6	z_1
$+z_4$	z_7	z_8
z_5	z_9	z_{10}
z_6	z_8	z_{10}
$+z_7$	z_4	z_{11}
$+z_8$	z_{11}	z_4
z_9	z_{11}	z_1
z_{10}	z_{12}	z_5
$+z_{11}$	z_8	z_7
$+z_{12}$	z_7	z_3

Here is what FA_3 may look like:

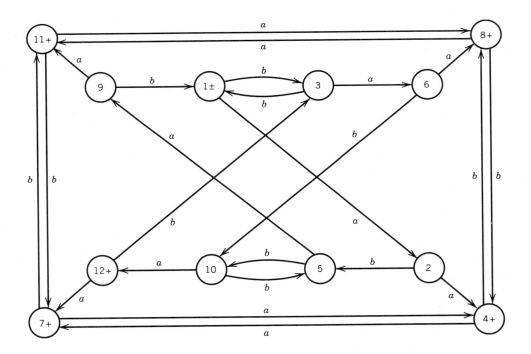

If a string traces through this machine and ends up at a final state, it means that it would also end at a final state either on machine FA_1 or on machine FA_2. Also, any string accepted by either FA_1 or FA_2 will be accepted by this FA_3.

ALGORITHM

The general description of the algorithm we employed earlier is as follows. Starting with two machines, FA_1 with states $x_1, x_2, x_3, \ldots$ and FA_2 with states $y_1, y_2, y_3, \ldots$, build a new machine FA_3 with states $z_1, z_2, z_3, \ldots$, where each z is of the form "$x_{\text{something}}$ or $y_{\text{something}}$." The combination state x_{start} or y_{start} is the $-$ state of the new FA. If either the x part or the y part is a final state, then the corresponding z is a final state. To go from one z to another by reading a letter from the input string, we see what happens to the x part and the y part and go to the new z accordingly. We could write this as a formula:

$$z_{\text{new}} \text{ after letter } p = [x_{\text{new}} \text{ after letter } p \text{ on } FA_1] \text{ or } [y_{\text{new}} \text{ after letter } p \text{ on } FA_2]$$

Because there are only finitely many x's and y's, there can be only finitely many possible z's. Not all of them will necessarily be used in FA_3 if no input string beginning at $-$ can get to them. In this way, we can build a machine that can accept the sum of two regular expressions if we already know machines to accept each of the component regular expressions separately. ∎

EXAMPLE (Inside the proof of Theorem 6)

Let us go through this very quickly once more on the two machines:

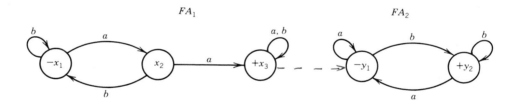

FA_1 accepts all words with a double a in them, and FA_2 accepts all words ending in b. The machine that accepts the union of the two languages for these two machines begins:

$$-z_1 = x_1 \quad \text{or} \quad y_1$$

In z_1 if we read an a, we go to x_2 or $y_1 = z_2$
In z_1 if we read a b, we go to x_1 or $y_2 = z_3$, which is a final state since y_2 is.

The partial picture of this machine is now

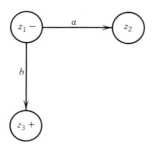

In z_2 if we read an a, we go to x_3 or $y_1 = z_4$, which is a final state because x_3 is.
In z_2 if we read a b, we go to x_1 or $y_2 = z_3$.

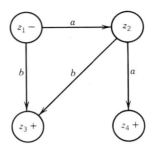

In z_3 if we read an a, we go to x_2 or $y_1 = z_2$.
In z_3 if we read a b, we go to x_1 or $y_2 = z_3$.
In z_4 if we read an a, we go to x_3 or $y_1 = z_4$.
In z_4 if we read a b, we go to x_3 or $y_2 = z_5$, which is a final state.
In z_5 if we read an a, we go to x_3 or $y_1 = z_4$.
In z_5 if we read a b, we go to x_3 or $y_2 = z_5$.

The whole machine looks like this:

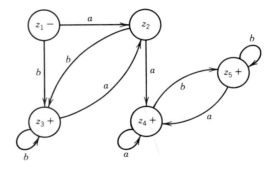

This machine accepts all words that have a double a *or* that end in b.
The seemingly logical possibility

$$z_6 = x_2 \quad \text{or} \quad y_2$$

does not arise. This is because to be in x_2 on FA_1 means the last letter read is an a. But to be in y_2 on FA_2 means the last letter read is a b. These cannot both be true at the same time, so no input string ever has the possibility of being in state z_6.   ∎

EXAMPLE   (Inside the proof of Theorem 6)

Let FA_1 be the machine below that accepts all words that end in a:

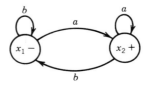

and let FA_2 be the machine below that accepts all words with an odd number of letters (odd length):

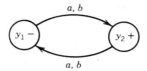

Using the algorithm produces the machine below that accepts all words that either have an odd number of letters or end in a:

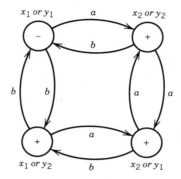

The only state that is not a + state is the − state. To get back to the start state, a word must have an even number of letters *and* end in b. ∎

EXAMPLE   (Inside the proof of Theorem 6)

Let FA_1 be

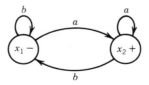

which accepts all words ending in a, and let FA_2 be

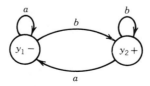

which accepts all words ending in b.
Using the algorithm, we produce

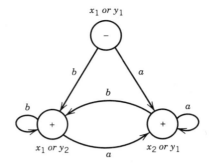

which accepts all words ending in a or b, that is, all words except Λ. Notice that the state x_2 or y_2 cannot be reached because x_2 means "we have just read an a" and y_2 means "we have just read a b." ∎

    There is an alternate procedure for producing the union-machine form two-component machines that has a more compact mathematical description, but whose disadvantages are well illustrated by the example we have just considered. Let FA_1 have states $x_1, x_2, \ldots$ and FA_2 have states $y_1, y_2, \ldots$. Then we can define FA_3 initially as having all the possible states x_i or y_j for all combinations of i and j. The number of states in FA_3 would always be the product of the number of states in FA_1 and the number of states in FA_2. For each state in FA_3 we could then, in any order, draw its a-edge and b-edge because they would go to already existing states. What we have done before is create new z-states as the need arose, as in the Japanese "just in time" approach to automobile manufacturing. This may seem a little haphazard, and we never really know when or whether the need for a new combination of x and y would arise. This alternate, more organized, approach has the advantage of knowing from the beginning just how many states and edges we will need to draw, always the pessimistic estimate of the largest possible number. For the example above, we would start with four possible states:

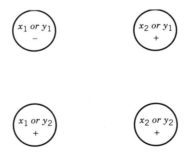

For each of these four states we would draw two edges, producing

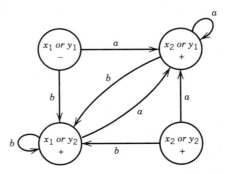

This is a perfectly possible FA for the union language $FA_1 + FA_2$. However, on inspection we see that its lower right-hand state is completely useless because it can never be entered by any string starting at $-$. It is not against the definition of an FA to have such a useless state, nor is it a crime. It is simply an example of the tradeoff between constructing states in our need-to-have policy versus the more universal-seeming all-at-once strategy.

By either algorithm, this concludes the proof of Rule 2.

We still have two rules to go.

Rule 3　If there is an FA_1 that accepts the language defined by the regular expression $\mathbf{r}_1$ and an FA_2 that accepts the language defined by the regular expression $\mathbf{r}_2$, then there is an FA_3 that accepts the language defined by the concatenation $\mathbf{r}_1\mathbf{r}_2$, the product language.

Proof of Rule 3

Again, we shall verify this rule by a constructive algorithm. We shall prove that such an FA_3 exists by showing how to construct it from FA_1 and FA_2. As usual, first we do an illustration; then we state the general principles, but our illustration here first is of what can go wrong, not what to do right.

Let L_1 be the language of all words with b as the second letter. One machine that accepts L_1 is FA_1:

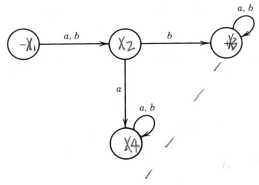

Let L_2 be the language of all words that have an odd number of a's. One machine for L_2 is FA_2:

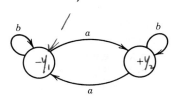

Now consider the input string *ababbaa*. This is a word in the product language L_1L_2, because it is the concatenation of a word in L_1 (*ab*) with a word in L_2 (*abbaa*). If we begin to run this string on FA_1, we would reach the $+$ state after the second letter. If we could now somehow automatically jump over into FA_2, we could begin running what is left of the input, *abbaa*, starting in the $-$ state. This remaining input is a word in L_2, so it will finish its path in the $+$ state of FA_2. Basically, this is what we want to build—an FA_3 that processes the first part of the input string as if it were FA_1; then when it reaches the FA_1 + state, it turns into the − state on FA_2. From there it continues processing the string until it reaches the + state on FA_2, and we can then accept the input.

Tentatively, let us say FA_3 looks something like this:

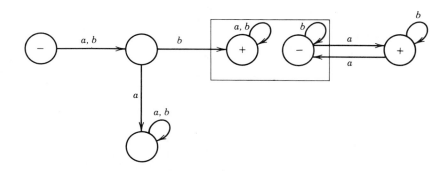

Unfortunately, this idea, though simple, does not work. We can see this by considering a different input string from the same product language. The word *ababbab* is also in $L_1 L_2$, because *abab* is in L_1 (it has b as its second letter) and *bab* is in L_2 (it has an odd number of a's).

If we run the input string *ababbab* first on FA_1, we get to the + state after two letters, but we must not say that we are finished yet with the L_1 part of the input. If we stopped running on FA_1 after *ab*, when we reached + in FA_1, the remaining input string *abbab* could not reach + on FA_2 because it has an even number of a's.

Remember that FA_1 accepts all words with paths that *end* at a final state. They could pass through that final state many times before *ending* there. This is the case with the input *abab*. It reaches + after two letters. However, we must continue to run the string on FA_1 for two more letters. We enter + three times. *Then* we can jump to FA_2 (whatever that means) and run the remaining string *bab* on FA_2. The input *bab* will then start on FA_2 in the − state and finish in the + state.

Our problem is this: How do we know when to jump from FA_1 to FA_2? With the input *ababbaa* we should jump when we first reach the + in FA_1. With the input *ababbab* (which differs only in the last letter), we have to stay in FA_1 until we have looped back to the + state some number of times before jumping to FA_2. How can a finite automaton, which must make a mandatory transition on each input letter without looking ahead to see what the rest of the string will be, know when to jump from FA_1 to FA_2?

This is a subtle point, and it involves some new ideas.

We have to build a machine that has the characteristic of starting out like FA_1 and following along it until it enters a final state at which time an option is reached. Either we continue along FA_1 waiting to reach another +, or else we switch over to the start state of FA_2 and begin circulating there. This is tricky, because the r_1 part of the input string can generate an arbitrarily long word if it has a star in it, and we cannot be quite sure of when to jump out of FA_1 and into FA_2. And what happens (heavens forfend) if FA_1 has more than one +?

Now let us illustrate how to build such an FA_3 for a specific example. The two machines we shall use are

$$FA_1 = \text{the machine that accepts only strings with a double } a \text{ in them}$$

and

$$FA_2 = \text{the machine that accepts all words that end in the letter } b$$

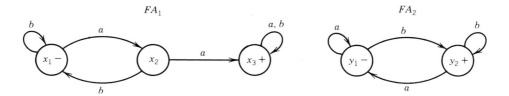

We shall start with the state z_1, which is exactly like x_1. It is a start state, and it means that the input string is being run on FA_1 alone. Unlike the union machine the string is not being run on FA_2 yet. From z_1 if we read a b, we must return to the same state x_1, which is z_1 again. From z_1 if we read an a, we must go to state x_2 because we are interested in seeing that the first section of the input string is a word accepted by FA_1. Therefore, z_2 is the same as x_2. From the state z_2 if we read a b, we must go back to z_1. Therefore, we have the relationships

$$z_1 = x_1$$
$$z_2 = x_2$$

The picture of FA_3 starts out just like the picture of FA_1:

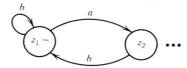

Now if we are in z_2 and we read an a, we must go to a new state z_3, which in some ways corresponds to the state x_3 in FA_1. However, x_3 has a dual identity. Either it means that we have reached a final state for the first half of the input as a word in the language for FA_1 and it is where we cross over and run the rest of the input string on FA_2, or else it is merely another state that the string must pass through to get eventually to its last state in FA_1. Many strings, some of which are accepted and some of which are rejected, pass through several + states on their way through any given machine.

If we are now in z_3 in its capacity as the final state of FA_1 for the first part of this input string, we must begin running the rest of the input string as if it were input of FA_2 beginning at state y_1. Therefore, the full meaning of being in z_3 is

$$z_3 = \begin{cases} x_3, \text{ and we are still running on } FA_1 \\ \qquad\qquad \text{or} \\ y_1, \text{ and we have begun to run on } FA_2 \end{cases}$$

Notice the similarity between this disjunctive (either/or) definition of z_3 and the disjunctive definitions for the z-states produced by the algorithm given for the addition of two FAs. There are also significant differences, as discussed next.

If we are in state z_3 and we read an a, we have now *three* possible interpretations for the state into which this puts us:

$$\begin{cases} \text{We are back in } x_3 \text{ continuing to run the string on } FA_1 \\ \qquad\qquad \text{or} \\ \text{we have just finished on } FA_1 \text{ and we are now in } y_1 \\ \text{beginning to run on } FA_2 \\ \qquad\qquad \text{or} \\ \text{we have looped from } y_1 \text{ back to } y_1 \text{ while already running on} \\ FA_2 \end{cases}$$

$$= x_3 \text{ or } y_1$$
(because being in y_1 is the same whether we are
there for the first time or not)
$$= z_3$$

Therefore, if we are in z_3 and we read an a, we loop back to z_3.

If we are in state z_3 and we read a b, we go to state z_4, which has the following meaning:

$$+z_4 = \begin{cases} \text{We are still in } x_3 \text{ continuing to run on } FA_1 \\ \qquad\qquad \text{or} \\ \text{we have just finished running on } FA_1 \text{ and are now in } y_1 \text{ on } FA_2 \\ \qquad\qquad \text{or} \\ \text{we are now in } y_2 \text{ on } FA_2, \text{ having reached there via } y_1 \end{cases}$$

$$= x_3 \quad \text{or} \quad y_1 \quad \text{or} \quad y_2$$

If an input string ends its path in this state z_4, that means that it could have been broken into two sections, the first going from x_1 to x_3 and the second from y_1 to y_2; therefore, it must be accepted, so z_4 is a final state.

So far, our machine looks like this:

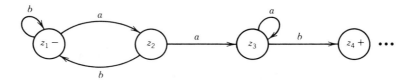

If we are in z_4 and we read an a, our choices are

$$\begin{cases} \text{remaining in } x_3 \text{ and continuing to run on } FA_1 \\ \qquad\qquad \text{or} \\ \text{having just finished } FA_1 \text{ and beginning at } y_1 \\ \qquad\qquad \text{or} \\ \text{having moved from } y_2 \text{ back to } y_1 \text{ in } FA_2 \end{cases}$$

$$= x_3 \quad \text{or} \quad y_1$$

However, this is exactly the definition of z_3 again. So, in summary, if we are in z_4 and read an a, we go back to z_3.

If we are in z_4 and read a b, our choices are

$$\begin{cases} \text{remaining in } x_3 \text{ and continuing to run on } FA_1 \\ \qquad\qquad \text{or} \\ \text{having just finished } FA_1 \text{ and beginning at } y_1 \\ \qquad\qquad \text{or} \\ \text{having looped back from } y_2 \text{ to } y_2 \text{ running on } FA_2 \end{cases}$$

$$= x_3 \quad \text{or} \quad y_1 \quad \text{or} \quad y_2$$
$$= z_4$$

Accordingly, if we are in z_4 and read a b, we loop back to z_4.

The whole machine then looks like this:

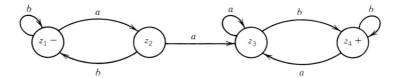

Thus, we have produced a machine that accepts exactly those strings that have a front section with a double a followed by a back section that ends in b. This we can see because without a double a we never get to z_3 and we end in z_4 only if the whole word ends in b.

ALGORITHM

In general, we can describe the algorithm for forming the machine FA_3 as follows. First, we make a z-state for every nonfinal x-state in FA_1 reached before ever hitting a final state on FA_1. For each final state in FA_1, we establish a z-state that expresses the options that we are continuing on FA_1 or are beginning on FA_2.

$$\left\{ \begin{array}{l} \text{Are in } x_{\text{something}}, \text{ which is a } + \text{ state but still} \\ \text{continuing on } FA_1 \\ \qquad\qquad\qquad \text{or} \\ \text{have finished the } FA_1 \text{ part of the input string and} \\ \text{have jumped to } y_1 \text{ to commence tracing the remainder of} \\ \text{the input string on } FA_2 \end{array} \right.$$

After we have reached a jump-to-FA_2 state, any other state we reach has an x and a y possibility like the z-states in the union machine, with the additional possibility that every time we hit yet another final state on the FA_1-machine, we may again exercise the option of jumping to y_1. This means that every time we pass through a final state while processing the FA_1 part of the input string, we jettison an alter-ego jumping to y_1 that runs around on the FA_2-machine. These little mice tracing paths on FA_2 each start at y_1 but at different points in the input string, at any future instant they may be at several different y-states on FA_2. Every z-state therefore can have the nature of one and only one x-state, but a whole set of possible y-states.

So, the full nature of a z-state is

$$\left\{ \begin{array}{l} \text{are in } x_{\text{something}} \text{ continuing on } FA_1 \\ \qquad\qquad\qquad \text{or} \\ \text{are in a set of } y_{\text{something}} \text{ continuing on } FA_2 \end{array} \right.$$

There are clearly only finitely many possibilities for such z-states, so FA_3 is a finite machine. The transition from one z-state to another for each letter of the alphabet is determined uniquely by the transition rules in FA_1 and FA_2. One set of y's will move to another set of y's along their a-edges or b-edges. So, FA_3 is a well-defined finite automaton that clearly does what we want; that is, it accepts only strings that first reach a final state on FA_1, jump to y_1, and then reach a final state on FA_2.

We still have to decide which states in the new FA are final states. Clearly, to be in FA_1FA_2 means to end in a final state in FA_2, so any z-state is a final state if it contains a y-machine final state as a possible position for the input. This completes the algorithm. ∎

EXAMPLE   (Inside the proof of Theorem 6)

Let us illustrate this algorithm to construct the machine for the product of the languages of L_1, all words that start with a b, and L_2, all words that end with a b.

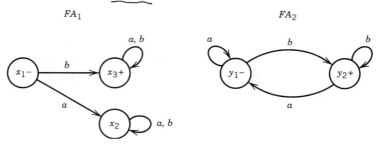

Initially, we must begin in x_1, which we shall just call z_1. If we read an a, we go to x_2, which we may as well call z_2. If we read a b, we go to x_3, which being a final state means that we have the option of jumping to y_1, an option we do not necessarily have to exercise at this moment.

$$z_3 = x_3 \quad \text{or} \quad y_1$$

From z_2, like x_2, both an a or a b take us back to z_2.

In z_3 if we are in the x_3 condition and we read an a, we stay in x_3 or we now choose (because x_3 is a final state) to jump to y_1. If we were in z_3 in the y_1 condition already and we read an a, we would loop back to y_1 on the FA_2-machine. In any of these three eventualities, if we are in z_3 and we read an a, we end up at either x_3 or y_1; in other words, from z_3 we go back to z_3.

If we are in z_3 and we read a b, a different event takes place. If the z_3 meant x_3, we either stay there or use the occasion to jump to y_1. If we were in z_3 already in y_1, then the b would necessarily take us to y_2. Therefore, we need a new state:

$$z_4 = x_3 \quad \text{or} \quad y_1 \quad \text{or} \quad y_2$$

If the input string processing ends in this state, then it should be accepted because it may have gotten to the final state on the FA_2-machine. So, z_4 is a final state for FA_3.

What happens if we are in z_4 and we read an a?

x_3 goes to x_3, staying on FA_1

or

x_3 goes to x_3, then jumps to y_1 on FA_2

or

y_1 stays in y_1

or

y_2 goes to y_1

So from z_4 an a takes us to x_3 or y_1, which is z_3.

What happens if we are in z_4 and we read the input letter b?

x_3 goes to x_3, staying on FA_1

or

x_3 goes to x_3, which jumps to y_1

or

y_1 goes to y_2

or

y_2 loops back to y_2

So from z_4 a b will loop us back to z_4.

The complete picture of the machine then looks like this:

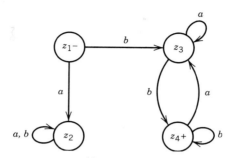

It is fairly evident that this is a decent machine for all words that both begin and end with the letter b, which is what the product of the two languages would be. Notice that the word b itself is not accepted. Even though it begins and ends with the letter b, they are the same letter b and therefore it cannot be factored into b-beginning and b-ending strings.

What if we were to multiply these languages in the opposite order: all words that end in b times all words that begin with a b. The resultant language should be that of all words with a double b in them. To build the machine, we multiply FA_2 times FA_1:

$$z_1 = y_1$$

An a from z_1 will take us back to z_1. A b will take us to

$$z_2 = y_2 \quad \text{or} \quad x_1 \quad \text{(because } y_2 \text{ is a final state for the first machine)}$$

From z_2 an a will take us to y_1 or x_2, not x_1, because y_1 is not a final state on the first machine:

$$z_3 = y_1 \quad \text{or} \quad x_2$$

From z_2 a b will take us from y_2 back to y_2, or y_2 back to y_2 and then jump to x_1, or x_1 to x_3. This is a new state:

$$z_4 = y_2 \quad \text{or} \quad x_1 \quad \text{or} \quad x_3$$

From z_3 an a will take us from y_1 to y_1, or x_2 to x_2. So, z_3 has an a-loop.

From z_3 a b will take us from y_1 to y_2, or y_1 to y_2 to x_1, or x_2 to x_2. This is a new state:

$$z_5 = y_2 \quad \text{or} \quad x_1 \quad \text{or} \quad x_2$$

From z_4 an a will take us from y_2 to y_1, or x_1 to x_2, or x_3 to x_3. This is also a new state:

$$z_6 = y_1 \quad \text{or} \quad x_2 \quad \text{or} \quad x_3$$

From z_4 a b will take us from y_2 to y_2, or y_2 to y_2 to x_1, or x_1 to x_3, or x_3 to x_3, which is z_4.

From z_5 an a will take us from y_2 to y_1, x_1 to x_2, x_2 to x_2, which is just z_3 again.

From z_5 a b will take us from y_2 to y_2, y_2 to y_2 to x_1, x_1 to x_3, x_2 to x_2, which is a new state:

$$z_7 = y_2 \quad \text{or} \quad x_1 \quad \text{or} \quad x_2 \quad \text{or} \quad x_3$$

From z_6 an a will loop us back to z_6 for each of its three components.

From z_6 a b will take us from y_1 to y_2, y_1 to y_2 to x_1, x_2 to x_2, x_3 to $x_3 = z_7$.

From z_7 an a will take us from y_1 to y_1, x_1 to x_2, x_2 to x_2, x_3 to $x_3 = z_6$.
From z_7 a b will take us from y_2 to y_2, y_2 to y_2 to x_1, x_1 to x_3, x_2 to x_2, x_3 to $x_3 = z_7$.

Therefore, the machine is finished.

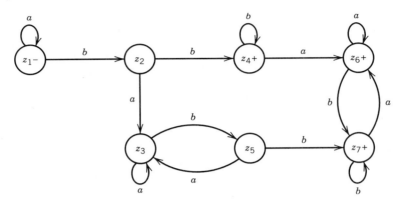

The only final states are those that contain the possibility of x_3. It is very clear that this machine accepts all words with a double b in them, but it is obviously not the most efficient machine to do so. ∎

While we were working the last example, we may have begun to loose faith in the finiteness of the algorithm; new (and needless) states kept arising. Yet, every state of the z-machine had the identity of a single y-state and a subset of x-states. There are finitely many possibilities for each of these and therefore finitely many possibilities for them jointly. The algorithm must always work and must always terminate.

EXAMPLE   (Inside the proof of Theorem 6)

Let FA_1 be

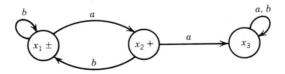

which accepts the language L_1 of all words that do *not* contain the substring aa.
   Let FA_2 be

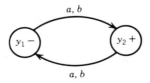

which accepts the language L_2 of all words with an odd number of letters.
   Using the preceding algorithm, we produce the following machine to accept the product language $L_1 L_2$:

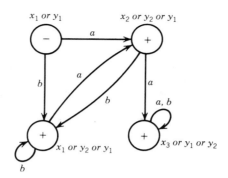

All states except the − state are final states. The − state is left the instant an input letter is read, and it can never be reentered. Therefore, the language this machine accepts is all words but Λ. This actually *is* the product language L_1L_2, because if a word w has an odd number of letters, we can factor it as $(\Lambda)(w)$, where Λ is in L_1 and w is in L_2. While if it has an even (not 0) number of letters, we factor it as

$$w = \text{(first letter)(the rest)}$$

where (first letter) must be in L_1 (cannot contain aa) and (the rest) is in L_2. Only the word Λ cannot be factored into a part in L_1 and a part in L_2. ∎

We are now ready for our last rule.

Rule 4　If **r** is a regular expression and FA_1 is a finite automaton that accepts exactly the language defined by **r**, then there is an FA called FA_2 that will accept exactly the language defined by **r***.

Proof of Rule 4

The language defined by **r*** must always contain the null word. To accept the null string Λ, we must indicate that the start state is also a final state. This could be an important change in the machine FA_1, because strings that return to x_1 might not have been accepted before. They may not be in the language of the expression **r**. The building of our new machine must be done carefully.

We shall, as in the other cases, first illustrate the algorithm for manufacturing this machine with a simple example. We cannot use most of the examples we have seen recently because their closure is not different from themselves (except for the possibility of including the word Λ). This is just a curious accident of these examples and not usual for regular expressions. The concatenation of several strings of words ending in b is itself a word ending in b. The concatenation of several strings containing aa is itself a string containing aa. The concatenation of arbitrarily many EVEN-EVEN strings is itself an EVEN-EVEN string.

Let us consider the regular expression

$$\mathbf{r} = \mathbf{a^* + aa^*b}$$

The language defined by **r** is all strings of only a's and the strings of some (not 0) a's ending in a single b. The closure of this language is defined by $(\mathbf{a^* + aa^*b})^*$, which includes all words in which each b has an a on its left. Here, **r*** is clearly not equal to **r**, because such words as aba and $ababaaa$ are in **r*** but not in the language of **r**. The language of **r*** is all strings without a double b that do not begin with b.

The machine we use to accept **r** is FA_1 pictured below:

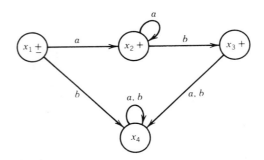

Notice that x_4 is a reject state. Any string that enters it stays there and is eventually rejected. A word that goes to x_2 and stops there is a word of all a's and it is accepted. To get to x_3 and stop there, we need exactly one b after the a's. It is true that x_1 is also a final state, but the only word that ends there is Λ.

The machine we shall build, FA_2, to accept the language defined by **r*** begins as follows:

$$\pm z_1 = x_1$$

If we are in z_1 and read a b, we go to the reject state x_4, which we call z_2.

$$z_2 = x_4$$

If we are in z_1 and read an a, we go to z_3, which means a little more than x_2 alone.

$$+z_3 = \begin{cases} x_2 \text{ and we continue processing the middle of a longer factor} \\ \text{of type } \mathbf{r} \text{ that is not yet complete and that itself may be only} \\ \text{one of many substrings of type } \mathbf{r} \text{ that the input word is composed of} \\ \qquad\qquad\qquad\qquad \text{or} \\ \text{we have just accepted a section of the input string as being} \\ \text{in the proper form for } \mathbf{r} \text{ and now we should consider ourselves} \\ \text{to be back in } x_1, \text{ starting fresh on the next section of the input string} \end{cases}$$

$$+z_3 = x_2 + x_1$$

What we are trying to say here is that while we are scanning the input string, we may have arrived at a break between one factor of type **r** and another factor of type **r**, in which case the first ends correctly at a + and the second should begin at the −. However, a factor of type **r** does not have to stop at the first + that it comes to. It may terminate at the fourth +, and the new type **r** factor may then pick up at the −. So, this jump is only an option, not necessary.

As we saw with the product of two machines when we hit a + on the first machine, we can continue on that machine or jump to the − on the second. Here when we hit a +, we can also jump back to the − (on the same machine), or we can ignore the + status of the state and continue processing, or (a new option) we can end completely.

This situation is like a bus with passengers. At each stop (final state), there is the possibility that some people get off, while others stay on the bus waiting for their correct later stops. Those that get off may jump back to start and get on another bus immediately. We are trying to trace where all these people could be at any given time. Where they are must be some collection of bus stops (states), and they are either finished, still inside the bus riding, or back at start, ready to catch another bus.

If we ever get to z_2, the total input is to be rejected, so we stay at z_2. We know this mechanically (which means here that we know it without any intelligent insight, which is important because we should never need anything that the algorithm does not automatically provide) because x_4 loops back to x_4 by a and b and therefore z_2 must do the same.

If we are in z_3 and we read a b, we go different places depending on which clause in the definition of z_3 was meant in a particular case. If z_3 meant x_2, we now go to x_3, but if z_3 meant that we are back in x_1, then we now go to x_4. Therefore, we have a new state. However, even when we are in x_3, we could be there in two ways. We could be continuing to run a string on FA_1 and proceed as normal, or else we could have just accepted a part of the string and we are starting to process the next section from scratch at x_1. Therefore, z_4 has a triple meaning:

$$+z_4 = x_1 \quad \text{or} \quad x_3 \quad \text{or} \quad x_4$$

Because x_3 is an accept state, z_4 can also accept a string that ends its path there.

Where do we go if we are in z_3 and we read an a? If we were in x_2, we stay there, whereas if we were back in x_1, we would go to x_2. Remember again that every $+$ state is also automatically a possible restart state jumping back to x_1. Therefore, we return to z_3.

If we are in z_4 and we read a b, whether we are in x_1, x_3, or x_4, we definitely go to x_4, which is z_2.

If we are in z_4 and we read an a, we go (if we were in x_1) to x_2, or (if we were in x_3) to x_4, or (if we were in x_4) to x_4. Therefore, we are in a new state:

$$+z_5 = x_1 \quad \text{or} \quad x_2 \quad \text{or} \quad x_4$$

which must be a final state because x_2 is.

From z_5 an a gets us to (x_1 or x_2 or x_4), which is z_5 itself, whereas a b gets us to (x_1 or x_3 or x_4), which is z_4 again.

This finishes the description of the whole machine. It is pictured below:

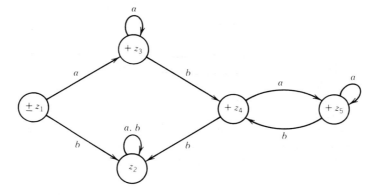

This is not actually a bad machine for the language defined by

$$(\mathbf{a}^* + \mathbf{aa}^*\mathbf{b})^*$$

ALGORITHM   (incomplete)

The general rule for this algorithm is that each z-state corresponds to some collection of x-states. We must remember each time we reach a final state it is *possible* that we have to start over again at x_1. There are only finitely many possible collections of x-states, so the machine produced by this algorithm has only finitely many states. The transitions from one collection of x-states to another based on reading certain input letters is determined completely by the transition rules for FA_1. ■

EXAMPLE

The machine below accepts all strings that end in a:

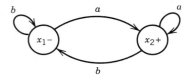

If we mechanically follow the incomplete algorithm, we would have built a machine with three states: x_1, x_2, and x_1 or x_2. Because x_2 is a + state, every time an input string path enters x_2, it could possibly be deemed to have just accepted an **r** segment and then jump to x_1 to continue processing the next syllable from start again. So, there are really only two states used in this FA*. The edges can be deduced to run as shown below:

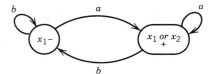

To decide which are the final states, the rule tells us that since x_2 is the only final state in the original FA (therefore, the only final states in the FA*-machine are those including the possibility of x_2), this is only the right-hand state. But now Λ is not accepted by this machine. Actually, all the other words in **r*** are accepted by this machine. If we simply stick a + in the start state, then all the states in the resultant machine are final and the machine would accept every input string. But this is not the correct machine for the language **r***, which does not contain the word bbb, for example. ∎

The proper procedure is to always begin the FA*-machine with a special ± start state that exists in addition to all the states that are subsets of x's. This start state should have exiting a- and b-edges going to the same x's that the old start state did, but this new state has no incoming edges at all. The old start state, say, it was x_1, still appears in the new machine but not as a start state, just once as itself alone and many times in combination with other x's. If the old start state was not a + state, landing in this state, or states with this alternative, will not create acceptance for strings that were not previously accepted.

The Kleene closure of the machine shown above is more accurately this:

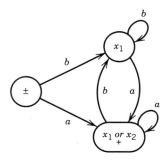

There is another possible way of resolving this difficulty. Because the FA produced by the first draft of our algorithm was perfectly fine except for the possibility of omitting Λ, we might have corrected the problem by using a combination of Rules 1 and 2 as follows. From Rule 1 we could take the FA that accepts only Λ and from Rule 2 we could have added the Λ-FA to the FA* produced by the algorithm and thus patch up the problem by adding the missing word. This new machine would have not just one additional state, but would have as many as twice the number of states in FA*. That makes this suggestion a wasteful but mathematically adequate resolution. Either way, the algorithm is now complete and correct.

ALGORITHM   (for real)

Given an FA whose states are $x_1, x_2, \ldots$, an FA that accepts the Kleene closure of the language of the original machine can be built as follows:

> Step 1   Create a state for every subset of x's. Cancel any subset that contains a final x-state, but does not contain the start state.

> Step 2   For all the remaining nonempty states, draw an a-edge and a b-edge to the collection of x-states reachable in the original FA from the component x's by a- and b-edges, respectively.

> Step 3   Call the null subset a $\pm$ state and connect it to whatever states the original start state is connected to by a- and b-edges, even possibly the start state itself.

> Step 4   Finally, put $+$ signs in every state containing an x-component that is a final state of the original FA.   ◼

This algorithm will always produce an FA, and the FA it produces satisfies our requirements.   ◼

EXAMPLE

Consider the regular expression

$$\mathbf{r = aa^*bb^*}$$

This defines the language of all words where all the a's (of which there is at least one) come before all the b's (of which there is at least one).

One FA that accepts this language is

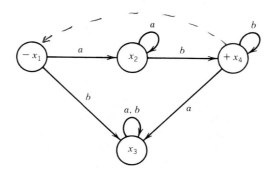

Now let us consider the language defined by $\mathbf{r}^*$:

$$\mathbf{r^* = (aa^*bb^*)^*}$$

This is a collection of a's, then b's, then a's, then b's, and so on. Most words fit this pattern. In fact, the only strings not in this language are those that start with a b and those that end with an a. All other strings are words defined by $\mathbf{r}^*$. Thus, $\mathbf{r}^*$ is almost equivalent to

$$\mathbf{a(a + b)^*b}$$

For example, *aababbb* is in $\mathbf{r}^*$ because (*aab*) is in $\mathbf{r}$ and (*abbb*) is in $\mathbf{r}$. (Every string in $\mathbf{r}^*$ can be *uniquely* factored into its substrings of type $\mathbf{r}$, but this is a side issue.) The string *abba* is definitely not in $\mathbf{r}^*$ because it ends in a.

Now let us build an FA for $\mathbf{r}^*$. Let us first see what goes wrong if we try to follow the incomplete form of the algorithm. We begin with the start state:

$$-z_1 = x_1$$

Reading an a takes us to

$$z_2 = x_2$$

Reading a b in state z_1 takes us to

$$z_3 = x_3$$

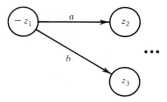

Like its counterpart x_3, z_3 is a point of no return (abandon all hope, ye that enter).

From z_2 if we read an a, we return to z_2, just as with x_2. From z_2 if we read a b, we proceed to a new state called z_4.

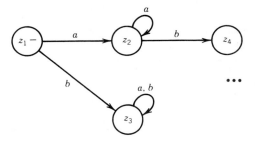

However, z_4 is not just x_4. Why? Because when we are processing the string *ababb* and we get to z_4, we may have just accepted the first factor (*ab*) as being of the form $\mathbf{r}$ and be about to process the second factor starting again in the state x_1. On the other hand, if we are processing the string *abbab* and we have only read the first two letters, even though we are in z_4, we have not completed reading the whole first factor of type $\mathbf{r}$. Therefore,

$$+z_4 = x_1 \quad \text{or} \quad x_4$$

Because it is possible to end here and accept a string, this must be a final state, but we must have the option of continuing to read another factor (substring) of type $\mathbf{r}$, or to finish reading a factor we are in the middle of. If we are in z_4 and we read an a, we go to x_3 (if we were in x_4) or x_2 (if we were in x_1). Therefore, we could say that we are going to a new state:

$$z_5 = x_2 \quad \text{or} \quad x_3$$

However, the option of being in x_3 is totally worthless. If we ever go there, we cannot accept the string. Remember x_3 is Davy Jones's locker. No string that gets there ever leaves or is ever accepted. So, if we are interested in the paths by which strings can be accepted, we need only consider that when in z_4, if we read an a, it is because we were in the x_1 part of z_4, not the x_4 part. This a, then, takes us back to z_2. (This is a touch of extra insight not actually provided by the algorithm. The algorithm requires us blindly to form a new state, z_5. We shall build both machines, the smart one and the algorithm one.)

If we are in z_2 and we read a b, we go to x_4 (if we were in x_4) or x_3 (if we were in x_1). Again, we need not consider the option of going to x_3 (the suicide option), because a path going there could accept no words. So, instead of inventing a new state,

$$z_6 = x_1 \quad \text{or} \quad x_3 \quad \text{or} \quad x_4$$

which the preceding algorithm tells us to construct, we can simply assume that from z_4 a b always takes us to x_4. This is, of course, really the combination (x_4 or x_1) because we could now continue the processing of the next letter as if it were in the state x_1 having just accepted a factor of type **r**. This is the case with the word *abbab*.

These options, x_1 or x_4, are already the definition of state z_4, so we have finished our machine.

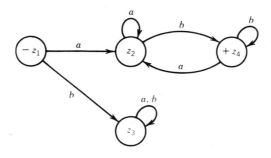

If we had mechanically followed the algorithm in the proof, we would have constructed

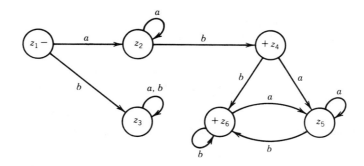

For some applications, it may be important to construct the entire machine mechanically as above because accepting an input string in z_4 may somehow be different from accepting it in z_6 (the cost could be different, or the storage space, etc.). For our simple purposes, there is no difference between these two machines except that the first one requires cleverness, which is never allowed in a proof by constructive algorithm.

In both of these diagrams, it is clear that in order to be accepted, the only conditions a string must satisfy are that it begin with an a and end with a b. Therefore, because we understand the language **r*** and we understand these two machines, we know that they truly represent the language **r*** as desired.

Before we feel completely satisfied with ourselves, we should realize that neither of the machines we have built accepts the word Λ, which *must* be in the closure of any language.

The incomplete algorithm succeeds only in cases of final and nonreenterable start states. For all other machines the real algorithm is necessary.

What went wrong was at the very beginning, when we said that z_1 was the equivalent of x_1. This is true only when x_1 is also a final state, because otherwise z_1, which must be a final state, cannot be its true twin. z_1 can act like x_1 in all other respects as a starting state for the acceptance of a word on FA_1, but because z_1 *must* be a final state, we cannot simply posit its equivalence to x_1. What we need are two states that are like x_1. One of them will be x_1 *and* a final state, whereas the other will be x_1 *and* a nonfinal state. The reason we may need a state like x_1 that is not a final state is that in the running of an input string of FA_1 we may be required to reenter the state x_1 several times. If x_1 is not a final state in FA_1, but we convert it into z_1, which is a final state, then when an input string ends in x_1 on FA_1 and is not accepted on FA_1, we do not want mistakenly to say that it ends in z_1, which then causes it to be accepted on FA_2. In the machine we have at present, this is no problem because the state x_1 on FA_1 can never be reentered (no edges go into x_1). Therefore, we can say that the z_1 we have is sufficient to represent x_1 in all its uses. An accurate machine for the language defined by **(aa*bb*)*** is

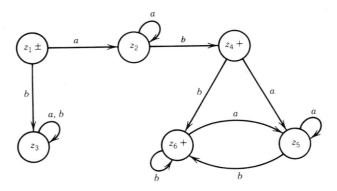

To illustrate the possible need for two different states representing x_1, we have to start with a machine that does not accept Λ, but that does allow the state x_1 to be reentered in the path for some input words.

EXAMPLE

One such FA is the one below, which accepts the language of all words with an odd number of b's:

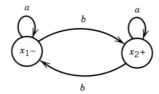

Let us practice our algorithm on this machine.

The first state we want is z_1, which must be like x_1 except that it is also a final state. If we are in z_1 and we read an a, we come back to x_1, but this time in its capacity as a nonfinal state. We have to give a different name to this state; let us call it z_2.

$$z_1 = x_1 \text{ and a final state}$$
$$z_2 = x_1 \text{ and a nonfinal state}$$

If we are in z_1 and we read a b, we must go to a state like x_2. Now because x_2 is a final state, we must also include the possibility that once we enter x_2, we immediately proceed as if we were back in x_1. Therefore, the state z_3 that we go to is simply x_1 or x_2 and a final state because of x_2.

At this point, the machine looks like this:

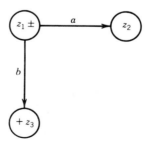

If we are in z_2 and we read an a, we stay in z_2. If we are in z_2 and we read a b, we go to z_3. If we are in z_3 and we read an a, it will take us back to z_3, because if we were in x_1, we would stay in x_1, and if we were in x_2, we would stay in x_2. If we are in z_3 and we read a b, then we also return to z_3, because if we were in x_1, then we would go to x_2, and if we were in x_2, we would go to x_1. The whole machine is shown on the next page:

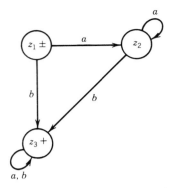

The only words not accepted by this machine are words of solid a's. All other words are clearly the concatenation of substrings with one b each and are therefore in the closure of the language of FA_1.

This is another example of how the null string is a royal pain in the neck. One regular expression defining the language of all words with an odd number of b's is

$$r = a*b(a*ba*b)*a*$$

Therefore, the regular expression

$$r* = [a*b(a*ba*b)*a*]*$$

defines the language of all words that are not of the form $aa*$. Another regular expression for this language is

$$\Lambda + (a + b)*b(a + b)*$$

Therefore,

$$\Lambda + (a + b)*b(a + b)* = [a*b(a*ba*b)*a*]*$$

It is hard to imagine an algebraic proof of this equation. The problem of determining when two regular expressions define the same language will be discussed in Chapter 11. ■

We have now developed algorithms that, when taken together, finish the proof of Part 3 of Kleene's theorem. (We have been in the middle of this project for so long it is possible to lose our perspective.)

Because of Rules 1, 2, 3, and 4, we know that all regular expressions have corresponding finite automata that give the same language. This is because while we are building the regular expression from the elementary building blocks by the recursive definition, we can simultaneously be building the corresponding FA from the four preceding algorithms. This is a powerful example of the strength of recursive definitions.

As an example, suppose we want to find an FA to accept the language for the regular expression $(ab)*a(ab + a*)*$. Because this is a regular expression, it can be built up by repeated applications of the rules: any letter, sum, product, star.

The lengthy process of expression and machine-building can proceed as follows: a is a letter in the alphabet, so there is an FA that accepts it called FA_1. Now b is a letter in the alphabet, so there is a machine that accepts it, FA_2. Then ab is the language of the product of the two machines FA_1 and FA_2, so there is a machine to accept it, FA_3. Then $(ab)*$ is the language of the closure of the machine FA_3, so there is a machine to accept it; call it FA_4.

Now $a*$ is the language of the closure of the machine FA_1, so there is an FA to accept it called FA_5. Now **ab** + **a*** is the language of the sum of FA_3 and FA_5, so there is a machine to accept it, FA_6. Now (**ab** + **a***)* is the language of the closure of FA_6; therefore, there is a machine to accept it, FA_7. Now **a**(**ab** + **a***)* is the product of FA_1 and FA_7, so there is a machine to accept it, FA_8. Now (**ab**)***a**(**ab** + **a***)* is the product of machines FA_4 and FA_8; call it FA_9. Done.

All regular expressions can be handled the same way. We have shown that every language accepted by an FA can be accepted by a TG, every language accepted by a TG can be defined by a regular expression, and every language defined by a regular expression can be accepted by an FA. This concludes the proof of all of Kleene's theorem. ■

The proof has been **constructive,** which means that we have not only shown that there is a correspondence between regular expressions, FAs and TGs, but we have also shown exactly how to find examples of the things that correspond. Given any one, we can build the other two using the techniques outlined in the preceding proof.

Because TGs seem more understandable, we often work with them instead of struggling with the rigors of FAs (especially having to specify what happens in every state to every letter).

The biggest surprise of this theorem may be that TGs are not any more powerful than FAs in the sense that there are no extra languages that TGs can accept that FAs could not handle already. This is too bad because we shall soon show that there are some languages that FAs cannot accept, and we shall need a more powerful type of machine than a TG to deal with them.

Even though with a TG we had the right to exercise some degree of judgment—we made some decisions about sectioning the reading of the input string—we could do no better than a purely automatic robot like an FA. The human input factor was worth essentially nothing.

⚜ NONDETERMINISTIC FINITE AUTOMATA

Now that we have shown how a possibly nondeterministic machine like a TG can be turned (by a deterministic algorithmic procedure) into a deterministic machine, an FA, we may introduce a conceptual machine that occurs in practice more frequently than the TG, but that shares with it the property of being nondeterministic.

DEFINITION

A **nondeterministic finite automaton** is a TG with a unique start state with the property that each of its edge labels is a single alphabet letter. It is given the acronym NFA. Sometimes, to distinguish them from NFAs, the regular deterministic finite automata are referred to as DFAs. ■

We defined NFAs as a type of TGs, but we might just as easily have started with the concept of FA and expanded their scope by allowing arbitrarily many a- and b-edges coming out of each state. The result would be the same, but then we would have to restate the notion of acceptance of an input string for a nondeterministic machine as the existence of any one possible path to +. We would also have to rehash the possibility of crashing and its inconclusive consequences.

EXAMPLE

These are all NFAs:

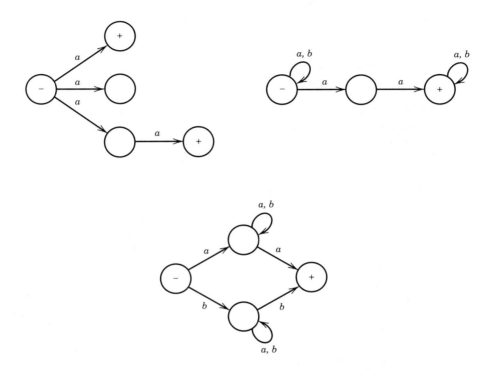

NFAs were invented by Michael Oser Rabin and Dana Scott in 1959. ∎

EXAMPLE

One possible use of the NFA is to eliminate all loop states in a given FA. Instead of the situation

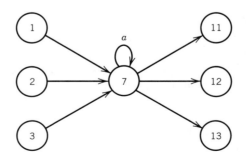

we can invent a twin for state 7, called 7′, and instead of being in state 7 and looping back to it, we can jump from 7 to 7′, and back and forth if we want.

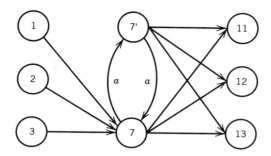

The advantage of this NFA is that the fact of whether looping in state 7 occurs for a given input is recorded in whether the path the input follows goes through state 7' or not. In a computer program, state 7' may set a flag alerting one to the incidence of looping. ■

EXAMPLE

If we are looking for a machine to define the language of all strings with a triple a followed by a triple b, we could design the NFA:

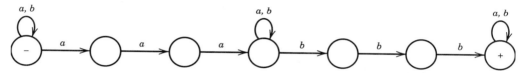

There is one thing that we must notice about this machine; it will also accept words in which some bbb can occur before the first aaa (by looping at the − state) and then has another bbb later. If the language we were interested in was more precisely the set of all strings in which the *first* triple b is preceded by a triple a, we need the more complex machine below:

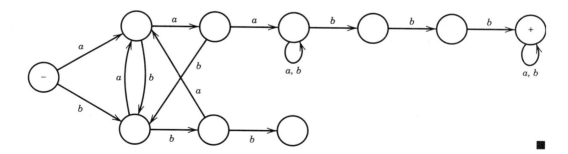

■

Because an NFA is a type of TG and Kleene's theorem (p. 92) shows us by constructive algorithm how to convert TGs into FAs, it follows that all NFAs can be converted into FAs that accept the same language. Clearly, all FAs can be considered NFAs that do not make use of the option of extra freedom of edge production. So as language acceptors, NFA = FA.

THEOREM 7

For every NFA, there is some FA that accepts exactly the same language.

PROOF 1   (the slick proof)

Using the algorithms in Part 2 of the proof of Kleene's theorem, convert the NFA into a regular expression by state bypass operations. Once we have a regular expression defining the same language, use the four rules in Part 3 of the proof to construct an FA that accepts the same language as the regular expression.   ∎

This proof is short and sweet but needlessly overcumbersome in practice, so we present another proof that is based on a specialized (yet familiar-sounding) constructive algorithm allowing us to go from NFA to FA without passing through an avatar of regular expression.

PROOF 2 OF THEOREM 7

The constructive algorithm we suggest is reminiscent of the algorithm of Part 3, Rule 4, of Kleene's theorem. This is the one that started with an FA and produced an FA*. It did so by realizing that at any stage in the processing of the input string, the path might have taken various branches and so might currently be in any of a collection of possible x-states. Nondeterminism produces exactly the same degree of uncertainty. Thus, the states in the FA that we are going to produce will also be collections of states from the original NFA. For every collection of states from the old machine

$$x_{\text{this}} \quad \text{or} \quad x_{\text{that}} \quad \text{or} \quad \cdot \cdot \cdot x_{\text{the other}}$$

the new state that an a-edge (or a b-edge) will take us to is just the collection of possibilities that can result from being in x_{this} and taking an a-edge, or being in x_{that} and taking an a-edge, and so on. The start state of the new FA is the same old start state we had to begin with in the NFA and its a-edge goes to the collection of x-states that can be reached by an a-edge from start in the NFA. Because there may be no a-edges leaving the start state in the NFA (or leaving any other particular state), the collection of x-states reached by an a-edge in this case must be the null collection (ϕ). In the final FA, this state has of necessity an a, b loop going back to itself. The ϕ state in the FA is not a final state because the final states (as always before) are all the collections of x-states from the original machine that include an old final state among them.   ∎

EXAMPLE

When we convert the NFA on the left below, the algorithm produces the one on the right:

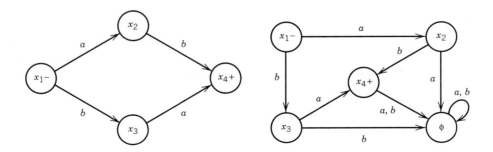

∎

EXAMPLE

A simple NFA that accepts the language {bb bbb} is

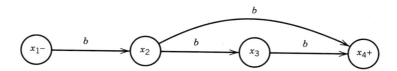

The algorithm in Proof 2 converts this to the FA:

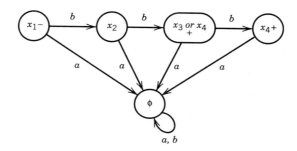

EXAMPLE

One NFA that accepts all inputs with a bb in them is

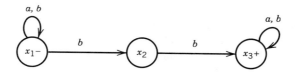

This converts to the FA:

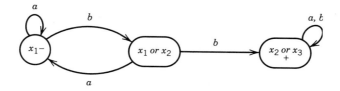

EXAMPLE

One NFA that accepts all inputs with a triple letter is

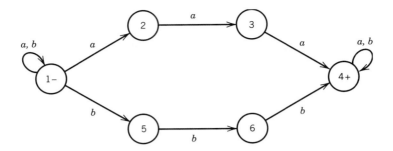

By the algorithm, it becomes

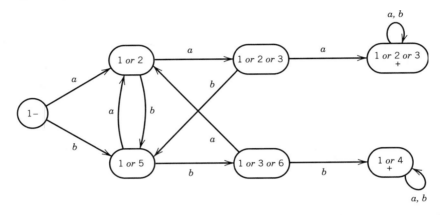

Even though both machines have the same number of states, the "meaning" of the language is easier to determine from the NFA.   ∎

⚜ NFAs AND KLEENE'S THEOREM

Our approach to Kleene's theorem, Part 3, was to build FAs analogous to the building of regular expressions, by union, multiplication, and closure. The proofs that $FA_1 + FA_2$, $FA_1 FA_2$, and $FA_1{}^*$ were all equivalent to other FAs could have been done differently (not necessarily better) by employing NFAs in the process.

For example, Rule 1 states that there are FAs for languages $\{a\}$, $\{b\}$, and $\{\Lambda\}$. Below is an alternate method of proving this.

PROOF 2, THEOREM 6, PART 3, RULE 1

Step 1   The three languages in question can all be accepted by the NFAs below:

Step 2   Because by Theorem 7 on p. 137, for every NFA there is an equivalent FA, there must be FAs for these three languages as well.   ∎

In general, we must be careful when using Theorem $(X + 1)$ to prove Theorem (X)

to be sure that we did not already use Theorem (X) first in the proof of Theorem $(X + 1)$. However, if we examine the proof of Theorem 7, we see that it was similar to, but did not employ, Theorem 6 (p. 92).

PROOF 2, THEOREM 6, PART 3, RULE 2

Given FA_1 and FA_2, we shall construct an algorithm for producing a union machine $FA_1 + FA_2$ by two steps:

Step 1   Introduce a new and unique start state with two outgoing a-edges and two outgoing b-edges but no incoming edges. Connect them to the states that the start states of FA_1 and FA_2 are already connected to. Do not eliminate the start states of FA_1 and FA_2, but erase their $-$ signs, leaving all their edges intact. The new machine is an NFA that clearly accepts exactly language(FA_1) + language(FA_2).

Step 2   Using the algorithm of Theorem 7, convert the NFA into an FA.   ■

EXAMPLE

We only need to illustrate step 1 because step 2 has already been conquered. Consider

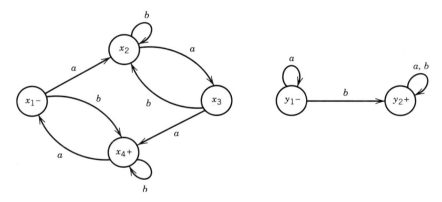

The NFA that is their a sum is

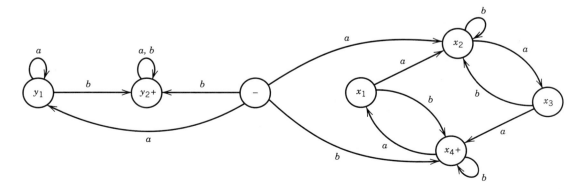

  ■

Rules 3 and 4 of Part 3 of Kleene's theorem can also be proven using Theorem 7, but this we leave for the problems section.

⚜ PROBLEMS

1. Using the bypass algorithm in the proof of Theorem 6, Part 2, convert each of the following TGs into regular expressions:

(i)

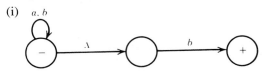

(ii)

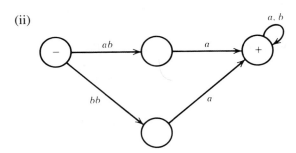

(iii)

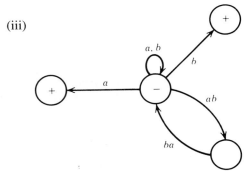

(iv)

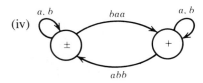

(v)

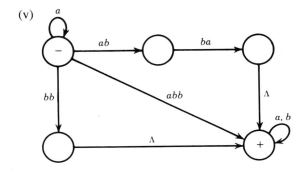

(vi)

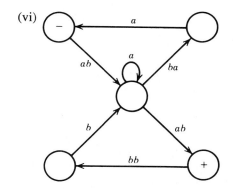

2. In Chapter 5, Problem 10, we began the discussion of all possible FAs with two states. Write a regular expression for each machine of type 2 and type 3 by using the conversion algorithm described in the proof of Theorem 6, Part 2. Even though there is no algorithm for recognizing the languages, try to identify as many as possible in the attempt to discover how many different languages can be accepted by a two-state FA.

For Problems 3 through 12, use the following machines:

FA_1

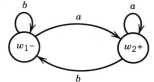

FA_2

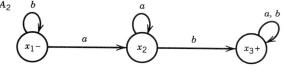

FA_3

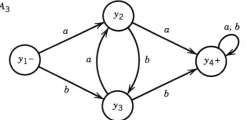

FA_4

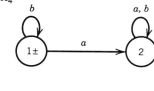

3. Using the algorithm of Kleene's theorem, Part 3, Rule 2, Proof 1, construct FAs for the following union languages:
   (i) $FA_1 + FA_2$
   (ii) $FA_1 + FA_3$
   (iii) $FA_2 + FA_3$

4. Using the algorithm of Kleene's theorem, Part 3, Rule 2, Proof 2, construct NFAs for the following languages:
   (i) $FA_1 + FA_2$
   (ii) $FA_1 + FA_3$
   (iii) $FA_2 + FA_3$

5. Using the algorithm of Theorem 6, Part 3, Rule 3, construct FAs for the following product languages:
   (i) $FA_1 FA_2$

    (ii) $FA_1\, FA_3$
    (iii) $FA_1\, FA_1$
    (iv) $FA_2\, FA_1$
    (v) $FA_2\, FA_2$

6. Using the algorithm of Part 3, Rule 4, construct FAs for the following languages:

    (i) $(FA_1)^*$
    (ii) $(FA_2)^*$

7. We are now interested in proving Part 3, Rule 3, of Kleene's theorem by NFAs. The basic theory is that when we reach any $+$ state in FA_1, we could continue to FA_1 by following its a-edge and b-edge, or we could pretend that we have jumped to FA_2 by following the a-edge and b-edge coming out of the start state on FA_2. We do not change any states or edges in either machine; we merely add some new (nondeterministic) edges from $+$ states in FA_1 to the destination states of FA_2's start state. Finally, we erase the $+$'s from FA_1 and the $-$ sign from FA_2 and we have the desired NFA.
    Let us illustrate this by multiplying FA_1 and FA_2 above.

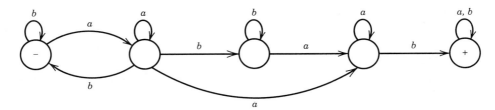

Find NFAs for the following product languages:

    (i) $FA_1\, FA_1$
    (ii) $FA_1\, FA_3$
    (iii) $FA_2\, FA_2$

8. Take the three NFAs in Problem 7 above and convert them into FAs by the algorithm of Theorem 7.

9. We can use NFAs to prove Theorem 6, Part 3, Rule 4, as well. The idea is to allow a nondeterministic jump from any $+$ state to the states reachable from the $-$ state by a- and b-edges.

    (i) Provide the details for this proof by constructive algorithm.
    (ii) Draw the resultant NFA for $(FA_1)^*$.
    (iii) Draw the resultant NFA for $(FA_2)^*$.
    (iv) Draw the resultant NFA for $(FA_3)^*$.

10. Convert the machines in Problem 9(ii) and (iii) above to FAs by the algorithm in the proof of Theorem 7.

11. Find FAs for the following languages:

    (i) $FA_4\, FA_4$
    (ii) $(FA_4)^*$

12. (i) Is the machine for $FA_1\, FA_1$ (Problem 5) the same as the machine for $(FA_1)^*$ (Problem 6)? Are the languages the same?
    (ii) Is the machine for $FA_4\, FA_4$ the same as the machine for $(FA_4)^*$ (Problem 11)? Are the languages the same?

13. (i) For the examples derived earlier, which algorithmic method produces product machines with fewer states, the direct (Problem 5) or the NFA (Problem 8)?

    (ii) If some automaton, FA_1, has n states and some other automaton, FA_2, has m states, what are the maximum number of states possible in each of the machines corresponding to $FA_1 + FA_2$, $FA_1 FA_2$, $(FA_1)^*$ that are produced.

    (a) By the subset method described in the proof of Kleene's theorem.

    (b) By building NFAs and then converting them into FAs.

14. Convert each of the following NFAs into FAs using the constructive algorithm presented in Proof 2 of Theorem 7.

    (i)

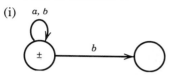

    (ii)

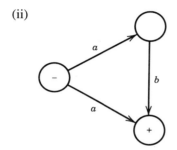

    (iii)

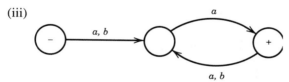

    (iv)

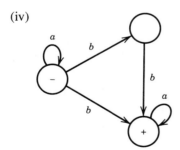

    (v)

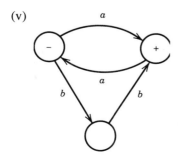

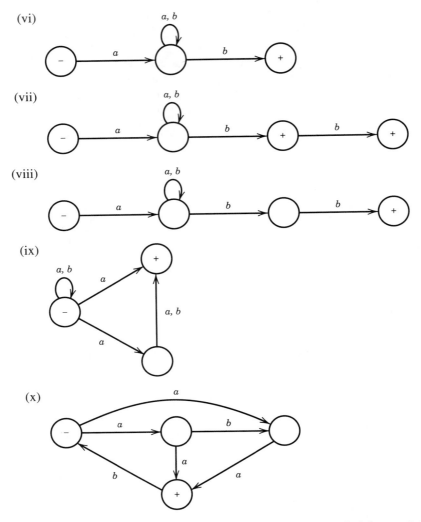

For Problems 15 through 17, let us now introduce a machine called "**a nondeterministic fi-nite automaton with null string labels,**" abbreviated **NFA-Λ**. This machine follows the same rules as an NFA except that we are allowed to have edges labeled **Λ**.

15. Show that it is possible to use a technique analogous to that used in Proof 2 of Theorem 7 to constructively convert an NFA-**Λ** into an FA by explicitly giving the steps of the conversion process.

16. Convert the following NFA-**Λ**'s into FAs using the algorithm invented in Problem 15:

(i)

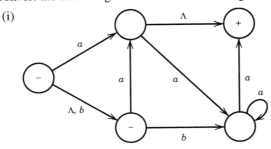

(ii)

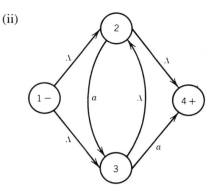

(iii)

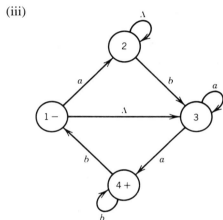

17. Using the result in Problem 15, find a third proof of Part 3 of Kleene's theorem:

    (i) Rule 2

    (ii) Rule 3

    (iii) Rule 4

18. (i) Find two different machines FA_1 and FA_2 such that the languages accepted by $FA_1 + FA_2$ and $FA_1 FA_2$ are the same, yet the machines generated by the algorithm in the proof of Theorem 6 are different.

    (ii) Find two different machines FA_1 and FA_2 such that the algorithm in the proof of Theorem 6 creates the same machine for $(FA_1)^*$ and $(FA_2).^*$

19. For the language accepted by the following machine, find a different FA with four states. Find an NFA that accepts the same language and has only seven edges (where edges with two labels are counted twice).

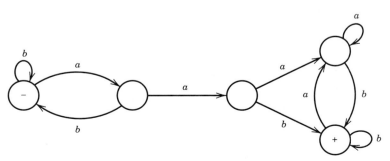

20. A one-person game can be converted into an NFA as follows. Let every possible board situation be a state. If any move (there may be several types of moves, but we are not interested in distinguishing among them) can change some state x into some state y, then draw an edge from x to y and label it m. Label the initial position $-$ and the winning positions $+$. "This game can be won in five moves" is the same as saying, "m^5 is accepted by this NFA." Once we have the NFA, we use the algorithm of Chapter 7 to convert it into a regular expression. The language it represents tells us how many moves are in each winning sequence.

Let us do this with the following example. The game of Flips is played with three coins. Initially, they are all heads. A move consists of flipping two coins simultaneously from whatever they were to the opposite side. For example, flipping the end coins changes THH into HHT. We win when all three coins are tails. There are eight possible states: HHH, HHT, . . . TTT. The only $-$ is HHH; the only $+$ is TTT. Draw this NFA, labeling any edge that can flip between states with the letter m.

Convert this NFA into a regular expression. Is m^3 or m^5 in the language of this machine? The shortest word in this language is the shortest solution of this puzzle. What is it?

CHAPTER 8

Finite Automata with Output

⚜ MOORE MACHINES

In our discussion of finite automata in Chapter 5, our motivation was in part to begin to design a mathematical model for a computer. We said that the input string represents the program and input data. Reading the letters from the string is analogous to executing instructions in that it changes the state of the machine; that is, it changes the contents of memory, changes the control section of the computer, and so on. Part of this "and so on," that was not made explicit before, is the question of output. We mentioned that we could consider the output as part of the total state of the machine. This could mean two different things: one, that to enter a specific computer state means change to memory a certain way and print a specific character; or two, that a state includes both the present condition of memory plus the total output thus far. In other words, the state could reflect (in addition to the status of the running program) (i) what we are now printing or (ii) what we have printed in total. One natural question to ask is, "If we have these two different models, do these machines have equal power or are there some tasks that one can do that the other cannot?"

The only explicit task a machine has done so far is to recognize a language. Computers, as we know, often have the more useful function of performing calculations and conveying results. In this chapter, we expand the notion of machine task.

If we assume that all the printing of output is to be done at the end of the program run, at which time we have an instruction that dumps a buffer that has been assembled, then we have a maximum on the number of characters that the program can print, namely, the size of the buffer. However, theoretically we should be able to have outputs of any finite length. For example, we might simply want to print out a copy of the input string, which could itself be arbitrarily long.

These are questions that have to be faced if we are to claim that our mathematical models of FAs and TGs represent actual physical machines. In this chapter, we shall investigate two different models for FAs with output capabilities. These were created by G. H. Mealy (1955) and, independently, by E. F. Moore (1956). The original purpose of the inventors was to design a mathematical model for sequential circuits, which are only one component of the architecture of a whole computer. It is an important component and, as we shall see, acts as a machine all by itself. We shall present these two models, prove that they are equivalent, and give some examples of how they arise in the "logic" section of a computer.

DEFINITION

A **Moore machine** is a collection of five things:

1. A finite set of states $q_0, q_1, q_2, \ldots$, where q_0 is designated as the start state.
2. An alphabet of letters for forming the input string

$$\Sigma = \{a \quad b \quad c \ldots\}$$

3. An alphabet of possible output characters

$$\Gamma = \{x \quad y \quad z \ldots\}$$

4. A transition table that shows for *each* state and *each* input letter what state is reached next.
5. An output table that shows what character from Γ is printed by each state as it is entered.   ■

Notice that we did not assume that the input alphabet Σ is the same as the output alphabet Γ. When dealing with contemporary machines, both input and output are usually encoded strings of 0's and 1's. However, we may interpret the input bit strings as instructions in a programming language followed by the data to be processed. We may also wish to group the strings of output bits into codes for typewriter characters. We discuss whether it is necessary to have more than two letters in an alphabet in Chapter 23.

To keep the output alphabet separate from the input alphabet, we give it a different name, Γ instead of Σ, and for its letters we use symbols from the other end of the Latin alphabet: $\{x \quad y \quad z \ldots\}$ or numbers $\{0 \quad 1 \ldots\}$ instead of $\{a \quad b \quad c \ldots\}$. Moreover, we refer to the input symbols (as we always have) as **letters,** whereas we call the output symbols **characters.**

As we shall see from our circuitry examples, the knowledge of which state is the start state is not always important in applications. If the machine is run several times, it may continue from where it left off rather than restart. Because of this, we can define the Moore machine in two ways: Either the first symbol printed is the character always specified in the start state, or else it is the character specified in the next state, which is the first state *chosen* by the input. We shall adopt the policy that a Moore machine always begins by printing the character dictated by the mandatory start state. This difference is not significant. If the input string has seven letters, then the output string will have eight characters because it includes eight states in its path.

Because the word "outputted" is so ugly, we shall say "printed" instead, even though we realize that the output device does not technically have to be a printer.

A Moore machine does not define a language of accepted words, because every possible input string creates an output string and there is no such thing as a final state. The processing is terminated when the last input letter is read and the last output character is printed. Nevertheless, there are several subtle ways to turn Moore machines into language-definers.

Moore machines have pictorial representations very similar to their cousins, the FAs. We start with little circles depicting the states and directed edges between them labeled with input letters. The difference is that instead of having only the name of the state inside the little circle, we also specify the output character printed by that state. The two symbols inside the circle are separated by a slash "/". On the left side is the name of the state and on the right is the output from that state.

EXAMPLE

Let us consider an example defined first by a table:

$$\text{Input alphabet:} \quad \Sigma = \{a \quad b\}$$
$$\text{Output alphabet:} \quad \Gamma = \{0 \quad 1\}$$
$$\text{Names of states:} \quad q_0, q_1, q_2, q_3 \quad (q_0 = \text{start state})$$

Transition Table

Old State	Output by the Old State	New State	
		After Input a	After Input b
$- q_0$	1	q_1	q_3
q_1	0	q_3	q_1
q_2	0	q_0	q_3
q_3	1	q_3	q_2

The pictorial representation of this Moore machine is

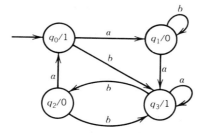

In Moore machines, so much information is written inside the state circles that there is no room for the minus sign indicating the start state. We usually indicate the start state by an outside arrow as shown above. As mentioned before, there is no need for any plus signs either.

Let us trace the operation of this machine on the input string *abab*. We always start this machine off in state q_0, which automatically prints out the character 1. We then read the first letter of the input string, which is an *a* and which sends us to state q_1. This state tells us to print a 0. The next input letter is a *b*, and the loop shows that we return to state q_1. Being in q_1 again, we print another 0. Then we read an *a*, go to q_3, and print a 1. Next, we read a *b*, go to q_2, and print a 0. This is the end of the run. The output sequence has been 10010. ∎

EXAMPLE

Suppose we were interested in knowing exactly how many times the substring *aab* occurs in a long input string. The following Moore machine will "count" this for us:

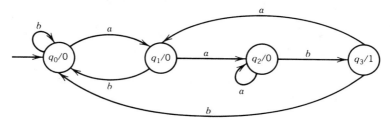

Every state of this machine prints out the character 0 except for state q_3, which prints a 1. To get to state q_3, we must have come from state q_2 and have just read a b. To get to state q_2, we must have just read at least two a's in a row, having started in any state. After finding the substring aab and tallying a 1 for it, we begin to look for the next aab. If we read a b, we start the search in q_0; if we read an a, we start in q_1. The number of substrings aab in the input string will be exactly the number of 1's in the output string.

Input		a	a	a	b	a	b	b	a	a	b	b
State	q_0	q_1	q_2	q_2	q_3	q_1	q_0	q_0	q_1	q_2	q_3	q_0
Output	0	0	0	0	1	0	0	0	0	0	1	0

■

The example above is part of a whole class of useful Moore machines. Given a language L and an FA that accepts it, if we add the printing instruction 0 to any nonfinal state and 1 to each final state, the 1's in any output sequence mark the end position of all substrings of the input string starting from the first letter that are words in L. In this way, a Moore machine can be said to *define* the language of all input strings whose output ends in a 1. The machine above with $q_0 = -$, $q_3 = +$ accepts all words that end in aab.

⚜ MEALY MACHINES

Our next subject is another variation of the FA called the **Mealy machine.** A Mealy machine is like a Moore machine except that now we do our printing while we are traveling along the edges, not in the states themselves. If we are in state q_4 and we are proceeding to q_7, we do not simply print what q_7 tells us. What we print depends on the edge we take. If there are two different edges from q_4 to q_7, one an a-edge and one a b-edge, it is possible that they will have different printing instructions for us. We take no printing instructions from the state itself.

DEFINITION

A **Mealy machine** is a collection of four things:

1. A finite set of states $q_0, q_1, q_2, \ldots$, where q_0 is designated as the start state.
2. An alphabet of letters $\Sigma = \{a \quad b \ldots\}$ for forming input strings.
3. An alphabet of output characters $\Gamma = \{x \quad y \quad z \ldots\}$.
4. A pictorial representation with states represented by small circles and directed edges indicating transitions between states. Each edge is labeled with a compound symbol of the form i/o, where i is an input letter and o is an output character. *Every* state must have exactly one outgoing edge for *each* possible input letter. The edge we travel is determined by the input letter i. While traveling on the edge, we must print the output character o.   ■

We have for the sake of variation defined a Mealy machine by its pictorial representation. One reason for this is that the table definition is not as simple as that for a Moore machine (see the Problem section, later).

EXAMPLE

The following picture represents a Mealy machine:

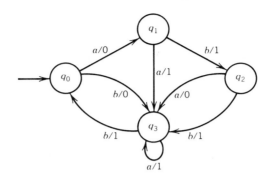

Notice that when we arrive in state q_3 we may have just printed a 1 or a 0. If we came from state q_0 by the b-road, we printed a 0. If we got there from q_1 by the a-road, we printed a 1. If we got there from q_2, it depends on whether we took the a-road and printed a 0 or the b-road and printed a 1. If we were in q_3 already and looped back on the input a, we then printed a 1. Every time we enter q_1, we have just printed a 0; this time it is possible to tell this information from the destination state alone.

Let us trace the running of this machine on the input sequence $aaabb$. We start in state q_0. In distinction to the Moore machine, here we do not have to print the same character each time we start up, even before getting a look at the input. The first input letter is an a, which takes us to q_1 and prints a 0. The second letter is an a, which takes us to q_3 and prints a 1. The third letter is an a, which loops us back to q_3 and prints a 1. The fourth letter is a b, which takes us back to q_0 and prints a 1. The fifth letter is a b, which takes us to q_3 and prints a 0. The output string for this input is 01110. ■

Notice that in a Mealy machine the output string has the same number of characters as the input string has letters. As with the Moore machine, the Mealy machine does not define a language by accepting and rejecting input strings, so it has no final states. However, we will see shortly that there is a sense in which it can recognize a language.

If there are two edges going in the same direction between the same pair of states, we can draw only one arrow and represent the choice of label by the usual comma.

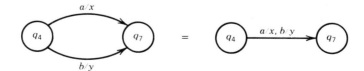

EXAMPLE

One simple example of a useful Mealy machine is one that prints out the 1's complement of an input bit string. This means that we want to produce a bit string that has a 1 wherever the input string has a 0 and a 0 wherever the input has a 1. For example, the input 101 should become the output 010. One machine that does this is shown on the next page.

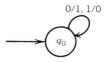

If the input is 001010, the output is 110101. This is a case where the input alphabet and output alphabet are both {0   1}. ∎

EXAMPLE

We now consider a Mealy machine called the **increment machine** that assumes that its input is a binary number and prints out the binary number that is one larger. We assume that the input bit string is a binary number fed in backward, that is, units digit first (then 2's digit, 4's digit, . . .). The output string will be the binary representation of the number one greater and will also be generated right to left.

The machine will have three states: start, owe-carry, no-carry. The owe-carry state represents the overflow when two bits equal to 1 are added—we print a 0 and we carry a 1.

From the start state, we read the first bit. If we read in a 0, we print a 1 and we do not owe a carry bit. If we read a 1, we print a 0 and we do owe a carry bit. If at any point in the process we are in no-carry (which means that we do not owe a carry), we print the next bit just as we read it and remain in no-carry. However, if at some point in the process we are in owe-carry, the situation is different. If we read a 0, we print a 1 and go to the no-carry state. If we are in owe-carry and we read a 1, we print a 0 and we loop back to owe-carry. The complete picture for this machine is

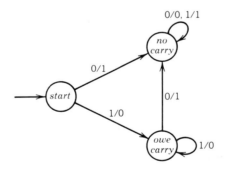

Let us watch this machine in action on the binary representation for the number 11, 1011. The string is fed into the machine as 1101 (backwards). The first 1 causes a 0 to be printed and sends us to owe-carry. The next 1 causes a 0 to be printed and loops back to owe-carry. The next input letter is a 0 and causes a 1 to be printed on our way to no-carry. The next bit, 1, is printed out, as it is fed in, on the no-carry loop. The total output string is 0011, which when reversed is 1100, and is, as desired, the binary representation for the number 12.

As simple as this machine is, it can be simplified even further (see Problem 7).

This machine has the typical Mealy machine property that the output string is exactly as long as the input string. This means that if we ran this incrementation machine on the input 1111, we would get 0000. We must interpret the owe-carry state as an overflow situation if a string ever ends there. ∎

There is a connection between Mealy machines and sequential circuits (which we touch on at the end of this chapter) that makes them a very valuable component of computer theory. The two examples we have just presented are also valuable to computing. Once we have an incrementer, we can build a machine that can perform the addition of binary numbers, and then we can use the 1's complementing machine to build a subtracting machine based on the following principle:

> *If* a *and* b *are strings of bits, then the subtraction* a − b *can be performed by*
> *(1) adding the 1's complement of* b *to* a, *ignoring any overflow digit, and*
> *(2) incrementing the results by 1.*

For example,

$$14 - 5 \text{ (decimal)} = 1110 - 0101 \text{ (binary)}$$
$$= 1110 + 1\text{'s complement of } 0101 + 1 \text{ (binary)}$$
$$= 1110 + 1010 + 1 \text{ (binary)}$$
$$= [1]1001 \text{ binary} = 9 \text{ (decimal) (dropping the } [1])$$
$$18 - 7 = 10010 - 00111 = 10010 + 11000 + 1$$
$$= [1]01011 = 01011 = 11 \text{ (decimal)}$$

The same trick works in decimal notation if we use 9's complements, that is, replace each digit d in the second number by the digit $(9 - d)$. For example, $46 - 17 \rightarrow 46 + 82 + 1 = [1]29 \rightarrow 29$.

EXAMPLE

Even though a Mealy machine does not accept or reject an input string, it can recognize a language by making its output string answer some questions about the input. We have discussed before the language of all words that have a double letter in them. The Mealy machine below will take a string of a's and b's and print out a string of 0's and 1's such that if the nth output character is a 1, it means that the nth input letter is the second in a pair of double letters. For example, *ababbaab* becomes 00001010 with 1's in the position of the second of each pair of repeated letters.

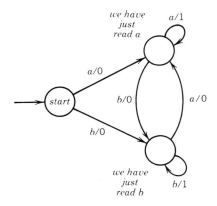

This is similar to the Moore machine that recognized the number of occurrences of the substring *aab*. This machine recognizes the occurrences of *aa* or *bb*. Notice that the triple-letter word *aaa* produces the output 011 since the second and third letters are both the back end of a pair of double *a*'s.   ∎

 MOORE = MEALY

So far, our definition of the equivalence of two machines has been that they accept the same language. In this sense, we cannot compare a Mealy machine and a Moore machine. However, we may say that two output automata are equivalent if they always give the same output string when presented with the same input string. In this way, two Mealy machines may be equivalent and two Moore machines may be equivalent, but a Moore machine can never be directly equivalent to a Mealy machine because the length of the output string from a Moore machine is one longer than that from a Mealy machine given the same input. The problem is that a Moore machine always begins with one automatic start symbol.

To get around this difficulty, we define a Mealy machine to be equivalent to a Moore machine whenever they always result in the same output if the automatic start symbol for the Moore machine is deleted from the front of the output.

DEFINITION

Given the Mealy machine *Me* and the Moore machine *Mo*, which prints the automatic start-state character *x*, we will say that these two machines are **equivalent** if for every input string the output string from *Mo* is exactly *x* concatenated with the output from *Me*.   ∎

Rather than debate the merits of the two types of machines, we prove that for every Moore machine there is an equivalent Mealy machine and for every Mealy machine there is an equivalent Moore machine. We can then say that the two types of machines are functionally equivalent.

THEOREM 8

If *Mo* is a Moore machine, then there is a Mealy machine *Me* that is equivalent to it.

PROOF

The proof will be by constructive algorithm.

Consider any particular state in *Mo*—call it q_4. It gives instructions to print a certain character—call it *t*. Let us consider all the edges that enter this state. Each of them is labeled with an input letter. Let us change this. Let us relabel all the edges coming into q_4. If they were previously labeled *a* or *b* or *c* . . . , let them now be labeled *a/t* or *b/t* or *c/t* . . . and let us erase the *t* from inside the state q_4. This means that we shall be printing a *t* on the incoming edges before they enter q_4.

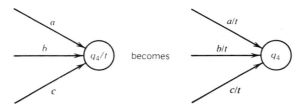

We leave the outgoing edges from q_4 alone. They will be relabeled to print the character associated with the state to which they lead.

   If we repeat this procedure for every state $q_0, q_1, \ldots$, we turn Mo into a Mealy machine Me. As we move from state to state, the things that get printed are exactly what Mo would have printed itself.

   The symbol that used to be printed automatically when the machine started in state q_0 is no longer the first output character, but this does not stop the rest of the output string from being the same.

                                                                                                    ■

   Therefore, every Mo is equivalent to some Me.

EXAMPLE

Below, a Moore machine is converted into a Mealy machine by the algorithm of the proof above:

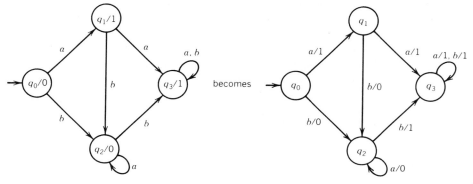

                                                                                                    ■

THEOREM 9

For every Mealy machine Me, there is a Moore machine Mo that is equivalent to it.

PROOF

Again, the proof will be by constructive algorithm.

   We cannot just do the reverse of the previous procedure. If we were to try to push the printing instruction from the edge as it is in Me to the inside of the state as it should be for a Moore machine, we might end up with a conflict. Two edges might come into the same state but have different printing instructions, as in this example:

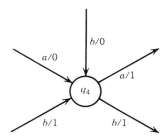

What we need then are twin copies of the same state. The edge $a/0$ will go into q_4^1 (q_4 copy 1, a state that prints a 0) and the edge $b/1$ will go into q_4^2 (q_4 copy 2, a state that prints a 1). The edge labeled $b/0$ will also go into q_4^1. Inside these states, we include the printing instructions $q_4^1/0$ and $q_4^2/1$. The arrows coming out of each of these copies of what used to be q_4 must be the same as the edges coming out of q_4 originally. We get two sets of the output edges each equal to the original outgoing edges, but the one set of original incoming edges is divided between the two copies. The example above becomes

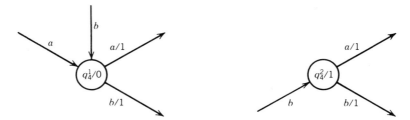

The instruction to print a 0 or a 1 is now found inside the state, not along the edge.

Leaving the outgoing edges the way they were is only temporary as they themselves will soon be changed.

State by state we repeat this procedure. If all the edges coming into the object state have the same printing instruction, then we can simply move that printing instruction into the state. This does not affect the edges coming out of the state:

If there are multiple possibilities for printing as we enter a given state, then we need a copy of the state for each character we might have been instructed to print. (We may need as many copies as there are characters in Γ.) All the edges that entered a certain state that used to be labeled

something/t

now lead into the copy of that state that instructs us to print the character t. Each of the copies of the original state retains a complete set of the original outgoing edges. The labels on the incoming edges lose their printing instructions. The letters on the outgoing edges retain them a while longer, if they have not lost them already. This algorithm slowly turns a Mealy into a Moore state by state.

One interesting consequence of this algorithm is that an edge that was a loop in *Me* may become two edges in *Mo* — one edge that is not a loop and one that is. For example,

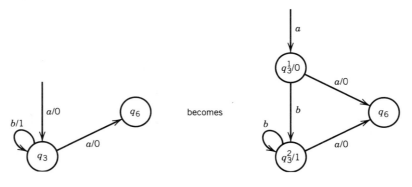

What happens in the preceding example is that the edge labeled $a/0$ has to enter a version of q_3 that prints a 0. We call this $q_3^1/0$. The loop labeled $b/1$ at q_3 has to enter a version of q_3 that prints a 1. We call this $q_3^2/1$. When we enter q_3 from the edge $a/0$, we enter $q_3^1/0$, but we must also be able to loop with b's while staying in a q_3-like state. Therefore, an edge labeled b must connect $q_3^1/0$ to $q_3^2/1$. Because we must be allowed to repeat as many b's as we want, there must be a b-loop at the state $q_3^2/1$. Each b-loop we go around prints another 1 when it reenters q_3^2. As with all such clones of an original state, they must both be connected to q_6 by $a/0$.

If there is ever a state that has no edges entering it, we can assign it any printing instruction we want, even if this state is the start state.

Let us repeat this process for each state of Me, $q_0, q_1, \ldots$. This will produce Mo. If we have to make copies of the start state in Me, we can let any one of them be the start state in Mo because they all give the identical directions for proceeding to other states. Having a choice of start states means that the conversion of Me into Mo is not unique. We should expect this because any Me is equivalent to more than one Mo. It is equivalent to the Mo with automatic start symbol 0, or to the Mo with automatic start symbol 1, ...

When we start up the machine initially, we print some unpredictable character, specified by the start state, that does not correspond to any output from Me, because Me never prints before reading an input letter. But we allowed for this discrepancy in the definition of equivalence, so there is no problem. ■

Together, Theorems 8 and 9 (pp. 156 and 157) allow us to say

$$Me = Mo$$

When we went from Mo to Me, we kept the same number of states and same number of edges. When we go from Me to Mo, these can both increase drastically.

EXAMPLE

Let us start with the following Mealy machine:

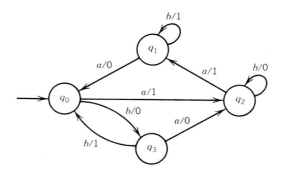

We can begin the conversion process anywhere because the algorithm does not specify the order of replacing states; so let us first consider the state q_0. Two edges come into this state, one labeled $a/0$ and one labeled $b/1$. Therefore, we need two copies of this state: one that prints a 0 (called q_0^1) and one that will print a 1 (called q_0^2). Both these states must be connected to q_2 through an edge labeled $a/1$ and to q_3 through an edge labeled $b/0$. There is no loop at q_0, so these two clones of q_0 are not connected to each other. The machine becomes

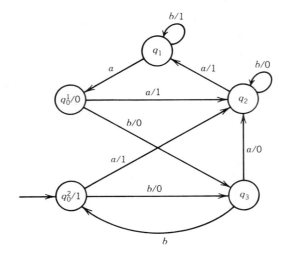

We must select the start state for the new machine, so let us arbitrarily select q_0^2. Notice that we now have two edges that cross. This sometimes happens, but aside from making a messier picture, there is no real problem in understanding which edge goes where. Notice that the edge from q_1 to q_0, which used to be labeled $a/0$, is now only labeled a because the instruction to print the 0 is found in the state $q_0^1/0$. The same is true for the edge from q_3 to q_0^2, which also loses its printing instruction.

State q_1 has only two edges coming into it: one from q_2 labeled $a/1$ and a loop labeled $b/1$. So whenever we enter q_1, we are always printing a 1. We have no trouble here transferring the print instructions from the edges into the state. The machine now looks like this:

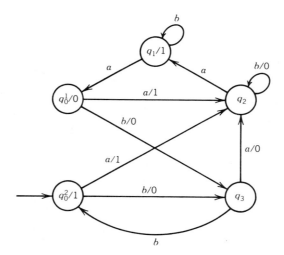

What we have now is a partially converted machine or hybrid. We could run an input string on this machine, and it would give us the same output as the original Me. The rules are that if an edge says print, then print; if a state says print, then print. If not, do not.

Let us continue the conversion. State q_3 is easy to handle. Two edges come into it, both labeled $b/0$, so we change the state to $q_3/0$ and simplify the edge labels to b alone:

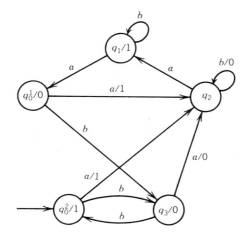

The only job left is to convert state q_2. It has some 0-printing edges entering it and some 1-printing edges (actually two of each, counting the loop). Therefore, we must split it into two copies, q_2^1 and q_2^2. Let the first print a 0 and the second print a 1. The two copies will be connected by a b-edge going from q_2^2 to q_2^1 (to print a 0). There will also be a b-loop at q_2^1. The final machine is

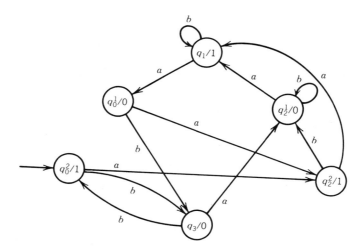

⚜ TRANSDUCERS AS MODELS OF SEQUENTIAL CIRCUITS

The student of computer science may already have met these machines in courses on computer logic or architecture. They are commonly used to describe the action of sequential circuits that involve flip-flops and other feedback electronic devices for which the output of the circuit is not only a function of the specific instantaneous inputs, but also a function of the previous state of the system. The total amount of history of the input string that can be "remembered" in a finite automaton is bounded by a function of the number of states the automaton has. Automata with input and output are sometimes called **transducers** because of their connection to electronics.

EXAMPLE

Let us consider an example of a simple sequential circuit. The box labeled NAND means "not and." Its output wire carries the complement of the Boolean AND of its input wires. The output of the box labeled DELAY is the same as its previous input. It delays transmission of the signal along the wire by one step (clock pulse). The DELAY is sometimes called a D flip-flop. The AND and OR are as usual. Current in a wire is denoted by the value 1, no current by 0.

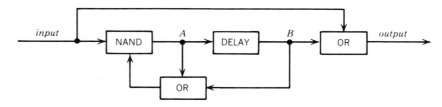

We identify four states based on whether or not there is current at points A and B in the circuit:

$$q_0 \text{ is } A = 0, \quad B = 0$$
$$q_1 \text{ is } A = 0, \quad B = 1$$
$$q_2 \text{ is } A = 1, \quad B = 0$$
$$q_3 \text{ is } A = 1, \quad B = 1$$

The operation of this circuit is such that after an input of 0 or 1, the state changes according to the following rules:

$$\text{New } B = \text{old } A$$
$$\text{New } A = (\text{input}) \quad \text{NAND} \quad (\text{old } A \text{ OR old } B)$$
$$\text{Output} = (\text{input}) \quad \text{OR} \quad (\text{old } B)$$

At a sequence of discrete pulses of a time clock a string of input is received, the state changes, and output is generated.

Suppose we are in state q_0 and we receive the input 0:

$$\text{New } B = \text{old } A = 0$$
$$\text{New } A = (\text{input}) \quad \text{NAND} \quad (\text{old } A \text{ OR old } B)$$
$$= (0) \text{ NAND} \quad (0 \text{ OR } 0)$$
$$= 0 \text{ NAND } 0$$
$$= 1$$
$$\text{Output} = 0 \text{ OR } 0 = 0$$

The new state is q_2 (because new $A = 1$, new $B = 0$).
If we are in state q_0 and we receive the input 1,

$$\text{New } B = \text{old } A = 0$$
$$\text{New } A = 1 \text{ NAND } (0 \text{ OR } 0) = 1$$
$$\text{Output} = 1 \text{ OR } 0 = 1$$

The new state is q_2 (because the new $A = 1$ and the new $B = 0$).
    If we are in q_1 and we receive the input 0:

$$\text{New } B = \text{old } A = 0$$
$$\text{New } A = 0 \text{ NAND } (0 \text{ OR } 1) = 1$$
$$\text{Output} = 0 \text{ OR } 1 = 1$$

The new state is q_2.
    If we are in q_1 and we receive the input 1,

$$\text{New } B = \text{old } A = 0$$
$$\text{New } A = 1 \text{ NAND } (0 \text{ OR } 1) = 0$$
$$\text{Output} = 1 \text{ OR } 1 = 1$$

The new state is q_0.
    If we are in state q_2 and we receive the input 0,

$$\text{New } B = \text{old } A = 1$$
$$\text{New } A = 0 \text{ NAND } (1 \text{ OR } 0) = 1$$
$$\text{Output} = 0 \text{ OR } 0 = 0$$

The new state is q_3.
    If we are in q_2 and we receive the input 1,

$$\text{New } B = \text{old } A = 1$$
$$\text{New } A = 1 \text{ NAND } (1 \text{ OR } 0) = 0$$
$$\text{Output} = 1 \text{ OR } 0 = 1$$

The new state is q_1
    If we are in q_3 and we receive the input 0,

$$\text{New } B = \text{old } A = 1$$
$$\text{New } A = 0 \text{ NAND } (1 \text{ OR } 1) = 1$$
$$\text{Output} = 0 \text{ OR } 1 = 1$$

The new state is q_3
    If we are in q_3 and we receive the input 1,

$$\text{New } B = \text{old } A = 1$$
$$\text{New } A = 1 \text{ NAND } (1 \text{ OR } 1) = 0$$
$$\text{Output} = 1 \text{ OR } 1 = 1$$

The new state is q_1.

| | After Input 0 | | After Input 1 | |
Old State	New State	Output	New State	Output
q_0	q_2	0	q_2	1
q_1	q_2	1	q_0	1
q_2	q_3	0	q_1	1
q_3	q_3	1	q_1	1

    The action of this sequential feedback circuit is equivalent to the following Mealy machine:

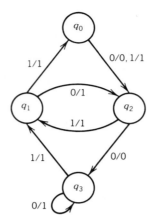

If we input two 0's no matter which state we started from, we will get to state q_3. From there, the input string 011011 will cause the output sequence 111011. ∎

Comparison Table for Automata

	FA	TG	NFA	NFA-Λ	MOORE	MEALY
Start states	One	One or more	One	One	One	One
Final states	Some or none	Some or none	Some or none	Some or none	None	None
Edge labels	Letters from Σ	Words from Σ*	Letters from Σ	Letters from Σ and Λ	Letters from Σ	i/o i from Σ o from Γ
Number of edges from each state	One for each letter in Σ	Arbitrary	Arbitrary	Arbitrary	One for each letter in Σ	One for each letter in Σ
Deterministic	Yes	No	No	No	Yes	Yes
Output	No	No	No	No	Yes	Yes
Page defined	53	79	135	146	150	152

⚜ PROBLEMS

1. Each of the following is a Moore machine with alphabet $\Sigma = \{a \quad b\}$ and output alphabet $\Gamma = \{0 \quad 1\}$. Given the transition and output tables, draw the machines.

(i)

	a	b	Output
q_0	q_1	q_2	1
q_1	q_1	q_1	0
q_2	q_1	q_0	1

(ii)

	a	b	Output
q_0	q_0	q_2	0
q_1	q_1	q_0	1
q_2	q_2	q_1	1

(iii)

	a	b	Output
q_0	q_0	q_1	1
q_1	q_0	q_2	0
q_2	q_2	q_2	1
q_3	q_1	q_1	0

(iv)

	a	b	Output
q_0	q_3	q_2	0
q_1	q_1	q_0	0
q_2	q_2	q_3	1
q_3	q_0	q_1	0

(v)

	a	b	Output
q_0	q_1	q_2	0
q_1	q_2	q_3	0
q_2	q_3	q_4	1
q_3	q_4	q_4	0
q_4	q_0	q_0	0

2. (i) Based on the table representation for Moore machines, how many different Mo's are there with four states?

(ii) How many different Moore machines are there with n states?

3. For each of the following Moore machines, construct the transition and output tables:

(i)

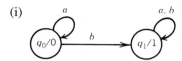

(ii)

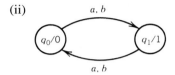

(iii)

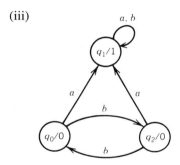

(iv)

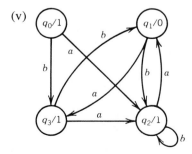

(v)

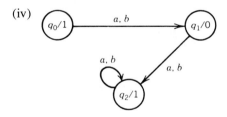

4. On each of the Moore machines in Problems 1 and 3, run the input sequence *aabab*. What are their respective outputs?

5. Suppose we define a Less machine to be a Moore machine that does not automatically print the character of the start state. The first character it prints is the character of the second state it enters. From then on, for every state it enters it prints a character, even when it reenters the start state. In this way, the input string gets to have some say in what the first character printed is going to be. Show that these Less machines are equivalent to Mealy machines in the direct sense, that is, for every Less machine there is a Mealy machine that has the same output for every input string.

6. Mealy machines can also be defined by transition tables. The rows and the columns are both labeled with the names of the states. The entry in the table is the label of the edge (or edges) going from the row state to the column state (if there is no such edge, this entry is blank).

Construct the transition table for each of the four Mealy machines shown below:

(i)
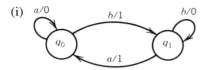

(ii)
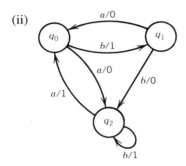

(iii)
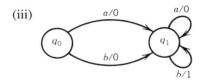

(iv)
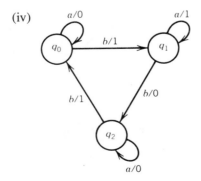

7. The example of the increment machine on p. 154 used three states to perform its job. Show that two states are all that are needed.

8. Convert the Moore machines in Problem 3 into Mealy machines.

9. Convert the Mealy machines in Problem 6 into Moore machines.

10. Draw a Mealy machine equivalent to the following sequential circuit:

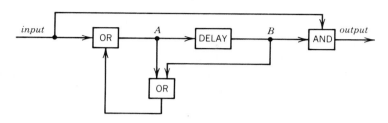

11. Construct a Mealy machine that produces an output string of solid 1's no matter what the input string is.

12.   (i) Design a machine to perform a parity check on the input string; that is, the output string ends in 1 if the total number of 1-bits in the input string is odd and 0 if the total number of 1-bits in the input string is even (the front part of the output string is ignored).

  (ii) In your answer to (i), did you choose a Mealy or Moore machine and why was that the right choice?

13. Given a bit string of length n, the shift-left-cyclic operation places the first bit at the end, leaving the rest of the bits unchanged. For example, SLC (100110) = 001101.

  (i) Build a Mealy machine with input and output alphabet {0 1 $} such that for any bit string x when we input the $n + 1$ bits $x\$$, we get as output the $n + 1$ bit string \$ SLC(x).

  (ii) Explain why this cannot be done without a \$.

For Problems 14 through 16, let $(Me)^2$ mean that given a Mealy machine, an input string is processed and then the output string is immediately fed into the machine (as input) and re-processed. Only this second resultant output is considered the final output of $(Me)^2$. If the final output string is the same as the original input string, we say that $(Me)^2$ has an identity property. Symbolically, we write $(Me)^2$ = identity.

14. Let Me_1 be the identity Mealy machine that looks like this:

0/0, 1/1

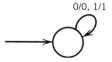

Let Me_2 be the 1's complement Mealy machine pictured below:

0/1, 1/0

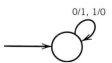

Prove that both $(Me_1)^2$ and $(Me_2)^2$ have the identity property that the result of processing any bit string is the original string again.

15. Show that the following machine also has this identity property:

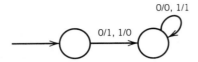

16. Find yet another Mealy machine with this identity property.

For Problems 17 and 18, similarly, given two Mealy machines, let $(Me_1)(Me_2)$ mean that an input string is processed on Me_1 and then the output string is immediately fed into Me_2 (as input) and reprocessed. Only this second resultant output is considered the final output of $(Me_1)(Me_2)$. If the final output string is the same as the original input string, we say that $(Me_1)(Me_2)$ has the identity property, symbolically written $(Me_1)(Me_2) =$ identity.

   Given two specific machines such that $(Me_1)(Me_2)$ reproduces the original bit string, we aim to prove (in the following two problems) that $(Me_2)(Me_1)$ must necessarily also have this property.

17. Show that the 2^n possible n-bit strings when fed into Me_1 give 2^n different outputs.

18. Take the equality $(Me_1)(Me_2) =$ identity. Multiply both sides by Me_1 to get $(Me_1)(Me_2)(Me_1) =$ identity $(Me_1) = Me_1$. This means that $(Me_2)(Me_1)$ takes all outputs from Me_1 and leaves them unchanged. Show that this observation completes the proof.

19. You are given these two Mealy machines:

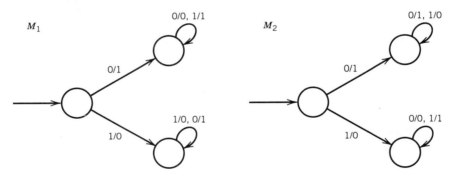

Notice that they are indeed different and show that each is the inverse machine of the other, that means that
$$(Me_1)(Me_2) = \text{identity} = (Me_2)(Me_1)$$

20. Prove that there is no Mealy machine that reverses an input string, that is,
$Me(s) =$ transpose(s).

CHAPTER 9

Regular
Languages

⚜ CLOSURE PROPERTIES

A language that can be defined by a regular expression is called a **regular language.** In the next chapter, we address the important question, "Are all languages regular?" The answer is no. But before beginning to worry about how to prove this fact, we shall discuss in this chapter some of the properties of the class of all languages that are regular.

The information we already have about regular languages is summarized in the following theorem.

THEOREM 10

If L_1 and L_2 are regular languages, then $L_1 + L_2, L_1L_2$, and L_1^* are also regular languages.

Remark

$L_1 + L_2$ means the language of all words in either L_1 or L_2. L_1L_2 means the language of all words formed by concatenating a word from L_1 with a word from L_2. L_1^* means strings that are the concatenation of arbitrarily many factors from L_1. The result stated in this theorem is often expressed by saying: The set of regular languages is *closed* under union, concatenation, and Kleene closure.

PROOF 1   (by regular expressions)

If L_1 and L_2 are regular languages, there are regular expressions $\mathbf{r}_1$ and $\mathbf{r}_2$ that define these languages. Then $(\mathbf{r}_1 + \mathbf{r}_2)$ is a regular expression that defines the language $L_1 + L_2$. The language L_1L_2 can be defined by the regular expression $\mathbf{r}_1\mathbf{r}_2$. The language L_1^* can be defined by the regular expression $(\mathbf{r}_1)^*$. Therefore, all three of these sets of words are definable by regular expressions and so are themselves regular languages.   ■

The proof of Theorem 10 above uses the fact that L_1 and L_2 must be definable by regular expressions if they are regular languages. Regular languages can also be defined in terms of machines, and as it so happens, machines can also be used to prove this theorem.

PROOF 2   (by machines)

Because L_1 and L_2 are regular languages, there must be TGs that accept them. Let TG_1 accept L_1 and TG_2 accept L_2. Let us further assume that TG_1 and TG_2 each have a unique start state and a unique separate final state. If this is not the case originally, we can modify the TGs so that it becomes true as in Theorem 6, Part 2 of the proof (p. 93).

The TG described below accepts the language $L_1 + L_2$:

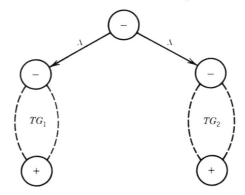

Starting at the $-$ of TG_1, our only option is to follow a path on TG_1. Starting at the $-$ of TG_2, we can only follow a path on TG_2. Starting at the new $-$ state, we must choose to go to one machine or the other; once there, we stay there. This machine proves that $L_1 + L_2$ is regular.

The TG described below accepts the language L_1L_2:

where 1 is the former $+$ of TG_1 and 2 is the former $-$ of TG_2.

The TG described below accepts the language L_1^*:

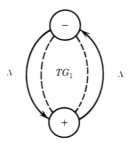

Here, we begin at the $-$ of TG_1 and trace a path to the $+$ of TG_1. At this point, we could stop and accept the string or jump back, at no cost, to the $-$ of TG_1 and run another segment of the input string back down to $+$. We can repeat this process as often as we want. The edge that goes directly from $-$ to $+$ allows us to accept the word Λ, but otherwise it has no effect on the language accepted.

There is a small problem here if the START state has internal edges leading back to it. In such a case, we must add a duplicate start state. All the TGs in this proof could be replaced with FA-Λ's that could then be converted into FAs by the algorithm of Theorem 7. ∎

EXAMPLE

Let the alphabet be $\Sigma = \{a \quad b\}$ and

L_1 = all words of two or more letters that begin and end with the same letter

and

L_2 = all words that contain the substring *aba*

For these languages, we will use the following TGs and regular expressions:

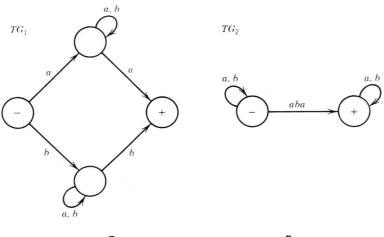

$$\mathbf{r}_1$$
$$\mathbf{a(a + b)^*a + b(a + b)^*b}$$

$$\mathbf{r}_2$$
$$\mathbf{(a + b)^*aba(a + b)^*}$$

The language $L_1 + L_2$ is regular because it can be defined by the regular expression

$$\mathbf{[a(a + b)^*a + b(a + b)^*b] + [(a + b)^*aba(a + b)^*]}$$

(for the purpose of clarity, we have employed brackets instead of nested parentheses) and is accepted by the TG:

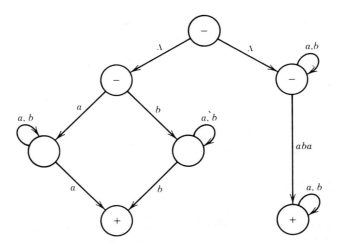

The language L_1L_2 is regular because it can be defined by the regular expression

$$[a(a + b)*a + b(a + b)*b] \quad [(a + b)*aba(a + b)*]$$

and is accepted by the TG

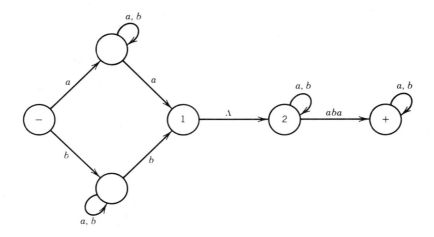

The language L_1^* is regular because it can be defined by the regular expression

$$[a(a + b)*a + b(a + b)*b]*$$

and is accepted by the TG

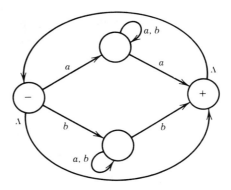

COMPLEMENTS AND INTERSECTIONS

DEFINITION

If L is a language over the alphabet Σ, we define its **complement,** L', to be the language of all strings of letters from Σ that are not words in L. ∎

Many authors use the bar notation $\overline{L}$ to denote the complement of the language L, but as with most writing for computers, we will use the form more easily typed.

EXAMPLE

If L is the language over the alphabet $\Sigma = \{a \quad b\}$ of all words that have a double a in them, then L' is the language of all words that do not have a double a. ■

It is important to specify the alphabet Σ, or else the complement of L might contain *cat*, *dog*, *frog*, . . . , because these are definitely not strings in L.

Notice that the complement of the language L' is the language L. We could write this as

$$(L')' = L$$

This is a theorem from set theory that is not restricted only to languages.

THEOREM 11

If L is a regular language, then L' is also a regular language. In other words, the set of regular languages is closed under complementation.

PROOF

If L is a regular language, we know from Kleene's theorem that there is some FA that accepts the language L. Some of the states of this FA are final states and, most likely, some are not. Let us reverse the final status of each state; that is, if it was a final state, make it a nonfinal state, and if it was a nonfinal state, make it a final state. If an input string formerly ended in a nonfinal state, it now ends in a final state and vice versa. This new machine we have built accepts all input strings that were not accepted by the original FA (all the words in L') and rejects all the input strings that the FA used to accept (the words in L). Therefore, this machine accepts exactly the language L'. So, by Kleene's theorem, L' is regular. ■

Notice that even the final status of the $-$ state gets reversed: $- \leftrightarrow \pm$.

EXAMPLE

An FA that accepts only the strings *aba* and *abb* is shown below:

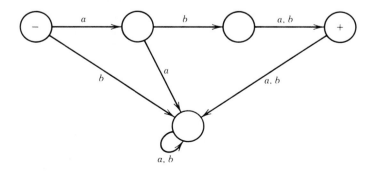

An FA that accepts all strings other than *aba* and *abb* is shown on the next page.

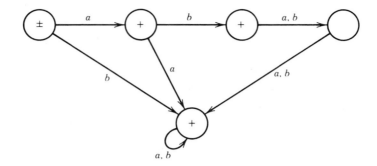

THEOREM 12

If L_1 and L_2 are regular languages, then $L_1 \cap L_2$ is also a regular language. In other words, the set of regular languages is closed under intersection.

PROOF

By DeMorgan's law for sets of any kind (regular languages or not):

$$L_1 \cap L_2 = (L_1' + L_2')'$$

This is illustrated by the Venn diagrams below:

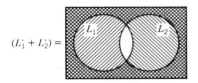   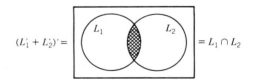

This means that the language $L_1 \cap L_2$ consists of all words that are not in either L_1' or L_2'. Because L_1 and L_2 are regular, then so are L_1' and L_2'. Since L_1' and L_2' are regular, so is $L_1' + L_2'$. And because $L_1' + L_2'$ is regular, then so is $(L_1' + L_2')'$, which means $L_1 \cap L_2$ is regular. ■

This is a case of "the proof is quicker than the eye." When we start with two languages L_1 and L_2, which are known to be regular because they are defined by FAs, finding the FA for $L_1 \cap L_2$ is not as easy as the proof makes it seem. If L_1 and L_2 are defined by regular expressions, finding $L_1 \cap L_2$ can be even harder. However, all the algorithms that we need for these constructions have already been developed.

EXAMPLE

Let us work out one example in complete detail. We begin with two languages over $\Sigma = \{a \quad b\}$.

$$L_1 = \text{all strings with a double } a$$
$$L_2 = \text{all strings with an even number of } a\text{'s}$$

These languages are not the same, because *aaa* is in L_1 but not in L_2 and *aba* is in L_2 but not in L_1.

They are both regular languages because they are defined by the following regular expressions (among others):

$$\mathbf{r}_1 = (\mathbf{a} + \mathbf{b})^*\mathbf{aa}(\mathbf{a} + \mathbf{b})^*$$

$$\mathbf{r}_2 = \mathbf{b}^*(\mathbf{ab}^*\mathbf{ab}^*)^*$$

The regular expression $\mathbf{r}_2$ is somewhat new to us. A word in the language L_2 can have some *b*'s in the front, but then whenever there is an *a*, it is balanced (after some *b*'s) by another *a*. This gives us factors of the form $(\mathbf{ab}^*\mathbf{ab}^*)$. The word can have as many factors of this form as it wants. It can end in an *a* or a *b*.

Because these two languages are regular, Kleene's theorem says that they can also be defined by FAs. The two smallest of these are

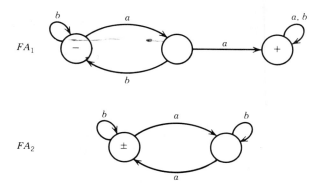

In the first machine, we stay in the start state until we read our first *a*; then we move to the middle state. This is our opportunity to find a double *a*. If we read another *a* from the input string while in the middle state, we move to the final state where we remain. If we miss our chance and read a *b*, we go back to $-$. If we never get past the middle state, the word has no double *a* and is rejected. We have seen this before.

The second machine switches from the left state to the right state or from the right state to the left state every time it reads an *a*. It ignores all *b*'s. If the string begins on the left and ends on the left, it must have made an even number of left/right switches. Therefore, the strings this machine accepts are exactly those in L_2. We have also seen this before.

Now the first step in building the machine (and regular expression) for $L_1 \cap L_2$ is to find the machines that accept the complementary languages L_1' and L_2'. Although it is not necessary for the successful execution of the algorithm, the English description of these languages is

$$L_1' = \text{all strings that do not contain the substring } aa$$

$$L_2' = \text{all strings having an odd number of } a\text{'s}$$

In the proof of the theorem where the complement of a regular language is regular, we gave the algorithm for building the machines that accept these languages. All that we have to do is reverse what is a final state and what is not a final state. The machines for these languages are then

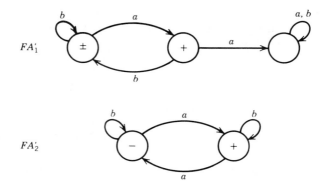

Even if we are going to want both the regular expression and the FA for the intersection language, we do not need to find the regular expressions that go with these two component machines. However, it is good exercise and the algorithm for doing this was presented as part of the proof of Kleene's theorem. Recall that we go through stages of transition graphs with edges labeled by regular expressions. FA_1' becomes

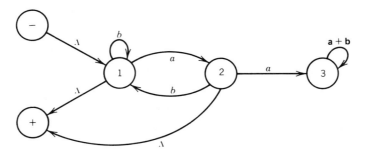

State 3 is part of no path from $-$ to $+$, so it can be dropped. To bypass state 2, we need to join the incoming a-edge with both outgoing edges (b-edge to 1 and Λ-edge to $+$). When we add the two loops, we get $\mathbf{b} + \mathbf{ab}$ and the sum of the two edges from 1 to $+$ is $\mathbf{a} + \Lambda$, so the machine looks like this:

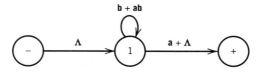

The last step is to bypass state 1. To do this, we concatenate the incoming Λ-label with the loop label starred $(\mathbf{b} + \mathbf{ab})^*$ concatenated with the outgoing $(\mathbf{a} + \Lambda)$-label to produce one edge from $-$ to $+$ with the regular expression for L_1'.

$$\mathbf{r_1'} = (\mathbf{b} + \mathbf{ab})^*(\mathbf{a} + \Lambda)$$

Let us now do the same thing for the language L_2'. FA_2' becomes

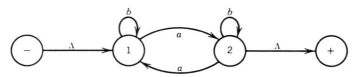

Let us start the simplification of this picture by eliminating state 2. There is one incoming edge, a loop, and two outgoing edges, so we need to replace them with only two edges: The path 1-2-2-1 becomes a loop at 1 and the path 1-2-2-+ becomes an edge from 1 to +. After bypassing state 2 and adding the two loop labels, we have

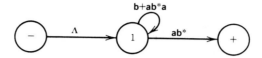

We can now eliminate state 1 and we have

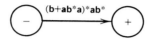

which gives us the regular expression

$$r_2' = (b + ab^*a)^*ab^*$$

This is one of several regular expressions that define the language of all words with an odd number of a's. Another is

b*ab*(ab*ab*)*

which we get by adding the factor **b*a** in front of the regular expression for L_1. This works because words with an odd number of a's can be interpreted as **b*a** in front of words with an even number of a's. The fact that these two different regular expressions define the same language is not obvious. The question, "How can we tell when two regular expressions are equal?", will be answered in Chapter 11.

We now have regular expressions for L_1' and L_2', so we can write the regular expression for $L_1' + L_2'$. This will be

$$r_1' + r_2' = (b + ab)^*(\Lambda + a) + (b + ab^*a)^*ab^*$$

We must now go in the other direction and make this regular expression into an FA so that we can take its complement to get the FA that defines $L_1 \cap L_2$.

To build the FA that corresponds to a complicated regular expression is no picnic, as we remember from the proof of Kleene's theorem, but it can be done. However not by anybody as reasonable as ourselves. Clever people like us can always find a better way.

An alternative approach is to make the machine for $L_1' + L_2'$ directly from the machines for L_1' and L_2' without resorting to regular expressions.

Let us label the states in the two machines for FA_1' and FA_2' as shown:

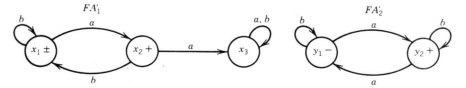

where the start states are x_1 and y_1 and the final states are x_1, x_2, and y_2. The six possible combination states are

$z_1 = x_1$ or y_1 start, final   (words ending here are accepted in FA_1')

$z_2 = x_1$ or y_2 final   (words ending here are accepted on FA_1' and FA_2')

$z_3 = x_2$ or y_1 final   (words ending here are accepted on FA_1')
$z_4 = x_2$ or y_2 final   (words ending here are accepted on FA_1' and FA_2')
$z_5 = x_3$ or y_1 not final on either machine
$z_6 = x_3$ or y_2 final   (words ending here are accepted on FA_2')

The transition table for this machine is

	a	b
$\pm z_1$	z_4	z_1
$+ z_2$	z_3	z_2
$+ z_3$	z_6	z_1
$+ z_4$	z_5	z_2
z_5	z_6	z_5
$+ z_6$	z_5	z_6

And so the union machine can be pictured like this:

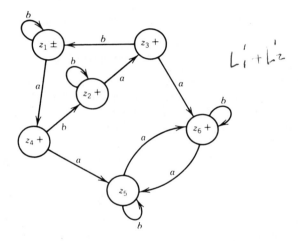

$$L_1' + L_2'$$

This is an FA that accepts the language $L_1' + L_2'$. If we reverse the status of each state from final to nonfinal and vice versa, we produce an FA for the language $L_1 \cap L_2$. This is it:

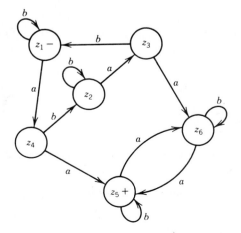

Bypassing z_2 and z_6 gives

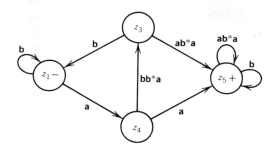

Then bypassing z_3 gives

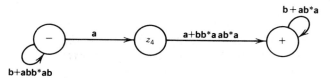

So, the whole machine reduces to the regular expression

$$L_1 \cap L_2 = \text{(b + abb*ab)*a(a + bb*aab*a)(b + ab*a)*}$$

Even though we know this expression must be our answer because we know how it was derived, let us try to analyze it anyway to see whether we can understand what this language means in some more intuitive sense.

As it stands, there are four factors (the second is just an **a** and the first and fourth are starred). Every time we use one of the options from the two end factors, we incorporate an even number of a's into the word (either none or two). The second factor gives us an odd number of a's (exactly one). The third factor gives us the option of taking either one or three a's. In total, the number of a's must be even. So, all the words in this language are in L_2.

The second factor gives us an a, and then we must immediately concatenate this with one of the choices from the third factor. If we choose the a, then we have formed a double a. If we choose the other expression, **bb*aab*a**, then we have formed a double a in a different way. By either choice, the words in this language all have a double a and are therefore in L_1.

This means that all the words in the language of this regular expression are contained in the language $L_1 \cap L_2$. But are *all* the words in $L_1 \cap L_2$ included in the language of this expression?

The answer to this is yes. Let us look at any word that is in $L_1 \cap L_2$. It has an even number of a's and a double a somewhere in it. There are two possibilities to consider separately:

1. Before the first double a, there are an even number of a's.
2. Before the first double a, there are an odd number of a's.

Words of type 1 come from the expression below:

(even number of a's but not doubled)(first aa)(even number of a's may be doubled)
$$= \text{(b + abb*ab)*(aa)(b + ab*a)*}$$
$$= \text{type 1}$$

Notice that the third factor defines the language L_1 and is a shorter expression than the $\mathbf{r}_1$ we used above.

Words of type 2 come from the expression

(odd number of not doubled a's)(first aa)(odd number of a's may be doubled)

Notice that the first factor must end in b, because none of its a's are part of a double a.

$$= [(b + abb^*ab)^*abb^*]aa[b^*a(b + ab^*a)^*]$$
$$= (b + abb^*ab)^*(a)(bb^*aab^*a)(b + ab^*a)^*$$
$$= \text{type 2}$$

Adding type 1 and type 2 together (and factoring out like terms using the distributive law), we obtain the same expression we got from the algorithm. We now have two proofs that this is indeed a regular expression for the language $L_1 \cap L_2$.

This completes the calculation that was started on p. 174.   ■

The proofs of the last three theorems are a tour de force of technique. The first was proved by regular expressions and TGs, the second by FAs, and the third by a Venn diagram.

We must confess now that the proof of the theorem that the intersection of two regular languages is again a regular language was an evil pedagogical trick. The theorem is not really as difficult as we made it seem. We chose the hard way to do things because it was a good example of mathematical thinking: *Reduce the problem to elements that have already been solved.*

This procedure is reminiscent of a famous story about a theoretical mathematician. Professor X is surprised one day to find his desk on fire. He grabs the extinguisher and douses the flames. The next day, he looks up from his book to see that his wastepaper basket is on fire. Quickly, he takes the basket and empties it onto his desk, which begins to burn. Having thus reduced the problem to one he has already solved, he goes back to his reading. (The students who find this funny are probably the ones who have been setting the fires in his office.)

The following is a more direct proof that the intersection of two regular languages is regular.

GOOD PROOF OF THEOREM 12

Let us recall the method we introduced to produce the union-machine FA_3 that accepts any string accepted by either FA_1 or FA_2.

To prove this, we showed how to build a machine with states z_1, z_2, . . . of the form $x_{\text{something}}$ if the input is running on FA_1 or $y_{\text{something}}$ if the input is running on FA_2. If either the x-state or the y-state was a final state, we made the z-state a final state.

Let us now build the exact same machine FA_3, but let us change the designation of final states. Let the z-state be a final state only if *both* the corresponding x-state *and* the corresponding y-state are final states. Now FA_3 accepts only strings that reach final states simultaneously on both machines.

The words in the language for FA_3 are words in both the languages for FA_1 and FA_2. This is therefore a machine for the intersection language.   ■

Not only is the proof shorter but also the construction of the machine has fewer steps.

EXAMPLE

In the proof of Kleene's theorem, we took the sum of the machine that accepts words with a double a,

	a	*b*
$-x_1$	x_2	x_1
x_2	x_3	x_1
$+x_3$	x_3	x_3

and the machine that accepts all words in EVEN-EVEN,

	a	*b*
$\pm y_1$	y_3	y_2
y_2	y_4	y_1
y_3	y_1	y_4
y_4	y_2	y_3

The resultant union-machine was

	a	*b*	Old States
$\pm z_1$	z_2	z_3	x_1 or y_1
z_2	z_4	z_5	x_2 or y_3
z_3	z_6	z_1	x_1 or y_2
$+z_4$	z_7	z_8	x_3 or y_1
z_5	z_9	z_{10}	x_1 or y_4
z_6	z_8	z_{10}	x_2 or y_4
$+z_7$	z_4	z_{11}	x_3 or y_3
$+z_8$	z_{11}	z_4	x_3 or y_2
z_9	z_{11}	z_1	x_2 or y_2
z_{10}	z_{12}	z_5	x_1 or y_3
$+z_{11}$	z_8	z_7	x_3 or y_4
$+z_{12}$	z_7	z_3	x_2 or y_1

The intersection machine is identical to this except that it has only one final state. In order for the z-state to be a final state, both the x- and y-states must be final states. If FA_1 and FA_2 have only one final state, then FA_3 can have only one final state (if it can be reached at all). The only final state in our FA_3 is z_4, which is x_3 or y_1.

This complicated machine is pictured below:

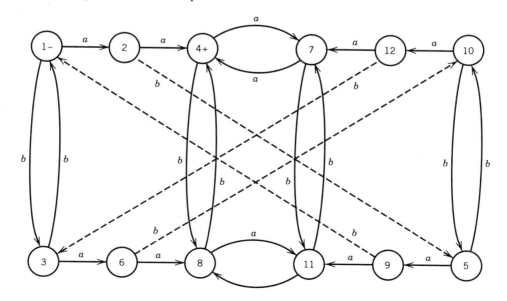

The dashed lines are perfectly good edges, but they have to cross other edges. With a little imagination, we can see how this machine accepts all EVEN-EVEN with a double a. All north–south changes are caused by b's, all east–west by a's. To get into the inner four states takes a double a. ∎

EXAMPLE

Let us rework the example in the first proof once again, this time by the quick method. This is like the citizens of the fabled city of Chelm who on learning that they did not have to carry all their logs down from the top of the mountain were so overjoyed that they carried them all back up again so that they could use the clever work-saving method of rolling them down.

$$L_1 = \text{all strings with a double } a$$

FA_1

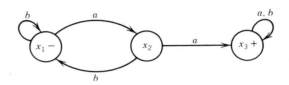

$$L_2 = \text{all strings with an even number of } a\text{'s}$$

FA_2

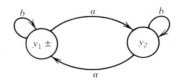

The machine that simulates the same input running on both machines at once is

	a	b	Old States
$-z_1$	z_4	z_1	x_1 or y_1
z_2	z_3	z_2	x_1 or y_2
z_3	z_6	z_1	x_2 or y_1
z_4	z_5	z_2	x_2 or y_2
$+z_5$	z_6	z_5	x_3 or y_1
z_6	z_5	z_6	x_3 or y_2

To be accepted by FA_1, an input string must have its path end in x_3. To be accepted by FA_2, an input string must have its path end in y_1. To be accepted by both machines at once, an input string on the z-machine, starting its processing in z_1, must end its path in state z_5 and only z_5.

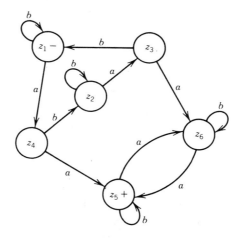

FIGURE 2 machine

EXAMPLE

Let us work through one last example of intersection. Our two languages will be

$$L_1 = \text{all words that begin with an } a$$
$$L_2 = \text{all words that end with an } a$$
$$\mathbf{r_1} = \mathbf{a(a + b)*}$$
$$\mathbf{r_2} = \mathbf{(a + b)*a}$$

The intersection language will be

$$L_1 \cap L_2 = \text{all words that begin and end with the letter } a$$

The language is obviously regular because it can be defined by the regular expression

$$\mathbf{a(a + b)*a + a}$$

Note that the first term requires that the first and last a's be different, which is why we need the second choice "+ **a**."

In this example, we were lucky enough to "understand" the languages, so we could concoct a regular expression that we "understand" represents the intersection. In general, this does not happen, so we follow the algorithm presented in the proof, which we can execute even without the benefit of understanding. (Although the normal quota of insights per human is one per year, the daily adult requirement of interpreting regular expressions is even lower.)

For this, we must begin with FAs that define these languages:

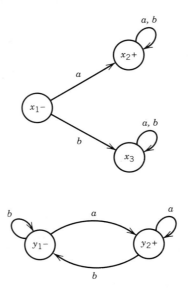

As it turns out, even though the two regular expressions are very similar, the machines are very different. There is a three-state version of FA_2, but no two-state version of FA_1.

We now build the transition table of the machine that runs its input strings on FA_1 and FA_2 simultaneously:

	State	Read a	Read b
$-z_1$	x_1 or y_1	x_2 or y_2	x_3 or y_1
z_2	x_2 or y_2	x_2 or y_2	x_2 or y_1
z_3	x_3 or y_1	x_3 or y_2	x_3 or y_1
z_4	x_2 or y_1	x_2 or y_2	x_2 or y_1
z_5	x_3 or y_2	x_3 or y_2	x_3 or y_1

The machine looks like this:

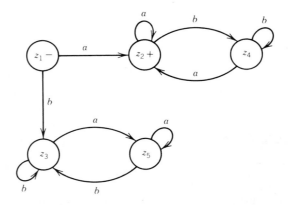

If we are building the machine for

$$L_1 + L_2 = \text{all words in either } L_1 \text{ or } L_2 \text{ or in both}$$

we would put $+$'s at any state representing acceptance by L_1 or L_2, that is, any state with an x_2 or a y_2:

$$z_2 +$$
$$z_4 +$$
$$z_5 +$$

Because we are instead constructing the machine for

$$L_1 \cap L_2 = \text{all words in both } L_1 \text{ and } L_2$$

we put a $+$ only in the state that represents acceptance by both machines at once:

$$z_2 + = x_2 \quad \text{or} \quad y_2$$

Strings ending here are accepted if being run on FA_1 (by ending in x_2) *and* if being run on FA_2 (by ending in y_2). ■

Do not be fooled by this slight confusion:

$$\cancel{\times} \left(z_2 = x_2 \; \boxed{\text{or}} \; y_2 = \text{accepted by } FA_1 \; \widehat{\text{and}} \; FA_2 \right)$$

The poor plus sign is perilously overworked.

$2 + 2$	(sometimes read "2 <u>and</u> 2 are 4")
$(a + b)*$	(*a* <u>or</u> *b* repeated as often as we choose)
a^+	(a string of at least one *a*)
$L_1 + L_2$	(all words in L_1 <u>or</u> L_2)
$+ z_2, z_2 +$	(z_2 is a final state, the machine accepts input strings if they end here)
$1 + 1 = 2$	Arithmetic
$1 + 1 = 10$	Binary
$1 + 1 = 0$	<u>Modulo 2</u>
$1 + 1 = 1$	Boolean

If humans were not smarter than machines, they could never cope with the mess they make of their own notation.

⚜ PROBLEMS

For each of the following pairs of regular languages, find a regular expression and an FA that each define $L_1 \cap L_2$:

L_1	L_2
1. $(a + b)*a$	$b(a + b)*$
2. $(a + b)*a$	$(a + b)*aa(a + b)*$
3. $(a + b)*a$	$(a + b)*b$
4. $(a + b)b(a + b)*$	$b(a + b)*$
5. $(a + b)b(a + b)*$	$(a + b)*aa(a + b)*$
6. $(a + b)b(a + b)*$	$(a + b)*b$
7. $(b + ab)*(a + \Lambda)$	$(a + b)*aa(a + b)*$
8. $(b + ab)*(a + \Lambda)$	$(b + ab*a)*ab*$
9. $(b + ab)*(a + \Lambda)$	$(a + ba)*a$
10. $(ab*)*$	$b(a + b)*$

11. (ab*)*   a(a + b)*

12. (ab*)*   (a + b)*aa(a + b)*

13. All strings of even length   b(a + b)*
    = (aa + ab + ba + bb)*

14. Even-length strings   (a + b)*aa(a + b)*

15. Even-length strings   (b + ab)*(a + Λ)

16. Odd-length strings   a(a + b)*

17. Even-length strings   EVEN-EVEN

18. (i) Even-length strings   Strings with an even number of *a*'s
    (ii) Even-length strings   Strings with an odd number of *a*'s

19. (i) Even-length strings   Strings with an odd number of *a*'s and an odd number of *b*'s
    (ii) Even-length strings   Strings with an odd number of *a*'s and an even number of *b*'s

20. We have seen that because the regular languages are closed under union and complement, they must be closed under intersection. Find a collection of languages that is closed under union and intersection but *not* under complement.

CHAPTER 10

Nonregular Languages

⚜ THE PUMPING LEMMA

By using FAs and regular expressions, we have been able to define many languages. Although these languages have had many different structures, they took only a few basic forms: languages with required substrings, languages that forbid some substrings, languages that begin or end with certain strings, languages with certain even/odd properties, and so on. We will now turn our attention to some new forms, such as the language PALINDROME of Chapter 3 or the language PRIME of all words a^p, where p is a prime number. In this chapter, we shall see that neither of these is a regular language. We can describe them in English, but they cannot be defined by an FA. More powerful machines are needed to define them, machines that we build in later chapters.

DEFINITION

A language that cannot be defined by a regular expression is called a **nonregular** language.

■

By Kleene's theorem, a nonregular language can also not be accepted by any FA or TG. All languages are either regular or nonregular; none are both.

Let us first consider a simple case. Let us define the language L.

$$L = \{\Lambda \quad ab \quad aabb \quad aaabbb \quad aaaabbbb \quad aaaaabbbbb \ldots \}$$

We could also define this language by the formula

$$L = \{a^n b^n \quad \text{for} \quad n = 0 \quad 1 \quad 2 \quad 3 \quad 4 \quad 5 \ldots \}$$

or for short

$$L = \{a^n b^n\}$$

When the range of the abstract exponent n is unspecified, we mean to imply that it is 0, 1, 2, 3, ...

We shall now show that this language is nonregular. Let us note, though, that it is a subset of many regular languages, such as **a*b***, which, however, also includes such strings as *aab* and *bb* that $\{a^n b^n\}$ does not.

Let us be very careful to note that $\{a^n b^n\}$ is not a regular expression. It involves the symbols { } and n that are not in the alphabet of regular expressions. This is a language-defining expression that is not regular. Just because this is not a regular expression does not mean that none exists; this we shall now prove.

Suppose on the contrary that this language were regular. Then there would have to exist some FA that accepts it. Let us picture one of these FAs (there might be several) in our mind. This FA might have many states. Let us say that it has 95 states, just for the sake of argument. Yet, we know it accepts the word $a^{96} b^{96}$. The first 96 letters of this input string are all a's and they trace a path through this machine. The path cannot visit a new state with each input letter read because there are only 95 states. Therefore, at some point the path returns to a state that it has already visited. The first time it was in that state it left by the a-road. The second time it is in that state it leaves by the a-road again. Even if it only returns once, we say that the path contains a circuit in it. (A **circuit** is a loop that can be made of several edges.) First, the path wanders up to the circuit and then it starts to loop around the circuit, maybe many times. It cannot leave the circuit until a b is read from the input. Then the path can take a different turn. In this hypothetical example, the path could make 30 loops around a three-state circuit before the first b is read.

After the first b is read, the path goes off and does some other stuff following b-edges and eventually winds up at a final state where the word $a^{96} b^{96}$ is accepted.

Let us, for the sake of argument again, say that the circuit that the a-edge path loops around has seven states in it. The path enters the circuit, loops around it madly, and then goes off on the b-line to a final state. What would happen to the input string $a^{96+7} b^{96}$? Just as in the case of the input string $a^{96} b^{96}$, this string would produce a path through the machine that would walk up to the same circuit (reading only a's) and begin to loop around it in exactly the same way. However, the path for $a^{96+7} b^{96}$ loops around this circuit one more time than the path for $a^{96} b^{96}$ — precisely one extra time. Both paths, at exactly the same state in the circuit, begin to branch off on the b-road. Once on the b-road, they both go the same 96 b-steps and arrive at the same final state. But this would mean that the input string $a^{103} b^{96}$ is accepted by this machine. However, that string is not in the language $L = \{a^n b^n\}$.

This is a contradiction. We assumed that we were talking about an FA that accepts exactly the words in L and then we were able to prove that the same machine accepts some word that is not in L. This contradiction means that the machine that accepts exactly the words in L does not exist. In other words, L is nonregular.

Let us review what happened. We chose a word in L that was so large (had so many letters) that its path through the FA had to contain a circuit. Once we found that some path with a circuit could reach a final state, we asked ourselves what happens to a path that is just like the first one, but that loops around the circuit one extra time and then proceeds identically through the machine. The new path also leads to the same final state, but it is generated by a different input string — an input string not in the language L.

Perhaps the following picture can be of some help in understanding the idea behind this discussion. Let the path for $a^9 b^9$ be

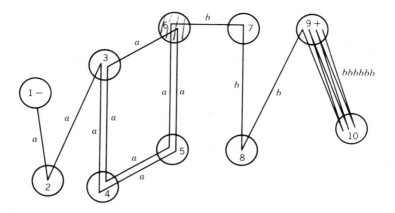

We have not indicated all the edges in this FA, only those used in the path of the word a^9b^9. State 6 is the only state for which we see both an a-exit edge and a b-exit edge.

In the path this input string takes to acceptance, we find two circuits: the a-circuit 3-4-5-6 and the b-circuit 9-10. Let us concentrate on the a-circuit. What would be the path through this FA of the input string $a^{13}b^9$? The path for $a^{13}b^9$ would begin with the same nine steps as the path for a^9b^9 ending after nine steps in state 6. The input string a^9b^9 now gives us a b to read, which makes us go to state 7. However, the path for $a^{13}b^9$ still has four more a-steps to take, which is one more time around the circuit, and then it follows the nine b-steps.

The path for $a^{13}b^9$ is shown below:

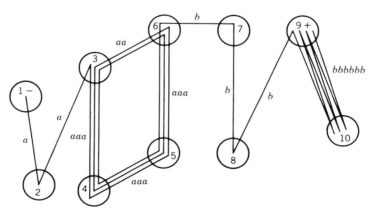

Let us return to our first consideration.

With the assumptions we made above (that there were 95 states and that the circuit was 7 states long), we could also say that $a^{110}b^{96}$, $a^{117}b^{96}$, $a^{124}b^{96}$, ... are also accepted by this machine.

They can all be written in this form:

$$a^{96}(a^7)^m b^{96}$$

where m is any integer 0, 1, 2, 3, ... If m is 0, the path through this machine is the path for the word $a^{96}b^{96}$. If m is 1, the path looks the same, but it loops the circuit one more time. If $m = 2$, the path loops the circuit two more times. In general, $a^{96}(a^7)^m b^{96}$ loops the circuit exactly m more times. After doing this looping, it gets off the circuit at exactly the same place $a^{96}b^{96}$ does and proceeds along exactly the same route to the final state. All these words, though not in L, must be accepted.

Suppose that we had considered a different machine to accept the language L, perhaps a machine that has 732 states. When we input the word $a^{733}b^{733}$, the path that the a's take must contain a circuit. We choose the word $a^{733}b^{733}$ to be efficient. The word $a^{9999}b^{9999}$ also must loop around a circuit in its a-part of the path. Suppose the circuit that the a-part follows has 101 states. Then $a^{733+101}b^{733}$ would also have to be accepted by this machine, because its path is the same in every detail except that it loops the circuit one more time. This second machine must also accept some strings that are not in L:

$$a^{834}b^{733} \qquad a^{935}b^{733} \qquad a^{1036}b^{733}. \ . \ .$$
$$= a^{733}(a^{101})^m b^{733} \quad \text{for} \quad m = 1 \quad 2 \quad 3 \ . \ . \ .$$

For each different machine we suggest to define L, there is a different counterexample proving that it accepts more than just the language L.

There are machines that include L in the language they accept, but for each of them there are infinitely many extra words they must also accept.

All in all, we can definitely conclude that there is no FA that accepts all the strings in L and only the strings in L. Therefore, L is nonregular.

The reason why we cannot find an FA that accepts L is not because we are stupid, but because none can exist.

The principle we have been using to discuss the language L above can be generalized so that it applies to consideration of other languages. It is a tool that enables us to prove that certain other languages are also nonregular. We shall now present the generalization of this idea, called the **pumping lemma** for regular languages, which was discovered by Yehoshua Bar-Hillel, Micha A. Perles, and Eliahu Shamir in 1961.

The name of this theorem is interesting. It is called "pumping" because we pump more stuff into the middle of the word, swelling it up without changing the front and the back part of the string. It is called a "lemma" because, although it is a theorem, its main importance is as a tool in proving other results of more direct interest; namely, it will help us prove that certain specific languages are nonregular.

THEOREM 13

Let L be any regular language that has infinitely many words. Then there exist some three strings x, y, and z (where y is not the null string) such that all the strings of the form

$$xy^n z \quad \text{for} \quad n = 1 \quad 2 \quad 3 \ . \ . \ .$$

are words in L.

PROOF

If L is a regular language, then there is an FA that accepts exactly the words in L. Let us focus on one such machine. Like all FAs, this machine has only finitely many states. But L has infinitely many words in it. This means that there are arbitrarily long words in L. (If there were some maximum on the length of all the words in L, then L could have only finitely many words in total.)

Let w be some word in L that has more letters in it than there are states in the machine we are considering. When this word generates a path through the machine, the path cannot visit a new state for each letter because there are more letters than states. Therefore, it must at some point revisit a state that it has been to before. Let us break the word w up into three parts:

Part 1   Call part x all the letters of w starting at the beginning that lead up to the first state that is revisited. Notice that x may be the null string if the path for w revisits the start state as its first revisit.

Part 2   Starting at the letter after the substring x, let y denote the substring of w that travels around the circuit coming back to the same state the circuit began with. Because there must be a circuit, y cannot be the null string. y contains the letters of w for exactly one loop around this circuit.

Part 3   Let z be the rest of w starting with the letter after the substring y and going to the end of the string w. This z could be null. The path for z could also possibly loop around the y-circuit or any other. What z does is arbitrary.

Clearly, from the definition of these three substrings

$$w = xyz$$

and w is accepted by this machine.

What is the path through this machine of the input string

$$xyyz?$$

It follows the path for w in the first part x and leads up to the beginning of the place where w looped around a circuit. Then like w, it inputs the string y, which causes the machine to loop back to this same state again. Then, again like w, it inputs a string y, which causes the machine to loop back to this same state yet another time. Then, just like w, it proceeds along the path dictated by the input string z and so ends on the same final state that w did. This means that $xyyz$ is accepted by this machine, and therefore it must be in the language L.

If we traced the paths for $xyyz$, $xyyyz$, and $xyyyyyyyyyyyyz$, they would all be the same. Proceed up to the circuit. Loop around the circuit some number of times. Then proceed to the final state. All these must be accepted by the machine and therefore are all in the language L. In fact, L must contain all strings of the form:

$$xy^n z \quad \text{for} \quad n = 1 \ \ 2 \ \ 3 \ . \ . \ .$$

as the theorem claims.

Perhaps these pictures can be helpful in understanding the argument above:

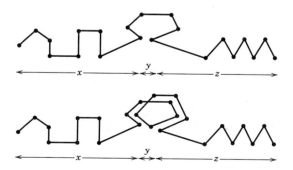

Notice that in this theorem it does not matter whether there is another circuit traced in the z-part or not. All we need to do is find one circuit, and then we keep pumping it for all it is worth.

Notice also that we did not assume that the x-, y-, or z-parts were repetitions of the same letter, as was the case in our discussion of $\{a^n b^n\}$. They could have been any arbitrary strings.   ■

EXAMPLE

Let us illustrate the action of the pumping lemma on a concrete example of a regular language. The machine below accepts an infinite language and has only six states:

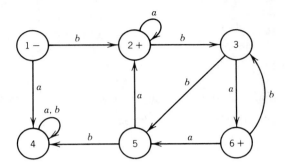

Any word with six or more letters must correspond to a path that includes a circuit. Some words with fewer than six letters correspond to paths with circuits, such as *baaa*. The word we will consider in detail is

$$w = bbbababa$$

which has more than six letters and therefore includes a circuit. The path that this word generates through the FA can be decomposed into three stages.

The first part, the x-part, goes from the $-$ state up to the first circuit. This is only one edge and corresponds to the letter b alone. The second stage is the circuit around states 2, 3, and 5. This corresponds to edges labeled b, b, and a. We therefore say that the substring *bba* is the y-part of the word w. After going around the circuit, the path proceeds to states 3, 6, 3, and 6. This corresponds to the substring *baba* of w, which constitutes the z-part:

$$w = b \quad bba \quad baba$$
$$x \quad\quad y \quad\quad z$$

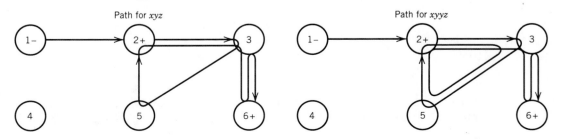

Now let us ask what would happen to the input string $xyyz$.

$$x \quad y \quad y \quad z = b \quad bba \quad bba \quad baba$$

This is what happens!

The same thing happens with $xyyyz$, $xyyyyz$, and in general for xy^nz. This is all that the pumping lemma says. ■

EXAMPLE

Suppose for a moment that we did not already have a discussion of the language

$$L = \{a^nb^n \quad \text{for} \quad n = 0 \quad 1 \quad 2 \quad 3 \ldots\}$$

Let us see how we could apply the pumping lemma directly to this case.

The pumping lemma says that there must be strings x, y, and z such that all words of the form xy^nz are in L. Is this possible? A typical word of L looks like

$$aaa \ldots aaaabbbb \ldots bbb$$

How do we break this into three pieces conformable to the roles x, y, and z? If the middle section y is going to be made entirely of a's, then when we pump it to $xyyz$, the word will have more a's than b's, which is not allowed in L. Similarly, if the middle part, y, is composed of only b's, then the word $xyyz$ will have more b's than a's. The solution is that the y-part must have some positive number of a's and some positive number of b's. This would mean that y contains the substring ab. Then $xyyz$ would have two copies of the substring ab. But every word in L contains the substring ab exactly once. Therefore, $xyyz$ cannot be a word in L. This proves that the pumping lemma cannot apply to L and therefore L is not regular. ■

EXAMPLE

Once we have shown that the language $\{a^nb^n\}$ is nonregular, we can show that the language EQUAL, of all words with the same total number of a's and b's, is also nonregular. (Note that the numbers of a's and b's do not have to be even, they just have to be the same.)

$$\text{EQUAL} = \{\Lambda \quad ab \quad ba \quad aabb \quad abab \quad abba \quad baab \quad baba \quad bbaa \quad aaabbb \ldots\}$$

The language $\{a^nb^n\}$ is the intersection of all words defined by the regular expression $\mathbf{a^*b^*}$ and the language EQUAL:

$$\{a^nb^n\} = \mathbf{a^*b^*} \cap \text{EQUAL}$$

Now if EQUAL were a regular language, then $\{a^nb^n\}$ would be the intersection of two regular languages and by Theorem 12 on p. 174 it would have to be regular itself. Because $\{a^nb^n\}$ is not regular, EQUAL cannot be. ■

For the example $\{a^nb^n\}$, and in most common instances, we do not need the full force of the pumping lemma as stated. It is often just as decisive to say that w can be decomposed into xyz, where $xyyz$ is also in the language. The fact that xy^nz is in the language for all $n > 2$ is also interesting and will be quite useful when we discuss whether certain languages are finite or infinite, but often $n = 2$ is adequate to show that a given language is nonregular.

EXAMPLE

Consider the language $a^nba^n = \{b \quad aba \quad aabaa \ldots\}$. If this language were regular, then there would exist three strings x, y, and z such that xyz and $xyyz$ were both words in this language. We can show that this is impossible:

Observation 1: If the *y* string contained the *b*, then *xyyz* would contain two *b*'s, which no word in this language can have.

Observation 2: If the *y* string is all *a*'s, then the *b* in the middle of the word *xyz* is in the *x*-side or *z*-side. In either case, *xyyz* has increased the number of *a*'s either in front of the *b* or after the *b*, but not both.

Conclusion 1: Therefore, *xyyz* does not have its *b* in the middle and is not in the form a^nba^n.

Conclusion 2: This language cannot be pumped and is therefore not regular.   ∎

EXAMPLE

Consider the language $a^nb^nab^{n+1}$ for $n = 1, 2, 3 \ldots$. The first two words of this infinite language are *ababb* and *aabbabbb*. We are going to show that this language too is not regular by showing that if *xyz* is in this language for any three strings *x*, *y*, and *z*, then *xyyz* is not in this language:

Observation 1: For every word in this language, if we know the total number of *a*'s, we can calculate the exact number of *b*'s (twice the total number of *a*'s − 1). And conversely, if we know the total number of *b*'s, we can uniquely calculate the number of *a*'s (add 1 and divide by 2). So, no two different words have the same number of *a*'s or *b*'s.

Observation 2: All words in this language have exactly two substrings equal to *ab* and one equal to *ba*.

Observation 3: If *xyz* and *xyyz* are both in this language, then *y* cannot contain either the substring *ab* or the substring *ba* because then *xyyz* would have too many.

Conclusion 1: Because *y* cannot be **Λ**, it must be a solid clump of *a*'s or a solid clump of *b*'s; any mixture contains the substrings forbidden to it in observation 3.

Conclusion 2: If *y* is solid *a*'s, then *xyz* and *xyyz* are different words with the same total *b*'s, violating observation 1. If *y* is solid *b*'s, then *xyz* and *xyyz* are different words with the same number of *a*'s violating observation 1.

Conclusion 3. It is impossible for both *xyz* and *xyyz* to be in this language for any strings *x*, *y*, and *z*. Therefore, the language is unpumpable and not regular.   ∎

The proof that we gave of the pumping lemma actually proved more than was explicitly stated in the lemma. By the method of proof that we used, we showed additionally that the string *x* and the string *y* together do not have any more letters than the machine in question has states. This is because as we proceed through *x* and *y*, we visit our first repeated state at the end of *y*; before that, all the states were entered only once each.

The same argument that proved Theorem 13 (see p. 190) proves the stronger theorem below.

THEOREM 14

Let *L* be an infinite language accepted by a finite automaton with *N* states. Then for all words *w* in *L* that have more than *N* letters, there are strings *x*, *y*, and *z*, where *y* is not null and length(*x*) + length(*y*) does not exceed *N* such that

$$w = xyz$$

and all strings of the form

$$xy^n z \quad (\text{for} \quad n = 1 \quad 2 \quad 3 \ldots)$$

are in L.

∎

We put the end-of-proof symbol ∎ right after the statement of the theorem to indicate that we have already provided a proof of this result.

The purpose of stressing the question of length is illustrated by our next example.

EXAMPLE

We shall show that the language PALINDROME is nonregular. We cannot use the first version of the pumping lemma to do this because the strings

$$x = a, \quad y = b, \quad z = a$$

satisfy the lemma and do not contradict the language. All words of the form

$$xy^n z = ab^n a$$

are in PALINDROME.

However, let us consider one of the FAs that might accept this language. Let us say that the machine we have in mind has 77 states. Now the palindrome

$$w = a^{80} b a^{80}$$

must be accepted by this machine because it is a palindrome. Because it has more letters than the machine has states, we can break w into the three parts: x, y, and z. But because the length of x and y must be in total 77 or less, they must both be made of solid a's, because the first 77 letters of w are all a's. That means when we form the word $xyyz$, we are adding more a's to the front of w. But we are not adding more a's to the back of w because all the rear a's are in the z-part, which stays fixed at 80 a's. This means that the string $xyyz$ is not a palindrome because it will be of the form

$$a^{\text{more than } 80} b a^{80}$$

But the second version of the pumping lemma says that PALINDROME has to include this string. Therefore, the second version does not apply to the language PALINDROME, which means that PALINDROME is nonregular.

Obviously, this demonstration did not really rely on the number of states in the hypothetical machine being 77. Some people think that this argument would be more mathematically sound if we called the number of states m. This is silly.

∎

EXAMPLE

Let us consider the language

$$\text{PRIME} = \{a^p \text{ where } p \text{ is a prime}\}$$
$$= \{aa \quad aaa \quad aaaaa \quad aaaaaaa \ldots\}$$

Is PRIME a regular language? If it is, then there is some FA that accepts exactly these words. Let us keep one such automaton in mind. Let us suppose, for the sake of argument, that it has 345 states. Let us choose a prime number bigger than 345—for example, 347. Then a^{347} can be broken into parts x, y, and z such that $xy^n z$ is in PRIME for any value of n. The parts x, y, and z are all just strings of a's. Let us take the value of $n = 348$. By the pumping lemma, the word $xy^{348} z$ must be in PRIME. Now

$$xy^{348}z = xyzy^{347}$$

We can write this because the factors x, y, and z are all solid clumps of a's, and it does not matter in what order we concatenate them. All that matters is how many a's we end up with.

Let us write

$$xyzy^{347} = a^{347}y^{347}$$

This is because x, y, and z came originally from breaking up a^{347} into three parts. We also know that y is some (nonempty) string of a's. Let us say that $y = a^m$ for some integer m that we do not know.

$$a^{347}y^{347} = a^{347}(a^m)^{347}$$
$$= a^{347+347m}$$
$$= a^{347(m+1)}$$

These operations are all standard algebraic manipulations.

What we have arrived at is that there is an element in PRIME that is of the form a to the power $347(m + 1)$. Now because $m \neq 0$, we know that $347(m + 1)$ is not a prime number. But this is a contradiction, because all the strings in PRIME are of the form a^p, where the exponent is a prime number. This contradiction arose from the assumption that PRIME was a regular language. Therefore, PRIME is nonregular. ∎

⚜ THE MYHILL–NERODE THEOREM

The pumping lemma is negative in its application. It is used exclusively to show that certain languages are not regular because they cannot meet its requirements. We shall now introduce another method for saying that a given language might be nonregular but has a constructive aspect to it.

If we consider a particular FA, then each state, whether a final state or not, can be thought of as creating a society of a certain class of strings. Here, we are talking about strings, not only accepted words. Two strings can be said to both belong to the society of state x_4 if they both trace a path from start to x_4 even if the paths are very different. Similarly, every state defines a society. Because every one of the infinitely many possible input strings ends up at one of the finitely many states, some of these societies have infinite membership.

If string x and string y are in the same society, then for all other strings z, either both xz and yz are accepted by the machine or both are rejected. This simply depends on whether the string z traces a path from the mutual state of x and y to a final state.

Now let us consider this from the aspect of a regular language without reference to any one of the many FAs that recognize it.

THEOREM 15

Given a language L, we shall say that any two strings x and y are in the same class if for all possible strings z either both xz and yz are in L or both are not.

1. The language L divides the set of all possible strings into separate (mutually exclusive) classes.

2. If L is regular, the number of classes L creates is finite.

3. If the number of classes L creates is finite, then L is regular.

PROOF

What needs to be proven in Part 1 is that the description we gave of dividing into classes is not self-contradicting. An example of a bad way of dividing into classes is this: Say any two students at college are in the same class if they have taken a course together. A and B may have taken history together, B and C may have taken geography together, but A and C never took a class together. Then A, B, and C are not all in the same class. This cannot happen according to our definition of classes. If both AZ and BZ are always in L or not and if both BZ and CZ are always in L or not, then A, B, and C must all be in the same class. If S is in a class with X and S is also in a class with Y, then by the reasoning above X and Y must be in the same class. Therefore, S cannot be in two different classes. No string is in two different classes and by definition every string is in some class. Therefore, every string is in exactly one class.

To prove Part 2, we know that because L is regular, there is some FA that accepts L, and its finitely many states create a finite division of all strings into finitely many societies as described above. We still use the word society instead of classes since these societies are not actually identical to what we have defined as classes in the theorem. The problem is that two different states might define societies that are actually the same class. In the example below:

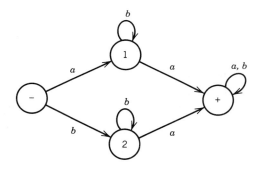

both states 1 and 2 have the property that any word in them when followed by string z will be accepted if z contains an a and rejected otherwise. These two societies are in the same class. It is true that the societies defined by the states in this machine are either separate classes in the sense of this theorem or can be grouped to form classes. In either case, the number of classes is not more than the number of societies and that is finite.

It should come as no surprise to us that the number of classes was not exactly the number of societies because the number of classes language L creates is dependent on L alone, whereas the number of societies depends on which FA we choose to recognize L.

We are going to prove Part 3 by what appears to be a constructive algorithm, but in fact it is not. This is because we will turn the set of finitely many classes that L creates into an FA, with each state representing one class. However, to be truly constructive, we have to know how to go from "L creates finitely many classes" to "these are the classes." This we have no idea how to do. What we will do is go from "these are the classes" to "here is the FA."

Let the finitely many classes be $C_1, C_2, \ldots$, where C_1 is the class containing Λ. We will turn this collection of classes into an FA by showing how to draw the edges between them and how to assign start and final states.

The start state must be C_1 because Λ begins and ends in the start state. Now we make another observation: If a class contains one word of L, then all the strings in the class are words in L. To prove this, let w be in class C_7 and a word in L, and let s be any other string in the class. Then letting $z = \Lambda$, we know that both $w\Lambda$ and $s\Lambda$ are either in L or not. Because $w\Lambda$ is in L, then so is $s\Lambda = s$. Therefore, some of the classes are completely contained in L and some have no L words. Label all those that are subsets of L with $+$'s. We should also note that all words in L are in the final states.

If x and y are two strings in class C_4, say, then by definition for all strings z, both xz and yz are in L or not. Also, both xa and ya must be in the same class because for all strings z, both xaz and yaz must be in L or not because az can be considered a tail added to x and y in class C_4. If we take every string in C_4 and add an a on the right, the resultant strings would therefore all be in the same class. Draw an a-edge from C_4 to this class. Similarly, draw all the a-edges and all the b-edges.

There is no guarantee that the picture which results is connected or has only enterable states, but it is an FA. Also, any string that can trace a path from the start to a final state must be in L and every string in L must end in a final state. Therefore, if a language creates a finite set of classes by the definition of the theorem, it is a regular language. ■

Myhill we have met before; Anil Nerode published this theorem in 1958.

First, we shall illustrate Part 3 with some examples. There are not many languages L for which we know what classes they create, but there are some.

EXAMPLE

Let us consider the language of all words that end in a. At first, it may seem that there is only one class here because for all x and y, both xz and yz end in a or not, depending on z alone. But this overlooks the fact that if z is Λ, then xz and yz are in the same class, depending on whether x and y end in a themselves. There are therefore two classes:

$$C_1 = \text{all strings that end in } a, \text{ a final state}$$
$$C_2 = \text{all strings that do not, the start state}$$

The FA is

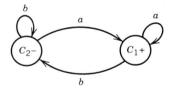

as we have seen before. ■

EXAMPLE

Let L be the language of all strings that contain a double a. There are three classes:

$$C_1 = \text{strings without } aa \text{ that end in } a$$
$$C_2 = \text{strings without } aa \text{ that end in } b \text{ or } \Lambda$$
$$C_3 = \text{strings with } aa, \text{ the final state}$$

States 1 and 2 are different because adding an a to any string in C_1 puts it in L, but it will not do the same for a string in C_2. Also, C_3 is different because adding $z = \Lambda$ to the strings in C_3 will put them in L, while it will not for strings in C_1 or C_2. As we have seen before, the machine is

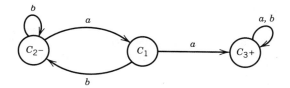

EXAMPLE

Working the algorithms of Theorem 15 (see p. 96) on the language EVEN-EVEN creates four obvious states:

$$C_1 = \text{EVEN-EVEN}$$
$$C_2 = \text{even } a\text{'s, odd } b\text{'s}$$
$$C_3 = \text{odd } a\text{'s, even } b\text{'s}$$
$$C_4 = \text{odd } a\text{'s, odd } b\text{'s}$$

Clearly, if x and y are in any one class, then both xz and yz are in L or not, depending on how many a's and b's z alone has. The FA is exactly the same as we have had before. ∎

For the purpose of this chapter, it was actually Part 2 that we were the most interested in, because it offers us a technique, different from the pumping lemma, for proving that certain languages are nonregular. If we can show that a given language L creates infinitely many classes, then we know L is nonregular.

EXAMPLE

To show that the language $a^n b^n$ is nonregular, we need only observe that the strings a, aa, aaa, $aaaa$, . . . are all in different classes because for each m, only a^m is turned into a word in L by $z = b^m$. ∎

EXAMPLE

To show that $a^n b a^n$ is nonregular, we note that the strings ab, aab, $aaab$, . . . are all in different classes because for each of them, one value of $z = a^m$ will produce a word in L and leave the others out of L. ∎

EXAMPLE

EQUAL is nonregular because, for each of the strings a, aa, aaa, $aaaa$, . . . , some value of $z = b^m$ will put it alone in EQUAL. ∎

EXAMPLE

PALINDROME is nonregular because ab, aab, $aaab$, . . . are all in different classes. For each of these, one value of $z = a^m$ will create a PALINDROME when added to it but to no other. ∎

EXAMPLE

Let us define the language DOUBLEWORD to be the collection of all words that are of the form SS, where S is any string of a's and b's. DOUBLEWORD starts out with these words: Λ *aa   bb   aabb   abab   baba   bbbb   aaaaaa* . . . . Let us use Theorem 15 to prove that the language DOUBLEWORD is nonregular. It is not so obvious when two strings are in different classes since strings can turn into doublewords in various ways. For example, $x = bb$ and $y = bbbb$ can each be turned into words in DOUBLEWORD using $z = x = bb$. However, the following infinite set of strings is easy to show as belonging to different classes: *ab   aab   aaab   aaaab* . . . . For any two strings x and y we choose from the set above, we let $z = x$ and find that xz is in DOUBLEWORD but not yz. Therefore, DOUBLEWORD creates infinitely many classes (at least one for each string above and maybe more) and is therefore nonregular. ∎

⚜ QUOTIENT LANGUAGES

Now that we have proven there are such things as nonregular languages, we have more respect for the theorem stating that the product of any two regular languages is always regular. We are also ready to approach the question of whether there is a corresponding division theorem; that is, can we prove that the quotient of two regular languages is regular?

There is a problem here regarding what it means to say that the language Q is the quotient of the two regular languages P and R. If we write

$$Q = R/P$$

whenever it is true that

$$PQ = R$$

then, in some cases, the symbol R/P does not determine a unique language. For example, if P, Q, and R are all the language $\mathbf{a}^*$, then it is true that

$$PQ = R$$

so therefore we may write

$$\mathbf{a}^* = \mathbf{a}^*/\mathbf{a}^*$$

On the other hand, if P and R are both the language $\mathbf{a}^*$, while Q is the language of the one word $\{\Lambda\}$, then $PQ = R$ is still true, which means we also have to write

$$\{\Lambda\} = \mathbf{a}^*/\mathbf{a}^*$$

Similarly, we can show that

$$\{\Lambda \quad a \quad aaaa \quad aaaaaaaa\} = \mathbf{a}^*/\mathbf{a}^*$$

There are infinitely many choices for the meaning of R/Q even in this simple case of the one-letter alphabet.

What happens if we do not use the division symbol itself as an operation to produce a unique language, but instead attempt to get around the ambiguity by proving that all these languages that could be interpreted as R/Q are regular? We could then make the following claim.

PSEUDOTHEOREM

If for three languages P, Q, and R we have

$$PQ = R$$

and P and R are regular, then Q must also be regular.

The reason that we have called this a pseudotheorem is that it is not true.

DISPROOF

Let us assume, for a moment, that this claim is true. Now let P be the language defined by the regular expression $\mathbf{a}^*$ and let Q be the product of $\{a^n b^n\}$ and $\mathbf{b}^*$ where we let n start from 0, which will allow the word Λ in the language. Now let R be the language defined by $\mathbf{a}^*\mathbf{b}^*$. In this case, it is true that

$$PQ = \mathbf{a}^*[\{a^n b^n\}\mathbf{b}^*]$$
$$= [\mathbf{a}^*\mathbf{b}^* = R$$

Because both P and R are regular, if the preceding claim is true, then Q must be regular. Now all we have to do to disprove the claim is show that this Q is not regular. This is not hard to do.

The language Q is the set of all strings of the form $a^x b^y$ where $x \leq y$. If Q were regular, it could be accepted by a certain FA with some fixed number of states; let us call it N. The word $a^N b^N$ is accepted by this machine in a path that contains a loop of solid a's. Cycling around this loop one extra time will create a path through the machine that leads to acceptance and corresponds to a word with more than N a's and only N b's. This word should not be in Q; therefore, no FA that can be imagined can accept exactly the language Q. So, Q is not regular, and the claim in the pseudotheorem is false.

Quod Erat Demolition

We do not need to abandon all hope of finding a result similar to a division theorem if we concentrate on the P factor and not the Q factor in the product. Let us imagine that we have a regular language R and some of its words end in a string that is a word in the language Q. If we focus our attention only on these words of R (the ones that end in a Q-word) and we define the language P to be the set of front-halves of these words, we can indeed prove that P is regular. Let us call these front-halves the prefixes that can be attached to *some* words in Q to obtain some words in R.

Let us state this cautiously.

DEFINITION

If R and Q are languages, then the language "the prefixes of Q in R," denoted by the symbolism

Pref(Q in R)

is the set of all strings of letters that can be concatenated to the front of some word in Q to produce some word in R.

We may write this as

Pref(Q in R) = the set of all strings p such that there exist words
q in Q and w in R such that $pq = w$ ∎

EXAMPLE

If Q is the language

$$\{aa \quad abaaabb \quad bbaaaaa \quad bbbbbbbbbb\}$$

and R is the language

$$\{b \quad bbbb \quad bbbaaa \quad bbbaaaaaa\}$$

then the language of the prefixes of Q in R is

$$\text{Pref}(Q \text{ in } R) = \{b \quad bbba \quad bbbaaa\}$$

because the first word in Q can be made into a word in R in two ways and the third word in Q can be made into a word in R in one way, whereas the other words in Q cannot be made into words in R by the addition of any possible prefixes. ■

We should note that Λ is only a word in the prefix language if Q and R have some words in common. It is also possible that no word of Q can be made into a word of R by the addition of a prefix. In this case, we say that the prefix language is empty, $\text{Pref}(Q \text{ in } R) = \phi$.

EXAMPLE

If $Q = \mathbf{ab}^*\mathbf{a}$ and $R = (\mathbf{ba})^*$, then the only word in Q that can be made into a word in R is aba because no word in R has a double letter and all other words in Q have. Also, aba can be made into a word in R by prefixing it with any word of the form $(\mathbf{ba})^*\mathbf{b}$. Therefore,

$$\text{Pref}[\mathbf{ab}^*\mathbf{a} \text{ in } (\mathbf{ba})^*] = (\mathbf{ba})^*\mathbf{b} \qquad ■$$

We can now prove a version of a division theorem that is at the same time less and more ambitious than we originally intended. It is disappointing in the sense that this prefix language does not actually give us a factorization of the language R into P times Q. In general,

$$\text{Pref}(Q \text{ in } R)Q \neq R$$

because many words of R may not be formed from words in Q by the addition of prefixes, and many words in Q may have nothing whatsoever to do with being parts of words in R. On the other hand, what we can show is that the prefix language is regular whenever R is regular *even if Q is not regular.*

THEOREM 16

If R is a regular language and Q is any language whatsoever, then the language

$$P = \text{Pref}(Q \text{ in } R)$$

is regular.

PROOF

Because R is a regular language, let us fix in our minds some FA that accepts R. This machine has one start state and possibly several final states. Now let s be any state in this machine (possibly the start or final state). Let us now process all the words from the language Q on this machine beginning in state s as if it actually were the start state. Either some word (or words) from the language Q will lead to a final state when traced through the FA or else no words from Q will end up in a final state. If any word in Q can begin in s and trace to a final state, paint the state s blue.

Let us make the same determination for all the states in the FA. If they end up blue, then some word from Q can start there and proceed to a final state. If they are not blue, then no word from Q can start there and go to a final state. What results is an FA with one start state and some or no blue states.

Let us now build a new machine from the one with which we started. Let this new machine have exactly the same states and edges as the original FA that accepts R. Let this new FA have the same state labeled start as in the original FA, but let the final states be all the blue states of the old FA and only those, no matter what their final status was in the original machine. We shall now show that the new FA accepts exactly the language $P = \text{Pref}(Q \text{ in } R)$.

To prove this, we have to observe two things: (1) Every word in P is accepted by this machine. (2) Every word accepted by this machine is in the language P.

If w is any word accepted by this machine, then when we trace its processing, beginning at the start state, the path of w will end in a final state, which on the original FA corresponds to a state painted blue. This state is blue because some word from Q (call it q) can start there and run to what was the final state on the original FA. This means that if the string wq was run on the original FA, it would be accepted, which in turn means that wq is in R and w is in P. So, we have shown that every word accepted by the machine is in P.

We now have to show that every word in P is, in fact, accepted by this machine. Let p be any word in P. Then by the definition there is a word q in Q and a word w in R, such that $pq = w$. This means that the string pq when run on the original FA leads from start to a final state. Let us trace this path and note where the processing of the p-part ends and the processing of the q-part begins. This will be at a state from which q runs to a final state, and it is therefore blue. This means that on the original machine the p-part traces from start to blue. Therefore, on the new FA the p-part traces from start to a final state. Thus, p is accepted by the new FA.

The language of this new machine is P, the whole P, and nothing but the P. Therefore, P is regular. ∎

We should take particular note of the fact that although this proof looks like a proof by constructive algorithm, it is not that at all. We glibly tossed in the phrase "process all the words from the language Q on this machine starting in state s . . . ." This is not easy to do if Q is an infinite language. This is indeed a weakness in practical terms, but it is not a flaw that invalidates the proof. It is still very much true that for each state s, either there is some word in Q that runs from there to a final state or else there is not. Therefore, every state of the machine is either definitely blue or definitely not blue. The trouble is that we have not provided a constructive method for deciding which. What we have proven is that there exists an FA that accepts the language $\text{Pref}(Q \text{ in } R)$ without having shown how to build one. This method of proof is called a nonconstructive existence proof, and as such, it is just like the proof of Part 3 of the Myhill–Nerode theorem.

⚜ PROBLEMS

1. Use the pumping lemma to show that each of these languages is nonregular:
   (i) $\{a^n b^{n+1}\} = \{abb \quad aabbb \quad aaabbbb . . .\}$
   (ii) $\{a^n b^n a^n\} = \{aba \quad aabbaa \quad aaabbbaaa \quad aaaabbbbaaaa . . .\}$
   (iii) $\{a^n b^{2n}\} = \{abb \quad aabbbb \quad aaabbbbbb . . .\}$
   (iv) $\{a^n b a^n\} = \{aba \quad aabaa \quad aaabaaa . . .\}$
   (v) $\{a^n b^n a^m \text{ where } n = 0, 1, 2, . . . \text{ and } m = 0, 1, 2, . . .\} = \{\Lambda \quad a \quad aa \quad ab \quad aaa \quad aba . . .\}$

2. Prove that the five languages in Problem 1 are nonregular using the Myhill–Nerode theorem.

3. Use the pumping lemma to prove that the language DOUBLEWORD from p. 200 is nonregular.

4. Define the language TRAILING-COUNT as any string s followed by a number of a's equal to length(s).

$$\text{TRAILING-COUNT} = \{aa \quad ba \quad aaaa \quad abaa \quad baaa \quad bbaa \quad aaaaaa \quad aabaaa$$
$$abaaaa \ . \ . \ .\}$$

Prove that this language is nonregular by the

(i) Pumping lemma.
(ii) Myhill–Nerode theorem.

5. Define the languages

$$\text{EVENPALINDROME} = \{\text{all words in PALINDROME that have even length}\}$$
$$= \{aa \quad bb \quad aaaa \quad abba \quad baab \quad bbbb . . .\}$$
$$\text{ODDPALINDROME} = \{\text{all words in PALINDROME that have odd length}\}$$

(i) Show that each is nonregular by the pumping lemma.
(ii) Show that each is nonregular by the Myhill–Nerode theorem.

6. Define the language SQUARE as follows:

$$\text{SQUARE} = \{a^n \text{ where } n \text{ is a square}\}$$
$$= \{a \quad aaaa \quad aaaaaaaaa . . .\}$$

This language could also be written as $\{a^{n^2}\}$.

(i) Use the pumping lemma to prove that SQUARE is nonregular.
(ii) Use the Myhill–Nerode theorem to prove that SQUARE is nonregular.

7. Define the language DOUBLESQUARE as follows:

$$\text{DOUBLESQUARE} = \{a^n b^n \text{ where } n \text{ is a square}\}$$
$$= \{ab \quad aaaabbbb \quad aaaaaaaaabbbbbbbbb \ . \ . \ .\}$$

Prove that DOUBLESQUARE is nonregular by the

(i) Pumping lemma.
(ii) Myhill–Nerode theorem.

8. Define the language DOUBLEPRIME as follows:

$$\text{DOUBLEPRIME} = \{a^p b^p \text{ where } p \text{ is any prime}\}$$
$$= \{aabb \quad aaabbb \quad aaaaabbbbb . . .\}$$

Prove that DOUBLEPRIME is nonregular by the

(i) Pumping lemma.
(ii) Myhill–Nerode theorem.

9. Define the language DOUBLEFACTORIAL as follows:

$$\text{DOUBLEFACTORIAL} = \{a^{n!} b^{n!}\}$$
$$= \{ab \quad aabb \quad aaaaaabbbbbb \ . \ . \ .\}$$

Prove that DOUBLEFACTORIAL is nonregular by the

(i) Pumping lemma.
(ii) Myhill–Nerode theorem.

10. Just for this problem, let the alphabet be $\Sigma = \{a \quad b \quad c\}$. Let us consider the language

$$a^n b^n c^n = \{abc \quad aabbcc \quad aaabbbccc \ldots\}$$

Prove that this language is nonregular by the

(i) Pumping lemma.
(ii) Myhill–Nerode theorem.

11. Let us revisit the language DOUBLEWORD from p. 200. Use the Myhill–Nerode theorem to show that this language is nonregular by showing that all the strings in **a*** are in different classes.

12. Let us consider the language of algebraic expression, ALEX, defined by the recursive definition on p. 29. We never attempted to give a regular expression for this language because it is nonregular. Prove this using the Myhill–Nerode theorem and the sequence

$$(x \qquad ((x \qquad (((x \ldots$$

13. Define the language MOREA as follows:

MOREA = (all strings of a's and b's in which the total number of a's is greater than the
total number of b's}

$$= \{a \quad aa \quad aab \quad aba \quad baa \quad aaab \quad aaba \ldots\}$$

(i) Use the fact that

$$\text{MOREA}' \cap \text{MOREB}' \cap (\mathbf{a} + \mathbf{b})^* = \text{EQUAL}$$

to prove that MOREA is nonregular (where MOREB has its obvious meaning).
(ii) Explain why the pumping lemma cannot be used to prove that MOREA is nonregular.
(iii) Show that MOREA can be shown to be nonregular by the Myhill–Nerode theorem by using the sequence

$$aab \quad aaab \quad aaaab \quad aaaaab \ldots$$

14. Let $L_1, L_2, L_3, \ldots$ be an infinite sequence of regular languages.

(i) Let L be the infinite union of all these languages taken together. Is L necessarily regular?
(ii) Is the infinite intersection of all these languages necessarily regular?

15. (i) Give an example of a regular language R and a nonregular language N such that $R + N$ is regular.
(ii) Give an example of a regular language R and a nonregular language N such that $R + N$ is nonregular.

16. Consider the following language:

$$\text{PRIME}' = \{a^n \text{ where } n \text{ is not a prime}\}$$
$$= \{\Lambda \quad a \quad aaaa \quad aaaaaa \quad aaaaaaaa \ldots\}$$

(i) Prove that PRIME' is nonregular.
(ii) Prove, however, that PRIME' *does* satisfy the pumping lemma.
(iii) How can this be?

17. (i) Show that if we add a finite set of words to a regular language, the result is a regular language.

   (ii) Show that if we subtract a finite set of words from a regular language, the result is a regular language.

   (iii) Show that if we add a finite set of words to a nonregular language, the result is a nonregular language.

   (iv) Show that if we subtract a finite set of words from a nonregular language, the result is a nonregular language.

18. The proof of Theorem 16 used FAs to show that the language P/Q is regular. Show that the language P/Q is regular using the Myhill–Nerode theorem instead.

19. Let us define the language PARENTHESES to be the set of all algebraic expressions from which everything but the parentheses have been deleted. For example, the expression $(3 + (4*7) + (8 + 9)) + (2 + 1)$ becomes the word $(()()) ()$.

   PARENTHESES = $\{\Lambda\quad ()\quad (())\quad ()()\quad ((()))\quad (())()\quad ()(())\quad ()()()\dots\}$

   (i) Show that this language is nonregular using the Myhill–Nerode theorem.

   (ii) Show that the pumping lemma cannot be successful in proving that this language is nonregular.

   (iii) If we convert the character "(" into the letter a and the character ")" into the letter b, show that PARENTHESES becomes a subset of the language EQUAL in which each word has the property that when read from left to right, there are never more b's than a's.

20. Consider what happens when an FA is built for an infinite language over the one-letter alphabet $\Sigma = \{a\}$. When the input is a string of a's that is longer than the number of states, the path it traces must take the form of some initial sequence of edges followed by a circuit. Because all the words in the language accepted by the machine are strings of a's, all the long words accepted by this FA follow the same path up to the circuit and then around and around as in the picture below:

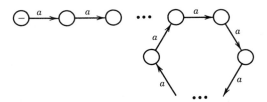

   Some of the states leading up to the circuit may be final states and some of the states in the circuit may be final states. This means that by placing + signs judiciously along a long path to the circuit, we can make the machine accept any finite set of words S_1. While going around the circuit the first time, the FA can accept another finite set of words S_2. If the length of the circuit is n, all words of the form a^n times a word in S_2 will also be accepted on the second go-round of the circuit.

   (i) Prove that if L is any regular language over the alphabet $\Sigma = \{a\}$, then there are two finite sets of words S_1 and S_2 and an integer n such that

$$L = S_1 + S_2(a^n)*$$

   (ii) Consider the language L defined as

$L = \{a^n$ where n is any integer with an even number of digits in base 10$\}$
$= \{\Lambda\quad a^{10}\quad a^{11}\quad a^{12}\dots\}$

   Prove that L is nonregular.

CHAPTER 11

Decidability

⚜ EQUIVALENCE 等价

In this part of the book, we have laid the foundations for the theory of finite automata. The pictures and tables that we have called "machines" can actually be built out of electronic components and operate exactly as we have described. Certain parts of a computer and certain aspects of a computer obey the rules we have made up for FAs. We have not yet arrived, though, at a mathematical model for a whole computer. That we shall present in Part III. But before we leave this topic, we have some unfinished business to clear up. Along the way, we asked some very basic questions that we deferred considering. We now face three of these issues:

1. How can we tell whether two regular expressions define the same language?
2. How can we tell whether two FAs accept the same language?
3. How can we tell whether the language defined by an FA has finitely many or infinitely many words in it, or any words at all, for that matter?

In mathematical logic, we say that a problem is **effectively solvable** if there is an algorithm that provides the answer in a finite number of steps, no matter what the particular inputs are. The maximum number of steps the algorithm will take must be predictable before we begin to execute the procedure. For example, if the problem was, "What is the solution to a quadratic equation?", then the quadratic formula provides an algorithm for calculating the answer in a predetermined number of arithmetic operations: four multiplications, two subtractions, one square root, and one division. The number of steps in the algorithm is never greater than this no matter what the particular coefficients of the polynomial are. Other suggestions for solving a quadratic equation (such as "keep guessing until you find a number that satisfies the equation") that do not guarantee to work in a fixed number of steps are not considered effective solutions, nor are methods that do not work in all cases (such as "try $x = 2$, it couldn't hurt").

DEFINITION

An effective solution to a problem that has a yes or no answer is called a **decision procedure**. A problem that has a decision procedure is called **decidable**. ∎

The first thing we want to decide is whether two regular expressions determine the exact same language. We might, very simply, use the two expressions to generate many words from each language until we find one that obviously is not in the language of the other. To be even more organized, we may generate the words in size order, smallest first. In practice, this method works fairly well, but there is no mathematical guarantee that we find such an obvious benchmark word at any time in the next six years. Suppose we begin with the two expressions

$$a(a + b)^* \quad \text{and} \quad (b + \Lambda)(baa + ba^*)^*$$

It is obvious that all the words in the language represented by the first expression begin with the letter a and all the words in the language represented by the second expression begin with the letter b. These expressions have no word in common; this fact is very clear. However, consider these two expressions:

$$(aa + ab + ba + bb)^* \quad \text{and} \quad ((ba + ab)^*(aa + bb)^*)^*$$

Both define the language of all strings over $\Sigma = \{a \quad b\}$ with an even number of letters. If we did not recognize this, how could we decide the question of whether they are equivalent? We could generate many examples of words from the languages each represents, but we would not find a difference. Could we then conclude that they are equivalent? It is logically possible that the smallest example of a word that is in one language but not in the other has 96 letters. Maybe the smallest example has 2 million letters. Generating words and praying for inspiration is not an effective procedure, and it does not decide the problem.

The following two expressions are even less clear:

$$((b^*a)^*ab^*)^* \quad \text{and} \quad \Lambda + a(a + b)^* + (a + b)^*aa(a + b)^*$$

They both define the language of all words that either start with an a or else have a double a in them somewhere or else are null. The suggestion that we should "interpret what the regular expressions mean and see whether or not they are the same" is, of course, hopeless.

Before we answer the first major question of this chapter, let us note that it is virtually the same as the second question. If we had a decision procedure to determine whether two regular expressions were equivalent, we could use it to determine whether two FAs were equivalent. First, we would convert the FAs into regular expressions and then decide about the regular expressions. The process of converting FAs into regular expressions is an effective procedure that we developed in the proof of Kleene's theorem in Chapter 7. The number of steps required can be predicted in advance based on the size of the machine to be converted. Since the conversion process eliminates at least one state with each step, a machine with 15 states will take at most 16 steps to convert into a regular expression (counting the step that creates a unique $-$ and a unique $+$).

Similarly, if we had an effective procedure to determine whether two FAs were equivalent, we could use it to decide the problem for regular expressions by converting them into FAs.

Fortunately, we have already developed all the algorithms necessary to decide the "equivalency problem" for FAs and thereby regular expressions. We need only recognize how to apply them.

Given two languages L_1 and L_2 defined by either regular expressions or FAs, we have developed (in Chapter 9) the procedures necessary to produce finite automata for the languages L_1', L_2', $L_1 \cap L_2'$, and $L_2 \cap L_1'$. Therefore, we can produce an FA that accepts the language

$$(L_1 \cap L_2') + (L_2 \cap L_1')$$

This machine accepts the language of all words that are in L_1 but not L_2, or else in L_2 but not L_1. If L_1 and L_2 are the same language, this machine cannot accept any words. If this machine accepts even one word, then L_1 is not equal to L_2, even if the one word is the null word. If L_1 is equal to L_2, then the machine for the preceding language accepts nothing at all.

To make this discussion into an effective decision procedure, we must show that we can tell by some algorithm when an FA accepts no words at all. This is not a very hard task, and there are several good ways to do it. We make a big fuss about this because it is so simple that it might seem unimportant, which is wrong. It is a basic question in its own right — not just as part of the decidability of the equivalence of regular languages.

The following subsections outline how to determine whether an FA accepts any words.

Method 1

Convert the FA into a regular expression. Every regular expression defines some words. We can prove this by an algorithm. First, delete all stars. Then for each + we throw away the right half of the sum and the + sign itself. When we have no more *'s or +'s, we remove the parentheses and we have a concatenation of a's, b's, and Λ's. These taken together form a word. For example,

$$\textbf{(a + \Lambda)(ab* + ba*)*(\Lambda + b*)*}$$

becomes (after we remove *'s)

$$\textbf{(a + \Lambda)(ab + ba)(\Lambda + b)}$$

which becomes (after we throw away right halves)

$$\textbf{(a)(ab)(\Lambda)}$$

which becomes (after we eliminate parentheses)

$$\textbf{a \quad ab \quad \Lambda}$$

which is the word

$$aab$$

This word must be in the language of the regular expression because the operations of choosing * to be power 1 and + to be the left half are both legal choices for forming words. If every regular expression defines at least one word, it *seems* at first glance that this means that every FA must accept at least one word. How then could we ever show that two languages are equal? If we first build an FA for the language

$$(L_1 \cap L_2') + (L_2 \cap L_1')$$

and then convert this machine into a regular expression, is it not true that, by the argument above we must find some word in the language of the regular expression, and therefore $L_1 \neq L_2$ no matter what they are? No. The hole in this reasoning is that the process of converting this FA into a regular expression breaks down. We come down to the last step where we usually have several edges running from $-$ to $+$ that we add together to form the regular expression

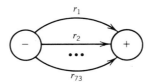

However, when we get to this last step, we suddenly realize that there are no paths from $-$ to $+$ at all.

This could happen theoretically in three different ways: The machine has no final states, such as this one:

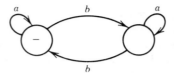

or the final state is disconnected from the start state, as with this one:

or the final state is unreachable from the start state, as with this one:

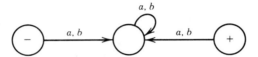

We shall see later in this chapter which of these situations does arise if the languages are actually equal.

Method 2

Examine the FA to see whether or not there is any path from − to +. If there is any path, then the machine must accept some words—for one, the word that is the concatenation of the labels of the edges in the path from − to + just discovered. In a large FA with thousands of states and millions of directed edges, it may be impossible to decide whether there is a path from − to + without the guidance of an effective procedure. One such procedure is this:

Step 1   Paint the start state blue.

Step 2   From every blue state, follow each edge that leads out of it and paint the destination state blue, then delete this edge from the machine.

Step 3   Repeat step 2 until no new state is painted blue, then stop.

Step 4   When the procedure has stopped, if any of the final states are painted blue, then the machine accepts some words and, if not, it does not.

Let us look at this procedure at work on the machine:

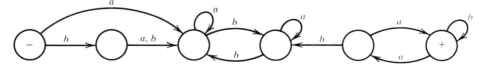

after step 1:

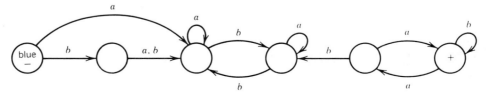

after step 2:

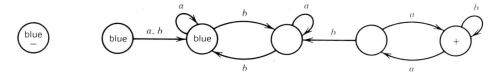

after step 2 again:

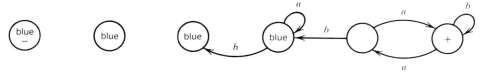

after step 2 again:

No new states were painted blue this time, so the procedure stops and we examine the + state. The + state is not blue, so the machine accepts no words.

While we were examining the second method, we might have noticed that step 2 cannot be repeated more times than there are total states in the machine. If the machine has N states, after N iterations of step 2 either they are all colored blue or we have already stopped. We can summarize this as a theorem.

THEOREM 17

Let F be an FA with N states. Then if F accepts any words at all, it accepts some word with N or fewer letters.

PROOF

The shortest path from $-$ to $+$ (if there is any) cannot contain a circuit because if we go from $-$ to state 7 and then around a circuit back to state 7 and then to $+$, it would have been shorter to go from $-$ to state 7 to $+$ directly. If there is a path from $-$ to $+$ without a circuit, then it can visit each state at most one time. The path can then have at most N edges and the word that generates it can have at most N letters. ∎

The proof actually shows that the shortest word must have at most $N - 1$ letters, because if the start state is a final state, then the word Λ is accepted and with $N - 1$ letters we can visit the other $N - 1$ states. The FA below has four states, but it accepts no word with fewer than three letters, so we see that the bound $N - 1$ is the best possible:

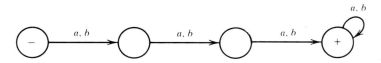

This gives us a third method for determining whether an FA accepts any words.

Method 3

Test all words with fewer than N letters by running them on the FA. If the FA accepts none of them, then it accepts no words at all. There are a predictable number of words to test, and each word takes a finite predictable time to run, so this is an effective decision procedure.

These methods are all effective; the question of which is more efficient is a whole other issue, one that we do not (often) raise in this book. As soon as we know that there is at least one way to accomplish a certain task, we lose interest because our ultimate concern is the question, "What can be done and what cannot?" The only motivation we have for investigating alternative methods is that maybe they can be generalized to apply to new problems that our first approach could not be extended to cover.

EXAMPLE

Let us illustrate the effective decision procedure described above that determines whether two regular expressions are equivalent. We shall laboriously execute the entire process on a very simple example. Let the two regular expressions be

$$\mathbf{r}_1 = \mathbf{a*} \quad \text{and} \quad \mathbf{r}_2 = \Lambda + \mathbf{aa*}$$

Luckily, in this case we can understand that these two define the same language. Let us see how the decision procedure proves this. Some machines for FA_1, FA_1', FA_2, and FA_2' are shown below:

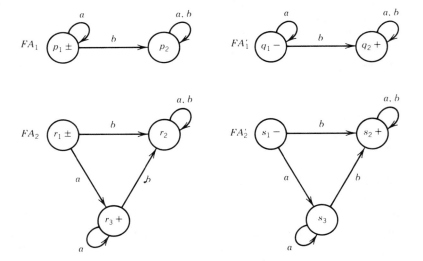

If we did not know how to produce these, algorithms in previous chapters would show us how. We have labeled the states with the letters p, q, r, and s for clarity. Instead of using the logical formula

$$(L_1 \cap L_2') + (L_2 \cap L_1')$$

we build our machine based on the equivalent set theory formula

$$(L_1' + L_2)' + (L_2' + L_1)'$$

The machine for the first half of this formula is $(FA_1' + FA_2)'$

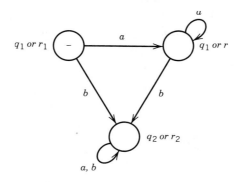

The machine for the second half is $(FA_2' + FA_1)'$

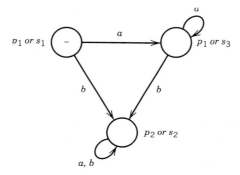

It was not an oversight that we failed to mark any of the states in these two machines with a +. Neither machine has any final states. For $(FA_1' + FA_2)'$ to have a final state, the machine $(FA_1' + FA_2)$ must have a nonfinal state. The start state for this machine is q_1 or r_1. From there, if we read an a, we go to q_1 or r_3, and if we read instead a b, we go to q_2 or r_2. If we ever get to q_2 or r_2, we must stay there. From q_1 or r_3 an input b takes us to q_2 or r_2 and an input a leaves us at q_1 or r_3. All in all, from $-$ we cannot get to any other combination of states, such as the potential q_2 or r_1 or q_1 or r_2. Now because q_2 is a + and r_1 and r_3 are both +, all three states (q_1 or r_1, q_1 or r_3, and q_2 or r_2) are +, which means that the complement has no final states.

The exact same thing is true for the machine for the second half of the formula. Clearly, if we added these two machines together, we would get a machine with nine states and no final state. Because it has no final state, it accepts no words and the two languages L_1 and L_2 are equivalent. This ends the decision procedure. There are no words in one language that are not in the other, so the two regular expressions define the same language and are equivalent. ∎

This example is a paradigm for the general situation. The machine for $(L_1' + L_2)'$ accepts only those words in L_1 but not L_2. If the languages are in fact equal, this machine will have no reachable final states. The same will be true for the machine for $(L_2' + L_1)'$. It will never be necessary to combine these two machines, because if either accepts a word, then $L_1 \neq L_2$.

When we listed three ways that a machine could accept no words, the first way was that there be no final states and the second and third ways were that the final states not be reachable from the start state. We counted these situations separately. When we form a machine by adding two machines together, we do not usually bother describing the states that are not reachable from the start state. The algorithm that we described in Chapter 7 never gets to consider combinations of states of the component machines that are never referred to. However, if we used a different algorithm, based on writing down the whole table of possible combinations and then drawing edges between the resultant states as indicated, we would, in this example, produce a picture with a final state but it would be unreachable from the start state. In the preceding example, the full machine for $(FA_1' + FA_2)'$ is this:

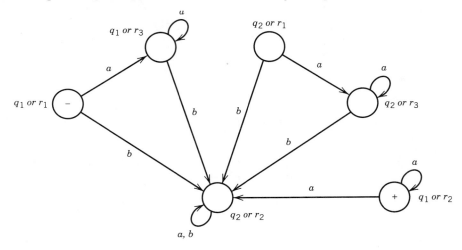

The only final state $(q_1 \; or \; r_2)$ cannot be reached from anywhere—in particular, not from the start state $(q_1 \; or \; r_1)$. So, the machine accepts no words.

We can summarize what we have learned so far in the following theorem.

THEOREM 18

There is an effective procedure to decide whether:

1. A given FA accepts any words.
2. Two FAs are equivalent.
3. Two regular expressions are equivalent.   ■

⚜ FINITENESS

Let us now answer our last question of decidability. How can we tell whether an FA, or regular expression, defines a finite language or an infinite language?

With regular expressions this is easy. The closure of any nonempty set, whether finite or infinite, is itself infinite. Even the closure of one letter is infinite. Therefore, if when building the regular expression from the recursive definition, we have ever had to use the closure operator, the resulting language is infinite. This can be determined by scanning the expression itself to see whether it contains the symbol *. If the regular expression does contain a *, then the language is infinite. The one exception to this rule is Λ*, which is just Λ. This one exception can, however, be very tricky. Of the two regular expressions

$$(\Lambda + a\Lambda^*)(\Lambda^* + \Lambda)^* \quad \text{and} \quad (\Lambda + a\Lambda)^*(\Lambda^* + \Lambda)^*$$

only the second defines an infinite language.

If the regular expression does not contain a *, then the language is necessarily finite. This is because the other rules of building regular expressions (any letter, sum, and product) cannot produce an infinite set from finite ones. Therefore, as we could prove recursively, the result must be finite.

If we want to decide this question for an FA, we could first convert it to a regular expression. On the other hand, there are ways to determine whether an FA accepts an infinite language without having to perform the conversion.

THEOREM 19

Let F be an FA with N states. Then:

1. If F accepts an input string w such that

$$N \leq \text{length}(w) < 2N$$

then F accepts an infinite language.

2. If F accepts infinitely many words, then F accepts some word w such that

$$N \leq \text{length}(w) < 2N$$

PROOF

1. The first version of the pumping lemma assumed the language was infinite, but for the second version this was not required, because a word is long enough to be pumped if it has more letters than the FA has states. If there is some word w with N or more letters, then by the second version of the pumping lemma, we can break it into three parts:

$$w = xyz$$

The infinitely many different words $xy^n z$ for $n = 1, 2, 3, \ldots$ are all accepted by F.

2. Now we are supposing that F does accept infinitely many words. Then it must accept a word so large that its path must contain a circuit, maybe several circuits. Each circuit can contain at most N states because F has only N states in total. Let us change the path of this long word by keeping the first circuit we come to and bypassing all the others. To bypass a circuit means to come up to it, go no more than part way around it, and leave at the first occurrence of the state from which the path previously exited.

   This one-circuit path corresponds to some word accepted by F. The word can have at most $2N$ letters, because at most N states are on the one circuit and at most N states are encountered off that circuit. If the length of this word is more than N, then we have found a word whose length is in the range that the theorem specifies. If, on the other hand, the length of this word is less than N, we can increase it by looping around the one circuit until the length is greater than N. The first time the length of the word (and path) becomes greater than N, it is still less than $2N$, because we have increased the word only by the length of the circuit, which is less than N. Eventually, we come to an accepted word with a length in the proper range. ∎

EXAMPLE

Consider this example:

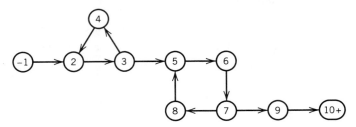

The first circuit is 2-3-4. It stays. The second circuit is 5-6-7-8. It is bypassed to become 5-6-7-9.

The path that used to be

$$1\text{-}2\text{-}3\text{-}4\text{-}2\text{-}3\text{-}5\text{-}6\text{-}7\text{-}8\text{-}5\text{-}6\text{-}7\text{-}8\text{-}5\text{-}6\text{-}7\text{-}9+$$

becomes

$$1\text{-}2\text{-}3\text{-}4\text{-}2\text{-}3\text{-}5\text{-}6\text{-}7\text{-}9+$$

This path contains 11 states. The total machine has N states where N is at least 10. If 11 is not in the range of N to $2N$ then continue to add three states by looping around 2-3-4 until the total path length is between N and $2N$. ■

This theorem provides us with an effective procedure for determining whether F accepts a finite language or an infinite language. We simply test the finitely many strings with lengths between N and $2N$ by running them on the machine and seeing whether any reach a final state. If none does, the language is finite. Otherwise, it is infinite.

THEOREM 20

There is an effective procedure to decide whether a given FA accepts a finite or an infinite language.

PROOF

If the machine has N states and the alphabet has m letters, then in total there are

$$m^N + m^{N+1} + m^{N+2} + \cdots + m^{2N-1}$$

different input strings in the range

$$N \le \text{length of string} < 2N$$

We can test them all by running them on the machine. If any are accepted, the language is infinite. If none are accepted, the language is finite. ■

It may often be more efficient to convert the FA to a regular expression, but so what?

In the case where the machine has three states and the alphabet has two letters, the number of strings we have to test is

$$2^3 + 2^4 + 2^5 = 8 + 16 + 32 = 56$$

which is not too bad. However, an FA with three states can be converted into a regular expression in very few steps.

⚜ PROBLEMS

For Problems 1 through 5, show by the method described in this chapter that the following pairs of FAs are equivalent:

1.

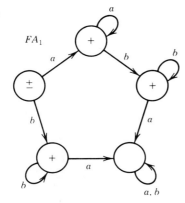

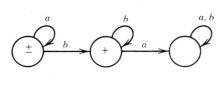

2.

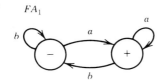

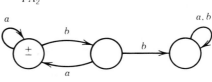

3.

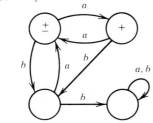

4.

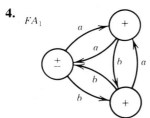

5. FA_1

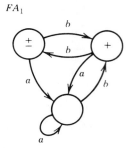

FA_2

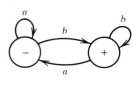

Why is this problem wrong? How can it be fixed?

6. Using the method of intersecting each machine with the complement of the other, show that

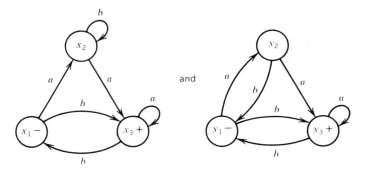

do not accept the same language.

7. Using the method of intersecting each machine with the complement of the other, show that

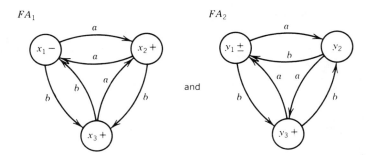

do not accept the same language.

8. List the 56 strings that will suffice to test whether a three-state FA over $\Sigma = \{a \quad b\}$ has a finite language.

By using blue paint, determine which of the following FAs accept any words:

9.

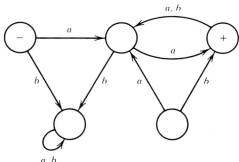

10.

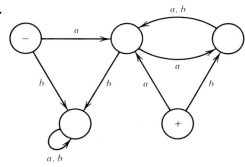

11.

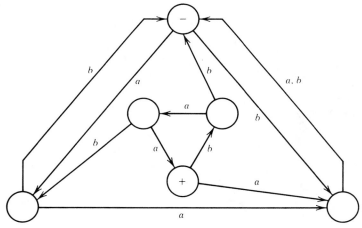

12.

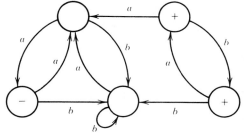

Which of the following FAs accepts a finite language and which an infinite one?

13.   (i)

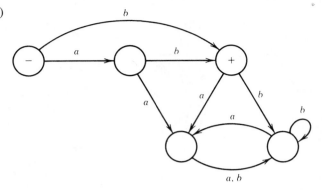

(ii)

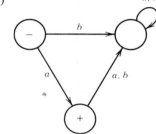

(iii)

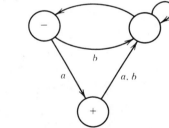

(iv)

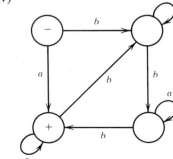

14. Without converting it into a regular expression or an FA, give an algorithm that decides whether a TG accepts any words.

15. Without converting it into a regular expression or an FA, give an algorithm that decides whether the language of an NFA is empty, finite, or infinite.

16. Do the same as Problem 15 for NFA-Λ's. Be careful. The machine

has an infinite language, whereas the machine

has a one-word language.

17. Consider the following simplified algorithm to decide whether an FA with exactly N states has an empty language:

   Step 1   Take the edges coming out of each final state and turn them into loops going back to the state they started from.

   Step 2   Relabel all edges with the letter x. (We now have an NFA.)

   Step 3   The original FA has a nonempty language if and only if this new NFA accepts the word x^N.

   Illustrate this algorithm and prove it always works.
   Is this an effective procedure?

18. By moving the start state, construct a decision procedure to determine whether a given FA accepts at least one word that starts with an a.

19. (i) Construct a decision procedure to determine whether a given FA accepts at least one word that contains the letter b.
   (ii) Construct a decision procedure to determine whether a given FA accepts some words of even length.

20. Given two regular expressions r_1 and r_2, construct a decision procedure to determine whether the language of r_1 is contained in the language of r_2.

PART II

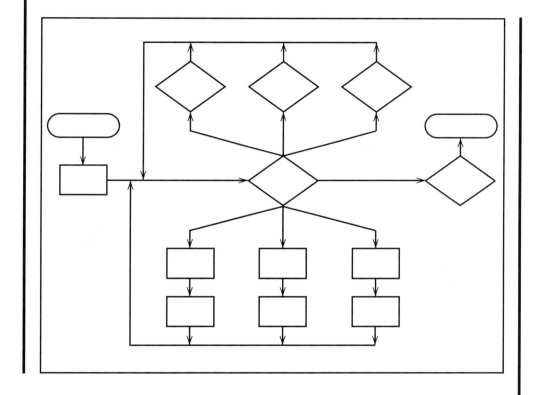

Pushdown
Automata
Theory

CHAPTER 12

Context-Free
Grammars

⚜ SYNTAX AS A METHOD FOR DEFINING LANGUAGES

Because of the nature of early computer input devices, such as keypunches, paper tape, magnetic tape, and typewriters, it was necessary to develop a way of writing complicated algebraic expressions in one line of standard typewriter symbols. Some few new symbols could be invented if necessary, but the whole expression had to be encoded in a way that did not require a multilevel display or depend on the perception of spatial arrangement. Formulas had to be converted into linear strings of characters.

Several of the adjustments that had to be made were already in use in the scientific literature for various other reasons. For example, the use of the slash as a divide sign was already accepted by the mathematical public. Most publishers had special symbols for the popular fractions such as $\frac{1}{2}$ and $\frac{1}{4}$, but eight-elevenths was customarily written as 8/11.

Still, before the days of the computer no one would ever have dreamed of writing a complicated compound fraction such as

$$\frac{\frac{1}{2} + 9}{4 + \frac{8}{21} + \frac{5}{3 + \frac{1}{2}}}$$

in the parentheses-laden one-line notation

$$((1/2) + 9)/(4 + (8/21) + (5/(3 + (1/2))))$$

The most important reason for not using the one-line version unless necessary is that in the two-dimensional version we can easily see that the number we are looking at is a little more than 9 divided by a little more than 5, so it obviously has a value between 1 and 2. Looking at the parentheses notation, we see that it is not even obvious which of the slash marks separates the numerator from the denominator of the major division.

How can a computer scan over this one-line string of typewriter characters and figure out what is going on? That is, how can a computer convert this string into its personal language of LOAD this, STORE that, and so on?

The conversion from a "high-level" language into a machine-executable language is done by a program called the **compiler.** This is a superprogram. Its input data are other programs. It processes them and prints out an equivalent program written in machine or assembler language. To do this, it must figure out in what order to perform the complicated set of arithmetic operations that it finds written out in the one-line formula. It must do this in a mechanical, algorithmic way. It cannot just look at the expression and understand it. Rules must be given by which this string can be processed—rules, perhaps, like those the machines of Part I could follow.

Along with evaluating those input strings that do have a meaning, we want our machine to be able to reject strings of symbols that make no sense as arithmetic expressions, such as "((9) + ". This input string should not take us to a final state in the machine. However, we cannot know that this is a bad input string until we have reached the last letter. If the + were changed to a), the formula would be valid. An FA that translated expressions into instructions simultaneously as it scanned left to right like a Mealy machine would already be turning out code before it realized that the whole expression is nonsense.

Before we try to build a compiling machine, let us return to the discussion of what is and what is not a valid arithmetic expression as defined in Chapter 3 by recursive definition (p. 25).

Rule 1   Any number is in the set *AE.*

Rule 2   If *x* and *y* are in *AE,* then so are

$$(x) \qquad -(x) \qquad (x + y) \qquad (x - y) \qquad (x * y) \qquad (x/y) \qquad (x ** y)$$

This time we have included parentheses around every component factor. This avoids the ambiguity of expressions like 3 + 4 * 5 and 8/4/2 by making them illegal. We shall present a more forgiving definition of this language later.

First, we must design a machine that can figure out how a given input string was built up from these basic rules. Then we should be able to translate this sequence of rules into an assembler language program, because all these rules are pure assembler language instructions (with the exception of exponentiation, which presents a totally different problem, but because this is not a course in compiler design, we ignore this embarrassing fact).

For example, if we present the input string

$$((3 + 4) * (6 + 7))$$

and the machine discovers that the way this can be produced from the rules is by the sequence

> 3 is in *AE*
> 4 is in *AE*
> (3 + 4) is in *AE*
> 6 is in *AE*
> 7 is in *AE*
> (6 + 7) is in *AE*
> ((3 + 4) * (6 + 7)) is in *AE*

we can therefore algorithmically convert this into

> LOAD 3 in register 1
> LOAD 4 in register 2
> ADD the contents of register 2 into register 1
> LOAD 6 in register 3
> LOAD 7 in register 4
> ADD the contents of register 3 into register 4
> MULTIPLY register 1 by register 4

or some such sequence of instructions depending on the architecture of the particular machine (not all computers have so many arithmetic registers or allow multiplication.

The hard part of the problem is to figure out by mechanical means how the input string can be produced from the rules. The second part—given the sequence of rules that create the expression, to convert it into a computer program to evaluate the expression—is easy.

The designers of the first high-level languages realized that the problem of interpreting algebra is analogous to the problem humans face hundreds of times every day when they decipher the grammatical structure of sentences that they hear or read in English. Here, we have again the ever-present parallelism: Recognizing the structure of a computer language instruction is analogous to recognizing the structure of a sentence in a human language.

Elementary school used to be called grammar school because one of the most important subjects taught was English grammar. A grammar is the set of rules by which the valid sentences in a language are constructed. The rules by which sentences are made are an example of an organically evolved recursive definition. Our ability to understand what a sentence means is based on our ability to understand how it could be formed from the rules of grammar. Determining how a sentence can be formed from the rules of grammar is called *parsing the sentence.*

When we hear or read a sentence in our native language, we do not go through a conscious act of parsing. Exactly why this is the case is a question for other sciences. Perhaps it is because we learned to speak as infants by a trial-and-error method that was not as mathematical and rigorous as the way in which we learn foreign languages later in life. When we were born, we spoke no language in which the grammar of our native tongue could be described to us. However, when we learn a second language, the rules of grammar for that language can be explained to us in English. How we can possibly learn our first language is a problem discussed by linguists, psychologists, philosophers, and worried parents. Whether the way we teach computers to speak is the same as the way humans learn is an interesting question, but beyond our present mandate.

Even though human languages have rules of grammar that can be stated explicitly, it is still true that many invalid sentences, those that are not, strictly speaking, grammatical, can be understood. Perhaps this is because there are tacit alternative rules of grammar that, although not taught in school, nevertheless are rules people live by. But this will not concern us either. No computer yet can forgive the mess, "Let *x* equal two times the radius times that funny looking Greek letter with the squiggly top that sounds like a pastry, you know what I mean?" The rules of computer language grammar are prescriptive—no ungrammatical strings are accepted.

Because the English word "grammar" can mean the study of grammar as well as the set of rules themselves, we sometimes refer to the *set of rules* as forming a **generative grammar.** This emphasizes the point that from them and a dictionary (the alphabet) we can generate all the sentences (words) in the language.

Let us look at the rule in English grammar that allows us to form a sentence by juxtaposing a noun and a verb (assuming that the verb is in the correct person and number). We might produce

Birds sing.

However, using the same rule might also produce

Wednesday sings.   or   *Coal mines sing.*

If these are not meant to be poetical or metaphoric, they are just bad sentences. They violate a different kind of rule of grammar, one that takes into account the meaning of words as well as their person, number, gender, and case.

Rules that involve the meaning of words we call **semantics** and rules that do not involve the meaning of words we call **syntax.** In English, the meaning of words can be relevant, but in arithmetic the meaning of numbers is rarely cataclysmic. In the high-level computer languages, one number is as good as another. If

$$X = B + 9$$

is a valid formulation, then so are

$$X = B + 8 \qquad X = B + 473 \qquad X = B + 9999$$

So long as the constants do not become so large that they are out of range, we do not try to divide by 0, take the square root of a negative number, and we do not mix fixed-point numbers with floating-point numbers in bad ways, one number is as good as another. It could be argued that such rules as "thou shalt not divide by zero" as well as the other restrictions mentioned are actually semantic laws, but this is another interesting point that we shall not discuss. In general, the rules of computer language grammar are all syntactic and not semantic, which makes the task of interpretation much easier.

There is another way in which the parsing of arithmetic expressions is easier than the parsing of English sentences. To parse the English sentence, "Birds sing.", it is necessary to look up in the dictionary whether "birds" is a noun or a verb. To parse the arithmetic expression "$(3 + 5)*6$", it is not necessary to know any other characteristics of the numbers 3, 5, and 6. We shall see more differences between simple languages and hard languages as we progress.

Let us go back to the analogy between computer languages and English. Some of the rules of English grammar are these:

1. A _sentence_ can be a _subject_ followed by a _predicate_.
2. A _subject_ can be a _noun-phrase_.
3. A _noun-phrase_ can be an _adjective_ followed by a _noun-phrase_.
4. A _noun-phrase_ can be an _article_ followed by a _noun-phrase_.
5. A _noun-phrase_ can be a _noun_.
6. A _predicate_ can be a _verb_ followed by a _noun-phrase_.
7. A _noun_ can be

$$apple \qquad bear \qquad cat \qquad dog$$

8. A _verb_ can be

$$eats \qquad follows \qquad gets \qquad hugs$$

9. An _adjective_ can be

$$itchy \qquad jumpy$$

10. An _article_ can be

$$a \qquad an \qquad the$$

Let us, for the moment, restrict the possibility of forming sentences to the laws stated above. Within this small model of English, there are hundreds of sentences we can form—for example,

The itchy bear hugs the jumpy dog.

The method by which this sentence can be generated is outlined here:

sentence ⇒ _subject_ _predicate_	Rule 1
⇒ _noun-phrase_ _predicate_	Rule 2
⇒ _noun-phrase_ _verb_ _noun-phrase_	Rule 6

$\Rightarrow$ *article noun-phrase verb noun-phrase*   Rule 4

$\Rightarrow$ *article adjective noun-phrase verb noun-phrase*   Rule 3

$\Rightarrow$ *article adjective noun verb noun-phrase*   Rule 5

$\Rightarrow$ *article adjective noun verb article noun-phrase*   Rule 4

$\Rightarrow$ *article adjective noun verb article adjective noun-phrase* Rule 3

$\Rightarrow$ *article adjective noun verb article adjective noun*   Rule 5

$\Rightarrow$ *the adjective noun verb article adjective noun*   Rule 10

$\Rightarrow$ *the itchy noun verb article adjective noun*   Rule 9

$\Rightarrow$ *the itchy bear verb article adjective noun*   Rule 7

$\Rightarrow$ *the itchy bear hugs article adjective noun*   Rule 8

$\Rightarrow$ *the itchy bear hugs the adjective noun*   Rule 10

$\Rightarrow$ *the itchy bear hugs the jumpy noun*   Rule 9

$\Rightarrow$ *the itchy bear hugs the jumpy dog*   Rule 7

A law of grammar is in reality a suggestion for possible substitutions. The arrow ($\Rightarrow$) indicates that a substitution was made according to the preceding rules of grammar. What happened above is that we started out with the initial symbol *sentence*. We then applied the rules for producing sentences listed in the generative grammar. In most cases, we had some choice in selecting which rule we wanted to apply. There is a qualitative distinction between the word "*noun*" and the word "*bear*." To show this, we have underlined the words that stand for parts of speech and are not to be considered themselves as words for the finished sentences. Of course, in the complete set of rules for English the words "verb," "adjective," and so on, are all perfectly good words and would be included in our final set of rules as usable words. They are all nouns. But in this model the term *verb* is a transitory place holder. It means, "stick a verb here." It *must* eventually be replaced to form a finished sentence.

Once we have put in the word "bear," we are stuck with it. No rule of grammar says that a bear can be replaced by anything else. The words that cannot be replaced by anything are called **terminals.** Words that must be replaced by other things we call **nonterminals.** We will give a more general definition of this shortly. The job of sentence production is not complete until all the nonterminals have been replaced with terminals.

Midway through the production procedure, we developed the sentence into as many nonterminals as it was going to become.

article adjective noun verb article adjective noun

From this point on, the procedure was only one of selecting which terminals were to be inserted in place of the nonterminals. This middle stage in which all the terminals are identified by their nonterminal names is the "grammatical parse" of the sentence. We can tell what noun each adjective modifies because we know how it got into the sentence in the first place. We know which noun-phrase produced it. "Itchy" modifies "bear" because they were both introduced by application of Rule 3.

We have allowed a noun-phrase to be an adjective followed by a noun-phrase. This could lead to

noun-phrase $\Rightarrow$ *adjective noun-phrase*
$\Rightarrow$ *adjective adjective noun-phrase*
$\Rightarrow$ *adjective adjective adjective noun-phrase*
$\Rightarrow$ *adjective adjective adjective noun*
$\Rightarrow$ *itchy adjective adjective noun*
$\Rightarrow$ *itchy itchy adjective noun*

$$\Rightarrow \textit{itchy itchy itchy } \underline{\textit{noun}}$$
$$\Rightarrow \textit{itchy itchy itchy bear}$$

If we so desired, we could produce 50 itchy's. Using the Kleene closure operator, we could write something like

$$\underline{\textit{noun-phrase}} \Rightarrow \underline{\textit{adjective}}^* \underline{\textit{noun}}$$

But now, we are getting ahead of ourselves.

The rules we have given for this simplified version of English allow for many dumb sentences, such as

Itchy the apple eats a jumpy jumpy jumpy bear.

Because we are not considering the limitations of semantics, diction, or good sense, we must consider this string of terminals as a legitimate sentence. This is what we mean by the phrase "formal language," which we used in Part I. It is a funny phrase because it sounds as if we mean the stuffy language used in aristocratic or diplomatic circles. In our case, it means only that any string of symbols satisfying the rules of grammar (syntax alone) is as good as any other. The word "formal" here means "strictly formed by the rules," not "highly proper." The Queen of England is unlikely to have made the remark above about itchy the apple.

We can follow the same model for defining arithmetic expressions. We can write the whole system of rules of formation as the list of possible substitutions shown below:

$$\underline{\text{Start}} \to (\underline{\text{AE}})$$
$$\underline{\text{AE}} \to (\underline{\text{AE}} + \underline{\text{AE}})$$
$$\underline{\text{AE}} \to (\underline{\text{AE}} - \underline{\text{AE}})$$
$$\underline{\text{AE}} \to (\underline{\text{AE}} * \underline{\text{AE}})$$
$$\underline{\text{AE}} \to \underline{\text{AE}} / \underline{\text{AE}})$$
$$\underline{\text{AE}} \to (\underline{\text{AE}} ** \underline{\text{AE}})$$
$$\underline{\text{AE}} \to (\underline{\text{AE}})$$
$$\underline{\text{AE}} \to -(\underline{\text{AE}})$$
$$\underline{\text{AE}} \to \underline{\text{ANY-NUMBER}}$$

Here, we have used the word "$\underline{\text{Start}}$" to begin the process, as we used the symbol "$\underline{\text{sentence}}$" in the sample of English. Aside from $\underline{\text{Start}}$, the only other nonterminal is $\underline{\text{AE}}$. The terminals are the phrase "$\underline{\text{ANY-NUMBER}}$" and the symbols

$$+ \quad - \quad * \quad / \quad ** \quad (\quad)$$

Either we could be satisfied that we know what is meant by the words "any number," or else we could define this phrase by a set of rules, thus converting it from a terminal into a nonterminal.

Rule 1 $\underline{\text{ANY-NUMBER}} \to \underline{\text{FIRST-DIGIT}}$
Rule 2 $\underline{\text{FIRST-DIGIT}} \to \underline{\text{FIRST-DIGIT}} \ \underline{\text{OTHER-DIGIT}}$
Rule 3 $\underline{\text{FIRST-DIGIT}} \to 1 \quad 2 \quad 3 \quad 4 \quad 5 \quad 6 \quad 7 \quad 8 \quad 9$
Rule 4 $\underline{\text{OTHER-DIGIT}} \to 0 \quad 1 \quad 2 \quad 3 \quad 4 \quad 5 \quad 6 \quad 7 \quad 8 \quad 9$

Rules 3 and 4 offer choices of terminals. We put spaces between them to indicate "choose one," but we soon shall introduce another disjunctive symbol.

We can produce the number 1066 as follows:

$\underline{\text{ANY-NUMBER}} \Rightarrow \underline{\text{FIRST-DIGIT}}$		Rule 1
$\Rightarrow \underline{\text{FIRST-DIGIT}} \ \underline{\text{OTHER-DIGIT}}$		Rule 2

⇒ <u>FIRST-DIGIT OTHER-DIGIT OTHER-DIGIT</u>	Rule 2
⇒ <u>FIRST-DIGIT OTHER-DIGIT OTHER-DIGIT OTHER-DIGIT</u>	Rule 2
⇒ 1066	Rule 3 and 4

Here, we have made all our substitutions of terminals for nonterminals in one fell swoop, but without any possible confusion. One thing we should note about the definition of <u>AE</u> is that some of the grammatical rules involve both terminals and nonterminals together. In English, the rules were either of the form

$$\text{One Nonterminal} \rightarrow \text{string of Nonterminals}$$

or

$$\text{One Nonterminal} \rightarrow \text{choice of terminals}$$

In our present study, we shall see that the form of the rules in the grammar has great significance.

The sequence of applications of the rules that produces the finished string of terminals from the starting symbol is called a **derivation** or a **generation** of the word. The grammatical rules are often referred to as **productions.** They all indicate possible substitutions. The derivation may or may not be unique, which means that by applying productions to the start symbol in two different ways, we may still produce the same finished product.

We are now ready to define the general concept of which all these examples have been special cases. We call this new structure a context-free grammar, or CFG. The full meaning of the term "context-free" will be made clear later. The concept of CFGs was invented by the linguist Noam Chomsky in 1956. Chomsky gave several mathematical models for languages, and we shall see more of his work later.

⚜ SYMBOLISM FOR GENERATIVE GRAMMARS

DEFINITION

A **context-free grammar, CFG,** is a collection of three things:

1. An alphabet Σ of letters called terminals from which we are going to make strings that will be the words of a language.
2. A set of symbols called nonterminals, one of which is the symbol S, standing for "start here."
3. A finite set of productions of the form

$$\text{One Nonterminal} \rightarrow \text{finite string of terminals and/or Nonterminals}$$

where the strings of terminals and nonterminals can consist of only terminals or of only nonterminals, or of any mixture of terminals and nonterminals or even the empty string. We require that at least one production has the nonterminal S as its left side.   ∎

So as not to confuse terminals and nonterminals, we always insist that nonterminals be designated by capital letters, whereas terminals are usually designated by lowercase letters and special symbols. In our example for English, we underlined the nonterminals, but this treatment is more standard.

DEFINITION

The **language generated** by a CFG is the set of all strings of terminals that can be produced from the start symbol S using the productions as substitutions. A language generated by a CFG is called a **context-free language,** abbreviated **CFL.** ∎

There is no great uniformity of opinion among experts about the terminology to be used here. The language generated by a CFG is sometimes called the **language defined** by the CFG, the **language derived** from the CFG, or the **language produced** by the CFG. This is similar to the problem with regular expressions. We should say "the language defined by the regular expression," although the phrase "the language of the regular expression" has a clear meaning.

EXAMPLE

Let the only terminal be a and the productions be

$$\text{Prod 1} \quad S \rightarrow aS$$
$$\text{Prod 2} \quad S \rightarrow \Lambda$$

If we apply production 1 six times and then apply production 2, we generate the following:

$$S \Rightarrow aS$$
$$\Rightarrow aaS$$
$$\Rightarrow aaaS$$
$$\Rightarrow aaaaS$$
$$\Rightarrow aaaaaS$$
$$\Rightarrow aaaaaaS$$
$$\Rightarrow aaaaaa\Lambda$$
$$= aaaaaa$$

This is a derivation of a^6 in this CFG. The string a^n comes from n applications of production 1 followed by one application of production 2. If we apply production 2 without production 1, we find that the null string is itself in the language of this CFG. Because the only terminal is a, it is clear that no words outside of **a*** can possibly be generated. The language generated by this CFG is exactly **a***. ∎

In the examples above, we used two different arrow symbols. The symbol "$\rightarrow$" we employ exclusively in the statement of the productions. It means "can be replaced by," as in $S \rightarrow aS$. The other arrow symbol "$\Rightarrow$" we employ between the unfinished stages in the generation of our word. It means "can develop into," as in $aaS \Rightarrow aaaS$. These "unfinished stages" are strings of terminals and nonterminals that we shall call **working strings.**

Notice that in this last example we have both $S \rightarrow aS$ as a production in the abstract and $S \Rightarrow aS$ as the first step in a particular derivation.

EXAMPLE

Let the only terminal be a and the productions be

$$\text{Prod 1} \quad S \rightarrow SS$$
$$\text{Prod 2} \quad S \rightarrow a$$
$$\text{Prod 3} \quad S \rightarrow \Lambda$$

In this language, we can have the following derivation:

$$S \Rightarrow SS$$
$$\Rightarrow SSS$$
$$\Rightarrow SaS$$
$$\Rightarrow SaSS$$
$$\Rightarrow \Lambda aSS$$
$$\Rightarrow \Lambda aaS$$
$$\Rightarrow \Lambda aa\Lambda$$
$$= aa$$

The language generated by this set of productions is also just the language **a***, but in this case the string *aa* can be obtained in many (actually infinitely many) ways. In the first example, there was a unique way to produce every word in the language. This also illustrates that the same language can have more than one CFG generating it. Notice above that there are two ways to go from *SS* to *SSS*—either of the first two *S*'s can be doubled.   ■

In the previous example, the only terminal is *a* and the only nonterminal is *S*. What then is Λ? It is not a nonterminal, because there is no production of the form

$$\Lambda \rightarrow \text{something}$$

Yet, it is not a terminal, because it vanishes from the finished string $\Lambda aa\Lambda = aa$. As always, Λ is a very special symbol and has its own status. In the definition of a CFG, we said a nonterminal could be replaced by any string of terminals and/or nonterminals, even the empty string. To replace a nonterminal by Λ is to delete it without leaving any tangible remains. For the nonterminal *N*, the production

$$N \rightarrow \Lambda$$

means that whenever we want, *N* can simply be deleted from any place in a working string.

EXAMPLE

Let the terminals be *a* and *b*, the only nonterminal be *S*, and the productions be

$$\text{P\scriptsize ROD}\ 1 \quad S \rightarrow aS$$
$$\text{P\scriptsize ROD}\ 2 \quad S \rightarrow bS$$
$$\text{P\scriptsize ROD}\ 3 \quad S \rightarrow a$$
$$\text{P\scriptsize ROD}\ 4 \quad S \rightarrow b$$

We can produce the word *baab* as follows:

$$S \Rightarrow bS \quad \text{(by P\scriptsize ROD}\ 2)$$
$$\Rightarrow baS \quad \text{(by P\scriptsize ROD}\ 1)$$
$$\Rightarrow baaS \quad \text{(by P\scriptsize ROD}\ 1)$$
$$\Rightarrow baab \quad \text{(by P\scriptsize ROD}\ 4)$$

The language generated by this CFG is the set of all possible strings of the letters *a* and *b* except for the null string, which we cannot generate.

We can generate any word by the following algorithm:

At the beginning, the working string is the start symbol *S*. Select a word to be generated. Read the letters of the desired word from left to right one at a time. If an *a* is read that is not the last letter of the word, apply PROD 1 to the working string. If a *b* is read that is not the last letter of the word, apply PROD 2 to the working string. If the last letter is read and it is an *a*, apply PROD 3 to the working string. If the last letter is read and it is a *b*, apply PROD 4 to the working string.

At every stage in the derivation before the last, the working string has the form

$$(\text{string of terminals}) \; S$$

At every stage in the derivation, to apply a production means to replace the final nonterminal *S*. Productions 3 and 4 can be used only once and only one of them can be used. For example, to generate *babb*, we apply in order productions 2, 1, 2, 4, as below:

$$S \Rightarrow bS \Rightarrow baS \Rightarrow babS \Rightarrow babb \qquad \blacksquare$$

EXAMPLE

Let the terminals be *a* and *b*, the nonterminals be *S*, *X*, and *Y*, and the productions be

$$S \rightarrow X$$
$$S \rightarrow Y$$
$$X \rightarrow \Lambda$$
$$Y \rightarrow aY$$
$$Y \rightarrow bY$$
$$Y \rightarrow a$$
$$Y \rightarrow b$$

All the words in this language are either of type *X*, if the first production in their derivation is

$$S \rightarrow X$$

or of type *Y*, if the first production in their derivation is

$$S \rightarrow Y$$

The only possible continuation for words of type *X* is the production

$$X \rightarrow \Lambda$$

Therefore, Λ is the only word of type *X*.

The productions whose left side is *Y* form a collection identical to the productions in the previous example except that the start symbol *S* has been replaced by the symbol *Y*. We can carry on from *Y* the same way we carried on from *S* before. This does not change the language generated, which contains only strings of terminals. Therefore, the words of type *Y* are exactly the same as the words in the previous example. That means that any string of *a*'s and *b*'s except the null string can be produced from *Y* as these strings were produced before from *S*.

Putting together the type *X* and the type *Y* words, we see that the total language generated by this CFG is all strings of *a*'s and *b*'s, null or otherwise. The language generated is **(a + b)***. $\qquad \blacksquare$

EXAMPLE

Let the terminals be *a* and *b*, the only nonterminal be *S*, and the productions be

$$S \rightarrow aS$$
$$S \rightarrow bS$$
$$S \rightarrow a$$
$$S \rightarrow b$$
$$S \rightarrow \Lambda$$

The word *ab* can be generated by the derivation

$$S \Rightarrow aS$$
$$\Rightarrow abS$$
$$\Rightarrow ab\Lambda$$
$$= ab$$

or by the derivation

$$S \Rightarrow aS$$
$$\Rightarrow ab$$

The language of this CFG is also $(\mathbf{a} + \mathbf{b})^*$, but the sequence of productions that is used to generate a specific word is not unique.

If we deleted the third and fourth productions, the language generated would be the same. ∎

EXAMPLE

Let the terminals be *a* and *b*, the nonterminals be *S* and *X*, and the productions be

$$S \rightarrow XaaX$$
$$X \rightarrow aX$$
$$X \rightarrow bX$$
$$X \rightarrow \Lambda$$

We already know from the previous example that the last three productions will allow us to generate any word we want from the nonterminal *X*. If the nonterminal *X* appears in any working string, we can apply productions to turn it into any string we want. Therefore, the words generated from *S* have the form

anything aa anything

or

$(\mathbf{a} + \mathbf{b})^*\mathbf{aa}(\mathbf{a} + \mathbf{b})^*$

which is the language of all words with a double *a* in them somewhere.

For example, to generate *baabaab,* we can proceed as follows:

$$S \Rightarrow XaaX \Rightarrow bXaaX \Rightarrow baXaaX \Rightarrow baaXaaX \Rightarrow baabXaaX$$
$$\Rightarrow baab\Lambda aaX \Rightarrow baabaaX \Rightarrow baabaabX \Rightarrow baabaab\Lambda = baabaab$$

There are other sequences that also derive the word *baabaab*. ∎

EXAMPLE

Let the terminals be *a* and *b*, the nonterminals be *S*, *X*, and *Y*, and the productions be

$$S \rightarrow XY$$
$$X \rightarrow aX$$
$$X \rightarrow bX$$
$$X \rightarrow a$$
$$Y \rightarrow Ya$$
$$Y \rightarrow Yb$$
$$Y \rightarrow a$$

What can be derived from X? Let us look at the X productions alone:

$$X \rightarrow aX$$
$$X \rightarrow bX$$
$$X \rightarrow a$$

Beginning with the nonterminal X and starting a derivation using the first two productions, we always keep a nonterminal X on the right end. To get rid of the X for good, we must eventually replace it with an a by the third production. We can see that any string of terminals that comes from X must end in an a and any words ending in an a can be derived from X in a unique fashion. For example, to derive the word $babba$ from X, we must proceed as follows:

$$X \Rightarrow bX \Rightarrow baX \Rightarrow babX \Rightarrow babbX \Rightarrow babba$$

Similarly, the words that can be derived from Y are exactly those that begin with an a. To derive $abbab$, for example, we can proceed:

$$Y \Rightarrow Yb \Rightarrow Yab \Rightarrow Ybab \Rightarrow Ybbab \Rightarrow abbab$$

When an X-part is concatenated with a Y-part, a double a is formed.

We can conclude that starting from S, we can derive only words with a double a in them, and all these words can be derived.

For example, to derive $babaabb$, fix we know that the X-part must end at the first a of the double a and that the Y-part must begin with the second a of the double a:

$$S \Rightarrow XY \Rightarrow bXY \Rightarrow baXY \Rightarrow babXY \Rightarrow babaY$$
$$\Rightarrow babaYb \Rightarrow babaYbb \Rightarrow babaabb$$

Therefore, this grammar generates the same language as the last, although it has more nonterminals and more productions. ∎

EXAMPLE

Let the terminals be a and b and the three nonterminals be S, BALANCED, and UNBALANCED. We treat these nonterminals as if they were each a single symbol and nothing more confusing. Let the productions be

$$S \rightarrow SS$$
$$S \rightarrow \text{BALANCED } S$$
$$S \rightarrow S \text{ BALANCED}$$
$$S \rightarrow \Lambda$$
$$S \rightarrow \text{UNBALANCED } S \text{ UNBALANCED}$$
$$\text{BALANCED} \rightarrow aa$$
$$\text{BALANCED} \rightarrow bb$$
$$\text{UNBALANCED} \rightarrow ab$$
$$\text{UNBALANCED} \rightarrow ba$$

We shall show that the language generated from these productions is the set of all words with an even number of a's and an even number of b's. This is our old friend, the language EVEN-EVEN.

To prove this, we must show two things: that all the words in EVEN-EVEN can be generated from these productions and that every word generated from these productions is, in fact, in the language EVEN-EVEN.

First, we show that every word in EVEN-EVEN can be generated by these productions. From our earlier discussion of the language EVEN-EVEN, we know that every word in this language can be written as a collection of substrings of

type aa   or   type bb   or   type(ab + ba)(aa + bb)*(ab + ba)

All three types can be generated from the nonterminal S from the preceding productions. The various substrings can be put together by repeated application of the production

$$S \rightarrow SS$$

This production is very useful. If we apply it four times, we can turn one S into five S's. Each of these S's can be a syllable of any of the three types. For example, the EVEN-EVEN word *aababbab* can be produced as follows:

$$
\begin{aligned}
S &\Rightarrow \text{BALANCED } S \\
&\Rightarrow aaS \\
&\Rightarrow aa \text{ UNBALANCED } S \text{ UNBALANCED} \\
&\Rightarrow aa \text{ ba } S \text{ UNBALANCED} \\
&\Rightarrow aa \text{ ba } S \text{ ab} \\
&\Rightarrow aa \text{ ba BALANCED } S \text{ ab} \\
&\Rightarrow aa \text{ ba bb } S \text{ ab} \\
&\Rightarrow aa \text{ ba bb } \Lambda \text{ ab} \\
&= aababbab
\end{aligned}
$$

To see that all the words that are generated by these productions are in the language EVEN-EVEN, we need only to observe that the unbalanced pairs are only added into the working string by one production and then they enter two at a time.

Therefore, the language generated by this CFG is exactly EVEN-EVEN.   ∎

So far, we have demonstrated several regular languages that could also be defined by CFGs. If all the languages that CFGs could generate were regular, this topic would have been included in Part I; therefore, the alert reader will expect that CFGs can also generate at least some nonregular languages too. The following examples show that this is, in fact, the case.

EXAMPLE

Let us consider the CFG

$$
\begin{aligned}
S &\rightarrow aSb \\
S &\rightarrow \Lambda
\end{aligned}
$$

We shall now show that the language generated by these productions is the canonical nonregular language $\{a^n b^n\}$. There is apparently only one nonterminal S and two terminals a and b (heretofore we have announced the terminals and nonterminals before stating the production set, yet this is one of those fastidiousnesses one quickly outgrows). As long as we continue to apply the first production, the working string produced will always have one and only one nonterminal in it and that will be a central S. Whenever we choose to employ the second production, the S drops out and what is left is a string of terminals that must then be a word generated by the grammar. The fact that the S always stays dead-center follows from the fact that production 1 always replaces the S with a string in which the S is again dead-center. So, if it used to be in the middle, it remains in the middle, and because it starts in the middle, it stays there, because the middle of the middle section is the middle of the string. On the right side of the S, we have nothing but a's, and on the left side of the S, we have nothing but b's. Therefore, after six applications of the first production, we must have the working string a^6Sb^6. If we apply the second production now, the word a^6b^6 would be produced.

$$S \Rightarrow aSb \Rightarrow aaSbb$$
$$\Rightarrow aaaSbbb \Rightarrow aaaaSbbbb$$
$$\Rightarrow aaaaaSbbbbb \Rightarrow aaaaaaSbbbbbb$$
$$\Rightarrow aaaaaabbbbbb$$

Clearly, if we use production 1 m times followed by production 2, the resultant word would be a^mb^m, and (what always must be made separately clear) every word of the form a^mb^m can be produced this way. Because a sequence of production 1's followed by a single production 2 is the only word-producing option for this grammar, we can conclude that the language it generates is exactly $\{a^nb^n\}$. ■

EXAMPLE

If we vary the rules of production slightly, we may arrive at this CFG:

$$S \rightarrow aSa$$
$$S \rightarrow bSb$$
$$S \rightarrow \Lambda$$

There are a great many similarities between this grammar and the previous one. Repeated applications of the first two rules will produce working strings with exactly one nonterminal, that is, S. Furthermore, this S begins in the middle of the working string and both rules of production replace it with strings in which it remains in the middle, and the middle of the middle is the middle of the working string, so S is always the unique and central nonterminal in all working strings.

Let us now note that the right side of each production is a palindrome (it reads the same backward and forward even if it does contain both terminals and a nonterminal). Let us also note that if a palindrome is inserted into the dead-center of another palindrome, the resultant string will again be a palindrome. Once we finally employ production rule 3 and delete the S, the final word will again be a palindrome. Therefore, all the words produced by this grammar will be in the language PALINDROME. However, it is not true that all the words in the language PALINDROME can be generated by this grammar. We must observe that palindromes come in two flavors: those with a unique central letter and those with even length that have no central letter. The language generated by this grammar is that of all palindromes with even length and no center letter called EVENPALINDROME (cf. p. 204). To prove that any word in EVENPALINDROME can be produced from this grammar, all we need to do is to take any evenpalindrome and show that it itself gives us a complete set of directions of how it is to be produced. These are the directions: Scan the first half of the word left to right. When we encounter an a, it is the instruction to apply production 1; when we encounter a b, it is the instruction to apply production 2; when we have finished the first half of the word, apply production 3. For example, if we start with the even palindrome *abbaabba*, the first half is *abba* and the rules of production to be applied are, in sequence, productions 1, 2, 2, 1, 3, as below:

$$S \Rightarrow aSa$$
$$\Rightarrow abSba$$
$$\Rightarrow abbSbba$$
$$\Rightarrow abbaSabba$$
$$\Rightarrow abbaabba$$

∎

EXAMPLE

The difference between EVENPALINDROME and ODDPALINDROME (whose definition is obvious) is that when we are finally ready to get rid of the S in the EVENPALINDROME working string, we must replace it with a Λ. If we were forced to replace it with an a or b instead, we would create a central letter and the result would be a grammar for ODDPALINDROME as follows:

$$S \Rightarrow aSa$$
$$S \Rightarrow bSb$$
$$S \Rightarrow a$$
$$S \Rightarrow b$$

If we allow the option of turning the central S into either Λ or a letter, we would have a grammar for the entire language PALINDROME:

$$S \Rightarrow aSa$$
$$S \Rightarrow bSb$$
$$S \Rightarrow a$$
$$S \Rightarrow b$$
$$S \Rightarrow \Lambda$$

∎

The languages $\{a^n b^n\}$ and PALINDROME are amazingly similar in grammatical structure, while the first is nearly a regular expression and the other is far from it.

EXAMPLE

One language that we demonstrated was nonregular, which had an appearance similar to $\{a^n b^n\}$, was $\{a^n b a^n\}$. This language too can be generated by a CFG

$$S \Rightarrow aSa$$
$$S \Rightarrow b$$

but the cousin language $\{a^n b a^n b^{n+1}\}$ cannot be generated by any CFG for reasons that we shall discuss a bit later.

∎

Let us consider one more example of a nonregular language that can be generated by a CFG.

EXAMPLE

Let the terminals be a and b, the nonterminals be S, A, and B, and the productions be

$$S \rightarrow aB$$
$$S \rightarrow bA$$
$$A \rightarrow a$$
$$A \rightarrow aS$$
$$A \rightarrow bAA$$
$$B \rightarrow b$$
$$B \rightarrow bS$$
$$B \rightarrow aBB$$

The language that this CFG generates is the language EQUAL of all strings that have an equal number of a's and b's in them. This language begins

EQUAL = {ab   ba   aabb   abab   abba   baab   baba   bbaa   aaabbb . . .}

(Notice that previously we included Λ in this language, but for now it has been dropped.)

Before we begin to prove that this CFG does generate exactly the language EQUAL, we should explain the rationale behind this set of productions. The basic idea is that if a word in EQUAL starts with an a, the remainder of the word is a string with the property that it has, in total, exactly one more b than a's. If the remainder has seven a's, then it must have eight b's, because otherwise $a(remainder)$ will not be in EQUAL. For this purpose, we introduce the nonterminal symbol B and we intend to write rules that will allow us to generate from B all strings with the property that they have exactly one more b than a's. Analogously, if a word in EQUAL starts with a b, it must be of the form bA, where from A we can generate any string that has in total one more a than b's.

To begin to find a method of generating all the strings that should be derivable from A, we note that if the A-string begins with the letter a, then the rest will be a word in EQUAL that is either derivable from S or is Λ. Otherwise, despite the fact that it has one more a than b's, it might still stubbornly insist on starting with a b. In this case, however, what remains is a string with the property that it now has *two* more a's than b's. We could be tempted to introduce a new symbol, say, A_2, as the nonterminal that would stand for these strings, but that would lead us down a path requiring more and more (eventually infinitely many) nonterminals. Instead, we make the useful observation that any string that contains two more a's than b's can be factored into the product of two type-A strings, each with exactly one more a than b's. To prove this, we scan the 2-a-heavy string from left to right until we find a factor that is of type A. We must eventually have the number of a's surpass the number of b's because otherwise it could not be 2-a-heavy. All the first instant the number of a's passes the number of b's in the scan (necessarily by exactly one extra), we have found an A-factor. Now what is left of the string is again a string that is only 1-a-heavy and is, therefore, itself a factor of type A. This is the reasoning behind the production $A \rightarrow bAA$.

The three productions for B are just symmetric to the A productions.

Now there is a little bit of a problem here because to produce EQUAL, we defined S to be bA, assuming that A does generate the 1-a-heavy strings, and later we defined A to be aS, assuming that S does generate only words in EQUAL. Is this reasoning not circular and therefore unsound? The answer is that once we know that S, A, and B do their intended jobs on short strings, we will be certain that they will continue to do their job on longer and longer strings. Let us discuss this in detail.

From the rules of production we can derive a from A and b from B and therefore both ab and ba come from S. Now using these building blocks, we can generate from $A \rightarrow aS$ both aab and aba, and from $A \rightarrow bAA$ we get baa. Therefore, all three-letter strings with two a's and one b can be derived from A. Similarly, all three-letter strings with two b's and one a can be derived from B.

Now we consider the four-letter strings. A and B generate only odd-length strings so all the relevant four-letter strings are the words in EQUAL. Once we know that all three-letter 1-a-heavy strings can be derived from A, we can safely conclude that all EQUAL words of four letters starting with a b can be derived from $S \rightarrow bA$. Similarly, once we know that all three-letter strings derivable from B are the 1-b-heavy strings, we conclude that $S \rightarrow aB$ gives all the four-letter words in EQUAL starting with an a and only those. So once we know that A and B are correct for three-letter words, we know that S is correct for four-letter words.

Now we bounce back to six-letter words. Starting with the knowledge that S produces all the two- and four-letter words in EQUAL, and that A and B generate all 1-a-heavy and 1-b-heavy words of length one and three, we have no trouble concluding that the correct and only the correct six-letter words are derived from A and B by the production rules. We could conclude that S generates all the six-letter words in EQUAL and only those, and so on.

The reasoning behind the productions is not circular but inductive. The S's in $S \rightarrow bA$ and $A \rightarrow aS$ are not the same S because the second one is two letters shorter. We could also see a parallel between this reasoning and recursive definitions: "If x has the property, then so does xx, and so on."

Therefore, all the words derivable from S are the words in EQUAL and all the words in EQUAL are generated by S. ∎

It is common for the same nonterminal to be the left side of more than one production. We now introduce the symbol " | ", a vertical line, to mean disjunction (or). Using it, we can combine all the productions that have the same left side. For example,

$$S \rightarrow aS$$
$$S \rightarrow \Lambda$$

can be written simply as

$$S \rightarrow aS \mid \Lambda$$

The CFG

$$S \rightarrow X$$
$$S \rightarrow Y$$
$$X \rightarrow \Lambda$$
$$Y \rightarrow aY$$
$$Y \rightarrow bY$$
$$Y \rightarrow a$$
$$Y \rightarrow b$$

can be written more compactly as

$$S \rightarrow X \mid Y$$
$$X \rightarrow \Lambda$$
$$Y \rightarrow aY \mid bY \mid a \mid b$$

The notation we are using for CFGs is practically universal with the following minor changes:

Some authors use the symbol

$$:: = \qquad \text{instead of} \qquad \rightarrow$$

Some authors call nonterminals **variables.**

Some authors use an epsilon, ϵ, or lambda, λ, instead of Λ to denote the null string.

Some authors indicate nonterminals by writing them in angle brackets:

$$\langle S \rangle \rightarrow \langle X \rangle \mid \langle Y \rangle$$
$$\langle X \rangle \rightarrow \Lambda$$
$$\langle Y \rangle \rightarrow a\langle Y \rangle \mid b\langle Y \rangle \mid a \mid b$$

We shall be careful to use capital letters for nonterminals and lowercase letters for terminals. Even if we did not do this, it would not be hard to determine when a symbol is a terminal. All symbols that do not appear as the left parts of productions are terminals with the exception of Λ.

Aside from these minor variations, we call this format—arrows, vertical bars, terminals, and nonterminals—for presenting a CFG the **BNF**, which stands for **Backus normal form** or **Backus–Naur form.** It was invented by John W. Backus for describing the high-level language ALGOL. Peter Naur was the editor of the report in which it appeared, and that is why BNF has two possible meanings.

A FORTRAN identifier (variable or storage location name) can, by definition, be up to six alphanumeric characters long but must start with a letter. We can generate the language of all FORTRAN identifiers by a CFG:

$$\underline{\text{IDENTIFIER}} \rightarrow \underline{\text{LETTER}} \; XXXXX$$
$$X \rightarrow \underline{\text{LETTER}} \mid \underline{\text{DIGIT}} \mid \Lambda$$
$$\underline{\text{LETTER}} \rightarrow A \mid B \mid C \mid \; . \; . \; . \; \mid Z$$
$$\underline{\text{DIGIT}} \rightarrow 0 \mid 1 \mid 2 \mid \; . \; . \; . \; \mid 9$$

Not just the language of identifiers but the language of all proper FORTRAN instructions can be defined by a CFG. This is also true of all the statements in the languages C, PASCAL, BASIC, PL/I, and so on. This is not an accident. As we shall see later, if we are given a word generated by a specified CFG, we can determine how the word was produced. This, in turn, enables us to understand the intended instruction of the word just as identifying the parts of speech helps us to understand the structure of an English sentence. A computer must determine the grammatical structure of a computer language statement before it can execute the instruction. Let us revisit our early school days.

⚜ TREES

In English grammar courses, we were taught how to diagram a sentence. This meant that we were to draw a **parse tree,** which is a picture with the base line divided into subject and predicate. All words or phrases modifying these were drawn as appendages on connecting lines. For example,

The quick brown fox jumps over the lazy dog.

becomes

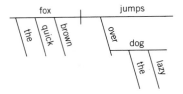

If the fox is dappled gray, then the parse tree would be

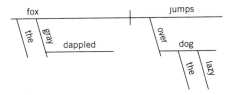

because dappled modifies gray and therefore is drawn as a branch off the gray line.

The sentence "I shot the man with the gun." can be diagrammed in two ways:

or

In the first diagram, "with the gun" explains *how* I shot. In the second diagram, "with the gun" explains *whom* I shot.

These diagrams turn a string of ambiguous symbols into an interpretable idea by identifying who does what to whom.

A famous case of ambiguity is the sentence "Time flies like an arrow." We humans have no difficulty identifying this as a poetic lament, technically a simile, meaning "Time passes all too quickly, just as a speeding arrow darts inexorably across the endless skies"—or some such euphuism.

This is diagrammed by the following parse tree:

Notice how the picture grows like a tree when "an" branches from "arrow." A graph theory tree, unlike an arboreal tree, can grow sideways or upside down.

A nonnative speaker of English with no poetry in her soul (a computer, e.g.) who has just yesterday read the sentence "Horse flies like a banana" might think the sentence should be diagrammed as

where she thinks "time flies" may have even shorter lives than drosophilae.

Looking in our dictionary, we see that "time" is also a verb, and if so in this case, the sentence could be in the imperative mood with the understood subject "you," in the same way that "you" is the understood subject of the sentence "Close the door." A race track tout may ask a jockey to do a favor and "Time horses like a trainer" for him. The computer might think this sentence should be diagrammed as

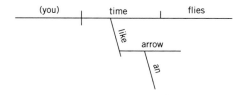

Someone is being asked to take a stopwatch and "time" some racing "flies" just as "an arrow" might do the same job, although one is unlikely to meet a straight arrow at the race track.

The idea of diagramming a sentence to show how it should be parsed carries over to CFGs. We start with the symbol S. Every time we use a production to replace a nonterminal by a string, we draw downward lines from the nonterminal to each character in the string.

Let us illustrate this on the CFG

$$S \rightarrow AA$$
$$A \rightarrow AAA \,|\, bA \,|\, Ab \,|\, a$$

We begin with S and apply the production $S \rightarrow AA$:

To the left-hand A, let us apply the production $A \rightarrow bA$. To the right-hand A, let us apply $A \rightarrow AAA$:

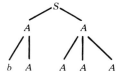

The b that we have on the bottom line is a terminal, so it does not descend further. In the terminology of trees, it is called a **terminal node.** Let the four A's, left to right, undergo the productions $A \rightarrow bA$, $A \rightarrow a$, $A \rightarrow a$, $A \rightarrow Ab$, respectively. We now have

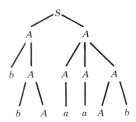

Let us finish off the generation of a word with the productions $A \rightarrow a$ and $A \rightarrow a$:

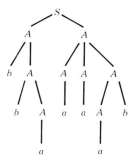

Reading from left to right, we see that the word we have produced is *bbaaaab*.

As was the case with diagramming a sentence, we understand more about the finished word if we see the whole tree. The third and fourth letters are both *a*'s, but they are produced by completely different branches of the tree.

These tree diagrams are called **syntax trees, parse trees, generation trees, production trees,** or **derivation trees.** The variety of terminology comes from the multiplicity of applications to linguistics, compiler design, and mathematical logic.

The only rule for formation of such a tree is that every nonterminal sprouts branches leading to every character in the right side of the production that replaces it. If the nonterminal *N* can be replaced by the string *abcde*,

$$N \rightarrow abcde$$

then in the tree we draw

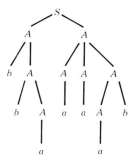

There is no need to put arrow heads on the edges because the direction of production is always downward.

EXAMPLE

One CFG for a subsystem of propositional calculus is

$$S \rightarrow (S) \,|\, S \supset S \,|\, \sim S \,|\, p \,|\, q$$

The only nonterminal is *S*. The terminals are $p \; q \sim \; \supset \; (\;)$, where "$\supset$" is today's symbol for implication.

In this grammar, consider the diagram

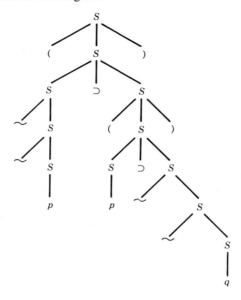

This is a derivation tree for the 13-letter word:

$$(\sim\sim p \supset (p \supset \sim\sim q))$$ ∎

We often say that to know the derivation tree for a given word in a given grammar is to understand the "meaning" of that word.

The concept of "meaning" is one that we shall not deal with in this book. We never presumed that the languages generated by our CFGs have any significance beyond being formal strings of symbols. However, in some languages the grammatical derivation of a string of symbols is important to us for reasons of computation. We shall soon see that knowing the tree helps us determine how to evaluate and compute.

⚜ ŁUKASIEWICZ NOTATION

Let us concentrate for a moment on an example of a CFG for a simplified version of arithmetic expressions:

$$S \rightarrow S + S \mid S * S \mid \underline{number}$$

Let us presume that we know precisely what is meant by "<u>number</u>."

We are all familiar with the ambiguity inherent in the expression

$$3 + 4 * 5$$

Does it mean $(3 + 4) * 5$, which is 35, or does it mean $3 + (4 * 5)$, which is 23?

In the language defined by this particular CFG, we do not have the option of putting in parentheses for clarification. Parentheses are not generated by any of the productions and are therefore not letters in the derived language. There is no question that $3 + 4 * 5$ is a word in the language of this CFG. The only question is what does this word intend in terms of calculation?

It is true that if we insisted on parentheses by using the grammar

$$S \rightarrow (S + S) \,|\, (S * S) \,|\, \underline{number}$$

we could not produce the string $3 + 4 * 5$ at all. We could only produce

$$S \Rightarrow (S + S) \Rightarrow (S + (S * S)) \Rightarrow \ldots \Rightarrow (3 + (4 * 5))$$

or

$$S \Rightarrow (S * S) \Rightarrow ((S + S) * S) \Rightarrow \ldots \Rightarrow ((3 + 4) * 5)$$

neither of which is an ambiguous expression.

   In the practical world, we do not need to use all these cluttering parentheses because we have adopted the convention of "hierarchy of operators," which says that $*$ is to be executed before $+$. This, unfortunately, is not reflected in either grammar. Later, we present a grammar that generates unambiguous arithmetic expressions that will mean exactly what we want them to mean without the need for burdensome parentheses. For now, we can only distinguish between these two possible meanings for the expression $3 + 4 * 5$ by looking at the two possible derivation trees that might have produced it:

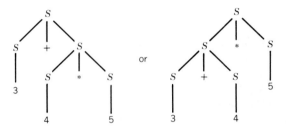

   We can evaluate an expression in parse-tree form from the tree picture itself by starting at the bottom and working our way up to the top, replacing each nonterminal as we come to it by the result of the calculation that it produces.

   This can be done as follows:

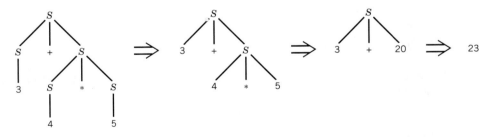

or

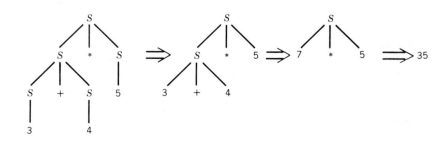

These examples show how the derivation tree can explain what the expression intends in much the same way that the parse trees in English grammar explain the intention of sentences.

In the special case of *this particular grammar* (not for CFGs in general), we can draw meaningful trees of terminals alone using the start symbol S only once. This will enable us to introduce a new notation for arithmetic expressions—one that has direct applications to computer science.

The method for drawing the new trees is based on the fact that $+$ and $*$ are binary operations that combine expressions already in the proper form. The expression $3 + (4 * 5)$ is a sum. A sum of what? A sum of a number and a product. What product? The product of two numbers. Similarly, $(3 + 4) * 5$ is a product of a sum and a number, where the sum is a sum of numbers. Notice the similarity to the original recursive definition of arithmetic expressions. These two situations are depicted in the following trees:

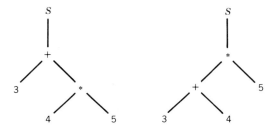

These are like derivation trees for the CFG

$$S \rightarrow S + S \mid S * S \mid \underline{\text{number}}$$

except that we have eliminated most of the S's. We have connected the branches directly to the operators instead.

The symbols $*$ and $+$ are no longer terminals, because they must be replaced by numbers. These are actually standard derivation trees taken from a new CFG in which S, $*$, and $+$ are nonterminals and $\underline{\text{number}}$ is the only terminal. The productions are

$S \rightarrow * \mid + \mid \underline{\text{number}}$
$+ \rightarrow + + \mid + * \mid + \underline{\text{number}} \mid * + \mid * * \mid * \underline{\text{number}} \mid \underline{\text{number}} + \mid \underline{\text{number}} * \mid \underline{\text{number}} \, \underline{\text{number}}$
$* \rightarrow + + \mid + * \mid + \underline{\text{number}} \mid * + \mid * * \mid * \underline{\text{number}} \mid \underline{\text{number}} + \mid \underline{\text{number}} * \mid \underline{\text{number}} \, \underline{\text{number}}$

As usual, $\underline{\text{number}}$ has been underlined because it is only one symbol in this case, our only terminal.

From these trees, we can construct a new notation for arithmetic expressions. To do this, we walk around the tree and write down the symbols, once each, as we encounter them. We begin our trip on the left side of the start symbol S heading south. As we walk around the tree, we always keep our left hand on the tree.

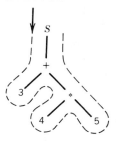

The first symbol we encounter on the first tree is $+$. This we write down as the first symbol of the expression in the new notation. Continuing to walk around the tree, keeping it on our left, we first meet 3, then $+$ again. We write down the 3, but this time we do not write down $+$ because we have already included it in the string we are producing. Walking some more, we meet $*$, which we write down. Then we meet 4, then $*$ again, then 5. So, we write down 4, then 5. There are no symbols we have not met, so our trip is done. The string we have produced is

$$+ 3 * 4\ 5$$

The second derivation tree when converted into the new notation becomes

$$* + 3\ 4\ 5$$

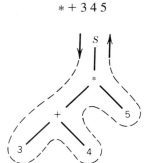

This tree-walking method produces a string of the symbols $+$, $*$, and <u>number</u>, which summarizes the picture of the tree and thus contains the information necessary to interpret the expression. This is information that is lacking in our usual representation of arithmetic expressions, unless parentheses are inserted. We shall show that these strings are unambiguous in that each determines a unique calculation without the need for establishing the hierarchical convention of times before plus. These representations are said to be in **operator prefix notation** because the operator is written in front of the operands it combines.

Since $S \rightarrow S + S$ has changed from

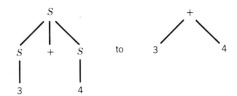

the left-hand tracing changes $3 + 4$ into $+\ 3\ 4$.

To evaluate a string of characters in this new notation, we proceed as follows. We read the string from left to right. When we find the first substring of the form

$$\text{operator-operand-operand}\quad \text{(call this o-o-o for short)}$$

we replace these three symbols with the one result of the indicated arithmetic calculation. We then rescan the string from the left. We continue this process until there is only one number left, which is the value of the entire original expression.

In the case of the expression $+\ 3\ *\ 4\ 5$, the first substring we encounter of the form operator-operand-operand is $*\ 4\ 5$, so we replace this with the result of the indicated multiplication, that is, the number 20. The string is now $+\ 3\ 20$. This itself is in the form o-o-o, and we evaluate it by performing the addition. When we replace this with the number 23, we see that the process of evaluation is complete.

In the case of the expression $* + 3\ 4\ 5$, the first o-o-o substring is $+ 3\ 4$. This we replace with the number 7. The string is then $* 7\ 5$, which itself is in the o-o-o form. When we replace this with 35, the evaluation process is complete.

Let us see how this process works on a harder example. Let us start with the arithmetic expression

$$((1 + 2) * (3 + 4) + 5) * 6$$

This is shown in normal notation, which is called **operator infix notation** because the operators are placed in between the operands. With infix notation, we often need to use parentheses to avoid ambiguity, as is the case with the expression above. To convert this to operator prefix notation, we begin by drawing its derivation tree:

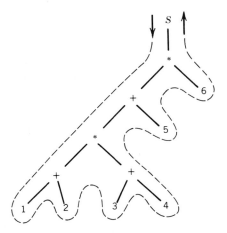

Reading around this tree gives the equivalent prefix notation expression

$$* + * + 1\ 2 + 3\ 4\ 5\ 6$$

Notice that the operands are in the same order in prefix notation as they were in infix notation; only the operators are scrambled and all parentheses are deleted.

To evaluate this string, we see that the first substring of the form operator-operand-operand is $+ 1\ 2$, which we replaced with the number 3. The evaluation continues as follows:

String	First o-o-o Substring
$* + * 3 + 3\ 4\ 5\ 6$	$+ 3\ 4$
$\Downarrow$	
$* + * 3\ 7\ 5\ 6$	$* 3\ 7$
$\Downarrow$	
$* + 21\ 5\ 6$	$+ 21\ 5$
$\Downarrow$	
$* 26\ 6$	$* 26\ 6$
$\Downarrow$	
156	

which is the correct value for the expression with which we started.

Because the derivation tree is unambiguous, the prefix notation is also unambiguous and does not rely on the tacit understanding of operator hierarchy or on the use of parentheses.

This clever parenthesis-free notational scheme was invented by the Polish logician Jan Łukasiewicz (1878–1956) and is often called Polish notation. There is a similar operator postfix notation, which is also called Polish notation, in which the operation symbols (+, *, . . .) come after the operands. This can be derived by tracing around the tree from the other side, keeping our right hand on the tree and then reversing the resultant string. Both these methods of notation are useful for computer science. Compilers often convert infix to prefix and then to assembler code. ∎

AMBIGUITY

EXAMPLE

Let us consider the language generated by the following CFG:

$$\text{PROD 1} \quad S \rightarrow AB$$
$$\text{PROD 2} \quad A \rightarrow a$$
$$\text{PROD 3} \quad B \rightarrow b$$

There are two different sequences of applications of the productions that generate the word *ab*. One is PROD 1, PROD 2, PROD 3. The other is PROD 1, PROD 3, PROD 2.

$$S \Rightarrow AB \Rightarrow aB \Rightarrow ab \qquad \text{or} \qquad S \Rightarrow AB \Rightarrow Ab \Rightarrow ab$$

However, when we draw the corresponding syntax trees, we see that the two derivations are essentially the same:

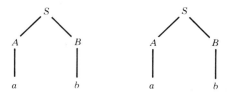

This example, then, presents no substantive difficulty because there is no ambiguity of interpretation. When all the possible derivation trees are the same for a given word, then the word is unambiguous. ∎

DEFINITION

A CFG is called **ambiguous** if for at least one word in the language that it generates there are two possible derivations of the word that correspond to different syntax trees. If a CFG is not ambiguous, it is called **unambiguous.** ∎

EXAMPLE

Let us reconsider the language PALINDROME, which we saw earlier can be generated by the CFG below:

$$S \rightarrow aSa \,|\, bSb \,|\, a \,|\, b \,|\, \Lambda$$

At every stage in the generation of a word by this grammar, the working string contains only the one nonterminal S smack dab in the middle. The word grows like a tree from the center out. For example,

$$\ldots baSab \Rightarrow babSbab \Rightarrow babbSbbab \Rightarrow babbaSabbab \ldots$$

When we finally replace S by a center letter (or Λ if the word has no center letter), we have completed the production of a palindrome. The word $aabaa$ has only one possible generation:

$$S \Rightarrow aSa$$
$$\Rightarrow aaSaa$$
$$\Rightarrow aabaa$$

If any other production were applied at any stage in the derivation, a different word would be produced. Every word in PALINDROME has a unique sequence of productions leading to it. As we read the first half left to right, an a means use $S \rightarrow aSa$, a b means use $S \rightarrow bSb$, and the middle letter determines the final production.

We see then that this CFG is unambiguous. ∎

EXAMPLE

The language of all nonnull strings of a's can be defined by a CFG as follows:

$$S \rightarrow aS \mid Sa \mid a$$

In this case, the word a^3 can be generated by four different trees:

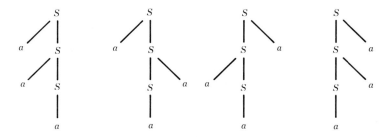

This CFG is therefore ambiguous.

However, the same language can also be defined by the CFG

$$S \rightarrow aS \mid a$$

for which the word a^3 has only one production:

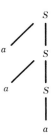

This CFG is not ambiguous. ∎

From this last example, we see that we must be careful to say that it is the CFG that is ambiguous, not that the language it generates is itself ambiguous.

THE TOTAL LANGUAGE TREE

So far in this chapter, we have seen that derivation trees carry with them an additional amount of information that helps resolve ambiguity in cases where interpretation is important. Trees can be useful in the study of formal grammars in other ways.

For example, it is possible to depict the generation of all the words in the language of a CFG simultaneously in one big (possibly infinite) tree.

DEFINITION

For a given CFG, we define a tree with the start symbol S as its root and whose nodes are working strings of terminals and nonterminals. The descendants of each node are all the possible results of applying every applicable production to the working string, one at a time. A string of all terminals is a terminal node in the tree.

The resultant tree is called the **total language tree** of the CFG. ∎

EXAMPLE

For the CFG

$$S \rightarrow aa \mid bX \mid aXX$$
$$X \rightarrow ab \mid b$$

the total language tree is

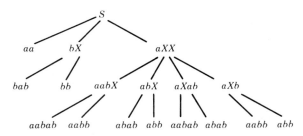

This total language has only seven different words. Four of its words (*abb*, *aabb*, *abab*, *aabab*) have two different possible derivations because they appear as terminal nodes in this total language tree in two different places. However, the words are not generated by two different derivation trees and the grammar is unambiguous. For example,

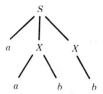

■

EXAMPLE

Consider the CFG

$$S \rightarrow aSb \,|\, bS \,|\, a$$

We have the terminal letters a and b and three possible choices of substitutions for S at any stage. The total tree of this language begins

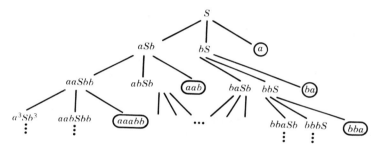

Here, we have circled the terminal nodes because they are the words in the language generated by this CFG. We say "begins" because since the language is infinite, the total language tree is too.

We have already generated all the words in this language with one, two, or three letters:

$$L = \{a \quad ba \quad aab \quad bba \ldots\}$$

These trees may get arbitrarily wide as well as infinitely long. ■

EXAMPLE

$$S \rightarrow SAS \,|\, b$$
$$A \rightarrow ba \,|\, b$$

Every string with some S's and some A's has many possible productions that apply to it, two for each S and two for each A:

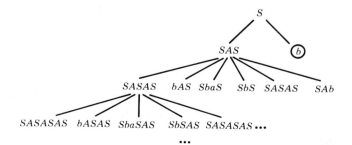

There are more words in this language, but we have not reached them yet. The word *bbb* will come up shortly. ∎

The essence of recursive definition comes into play in an obvious way when some nonterminal has a production with a right-side string containing its own name, as in this case:

$$X \rightarrow (\text{blah})X(\text{blah})$$

The total tree for such a language then must be infinite because it contains the branch

$$X \Rightarrow (\text{blah})X(\text{blah})$$
$$\Rightarrow (\text{blah})(\text{blah})X(\text{blah})(\text{blah})$$
$$\Rightarrow (\text{blah})^3X(\text{blah})^3$$
$$\cdots$$

This has a deep significance that will be important to us shortly.

Surprisingly, even when the whole language tree is infinite, the language may have only finitely many words.

EXAMPLE

Consider this CFG:

$$S \rightarrow X \mid b$$
$$X \rightarrow aX$$

The total language tree begins

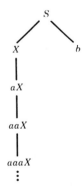

Clearly, the only word in this language is the single letter *b*. *X* is a bad mistake; it leads to no words, because once a working string has got *X*, it can never be cured of it. ∎

⚜ PROBLEMS

1. Consider the CFG

$$S \rightarrow aS \mid bb$$

Prove that this generates the language defined by the regular expression

a*bb

2. Consider the CFG

$$S \rightarrow XYX$$
$$X \rightarrow ax \,|\, bX \,|\, \Lambda$$
$$Y \rightarrow bbb$$

Prove that this generates the language of all strings with a triple b in them, which is the language defined by

$$(\mathbf{a} + \mathbf{b})^*\mathbf{bbb}(\mathbf{a} + \mathbf{b})^*$$

3. (i) Consider the CFG

$$S \rightarrow aX$$
$$X \rightarrow aX \,|\, bX \,|\, \Lambda$$

What is the language this CFG generates?

(ii) Consider the CFG

$$S \rightarrow XaXaX$$
$$X \rightarrow aX \,|\, bX \,|\, \Lambda$$

What is the language this CFG generates?

4. Consider the CFG

$$S \rightarrow SS \,|\, XaXaX \,|\, \Lambda$$
$$X \rightarrow bX \,|\, \Lambda$$

(i) Prove that X can generate any $\mathbf{b}^*$.
(ii) Prove that $XaXaX$ can generate any $\mathbf{b}^*\mathbf{ab}^*\mathbf{ab}^*$.
(iii) Prove that S can generate $(\mathbf{b}^*\mathbf{ab}^*\mathbf{ab}^*)^*$.
(iv) Prove that the language of this CFG is the set of all words in $(\mathbf{a} + \mathbf{b})^*$ with an even number of a's with the following exception: We consider the word Λ to have an even number of a's, as do all words with no a's, but of the words with no a's only Λ can be generated.
(v) Show how the difficulty in part (iv) can be alleviated by adding the production

$$S \rightarrow XS$$

5. Consider the CFG

$$S \rightarrow XbaaX \,|\, aX$$
$$X \rightarrow Xa \,|\, Xb \,|\, \Lambda$$

What is the language this generates? Find a word in this language that can be generated in two substantially different ways.

6. (i) Consider the CFG for "some English" given in this chapter. Show how these productions can generate the sentence

Itchy the bear hugs jumpy the dog.

(ii) Change the productions so that an article cannot come between an adjective and its noun.

(iii) Show how in the CFG for "some English" we can generate the sentence

The the the cat follows cat.

(iv) Change the productions again so that the same noun cannot have more than one article.

7. Find a CFG for each of the languages defined by the following regular expressions:

    (i) **ab***

    (ii) **a*b***

    (iii) **(baa + abb)***

8. Find CFGs for the following languages over the alphabet $\Sigma = \{a \quad b\}$:

    (i) All words in which the letter b is never tripled.

    (ii) All words that have exactly two or three b's.

    (iii) All words that do not have the substring ab.

    (iv) All words that do not have the substring baa.

    (v) All words that have different first and last letters:

$$\{ab \quad ba \quad aab \quad abb \quad baa \quad bba \ldots\}$$

9. Consider the CFG

$$S \rightarrow AA$$
$$A \rightarrow AAA$$
$$A \rightarrow bA \,|\, Ab \,|\, a$$

Prove that the language generated by these productions is the set of all words with an even number of a's, but not no a's. Contrast this grammar with the CFG in Problem 4.

10. Describe the language generated by the following CFG:

$$S \rightarrow SS$$
$$S \rightarrow XXX$$
$$X \rightarrow aX \,|\, Xa \,|\, b$$

11. Write a CFG to generate the language MOREA of all strings that have more a's than b's (not necessarily only one more, as with the nonterminal A for the language EQUAL, but any number more a's than b's).

$$\text{MOREA} = \{a \quad aa \quad aab \quad aba \quad baa \quad aaaa \quad aaab \ldots\}$$

12. Let L be any language. We have already defined the transpose of L to be the language of all the words in L spelled backward (see Chapter 6, Problem 17). Show that if L is a context-free language, then the transpose of L is context-free also.

13. In Chapter 10, Problem 4, we showed that the language

$$\text{TRAILING-COUNT} = \{sa^{\text{length}(s)} \quad \text{for all } s \text{ in } (\mathbf{a} + \mathbf{b})^*\}$$

is nonregular. Show however that it is context-free and generated by

$$S \rightarrow aSa \,|\, bSa \,|\, \Lambda$$

14. (i) In response to "Time flies like an arrow," the tout said, "My watch must be broken." How many possible interpretations of this reply are there?

    (ii) Chomsky found three different interpretations for "I had a book stolen." Explain them. Are their parsing trees different?

15. Below is a set of words and a set of CFGs. For each word, determine whether the word is in the language of *each* CFG and, if it is, draw a syntax tree to prove it.

    Words   **CFGs**

    (i) ab CFG 1. $S \rightarrow aSb \,|\, ab$

(ii) *aaaa*   CFG 2. $S \rightarrow aS \,|\, bS \,|\, a$
(iii) *aabb*
(iv) *abaa*   CFG 3. $S \rightarrow aS \,|\, aSb \,|\, X$
(v) *abba* $X \rightarrow aXa \,|\, a$
(vi) *baaa*
(vii) *abab*   CFG 4. $S \rightarrow aAS \,|\, a$
(viii) *bbaa* $A \rightarrow SbA \,|\, SS \,|\, ba$
(ix) *baab*
                     CFG 5. $S \rightarrow aB \,|\, bA$
                              $A \rightarrow a \,|\, aS \,|\, bAA$
                              $B \rightarrow b \,|\, bS \,|\, aBB$

16. Show that the following CFGs are ambiguous by finding a word with two distinct syntax trees:

(i) $S \rightarrow SaSaS \,|\, b$
(ii) $S \rightarrow aSb \,|\, Sb \,|\, Sa \,|\, a$
(iii) $S \rightarrow aaS \,|\, aaaS \,|\, a$
(iv) $S \rightarrow aS \,|\, aSb \,|\, X$
    $X \rightarrow Xa \,|\, a$
(v) $S \rightarrow AA$
    $A \rightarrow AAA \,|\, a \,|\, bA \,|\, Ab$

17. Show that the following CFGs that use Λ are ambiguous:

(i) $S \rightarrow XaX$
    $X \rightarrow aX \,|\, bX \,|\, \Lambda$
(ii) $S \rightarrow aSX \,|\, \Lambda$
    $X \rightarrow aX \,|\, a$
(iii) $S \rightarrow aS \,|\, bS \,|\, aaS \,|\, \Lambda$
(iv) Find unambiguous CFGs that generate these three languages.
(v) For each of these three languages, find an unambiguous grammar that generates exactly the same language except for the word Λ. Do this by not employing the symbol Λ in the CFGs at all.

18. Begin to draw the total language trees for the following CFGs until we can be sure we have found all the words in these languages with one, two, three, or four letters. Which of these CFGs are ambiguous?

(i) $S \rightarrow aS \,|\, bS \,|\, a$
(ii) $S \rightarrow aSaS \,|\, b$
(iii) $S \rightarrow aSa \,|\, bSb \,|\, a$
(iv) $S \rightarrow aSb \,|\, bX$
    $X \rightarrow bX \,|\, b$
(v) $S \rightarrow bA \,|\, aB$
    $A \rightarrow bAA \,|\, aS \,|\, a$
    $B \rightarrow aBB \,|\, bS \,|\, b$

19. Convert the following infix expressions into Polish notation:

(i) $1 * 2 * 3$
(ii) $1 * 2 + 3$
(iii) $1 * (2 + 3)$
(iv) $1 * (2 + 3) * 4$
(v) $((1 + 2) * 3) + 4$

(vi) $1 + (2 * (3 + 4))$
(vii) $1 + (2 * 3) + 4$

20. Invent a form of prefix notation for the system of propositional calculus used in this chapter that enables us to write all well-formed formulas without the need for parentheses (and without ambiguity).

CHAPTER 13

Grammatical Format

⚜ REGULAR GRAMMARS

Some of the examples of languages we have generated by CFGs have been regular languages; that is, they are definable by regular expressions. However, we have also seen some nonregular languages that can be generated by CFGs (PALINDROME and EQUAL).

What then is the relationship between regular languages and context-free grammars? Several possibilities come to mind:

1. All possible languages can be generated by CFGs.

2. All regular languages can be generated by CFGs, and so can some nonregular languages but not all possible languages.

3. Some regular languages can be generated by CFGs and some regular languages cannot be generated by CFGs. Some nonregular languages can be generated by CFGs and maybe some nonregular languages cannot.

Of these three possibilities, number 2 is correct. In this chapter, we shall indeed show that all regular languages can be generated by CFGs. We leave the construction of a language that cannot be generated by any CFG for Chapter 16.

Before we proceed to prove this, it will be useful for us to introduce the notion of a semiword.

DEFINITION

For a given CFG, a **semiword** is a string of terminals (maybe none) concatenated with exactly one nonterminal (on the right). In general, a semiword has the shape

$$(\text{terminal})(\text{terminal}) \ . \ . \ . \ (\text{terminal})(\text{Nonterminal}) \qquad ■$$

THEOREM 21

Given any FA, there is a CFG that generates exactly the language accepted by the FA. In other words, all regular languages are context-free languages.

PROOF

The proof will be by constructive algorithm. We shall show how to start with the FA and create one such CFG.

Step 1   The nonterminals in the CFG will be all the names of the states in the FA with the start state renamed S.

Step 2   For every edge

create the production

$$X \rightarrow aY \quad \text{or} \quad X \rightarrow aX$$

Do the same for b-edges.

Step 3   For every final state X, create the production

$$X \rightarrow \Lambda$$

Claim

This CFG generates exactly the language accepted by the original FA. To prove this claim, we must show that (i) every word accepted by the FA can be generated from the CFG and (ii) every word generated by the CFG is accepted by the FA.

Proof of (i)

Let w be some word, say, *abbaa*, accepted by the FA; then letter by letter, we can grow the path through the FA by a sequence of **semipaths**, the string read from the input so far followed by the name of the state to which the string takes us. The sequence of semipaths looks something like this:

	Semipaths
First start in S.	S
Then read an a and go to X.	aX
Then read a b and go to Y.	abY
. . .	. . .
Finally read an a and go to F.	$abbaaF$
F is a final state, so accept the word.	

This corresponds exactly to a derivation in the CFG of the word w through semiwords:

Production	Derivation
$S \rightarrow aX$	$S \Rightarrow aX$
$X \rightarrow bY$	$\Rightarrow abY$
. . .	. . .
	$\Rightarrow abbaaF$
$F \rightarrow \Lambda$	$\Rightarrow abbaa$

In summary, a word w accepted by the FA generates a sequence of step-by-step semi-paths, each one edge longer than the previous, that corresponds to a derivation of w through semiwords identical to the semipaths. Since the word w is accepted by the FA, its semipath ends in a final state. In the derivation, this is the same as replacing the last nonterminal of the last semiword with Λ and completing the generation of w.

EXAMPLE   (in the middle of the proof)

Consider the FA

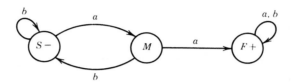

The CFG the algorithm tells us to create is

$$S \rightarrow aM$$
$$S \rightarrow bS$$
$$M \rightarrow aF$$
$$M \rightarrow bS$$
$$F \rightarrow aF$$
$$F \rightarrow bF$$
$$F \rightarrow \Lambda$$

The word *babbaaba* is accepted by this FA through this sequence of semipaths:

$$S$$
$$bS$$
$$baM$$
$$babS$$
$$babbS$$
$$babbaM$$
$$babbaaF$$
$$babbaabF$$
$$babbaabaF$$
$$babbaaba$$

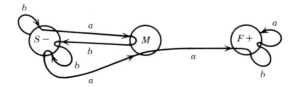

corresponding to the CFG derivation applying, in order, the productions $S \rightarrow bS$, $S \rightarrow aM$, $M \rightarrow bS$, $S \rightarrow bS$, $S \rightarrow aM$, $M \rightarrow aF$, $F \rightarrow bF$, $F \rightarrow aF$, $F \rightarrow \Lambda$.   ∎

Proof of (ii)

We now show that any word generated from the CFG created by the algorithm is accepted when run on the FA.

Because all the rules of production are of the form

$$\text{Nonterminal} \rightarrow \text{terminal Nonterminal}$$

there will always be one nonterminal in any working string in any derivation in this CFG, and that nonterminal will be on the extreme right end. Therefore, all derivations in this CFG are through working strings that are semiwords exclusively. Each derivation starts with an S and the sequence of semiwords corresponds to a growing sequence of semipaths through the FA. We can only end the generation of a word when we turn the final nonterminal into Λ, but this means that the state the semipath is in is a final state and the word generated is an input string accepted by the FA. ∎

EXAMPLE

The language of all words with an even number of a's (with at least some a's) can be accepted by this FA:

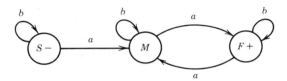

Calling the states S, M, and F as before, we have the following corresponding set of productions:

$$S \rightarrow bS \mid aM$$
$$M \rightarrow bM \mid aF$$
$$F \rightarrow bF \mid aM \mid \Lambda$$

We have already seen two CFGs for this language, but this CFG is substantially different. ∎

Theorem 21, on p. 259, was discovered (or perhaps invented) by Noam Chomsky and George A. Miller in 1958. They also proved the result below, which seems to be the flip side of the coin.

THEOREM 22

If all the productions in a given CFG fit one of the two forms:

$$\text{Nonterminal} \rightarrow \text{semiword}$$

or

$$\text{Nonterminal} \rightarrow \text{word}$$

(where the word may be Λ), then the language generated by this CFG is regular.

PROOF

We shall prove that the language generated by such a CFG is regular by showing that there is a TG that accepts the same language. We shall build this TG by constructive algorithm.

Let us consider a general CFG in this form:

$$N_1 \rightarrow w_1 N_2 \qquad N_7 \rightarrow w_{10}$$
$$N_1 \rightarrow w_2 N_3 \qquad N_{41} \rightarrow w_{23}$$
$$N_2 \rightarrow w_3 N_4 \qquad \cdots$$
$$\cdots$$

where the N's are the nonterminals, the w's are strings of terminals, and the parts $w_y N_z$ are the semiwords used in productions. One of these N's must be S. Let $N_1 = S$.

Draw a small circle for each N and one extra circle labeled $+$. The circle for S we label $-$.

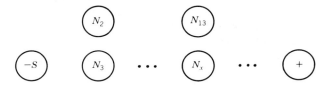

For every production rule of the form

$$N_x \rightarrow w_y N_z$$

draw a directed edge from state N_x to N_z and label it with the word w_y.

If $N_x = N_z$, the path is a loop. For every production rule of the form

$$N_p \rightarrow w_q$$

draw a directed edge from N_p to $+$ and label it with the word w_q, even if $w_q = \Lambda$.

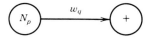

We have now constructed a transition graph. Any path in this TG from $-$ to $+$ corresponds to a word in the language of the TG (by concatenating labels) and simultaneously corresponds to a sequence of productions in the CFG generating the same word. Conversely, every production of a word in this CFG:

$$S \Rightarrow wN \Rightarrow wwN \Rightarrow wwwN \Rightarrow \cdots \Rightarrow wwwww$$

corresponds to a path in this TG from $-$ to $+$.

Therefore, the language of this TG is exactly the same as that of the CFG. Therefore, the language of the CFG is regular. ∎

We should note that the fact that the productions in some CFGs are all in the required format does not guarantee that the grammar generates any words. If the grammar is totally discombobulated, the TG that we form from it will be crazy too and may accept no words. However, if the grammar generates a language of some words, then the TG produced earlier for it will accept that same language.

DEFINITION

A CFG is called a **regular grammar** if each of its productions is of one of the two forms

$$\text{Nonterminal} \rightarrow \text{semiword}$$

or

$$\text{Nonterminal} \rightarrow \text{word}$$ ∎

The two previous proofs imply that all regular languages can be generated by regular grammars and all regular grammars generate regular languages.

We must be very careful not to be carried away by the symmetry of these theorems. Despite both theorems, it is still possible that a CFG that is not in the form of a regular grammar can generate a regular language. In fact, we have already seen many examples of this very phenomenon.

EXAMPLE

Consider the CFG

$$S \rightarrow aaS \,|\, bbS \,|\, \Lambda$$

This is a regular grammar and so we may apply the algorithm to it. There is only one nonterminal, S, so there will be only two states in the TG: $-$ and the mandated $+$. The only production of the form $N_p \rightarrow w_q$ is $S \rightarrow \Lambda$, so there is only one edge into $+$ and that is labeled Λ. The productions $S \rightarrow aaS$ and $S \rightarrow bbS$ are of the form $N_1 \rightarrow wN_2$, where the N's are both S. Because these are supposed to be made into paths from N_1 to N_2, they become loops from S back to S. These two productions will become two loops at $-$, one labeled aa and one labeled bb. The whole TG is shown below:

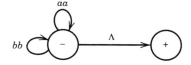

By Kleene's theorem (see Chapter 7), any language accepted by a TG is regular; therefore, the language generated by this CFG (which is the same) is regular. It corresponds to the regular expression $(\mathbf{aa} + \mathbf{bb})^*$. ∎

EXAMPLE

Consider the regular CFG

$$S \rightarrow aaS \,|\, bbS \,|\, abX \,|\, baX \,|\, \Lambda$$
$$X \rightarrow aaX \,|\, bbX \,|\, abS \,|\, baS$$

The algorithm tells us that there will be three states: $-, X, +$. Because there is only one production of the form

$$N_p \rightarrow w_q$$

there is only one edge into $+$. The TG is

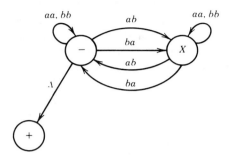

which we immediately see accepts our old friend, the language EVEN-EVEN. (Do not be fooled by the Λ edge to the $+$ state. It is the same as relabeling the $-$ state $\pm$.) ■

EXAMPLE

Consider the regular CFG

$$
\begin{aligned}
S &\rightarrow aA \mid bB \\
A &\rightarrow aS \mid a \\
B &\rightarrow bS \mid b
\end{aligned}
$$

The corresponding TG constructed by the algorithm in Theorem 22 (p. 262) is

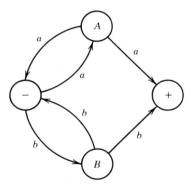

The language of this CFG is exactly the same as that of the CFG two examples ago, except that it does not include the word Λ. This language can be defined by the regular expression $(\mathbf{aa} + \mathbf{bb})^+$. ■

⚜ KILLING Λ-PRODUCTIONS

We have not yet committed ourselves to a definite stand on the social acceptability of **Λ-productions,** that is, productions of the form

$$N \rightarrow \Lambda$$

where N is any nonterminal. We have employed them, but we do not pay them equal wages. These Λ-productions will make our lives very difficult in the discussions to come, so we must ask ourselves, Do we need them at all?

Any context-free language in which Λ is a word must have some Λ-productions in its grammar since otherwise we could never derive the word Λ from S. This statement is obvious, but it should be given some justification. Mathematically, this is easy: We observe that Λ-productions are the only productions that shorten the working string. If we begin with the string S and apply only non-Λ-productions, we never develop a word of length 0.

However, there are some grammars that generate languages that do not include the word Λ, but that contain some Λ-productions anyway. One such CFG is

$$S \rightarrow aX$$
$$X \rightarrow \Lambda$$

Its language is the single word a. There are other CFGs that generate this same language that do not include any Λ-productions.

The following theorem, which is the work of Bar-Hillel, Perles, and Shamir, shows that Λ-productions are not necessary in a grammar for a context-free language that does not contain the word Λ. It proves an even stronger result.

THEOREM 23

If L is a context-free language generated by a CFG that includes Λ-productions, then there is a different context-free grammar that has no Λ-productions that generates either the whole language L (if L does not include the word Λ) or else generates the language of all the words in L that are not Λ.

PROOF

We prove this by providing a constructive algorithm that will convert a CFG that contains Λ-productions into a CFG that does not contain Λ-productions that still generates the same language with the possible exception of the word Λ.

Consider the purpose of the production

$$N \rightarrow \Lambda$$

If we apply this production to some working string, say, $abAbNaB$, we get $abAbaB$. In other words, the net result is to delete N from the working string. If N was just destined to be deleted, why did we let it get in there in the first place? Just because N will come out does not mean we could have avoided putting it in originally.

Consider the following CFG for EVENPALINDROME (the language of all palindromes with an even number of letters):

$$S \rightarrow aSa \mid bSb \mid \Lambda$$

In this grammar, we have the following possible derivation:

$$S \Rightarrow aSa$$
$$\Rightarrow aaSaa$$
$$\Rightarrow aabSbaa$$
$$\Rightarrow aabbaa$$

We obviously need the nonterminal S in the production process even though we delete it from the derivation when it has served its purpose.

The following rule *seems* to take care of using and deleting the nonterminals involved in Λ-productions.

Proposed Replacement Rule

If, in a certain CFG, there is a production of the form

$$N \rightarrow \Lambda$$

among the set of productions, where N is any nonterminal (even S), then we can modify the grammar by deleting this production and adding the following list of productions in its place.

For all productions of the form

$$X \rightarrow (\text{blah 1}) \; N \; (\text{blah 2})$$

where X is any nonterminal (even S or N) and where (blah 1) and (blah 2) are anything at all (even involving N), *add* the production

$$X \rightarrow (\text{blah 1})(\text{blah 2})$$

Notice that we do not delete the production $X \rightarrow (\text{blah 1})N(\text{blah 2})$, only the production $N \rightarrow \Lambda$.

For all productions that involve more than one N on the right side, add new productions that have the same other characters but that have all possible subsets of N's deleted.

For example, the production

$$X \rightarrow aNbNa$$

makes us add

$$X \rightarrow abNa \quad \text{(deleting only the first } N)$$
$$X \rightarrow aNba \quad \text{(deleting only the second } N)$$
$$X \rightarrow aba \quad \text{(deleting both } N\text{'s)}$$

Also, the possible production

$$X \rightarrow NN$$

makes us add

$$X \rightarrow N \quad \text{(deleting one } N)$$
$$X \rightarrow \Lambda \quad \text{(deleting both } N\text{'s)}$$

Instead of using a production with an N and then dropping the N later to form the word w, we simply use the correct form of the production with the appropriate N already dropped when generating w. There is then no need to remove N later and so no need for the Λ-production. This modification of the CFG will produce a new CFG that generates exactly the same words as the first grammar with the possible exception of the word Λ. This is the end of the proposed replacement rule.

Let us see what happens when we apply this replacement rule to the following CFG for EVENPALINDROME:

$$S \rightarrow aSa \mid bSb \mid \Lambda$$

We remove the production $S \rightarrow \Lambda$ and replace it with $S \rightarrow aa$ and $S \rightarrow bb$, which are the first two productions with the right-side S deleted.

The CFG is now

$$S \rightarrow aSa \mid bSb \mid aa \mid bb$$

which also generates EVENPALINDROME, except for the word Λ, which can no longer be derived.

For example, the following derivation is generated in the old CFG:

Derivation	Production Used
$S \Rightarrow aSa$	$S \rightarrow aSa$
$\Rightarrow aaSaa$	$S \rightarrow aSa$
$\Rightarrow aabSbaa$	$S \rightarrow bSb$
$\Rightarrow aabbaa$	$S \rightarrow \Lambda$

In the new CFG, we can combine the last two steps into one:

Derivation	Production Used
$S \Rightarrow aSa$	$S \rightarrow aSa$
$\Rightarrow aaSaa$	$S \rightarrow aSa$
$\Rightarrow aabbaa$	$S \rightarrow bb$

We do not eliminate the entire possibility of using S to form words.

We can now use this proposed replacement rule to describe an algorithm for eliminating all Λ-productions from a given grammar.

If a particular CFG has several nonterminals with Λ-productions, then we replace these Λ-productions one by one following the steps of the proposed replacement rule. As we saw, we will get more productions (new right sides by deleting some N's) but shorter derivations (by combining the steps that formerly employed Λ-productions). We end up with a CFG that generates the exact same language as the original CFG (with the possible exception of the word Λ) but that has no Λ-productions.

A little discussion is in order here to establish not only that the new CFG actually does generate all the non-Λ words the old CFG does but that it also generates no new words that the old CFG did not.

We must observe that the new rules of production added do not lead to the generation of any new words that were not capable of being generated from the old CFG. This is because the new production has the same affect as the application of two old rules and instead of using $X \rightarrow$ (new N-deleted string) we could employ these two steps $X \rightarrow$ (old string with N) and then $N \rightarrow \Lambda$.

Before we claim that this constructive algorithm provides the whole proof, we must ask whether or not it is *finite*. It seems that if we start with some nonterminals N_1, N_2, N_3, which have Λ-productions and we eliminate these Λ-productions one by one until there are none left, nothing can go wrong. Can it?

What can go wrong is that the proposed replacement rule may create *new* Λ-productions that cannot themselves be removed without again creating more. For example, in this grammar

$$S \rightarrow a \mid Xb \mid aYa$$
$$X \rightarrow Y \mid \Lambda$$
$$Y \rightarrow b \mid X$$

we have the Λ-production

$$X \rightarrow \Lambda$$

so by the replacement rule we can eliminate this production and put in its place the additional productions

$$S \rightarrow b \quad \text{(from } S \rightarrow Xb\text{)}$$

and

$$Y \rightarrow \Lambda \quad \text{(from } Y \rightarrow X\text{)}$$

But now we have created a new Λ-production that was not there before. So, we still have the same number of Λ-productions we started with. If we now use the proposed replacement rule to get rid of $Y \rightarrow \Lambda$, we get

$$S \rightarrow aa \quad \text{(from } S \rightarrow aYa\text{)}$$

and

$$X \rightarrow \Lambda \quad \text{(from } X \rightarrow Y\text{)}$$

But we have now recreated the production $X \rightarrow \Lambda$. So, we are back with our old Λ-production. In this particular case, the proposed replacement rule will never eliminate all Λ-productions even in hundreds of applications.

Therefore, unfortunately, we do not yet have a proof of this theorem. However, we can take some consolation in having created a wonderful illustration of the need for careful proofs. Never again will we think that the phrase "and so we see that the algorithm is finite" is a silly waste of words.

Despite the apparent calamity, all is not lost. We can perform an ancient mathematical trick and patch up the proof. The trick is to eliminate all the Λ-productions simultaneously.

DEFINITION   (inside the proof of Theorem 23)

In a given CFG, we call a nonterminal N **nullable** if

There is a production $N \rightarrow \Lambda$, or

There is a derivation that starts at N and leads to Λ:

$$N \Rightarrow \cdots \Rightarrow \Lambda \qquad \blacksquare$$

As we have seen, all nullable nonterminals are dangerous. We now state the careful formulation of the algorithm.

Modified Replacement Rule

1. Delete all Λ-productions.
2. Add the following productions: For every production

$$X \rightarrow \text{old string}$$

add new productions of the form $X \rightarrow \cdots$, where the right side will account for any modification of the old string that can be formed by deleting all possible subsets of nullable nonterminals, except that we do not allow $X \rightarrow \Lambda$ to be formed even if all the characters in this old string are nullable.

For example, in the CFG

$$S \rightarrow a \mid Xb \mid aYa$$
$$X \rightarrow Y \mid \Lambda$$
$$Y \rightarrow b \mid X$$

we find that X and Y are nullable. So when we delete $X \rightarrow \Lambda$, we have to check all productions that include X or Y to see what new productions to add:

Old Productions with Nullables	Productions Newly Formed by the Rule
$X \rightarrow Y$	Nothing
$X \rightarrow \Lambda$	Nothing
$Y \rightarrow X$	Nothing
$S \rightarrow Xb$	$S \rightarrow b$
$S \rightarrow aYa$	$S \rightarrow aa$

The new CFG is

$$S \rightarrow a \mid Xb \mid aYa \mid b \mid aa$$
$$X \rightarrow Y$$
$$Y \rightarrow b \mid X$$

It has no Λ-productions but generates the same language.

This modified replacement rule works the way we thought the first replacement rule would work, that is, by looking ahead at which nonterminals in the working string will be eliminated by Λ-productions and offering alternate substitutions in which the nullables have already been eliminated.

Before we conclude this proof, we should ask ourselves whether the modified replacement rule is really workable, that is, is it an effective procedure in the sense of our use of that term in Chapter 11? To apply the modified replacement rule, we must be able to identify all the nullable nonterminals at once. How can we do this if the grammar is complicated? For example, in the CFG

$$S \rightarrow Xay \mid YY \mid aX \mid ZYX$$
$$X \rightarrow Za \mid bZ \mid ZZ \mid Yb$$
$$Y \rightarrow Ya \mid XY \mid \Lambda$$
$$Z \rightarrow aX \mid YYY$$

all the nonterminals are nullable, as we can see from

$$S \Rightarrow ZYX \Rightarrow YYYYX \Rightarrow YYYYZZ \Rightarrow YYYYYYYZ \Rightarrow YYYYYYYYYY$$
$$\Rightarrow \cdots \Rightarrow \Lambda\Lambda\Lambda\Lambda\Lambda\Lambda\Lambda\Lambda\Lambda\Lambda = \Lambda$$

The solution to this problem is blue paint (the same shade used in Chapter 11). Let us start by painting all the nonterminals with Λ-productions blue. We paint every occurrence of them, throughout the entire CFG, blue. Now for step 2, we paint blue all nonterminals that produce solid blue strings. For example, if

$$S \rightarrow ZYX$$

and Z, Y, and X are all blue, then we paint S blue. Paint all other occurrences of S throughout the CFG blue too. As with the FAs, we repeat step 2 until nothing new is painted. At this point all nullable nonterminals will be blue.

This is an effective decision procedure to determine all nullables, and therefore the modified replacement rule is also effective.

This then successfully concludes the proof of this theorem.   ■

EXAMPLE

Let us consider the following CFG for the language defined by $(a + b)*a$:

$$S \rightarrow Xa$$
$$X \rightarrow aX \mid bX \mid \Lambda$$

The only nullable nonterminal here is X, and the productions that have right sides including X are:

Productions with Nullables	New Productions Formed by the Rule
$S \rightarrow Xa$	$S \rightarrow a$
$X \rightarrow aX$	$X \rightarrow a$
$X \rightarrow bX$	$X \rightarrow b$

The full new CFG is

$$S \rightarrow Xa \mid a$$
$$X \rightarrow aX \mid bX \mid a \mid b$$

To produce the word *baa*, we formerly used the derivation:

Derivation	Production Used
$S \Rightarrow Xa$	$S \rightarrow Xa$
$\Rightarrow bXa$	$X \rightarrow bX$
$\Rightarrow baXa$	$X \rightarrow aX$
$\Rightarrow baa$	$X \rightarrow \Lambda$

Now we combine the last two steps, and the new derivation in the new CFG is

$$
\begin{array}{ll}
S \Rightarrow Xa & S \rightarrow Xa \\
\Rightarrow bXa & X \rightarrow bX \\
\Rightarrow baa & X \rightarrow a
\end{array}
$$

Because Λ was not a word generated by the old CFG, the new CFG generates exactly the same language. ∎

EXAMPLE

Consider this inefficient CFG for the language defined by $(a + b)*bb(a + b)*$

$$S \rightarrow XY$$
$$X \rightarrow Zb$$
$$Y \rightarrow bW$$
$$Z \rightarrow AB$$
$$W \rightarrow Z$$
$$A \rightarrow aA \mid bA \mid \Lambda$$
$$B \rightarrow Ba \mid Bb \mid \Lambda$$

From X we can derive any word ending in b; from Y we can derive any word starting with b. Therefore, from S we can derive any word with a double b.

Obviously, A and B are nullable. Based on that, $Z \rightarrow AB$ makes Z also nullable. After that, we see that W is also nullable. X, Y, and S remain nonnullable. Alternately, of course, we could have arrived at this by azure artistry.

The modified replacement algorithm tells us to generate new productions to replace the Λ-productions as follows:

	Additional New Productions
Old	**Derived from Old**
$X \rightarrow Zb$	$X \rightarrow b$
$Y \rightarrow bW$	$Y \rightarrow b$
$Z \rightarrow AB$	$Z \rightarrow A$ and $Z \rightarrow B$
$W \rightarrow Z$	Nothing new
$A \rightarrow aA$	$A \rightarrow a$
$A \rightarrow bA$	$A \rightarrow b$
$B \rightarrow Ba$	$B \rightarrow a$
$B \rightarrow Bb$	$B \rightarrow b$

Remember, we do not eliminate all of the old productions, only the old Λ-productions.

The fully modified new CFG is

$$S \rightarrow XY$$
$$X \rightarrow Zb \mid b$$
$$Y \rightarrow bW \mid b$$
$$Z \rightarrow AB \mid A \mid B$$
$$W \rightarrow Z$$
$$A \rightarrow aA \mid bA \mid a \mid b$$
$$B \rightarrow Ba \mid Bb \mid a \mid b$$

Because Λ was not a word generated by the old CFG, the new CFG generates exactly the same language. ∎

⚜ KILLING UNIT PRODUCTIONS

We now eliminate another needless oddity that plagues some CFGs.

DEFINITION

A production of the form

$$\text{Nonterminal} \rightarrow \text{one Nonterminal}$$

is called a **unit production.** ∎

Bar-Hillel, Perles, and Shamir tell us how to get rid of these too.

THEOREM 24

If there is a CFG for the language L that has no Λ-productions, then there is also a CFG for L with no Λ-productions and no unit productions.

PROOF

This will be another proof by constructive algorithm.

First, we ask ourselves what is the purpose of a production of the form

$$A \rightarrow B$$

where A and B are nonterminals.

We can use it only to change some working string of the form

$$(\text{blah})A(\text{blah})$$

into the working string

$$(\text{blah})B(\text{blah})$$

Why would we want to do that? We do it because later we want to apply a production to the nonterminal B that is different from any that we could produce from A. For example,

$$B \rightarrow (\text{string})$$

so

$$(\text{blah})A(\text{blah}) \Rightarrow (\text{blah})B(\text{blah}) \Rightarrow (\text{blah})(\text{string})(\text{blah})$$

which is a change we could not make without using $A \rightarrow B$, because we had no production $A \rightarrow (\text{string})$.

It seems simple then to say that instead of unit productions all we need is $A \rightarrow (\text{string})$. We now formulate a replacement rule for eliminating unit productions.

Proposed Elimination Rule

If $A \rightarrow B$ is a unit production and all the productions starting with B are

$$B \rightarrow s_1 \mid s_2 \mid \ldots$$

where $s_1, s_2, \ldots$ are strings, then we can drop the production $A \rightarrow B$ and instead include these new productions:

$$A \rightarrow s_1 \mid s_2 \mid \ldots$$

Again, we ask ourselves, will repeated applications of this proposed elimination rule result in a grammar that does not include unit productions but defines exactly the same language?

The answer is that we still have to be careful. A problem analogous to the one that arose before can strike again.

The set of new productions we create may give us new unit productions. For example, if we start with the grammar

$$
\begin{aligned}
S &\rightarrow A \mid bb \\
A &\rightarrow B \mid b \\
B &\rightarrow S \mid a
\end{aligned}
$$

and we try to eliminate the unit production $A \rightarrow B$, we get instead

$$A \rightarrow S \mid a$$

to go along with the old productions we are retaining. The CFG is now

$$
\begin{aligned}
S &\rightarrow A \mid bb \\
A &\rightarrow b \mid a \mid S \\
B &\rightarrow S \mid a
\end{aligned}
$$

We still have three unit productions:

$$S \rightarrow A, \qquad A \rightarrow S, \qquad B \rightarrow S$$

If we now try to eliminate the unit production $B \rightarrow S$, we create the new unit production $B \rightarrow A$. If we then use the proposed elimination rule on $B \rightarrow A$, we will get back $B \rightarrow S$.

As was the case with Λ-productions, we must get rid of all unit productions in one fell swoop to avoid infinite circularity.

Modified Elimination Rule

For every pair of nonterminals A and B, *if* the CFG has a unit production $A \rightarrow B$ *or if* there is a chain of unit productions leading from A to B, such as

$$A \Rightarrow X_1 \Rightarrow X_2 \Rightarrow \cdots \Rightarrow B$$

where X_1, X_2 are some nonterminals, we *then* introduce new productions according to the following rule: If the nonunit productions from B are

$$B \rightarrow s_1 \mid s_2 \mid s_3 \mid \cdots$$

where s_1, s_2, and s_3 are strings, create the productions

$$A \rightarrow s_1 \mid s_2 \mid s_3 \mid \cdots$$

We do the same for all such pairs of A's and B's simultaneously. We can then eliminate all unit productions.

This is what we meant to do originally. If in the derivation for some word w the nonterminal A is in the working string and it gets replaced by a unit production $A \rightarrow B$, *or* by a sequence of unit productions leading to B, and further if B is replaced by the production $B \rightarrow s_4$, we can accomplish the same thing and derive the same word w by employing the production $A \rightarrow s_4$ directly in the first place.

This modified elimination rule avoids circularity by removing all unit productions at once. If the grammar contains no Λ-productions, it is not a hard task to find all sequences of unit productions $A \rightarrow S_1 \rightarrow S_2 \rightarrow \cdots \rightarrow B$, because there are only finitely many unit productions and they chain up in only obvious ways. In a grammar with Λ-productions and nullable nonterminals X and Y, the production $S \rightarrow ZYX$ is essentially a unit production. There are no Λ-productions allowed by the hypothesis of the theorem so no such difficulty is possible.

The modified method described in the proof is an effective procedure and it proves the theorem. ∎

EXAMPLE

Let us reconsider the troubling example mentioned in the proof above:

$$S \rightarrow A \mid bb$$
$$A \rightarrow B \mid b$$
$$B \rightarrow S \mid a$$

Let us separate the units from the nonunits:

Unit Productions	Decent Folks
$S \rightarrow A$	$S \rightarrow bb$
$A \rightarrow B$	$A \rightarrow b$
$B \rightarrow S$	$B \rightarrow a$

We list all unit productions and sequences of unit productions, one nonterminal at a time, tracing each nonterminal through each sequence it heads. Then we create the new productions that allow the first nonterminal to be replaced by any of the strings that could replace the last nonterminal in the sequence.

$$
\begin{array}{lll}
S \rightarrow A & \text{gives} & S \rightarrow b \\
S \rightarrow A \rightarrow B & \text{gives} & S \rightarrow a \\
A \rightarrow B & \text{gives} & A \rightarrow a \\
A \rightarrow B \rightarrow S & \text{gives} & A \rightarrow bb \\
B \rightarrow S & \text{gives} & B \rightarrow bb \\
B \rightarrow S \rightarrow A & \text{gives} & B \rightarrow b
\end{array}
$$

The new CFG for this language is

$$
\begin{array}{l}
S \rightarrow bb \mid b \mid a \\
A \rightarrow b \mid a \mid bb \\
B \rightarrow a \mid bb \mid b
\end{array}
$$

which had no unit productions.

Parenthetically, we may remark that this particular CFG generates a finite language since there are no nonterminals in any string produced from S. ∎

⚜ CHOMSKY NORMAL FORM

In our next result, we will separate the terminals from the nonterminals in CFG productions.

THEOREM 25

If L is a language generated by some CFG, then there is another CFG that generates all the non-Λ words of L, all of whose productions are of one of two basic forms:

$$
\begin{array}{l}
\text{Nonterminal} \rightarrow \text{string of only Nonterminals} \\
\text{Nonterminal} \rightarrow \text{one terminal}
\end{array}
$$

PROOF

The proof will be by constructive algorithm. Let us suppose that in the given CFG the nonterminals are $S, X_1, X_2, \ldots$.

Let us also assume that the terminals are a and b.

We now add two new nonterminals A and B and the productions

$$
\begin{array}{l}
A \rightarrow a \\
B \rightarrow b
\end{array}
$$

Now for every previous production involving terminals, we replace each a with the nonterminal A and each b with the nonterminal B. For example,

$$
X_3 \rightarrow X_4 a X_1 S b b X_7 a
$$

becomes

$$
X_3 \rightarrow X_4 A X_1 S B B X_7 A
$$

which is a string of solid nonterminals.

Even if we start with a string of solid terminals

$$X_6 \rightarrow aaba$$

we convert it into a string of solid nonterminals

$$X_6 \rightarrow AABA$$

All our old productions are now of the form

$$\text{Nonterminal} \rightarrow \text{string of Nonterminals}$$

and the two new productions are of the form

$$\text{Nonterminal} \rightarrow \text{one terminal}$$

Any derivation that formerly started with S and proceeded down to the word

$$aaabba$$

will now follow the same sequence of productions to derive the string

$$AAABBA$$

from the start symbol S. From here we apply $A \rightarrow a$ and $B \rightarrow b$ a number of times to generate the word $aaabba$. This convinces us that any word that could be generated by the original CFG can also be generated by the new CFG.

We must also note that any word generated by the new CFG could also be generated by the old CFG. Any derivation in the new CFG is a sequence of applications of those productions that are modified old productions and the two totally new productions from A and B. Because these two new productions are the replacement of one nonterminal by one terminal, nothing they introduce into the working string is itself replaceable. They do not interact with the other productions.

If the letters A and B were already nonterminals in the CFG to start with, then any two other unused symbols would serve as well. Therefore, this new CFG proves the theorem. ■

EXAMPLE

Let us start with the CFG

$$S \rightarrow X_1 \mid X_2 aX_2 \mid aSb \mid b$$
$$X_1 \rightarrow X_2 X_2 \mid b$$
$$X_2 \rightarrow aX_2 \mid aaX_1$$

After the conversion, we have

$S \rightarrow X_1$	$X_1 \rightarrow X_2 X_2$
$S \rightarrow X_2 AX_2$	$X_1 \rightarrow B$
$S \rightarrow ASB$	$X_2 \rightarrow AX_2$
$S \rightarrow B$	$X_2 \rightarrow AAX_1$
	$A \rightarrow a$
	$B \rightarrow b$

We have not employed the disjunction slash $\mid$, but instead have written out all the productions separately so that we may observe eight of the form

$$\text{Nonterminal} \rightarrow \text{string of Nonterminals}$$

and two of the form

$$\text{Nonterminal} \rightarrow \text{one terminal} \qquad \blacksquare$$

In all cases where the algorithm of the theorem is applied, the new CFG has the same number of terminals as the old CFG and more nonterminals (one new one for each terminal).

As with all our proofs by constructive algorithm, we have not said that this new CFG is the best example of a CFG that fits the desired format. We say only that it is *one* of those that satisfy the requirements.

One problem is that we may create unit productions where none existed before. For example, if we follow the algorithm to the letter of the law,

$$X \rightarrow a$$

will become

$$X \rightarrow A$$
$$A \rightarrow a$$

To avoid this problem, we should add a clause to our algorithm saying that any productions that we find that are already in one of the desired forms should be left alone: "If it ain't broke, don't fix it." Then we do not run the risk of creating unit productions (or Λ-productions for that matter).

EXAMPLE

One student thought that it was a waste of effort to introduce a new nonterminal to stand for a if the CFG already contained a production of the form nonterminal $\rightarrow a$. Why not simply replace all a's in long mixed strings by this nonterminal? For instance, why cannot

$$S \rightarrow Na$$
$$N \rightarrow a \mid b$$

become

$$S \rightarrow NN$$
$$N \rightarrow a \mid b$$

The answer is that bb is not generated by the first grammar, but it is by the second. The correct modified form is

$$S \rightarrow NA$$
$$N \rightarrow a \mid b$$
$$A \rightarrow a \qquad \blacksquare$$

EXAMPLE

The CFG

$$S \rightarrow XY$$
$$X \rightarrow XX$$
$$Y \rightarrow YY$$
$$X \rightarrow a$$
$$Y \rightarrow b$$

(which generates **aa*bb*** and which is already in the desired format) would, if we mindlessly attacked it with our algorithm, become

$$S \rightarrow XY$$
$$X \rightarrow XX$$
$$Y \rightarrow YY$$
$$X \rightarrow A$$
$$Y \rightarrow B$$
$$A \rightarrow a$$
$$B \rightarrow b$$

which is also in the desired format but has unit productions. When we get rid of the unit productions using the algorithm of Theorem 24 (p. 272), we return to the original CFG.

To the true theoretician, this meaningless waste of energy costs nothing. The goal was to *prove* the existence of an equivalent grammar in the specified format. The virtue here is to find the shortest, most understandable, and most elegant *proof,* not an algorithm with dozens of messy clauses and exceptions. The problem of finding the best such *grammar* is also a question theoreticians are interested in, but it is not the question presented in Theorem 25 (p. 275). ■

The purpose of Theorem 25 was to prepare the way for the following format and theorem developed by Chomsky.

DEFINITION

If a CFG has only productions of the form

Nonterminal $\rightarrow$ string of exactly two Nonterminals

or of the form

Nonterminal $\rightarrow$ one terminal

it is said to be in **Chomsky Normal Form,** or **CNF.** ■

THEOREM 26

For any context-free language L, the non-Λ words of L can be generated by a grammar in which all productions are in CNF.

Let us be careful to realize that any context-free language that does not contain Λ as a word has a CFG in CNF that generates exactly it. However, if a CFL contains Λ, then when its CFG is converted by the algorithms above into CNF, the word Λ drops out of the language, while all other words stay the same.

PROOF

The proof will be by constructive algorithm.

From Theorems 23 and 24 we know that there is a CFG for L (or for all L except Λ) that has no Λ-productions and no unit productions.

Let us suppose further that we start with a CFG for L that we have made to fit the form specified in Theorem 25. Let us suppose its productions are

$$S \rightarrow X_1 X_2 X_3 X_8 \qquad X_1 \rightarrow X_3 X_4 X_{10} X_4$$
$$S \rightarrow X_3 X_5 \qquad X_1 \rightarrow a$$
$$S \rightarrow b \qquad X_3 \rightarrow X_4 X_9$$
$$\cdots$$

The productions of the form

$$\text{Nonterminal} \rightarrow \text{one terminal}$$

we leave alone. We must now make the productions with right sides having many nonterminals into productions with right sides that have only two nonterminals.

For each production of the form

$$\text{Nonterminal} \rightarrow \text{string of Nonterminals}$$

we propose the following expansion that involves the introduction of the new nonterminals $R_1, R_2, \ldots$. The production

$$S \rightarrow X_1 X_2 X_3 X_8$$

should be replaced by

$$S \rightarrow X_1 R_1$$

where

$$R_1 \rightarrow X_2 R_3$$

and where

$$R_3 \rightarrow X_3 X_8$$

We use these new nonterminals nowhere else in the grammar; they are used solely to split this one production into small pieces. If we need to expand more productions, we introduce new R's with different subscripts.

Let us think of this as

$$S \rightarrow X_1(\text{rest}_1) \quad (\text{where rest}_1) = X_2 X_3 X_8)$$
$$(\text{rest}_1) \rightarrow X_2(\text{rest}_2) \quad (\text{where rest}_2) = X_3 X_8)$$
$$(\text{rest}_2) \rightarrow X_3 X_8$$

This trick works just as well if we start with an odd number of nonterminals on the right-hand side of the production:

$$X_8 \rightarrow X_2 X_1 X_1 X_3 X_9$$

should be replaced by

$$X_8 \rightarrow X_2 R_4 \quad (\text{where } R_4 = X_1 X_1 X_3 X_9)$$
$$R_4 \rightarrow X_1 R_5 \quad (\text{where } R_5 = X_1 X_3 X_9)$$
$$R_5 \rightarrow X_1 R_6 \quad (\text{where } R_6 = X_3 X_9)$$
$$R_6 \rightarrow X_3 X_9$$

In this way, we can convert productions with long strings of nonterminals into sequences of productions with exactly two nonterminals on the right side. As with the previous theorem, we are not finished until we have convinced ourselves that this conversion has not altered the language the CFG generates. Any word formerly generated is still generatable by virtually the same steps, if we understand that some productions have been expanded into several productions that must be executed in sequence.

For example, in a derivation where we previously employed the production

$$X_8 \rightarrow X_2 X_1 X_1 X_3 X_9$$

we must now employ the sequence of productions:

$$X_8 \rightarrow X_2 R_4$$
$$R_4 \rightarrow X_1 R_5$$
$$R_5 \rightarrow X_1 R_6$$
$$R_6 \rightarrow X_3 X_9$$

in exactly this order.

We must also show that with all these additional new nonterminals and productions we have not allowed any additional words to be generated. Let us observe that because the nonterminal R_5 occurs in only the two productions

$$R_4 \rightarrow X_1 R_5$$

and

$$R_5 \rightarrow X_1 R_6$$

any sequence of productions that generates a working string using R_5 must have used

$$R_4 \rightarrow X_1 R_5$$

to get R_5 into the working string, and

$$R_5 \rightarrow X_1 R_6$$

to remove it from the final string.

This combination has the net effect of a production like

$$R_4 \rightarrow X_1 X_1 R_6$$

Again, R_4 could have been introduced into the working string only by one specific production. Also, R_6 can be removed only by one specific production. In fact, the net effect of these R's must be the same as the replacement of X_8 by $X_2 X_1 X_1 X_3 X_9$. Because we use different R's in the expansion of each production, the new nonterminals (R's) cannot interact to give us new words. Each is on the right side of only one production and on the left side of only one production. The net effect must be like that of the original production.

The new grammar generates the same language as the old grammar and is in the desired form. ∎

EXAMPLE

Let us convert

$$S \rightarrow aSa \mid bSb \mid a \mid b \mid aa \mid bb$$

(which generates the language PALINDROME except for Λ) into CNF. This language is called NONNULLPALINDROME.

First, we separate the terminals from the nonterminal as in Theorem 25 (p. 275):

$$S \rightarrow ASA$$
$$S \rightarrow BSB$$
$$S \rightarrow AA$$

$$S \rightarrow BB$$
$$S \rightarrow a$$
$$S \rightarrow b$$
$$A \rightarrow a$$
$$B \rightarrow b$$

Notice that we are careful not to introduce the needless unit productions $S \rightarrow A$ and $S \rightarrow B$.

Now we introduce the R's:

$$S \rightarrow AR_1 \qquad S \rightarrow AA$$
$$R_1 \rightarrow SA \qquad S \rightarrow BB$$
$$S \rightarrow BR_2 \qquad S \rightarrow a$$
$$R_2 \rightarrow SB \qquad S \rightarrow b$$
$$A \rightarrow a$$
$$B \rightarrow b$$

This is in CNF, but it is quite a mess. Had we not seen how it was constructed, we would have some difficulty recognizing this grammar as a CFG for NONNULLPALIN-DROME.

If we include with this list of productions the additional production $S \rightarrow \Lambda$, we have a CFG for the entire language PALINDROME.

In languages without the word Λ, this procedure works smoothly. However, Λ is a word in PALINDROME, and adding the production $S \rightarrow \Lambda$ will incorporate this word without introducing any other (unwanted) words. ∎

EXAMPLE

Let us convert the CFG

$$S \rightarrow bA \mid aB$$
$$A \rightarrow bAA \mid aS \mid a$$
$$B \rightarrow aBB \mid bS \mid b$$

into CNF. Because we already use the symbols A and B in this grammar, let us call the new nonterminals we need to incorporate to achieve the form of Theorem 25 X (for a) and Y (for b).

The grammar becomes

$$S \rightarrow YA \qquad B \rightarrow XBB$$
$$S \rightarrow XB \qquad B \rightarrow YS$$
$$A \rightarrow YAA \qquad B \rightarrow b$$
$$A \rightarrow XS \qquad X \rightarrow a$$
$$A \rightarrow a \qquad Y \rightarrow b$$

Notice that we have left well enough alone in two instances:

$$A \rightarrow a \qquad \text{and} \qquad B \rightarrow b$$

We need to simplify only two productions:

$$A \rightarrow YAA \qquad \text{becomes} \qquad \begin{cases} A \rightarrow YR_1 \\ R_1 \rightarrow AA \end{cases}$$

and

$$B \rightarrow XBB \qquad \text{becomes} \qquad \begin{cases} B \rightarrow XR_2 \\ R_2 \rightarrow BB \end{cases}$$

The CFG has now become

$$
\begin{aligned}
S & \rightarrow YA \mid XB \\
A & \rightarrow YR_1 \mid XS \mid a \\
B & \rightarrow XR_2 \mid YS \mid b \\
X & \rightarrow a \\
Y & \rightarrow b \\
R_1 & \rightarrow AA \\
R_2 & \rightarrow BB
\end{aligned}
$$

which is in CNF. This is one of the more obscure grammars for the language EQUAL. ■

EXAMPLE

Consider the CFG

$$S \rightarrow aaaaS \mid aaaa$$

which generates the language a^{4n} for $n = 1, 2, 3, \ldots = \{a^4 \quad a^8 \quad a^{12} \ldots\}$. We convert this to CNF as follows: first into the form of Theorem 25

$$
\begin{aligned}
S & \rightarrow AAAAS \\
S & \rightarrow AAAA \\
A & \rightarrow a
\end{aligned}
$$

which in turn becomes

$$
\begin{aligned}
S & \rightarrow AR_1 \\
R_1 & \rightarrow AR_2 \\
R_2 & \rightarrow AR_3 \\
R_3 & \rightarrow AS \\
S & \rightarrow AR_4 \\
R_4 & \rightarrow AR_5 \\
R_5 & \rightarrow AA \\
A & \rightarrow a
\end{aligned}
$$

■

⚜ LEFTMOST DERIVATIONS

As the last topic in this chapter, we show that we can not only standardize the form of the grammar, but also the form of the derivations.

DEFINITION

The **leftmost nonterminal** in a working string is the first nonterminal that we encounter when we scan the string from left to right. ■

EXAMPLE

In the string *abNbaXYa*, the leftmost nonterminal is *N*.   ■

DEFINITION

If a word *w* is generated by a CFG by a certain derivation and at each step in the derivation, a rule of production is applied to the leftmost nonterminal in the working string; then this derivation is called a **leftmost derivation.**   ■

EXAMPLE

Consider the CFG

$$S \rightarrow aSX \mid b$$
$$X \rightarrow Xb \mid a$$

The following is a leftmost derivation:

$$S \Rightarrow aSX$$
$$\Rightarrow aaSXX$$
$$\Rightarrow aabXX$$
$$\Rightarrow aabXbX$$
$$\Rightarrow aababX$$
$$\Rightarrow aababa$$

At every stage in the derivation, the nonterminal replaced is the leftmost one.   ■

EXAMPLE

Consider the CFG

$$S \rightarrow XY$$
$$X \rightarrow XX \mid a$$
$$Y \rightarrow YY \mid b$$

We can generate the word *aaabb* through several different production sequences, each of which follows one of these two possible derivation trees:

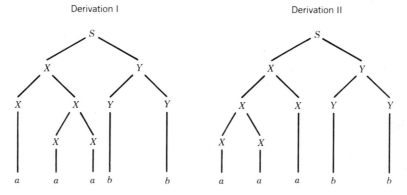

Derivation I   Derivation II

Each of these trees becomes a leftmost derivation when we specify in what order the steps are to be taken. If we draw a dotted line similar to the one that traces the Łukesiewicz notation for us, we see that it indicates the order of productions in the leftmost derivation. We number the nonterminals in the order in which we first meet them on the dotted line. This is the order in which they must be replaced in a leftmost derivation.

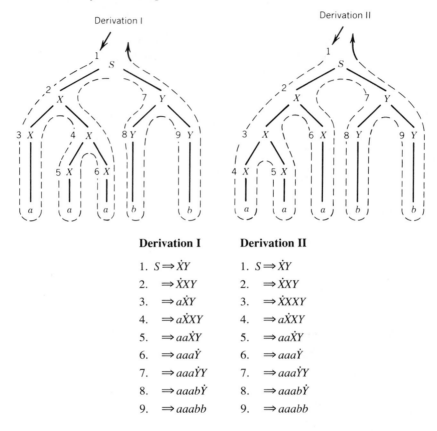

Derivation I	Derivation II
1. $S \Rightarrow \dot{X}Y$	1. $S \Rightarrow \dot{X}Y$
2. $\Rightarrow \dot{X}XY$	2. $\Rightarrow \dot{X}XY$
3. $\Rightarrow a\dot{X}Y$	3. $\Rightarrow \dot{X}XXY$
4. $\Rightarrow a\dot{X}XY$	4. $\Rightarrow a\dot{X}XY$
5. $\Rightarrow aa\dot{X}Y$	5. $\Rightarrow aa\dot{X}Y$
6. $\Rightarrow aaa\dot{Y}$	6. $\Rightarrow aaa\dot{Y}$
7. $\Rightarrow aaa\dot{Y}Y$	7. $\Rightarrow aaa\dot{Y}Y$
8. $\Rightarrow aaab\dot{Y}$	8. $\Rightarrow aaab\dot{Y}$
9. $\Rightarrow aaabb$	9. $\Rightarrow aaabb$

In each of these derivations, we have drawn a dot over the head of the leftmost nonterminal. It is the one that must be replaced in the next step if we are to have a leftmost derivation. ∎

The method illustrated above can be applied to any derivation in any CFG. It therefore provides a proof by constructive algorithm for the following theorem.

THEOREM 27

Any word that can be generated by a given CFG by some derivation also has a leftmost derivation.

EXAMPLE

Consider the CFG

$$S \rightarrow S \supset S \mid {\sim}S \mid (S) \mid p \mid q$$

To generate the symbolic logic formula

$$(p \supset (\sim p \supset q))$$

we use the following tree:

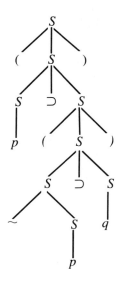

Remember that the terminal symbols are ( ) $\supset$ $\sim p$ q. Because the only nonterminal is S, we must always replace the leftmost S:

$$S \Rightarrow (\dot{S})$$
$$\Rightarrow (\dot{S} \supset S)$$
$$\Rightarrow (p \supset \dot{S})$$
$$\Rightarrow (p \supset (\dot{S}))$$
$$\Rightarrow (p \supset (\dot{S} \supset S))$$
$$\Rightarrow (p \supset (\sim \dot{S} \supset S))$$
$$\Rightarrow (p \supset (\sim p \supset \dot{S}))$$
$$\Rightarrow (p \supset (\sim p \supset q))$$

∎

⚜ PROBLEMS

1. Find CFGs that generate these regular languages over the alphabet $\Sigma = \{a \quad b\}$:

   (i) The language defined by $(\mathbf{aaa} + \mathbf{b})^*$.

   (ii) The language defined by $(\mathbf{a} + \mathbf{b})^*(\mathbf{bbb} + \mathbf{aaa})(\mathbf{a} + \mathbf{b})^*$.

  (iii) All strings without the substring aaa.

  (iv) All strings that end in b and have an even number of b's in total.

   (v) The set of all strings of odd length.

  (vi) All strings with exactly one a or exactly one b.

 (vii) All strings with an odd number of a's or an even number of b's.

2. For the seven languages of Problem 1, find CFGs for them that are in regular grammar format.

For the following CFGs, find regular expressions that define the same language and describe the language.

3. (i) $S \rightarrow aX \mid bS \mid a \mid b$
   $X \rightarrow aX \mid a$
   (ii) $S \rightarrow bS \mid aX \mid b$
   $X \rightarrow bX \mid aS \mid a$

4. (i) $S \rightarrow aaS \mid abS \mid baS \mid bbS \mid \Lambda$
   (ii) $S \rightarrow aB \mid bA \mid \Lambda$
   $A \rightarrow aS$
   $B \rightarrow bS$

5. (i) $S \rightarrow aB \mid bA$
   $A \rightarrow aB \mid a$
   $B \rightarrow bA \mid b$
   (ii) $S \rightarrow aS \mid bX \mid a$
   $X \rightarrow aX \mid bY \mid a$
   $Y \rightarrow aY \mid a$

6. (i) $S \rightarrow aS \mid bX \mid a$
   $X \rightarrow aX \mid bY \mid bZ \mid a$
   $Y \rightarrow aY \mid a$
   $Z \rightarrow aZ \mid bW$
   $W \rightarrow aW \mid a$
   (ii) $S \rightarrow bS \mid aX$
   $X \rightarrow bS \mid aY$
   $Y \rightarrow aY \mid bY \mid a \mid b$

7. (i) Starting with the alphabet

$$\Sigma = \{\mathbf{a} \quad \mathbf{b} \quad (\ ) \quad + \quad *\}$$

   find a CFG that generates all regular expressions.
   (ii) Is this language regular?

8. Despite the fact that a CFG is not in *regular form,* it still might generate a regular language. If so, this means that there is another CFG that defines the same language and *is* in regular form. For each of the examples below, find a regular form version of the CFG:

   (i) $S \rightarrow XYZ$
   $X \rightarrow aX \mid bX \mid \Lambda$
   $Y \rightarrow aY \mid bY \mid \Lambda$
   $Z \rightarrow aZ \mid \Lambda$
   (ii) $S \rightarrow XXX$
   $X \rightarrow aX \mid a$
   $Y \rightarrow bY \mid b$
   (iii) $S \rightarrow XY$
   $X \rightarrow aX \mid Xa \mid a$
   $Y \rightarrow aY \mid Ya \mid a$

9. Show how to convert a TG into a regular grammar without first converting it to an FA.

10. Let us, for the purposes of this problem only, allow a production of the form

$$N_1 \rightarrow \mathbf{r}N_2$$

where N_1 and N_2 are nonterminals and $\mathbf{r}$ is a regular expression. The meaning of this formula is that in any working string we may substitute for N_1 any string wN_2, where w is a word in the language defined by **r**. This can be considered a short hand way of writing an infinite family of productions, one for each word in the language of **r**.

Let a grammar be called *bad* if all its productions are of the two forms

$$N_1 \rightarrow \mathbf{r}N_2$$
$$N_3 \rightarrow \Lambda$$

Bad grammars generate languages the same way CFGs do.

Prove that even a bad grammar cannot generate a nonregular language, by showing how to construct one regular expression that defines the same language as the whole bad grammar.

11. Each of the following CFGs has a production using the symbol Λ and yet Λ is not a word in its language. Using the algorithm in this chapter, show that there are other CFGs for these languages that do not use Λ-productions:

   (i) $S \rightarrow aX \mid bX$
        $X \rightarrow a \mid b \mid \Lambda$
   (ii) $S \rightarrow aX \mid bS \mid a \mid b$
        $X \rightarrow aX \mid a \mid \Lambda$
   (iii) $S \rightarrow aS \mid bX$
        $X \rightarrow aX \mid \Lambda$
   (iv) $S \rightarrow XaX \mid bX$
        $X \rightarrow XaX \mid XbX \mid \Lambda$

12. (i) Show that if a CFG does not have Λ-productions, then there is another CFG that does have Λ-productions and generates the same language.
    (ii) Show that if a CFG does not have unit productions, then there is another CFG that does have unit productions and generates the same language.

13. Each of the following CFGs has unit productions. Using the algorithm presented in this chapter, find CFGs for these same languages that do not have unit productions.

   (i) $S \rightarrow aX \mid Yb$
        $X \rightarrow S$
        $Y \rightarrow bY \mid b$
   (ii) $S \rightarrow AA$
        $A \rightarrow B \mid BB$
        $B \rightarrow abB \mid b \mid bb$
   (iii) $S \rightarrow AB$
        $A \rightarrow B$
        $B \rightarrow aB \mid Bb \mid \Lambda$

14. Convert the following CFGs to CNF:

   (i) $S \rightarrow SS \mid a$
   (ii) $S \rightarrow aSa \mid SSa \mid a$
   (iii) $S \rightarrow aXX$
         $X \rightarrow aS \mid bS \mid a$
   (iv) $E \rightarrow E + E$
         $E \rightarrow E * E$
         $E \rightarrow (E)$
         $E \rightarrow 7$
         The terminals here are $+ * ( ) 7$.
   (v) $S \rightarrow ABABAB$

$A \rightarrow a \mid \Lambda$

$B \rightarrow b \mid \Lambda$

Note that Λ is a word in this language, but when converted into CNF, the grammar will no longer generate it.

(vi) $S \rightarrow SaS \mid SaSbS \mid SbSaS \mid \Lambda$

(vii) $S \rightarrow AS \mid SB$

$A \rightarrow BS \mid SA$

$B \rightarrow SS$

15. Convert the following CFGs with unit productions into CNF:

(i) $S \rightarrow X$

$X \rightarrow Y$

$Y \rightarrow Z$

$Z \rightarrow aa$

(ii) $S \rightarrow SS \mid A$

$A \rightarrow SS \mid AS \mid a$

16. If L is a CFL that contains the word Λ and we Chomsky-ize its CFG into CNF and then add on the sole extra production $S \rightarrow \Lambda$, do we now generate all of L and only L?

17. (i) Find the leftmost derivation for the word *abba* in the grammar

$$S \rightarrow AA$$
$$A \rightarrow aB$$
$$B \rightarrow bB \mid \Lambda$$

(ii) Find the leftmost derivation for the word *abbabaabbbabbab* in the CFG

$$S \rightarrow SSS \mid aXb$$
$$X \rightarrow ba \mid bba \mid abb$$

18. Given a CFG in CNF and restricting all derivations of words to being leftmost derivations, is it still possible that some word w has two nonidentical derivation trees? In other words, is it still possible that the grammar is ambiguous?

19. Prove that any word that can be generated by a CFG has a rightmost derivation.

20. Show that if L is any contex-free language that does not contain the word Λ, then there is a context-free grammar that generates L and has the property that the right-hand side of every production is a string that starts with a terminal. In other words, all productions are of the form

$$\text{Nonterminal} \rightarrow \text{terminal(arbitrary)}$$

CHAPTER 14

Pushdown Automata

⚜ A NEW FORMAT FOR FAs

In Chapter 13, we saw that the class of languages generated by CFGs is properly larger than the class of languages defined by regular expressions. This means that all regular languages can be generated by CFGs, and so can some nonregular languages (e.g., $\{a^n b^n\}$ and PALINDROME).

After introducing the regular languages defined by regular expressions, we found a class of abstract machines (FAs) with the following dual property: For each regular language, there is at least one machine that runs successfully only on the input strings from that language and for each machine in the class, the set of words it accepts is a regular language. This correspondence was crucial to our deeper understanding of this collection of languages. The pumping lemma, complements, intersection, decidability, and so on were all learned from the machine aspect, not from the regular expression. We are now considering a different class of languages but we want to answer the same questions, so we would again like to find a machine formulation. We are looking for a mathematical model of some class of machines that correspond analogously to CFLs; that is, there should be at least one machine that accepts each CFL and the language accepted by each machine is context-free. We want CFL-recognizers or CFL-acceptors just as FAs are regular language-recognizers and -acceptors. We are hopeful that an analysis of the machines will help us understand the class of context-free languages in a deeper, more profound sense, just as an analysis of FAs led to theorems about regular languages. In this chapter, we develop such a new type of machine. In the next chapter, we prove that these new machines do indeed correspond to CFLs in the way we desire. In subsequent chapters, we shall learn that the grammars have as much to teach us about the machines as the machines do about the grammars.

To build these new machines, we start with our old FAs and throw in some new gadgets that will augment them and make them more powerful. Such an approach does not necessarily always work—a completely different design may be required—but this time it will (it is a stacked deck).

What we shall do first is develop a slightly different pictorial representation for FAs, one that will be easy to augment with the new gizmos.

We have, so far, not given a name to the part of the FA where the input string lives while it is being run. Let us call this the **INPUT TAPE.** The INPUT TAPE must be long enough for any possible input, and because any word in **a*** is a possible input, the TAPE must be infinitely long (such a tape is very expensive). The TAPE has a first location for the first letter of the input, then a second location, and so on. Therefore, we say that the TAPE is infinite in one direction only. Some people use the silly term "half-infinite" for this condition (which is like being half sober).

We draw the TAPE as shown here:

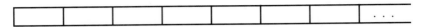

The locations into which we put the input letters are called cells. We name the cells with lowercase Roman numerals:

Below we show an example of an input TAPE already loaded with the input string *aaba*. The character Δ is used to indicate a blank in a TAPE cell.

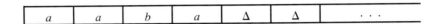

The vast majority (all but four) of the cells on the input TAPE are empty; that is, they are loaded with blanks, $\Delta\Delta$ . . . .

As we process this TAPE on the machine, we read one letter at a time and eliminate each as it is used. When we reach the first blank cell, we stop. We always presume that once the first blank is encountered, the rest of the TAPE is also blank. We read from left to right and never go back to a cell that was read before.

As part of our new pictorial representations for FAs, let us introduce the symbols

to streamline the design of the machine. The arrows (directed edges) into or out of these states can be drawn at any angle. The START state is like a − state connected to another state in a TG by a Λ-edge. We begin the process there, but we read no input letter. We just proceed immediately to the next state. A start state has no arrows coming into it.

An ACCEPT state is a shorthand notation for a dead-end final state—once entered, it cannot be left, such as

A REJECT state is a dead-end state that is not final:

Because we have used the adjective "final" to apply only to accepting states in FAs, we call the new ACCEPT and REJECT states "**halt** states." Previously, we could pass through a final state if we were not finished reading the input data; halt states cannot be traversed.

We are changing our diagrams of FAs so that every function a state performs is done by a separate box in the picture. The most important job performed by a state in an FA is to read an input letter and branch to other states depending on what letter has been read. To do this job from now on, we introduce the READ states. These are depicted as diamond-shaped boxes as shown below:

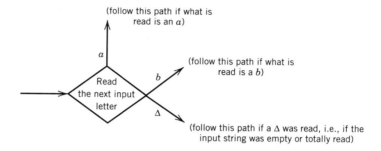

Here again, the directions of the edges in the picture above show only one of the many possibilities. When the character Δ is read from the TAPE, it means that we are out of input letters. We are then finished processing the input string. The Δ-edge will lead to ACCEPT if the state we have stopped in is a final state and to REJECT if the processing stops in a state that is not a final state. In our old pictures for FAs, we never explained how we knew we were out of input letters. In these new pictures, we can recognize this fact by reading a blank from the TAPE.

These suggestions have not altered the power of our machines. We have merely introduced a new pictorial representation that will not alter their language-accepting abilities.

The FA that used to be drawn like

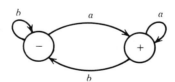

(the FA that accepts all words ending in the letter a) becomes, in the new symbolism, the machine below:

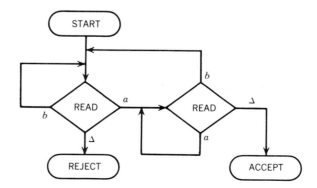

Notice that the edge from START needs no label because START reads no letter. All the other edges do require labels. We have drawn the edges as straight-line segments, not curves and loops as before. We have also used the electronic diagram notation for wires flowing into each other. For example,

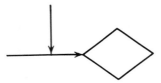

means

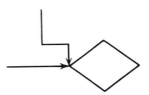

Our machine is still an FA. The edges labeled Δ are not to be confused with Λ-labeled edges. The Δ-edges lead only from READ boxes to halt states. We have just moved the $+$ and $-$ signs out of the circles that used to indicate properties of states and into adjoining ovals. The "states" are now only READ boxes and have no final/nonfinal status.

In the FA above, if we run out of input letters in the left READ state, we will find a Δ on the INPUT TAPE and so take the Δ-edge to REJECT. Reading a Δ in a READ state that corresponds to an FA final state, like the READ on the right, sends us to ACCEPT.

Let us give another example of the new pictorial notation.

EXAMPLE

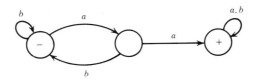

becomes

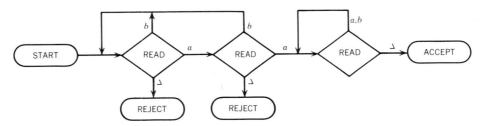

These pictures look more like the "flowcharts" we are familiar with than the old pictures for FAs did. The READ states are diamond-shaped because they are conditional branch instructions. The general study of the flowchart as a mathematical structure is part of computer theory, but beyond our intended scope.

⚜ ADDING A PUSHDOWN STACK

The reason we bothered to construct new pictures for FAs (which had perfectly good pictures already) is that it is now easier to make an addition to our machine called the **PUSHDOWN STACK,** or **PUSHDOWN STORE.** This is a concept we may have already met in a course on data structures.

A PUSHDOWN STACK is a place where input letters (or other information) can be stored until we want to refer to them again. It holds the letters it has been fed in a long column (as many letters as we want). The operation **PUSH** adds a new letter to the top of the column. The new letter is placed on top of the STACK, and all the other letters are pushed back (or down) accordingly. Before the machine begins to process an input string, the STACK is presumed to be empty, which means that every storage location in it initially contains a blank. If the STACK is then fed the letters a, b, c, d by the sequence of instructions

$$\text{PUSH } a$$
$$\text{PUSH } b$$
$$\text{PUSH } c$$
$$\text{PUSH } d$$

then the top letter in the STACK is d, the second is c, the third is b, and the fourth is a. If we now execute the instruction

$$\text{PUSH } b$$

the letter b will be added to the STACK on the top. The d will be pushed down to position 2, the c to position 3, the other b to position 4, and the bottom a to position 5.

One pictorial representation of a STACK with these letters in it is shown below. Beneath the bottom a, we presume that the rest of the STACK, which, like the INPUT TAPE, has infinitely many storage locations, holds only blanks.

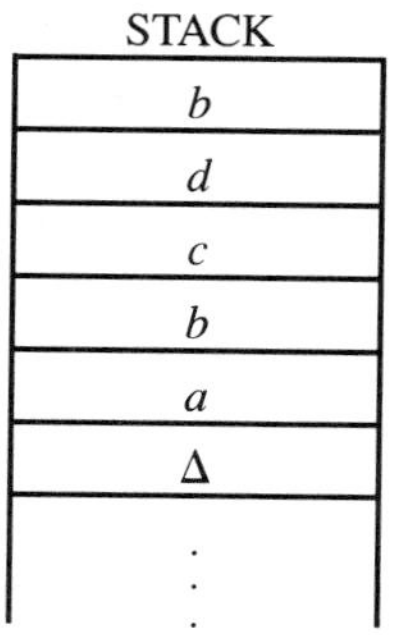

STACK

b
d
c
b
a
Δ

.
.
.

The instruction to take a letter out of the STACK is called **POP.** This causes the letter on the top of the STACK to be brought out of the STACK (popped). The rest of the letters are moved up one location each. A PUSHDOWN STACK is called a **LIFO** file, which stands for "the last in is the first out," like a narrow crowded elevator. It is not like the normal storage area of a computer, which allows random access (we can retrieve stuff from anywhere regardless of the order in which it was fed). A PUSHDOWN STACK lets us read only the top letter. If we want to read the third letter in the STACK, we must go POP, POP, POP, but then we have additionally popped out the first two letters and they are no longer in the STACK. We also have no simple instruction for determining the bottom letter in the STACK, for telling how many b's are in the STACK, and so forth. The only STACK operations allowed to us are PUSH and POP.

Popping an empty STACK, like reading an empty TAPE, gives us the blank character Δ.

We can add a PUSHDOWN STACK and the operations PUSH and POP to our new drawings of FAs by including as many as we want of the states

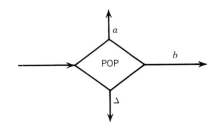

and

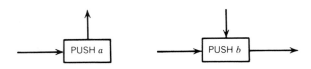

The edges coming out of a POP state are labeled in the same way as the edges from a READ state, one (for the moment) for each character that might appear in the STACK including the blank. Note that branching can occur at POP states but not at PUSH states. We can leave PUSH states only by the one indicated route, although we can enter a PUSH state from any direction.

When FAs have been souped up with a STACK and POP and PUSH states, we call them **pushdown automata,** abbreviated **PDAs.** These PDAs were introduced by Anthony G. Oettinger in 1961 and Marcel P. Schützenberger in 1963 and were further studied by Robert J. Evey, also in 1963.

The notion of a PUSHDOWN STACK as a data structure had been around for a while, but these mathematicians independently realized that when this memory structure is incorporated into an FA, its language-recognizing capabilities are increased considerably.

The precise definition will follow soon, after a few examples.

EXAMPLE

Consider the following PDA:

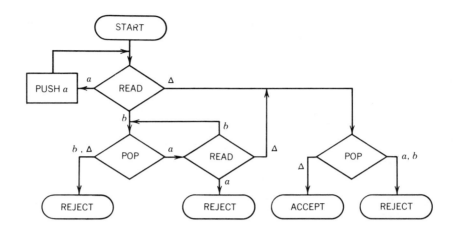

Before we begin to analyze this machine in general, let us see it in operation on the input string *aaabbb*. We begin by assuming that this string has been put on the TAPE. We always start the operation of the PDA with the STACK empty as shown:

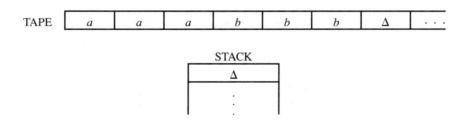

We must begin at START. From there we proceed directly into the upper left READ, a state that reads the first letter of input. This is an *a*, so we cross it off the TAPE (it has been read) and we proceed along the *a*-edge from the READ state. This edge brings us to the PUSH *a*-state that tells us to push an *a* onto the STACK. Now the TAPE and STACK look like this:

The edge from the PUSH a-box takes us back to the line feeding into the same READ box, so we return to this state. We now read another a and proceed as before along the a-edge to push it into the STACK. Again, we are returned to the READ box. Again, we read an a (our third) and, again, this a is pushed onto the STACK. The TAPE and STACK now look like this:

TAPE | $\not{a}$ | $\not{a}$ | $\not{a}$ | b | b | b | Δ | $\cdots$

STACK
| a |
| a |
| a |
| Δ |
| $\vdots$ |

After the third PUSH a, we are routed back to the same READ state again. This time, however, we read the letter b. This means that we take the b-edge out of this state down to the lower left POP. Reading the b leaves the TAPE like this:

TAPE | $\not{a}$ | $\not{a}$ | $\not{a}$ | $\not{b}$ | b | b | Δ | $\cdots$

The state POP takes the top element off the STACK. It is an a. It must be an a or a Δ because the only letters pushed onto the STACK in the whole program are a's. If it were a Δ or the impossible choice, b, we would have to go to the REJECT state. However, this time, when we pop the STACK, we get the letter a out, leaving the STACK like this:

STACK
| a |
| a |
| Δ |
| $\vdots$ |

Following the a-road from POP takes us to the other READ. The next letter on the TAPE to be read is a b. This leaves the TAPE like this:

TAPE | $\not{a}$ | $\not{a}$ | $\not{a}$ | $\not{b}$ | $\not{b}$ | b | Δ | $\cdots$

The b-road from the second READ state now takes us back to the edge feeding into the POP state. So, we pop the STACK again and get another a. The STACK is now down to only one a:

STACK
| a |
| Δ |
| $\vdots$ |

The *a*-line from POP takes us again to this same READ. There is only one letter left on the input TAPE, a *b*. We read it and leave the TAPE empty, that is, all blanks. However, the machine does not yet *know* that the TAPE is empty. It will discover this only when it next tries to read the TAPE and finds a Δ:

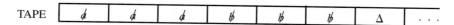

TAPE

The *b* that we just read loops us back into the POP state. We then take the last *a* from the STACK, leaving it also empty—all blanks:

STACK

Δ

The *a* takes us from POP to the right-side READ again. This time the only thing we can read from the TAPE is a blank, Δ. The Δ-edge takes us to the other POP on the right side. This POP now asks us to take a letter from the STACK, but the STACK is empty. Therefore, we say that we pop a Δ.

This means that we must follow the Δ-edge, which leads straight to the halt state ACCEPT. Therefore, the word *aaabbb* is accepted by this machine.

More than this can be observed. The language of words accepted by this machine is exactly

$$\{a^n b^n, \quad n = 0 \quad 1 \quad 2 \ldots\}$$

Let us see why.

The first part of the machine,

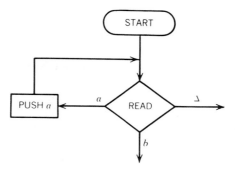

is a circuit of states that reads from the TAPE some number of *a*'s in a row and pushes them into the STACK. This is the only place in the machine where anything is pushed into the STACK. Once we leave this circuit, we cannot return, and the STACK contains everything it will ever contain.

After we have loaded the STACK with all the *a*'s from the front end of the input string, we read yet another letter from the input TAPE. If this character is a Δ, it means that the input word was of the form a^n, where *n* might have been 0 (i.e., some word in **a***).

If this is the input, we take the Δ-line all the way to the right-side POP state. This tests the STACK to see whether or not it has anything in it. If it has, we go to REJECT. If the STACK is empty at this point, the input string must have been the null word, Λ, which we accept.

Let us now consider the other logical possibility, that after loading the front *a*'s from the input (whether there are many or none) onto the STACK, we read a *b*. This must be the first *b* in the input string. It takes us to a new section of the machine into another small circuit.

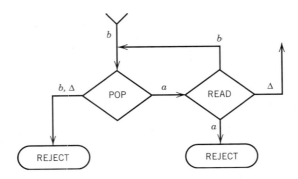

On reading this first b, we immediately pop the STACK. The STACK can contain some a's or only Δ's. If the input string started with a b, we would be popping the STACK without ever having pushed anything onto it. We would then pop a Δ and go to REJECT. If we pop a b, something impossible has happened. So, we go to REJECT and call the repairperson. If we pop an a, we go to the lower right READ state that asks us to read a new letter.

As long as we keep popping a's from the STACK to match the b's we are reading from the TAPE, we circle between these two states happily: POP a, READ b, POP a, READ b. If we pop a Δ from the STACK, it means that we ran out of STACK a's before the TAPE ran out of input b's. This Δ-edge brings us to REJECT. Because we entered this two-state circuit by reading a b from the TAPE before popping any a's, if the input is a word of the form $a^n b^n$, then the b's will run out first.

If while looping around this circuit, we hit an a on the TAPE, the READ state sends us to REJECT because this means the input is of the form

(some a's) (some b's) (another a) . . .

We cannot accept any word in which we come to an a after having read the first b. To get to ACCEPT, the second READ state must read a blank and send us to the second POP state. Reading this blank means that the word ends after its clump of b's. All the words accepted by this machine must therefore be of the form **a*b*** but, as we shall now see, only some of these words successfully reach the halt state ACCEPT.

Eventually, the TAPE will run out of letters and the READ state will turn up a blank. An input word of the form $a^n b^n$ puts n a's into the STACK. The first b read then takes us to the second circuit. After n trips around this circuit, we have popped the last a from the STACK and have read the other $(n-1)$ b's and a blank from the TAPE. We then exit this section to go to the last test.

We have exhausted the TAPE's supply of b's, so we should check to see

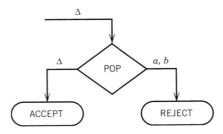

that the STACK is empty. We want to be sure we pop a Δ; otherwise, we reject the word because there must have been more a's in the front than b's in the back. For us to get to

ACCEPT, both TAPE and STACK must empty together. Therefore, the set of words this PDA accepts is exactly the language

$$\{a^n b^n, \quad n = 0 \quad 1 \quad 2 \quad 3 \ldots\}$$ ■

In the example above, we said that an a was read and then *it* was pushed onto the STACK. In reality (such as it is), the a that was read was consumed by traversing the a-edge. What was pushed was an unrelated a. PUSH states create matter out of thin air; they are not limited to what is read from the TAPE.

We have already shown that the language accepted by the PDA above could not be accepted by any FA, so pushdown automata *are* more powerful than finite automata. We can say *more* powerful because all regular languages can be accepted by some PDA because they can be accepted by some FA and an FA (in the new notation) is exactly like a PDA that never uses its STACK. Propriety dictates that we not present the formal proof of this fact until after we give the formal definition of the terms involved. We soon present the definition of PDAs (p. 307).

Let us take a moment to consider what makes these machines more powerful than FAs. The reason is that even though they too have only finitely many states to roam among, they do have an unlimited capacity for memory. It is a memory with restricted access but memory nonetheless. They can know where they have been and how often. The reason no FA could accept the language $\{a^n b^n\}$ was that for large enough n, the a^n part had to run around in a circuit and the machine could not keep track of how many times it had looped around. It could therefore not distinguish between $a^n b^n$ and some $a^m b^n$. However, the PDA has a primitive memory unit. It can keep track of how many a's are read at the beginning.

Is this mathematical model then as powerful as a whole computer? Not quite, but that goal will be reached eventually.

There are two points we must discuss. The first is that we need not restrict ourselves to using the same alphabet for input strings as we use for the STACK. In the example above, we could have read an a from the TAPE and then pushed an X into the STACK and let the X's count the number of a's. In this case, when we test the STACK with a POP state, we branch on X or Δ. The machine would then look like this:

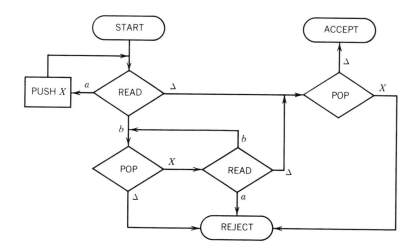

We have drawn this version of the PDA with some minor variations of display but no substantive change in function.

The READ states must provide branches for a, b, or Δ. The POP states must provide branches for X or Δ. We eliminated two REJECT states, by having all rejecting edges go into the same state.

When we do define PDAs, we shall require the specification of the TAPE alphabet Σ and the STACK alphabet Γ, which may be different. Although in Chapter 8 we used Γ to denote an output alphabet, we should not make the mistake of thinking that the STACK is an output device. It is an internal component of the PDA. We sometimes remember to call the things in Γ **characters** to distinguish them from input letters.

The second point that we should discuss is the possibility of nondeterminism. Because our goal is to produce a machine that recognizes all context-free languages just as an FA recognizes all regular languages, the addition of a simple STACK may not be enough. Consideration of the language PALINDROME will soon convince us that the new machines (PDAs) will have to be nondeterministic as well if they are to correspond to CFGs.

This is not like biology where we are discovering what is or is not part of a kangaroo; we are inventing these machines and we can put into them whatever characteristics we need. In our new notation, nondeterminism can be expressed by allowing more than one edge with the same label to leave either branching state, READ or POP.

A **deterministic PDA** is one (like the pictures we drew earlier) for which every input string has a unique path through the machine. A **nondeterministic PDA** is one for which at certain times we may have to choose among possible paths through the machine. We say that an input string is accepted by such a machine if *some* set of choices leads us to an ACCEPT state. If for *all possible* paths that a certain input string can follow it always ends at a REJECT state, then the string must be rejected. This is analogous to the definition of acceptance for nondeterministic TGs. As with TGs, nondeterminism here will also allow the possibility of too few as well as too many edges leading from a branch state. We shall have complete freedom not to put a b-edge leading out of a particular READ state. If a b is, by chance, read from the INPUT TAPE by that state, processing cannot continue. As with TGs, we say the machine **crashes** and the input is rejected. Having no b-edge leading out of a branch state (READ or POP) is the same as having exactly one b-edge that leads straight to REJECT.

We shall see that the PDAs that are equivalent to CFGs are the nondeterministic ones. For FAs, we found that nondeterminism (which gave us TGs and NFAs) did not increase the power of the machine to accept new languages. For PDAs, this is different. The following Venn diagram shows the relative power of these three types of machines:

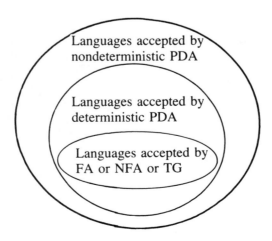

EXAMPLE

Let us introduce the language PALINDROMEX of all words of the form

$$s \; X \; \text{reverse}(s)$$

where s is any string in $(\mathbf{a} + \mathbf{b})^*$. The words in this language are

{X aXa bXb $aaXaa$ $abXba$ $baXab$ $bbXbb$ $aaaXaaa$ $aabXbaa$ . . .}

All these words are palindromes in that they read the same forward and backward. They all contain exactly one X, and this X marks the middle of the word. We can build a deterministic PDA that accepts the language PALINDROMEX. Surprisingly, it has the same basic structure as the PDA we had for the language $\{a^n b^n\}$.

In the first part of the machine, the STACK is loaded with the letters from the input string just as the initial a's from $a^n b^n$ were pushed onto the STACK. Conveniently for us, the letters go into the STACK first letter on the bottom, second letter on top of it, and so on until the last letter pushed in ends up on top. When we read the X, we know we have reached the middle of the input. We can then begin to compare the front half of the word (which is reversed in the STACK) with the back half (still on the TAPE) to see that they match.

We begin by storing the front half of the input string in the STACK with this part of the machine:

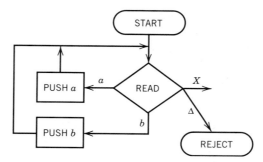

If we READ an a, we PUSH an a. If we READ a b, we PUSH a b, and on and on until we encounter the X on the TAPE.

After we take the first half of the word and stick it into the STACK, we have reversed the order of the letters and it looks exactly like the second half of the word. For example, if we begin with the input string

$$abbXbba$$

then at the moment we are just about to read the X, we have

TAPE | ∉ | ∌ | ∌ | X | b | b | a | Δ | . . .

STACK
b
b
a
Δ
⋮

Is it not amazing how palindromes seem perfect for PUSHDOWN STACKs?

When we read the X, we do not put it into the STACK. It is used up in the process of transferring us to phase two. This is where we compare what is left on the TAPE with what is in the STACK. In order to reach ACCEPT, these two should be the same letter for letter, down to the blanks.

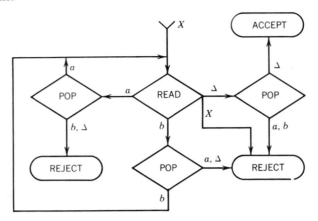

If we read an a, we had better pop an a (pop anything else and we REJECT), if we read a b, we had better pop a b (anything else and we REJECT), and if we read a blank, we had better pop a blank; when we do, we accept. If we ever read a second X, we also go to REJECT.

The machine we have drawn is deterministic. The input alphabet here is $\Sigma = \{a \quad b \quad X\}$, so each READ state has four edges coming out of it.

The STACK alphabet has two letters $\Gamma = \{a \quad b\}$, so each POP has three edges coming out of it. At each READ and each POP, there is only one direction the input can take. Each string on the TAPE generates a unique path through this PDA.

We can draw a less complicated picture for this PDA without the REJECT states if we do not mind having an input string *crash* when it has no path to follow.

The whole PDA (without REJECTs) is pictured below:

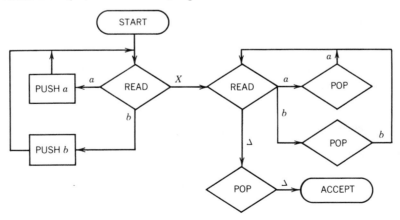

EXAMPLE

Let us now consider what kind of PDA could accept the language ODDPALINDROME. This is the language of all strings of a's and b's that are palindromes and have an odd number of letters. The words in this language are just like the words in PALINDROMEX except that the middle letter X has been changed into an a or a b.

$$\text{ODDPALINDROME} = \{a \quad b \quad aaa \quad aba \quad bab \quad bbb \ldots\}$$

The problem here is that the middle letter does not stand out, so it is harder to recognize where the first half ends and the second half begins. In fact, it is not only harder; it is impossible. A PDA, just like an FA, reads the input string sequentially from left to right and has no idea at any stage how many letters remain to be read. In PALINDROMEX, we knew that X marked the spot; now we have lost our treasure map. If we accidentally push into the STACK even one letter too many, the STACK will be larger than what is left on the TAPE and the front and back will not match. The algorithm we used to accept PALINDROMEX cannot be used without modification to accept ODDPALINDROME. We are not completely lost, though. The algorithm can be altered to fit our needs by introducing one nondeterministic jump. That we choose this approach does not mean that there is not a completely different method that might work deterministically, but the introduction of nondeterminism here seems quite naturally suited to our purpose.

Consider

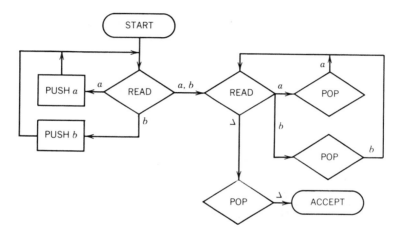

This machine is the same as the previous machine except that we have changed the X into the choice: a or b.

The machine is now nondeterministic because the left READ state has two choices for exit edges labeled a and two choices for b.

If we branch at the right time (exactly at the middle letter) along the former X-edge, we can accept all words in ODDPALINDROME. If we do not choose the right edge at the right time, the input string will be rejected even if it is in ODDPALINDROME. Let us recall, however, that for a word to be accepted by a nondeterministic machine (NFA, TG, or PDA), all that is necessary is that *some* choice of edges does lead to ACCEPT.

For every word in ODDPALINDROME, if we make the right choices, the path does lead to acceptance.

The word aba can be accepted by this machine if it follows the dotted path:

It will be rejected if it tries to push two, three, or no letters into the STACK before taking the right-hand branch to the second READ state.

We present a better method of tracking the action of a word on a PDA in the next example. ∎

Let us now consider a slightly different language.

EXAMPLE

Recall the language

$$\text{EVENPALINDROME} = \{s \; \text{reverse}(s), \quad \text{where } s \text{ is in } (\mathbf{a} + \mathbf{b})^*\}$$
$$= \{\Lambda \quad aa \quad bb \quad aaaa \quad abba \quad baab \quad bbbb \quad aaaaaa \ldots\}$$

This is the language of all palindromes with an even number of letters.
One machine to accept this language is pictured below:

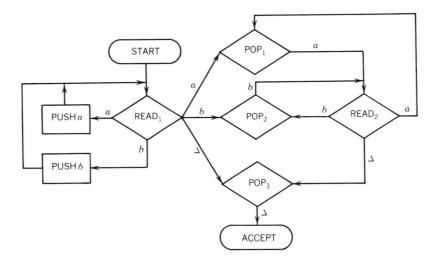

We have labeled the READ states 1 and 2 and the POP states 1, 2, and 3 so that we can identify them in discussion. These numbers do not indicate that we are to READ or POP more than one letter. They are only labels. Soda-POP, grand-POP, and POP-corn would do as well. The names will help us trace the path of an input string through the machine.

This machine is nondeterministic. At READ_1 when we read an a from the TAPE, we have the option of following an a-edge to PUSH a or an a-edge to POP_1. If we read a b in READ_1, we also have two alternatives: to go to PUSH b or to go to POP_2. If we read a Δ in READ_1, we have only one choice: to go to POP_3.

Let us take notice of what we have done here. In the PDA for PALINDROMEX, the X-edge took us into a second circuit, one that had the following form: read from TAPE → compare with STACK → read from TAPE → compare with STACK . . . . In this machine, we begin the process of "read from TAPE → compare with STACK" in READ_1. The first letter of the second half of the word is read in READ_1, then we immediately go to the POP that compares the character read with what is on top of the STACK. After this, we cycle $\text{READ}_2 \rightarrow \text{POP} \rightarrow \text{READ}_2 \rightarrow \text{POP} \rightarrow \ldots$ until both run out of letters simultaneously.

It will be easier to understand this machine once we see it in action. Let us run the string *babbab*. Initially, we have

TAPE	b	a	b	b	a	b	Δ	· · ·

STACK

Δ

$\vdots$

We can **trace** the path by which this input can be accepted by the successive rows in the table below:

STATE	STACK	TAPE
START	Δ · · ·	babbabΔ · · ·
READ₁	Δ · · ·	ƀabbabΔ · · ·
PUSH b	bΔ · · ·	ƀabbabΔ · · ·
READ₁	bΔ · · ·	ƀɑbbabΔ · · ·
PUSH a	abΔ · · ·	ƀɑbbabΔ · · ·
READ₁	abΔ · · ·	ƀɑƀbabΔ · · ·
PUSH b	babΔ · · ·	ƀɑƀbabΔ · · ·
READ₁	babΔ · · ·	ƀɑƀƀabΔ · · ·

If we are going to accept this input string, this is where we must make the jump out of the left circuit into the right circuit. The trace continues:

POP₂	abΔ · · ·	ƀɑƀƀabΔ · · ·
READ₂	abΔ · · ·	ƀɑƀƀɑbΔ · · ·
POP₁	bΔ · · ·	ƀɑƀƀɑbΔ · · ·
READ₂	bΔ · · ·	ƀɑƀƀɑƀΔ · · ·
POP₂	Δ · · ·	ƀɑƀƀɑƀΔ · · ·
READ₂	Δ · · ·	ƀɑƀƀɑƀɅ · · ·

(We have just read the first of the infinitely many blanks on the TAPE.)

POP₃	Δ · · · (Popping a blank from an empty stack still leaves blanks.)	ƀɑƀƀɑƀɅΔ · · · (Reading a blank from an empty tape still leaves blanks.)
ACCEPT	Δ · · ·	ƀɑƀƀɑƀɅ · · ·

Notice that to facilitate the drawing of this table, we have rotated the STACK so that it reads left to right instead of top to bottom.

Because this is a nondeterministic machine, there are other paths this input could have taken. However, none of them leads to acceptance.

Below we trace an unsuccessful path:

STATE	STACK	TAPE
START	Δ	*babbab*
READ$_1$ (We had no choice but to go here.)	Δ	$\not b abbab$
PUSH *b* (We could have chosen to go to POP$_2$ instead.)	*b* (We know there are infinitely many blanks underneath this *b*.)	$\not b abbab$ (Notice that the TAPE remains unchanged except by READ statements.)
READ$_1$ (We had no choice but to go here from PUSH *b*.)	*b*	$\not b \not a bbab$
POP$_1$ (Here, we exercised bad judgment and made a poor choice; PUSH *a* would have been better.)	Δ (When we pop the *b*, what is left is all Δ's.)	$\not b \not a bbab$
CRASH (This means that when we were in POP$_1$ and found a *b* on top of the STACK, we tried to take the *b*-edge out of POP$_1$. However, there is no *b*-edge out of POP$_1$.)		

Another unsuccessful approach to accepting the input *babbab* is to loop around the circuit READ$_1$ → PUSH six times until the whole string has been pushed onto the STACK. After this, a Δ will be read from the TAPE and we have to go to POP$_3$. This POP will ask if the STACK is empty. It will not be, so the path will CRASH right here.

The word Λ is accepted by this machine through the sequence

$$\text{START} \rightarrow \text{READ}_1 \rightarrow \text{POP}_3 \rightarrow \text{ACCEPT}$$ ■

As above, we shall not put all the ellipses (. . .) into the tables representing traces. We understand that the TAPE has infinitely many blanks on it without having to write

$$\not b \not a \not b babab\Delta \cdot \cdot \cdot$$

We shall see later why it is necessary to define PDAs as nondeterministic machines.

In constructing our new machines, we had to make several architectural decisions. Should we include a memory device?—yes. Should it be a stack, queue, or random access?—a stack. One stack or more?—one. Deterministic?—no. Finitely many states?—yes. Can we write on the INPUT TAPE?—no. Can we reread the input?—no. Remember that we are not trying to discover the structure of a naturally occurring creature; we are concocters trying to invent a CFL-recognizing machine. The test of whether our decisions are correct will come in the next chapter.

DEFINING THE PDA

We can now give the full definition of PDAs.

DEFINITION

A **pushdown automaton, PDA,** is a collection of eight things:

1. An alphabet Σ of input letters.
2. An input TAPE (infinite in one direction). Initially, the string of input letters is placed on the TAPE starting in cell i. The rest of the TAPE is blank.
3. An alphabet Γ of STACK characters.
4. A pushdown STACK (infinite in one direction). Initially, the STACK is empty (contains all blanks).
5. One START state that has only out-edges, no in-edges:

6. Halt states of two kinds: some ACCEPT and some REJECT. They have in-edges and no out-edges:

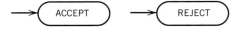

7. Finitely many nonbranching PUSH states that introduce characters onto the top of the STACK. They are of the form

where X is any letter in Γ.

8. Finitely many branching states of two kinds:
   (i) States that read the next unused letter from the TAPE

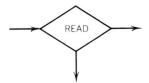

which may have out-edges labeled within letters from Σ and the blank character Δ, with no restrictions on duplication of labels and no insistence that there be a label for each letter of Σ, or Δ.

(ii) States that read the top character of the STACK

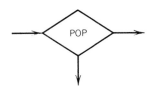

which may have out-edges labeled with the letters of Γ and the blank character Δ, again with no restrictions.

We further require that the states be connected so as to become a connected directed graph.

To **run** a string of input letters on a PDA means to begin from the START state and follow the unlabeled edges and those labeled edges that apply (making choices of edges when necessary) to produce a path through the graph. This path will end either at a halt state or will crash in a branching state when there is no edge corresponding to the letter/character read/popped. When letters are read from the TAPE or characters are popped from the STACK, they are used up and vanish.

An input string with a path that ends in ACCEPT is said to be **accepted.** An input string that can follow a selection of paths is said to be accepted if at least one of these paths leads to ACCEPT. The set of all input strings accepted by a PDA is called the **language accepted** by the PDA, or the **language recognized** by the PDA. ∎

We should make a careful note of the fact that we have allowed more than one exit edge from the START state. Because the edges are unlabeled, this branching has to be nondeterministic. We could have restricted the START state to only one exit edge. This edge could immediately lead into a PUSH state in which we would add some arbitrary symbol to the STACK, say, a *Weasel*. The PUSH *Weasel* would then lead into a POP state having several edges coming out of it all labeled *Weasel*. POP goes the *Weasel*, and we make our nondeterministic branching. Instead of this charade, we allow the START state itself to have several out-edges.

Even though these are nondeterministic like TGs, unlike TGs we do not allow edges to be labeled with words, only with single characters. Nor do we allow Λ-edges. Edges labeled with Δ are completely different.

We have not specified, as some authors do, that the STACK has to be empty at the time of accepting a word. Some go so far as to define acceptance by the STACK condition, as opposed to halt states. We shall address this point with a theorem later in this chapter.

EXAMPLE

Consider the language generated by the CFG

$$S \rightarrow S + S \,|\, S * S \,|\, 4$$

The terminals are $+$, $*$, and 4 and the only nonterminal is S.

The following PDA accepts this language:

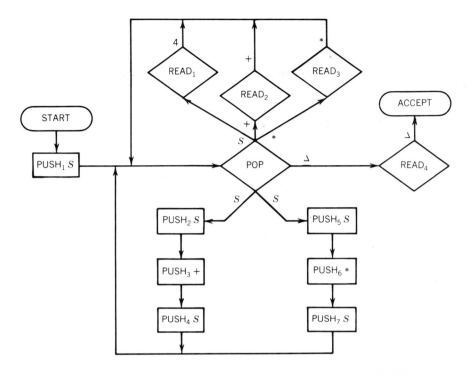

This is a funny-looking PDA with one POP, four READs, and seven PUSHs.

Instead of proving that this machine accepts exactly the language generated by this CFG, we only trace the acceptance of the string

$$4 + 4 * 4$$

This machine offers plenty of opportunity for making nondeterministic choices, almost all of them disastrous. The path we illustrate is one to acceptance.

STATE	STACK	TAPE
START	Δ	$4 + 4 * 4$
PUSH$_1$ S	S	$4 + 4 * 4$
POP	Δ	$4 + 4 * 4$
PUSH$_2$ S	S	$4 + 4 * 4$
PUSH$_3$ $+$	$+S$	$4 + 4 * 4$
PUSH$_4$ S	$S + S$	$4 + 4 * 4$
POP	$+S$	$4 + 4 * 4$
READ$_1$	$+S$	$+ 4 * 4$
POP	S	$+ 4 * 4$
READ$_2$	S	$4 * 4$
POP	Δ	$4 * 4$
PUSH$_5$ S	S	$4 * 4$

STATE	STACK	TAPE
PUSH$_6$ *	*S	4*4
PUSH$_7$ S	$S*S$	4*4
POP	*S	4*4
READ$_1$	*S	*4
POP	S	*4
READ$_3$	S	4
POP	Δ	4
READ$_1$	Δ	Δ
POP	Δ	Δ
READ$_4$	Δ	Δ
ACCEPT	Δ	Δ

Note that this time we have erased the TAPE letters read instead of striking them. ■

THEOREM 28

For every regular language L, there is some PDA that accepts it.

PROOF

We have actually discussed this matter already, but we could not formally prove anything until we had settled on the definition of a PDA.

Because L is regular, it is accepted by some FA. The constructive algorithm for converting an FA into an equivalent PDA was presented at the beginning of this chapter. ■

One important difference between a PDA and an FA is the length of the path formed by a given input. If a string of seven letters is fed into an FA, it follows a path exactly seven edges long. In a PDA, the path could be longer or shorter. The PDA below accepts the regular language of all words beginning with an a. But no matter how long the input string, the path is only one or two edges long.

Because we can continue to process the blanks on the TAPE even after all input letters have been read, we can have arbitrarily long or even infinite paths caused by very short input words. For example, the following PDA accepts only the word b, but it must follow a seven-edge path to acceptance:

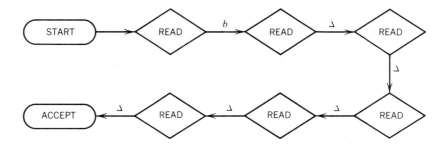

The following machine accepts all words that start with an a in a path of two edges and loops forever on any input starting with a b. (We can consider this an infinite path if we so desire.)

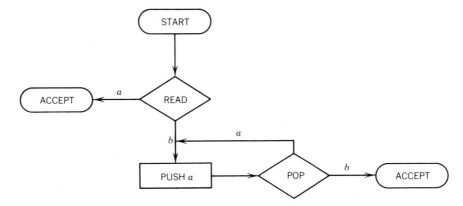

We shall be more curious about the consequences of infinite paths later.

The following result will be helpful to us in the next chapter.

THEOREM 29

Given any PDA, there is another PDA that accepts exactly the same language with the additional property that whenever a path leads to ACCEPT, the STACK and the TAPE contain only blanks.

PROOF

We present a constructive algorithm that will convert any PDA into a PDA with the property mentioned.

Whenever we have the machine part

we replace it with the following diagram:

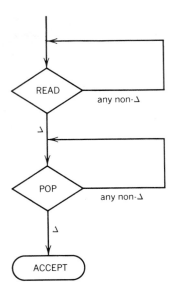

Technically speaking, we should have labeled the top loop "any letter in Σ" and the bottom loop "any character in Γ."

The new PDA formed accepts exactly the same language and finishes all successful runs with empty TAPE and empty STACK.   ■

⚜ PROBLEMS

In Problems 1 and 2, convert the following FAs into equivalent PDAs.

1.

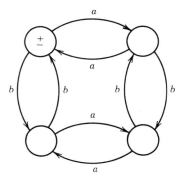

2.

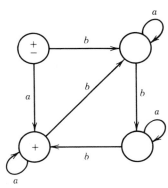

For Problems 3 and 4, consider the deterministic PDA:

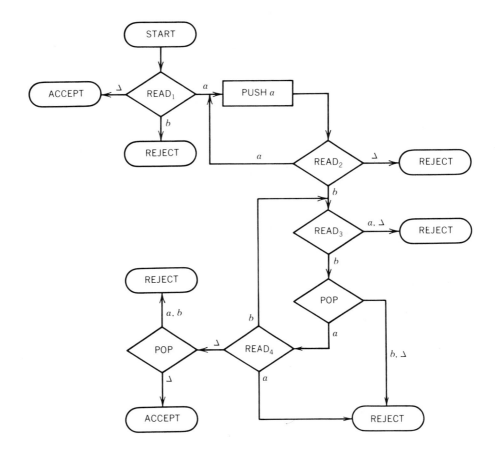

3. Using a trace table like those in this chapter, show what happens to the INPUT TAPE and STACK as each of the following words proceeds through the machine:

(i) *abb*
(ii) *abab*
(iii) *aabb*
(iv) *aabbbb*

4. (i) What is the language accepted by this PDA?
(ii) Find a CFG that generates this language.
(iii) Is this language regular?

5. Consider the following PDA:

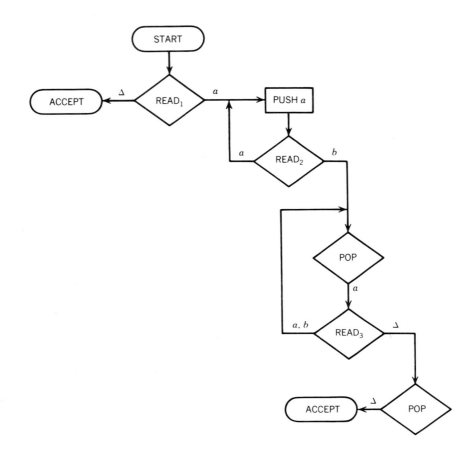

Trace the following words on this PDA:

(i) *aaabbb*
(ii) *aaabab*
(iii) *aaabaa*
(iv) *aaaabb*

6. (i) Prove that the language accepted by the machine in Problem 5 is

$$L = \{a^n S, \quad \text{where } S \text{ starts with } b \text{ and length}(S) = n\}$$

(ii) Find a CFG that defines the language in part (i).
(iii) Prove that the language of the machine in Problem 5 is not regular.

Consider the following PDA:

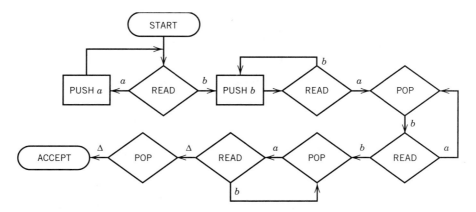

7. (i) This PDA is deterministic so it should be no problem to trace the inputs *aababb* and *abbbaaab* on it. Show that they lead to ACCEPT.
   (ii) Explain how this machine accepts the language $\{a^n b^m a^m b^n$, where n and m are independent integers, 2, 1$\}$.

8. (i) Show that the language $a^n b^m a^m b^n$ is context-free.
   (ii) Show that this language is nonregular.

   For Problems 9 through 11, consider the following nondeterministic PDA:

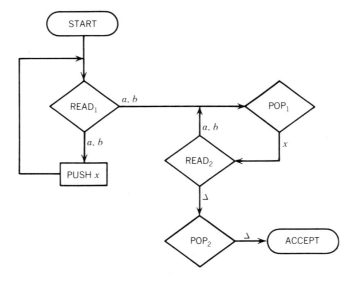

   In this machine, REJECT occurs when a string crashes. Notice here that the STACK alphabet is $\Gamma = \{x\}$.

9. (i) Show that the string *ab* can be accepted by this machine by taking the branch from $READ_1$ to POP_1 at the correct time.
   (ii) Show that the string *bbba* can also be accepted by giving the trace that shows when to take the branch.

10. Show that this PDA accepts the language of all words with an even number of letters (excluding Λ). Remember, it is also necessary to show that all words with odd length can never lead to ACCEPT.

11. Here we have a nondeterministic PDA for a language that could have been accepted by an FA. Find such an FA. Find a CFG that generates this language.

For Problems 12 and 13, consider the following nondeterministic PDA:

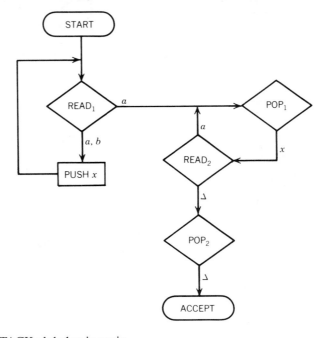

Here, the STACK alphabet is again

$$\Gamma = \{x\}$$

12. (i) Show that the word aa can be accepted by this PDA by demonstrating a trace of its path to ACCEPT.
    (ii) Show that the word $babaaa$ can be accepted by this PDA by demonstrating a trace of its path indicating exactly where we must take the branch from $READ_1$ to $READ_2$.
    (iii) Show that the string $babaaab$ cannot be accepted.
    (iv) Show that the string $babaaaa$ cannot be accepted.

13. Show that the language of this machine is

$$\text{TRAILINGCOUNT} = \{sa^{\text{length}(s)}\}$$
$$= \{\text{any string } s \text{ followed by as many } a\text{'s as } s \text{ has letters}\}$$

We know that this language is not regular from Chapter 10, Problem 4, that there is a CFG that generates it from Chapter 12, Problem 13.

14. Build a deterministic PDA to accept the language $\{a^n b^{n+1}\}$. (As always, when unspecified, the condition on n is assumed to be $n = 1, 2, 3, \ldots$.)

15. Let the input alphabet be $\Sigma = \{a \quad b \quad c\}$ and L be the language of all words in which all the a's come before the b's and there are the same number of a's as b's and arbitrarily

many c's that can be in front, behind, or among the a's and b's. Some words in L are *abc*, *caabcb*, *ccacaabcccbccbc*.

   (i) Write out all the words in this language with six or fewer letters.
   (ii) Show that the language L is not regular.
  (iii) Find a PDA (deterministic) that accepts L.
  (iv) Find a CFG that generates L.

16. Find a PDA (nondeterministic) that accepts all PALINDROME where the alphabet is $\Sigma = \{a \quad b\}$ by combining the EVENPALINDROME part with the ODDPALINDROME PDA. This is not the same machine for PALINDROME as produced in the next chapter—so do not cheat.

17. We have seen that an FA with N states can be converted into an equivalent PDA with N READ states (and no POP states). Show that for any FA with N states there is some PDA with only one READ state (and several POP states), but that uses N different STACK symbols and accepts the same language.

18. Let L be some regular language in which all the words happen to have an even length. Let us define the new language Twist(L) to be the set of all the words of L twisted, where by twisted we mean the first and second letters have been interchanged, the third and fourth letters have been interchanged, and so on. For example, if

$$L = \{ba \quad abba \quad babb \ \ . \ . \ .\}$$
$$\text{Twist}(L) = \{ab \quad baab \quad abbb \ \ . \ . \ .\}$$

Build a PDA that accepts Twist(L)

19. Given any language L that does not include Λ, let us define its cousin language $|L|$ as follows: For any string of a's and b's, if the word formed by concatenating the second, fourth, sixth, . . . letters of this string is a word in L, then the whole string is a word in $|L|$. For instance, if *bbb* is a word in L, then *ababbbb* and *bbababa* are both words in $|L|$.

   (i) Show that if there is some PDA that accepts L, then there is some PDA that accepts $|L|$.
  (ii) If L is regular, is $|L|$ necessarily regular too?

20. Let L be the language of all words that have the same number of a's and b's and that, as we read them from left to right, never have more b's than a's. For example,

$$abaaabbabb$$

is good but

$$abaabbba$$

is no good because at a certain point we had four b's but only three a's.

   In Chapter 10, Problem 19, we proved that this language is nonregular when we called it PARENTHESES.

   All the words in L with six letters are

$$aaabbb \quad aababb \quad aabbab$$
$$abaabb \quad ababab$$

   (i) Write out all the words in L with eight letters (there are 14).
   (ii) Find a PDA that accepts L.
  (iii) Prove that L is not regular.
  (iv) Find a CFG that defines L.

CHAPTER 15

CFG = PDA

♣ BUILDING A PDA FOR EVERY CFG

We are now ready to prove that the set of all languages accepted by PDAs is the same as the set of all languages generated by CFGs.

We prove this in two steps.

THEOREM 30

Given a CFG that generates the language L, there is a PDA that accepts exactly L.

THEOREM 31

Given a PDA that accepts the language L, there exists a CFG that generates exactly L.

These two important theorems were both discovered independently by Schützenberger, Chomsky, and Evey.

PROOF OF THEOREM 30

The proof will be by constructive algorithm. From Theorem 26 in Chapter 13 (p. 278), we can assume that the CFG is in CNF. (The problem of Λ will be handled later.)

Before we describe the algorithm that associates a PDA with a given CFG in its most general form, we shall illustrate it on one particular example. Let us consider the following CFG in CNF:

$$S \rightarrow SB$$
$$S \rightarrow AB$$
$$A \rightarrow CC$$
$$B \rightarrow b$$
$$C \rightarrow a$$

We now propose the following nondeterministic PDA:

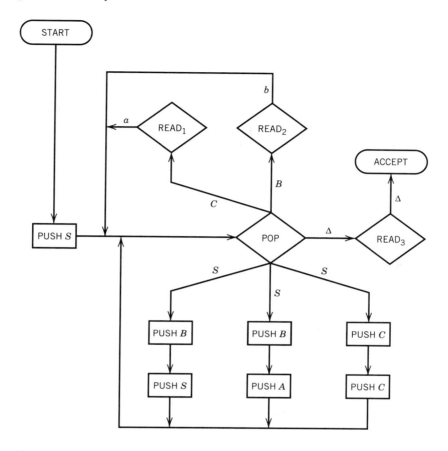

In this machine, the STACK alphabet is

$$\Gamma = \{S \quad A \quad B \quad C\}$$

whereas the TAPE alphabet is only

$$\Sigma = \{a \quad b\}$$

We begin by pushing the symbol S onto the top of the STACK. We then enter the busiest state of this PDA, the central POP. In this state, we read the top character of the STACK.

The STACK will always contain nonterminals exclusively. Two things are possible when we pop the top of the STACK. Either we replace the removed nonterminal with two other nonterminals, thereby simulating a production (these are the edges pointing downward), or else we do not replace the nonterminal at all but instead we go to a READ state, which insists we read a specific terminal from the TAPE or else it crashes (these edges point upward). To get to AC-CEPT, we must have encountered READ states that wanted to read exactly those letters that were originally on the INPUT TAPE in their exact order. We now show that to do this means we have simulated a leftmost derivation of the input string in this CFG.

Let us consider a specific example. The word *aab* can be generated by leftmost derivation in this grammar as follows:

Working-String Generation	Production Used	
$S \Rightarrow AB$	$S \rightarrow AB$	Step 1
$\Rightarrow CCB$	$A \rightarrow CC$	Step 2

$$\Rightarrow aCB \qquad C \rightarrow a \qquad \text{Step 3}$$
$$\Rightarrow aaB \qquad C \rightarrow a \qquad \text{Step 4}$$
$$\Rightarrow aab \qquad B \rightarrow b \qquad \text{Step 5}$$

In CNF, all working strings in leftmost derivations have the form

(string of terminals) (string of Nonterminals)

To run this word on this PDA, we must follow the same sequence of productions, keeping the STACK contents at all times the same as the string of nonterminals in the working string of the derivation.

We begin at START with

STACK		TAPE
Δ		aab

Immediately, we push the symbol S onto the STACK:

STACK		TAPE
S		aab

We then head into the central POP. The first production we must simulate is $S \rightarrow AB$. We pop the S and then we PUSH B, PUSH A, arriving at this:

STACK		TAPE
AB		aab

Note that the contents of the STACK are the same as the string of nonterminals in the working string of the derivation after step 1.

We again feed back into the central POP. The production we must now simulate is an $A \rightarrow CC$. This is done by popping the A and following the path PUSH C, PUSH C.

The situation is now

STACK		TAPE
CCB		aab

Notice that here again, the contents of the STACK are the same as the string of nonterminals in the working string of the derivation after step 2.

Again, we feed back into the central POP. This time we must simulate the production $C \rightarrow a$. We do this by popping the C and then reading the a from the TAPE. This leaves

STACK		TAPE
CB		ȼab

We do not keep any terminals in the STACK, only the nonterminal part of the working string. Again, the STACK contains the string of nonterminals in step 3 of the derivation. However, the terminal that would have appeared in front of these in the working string has been cancelled from the front of the TAPE. Instead of keeping the terminals in the STACK, we erase them from the INPUT TAPE to ensure a perfect match.

The next production we must simulate is another $C \rightarrow a$. Again, we POP C and READ a. This leaves

STACK	TAPE
B	a̸a̸b

Here again, we can see that the contents of the STACK are the string of nonterminals in the working string in step 4 of the derivation. The whole working string is *aaB*; the terminal part *aa* corresponds to what has been struck from the TAPE.

This time when we enter the central POP, we simulate the last production in the derivation, $B \rightarrow b$. We pop the *B* and read the *b*. This leaves

STACK	TAPE
Δ	a̸a̸b̸

This Δ represents the fact that there are no nonterminals left in the working string after step 5. This, of course, means that the generation of the word is complete.

We now reenter the POP, and we must make sure that both STACK and TAPE are empty:

$$POP\ \Delta \rightarrow READ_3 \rightarrow ACCEPT$$

The general principle is clear. To accept a word, we must follow its leftmost derivation from the CFG. If, in some CFG, the word is

ababbbaab

and at some point in its leftmost Chomsky derivation, we have the working string

ababbZWV

then at this point in the corresponding PDA-processing the status of the STACK and TAPE should be

STACK	TAPE
ZWV	a̸b̸a̸b̸b̸baab

the used-up part of the TAPE being the string of terminals and the contents of the STACK being the string of nonterminals of the working string. This process continues until we have derived the entire word. We then have

STACK	TAPE
Δ	a̸b̸a̸b̸b̸b̸a̸a̸b̸

At this point, we POP Δ, go to READ₃, and ACCEPT.

There is noticeable nondeterminism in this machine at the POP state. This parallels, reflects, and simulates the nondeterminism present in the process of generating a word. In a leftmost derivation, if we are to replace the nonterminal *N*, we have one possibility for each production that has *N* as the left side. Similarly, in this PDA we have one path leaving POP for each of these possible productions. Just as the one set of productions must generate any word in the language, the one machine must have a path to accept any legal word once it sits on the INPUT TAPE. The point is that the choices of which lines to take out of the central POP tell us how to generate the word through leftmost derivation, because each branch represents a production.

It should also be clear that any input string that reaches ACCEPT has gotten there by having each of its letters read by simulating Chomsky productions of the form

$$\text{Nonterminal} \rightarrow \text{terminal}$$

This means that we have necessarily formed a complete leftmost derivation of this word through CFG productions with no nonterminals left over in the STACK. Therefore, every word accepted by this PDA is in the language of the CFG.

One more example may be helpful. Consider the randomly chosen CFG (in CNF) below:

$$S \rightarrow AB \qquad B \rightarrow AB \qquad B \rightarrow a$$
$$A \rightarrow BB \qquad A \rightarrow a \qquad B \rightarrow b$$

We propose the following PDA:

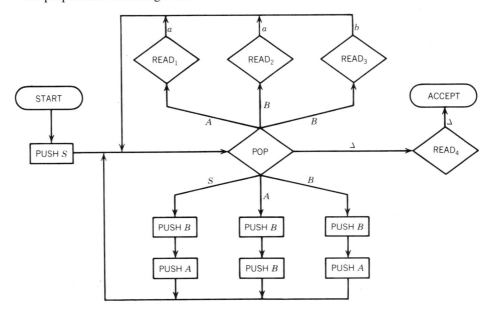

We shall trace simultaneously how the word *baaab* can be generated by this CFG and how it can be accepted by this PDA.

LEFTMOST DERIVATION	STATE	STACK	TAPE
	START	Δ	*baaab*
S	PUSH S	S	*baaab*
	POP	Δ	*baaab*
	PUSH B	B	*baaab*
$\Rightarrow AB$	PUSH A	AB	*baaab*
	POP	B	*baaab*
	PUSH B	BB	*baaab*
$\Rightarrow BBB$	PUSH B	BBB	*baaab*
	POP	BB	*baaab*

LEFTMOST DERIVATION	STATE	STACK	TAPE
$\Rightarrow bBB$	READ$_3$	BB	̶baaab
	POP	B	̶baaab
	PUSH B	BB	̶baaab
$\Rightarrow bABB$	PUSH A	ABB	̶baaab
	POP	BB	̶baaab
$\Rightarrow baBB$	READ$_1$	BB	̶b/aab
	POP	B	̶b̶aaab
$\Rightarrow baaB$	READ$_2$	B	̶b̶a̶aab
	POP	Δ	̶b̶a̶aab
	PUSH B	B	̶b̶a̶aab
$\Rightarrow baaAB$	PUSH A	AB	̶b̶a̶aab
	POP	B	̶b̶a̶aab
$\Rightarrow baaaB$	READ$_1$	B	̶b̶a̶a̶ab
	POP	Δ	̶b̶a̶a̶ab
$\Rightarrow baaab$	READ$_3$	Δ	̶b̶a̶a̶a̶b
	POP	Δ	̶b̶a̶a̶a̶b
	READ$_4$	Δ	̶b̶a̶a̶a̶b
	ACCEPT	Δ	̶b̶a̶a̶a̶b

At every stage, we have the following equivalence:

> Working string
>   = (letters cancelled from TAPE) (string of Nonterminals from STACK)

At the beginning, this means

> Working string $= S$
> Letters cancelled $=$ none
> String of Nonterminals in STACK $= S$

At the end, this means

> Working string $=$ the whole word
> Letters cancelled $=$ all
> STACK $= \Delta$

Now that we understand this example, we can give the rules for the general case.

ALGORITHM

If we are given a CFG in CNF as follows:

$$X_1 \rightarrow X_2 X_3$$
$$X_1 \rightarrow X_3 X_4$$

$$X_2 \rightarrow X_2 X_2$$
$$\cdot \; \cdot \; \cdot$$
$$X_3 \rightarrow a$$
$$X_4 \rightarrow a$$
$$X_5 \rightarrow b$$
$$\cdot \; \cdot \; \cdot$$

where the start symbol $S = X_1$ and the other nonterminals are $X_2, X_3, \ldots$, we build the following machine.

Begin with

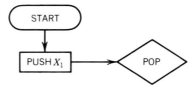

For each production of the form

$$X_i = X_j X_k$$

we include this circuit from the POP back to itself:

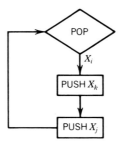

For all productions of the form

$$X_i \rightarrow b$$

we include this circuit:

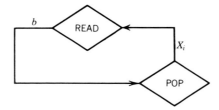

When the stack is finally empty, which means we have converted our last nonterminal to a terminal and the terminals have matched the INPUT TAPE, we follow this path:

From the reasons and examples given above, we know that all words generated by the

CFG will be accepted by this machine and all words accepted will have leftmost derivations in the CFG.

This does not quite finish the proof. We began by assuming that the CFG was in CNF, but there are some context-free languages that cannot be put into CNF. They are the languages that include the word Λ. In this case, we can convert all productions into one of the two forms acceptable to CNF, while the word Λ must still be included.

To include this word, we need to add another circuit to the PDA, a simple loop at the POP:

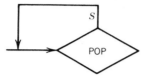

This kills the nonterminal S without replacing it with anything and the next time we enter the POP, we get a blank and proceed to accept the word. ■

EXAMPLE

The language PALINDROME (including Λ) can be generated by the following CFG in CNF (plus one Λ-production):

$$
\begin{array}{ll}
S \rightarrow AR_1 & S \rightarrow a \\
R_1 \rightarrow SA & S \rightarrow b \\
S \rightarrow BR_2 & A \rightarrow a \\
R_2 \rightarrow SB & B \rightarrow b \\
S \rightarrow AA & S \rightarrow \Lambda \\
S \rightarrow BB &
\end{array}
$$

The PDA that the algorithm in the proof of Theorem 30 instructs us to build is

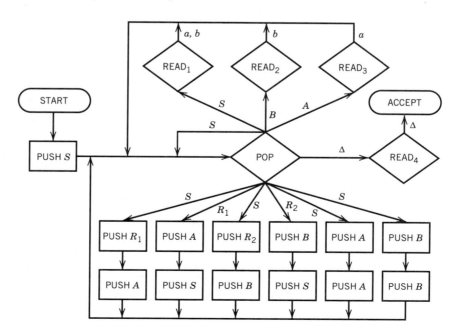

Let us examine how the input string *abaaba* is accepted by this PDA.

LEFTMOST DERIVATION	STATE	TAPE	STACK
	START	abaaba	Δ
	PUSH S	abaaba	S
	POP	abaaba	Δ
	PUSH R_1	abaaba	R_1
$S \Rightarrow AR_1$	PUSH A	abaaba	AR_1
	POP	abaaba	R_1
$\Rightarrow aR_1$	READ$_3$	ȧbaaba	R_1
	POP	ȧbaaba	Δ
	PUSH A	ȧbaaba	A
$\Rightarrow aSA$	PUSH S	ȧbaaba	SA
	POP	ȧbaaba	A
	PUSH R_2	ȧbaaba	R_2A
$\Rightarrow aBR_2A$	PUSH B	ȧbaaba	BR_2A
	POP	ȧbaaba	R_2A
$\Rightarrow abR_2A$	READ$_2$	ȧḃaaba	R_2A
	POP	ȧḃaaba	A
	PUSH B	ȧḃaaba	BA
$\Rightarrow abSBA$	PUSH S	ȧḃaaba	SBA
	POP	ȧḃaaba	BA
	PUSH A	ȧḃaaba	ABA
$\Rightarrow abAABA$	PUSH A	ȧḃaaba	AABA
	POP	ȧḃaaba	ABA
$\Rightarrow abaABA$	READ$_3$	ȧḃȧaba	ABA
	POP	ȧḃȧaba	BA
$\Rightarrow abaaBA$	READ$_3$	ȧḃȧȧba	BA
	POP	ȧḃȧȧba	A
$\Rightarrow abaabA$	READ$_2$	ȧḃȧȧḃa	A
	POP	ȧḃȧȧḃa	Δ
$\Rightarrow abaaba$	READ$_3$	ȧḃȧȧḃȧΔ	Δ
	POP	ȧḃȧȧḃȧΔ	Δ
	READ$_4$	ȧḃȧȧḃȧΔ	Δ
	ACCEPT	ȧḃȧȧḃȧΔ	Δ

Notice how different this is from the PDAs we developed in Chapter 14 for the languages EVENPALINDROME and ODDPALINDROME. ∎

⚜ BUILDING A CFG FOR EVERY PDA

Now we have to prove the other half of the equivalence theorem, that every language accepted by a PDA is context-free.

PROOF OF THEOREM 31

This is a long proof by constructive algorithm. In fact, it is unquestionably the most torturous proof in this book; parental consent is required. We shall illustrate each step with a particular example. It is important, though, to realize that the algorithm we describe operates successfully on all PDAs and we are not merely proving this theorem for one example alone.

The requirements for a proof are that it convinces and explains. The following arguments should do both if we are sufficiently perseverant.

Before we can convert a PDA into a CFG, we have to convert it into a standard form, which we call **conversion form**. To achieve this conversion form, it is necessary for us to introduce a new "marker state" called a **HERE** state. We can put the word HERE into a box shaped like a READ state in the middle of any edge and we say that we are passing through that state any time we travel on the edge that it marks. Like the READ and POP states, the HERE states can be numbered with subscripts.

One use of a HERE state is so that

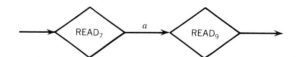

can become

Notice that a HERE state does not read the TAPE nor pop the STACK. It just allows us to describe being on the edge as being in a state. A HERE state is a legal fiction—a state with no status, but we do permit branching to occur at such points. Because the edges leading out of HERE states have no labels, this branching is necessarily nondeterministic.

DEFINITION   (inside the proof of Theorem 31)

A PDA is in **conversion form** if it meets all the following conditions:

1. There is only one ACCEPT state.
2. There are no REJECT states.
3. Every READ or HERE is followed immediately by a POP; that is, every edge leading out of any READ or HERE state goes directly into a POP state.

4. No two POPs exist in a row on the same path without a READ or HERE between them whether or not there are any intervening PUSH states. (POPs must be separated by READs or HEREs.)

5. All branching, deterministic, or nondeterministic, occurs at READ or HERE states, none at POP states, and every edge has only one label (no multiple labels).

6. Even before we get to START, a "bottom of STACK" symbol, $, is placed on the STACK. If this symbol is ever popped in the processing, it must be replaced immediately. The STACK is never popped beneath this symbol. Right before entering ACCEPT, this symbol is popped out and left out.

7. The PDA must begin with the sequence

8. The entire input string must be read before the machine can accept the word.   ■

It is now our job to show that all the PDAs as we defined them before can be made over into conversion form without affecting the languages they accept.

Condition 1 is easy to accommodate. If we have a PDA with several ACCEPT states, let us simply erase all but one of them and have all the edges that formerly went into the others feed into the one remaining.

Condition 2 is also easy. Because we are dealing with nondeterministic machines, if we are at a state with no edge labeled with the character we have just read or popped, we simply crash. For an input string to be accepted, there must be a safe path to ACCEPT; the absence of such a path is tantamount to REJECT. Therefore, we can erase all REJECT states and the edges leading to them without affecting the language accepted by the PDA.

Now let us consider condition 3. A READ in a certain PDA might not have a POP immediately following it; we might find something like this:

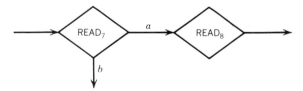

What we do is insert a POP and immediately put back on the STACK whatever might have been removed by this additional POP.

We need to have a PUSH for every letter of Γ every time we do this:

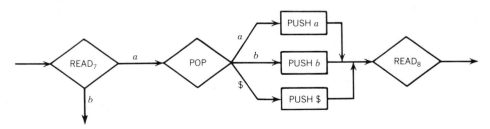

This looks like a silly waste of states, but it does mean that we can satisfy condition 3 without changing the language accepted.

We may need to insert some HERE states to satisfy condition 4:

becomes

To satisfy condition 5, we must convert all branching at POP states into branching at READ or HERE states. This is done as follows:

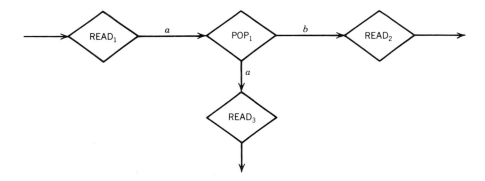

becomes

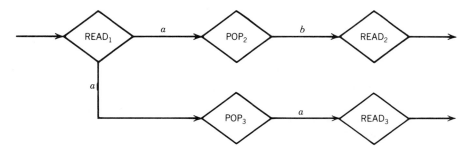

If the POP_1 state in the original picture was going to pop a b and branch to $READ_2$, then in the following modified version, its path through the machine must be the one that at $READ_1$ takes the a-edge to POP_2, not the a-edge to POP_3. If an a was going to be popped by POP_1, the path to POP_3 has to be taken to avoid crashing. All paths through these two segments of PDAs are the same, but in the second picture the deterministic branching at POP_1 has been replaced by nondeterministic branching at $READ_1$.

We must also modify the funny extra POP x–PUSH x situations that we introduced for condition 3. Instead of using

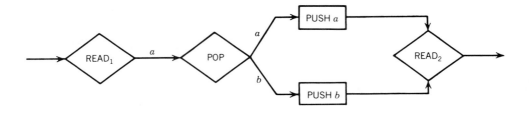

which entailed branching at the POP state, we must use the equivalent:

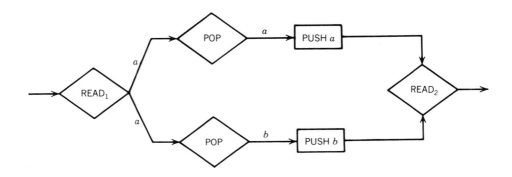

Instead of a deterministic branch at a POP state, we have made a nondeterministic branch at a READ or HERE state.

Condition 6 is another easy one. We simply presume that the STACK initially looks like

STACK

$
Δ

When we change a PDA into conversion form, we must also remember that instead of popping a Δ from an empty STACK, we shall find the symbol $. If we wanted (for some reason) to POP several Δ's off of an empty STACK, we shall have to be satisfied with several POP $-PUSH $ combinations. They work just as well.

If we ever have a PDA that wants to accept an input string without emptying the whole STACK (including $), we could just insert some states that empty the STACK harmlessly right before the ACCEPT, exactly as we did in the proof of Theorem 29 (p. 311).

Condition 7 makes no new demands if the STACK already satisfies condition 6. Condition 8 can be satisfied by the algorithm of Theorem 29 from Chapter 14.

Now let us take a whole PDA and change it into conversion form. The PDA we use is one that accepts the language

$$\{a^{2n}b^n\} = \{aab \quad aaaabb \quad aaaaaabbb \ldots\}$$

The PDA is

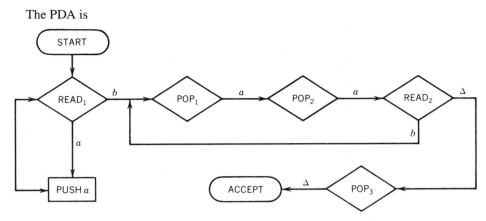

Every a from the beginning of the INPUT TAPE is pushed onto the STACK. Then for every b that follows, two a's are popped. Acceptance comes if both TAPE and STACK empty at the same time. The words accepted must therefore be of the form $a^{2n}b^n$ for $n = 1, 2, 3, \ldots$.

Here, we have already deleted the REJECT state and useless READ and POP alternative edges. To make this PDA satisfy all the conditions for conversion form, we must remake it into

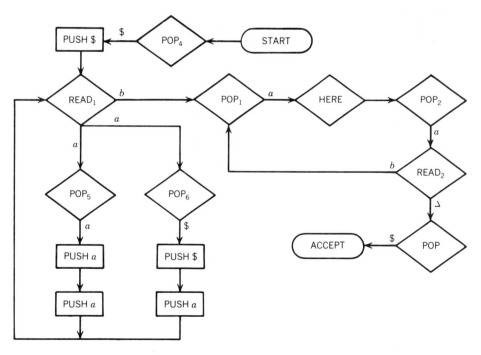

To begin with, we must start with the sequence demanded by condition 7. This makes us insert a new POP state called POP_4. Now in the original machine, we began a circuit $READ_1$–PUSH a–$READ_1$–PUSH a . . . . Because of condition 3, every READ must be followed by a POP so the pair $READ_1$–PUSH a must become $READ_1$–POP_5--PUSH a–PUSH a. The first PUSH is to return the a that was popped out. The second PUSH $adds$ the a to the STACK. The first time through this loop, the top of the STACK does not contain an a yet and what is popped is the \$, which must immediately be returned to the STACK.

This is the purpose of the nondeterministic branch POP_6–PUSH $\$$–PUSH a. This branch also *adds* an a to the STACK. This branch will be taken the first time out of $READ_1$, but if ever again, it will cause a CRASH and lead to the acceptance of no new words.

The next violation of conversion form in the original picture was that POP_1 was immediately followed by POP_2 without a READ in between. This is fixed by inserting a HERE. (There is only one HERE state in this whole machine, so there is no reason to number it.)

The last change is that instead of POP_3 finding a blank, it should find the stack-end symbol $\$$.

The new form of this PDA obviously accepts exactly the same language as before, $\{a^{2n}b^n\}$.

Now that we have put this PDA into conversion form, we can explain why we ever wanted to impose these eight conditions on a poor helpless machine. Any PDA in conversion form can be considered as a collection of primitive parts, or **path segments,** each of the following form:

FROM	TO	READ	POP	PUSH
START or READ or HERE	READ or HERE or ACCEPT	One or no input letters	Exactly one STACK character	Any string onto the STACK

The states START, READ, HERE, and ACCEPT are called the **joints** of the machine. Between two consecutive joints on a path, exactly one character is popped and any arbitrary number can be pushed. Because no edge has a multiple label, between any two joints the machine can read no letters at all from the INPUT TAPE or else exactly one specified letter. This was the purpose of imposing all the conversion conditions.

The PDA above can be drawn as a set of joints with "arcs" (path segments) between them much like a TG:

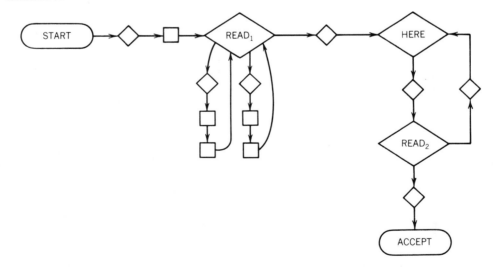

Once a PDA is in conversion form, we can describe the entire machine as a list of all the primitive joint-to-joint path segments (the "arcs" mentioned above). Such a list is called a **summary table.** A summary table for a PDA satisfies the same purpose as a transition table for an FA. It explains the total action on the inputs without recourse to pictorial representation. This may seem like a step backward, because the pictures make more sense than the tables—which is why we do not commonly use tables for FAs. However, for the purpose of completing the proof of Theorem 31 (which is what we are still in the midst of doing), the summary table will be very useful.

The PDA we have just converted corresponds to the following summary table:

FROM Where	TO Where	READ What	POP What	PUSH What	ROW Number
START	READ$_1$	Λ	$	$	1
READ$_1$	READ$_1$	a	$	$a$$	2
READ$_1$	READ$_1$	a	a	aa	3
READ$_1$	HERE	b	a	—	4
HERE	READ$_2$	Λ	a	—	5
READ$_2$	HERE	b	a	—	6
READ$_2$	ACCEPT	Δ	$	—	7

In the last column we have assigned a number to each row for our future purposes. Each path segment corresponds to one row of the table.

Notice that in Row$_2$ we summarized

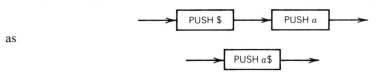

as

because it means add the $ first, then the a.

In our definition of conversion form, we made sure that all branching occurs at the joints READ and HERE. This means that no branching can occur in the middle of any row of the summary table.

Every word that can be accepted by the PDA corresponds to some path from START to ACCEPT. We can view these paths as made up not of the components "edges" but of the components "rows of summary table." A path is then broken into a sequence of these path segments.

For example, in the PDA above the word $aaaabb$ can be accepted by the machine through the path

START–POP$_4$–PUSH $–READ$_1$–POP$_6$–PUSH $–PUSH a–READ$_1$–POP$_5$–PUSH
a–PUSH a–READ$_1$–POP$_5$–PUSH a–PUSH a–READ$_1$–POP$_5$–PUSH a–PUSH
a–READ$_1$–POP$_1$–HERE–POP$_2$–READ$_2$–POP$_1$–HERE–POP$_2$–READ$_2$–POP$_3$–ACCEPT

This is a nondeterministic machine, and there are other paths that this input could take, but they all crash somewhere; only this path leads to acceptance. Instead of this long list of states, we could describe the path of this word through the machine as a sequence of rows from the summary table. The path above can be described as

Row$_1$–Row$_2$–Row$_3$–Row$_3$–Row$_3$–Row$_4$–Row$_5$–Row$_6$–Row$_5$–Row$_7$

Let us repeat that acceptance by a PDA is determined by the existence of a path from START to ACCEPT. In FAs, paths correspond in a natural fashion to strings of letters. In a PDA paths correspond in a natural way to strings of rows from the summary table.

The approach that we have taken for PDAs is to define them originally by a pictorial representation and imagine a correspondence between input strings and paths through the machine-graph. To abstract the grammar (CFG) of the language that the PDA accepts, we have had to begin by changing our PDAs first into conversion form and then into summary tables. This is to make an algebraic nonpictorial representation of our PDAs that we can then convert into a grammar. Most authors define PDAs originally as summary tables of some kind and the pictorial representations as directed graphs are rarely given. The proof of Theorem 31 in such a treatment is much shorter, because the proof can begin at the point we have just reached. Something is lost, though, in not seeing a PDA as a picture. This is best illustrated by comparing the preceding summary table with the first pictorial representation of the PDA. It is much easier to understand the looping and the language from the picture.

As definitions, both the pictures and the tables describe the same type of language-accepting device. The question of which is superior cannot be answered without knowing the specific application. Our application is education and the most understandable formulation is the best.

Notice that the HERE state reads nothing from the TAPE, so we have put Λ in the "READ What" column. We could put a dash or a ϕ there just as well. A blank (Δ) would be wrong, because it means something else; to say that we read a Δ means the TAPE must be empty. A Λ on the other hand means, by convention, that we do not read the TAPE.

The order in which we put the rows in the summary table does not matter as long as every path segment of the PDA between two consecutive joints is represented as some row.

The summary table carries in it all the information that is found in the pictorial representation of the PDA. Every path through the PDA is a sequence of rows of the summary table. However, not every sequence of rows from the summary table represents a viable path. Right now it is very important for us to determine which sequences of rows *do* correspond to possible paths through the PDA, because the *paths* are directly related to the language accepted.

Some sequences of rows are impossible; for example, we cannot immediately follow Row_4 with Row_6 because Row_4 leaves us in HERE, while Row_6 begins in READ_2. We must always be careful that the end joints connect up logically.

This requirement is necessary but not sufficient to guarantee that a sequence of rows can be a path. Row_1 leaves us in READ_1 and Row 3 starts in READ_1, yet $\text{Row}_1 - \text{Row}_3$ cannot be the beginning of a path. This is because Row_1 pushes a $, whereas Row_3, which pops an a, obviously presumes that the top of the STACK is an a. We must have some information about the STACK before we can string together rows.

Even if we arranged the rows so that the pushes and pops match up, we still might get into trouble. A path formed by a sequence of rows with four Row_3's and six Row_5's is impossible. This is true for a subtle reason. Six Row_5's will pop six a's from the STACK; however, because Row_2 can only be used once to obtain one a in the STACK and four Row_3's can contribute only four more a's to the STACK, we are short one a.

The question of which sequences of rows make up a path is very tricky. To represent a path, a sequence of rows must be **joint-consistent** (the rows meet up end to end) and **STACK-consistent** (when a row pops a character, it should be there, at the top of the STACK).

Let us now define the **row language** of a particular PDA represented by a summary table. It is the language whose alphabet letters are the names of the rows in the summary table:

$$\Sigma = \{\text{Row}_1 \quad \text{Row}_2 \quad \ldots \quad \text{Row}_7\}$$

and has as legal words all those sequences of alphabet letters that correspond to paths from START to ACCEPT that might possibly be followed by some input strings, that is, all sequences from START to ACCEPT that are joint-consistent and STACK-consistent.

Clearly, all valid words in this language begin with Row_1 and end with Row_7, but as we saw above, there are more requirements than just those.

Consider, for example,

$$\text{Row}_5\text{Row}_5\text{Row}_3\text{Row}_6$$

This is a string of length 4, but this string is not a word in the row language for three reasons: (1) It does not represent a path that begins with START or ends with ACCEPT; (2) it is not joint-consistent; (3) it is not STACK-consistent.

Not only are we going to look for rules to tell us which strings of rows are words, but we shall produce a CFG for the row language. From this CFG, we can produce another CFG, a grammar for the language of strings of a's and b's accepted by the original PDA.

Let us pause here to outline the global strategy of this proof:

1. We start with any PDA drawn as defined in Chapter 14.

2. We redraw the PDA to meet the requirements of conversion form.

3. From the machine in conversion form, we build a summary table and number the rows.

4. Every word accepted by the PDA corresponds to at least one path from START to ACCEPT and, as we shall soon see, every STACK-consistent path from START to ACCEPT corresponds to some word. Therefore, we define the row language to be the set of all sequences of rows that correspond to paths.

5. We determine a CFG that generates all the words in the row language.

6. We convert this CFG for the row language into a CFG that generates all the words in the original language of a's and b's that are accepted by the PDA, thus proving Theorem 31.

We are now up to step 5.

We had to build half this house before we could take our first look at the blueprints.

One thing we have to do is to keep track of the contents of the STACK. Since we are going to want to produce a CFG that generates the row language, we need to introduce nonterminals that contain the information we need to ensure joint- and STACK-consistency. We have to know about the beginning and end positions of the path segments to which certain row strings correspond and about the contents of the STACK. It is not necessary to maintain any information about what characters are read from the TAPE. If what is on the TAPE is what the rows want to read, then the input string will be accepted. Once we know what the rows are, we can find an input word that gives them what they want to read. We shall see the implications of this observation later, but every joint- and STACK-consistent path actually is the path through the PDA taken by some input string.

The nonterminals in the row language grammar have the following form:

$$\text{Net}(X, Y, Z)$$

where the X and Y can be any joint; START, READ, HERE, or ACCEPT, and Z is any character from the stack alphabet Γ. This whole expression is *one* nonterminal even though it is at least 10 printer's symbols long. These odd nonterminals stand for the following:

There is some path going from joint X *to joint* Y, *perhaps passing through some other joints (READ or HERE states), which has the net effect on the STACK of removing the symbol* Z, *where by "net effect" we mean that although there might be extra things put onto the STACK during the path, they are eventually removed and the STACK is never popped below the initial* Z *that is on the top of the STACK to begin with, and that is popped out somewhere along the way.*

We have never seen a nonterminal be such a complicated-looking item as $\text{Net}(X, Y, Z)$, but we have had nonterminals before with meanings that could be expressed in a sentence (as in the CFG for EQUAL).

This complicated description of the "net effect" on the STACK means, for instance, that the sequence of the STACK operations:

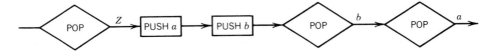

has the net effect of popping one Z because it represents these stack states:

The net STACK effect is the same as the simple POP Z, and no character was presumed to be in the STACK below the top Z. The symbol "?" here represents the unknown and unexamined part of the STACK. The picture

by itself is also an acceptable sequence for a STACK operation governed by a nonterminal $\text{Net}(X, Y, Z)$.

However,

is not, because it presupposes knowledge about what is in the STACK under the top Z. If there were a b under the Z initially, this sequence would fail (crash). We never presume knowledge of what is available in the STACK in the statement $\text{Net}(X, Y, Z)$ beyond knowing that Z is on top.

For a given PDA, some sets of all the possible sentences $\text{Net}(X, Y, Z)$ are true and some are false. Our job, given a PDA, is to determine which Net statements are true and how they fit together. To do this, we must first examine every row of the table to see which ones have the net effect of popping exactly one letter. There are other paths that are composed of several rows that can also be described by a single Net statement, but we shall discover these by a separate procedure later.

Let us recall the summary table that we have developed for the PDA for the language $\{a^{2n}b^n\}$. Row_4 of this table says essentially

$$\text{Net}(\text{READ}_1, \text{HERE}, a)$$

which means, "We can go from READ_1 to HERE at the total cost of popping an a from the top of the stack."

In other words, Row_4 is a single Net row. However, let us suppose that we have a row in the summary table for some arbitrary PDA that looks like this:

FROM	TO	READ	POP	PUSH	ROW
READ$_9$	READ$_3$	b	b	abb	11

As it stands, Row$_{11}$ is not a Net-style sentence because the trip from READ$_9$ to READ$_3$ does not subtract one letter from the STACK; the net effect is rather that it adds two. However, there is a particular way that Row$_{11}$ can interact with some other Net-style sentences. For instance, if we knew that the following three nonterminals could be realized as path segments for this machine

$$\text{Net(READ}_3, \text{READ}_7, a) \text{ Net(READ}_7, \text{READ}_1, b) \text{ Net(READ}_1, \text{READ}_8, b)$$

then, using Row$_{11}$, we could conclude that the nonterminal

$$\text{Net(READ}_9, \text{READ}_8, b)$$

could also be realized as a path segment. This is because we can go first from READ$_9$ to READ$_3$ using Row$_{11}$, which eats the b at the top of the STACK but leaves the letters abb in its place, with the net effect of adding ab. The first a takes us from READ$_3$ to READ$_7$ by the path implied by Net(READ$_3$, READ$_7$, a). The next b takes us from READ$_7$ along some path to READ$_1$, as guaranteed by Net(READ$_7$, READ$_1$, b). Then the last b takes us from READ$_1$ to READ$_8$ by some path guaranteed by the last Net. The total cost of the trip has been the top b. Thanks to the abb we added, during this whole trip we have never popped the STACK beneath the top b.

Let us write this as

$$\text{Net(READ}_9, \text{READ}_8, b)$$
$$\rightarrow \text{Row}_{11}\text{Net(READ}_3, \text{READ}_7, a)\text{Net(READ}_7, \text{READ}_1, b)\text{Net(READ}_1, \text{READ}_8, b)$$

In other words, the sentence that says that we can go from READ$_9$ to READ$_8$ at the cost of b can be replaced by the concatenation of the sentences Row$_{11}$, Net . . . Net . . . Net . . . .

This will be a production in our row language. We begin with the nonterminal Net(READ$_9$, READ$_8$, b), and we produce a string that has one terminal, Row$_{11}$, and some nonterminals, Net . . . Net . . . Net . . . . Notice that Row$_{11}$ takes us from READ$_9$ to READ$_3$, the first Net from READ$_3$ to READ$_7$, the second from READ$_7$ to READ$_1$, and the last from READ$_1$ to READ$_8$, giving us the trip promised on the left side of the production at the appropriate cost.

This hypothetical Row$_{11}$ that we are presuming exists for some PDA could also be used in other productions—for example,

$$\text{Net(READ}_9, \text{READ}_{10}, b)$$
$$\rightarrow \text{Row}_{11}\text{Net(READ}_3, \text{READ}_2, a)\text{Net(READ}_2, \text{READ}_2, b)\text{Net(READ}_2, \text{READ}_{10}, b)$$

assuming, of course, that these additional Net's are available, by which we mean realizable by actual paths.

The general formulation for creating productions from rows of the summary table is as follows:

If the summary table includes the row

FROM	TO	READ	POP	PUSH	ROW
READ$_x$	READ$_y$	u	w	$m_1m_2, \ldots, m_n$	i

then for any sequence of joint states, $S_1, S_2, \ldots, S_n$, we include the row language CFG production

$$\text{Net}(\text{READ}_x, S_n, w) \rightarrow \text{Row}_i \text{Net}(\text{READ}_y, S_1, m_1) \ \ldots \ \text{Net}(S_{n-1}, S_n, m_n)$$

This is a great number of productions and a large dose of generality all at once. Let us illustrate the point on an outrageous, ludicrous example.

Suppose that someone offered us a ride from Philadelphia to L.A. if we would trade him our old socks for his sunglasses and false teeth. We would say "terrific" because we could then go from Philadelphia to Denver for the price of the old socks. How? First, we get a ride to L.A. by trading the socks to him for the sunglasses and false teeth. Then, we find someone who will drive us from L.A. to Chicago for a pair of sunglasses and another nice guy who will drive us from Chicago to Denver for a pair of false teeth.

FROM	TO	READ	POP	PUSH	ROW
Phil.	L.A.	anything	socks	sunglasses, false teeth	77

$$\text{Net}(\text{Phil., Denver, socks}) \rightarrow \text{Row}_{77}\text{Net}(\text{L.A., Chi., shades})\text{Net}(\text{Chi., Denver, teeth})$$

The fact that we have written this production does not mean that it can ever be part of the derivation of an actual word in the row language. The idea might look good on paper, but where do we find the clown who will drive us from Chicago to Denver for the used choppers?

So too with the other productions formed by this general rule.

We can replace Net(this and that) with Net(such and such), but can we ever boil it all down to a string of rows? We have seen in working with CFGs in general that replacing one nonterminal with a string of others does not always lead to a word in the language.

In the example of the PDA for which we built the summary table, Row_3 says that we can go from READ_1 back to READ_1 and replace an a with aa. This allows the formation of many productions of the form

$$\text{Net}(\text{READ}_1, X, a) \rightarrow \text{Row}_3\text{Net}(\text{READ}_1, Y, a)\text{Net}(Y, X, a)$$

where X and Y could be READ_1, READ_2, or READ_3—or even HERE. Also, X could be ACCEPT, as in this possibility:

$$\text{Net}(\text{READ}_1, \text{ACCEPT}, a) \rightarrow \text{Row}_3\text{Net}(\text{READ}_1, \text{READ}_2, a)\text{Net}(\text{READ}_2, \text{ACCEPT}, a)$$

There are three rules for creating productions in what we shall prove is a CFG for the row language of a PDA presented to us in a summary table.

Rule 1　We have the nonterminal S, which starts the whole show, and the production

$$S \rightarrow \text{Net}(\text{START, ACCEPT, \$})$$

which means that we can consider any total path through the machine as a trip from START to ACCEPT at the cost of popping one symbol, $, and never referring to the STACK below $.

This rule is the same for all PDAs.

Rule 2　For every row of the summary table that has no PUSH entry, such as

FROM	TO	READ	POP	PUSH	ROW
X	Y	anything	Z	—	i

we include the production

$$\text{Net}(X, Y, Z) \rightarrow \text{Row}_i$$

This means that $\text{Net}(X, Y, Z)$, which stands for the hypothetical trip from X to Y at the net cost Z, is really possible by using Row_i alone. It is actualizable in this PDA.

Let us remember that because this is the row language we are generating, this production is in the form

$$\text{Nonterminal} \rightarrow \text{terminal}$$

In general, we have no guarantee that there are any such rows that push nothing, but if no row decreases the size of the STACK, it can never become empty and the machine will never accept any words.

For completeness we restate the expansion rule above.

Rule 3   For each row in the summary table that has some PUSH, we introduce a whole family of productions. For every row that pushes n characters onto the STACK, such as

FROM	TO	READ	POP	PUSH	ROW
X	Y	anything	Z	$m_1, \ldots, m_n$	i

for *all sets* of n READ, HERE, or ACCEPT states $S_1, \ldots,$, we create the productions

$$\text{Net}(X, S_n, Z) \rightarrow \text{Row}_i \text{Net}(Y, S_1, m_1) \ \ldots \ \text{Net}(S_{n-1}, S_n, m_n)$$

Remember the fact that we are creating productions does not mean that they are all useful in the generation of words. We merely want to guarantee that we get *all* the useful productions, and the useless ones will not hurt us.

No other productions are necessary.

We shall prove in a moment that these are all the productions in the CFG defining the row language. That is, the language of all sequences of rows representing every word accepted by the machine can be generated by these productions from the start symbol S.

Many productions come from these rules. As we have observed, not all of them are used in the derivation of words because some of these Net variables can never be realized as actual paths, just as we could include the nonterminal Net(NY, L.A., 5¢) in the optimistic hope that some airline will run a great sale. Only those nonterminals that can be replaced eventually by strings of solid terminals will ever be used in producing words in the row language. This is like the case with this CFG:

$$S \rightarrow X \mid Y$$
$$X \rightarrow aXX$$
$$Y \rightarrow ab$$

The production $X \rightarrow aXX$ is totally useless in producing words.

We shall now prove that this CFG with all the Net's is exactly the CFG for the row language. To do that, we need to show two things: First, every string generated by the CFG is a string of rows representing an actual path through the PDA from START to ACCEPT and, second, all the paths corresponding to accepted input strings are equivalent to row words generated by this CFG.

Before we consider this problem in the abstract, let us return to the concrete illustration of the summary table for the PDA that accepts

$$\{a^{2n}b^n\}$$

We shall make a complete list of all the productions that can be formed from the rows of the summary table using the three preceding rules.

Rule 1, always, gives us only the production

PROD 1 $S \rightarrow$ Net(START, ACCEPT, $)

Rule 2 applies to rows 4, 5, 6, and 7, creating the productions

PROD 2   Net(READ$_1$, HERE, a) $\rightarrow$ Row$_4$
PROD 3   Net(HERE, READ$_2$, a) $\rightarrow$ Row$_5$
PROD 4   Net(READ$_2$, HERE, a) $\rightarrow$ Row$_6$
PROD 5   Net(READ$_2$, ACCEPT, $) $\rightarrow$ Row$_7$

Finally, Rule 3 applies to rows 1, 2, and 3. When applied to Row$_1$, it generates

Net(START, X, $) $\rightarrow$ Row$_1$Net(READ$_1$, X, $)

where X can take on the different values READ$_1$, READ$_2$, HERE, or ACCEPT. This gives us these four new productions:

PROD 6   Net(START, READ$_1$, $) $\rightarrow$ Row$_1$Net(READ$_1$, READ$_1$, $)
PROD 7   Net(START, READ$_2$, $) $\rightarrow$ Row$_1$Net(READ$_1$, READ$_2$, $)
PROD 8   Net(START, HERE, $) $\rightarrow$ Row$_1$Net(READ$_1$, HERE, $)
PROD 9   Net(START, ACCEPT, $) $\rightarrow$ Row$_1$Net(READ$_1$, ACCEPT, $)

When applied to Row$_2$, Rule 3 generates

Net(READ$_1$, X, $) $\rightarrow$ Row$_2$Net(READ$_1$, Y, a)Net(Y, X, $)

where X can be any joint state but START, and Y can be any joint state but START or ACCEPT (because we cannot return to START or leave ACCEPT).

The new productions derived from Row$_2$ are of the form above with all possible values for X and Y:

PROD 10   Net(READ$_1$, READ$_1$, $)
             $\rightarrow$ Row$_2$Net(READ$_1$, READ$_1$, a)Net(READ$_1$, READ$_1$, $)
PROD 11   Net(READ$_1$, READ$_1$, $)
             $\rightarrow$ Row$_2$Net(READ$_1$, READ$_2$, a)Net(READ$_2$, READ$_1$, $)
PROD 12   Net(READ$_1$, READ$_1$, $)
             $\rightarrow$ Row$_2$Net(READ$_1$, HERE, a)Net(HERE, READ$_1$, $)
PROD 13   Net(READ$_1$, READ$_2$, $)
             $\rightarrow$ Row$_2$Net(READ$_1$, READ$_1$, a)Net(READ$_1$, READ$_2$, $)
PROD 14   Net(READ$_1$, READ$_2$, $)
             $\rightarrow$ Row$_2$Net(READ$_1$, READ$_2$, a)Net(READ$_2$, READ$_2$, $)
PROD 15   Net(READ$_1$, READ$_2$, $)
             $\rightarrow$ Row$_2$Net(READ$_1$, HERE, a)Net(HERE, READ$_2$, $)
PROD 16   Net(READ$_1$, HERE, $)
             $\rightarrow$ Row$_2$Net(READ$_1$, READ$_1$, a)Net(READ$_1$, HERE, $)

PROD 17   Net(READ$_1$, HERE, \$)
            $\rightarrow$ Row$_2$Net(READ$_1$, READ$_2$, a)Net(READ$_2$, HERE, \$)
PROD 18   Net(READ$_1$, HERE, \$)
            $\rightarrow$ Row$_2$Net(READ$_1$, HERE, a)Net(HERE, HERE, \$)
PROD 19   Net(READ$_1$, ACCEPT, \$)
            $\rightarrow$ Row$_2$Net(READ$_1$, READ$_1$, a)Net(READ$_1$, ACCEPT, \$)
PROD 20   Net(READ$_1$, ACCEPT, \$)
            $\rightarrow$ Row$_2$Net(READ$_1$, READ$_2$, a)Net(READ$_2$, ACCEPT, \$)
PROD 21   Net(READ$_1$, ACCEPT, \$)
            $\rightarrow$ Row$_2$Net(READ$_1$, HERE, a)Net(HERE, ACCEPT, \$)

When Rule 3 is applied to Row$_3$, it generates productions of the form

$$\text{Net(READ}_1, X, a) \rightarrow \text{Row}_3\text{Net(READ}_1, Y, a)\text{Net}(Y, X, a)$$

where X can be READ$_1$, READ$_2$, HERE, or ACCEPT and Y can only be READ$_1$, READ$_2$, or HERE.

This gives 12 new productions:

PROD 22   Net(READ$_1$, READ$_1$, a)
            $\rightarrow$ Row$_3$Net(READ$_1$, READ$_1$, a)Net(READ$_1$, READ$_1$, a)
PROD 23   Net(READ$_1$, READ$_1$, a)
            $\rightarrow$ Row$_3$Net(READ$_1$, READ$_2$, a)Net(READ$_2$, READ$_1$, a)
PROD 24   Net(READ$_1$, READ$_1$, a)
            $\rightarrow$ Row$_3$Net(READ$_1$, HERE, a)Net(HERE, READ$_1$, a)
PROD 25   Net(READ$_1$, READ$_2$, a)
            $\rightarrow$ Row$_3$Net(READ$_1$, READ$_1$, a)Net(READ$_1$, READ$_2$, a)
PROD 26   Net(READ$_1$, READ$_2$, a)
            $\rightarrow$ Row$_3$Net(READ$_1$, READ$_2$, a)Net(READ$_2$, READ$_2$, a)
PROD 27   Net(READ$_1$, READ$_2$, a)
            $\rightarrow$ Row$_3$Net(READ$_1$, HERE, a)Net(HERE, READ$_2$, a)
PROD 28   Net(READ$_1$, HERE, a)
            $\rightarrow$ Row$_3$Net(READ$_1$, READ$_1$, a)Net(READ$_1$, HERE, a)
PROD 29   Net(READ$_1$, HERE, a)
            $\rightarrow$ Row$_3$Net(READ$_1$, READ$_2$, a)Net(READ$_2$, HERE, a)
PROD 30   Net(READ$_1$, HERE, a)
            $\rightarrow$ Row$_3$Net(READ$_1$, HERE, a)Net(HERE, HERE, a)
PROD 31   Net(READ$_1$, ACCEPT, a)
            $\rightarrow$ Row$_3$Net(READ$_1$, READ$_1$, a)Net(READ$_1$, ACCEPT, a)
PROD 32   Net(READ$_1$, ACCEPT, a)
            $\rightarrow$ Row$_3$Net(READ$_1$, READ$_2$, a)Net(READ$_2$, ACCEPT, a)
PROD 33   Net(READ$_1$, ACCEPT, a)
            $\rightarrow$ Row$_3$Net(READ$_1$, HERE, a)Net(HERE, ACCEPT, a)

This is the largest CFG we have ever tried to handle. We have

         7 terminals: Row$_1$, Row$_2$, . . . , Row$_7$
29 nonterminals: S, 16 of the form Net(, , \$)
                        12 of the form Net(, , a)
   33 productions: PROD 1, . . . , PROD 33

We know that not all these will occur in an actual derivation starting at S. For example, Net(READ$_2$, ACCEPT, a) cannot happen, because to go from READ$_2$ to ACCEPT, we must pop a \$, not an a.

To see which productions can lead toward words, let us begin to draw the leftmost total language tree of the row language. By "leftmost" we mean that from every working-string node we make one branch for each production that applies to the leftmost nonterminal. Branching only on the leftmost nonterminal avoids considerable duplication without losing any words of the language, because all words that can be derived have leftmost derivations (Theorem 27 on p. 284).

In this case, the tree starts simply as

$$S$$
$$\downarrow$$
$$\text{Net(START, ACCEPT, \$)} \tag{1}$$
$$\downarrow$$
$$\text{Row}_1\text{Net(READ}_1\text{, ACCEPT, \$)} \tag{1, 9}$$

This is because the only production that has S as its left-hand side is PROD 1. The only production that applies after that is PROD 9. The numbers in parentheses at the right show which sequence of productions was used to arrive at each node in the tree. The leftmost (and only) nonterminal now is Net(READ$_1$, ACCEPT, $). There are exactly three productions that can apply here: PROD 19, PROD 20, and PROD 21. So, the tree now branches as follows:

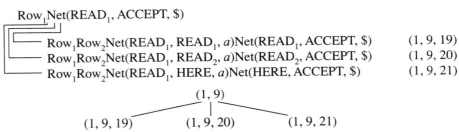

Row$_1$Net(READ$_1$, ACCEPT, $)

Row$_1$Row$_2$Net(READ$_1$, READ$_1$, a)Net(READ$_1$, ACCEPT, $)	(1, 9, 19)
Row$_1$Row$_2$Net(READ$_1$, READ$_2$, a)Net(READ$_2$, ACCEPT, $)	(1, 9, 20)
Row$_1$Row$_2$Net(READ$_1$, HERE, a)Net(HERE, ACCEPT, $)	(1, 9, 21)

(1, 9)

(1, 9, 19)   (1, 9, 20)   (1, 9, 21)

Let us consider the branch (1, 9, 19). Here, the leftmost nonterminal is Net(READ$_1$, READ$_1$, a). The productions that apply to this nonterminal are PROD 22, PROD 23, and PROD 24. Application of PROD 23 gives us an expression that includes Net(READ$_2$, READ$_1$, a), but there is no production for which this Net is the left-hand side. (This corresponds to the fact that there are no paths from READ$_2$ to READ$_1$ in this PDA.) Therefore, PROD 23 can never be used in the formation of a word in this row language.

This is also true of PROD 24, which creates the expression Net(HERE, READ$_1$, a). No matter how many times we apply PROD 22, we still have a factor of Net(READ$_1$, READ$_1$, a). There is no way to remove this nonterminal from a working string. Therefore, any branch incorporating this nonterminal can never lead to a string of only terminals. The situation is similar to this CFG:

$$S \rightarrow b \mid X$$
$$X \rightarrow aX$$

We can never get rid of the X. So, we get no words from starting with $S \rightarrow X$. Therefore, we might as well drop this nonterminal from consideration.

We could produce just as many words in the row language if we dropped PROD 22, PROD 23, and PROD 24. Therefore, we might as well eliminate PROD 19, because this created the situation that led to these productions, and it can give us no possible lines, only hopeless ones. We now see that we might as well drop the whole branch (1, 9, 19).

Now let us examine the branch (1, 9, 20). The leftmost nonterminal here is Net(READ$_1$, READ$_2$, a). The productions that apply to this nonterminal are PROD 25, PROD 26, and PROD 27.

Of these, PROD 25 generates a string that involves Net(READ$_1$, READ$_1$, a), which we saw before led to the death of the branch (1, 9, 19). So, PROD 25 is also poison.

We have no reason at the moment not to apply PROD 26 or PROD 27. The tree, therefore, continues:

$$(1, 9, 20)$$

Row$_1$Row$_2$Row$_3$Net(READ$_1$, READ$_2$, a)Net(READ$_2$, READ$_2$, a)Net(READ$_2$, ACCEPT, $)   (1, 9, 20, 26)
Row$_1$Row$_2$Row$_3$Net(READ$_1$, HERE, a)Net(HERE, READ$_2$, a)Net(READ$_2$, ACCEPT, $)   (1, 9, 20, 27)

$$(1, 9, 20)$$

$$(1, 9, 20, 26) \qquad (1, 9, 20, 27)$$

Let us continue the process along one branch of the tree:

$$(1, 9, 20, 27)$$
$$\downarrow$$
Row$_1$Row$_2$Row$_3$Row$_4$Net(HERE, READ$_2$, a)Net(READ$_2$, ACCEPT, $)   (1, 9, 20, 27, 2)
$$\downarrow$$
Row$_1$Row$_2$Row$_3$Row$_4$Row$_5$Net(HERE, ACCEPT, $)   (1, 9, 20, 27, 2, 3)
$$\downarrow$$
Row$_1$Row$_2$Row$_3$Row$_4$Row$_5$Row$_7$ (1, 9, 20, 27, 2, 3, 5)

This is the shortest word in the entire row language. The total language tree is infinite.

In this particular case, the proof that this is the CFG for the row language is easy, and it reflects the ideas in the general proof that the CFG formed by the three rules we stated is the desired CFG.

For one thing, it is clear that every derivation from these rules is a sequence of rows of the summary table that is joint- and STACK-consistent and therefore represents a real path through the PDA.

Now we have to explain why every path through the PDA is derivable from the set of productions that these rules create.

Every word accepted by the PDA is accepted through some path. Every particular path is associated with a specific sequence of STACK fluctuations (like a stock value going up and down). Every fluctuation is a Net nonterminal. It is either directly the equivalent of a Row terminal (if it represents a simple segment in the path), or it can be broken down into a sequence of smaller STACK fluctuations. There are rules of production that parallel this decomposition which break the Net nonterminal into a sequence of the other corresponding Net nonterminals. These smaller fluctuations, in turn, can continue to be resolved until we hit only nondecomposable Row terminals, and this sequence of terminals is the path. Therefore, every path through the PDA can be generated from our grammar.

Let us recapitulate the algorithm:

1. Starting with any PDA as defined in the previous section, we can convert it into conversion form without changing its language.

2. From conversion form, we can build a summary table that has all the information about the PDA broken into rows, each of which describes a simple path between joint states (READ, HERE, START, and ACCEPT). The rows are of the form

FROM	TO	READ	POP	PUSH	ROW

3. There is a set of rules describing how to create a CFG for the language whose words are all the row sequences corresponding to all the paths through the PDA that can be taken by input strings on their way to acceptance.

The rules create productions of three forms:

Rule 1 $S \rightarrow$ Net(START, ACCEPT, $)

Rule 2 $\text{Net}(X, Y, Q) \rightarrow \text{Row}_i$

Rule 3 $\text{Net}(A, B, C) \rightarrow \text{Row}_i \text{Net}(A, X, Y) \ \ldots \ \text{Net}(Q, B, W)$

What we need now to complete the proof of Theorem 31 is to create the CFG that generates the *language* accepted by the PDA—not just its row language which is the path language, but the language of strings of a's and b's.

We can finish this off in one simple step. In the summary table, every row had an entry that we have ignored until now, that is, the READ column.

Every row reads a, b, Λ, or Δ from the INPUT TAPE. There is no ambiguity because an edge from a READ state cannot have two labels. So, every row sequence corresponds to a sequence of letters read from the INPUT TAPE. We can convert the row language into the language of the PDA by adding to the CFG for the row language the set of productions created by a new rule, Rule 4.

Rule 4   For every row

FROM	TO	READ	POP	PUSH	ROW
A	B	C	D	$EFGH$	I

create the production

$$\text{Row}_I \rightarrow C$$

For example, in the summary table for the PDA that accepts that language $\{a^{2n}b^n\}$, we have seven rows. Therefore, we create the following seven new productions:

PROD 34 $\text{Row}_1 \rightarrow \Lambda$
PROD 35 $\text{Row}_2 \rightarrow a$
PROD 36 $\text{Row}_3 \rightarrow a$
PROD 37 $\text{Row}_4 \rightarrow b$
PROD 38 $\text{Row}_5 \rightarrow \Lambda$
PROD 39 $\text{Row}_6 \rightarrow b$
PROD 40 $\text{Row}_7 \rightarrow \Delta$

The symbols, Row_1, Row_2, . . . that used to be terminals in the row language are now nonterminals. From every row sequence we can produce a word. For example,

$$\text{Row}_1 \text{Row}_2 \text{Row}_3 \text{Row}_4 \text{Row}_5 \text{Row}_7$$

becomes

$$\Lambda aab \Lambda \Delta$$

Treating Δ like a Λ (to be painfully technical, by the production $\Delta \rightarrow \Lambda$), we have the word

$$aab$$

Clearly, this word can be accepted by this PDA by following the path

$$\text{Row}_1 - \text{Row}_2 - \text{Row}_3 - \text{Row}_4 - \text{Row}_5 - \text{Row}_7$$

The derivations of the words from the productions of this CFG not only tell us which words are accepted by this PDA, but also indicate a *path* by which the words may be accepted, which may be useful information.

Remember that because this is a nondeterministic machine, there may be several paths that accept the same word. But for every legitimate word there will be at least one complete path to ACCEPT.

The language generated by this CFG is exactly the language accepted by the PDA originally. Therefore, we may say that for any PDA there is a CFG that generates the same language the machine accepts. ∎

EXAMPLE

We shall now illustrate the complete process of equivalence, as given by the two theorems in this chapter, on one simple example. We shall start with a CFG and convert it into a PDA (using the algorithm of Theorem 30), and we then convert this very PDA back into a CFG (using the algorithm of Theorem 31).

The language of this illustration is the collection of all strings of an even number of a's:

$$\text{EVENA} = (aa)^+ = a^{2n} = \{aa \quad aaaa \quad aaaaaa \ldots\}$$

One obvious grammar for this language is

$$S \rightarrow SS \mid aa$$

The leftmost total language tree begins:

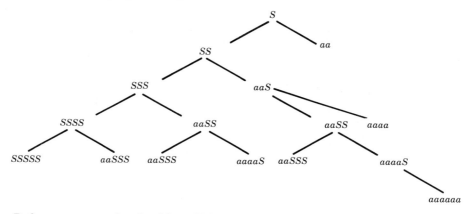

Before we can use the algorithm of Theorem 30 to build a PDA that accepts this language, we must put it into CNF. We therefore first employ the algorithm of Theorem 26, (p. 278).

$$S \rightarrow SS \mid AA$$
$$A \rightarrow a$$

The PDA we produce by the algorithm of Theorem 30 is

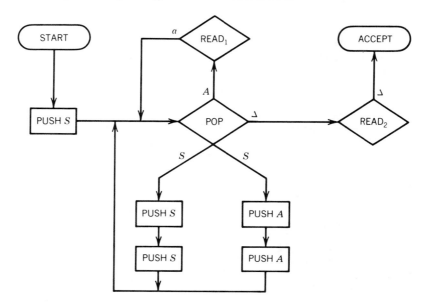

We shall now use the algorithm of Theorem 31 to turn this machine back into a CFG. First, we must put this PDA into conversion form:

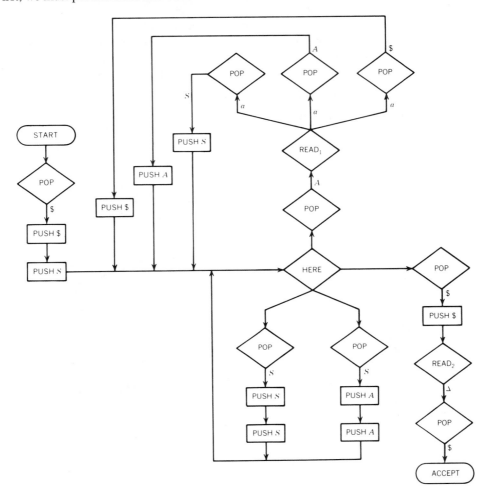

Notice that the branching that used to take place at the grand central POP must now take place at the grand central HERE. Notice also that because we insist there be a POP after every READ, we must have three POPs following READ$_1$. Who among us is so brazen as to claim to be able to glance at this machine and identify the language it accepts?

The next step is to put this PDA into a summary table:

FROM	TO	READ	POP	PUSH	ROW
START	HERE	Λ	$	S$	1
HERE	HERE	Λ	S	SS	2
HERE	HERE	Λ	S	AA	3
HERE	READ$_1$	Λ	A	—	4
READ$_1$	HERE	a	S	S	5
READ$_1$	HERE	a	$	$	6

FROM	TO	READ	POP	PUSH	ROW
READ$_1$	HERE	a	A	A	7
HERE	READ$_2$	Λ	$	$	8
READ$_2$	ACCEPT	Δ	$	—	9

We are now ready to write out all the productions in the row language. We always begin with the production from Rule 1:

$$S \rightarrow \text{Net(START, ACCEPT, \$)}$$

There are two rows with no PUSH parts, and they give us by Rule 2

$$\text{Net(HERE, READ}_1, A) \rightarrow \text{Row}_4$$
$$\text{Net(READ}_2, \text{ACCEPT, \$)} \rightarrow \text{Row}_9$$

From Row$_1$, we get 12 productions of the form

$$\text{Net(START}, X, \$) \rightarrow \text{Row}_1\text{Net(HERE}, Y, S)\text{Net}(Y, X, \$)$$

where X = HERE, READ$_1$, READ$_2$, or ACCEPT and Y = HERE, READ$_1$, or READ$_2$.
From Row$_2$, we get eight productions of the form

$$\text{Net(HERE}, X, S) \rightarrow \text{Row}_2\text{Net(HERE}, Y, S)\text{Net}(Y, X, S)$$

where X = HERE, READ$_1$, READ$_2$, or ACCEPT and Y = HERE or READ$_1$.
From Row$_3$, we get eight productions of the form

$$\text{Net(HERE}, X, S) \rightarrow \text{Row}_3\text{Net(HERE}, Y, A)\text{Net}(Y, X, A)$$

where X = HERE, READ$_1$, READ$_2$, or ACCEPT and Y = HERE or READ$_1$.
From Row$_5$, we get the four productions

$$\text{Net(READ}_1, X, S) \rightarrow \text{Row}_5\text{Net(HERE}, X, S)$$

where X = HERE, READ$_1$, READ$_2$, or ACCEPT.
From Row$_6$, we get the four productions

$$\text{Net(READ}_1, X, \$) \rightarrow \text{Row}_6\text{Net(HERE}, X, \$)$$

where X = HERE, READ$_1$, READ$_2$, or ACCEPT.
From Row$_7$, we get the four productions

$$\text{Net(READ}_1, X, A) \rightarrow \text{Row}_7\text{Net(HERE}, X, A)$$

where X = HERE, READ$_1$, READ$_2$, or ACCEPT.
From Row$_8$, we get the one production

$$\text{Net(HERE, ACCEPT, \$)} \rightarrow \text{Row}_8\text{Net(READ}_2, \text{ACCEPT, \$)}$$

All together, this makes a grammar of 44 productions for the row language.
To obtain the grammar for the actual language of the PDA, we must also include the following productions:

$$\text{Row}_1 \rightarrow \Lambda$$
$$\text{Row}_2 \rightarrow \Lambda$$
$$\text{Row}_3 \rightarrow \Lambda$$
$$\text{Row}_4 \rightarrow \Lambda$$
$$\text{Row}_5 \rightarrow a$$

$$\text{Row}_6 \rightarrow a$$
$$\text{Row}_7 \rightarrow a$$
$$\text{Row}_8 \rightarrow \Lambda$$
$$\text{Row}_9 \rightarrow \Lambda$$

This is not exactly the two-production grammar for EVENA we started with. We seem to have made a profit. ■

Before finishing our discussion of Theorem 31, we should say a word about condition 8 in the definition of conversion form. On the surface, it seems that we never made use of this property of the PDA in our construction of the CFG. We did not. However, it is an important factor in showing that the CFG generates the language accepted by the machine. According to our definition of PDA, it is possible for a machine to accept an input string without reading the whole string. Because the final strings come from the row language, and represent paths to ACCEPT, only that part of the input string corresponding to a path to ACCEPT could be generated by the grammar. If a particular input is only accepted by paths that do not read all its letters, then the grammar resulting from the conversion algorithm would not generate this word.

⚜ PROBLEMS

For each of the CFGs below in Problems 1 through 8, construct a PDA that accepts the same language they generate, using the algorithm of Theorem 30).

1. (i) $S \rightarrow aSbb \mid abb$
     (ii) $S \rightarrow SS \mid a \mid b$

2. $S \rightarrow XaaX$
     $X \rightarrow aX \mid bX \mid \Lambda$

3. $S \rightarrow aS \mid aSbS \mid a$

4. $S \rightarrow XY$
     $X \rightarrow aX \mid bX \mid a$
     $Y \rightarrow Ya \mid Yb \mid a$

5. $S \rightarrow Xa \mid Yb$
     $X \rightarrow Sb \mid b$
     $Y \rightarrow Sa \mid a$

6. (i) $S \rightarrow Saa \mid aSa \mid aaS$
     (ii) How many words of length 12 are there in this language?

7. (i) $S \rightarrow (S)(S) \mid a$
        Parentheses are terminals here.
     (ii) How many words are there in this language with exactly four a's?

8. (i) $S \rightarrow XaY \mid YbX$
         $X \rightarrow YY \mid aY \mid b$
         $Y \rightarrow b \mid bb$
     (ii) Draw the total language tree.

9. Explain briefly why it is not actually necessary to convert a CFG into CNF to use the algorithm of Theorem 30 to build a PDA that accepts the same language.

10. Let us consider the set of all regular expressions to be a language over the alphabet

$$\Sigma = \{a \quad b \quad (\quad) \quad + \quad * \quad \Lambda\}$$

Let us call this language REGEX.

   (i) Prove that REGEX is nonregular if you don't do this already on p. 286.
  (ii) Prove that REGEX is context-free by producing a grammar for it.
 (iii) Draw a PDA that accepts REGEX.
 (iv) Draw a deterministic PDA that accepts REGEX.

11. (i) Draw a PDA in conversion form that has twice as many READ states as POP states.
   (ii) Draw a PDA in conversion form that has twice as many POP states as READ states.

12. (i) In a summary table for a PDA, can there be more rows with PUSH than rows with no PUSH?
  (ii) In a summary table for a PDA, can there be more rows that PUSH more than one letter than there are rows that PUSH no letter?
 (iii) On a path through a PDA generated by a word in the language of the PDA, can there be more rows that PUSH more than one letter than rows that PUSH no letters?

13. Consider this PDA:

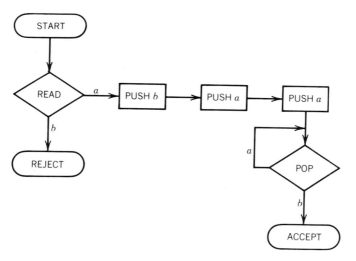

   (i) What is the language of words it accepts?
  (ii) Put it into conversion form.
 (iii) Build a summary table for this PDA.

14. (i) Write out the CFG for the row language of the PDA in Problem 13.
  (ii) Write out the CFG for the language accepted by this machine.

15. Starting with the CFG for $\{a^n b^n\}$

$$S \rightarrow aSb \mid ab$$

  (i) Put this CFG into CNF.
 (ii) Take this CNF and make a PDA that accepts this language.

16. (i) Take the PDA of Problem 15 and put it into conversion form. (Feel free to eliminate useless paths and states.)
  (ii) Build a summary table for this PDA.

17. (i) From the summary table produced in Problem 15, write out the productions of the CFG that generate the row language of the PDA.

    (ii) Convert this to the CFG that generates the actual language of the PDA (not the row language).

18. Prove that every context-free language over the alphabet $\Sigma = \{a \quad b\}$ can be accepted by a PDA with three READ states.

19. Prove that for any PDA there is another PDA that accepts exactly the same language but has only one POP state.

20. Show that if the algorithm of Theorem 31 produces a deterministic PDA, then the language has only one word in it.

CHAPTER 16

Non-Context-Free Languages

⚜ SELF-EMBEDDEDNESS

We are now going to answer the most important question about context-free languages: Are all languages context-free? As any student who realizes that we are only in Part II of a three-part book knows, the answer is no.

To prove this, we have to make a very careful study of the mechanics of word production from grammars. Let us consider a CFG that is in Chomsky Normal Form. All its productions are of the two forms

$$\text{Nonterminal} \rightarrow \text{Nonterminal Nonterminal}$$
$$\text{Nonterminal} \rightarrow \text{terminal}$$

THEOREM 32

Let G be a CFG in Chomsky Normal Form. Let us call the productions of the form

$$\text{Nonterminal} \rightarrow \text{Nonterminal Nonterminal}$$

live and the productions of the form

$$\text{Nonterminal} \rightarrow \text{terminal}$$

dead.

If we are restricted to using the live productions at most once each, we can generate only finitely many words.

PROOF

The question we shall consider is: How many nonterminals are there in the working strings at different stages in the production of a word?

Suppose we start (in some abstract CFG in CNF that we need not specify) with

$$S \Rightarrow AB$$

351

The right side, the working string, has exactly two nonterminals. If we apply the live production

$$A \rightarrow XY$$

we get

$$\Rightarrow XYB$$

which has three nonterminals. Now applying the dead production

$$X \rightarrow b$$

we get

$$\Rightarrow bYB$$

with two nonterminals. But now applying the live production

$$Y \rightarrow SX$$

we get

$$\Rightarrow bSXB$$

with three nonterminals again.

Every time we apply a live production, we increase the number of nonterminals by one. Every time we apply a dead production, we decrease the number of nonterminals by one. Because the net result of a derivation is to start with one nonterminal S and end up with none (a word of solid terminals), the net effect is to lose a nonterminal. Therefore, in all cases, to arrive at a string of only terminals, we must apply one more dead production than live production. This is true no matter in what order the productions are applied.

For example (again these derivations are in some arbitrary, uninteresting CFGs in CNF),

$S \Rightarrow b$	$S \Rightarrow XY$	$S \Rightarrow AB$
	$\Rightarrow aY$	$\Rightarrow XYB$
	$\Rightarrow aa$	$\Rightarrow bXB$
		$\Rightarrow bSXB$
or	or	$\Rightarrow baXB$
		$\Rightarrow baaB$
		$\Rightarrow baab$
0 live	1 live	3 live
1 dead	2 dead	4 dead

Let us suppose that the grammar G has exactly

$$p \text{ live productions}$$

and

$$q \text{ dead productions}$$

Because any derivation that does not reuse a live production can have at most p live productions, it must have at most $(p + 1)$ dead productions. Each letter in the final word comes from the application of some dead production. Therefore, all words generated from G without repeating any live productions have at most $(p + 1)$ letters in them.

Therefore, we have shown that the words of the type described in this theorem cannot be more than $(p + 1)$ letters long. Therefore, there can be at most finitely many of them. ∎

Notice that this proof applies to any derivation, not just leftmost derivations.

When we start with a CFG in CNF, in *all* leftmost derivations, each intermediate step is a working string of the form

$$\Rightarrow \text{(string of solid terminals) (string of solid Nonterminals)}$$

This is a special property of *leftmost Chomsky working strings* as we saw on p. 284. Let us consider some arbitrary, unspecified CFG in CNF.

Suppose that we employ some live production, say,

$$Z \rightarrow XY$$

twice in the derivation of some word w in this language. That means that at one point in the derivation, just before the duplicated production was used the first time, the leftmost Chomsky working string had the form

$$\Rightarrow (s_1)Z(s_2)$$

where s_1 is a string of terminals and s_2 is a string of nonterminals. At this point, the leftmost nonterminal is Z. We now replace this Z with XY according to the production and continue the derivation. Because we are going to apply this production again at some later point, the leftmost Chomsky working string will sometimes have the form

$$\Rightarrow (s_1)(s_3)Z(s_4)$$

where s_1 is the same string of terminals unchanged from before (once the terminals have been derived in the front, they stay put; nothing can dislodge them), s_3 is a newly formed string of terminals, and s_4 is the string of nonterminals remaining (it is a suffix of s_2). We are now about to apply the production $Z \rightarrow XY$ for the second time.

Where did this second Z come from? Either the second Z is a **tree descendant** of the first Z, or else it comes from something in the old s_2. By the phrase "tree descendant," we mean that in the derivation tree there is an ever-downward path from one Z to the other.

Let us look at an example of each possibility.

Case 1

In the arbitrary grammar

$$S \rightarrow AZ$$
$$Z \rightarrow BB$$
$$B \rightarrow ZA$$
$$A \rightarrow a$$
$$B \rightarrow b$$

as we proceed with the derivation of some word, we find

$$S \Rightarrow AZ$$
$$\Rightarrow aZ$$
$$\Rightarrow aBB$$
$$\Rightarrow abB$$
$$\Rightarrow abZA$$
$$\cdots$$

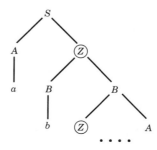

As we see from the derivation tree, the second Z was derived (descended) from the first. We can see this from the diagram because there is a downward path from the first Z to the second.

On the other hand, we could have something like in Case 2.

Case 2

In the arbitrary grammar

$$S \rightarrow AA$$
$$A \rightarrow BC$$
$$C \rightarrow BB$$
$$A \rightarrow a$$
$$B \rightarrow b$$

as we proceed with the derivation of some word, we find

$$S \Rightarrow AA$$
$$\Rightarrow BCA$$
$$\Rightarrow bCA$$
$$\Rightarrow bBBA$$

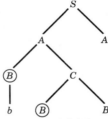

Two times the leftmost nonterminal is B, but the second B is not descended from the first B in the tree. There is no downward tree path from the first B to the second B.

Because a grammar in CNF replaces every nonterminal with one or two symbols, the derivation tree of each word has the property that every mode has one or two descendants. Such a tree is called a **binary tree** and should be very familiar to students of computer science.

When we consider the derivation tree, we no longer distinguish leftmost derivations from any other sequence of nonterminal replacements.

We shall now show that in an infinite language we can always find an example of Case 1.

THEOREM 33

If G is a CFG in CNF that has p live productions and q dead productions, and if w is a word generated by G that has more than 2^p letters in it, then somewhere in every derivation tree for w there is an example of some nonterminal (call it Z) being used twice where the second Z is descended from the first Z.

PROOF

Why did we include the arithmetical condition that

$$\text{length}(w) > 2^p ?$$

This condition ensures that the production tree for w has more than p rows (generations). This is because at each row in the derivation tree the number of symbols in the working string can at most double the last row.

For example, in some abstract CFG in CNF we may have a derivation tree that looks like this:

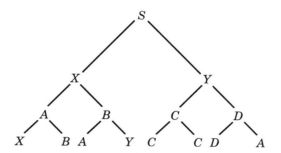

(In this figure, the nonterminals are chosen completely arbitrarily.) If the bottom row has more than 2^p letters, the tree must have more than $p + 1$ rows.

Let us consider any terminal that was one of the letters formed on the bottom row of the derivation tree by a dead production, say,

$$X \rightarrow b$$

The letter b is not necessarily the rightmost letter in w, but it is a letter formed after more than p generations of the tree. This means that it has more than p direct ancestors up the tree.

From the letter b, we trace our way back up through the tree to the top, which is the start symbol S. In this backward trace, we encounter one nonterminal after another in the inverse order in which they occurred in the derivation. Each of these nonterminals represents a production. If there are more than p rows to retrace, then there have been more than p productions in the ancestor path from b to S.

But there are only p different live productions possible in the grammar G, so if more than p have been used in this ancestor path, then some live productions have been used more than once.

The nonterminal on the left side of this repeated live production has the property that it occurs twice (or more) on the descent line from S to b. This then is a nonterminal that proves our theorem.

Before stamping the end-of-proof box, let us draw an illustration, a totally arbitrary tree for a word w in a grammar we have not even written out:

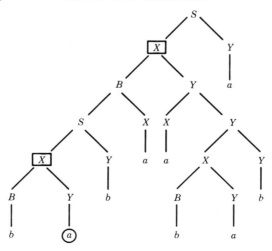

The word w is *babaababa*. Let us trace the ancestor path of the circled terminal a from the bottom row up:

> a came from Y by the production $Y \rightarrow a$
> Y came from X by the production $X \rightarrow BY$
> X came from S by the production $S \rightarrow XY$
> S came from B by the production $B \rightarrow SX$
> B came from X by the production $X \rightarrow BY$
> X came from S by the production $S \rightarrow XY$

If the ancestor chain is long enough, one production must be used twice. In this example, both $X \rightarrow BY$ and $S \rightarrow XY$ are used twice. The two X's that have boxes drawn around them satisfy the conditions of the theorem. One of them is descended from the other in the derivation tree of w. ∎

DEFINITION

In a given derivation of a word in a given CFG, a nonterminal is said to be **self-embedded** if it ever occurs as a tree descendant of itself. ∎

Theorem 33 (p. 354) says that in any CFG all sufficiently long words have leftmost derivations that include a self-embedded nonterminal.

EXAMPLE

Consider the CFG for NONNULLPALINDROME in CNF:

$$
\begin{array}{ll}
S \rightarrow AX & S \rightarrow b \\
X \rightarrow SA & S \rightarrow AA \\
S \rightarrow BY & S \rightarrow BB \\
Y \rightarrow SB & A \rightarrow a \\
S \rightarrow a & B \rightarrow b
\end{array}
$$

There are six live productions, so according to Theorem 33, it would require a word of more than $2^6 = 64$ letters to *guarantee* that each derivation has a self-embedded nonterminal in it.

If we are only looking for one example of a self-embedded nonterminal, we can find such a tree much more easily than that. Consider this derivation tree for the word *aabaa*:

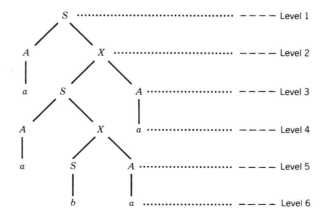

This tree has six levels, so it cannot quite *guarantee* a self-embedded nonterminal, but it has one anyway. Let us begin with the *b* on level 6 and trace its path back up to the top:

"The *b* came from *S* which came from *X*, which came
from *S*, which came from *X*, which came from *S*."

In this way, we find that the production $X \rightarrow SA$ was used twice in this tree segment:

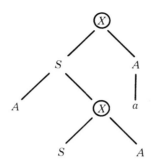

The tree above proceeds from *S* down to the first *X*. Then from the *second X* the tree proceeds to the final word. But once we have reached the second *X*, instead of proceeding with the generation of the word as we have it here, we could instead have repeated the same sequence of productions that the first *X* initiated, thereby arriving at a third *X*. The second can cause the third exactly as the first caused the second. From this third *X*, we could proceed to a final string of all terminals in a manner exactly as the second *X* did.

Let us review this logic more slowly. The first *X* can start a subtree that produces the second *X*, and the second *X* can start a subtree that produces all terminals, but it does not have to. *Instead, the second X can begin a subtree exactly like the first X. This will then produce a third X.* From this third *X*, we can produce a string of all terminals as the second *X* used to.

Original tree with
X-subtree indicated

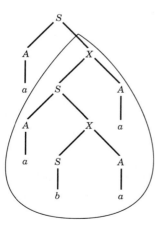

Modified tree with the whole *X*-subtree
hanging from where the second *X* was

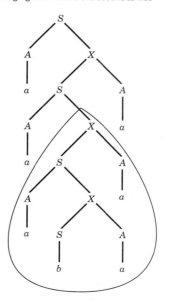

This modified tree *must* be a completely acceptable derivation tree in the original language because each node is still replaced by one or two nodes according to the rules of production found in the first tree.

The modified tree still has a last X and we can play our trick again. Instead of letting this X proceed to a subword as in the first tree, we can replace it by yet another copy of the original X-subtree.

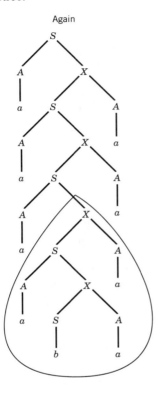

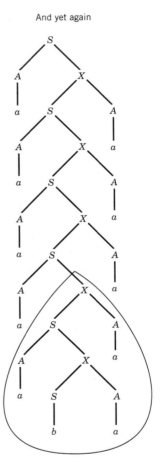

All these trees must be derivation trees of some words in the language in which the original tree started because they reflect only those productions already present in the original tree, just in a different arrangement. We can play this trick as many times as we want, but what words will we then produce?

The original tree produced the word *aabaa*, but it is more important to note that from S we could produce the working string aX, and from this X we could produce the working string aXa. Then from the second X we eventually produced the subword *ba*.

Let us introduce some new notation to facilitate our discussion.

DEFINITION

Let us introduce the notation $\overset{*}{\Rightarrow}$ to stand for the phrase "can eventually produce." It is used in the following context: Suppose in a certain CFG the working string S_1 can produce the working string S_2, which in turn can produce the working string S_3 . . . , which in turn can produce the working string S_n:

$$S_1 \Rightarrow S_2 \Rightarrow S_3 \Rightarrow \cdots \Rightarrow S_n$$

Then we can write

$$S_1 \overset{*}{\Rightarrow} S_n$$

■

Using this notation, we can write that in this CFG the following are true:

$$S \overset{*}{\Rightarrow} aX, \qquad X \overset{*}{\Rightarrow} aXa, \qquad X \overset{*}{\Rightarrow} ba$$

It will be interesting for us to reiterate the middle step since if $X \overset{*}{\Rightarrow} aXa$, then

$$X \overset{*}{\Rightarrow} aaXaa \qquad \text{and} \qquad X \overset{*}{\Rightarrow} aaaXaaa \quad \text{and so on}$$

In general,

$$X \overset{*}{\Rightarrow} a^n X a^n$$

We can then produce words in this CFG starting with $S \Rightarrow aX$ and finishing with $X \Rightarrow ba$ with these extra iterations in the middle:

$$S \overset{*}{\Rightarrow} aX \overset{*}{\Rightarrow} aaXa \overset{*}{\Rightarrow} aabaa$$
$$S \overset{*}{\Rightarrow} aX \overset{*}{\Rightarrow} aaaXaa \overset{*}{\Rightarrow} aaabaaa$$
$$S \overset{*}{\Rightarrow} aX \overset{*}{\Rightarrow} aaaaXaaa \overset{*}{\Rightarrow} aaaabaaaa$$
$$S \overset{*}{\Rightarrow} aX \overset{*}{\Rightarrow} aa^n X a^n \overset{*}{\Rightarrow} aa^n baa^n$$

Given any derivation tree in any CFG with a self-embedded nonterminal, we can use the iterative trick above to produce an infinite family of other words in the language. ■

EXAMPLE

For the arbitrary CFG,

$$S \to AB$$
$$A \to BC$$
$$C \to AB$$
$$A \to a$$
$$B \to b$$

One possible derivation tree is

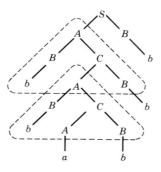

In this case, we find the self-embedded nonterminal A in the dashed triangle. Not only is A self-embedded, but it has already been used twice the same way (two identical dashed triangles).

Again, we have the option of repeating the sequence of productions in the triangle as many times as we want:

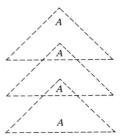

Each iteration will produce new and longer words, all of which must belong to the original language.

This is why in the last theorem it was important that the repeated nonterminals be along the same line of descent. ∎

⚜ THE PUMPING LEMMA FOR CFLs

This entire situation is analogous to the multiply reiterative pumping lemma of Chapter 10, so it should be no surprise that this technique was discovered by the same people: Bar-Hillel, Perles, and Shamir. The following theorem, called "the pumping lemma for context-free languages," states the consequences of reiterating a sequence of productions from a self-embedded nonterminal.

THEOREM 34

If G is any CFG in CNF with p live productions and w is any word generated by G with length greater than 2^p, then we can break up w into five substrings:

$$w = uvxyz$$

such that x is not Λ and v and y are not both Λ and such that all the words

$$\left. \begin{matrix} uvxyz \\ uvvxyyz \\ uvvvxyyyz \\ uvvvvxyyyyz \\ \cdots \cdots \end{matrix} \right\} = uv^nxy^nz \quad \text{for } n = 1 \quad 2 \quad 3 \ldots$$

can also be generated by G.

PROOF

From our previous theorem, we know that if the length of w is greater than 2^p, then there are always self-embedded nonterminals in any derivation tree for w.

Let us now fix in our minds one specific derivation of w in G. Let us call one self-embedded nonterminal P, whose first production is $P \rightarrow QR$.

Let us suppose that the tree for w looks like this:

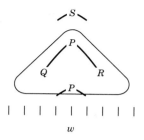

The triangle indicated encloses the whole part of the tree generated from the first P down to where the second P is produced.

Let us divide w into these five parts:

u = the substring of all the letters of w generated to the left of the triangle above (this may be Λ)

v = the substring of all the letters of w descended from the first P but to the left of the letters generated by the second P (this may be Λ)

x = the substring of w descended from the lower P (this may not be Λ because this nonterminal must turn into some terminals)

y = the substring of w of all letters generated by the first P but to the right of the letters descending from the second P (this may be Λ, but as we shall see, not if $v = \Lambda$)

z = the substring of all the letters of w generated to the right of the triangle (this may be Λ)

Pictorially,

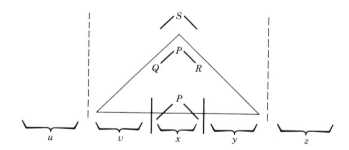

For example, the following is a complete tree in an unspecified grammar:

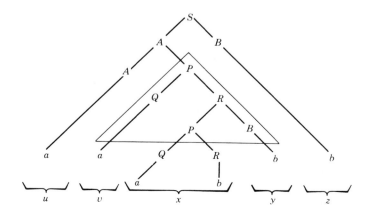

It is possible that either u or z or both might be Λ, as in the following example where S is itself the self-embedded nonterminal and all the letters of w are generated inside the triangle:

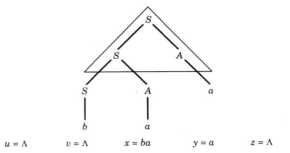

$$u = \Lambda \qquad v = \Lambda \qquad x = ba \qquad y = a \qquad z = \Lambda$$

However, either v is not Λ, y is not Λ, or both are not Λ. This is because in the picture

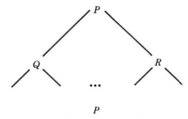

even though the lower P can come from the upper Q or from the upper R, there must still be some other letters in w that come from the other branch, the branch that does not produce this P.

This is important, because if it were ever possible that

$$v = y = \Lambda$$

then

$$uv^n xy^n z$$

would not be an interesting collection of words.

Now let us ask ourselves, what happens to the end word if we change the derivation tree by reiterating the productions inside the triangle? In particular, what is the word generated by this doubled tree?

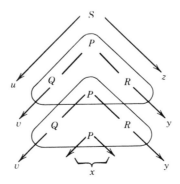

As we see can from the picture, we shall be generating the word

$$uvvxyyz$$

Remember that u, v, x, y, and z are all strings of a's and b's, and this is another word generated by the same grammar. The u-part comes from S to the left of the whole triangle. The first v is what comes from inside the first triangle to the left of the second P. The second v comes from the stuff in the second triangle to the left of the third P. The x-part comes from the third P. The first y-part comes from the stuff in the second triangle to the right of the third P. The second y comes from the stuff in the first triangle to the right of the second P. The z, as before, comes from S from the stuff to the right of the first triangle.

If we tripled the triangle, we would get

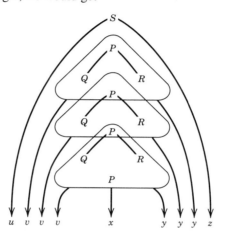

which is a derivation tree for the word

$$uvvvxyyyz$$

which must therefore also be in the language generated by G.

In general, if we repeat the triangle n times, we get a derivation tree for the word

$$uv^n xy^n z$$

which must therefore also be in the language generated by G. ■

We can also use our $\overset{*}{\Rightarrow}$ symbol to provide an algebraic proof of this theorem.

$$S \overset{*}{\Rightarrow} uPz \overset{*}{\Rightarrow} uvPyz \overset{*}{\Rightarrow} uvxyz = w$$

This new symbol is the nexus of two of our old concepts: the derivation $\Rightarrow$ and the closure *, meaning as many repetitions as we want. The idea of "eventually producing" was inherent in our concept of nullable. Using our new symbolism, we can write

N is **nullable** if $N \overset{*}{\Rightarrow} \Lambda$

We can also give an algebraic definition of self-embedded nonterminals.

DEFINITION (Second)

In a particular CFG, a nonterminal N is called **self-embedded** in the derivation of a word w if there are strings of terminals v and y not both null, such that

$$N \overset{*}{\Rightarrow} vNy$$

■

PROOF 2

If P is a self-embedded nonterminal in the derivation of w, then

$$S \overset{*}{\Rightarrow} uPz$$

for some u and z, both substrings of w. Also,

$$P \overset{*}{\Rightarrow} vPy$$

for some v and y, both substrings of w, and finally,

$$P \overset{*}{\Rightarrow} x$$

another substring of w.

But we may also write

$$
\begin{aligned}
S &\overset{*}{\Rightarrow} uPz \\
&\overset{*}{\Rightarrow} uvPyz \\
&\overset{*}{\Rightarrow} uvvPyyz \\
&\overset{*}{\Rightarrow} uvvvPyyyz \\
&\overset{*}{\Rightarrow} uv^nPy^nz \quad \text{(for any } n) \\
&\overset{*}{\Rightarrow} uv^nxy^nz
\end{aligned}
$$

So, this last set of strings are all words derivable in the original CFG.   ■

Some people are more comfortable with the algebraic argument and some are more comfortable reasoning from diagrams. Both techniques can be mathematically rigorous and informative. There is no need for a blood feud between the two camps.

EXAMPLE

We shall analyze a specific case in detail and then consider the situation in its full generality. Let us consider the following CFG in CNF:

$$
\begin{aligned}
S &\rightarrow PQ \\
Q &\rightarrow QS \mid b \\
P &\rightarrow a
\end{aligned}
$$

The word $abab$ can be derived from these productions by the following derivation tree:

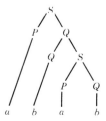

Here, we see three instances of self-embedded nonterminals. The top S has another S as a descendant. The Q on the second level has two Q's as descendants, one on the third level and one of the fourth level. Notice, however, that the two P's are not descended one from the other, so neither is self-embedded. For the purposes of our example, we shall focus on the self-embedded Q's of the second and third levels, although it would be just as good to look at the self-embedded S's. The first Q is replaced by the production $Q \rightarrow QS$, whereas the second is replaced by the production $Q \rightarrow b$. Even though the two Q's are not replaced by the same productions, they are self-embedded and we can apply the technique of this theorem.

If we draw this derivation:

$$S \Rightarrow PQ$$
$$\Rightarrow aQ$$
$$\Rightarrow aQS$$
$$\Rightarrow abS$$
$$\Rightarrow abPQ$$
$$\Rightarrow abaQ$$
$$\Rightarrow abab$$

we can see that the word w can be broken into the five parts $uvxyz$ as follows:

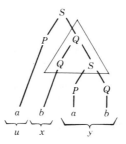

We have located a self-embedded nonterminal Q and we have drawn a triangle enclosing the descent from Q to Q. The u-part is the part generated by the tree to the left of the triangle. This is only the letter a. The v-part is the substring of w generated inside the triangle to the left of the repeated nonterminal. Here, however, the repeated nonterminal Q is the leftmost character on the bottom of the triangle. Therefore, $v = \Lambda$. The x-part is the substring of w descended directly from the second occurrence of the repeated nonterminal (the second Q). Here, that is clearly the single letter b. The y-part is the rest of w generated inside the triangle, that is, whatever comes from the triangle to the right of the repeated nonterminal. In this example, this refers to the substring ab. The z-part is all that is left of w, that is, the substring of w that is generated to the right of the triangle. In this case, that is nothing, $z = \Lambda$.

$$u = a, \qquad v = \Lambda, \qquad x = b, \qquad y = ab, \qquad z = \Lambda$$

The following diagram shows what would happen if we repeated the triangle from the second Q just as it descends from the first Q:

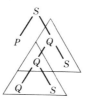

If we now fill in the picture by adding the terminals that descend from the P, Q, and S's, as we did in the original tree, we complete the new derivation tree as follows:

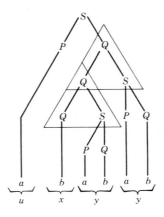

Here, we can see that the repetition of the triangle does not affect the u-part. There was one u-part and there still is only one u-part. If there were a z-part, that too would be left alone, because these are defined outside the triangle. There is no v-part in this example, but we can see that the y-part (its right-side counterpart) has become doubled. Each of the two triangles generates exactly the same y-part. In the middle of all this, the x-part has been left alone. There is still only one bottom repeated nonterminal from which the x-part descends. The word with this derivation tree can be written as $uvvxyyz$:

$$uvvxyyz = a\Lambda\Lambda babab\Lambda$$
$$= ababab$$

If we had tripled the triangle instead of only doubling it, we would obtain

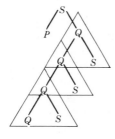
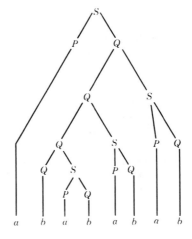

This word we can easily recognize as

$$uvvvxyyyz = a\Lambda\Lambda\Lambda bababab\Lambda$$

In general, after n iterations of the triangle, we obtain a derivation of the word

$$uv^n xy^n z$$

■

We draw one last generalized picture:

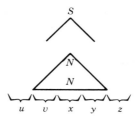

Pumped twice, it becomes

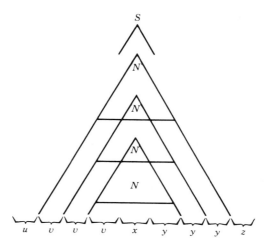

As before, the reason this is called the pumping lemma and not the pumping theorem is that it is to be used for some presumedly greater purpose. In particular, it is used to prove that certain languages are not context-free or, as we shall say, they are **non-context-free.**

EXAMPLE

Let us consider the language

$$\{a^n b^n a^n \quad \text{for } n = 1 \quad 2 \quad 3 \ldots\}$$
$$= \{aba \quad aabbaa \quad aaabbbaaa \ldots\}$$

Let us think about how this language could be accepted by a PDA. As we read the first a's, we must accurately store the information about exactly how many a's there were, because $a^{100}b^{99}a^{99}$ must be rejected but $a^{99}b^{99}a^{99}$ must be accepted. We can put this count into the STACK. One obvious way is to put the a's themselves directly into the STACK, but there may be other ways of doing this. Next, we read the b's and we have to ask the STACK whether or not the number of b's is the same as the number of a's. The problem is that asking the STACK this question makes the STACK forget the answer afterward, because we pop stuff out and cannot put it back. There is no temporary storage possible for the information that we have popped out. The method we used to recognize the language $\{a^n b^n\}$ was to store the a's in the STACK and then destroy them one for one with the b's. After we have checked that we have the correct number of b's, the STACK is empty. No record remains of how many a's there were originally. Therefore, we can no longer check whether the last clump of a's in $a^n b^n a^n$ is the correct size. In answering the question for the b's, the information was lost. This STACK is like a student who forgets the entire course after the final exam.

All we have said so far is, "We don't see how this language can be context-free because we cannot think of a PDA to accept it." This is, of course, no proof. Maybe someone smarter can figure out the right PDA.

Suppose we try this scheme. For every a we read from the initial cluster, we push two a's into the STACK. Then when we read b's, we match them against the first half of the a's in the STACK. When we get to the last clump of a's, we have exactly enough left in the STACK to match them also. The proposed PDA is this:

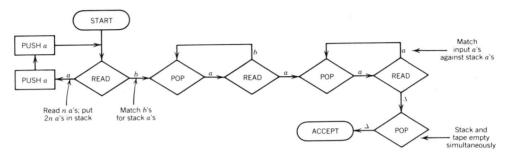

The problem with this idea is that we have no way of checking to be sure that the b's use up exactly *half* of the a's in the STACK. Unfortunately, the word $a^{10}b^8a^{12}$ is also accepted by this PDA. The first 10 a's are read and 20 are put into the STACK. Next, 8 of these are matched against b's. Finally, the 12 final a's match the a's remaining in the STACK and the word is accepted even though we do not want it in our language.

The truth is that nobody is ever going to build a PDA that accepts this language. This can be proven using the pumping lemma. In other words, we can prove that the language $\{a^nb^na^n\}$ is non-context-free.

To do this, let us assume that this language could be generated by some CFG in CNF. No matter how many live productions this grammar has, some word in this language is bigger than 2^p. Let us assume that the word

$$w = a^{200}b^{200}a^{200}$$

is big enough (if it is not, we have got a bag full of much bigger ones).

Now we show that *any* method of breaking w into five parts

$$w = uvxyz$$

will mean that

$$uv^2xy^2z$$

cannot be in $\{a^nb^na^n\}$.

There are many ways of demonstrating this, but let us take the quickest method.

Observation

All words in $\{a^nb^na^n\}$ have exactly one occurrence of the substring ab no matter what n is. Now if either the v-part or the y-part has the substring ab in it, then

$$uv^2xy^2z$$

will have more than one substring of ab, and so it cannot be in $\{a^nb^na^n\}$. Therefore, neither v nor y contains ab.

Observation

All words in $\{a^nb^na^n\}$ have exactly one occurrence of the substring ba no matter what n is. Now if either the v-part or the y-part has the substring ba in it, then

$$uv^2xy^2z$$

has more than one such substring, which no word in $\{a^n b^n a^n\}$ does. Therefore, neither v nor y contains ba.

Conclusion

The only possibility left is that v and y must be all a's, all b's, or Λ. Otherwise, they would contain either ab or ba. But if v and y are blocks of one letter, then

$$uv^2xy^2z$$

has increased one or two clumps of solid letters (more a's if v is a's, etc.). However, there are three clumps of solid letters in the words in $\{a^n b^n a^n\}$, and not all three of those clumps have been increased equally. This would destroy the form of the word.

For example, if

$$a^{200}b^{200}a^{200} = \underbrace{a^{200}b^{70}}_{u}\ \underbrace{b^{40}}_{v}\ \underbrace{b^{90}a^{82}}_{x}\ \underbrace{a^3}_{y}\ \underbrace{a^{115}}_{z}$$

then

$$uv^2xy^2z = (a^{200}b^{70})(b^{40})^2(b^{90}a^{82})\ (a^3)^2(a^{115})$$
$$= a^{200}b^{240}a^{203}$$
$$\neq a^n b^n a^n \text{ for any } n$$

The b's and the second clump of a's were increased, but not the first a's so the exponents are no longer the same.

We must emphasize that there is *no possible* decomposition of this w into $uvxyz$. It is not good enough to show that *one* partition into five parts does not work. It should be understood that we have shown that *any* attempted partition into $uvxyz$ must fail to have $uvvxyyz$ in the language.

Therefore, the pumping lemma cannot successfully be applied to the language $\{a^n b^n a^n\}$ at all. But the pumping lemma *does* apply to all context-free languages.

Therefore, $\{a^n b^n a^n\}$ is not a context-free language.   ■

EXAMPLE

Let us take, just for the duration of this example, a language over the alphabet $\Sigma = \{a \quad b \quad c\}$. Consider the language

$$\{a^n b^n c^n \text{ for } n = 1 \quad 2 \quad 3 \ . \ . \ .\}$$
$$= \{abc \quad aabbcc \quad aaabbbccc \ . \ . \ .\}$$

We shall now prove that this language is non-context-free.

Suppose it were context-free and suppose that the word

$$w = a^{200}b^{200}c^{200}$$

is large enough so that the pumping lemma applies to it. (That means larger than 2^p, where p is the number of live productions.) We shall now show that no matter what choices are made for the five parts u, v, x, y, z,

$$uv^2xy^2z$$

cannot be in the language.

Again, we begin with an observation.

Observation

All words in $a^n b^n c^n$ have:

> Only one substring ab
>
> Only one substring bc
>
> No substring ac
>
> No substring ba
>
> No substring ca
>
> No substring cb

no matter what n is.

Conclusion

If v or y is not a solid block of one letter (or Λ), then

$$uv^2xy^2z$$

would have more of some of the two-letter substrings ab, ac, ba, bc, ca, cb than it is supposed to have. On the other hand, if v and y are solid blocks of one letter (or Λ), then one or two of the letters a, b, c would be increased in the word $uvvxyyz$, whereas the other letter (or letters) would not increase in quantity. But all the words in $a^n b^n c^n$ have equal numbers of a's, b's, and c's. Therefore, the pumping lemma cannot apply to the language $\{a^n b^n c^n\}$, which means that this language is non-context-free. ∎

Theorem 34 and Theorem 13 (initially discussed on pp. 360 and 190, respectively) have certain things in common. They are both called a "pumping lemma," and they were both proven by Bar-Hillel, Perles, and Shamir. What else?

THEOREM 13

It w is a word in a regular language L and w is *long enough,* then w can be decomposed into three parts: $w = xyz$, such that all the words $xy^n z$ must also be in L.

THEOREM 34

If w is a word in a context-free language L and w is *long enough,* then w can be decomposed into five parts: $w = uvxyz$, such that all the words $uv^n xy^n x$ must also be in L.

The proof of Theorem 13 is that the path for w must be so long that it contains a sequence of edges that we can repeat indefinitely. The proof of Theorem 34 is that the derivation for w must be so long that it contains a sequence of productions that we can repeat indefinitely.

We use Theorem 13 to show that $\{a^n b^n\}$ is not regular because it cannot contain both xyz and $xyyz$. We use Theorem 34 to show that $\{a^n b^n a^n\}$ is not context-free because it cannot contain both $uvxyz$ and $uvvxyyz$.

One major difference is that the pumping lemma for regular languages acts on the machines, whereas the pumping lemma for context-free languages acts on the algebraic representation, the grammar.

There is one more similarity between the pumping lemma for context-free languages and the pumping lemma for regular languages. Just as Theorem 13 required Theorem 14 to finish the story, so Theorem 34 requires Theorem 35 to achieve its full power.

Let us look in detail at the proof of the pumping lemma. We start with a word w of more than 2^p letters. The path from some bottom letter back up to S contains more nonterminals than there are live productions. Therefore, some nonterminal is repeated along the path. Here is the new point: If we look for the *first* repeated nonterminal backing up from the letter, the second occurrence will be within p steps up from the terminal row (the bottom). Just because we said that length$(w) > 2^p$ does not mean it is only a little bigger. Perhaps length$(w) = 10^p$. Even so, the upper of the first self-embedded nonterminal pair scanning from the bottom encountered is within p steps of the bottom row in the derivation tree.

What significance does this have? It means that the total output of the upper of the two self-embedded nonterminals produces a string not longer than 2^p letters in total. The string it produces is vxy. Therefore, we can say that

$$\text{length}(vxy) < 2^p$$

This observation turns out to be very useful, so we call it a theorem: the pumping lemma with length.

THEOREM 35

Let L be a CFL in CNF with p live productions.

Then any word w in L with length $> 2^p$ can be broken into five parts:

$$w = uvxyz$$

such that

$$\text{length}(vxy) \le 2^p$$
$$\text{length}(x) > 0$$
$$\text{length}(v) + \text{length}(y) > 0$$

and such that all the words

$$\left. \begin{array}{l} uvvxyyz \\ uvvvxyyyz \\ uvvvvxyyyyz \\ \cdot \ \cdot \ \cdot \end{array} \right\} \quad uv^nxy^nz$$

are in the language L. ∎

The discussion above has already proven this result.

We now demonstrate one application of a language that cannot be shown to be non-context-free by Theorem 34, but can be by Theorem 35.

EXAMPLE

Let us consider the language

$$L = \{a^nb^ma^nb^m\}$$

where n and m are integers $1, 2, 3, \ldots$ and n does not necessarily equal m.

$$L = \{abab \quad aabaab \quad abbabb \quad aabbaabb \quad aaabaaab \ldots\}$$

If we tried to prove that this language was non-context-free using Theorem 34 (p. 360) we could have

$$u = \Lambda$$
$$v = \text{first } a\text{'s} = a^s$$
$$x = \text{middle } b\text{'s} = b^t$$
$$y = \text{second } a\text{'s} = a^s$$
$$z = \text{last } b\text{'s} = b^t$$
$$uv^n xy^n z = \Lambda(a^s)^n b^t (a^s)^n b^t$$

all of which *are* in *L*. Therefore, we have no contradiction and the pumping lemma does apply to *L*.

Now let us try the pumping lemma with length approach. If *L* did have a CFG that generates it, let that CFG in CNF have *p* live productions. Let us look at the word

$$a^{2^p} b^{2^p} a^{2^p} b^{2^p}$$

This word has length long enough for us to apply Theorem 35 to it. But from Theorem 35, we know that

$$\text{length}(vxy) < 2^p$$

so *v* and *y* cannot be solid blocks of one letter separated by a clump of the other letter, because the separator letter clump is longer than the length of the whole substring *vxy*.

By the usual argument (counting substrings of "*ab*" and "*ba*"), we see that *v* and *y* must be one solid letter. But because of the length condition, all the letters must come from the same clump. Any of the four clumps will do.

However, this now means that *uvvxyyz* is not of the form

$$a^n b^m a^n b^m$$

but must also be in *L*. Therefore, *L* is non-context-free. ∎

EXAMPLE

Let us consider the language

$$\text{DOUBLEWORD} = \{ss \quad \text{where } s \text{ is any string of } a\text{'s and } b\text{'s}\}$$
$$= \{\Lambda \quad aa \quad bb \quad aaaa \quad abab \quad baba \quad bbbb \ . \ . \ .\}$$

In Chapter 10, p. 200, we showed that DOUBLEWORD is nonregular. Well even more is true. DOUBLEWORD is not even context-free. We shall prove this by contradiction.

If DOUBLEWORD were generated by a grammar with *p* live productions, then any word with length greater than 2^p can be pumped, that is, decomposed into five strings *uvxyz* such that *uvvxyyz* is also in DOUBLEWORD and length(*vxy*) < 2^p.

Let *n* be some integer greater than 2^p and let our word to be pumped be

$$w = a^n b^n a^n b^n$$

which is clearly in DOUBLEWORD and more than long enough. Now because length(*vxy*) is less than 2^p, it is also less than *n*. If the *vxy* section is contained entirely in one solid letter clump, then replacing it with *vvxyy* will increase only one clump and not the others, thus breaking the pattern and the pumped word would not be in DOUBLEWORD. Therefore, we can conclude that the *vxy* substring spans two clumps of letters. Notice that it cannot be long enough to span three clumps. This means the *vxy* contains a substring *ab* or a substring *ba*. When we form *uvvxyyz*, it may then no longer be in the form *a*b*a*b**, but it might still be in DOUBLEWORD. However, further analysis will show that it cannot be.

It is possible that the substring *ab* or *ba* is not completely inside any of the parts *v*, *x*, or *y* but lies between them. In this case, *uvvxyyz* leaves the pattern *a*b*a*b** but increases two consecutive clumps in size. Any way of doing this would break the pattern of *ss* of DOUBLEWORD. This would also be true if the *ab* or *ba* were contained within the *x*-part. So, the *ab* or *ba* must live in the *v*- or *y*-part.

Let us consider what would happen if the *ab* were in the *v*-part. Then *v* is of the form a^+b^+. So, *vxy* would lie between some a^n and b^n. Because the *v*-part contains the substring *ab*, the *xy*-part would lie entirely within the b^n. (Notice that it cannot stretch to the next a^n since its total length is less than *n*.) Therefore, *x* and *y* are both strings of *b*'s that can be absorbed by the *b** section on their right. Also, *v* starts with some *a*'s that can be absorbed by the *a** section on its left. Thus, *uvvxyyz* is of the form

$$\underbrace{a^*}_{u}\ \underbrace{a^+b^+a^+b^+}_{vv}\ \underbrace{b^*}_{xyy}\ \underbrace{b^*a^nb^n}_{z}$$
$$= a^*b^+a^+b^+a^+b^+$$

If *S* begins and ends with different letters, then *SS* has an even number of *a* clumps and an even number of *b* clumps. If *S* begins and ends with the same letter, then *SS* will have an odd number of clumps of that letter but an even number of clumps of the other letter. In any case, *SS* cannot have an odd number of clumps of both letters, and this string is not in DOUBLEWORD.

The same argument holds if the *ab* or *ba* substring is in the *y*-part. Therefore, *w* cannot be pumped and therefore DOUBLEWORD is non-context-free. ∎

⚜ PROBLEMS

1. Study this CFG for EVENPALINDROME:

$$S \to aSa$$
$$S \to bSb$$
$$S \to \Lambda$$

List all the derivation trees in this language that do not have two equal nonterminals on the same line of descent, that is, that do not have a self-embedded nonterminal.

2. Consider the CNF for NONNULLEVENPALINDROME given below:

$$S \to AX$$
$$X \to SA$$
$$S \to BY$$
$$Y \to SB$$
$$S \to AA$$
$$S \to BB$$
$$A \to a$$
$$B \to b$$

   (i) Show that this CFG defines the language it claims to define.
   (ii) Find all the derivation trees in this grammar that do not have a self-embedded non-terminal.
   (iii) Compare this result with Problem 1.

3. The grammar defined in Problem 2 has six live productions. This means that the second theorem of this section implies that all words of more than $2^6 = 64$ letters must have a self-embedded nonterminal. Find a better result. What is the smallest number of letters that guarantees that a word in this grammar has a self-embedded nonterminal in each of its derivations. Why does the theorem give the wrong number?

4. Consider the grammar given below for the language defined by **a*ba***:

$$S \rightarrow AbA$$
$$A \rightarrow Aa \mid \Lambda$$

   (i) Convert this grammar to one without Λ-productions.
   (ii) Chomsky-ize this grammar.
   (iii) Find all words that have derivation trees that have no self-embedded nonterminals.

5. Consider the grammar for $\{a^n b^n\}$:

$$S \rightarrow aSb \mid ab$$

   (i) Chomsky-ize this grammar.
   (ii) Find all derivation trees that do not have self-embedded nonterminals.

6. Instead of the concept of *live productions* in CNF, let us define a *live nonterminal* to be one appearing at the left side of a live production. A *dead nonterminal N* is one with only productions of the single form

$$N \rightarrow \text{terminal}$$

   If m is the number of live nonterminals in a CFG in CNF, prove that any word w of length more than 2^m will have self-embedded nonterminals.

7. Illustrate the theorem in Problem 6 on the CFG in Problem 2.

8. Apply the theorem of Problem 6 to the following CFG for NONNULLPALINDROME:

$$
\begin{array}{ll}
S \rightarrow AX & S \rightarrow a \\
X \rightarrow SA & S \rightarrow b \\
S \rightarrow BY & A \rightarrow a \\
Y \rightarrow SB & B \rightarrow b \\
S \rightarrow AA & \\
S \rightarrow BB &
\end{array}
$$

9. Prove that the language

$$\{a^n b^n a^n b^n \quad \text{for } n = 1 \; 2 \; 3 \; 4 \ldots\}$$
$$= \{abab \quad aabbaabb \ldots\}$$

   is non-context-free.

10. Prove that the language

$$\{a^n b^n a^n b^n a^n \quad \text{for } n = 1 \; 2 \; 3 \; 4 \ldots\}$$
$$= \{ababa \quad aabbaabbaa \ldots\}$$

   is non-context-free.

11. Let L be the language of all words of any of the following forms:

$$\{a^n \quad a^n b^n \quad a^n b^n a^n \quad a^n b^n a^n b^n \quad a^n b^n a^n b^n a^n \ldots \quad \text{for } n = 1 \; 2 \; 3 \ldots\}$$
$$= \{a \quad aa \quad ab \quad aaa \quad aba \quad aaaa \quad aabb \quad aaaaa \quad ababa \quad aaaaaa \quad aaabbb$$
$$\quad aabbaa \ldots\}$$

   (i) How many words does this language have with 105 letters?
   (ii) Prove that this language is non-context-free.

12. Is the language

$$\{a^n b^{3n} a^n \quad \text{for } n = 1 \quad 2 \quad 3 \ldots\}$$
$$= \{abbba \quad aabbbbbbaa \ldots\}$$

context-free? If so, find a CFG for it. If not, prove so.

13. Consider the language

$$\{a^n b^n c^m \quad \text{for } n, m = 1 \quad 2 \quad 3 \ldots, \quad n \text{ not necessarily } = m\}$$
$$= \{abc \quad abcc \quad aabbc \quad abccc \quad aabbcc \ldots\}$$

Is it context-free? Prove that your answer is correct.

14. Show that the language

$$\{a^n b^n c^n d^n \quad \text{for } n = 1 \quad 2 \quad 3 \ldots\}$$
$$= \{abcd \quad aabbccdd \ldots\}$$

is non-context-free.

15. Why does the pumping lemma argument not show that the language PALINDROME is not context-free? Show how v and y can be found such that $uv^n xy^n z$ are all also in PALINDROME no matter what the word w is.

16. Let VERYEQUAL be the language of all words over $\Sigma = \{a \quad b \quad c\}$ that have the same number of a's, b's, and c's.

$$\text{VERYEQUAL} = \{abc \quad acb \quad bac \quad bca \quad cab \quad cba \quad aabbcc \quad aabcbc \ldots\}$$

Notice that the order of these letters does not matter. Prove that VERYEQUAL is non-context-free.

17. The language EVENPALINDROME can be defined as all words of the form

$$s \text{ reverse}(s)$$

where s is any string of letters from $(\mathbf{a} + \mathbf{b})^*$. Let us define the language UPDOWNUP as

$$L = \{\text{all words of the form } s(\text{reverse}(s)) s \quad \text{where } s \text{ is in } (\mathbf{a} + \mathbf{b})^*\}$$
$$= \{aaa \quad bbb \quad aaaaaa \quad abbaab \quad baabba \quad bbbbbb \ldots aaabbaaaaaab \ldots\}$$

Prove that L is non-context-free.

18. Using an argument similar to the one on p. 195, show that the language

$$\text{PRIME} = \{a^p \quad \text{where } p \text{ is a prime}\}$$

is non-context-free.

19. Using an argument similar to the one for Chapter 10, Problem 6(i), prove that

$$\text{SQUARE} = \{a^n \quad \text{where } n = 1 \quad 2 \ldots\}$$

is non-context-free.

20. Problems 18 and 19 are instances of one larger principle. Prove:

Theorem

If L is a language over the one-letter alphabet $\Sigma = \{a\}$ and L can be shown to be non-regular using the pumping lemma for regular languages, then L can be shown to be non-context-free using the pumping lemma for CFLs.

CHAPTER 17

Context-Free Languages

⚜ CLOSURE PROPERTIES

In Part I, we showed that the union, the product, the Kleene closure, the complement, and the intersection of regular languages are all regular. We are now at the same point in our discussion of context-free languages. In this section, we prove that the union, the product, and the Kleene closure of context-free languages are context-free. What we shall not do is show that the complement and intersection of context-free languages are context-free. Rather, we show in the next section that this is not true in general.

THEOREM 36

If L_1 and L_2 are context-free languages, then their union, $L_1 + L_2$, is also a context-free language. In other words, the context-free languages are closed under union.

PROOF 1 (by grammars)

This will be a proof by constructive algorithm, which means that we shall show how to create the grammar for $L_1 + L_2$ out of the grammars for L_1 and L_2.

Because L_1 and L_2 are context-free languages, there must be some CFGs that generate them.

Let the CFG for L_1 have the start symbol S and the nonterminals $A, B, C, \ldots$. Let us change this notation a little by renaming the start symbol S_1 and the nonterminals $A_1, B_1, C_1, \ldots$. All we do is add the subscript 1 onto each character. For example, if the grammar were originally

$$S \rightarrow aS \mid SS \mid AS \mid \Lambda$$
$$A \rightarrow AA \mid b$$

it would become

$$S_1 \rightarrow aS_1 \mid S_1 S_1 \mid A_1 S_1 \mid \Lambda$$
$$A_1 \rightarrow A_1 A_1 \mid b$$

where the new nonterminals are S_1 and A_1.

Notice that we leave the terminals alone. Clearly, the language generated by this CFG from S_1 is the same as before, because the added 1's do not affect the strings of terminals derived.

Let us do something comparable to a CFG that generates L_2. We add a subscript 2 to each nonterminal symbol. For example,

$$S \rightarrow AS \mid SB \mid \Lambda$$
$$A \rightarrow aA \mid a$$
$$B \rightarrow bB \mid b$$

becomes

$$S_2 \rightarrow A_2 S_2 \mid S_2 B_2 \mid \Lambda$$
$$A_2 \rightarrow aA_2 \mid a$$
$$B_2 \rightarrow bB_2 \mid b$$

Again, we should note that this change in the names of the nonterminals has no effect on the language generated.

Now we build a new CFG with productions and nonterminals that are those of the rewritten CFG for L_1 and the rewritten CFG for L_2, plus the new start symbol S and the additional production

$$S \rightarrow S_1 \mid S_2$$

Because we have been careful to see that there is no overlap in the use of nonterminals, once we begin $S \rightarrow S_1$, we cannot then apply any productions from the grammar for L_2. All words with derivations that start $S \rightarrow S_1$ belong to L_1, and all words with derivations that begin $S \rightarrow S_2$ belong to L_2.

All words from both languages can obviously be generated from S. Because we have created a CFG that generates the language $L_1 + L_2$, we conclude it is a context-free language. ∎

EXAMPLE

Let L_1 be PALINDROME. One CFG for L_1 is

$$S \rightarrow aSa \mid bSb \mid a \mid b \mid \Lambda$$

Let L_2 be $\{a^n b^n\}$. One CFG for L_2 is

$$S \rightarrow aSb \mid \Lambda$$

Theorem 36 recommends the following CFG for $L_1 + L_2$:

$$S \rightarrow S_1 \mid S_2$$
$$S_1 \rightarrow aS_1 a \mid bS_1 b \mid a \mid b \mid \Lambda$$
$$S_2 \rightarrow aS_2 b \mid \Lambda$$

∎

No guarantee was made in this proof that the grammar proposed for $L_1 + L_2$ was the simplest or most intelligent CFG for the union language, as we can see from the following.

EXAMPLE

One CFG for the language EVENPALINDROME is

$$S \rightarrow aSa \mid bSb \mid \Lambda$$

One CFG for the language ODDPALINDROME is

$$S \rightarrow aSa \mid bSb \mid a \mid b$$

Using the algorithm of the preceding proof, we produce the following CFG for PALINDROME:

PALINDROME = EVENPALINDROME + ODDPALINDROME

$$
\begin{aligned}
S &\rightarrow S_1 \mid S_2 \\
S_1 &\rightarrow aS_1a \mid bS_1b \mid \Lambda \\
S_2 &\rightarrow aS_2a \mid bS_2b \mid a \mid b
\end{aligned}
$$

We have seen more economical grammars for this language before. ■

No stipulation was made in this theorem that the set of terminals for the two languages had to be the same.

EXAMPLE

Let L_1 be PALINDROME over the alphabet $\Sigma_1 = \{a \quad b\}$, whereas let L_2 be $\{c^n d^n\}$ over the alphabet $\Sigma_2 = \{c \quad d\}$. Then one CFG that generates $L_1 + L_2$ is

$$
\begin{aligned}
S &\rightarrow S_1 \mid S_2 \\
S_1 &\rightarrow aS_1a \mid bS_1b \mid a \mid b \mid \Lambda \\
S_2 &\rightarrow cS_2d \mid \Lambda
\end{aligned}
$$

This is a language over the alphabet $\{a \quad b \quad c \quad d\}$. ■

In the proof of Theorem 36, we made use of the fact that context-free languages are generated by context-free grammars. However, we could also have proven this result using the alternative fact that context-free languages are those accepted by PDAs.

PROOF 2   (by machines)

Because L_1 and L_2 are context-free languages, we know (from the previous chapter) that there is a PDA_1 that accepts L_1 and a PDA_2 that accepts L_2.

We can construct a PDA_3 that accepts the language of $L_1 + L_2$ by amalgamating the START states of these two machines. This means that we draw only one START state and from it come all the edges that used to come from either prior START state.

becomes

In PDA_3

Once an input string starts on a path on this combined machine, it follows the path either entirely within PDA_1 or entirely within PDA_2 because there are no cross-over edges.

Any input reaching an ACCEPT state has been accepted by one machine or the other and so is in L_1 or L_2. Also, any word in $L_1 + L_2$ can find its old path to acceptance on the subpart of PDA_3 that resembles PDA_1 or PDA_2. ∎

Notice how the nondeterminism of the START state is important in the proof above. We could also do this amalgamation of machines using a single-edge START state by weaseling our way out, as we saw in Chapter 14.

EXAMPLE

Consider these two machines:

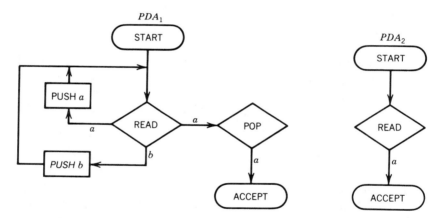

PDA_1 accepts the language of all words that contain a double a. PDA_2 accepts all words that begin with an a. The machine for $L_1 + L_2$ is

PDA_3

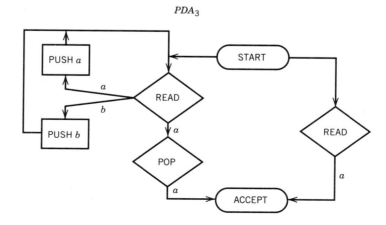

Notice that we have drawn PDA_3 with only one ACCEPT state by combining the ACCEPT states from PDA_1 and PDA_2.

This was not mentioned in the algorithm in the proof, but it only simplifies the picture without changing the substance of the machine.   ■

THEOREM 37

If L_1 and L_2 are context-free languages, then so is L_1L_2. In other words, the context-free languages are closed under product.

PROOF 1   (by grammars)

Let CFG_1 and CFG_2 be context-free grammars that generate L_1 and L_2, respectively. Let us begin with the same trick we used last time: putting a 1 after every nonterminal in CFG_1 (including S) and a 2 after every nonterminal in CFG_2.

Now we form a new CFG using all the old productions in CFG_1 and CFG_2 and adding the new START symbol S and the production

$$S \rightarrow S_1 S_2$$

Any word generated by this CFG has a front part derived from S_1 and a rear derived from S_2. The two sets of productions cannot cross over and interact with each other because the two sets of nonterminals are completely disjoint. It is therefore in the language L_1L_2.

The fact that any word in L_1L_2 can be derived in this grammar should be no surprise.   ■

(We have taken a little liberty with mathematical etiquette in our use of the phrase ". . . should be no surprise." It is more accepted practice to use the cliches "obviously . . . ," or "clearly . . . ," or "trivially. . . ." But it is only a matter of style. A proof only needs to explain enough to be convincing. Other virtues a proof might have are that it be interesting, lead to new results, or be constructive. The proof above is at least the latter.)

EXAMPLE

Let L_1 be PALINDROME and CFG_1 be

$$S \rightarrow aSa \mid bSb \mid a \mid b \mid \Lambda$$

Let L_2 be $\{a^n b^n\}$ and CFG_2 be

$$S \rightarrow aSb \mid \Lambda$$

The algorithm in the proof recommends the CFG

$$S \rightarrow S_1 S_2$$
$$S_1 \rightarrow aS_1a \mid bS_1b \mid a \mid b \mid \Lambda$$
$$S_2 \rightarrow aS_2b \mid \Lambda$$

for the language $L_1 L_2$. ∎

(?) PROOF 2 (by machines)

For the previous theorem we gave two proofs: one grammatical and one mechanical. There is an obvious way to proceed to give a machine proof for this theorem too. The front end of the word should be processed by one PDA and the rear end of the word processed on the second PDA. Let us see how this idea works out.

If we have PDA_1 that accepts L_1 and PDA_2 that accepts L_2, we can try to build the machine PDA_3 that accepts $L_1 L_2$ as follows.

Draw a black dot. Now take all the edges of PDA_1 that feed into any ACCEPT state and redirect them into the dot. Also take all the edges that come from the START state of PDA_2 and draw them coming out of the dot. Erase the old PDA_1 ACCEPT and the old PDA_2 START states.

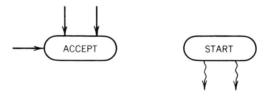

becomes

This kind of picture is not legal in a pushdown automaton drawing because we did not list "a black dot" as one of the pieces in our definition of PDA. The black dot is not necessary. We wish to connect every state that leads to ACCEPT-PDA_1 to every state in PDA_2 that comes from START-PDA_2. We can do this by edges drawn directly pointing from one machine to another. Alternately, the edges from PDA_1 can lead into a new artificial state: PUSH OVER, which is followed immediately by POP OVER whose nondeterministic edges, all labeled OVER, continue to PDA_2. Let us call this the black dot.

For an input string to be accepted by the new PDA, its path must first reach the black dot and then proceed from the dot to the ACCEPT states of PDA_2. There is no path from the START (of PDA_1) to ACCEPT (of PDA_2) without going through the dot. The front substring with a path that leads up to the dot would be accepted by PDA_1, and the remaining substring with a path that leads from the dot to ACCEPT would be accepted by PDA_2. Therefore, all words accepted by this new machine are in the language $L_1 L_2$.

It is also obvious that any word in $L_1 L_2$ is accepted by this new machine.

Not so fast.

We did not put an end-of-proof mark, ■, after the last sentence because the proof actually is not valid. It certainly sounds valid. But it has a subtle flaw, which we shall illustrate.

When an input string is being run on PDA_1 and it reaches ACCEPT, we may not have finished reading the entire INPUT TAPE. The two PDAs that were given in the preceding example (which we have redrawn below) illustrate this point perfectly. In the first, we reach the ACCEPT state right after reading a double a from the INPUT TAPE. The word $baabbb$ will reach ACCEPT on this machine while it still has three b's unread.

The second machine presumes that it is reading the first letter of the L_2 part of the string and checks to be sure that the very first letter it reads is an a.

If we follow the algorithm as stated earlier, we produce the following. From

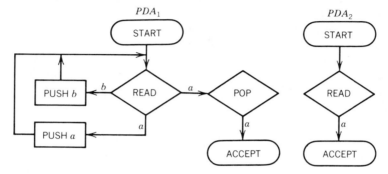

we get

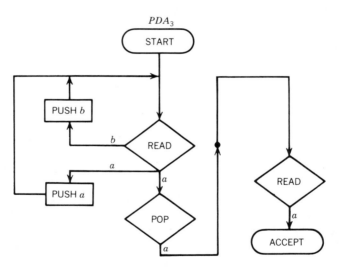

The resultant machine will reject the input string $(baabbb)(aa)$ even though it is in the language L_1L_2 because the black dot is reached after the third letter and the next letter it reads is a b, not the desired a, and the machine will crash. Only words containing aaa are accepted by this machine.

For this technique to work, we must insist that PDA_1, which accepts L_1, have the property that it reads the whole input string before accepting. In other words, when the ACCEPT state is encountered, there must be no unread input left. What happens if we try to modify PDA_1 to meet this requirement? Suppose we use PDA_1 version 2 as on the next page, which employs a technique from the proof of Theorem 29 (p. 311):

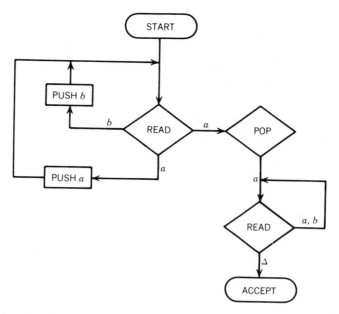

This machine does have the property that when we get to ACCEPT, there is nothing left on the TAPE. This is guaranteed by the READ loop right before ACCEPT. However, when we process the input $(baabbb)(aa)$, we shall read all eight letters before reaching ACCEPT and there will be nothing left to process on PDA_2 because we have *insisted* that the TAPE be exhausted by the first machine. Perhaps it is better to leave the number of letters read before the first ACCEPT up to the machine to decide nondeterministically.

If we try to construct PDA_3 as shown below using the modified PDA_1, with a nondeterministic feed into the black dot, we have another problem.

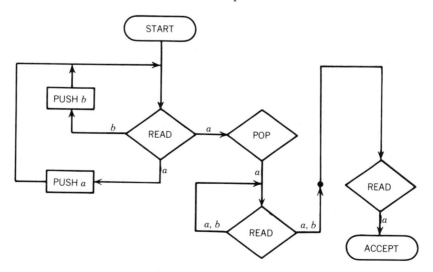

This conglomerate will accept the input $(baabbb)(bba)$ by reading the first two b's of the second factor in the PDA_1 part and then branching through the black dot to read the last letter on the second machine. However, this input string actually is in the language L_1L_2, because it is also of the form $(babbbbb)(a)$.

So this PDA_3 version works in this particular instance, but does it work in *all cases*? Are we convinced that even though we have incorporated some nondeterminism, there are no un-desirable strings accepted?

As it stands, the preceding discussion is no proof. Luckily, this problem does not affect the first proof, which remains valid. This explains why we put the "?" in front of the word "proof" earlier. No matter how rigorous a proof appears, or how loaded with mathematical symbolism, it is always possible for systematic oversights to creep in undetected. The reason we have proofs at all is to try to stop this. But we never really know. We can never be sure that human error has not made us blind to substantial faults. The best we can do, even in purely symbolic abstract mathematics, is to try to be very, very clear and complete in our arguments, to try to *understand* what is going on, and to try many examples.

THEOREM 38

If L is a context-free language, then $L*$ is one too. In other words, the context-free languages are closed under the Kleene star.

PROOF

Let us start with a CFG for the language L. As always, the start symbol for this language is the symbol S. Let us as before change *this symbol* (but no other nonterminals) to S_1 throughout the grammar. Let us then add to the list of productions the new production

$$S \rightarrow S_1 S \mid \Lambda$$

Now we can, by repeated use of this production, start with S and derive

$$S \Rightarrow S_1 S \Rightarrow S_1 S_1 S \Rightarrow S_1 S_1 S_1 S \Rightarrow S_1 S_1 S_1 S_1 S \Rightarrow S_1 S_1 S_1 S_1 S_1$$
$$S \overset{*}{\Rightarrow} S_1^{\ n}$$

Following each of these S_1's independently through the productions of the original CFG, we can form any word in $L*$ made up of n concatenated words from L. To convince ourselves that the productions applied to the various separate word factors do not interfere in undesired ways, we need only think of the derivation tree. Each of these S_1's is the root of a distinct branch. The productions along one branch of the tree do not affect those on another. Similarly, any word in $L*$ can be generated by starting with enough copies of S_1. ∎

EXAMPLE

If the CFG is

$$S \rightarrow aSa \mid bSb \mid a \mid b \mid \Lambda$$

(which generates PALINDROME), then one possible CFG for PALINDROME* is

$$S \rightarrow XS \mid \Lambda$$
$$X \rightarrow aXa \mid bXb \mid a \mid b \mid \Lambda$$

Notice that we have used the symbol X instead of the nonterminal S_1, which was indicated in the algorithm in the proof. Of course, this makes no difference. ∎

⚜ INTERSECTION AND COMPLEMENT

Here is a pretty wishy-washy result.

THEOREM 39

The intersection of two context-free languages may or may not be context-free.

PROOF

We shall break this proof into two parts: may and may not.

May

All regular languages are context-free (Theorem 21, p. 259). The intersection of two regular languages is regular (Theorem 12, p. 174). Therefore, if L_1 and L_2 are regular and context-free, then

$$L_1 \cap L_2$$

is both regular and context-free.

May Not

Let

$L_1 = \{a^n b^n a^m,$ where $n, m = 1$ 2 3 . . . , but n is not necessarily the same as $m\}$
$= \{aba \quad abaa \quad aabba \ . \ . \ .\}$

To prove that this language is context-free, we present a CFG that generates it:

$$S \rightarrow XA$$
$$X \rightarrow aXb \mid ab$$
$$A \rightarrow aA \mid a$$

We could alternately have concluded that this language is context-free by observing that it is the product of the CFL $\{a^n b^n\}$ and the regular language aa^*. Let

$L_2 = \{a^n b^m a^m,$ where $n, m = 1$ 2 3 . . . , but n is not necessarily the same as $m\}$
$= \{aba \quad aaba \quad abbaa \ . \ . \ .\}$

Be careful to notice that these two languages are different.

To prove that this language is context-free, we present a CFG that generates it:

$$S \rightarrow AX$$
$$X \rightarrow bXa \mid ba$$
$$A \rightarrow aA \mid a$$

Alternately, we could observe that L_2 is the product of the regular language aa^* and the CFL $\{b^n a^n\}$.

Both languages are context-free, but their intersection is the language

$$L_3 = L_1 \cap L_2 = \{a^n b^n a^n \quad \text{for } n = 1 \quad 2 \quad 3 \ . \ . \ .\}$$

because any word in both languages has as many starting a's as middle b's (to be in L_1) and as many middle b's as final a's (to be in L_2).

But on p. 367, we proved that this language is non-context-free. Therefore, the intersection of two context-free languages can be non-context-free. ∎

EXAMPLE (May)

If L_1 and L_2 are two CFLs and if L_1 is contained in L_2, then the intersection is L_1 again, which is still context-free, for example,

$$L_1 = \{a^n \quad \text{for } n = 1 \quad 2 \quad 3 \ldots \}$$
$$L_2 = \text{PALINDROME}$$

L_1 is contained in L_2; therefore,

$$L_1 \cap L_2 = L_1$$

which is context-free.

Notice that in this example we do not have the intersection of two regular languages since PALINDROME is nonregular. ∎

EXAMPLE (May)

Let

$$L_1 = \text{PALINDROME}$$
$$L_2 = \text{language of } \mathbf{a^+b^+a^+} = \text{language of } \mathbf{aa*bb*aa*}$$

In this case,

$$L_1 \cap L_2$$

is the language of all words with as many final a's as initial a's with only b's in between.

$$L_1 \cap L_2 = \{a^n b^m a^n \quad n, m = 1 \quad 2 \quad 3 \ldots, \quad \text{where } n \text{ is not necessarily equal to } m\}$$
$$= \{aba \quad abba \quad aabaa \quad aabbaa \ldots\}$$

This language is still context-free because it can be generated by the grammar

$$S \rightarrow aSa \mid B$$
$$B \rightarrow bB \mid b$$

or accepted by this PDA:

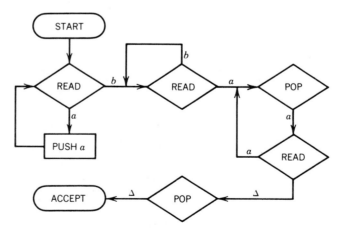

First, all the front a's are put into the STACK. Then the b's are consumed and ignored. Then we alternately READ and POP a's until both the INPUT TAPE and STACK run out simultaneously.

Again note that these languages are not both regular (one is, one is not). ∎

We mention that these two examples are not purely regular languages because the proof of the theorem as given might have conveyed the wrongful impression that the intersection of CFLs is a CFL only when the CFLs are regular.

EXAMPLE   (May Not)

Let L_1 be the language

> EQUAL = all words with the same number of a's and b's

We know this language is context-free because we have seen a grammar that generates it (p. 239):

$$S \rightarrow bA \mid aB$$
$$A \rightarrow bAA \mid aS \mid a$$
$$B \rightarrow aBB \mid bS \mid b$$

Let L_2 be the language

$$L_2 = \{a^n b^m a^n \quad n, m = 1 \quad 2 \quad 3 \ldots, \quad n = m \text{ or } n \neq m\}$$

The language L_2 was shown to be context-free in the previous example. Now

$$L_3 = L_1 \cap L_2 = \{a^n b^{2n} a^n \quad \text{for } n = 1 \quad 2 \quad 3 \ldots\}$$
$$= \{abba \quad aabbbbaa \ldots\}$$

To be in L_1 = EQUAL, the b-total must equal the a-total, so there are $2n$ b's in the middle if there are n a's in the front and the back.

We use the pumping lemma of Chapter 16 to prove that this language is non-context-free.

As always, we observe that the sections of the word that get repeated cannot contain the substrings ab or ba, because all words in L_3 have exactly one of each substring. This means that the two repeated sections (the v-part and y-part) are each a clump of one solid letter. If we write some word w of L_3 as

$$w = uvxyz$$

then we can say of v and y that they are either all a's or all b's or one is Λ. However, if one is solid a's, that means that to remain a word of the form $a^n b^m a^n$, the other must also be solid a's because the front and back a's must remain equal. But then we would be increasing both clumps of a's without increasing the b's, and the word would then not be in EQUAL. If neither v nor y have a's, then they increase the b's without the a's and again the word fails to be in EQUAL.

Therefore, the pumping lemma cannot apply to L_3, so L_3 is non-context-free.   ■

The question of when the intersection of two CFLs is a CFL is apparently very interesting. If an algorithm were known to answer this question, it would be printed right here. Instead, we shall move on to the question of complements.

The story of complements is similarly indecisive.

THEOREM 40

The complement of a context-free language may or may not be context-free.

PROOF

The proof occurs in two parts.

May

If L is regular, then L' is also regular and both are context-free.

May Not

This is one of our few proofs by indirect argument.

Suppose the complement of *every* context-free language were context-free. Then if we started with two such languages, L_1 and L_2, we would know that L_1' and L_2' are also context-free. Furthermore,

$$L_1' + L_2'$$

would have to be context-free by Theorem 36 (p. 376).

Not only that, but

$$(L_1' + L_2')'$$

would also have to be context-free, as the complement of a context-free language. But,

$$(L_1' + L_2')' = L_1 \cap L_2$$

and so then the intersection of L_1 and L_2 must be context-free. But L_1 and L_2 are any arbitrary CFLs, and therefore *all* intersections of context-free languages would have to be context-free. But by the previous theorem, we know that this is not the case.

Therefore, not all context-free languages have context-free complements. ∎

EXAMPLE   (May)

All regular languages have been covered in the proof above. There are also some nonregular but context-free languages that have context-free complements. One example is the language of palindromes with an X in the center, PALINDROMEX. This is a language over the alphabet $\Sigma = \{a \quad b \quad X\}$:

$$= \{wX\ reverse(w), \quad \text{where } w \text{ is any string in } (\mathbf{a} + \mathbf{b})^*\}$$
$$= \{X \quad aXa \quad bXb \quad aaXaa \quad abXba \quad baXab \quad bbXbb \ . \ . \ .\}$$

This language can be accepted (as we have seen in Chapter 14 p. 301) by a deterministic PDA such as the one below:

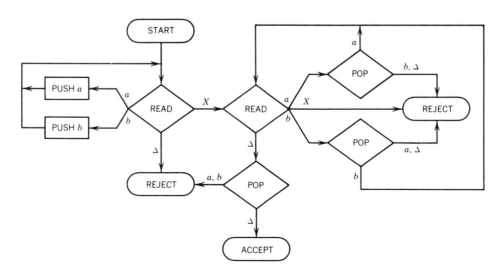

Because this is a deterministic machine, every input string determines a unique path from START to a halt state, either ACCEPT or REJECT. We have drawn in all possible branching edges so that no input crashes. The strings not accepted all go to REJECT. In every loop, there is a READ statement that requires a fresh letter of input so that no input string can loop forever. (This is an important observation, although there are other ways to guarantee no infinite looping.)

To construct a machine that accepts exactly those input strings that this machine rejects, all we need to do is reverse the status of the halt states from ACCEPT to REJECT and vice versa. This is the same trick we pulled on FAs to find machines for the complement language.

In this case, the language L' of all input strings over the alphabet $\Sigma = \{a \quad b \quad X\}$ that are not in L is simply the language accepted by

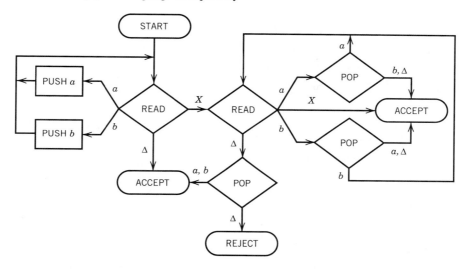

We may wonder why this trick cannot be used to prove that the complement of any context-free language is context-free, because they all can be defined by PDAs. The answer is *nondeterminism*.

If we have a nondeterministic PDA, then the technique of reversing the status of the halt states fails. In a nondeterministic PDA, a word may have two possible paths, the first of which leads to ACCEPT and the second of which leads to REJECT. We accept this word because there is at least one way it can be accepted. Now if we reverse the status of each halt state, we still have two paths for this word: The first now leads to REJECT and the second now leads to ACCEPT. Again, we have to accept this word since at least one path leads to ACCEPT. The same word cannot be in both a language and its complement, so the halt-status-reversed PDA does not define the complement language.

We still owe an example of a context-free language with a complement that is non-context-free.

EXAMPLE   (May Not)

Whenever we are asked for an example of a non-context-free language, $\{a^n b^n a^n\}$ springs to mind. We seem to use it for everything. Surprisingly enough, its complement is context-free, as we shall now show, by taking the union of seven CFLs.

This example takes several steps. First, let us define the language M_{pq} as follows:

$$M_{pq} = \{a^p b^q a^r, \quad \text{where } p, q, r = 1 \quad 2 \quad 3 \ldots, \quad \text{but } p > q \text{ while } r \text{ is arbitrary}\}$$
$$= \{aaba \quad aaaba \quad aabaa \quad aaabaa \quad aaabba \ldots\}$$

We know this language is context-free because it is accepted by the following CFG:

$$S \rightarrow AXA$$
$$X \rightarrow aXb \mid ab$$
$$A \rightarrow aA \mid a$$

The X-part is always of the form $a^n b^n$, and when we attach the A-parts, we get a string defined by the expression

$$(\mathbf{aa^*})(a^n b^n)(\mathbf{aa^*}) = a^p b^q a^r, \quad \text{where } p > q$$

(*Note:* We are mixing regular expressions with things that are not regular expressions, but the meaning is clear anyway.)

This language can be shown to be context-free in two other ways. We could observe that M_{pq} is the product of the three languages $\mathbf{a^+}$, $\{a^n b^n\}$, and $\mathbf{a^+}$:

$$M_{pq} = (\mathbf{a^+})(a^n b^n)(\mathbf{a^+})$$

Because the product of two context-free languages is context-free, so is the product of three context-free languages.

We could also build a PDA to accept it. The machine would have three READ statements. The first would read the initial clump of a's and push them into the STACK. The second would read b's and correspondingly pop a's. When the second READ hits the first a of the third clump, it knows the b's are over, so it pops another a to be sure the initial clump of a's (in the STACK) was larger than the clump of b's. Even when the input passes this test, the machine is not ready to accept. We must be sure that there is nothing else on the INPUT TAPE but unread a's. If there is a b hiding behind these a's, the input must be rejected. We therefore move into the third READ state that loops as long as a's are read, crashes if a b is read, and accepts as soon as a blank is encountered.

Let us also define another language:

$$M_{qp} = \{a^p b^q a^r, \quad \text{where } p, q, r = 1 \quad 2 \quad 3 \ldots, \quad \text{but } q > p \text{ while } r \text{ is arbitrary}\}$$
$$= \{abba \quad abbaa \quad abbba \quad abbaaa \quad aabbba \ldots\}$$

This language too is context-free because it can be generated by

$$S \rightarrow XBA$$
$$X \rightarrow aXb \mid ab$$
$$B \rightarrow bB \mid b$$
$$A \rightarrow aA \mid a$$

which we can interpret as

$$X \overset{*}{\Rightarrow} a^n b^n$$
$$B \overset{*}{\Rightarrow} \mathbf{b^+}$$
$$A \overset{*}{\Rightarrow} \mathbf{a^+}$$

Together, this gives

$$(a^n b^n)(\mathbf{bb^*})(\mathbf{aa^*}) = a^p b^q a^r, \quad \text{where } q > p$$

Let us also define the language

$$M_{pr} = \{a^p b^q a^r, \quad \text{where } p, q, r = 1 \quad 2 \quad 3 \dots, \quad \text{but } p > r \text{ while } q \text{ is arbitrary}\}$$
$$= \{aaba \quad aaaba \quad aabba \quad aaabaa \dots\}$$

This language is also context-free, because it can be generated by the CFG.

$$S \rightarrow AX$$
$$X \rightarrow aXa \mid aBa$$
$$B \rightarrow bB \mid b$$
$$A \rightarrow aA \mid a$$

First, we observe

$$A \overset{*}{\Rightarrow} \mathbf{a}^+ \qquad \text{and} \qquad B \overset{*}{\Rightarrow} \mathbf{b}^+$$

Therefore, the X-part is of the form

$$a^n \mathbf{bb}^* a^n$$

So, the words generated are of the form

$$(\mathbf{aa}^*)(a^n \mathbf{bb}^* a^n) = a^p b^q a^r, \quad \text{where } p > r$$

Let us also define the language

$$M_{rp} = \{a^p b^q a^r, \quad \text{where } p, q, r = 1 \quad 2 \quad 3 \dots, \quad \text{but } r > p \text{ while } q \text{ is arbitrary}\}$$
$$= \{abaa \quad abaaa \quad aabaaa \quad abbaaa \dots\}$$

One CFG for this language is

$$S \rightarrow XA$$
$$X \rightarrow aXa \mid aBa$$
$$B \rightarrow bB \mid b$$
$$A \rightarrow aA \mid a$$

which gives

$$A \overset{*}{\Rightarrow} \mathbf{a}^+$$
$$B \overset{*}{\Rightarrow} \mathbf{b}^+$$
$$X \overset{*}{\Rightarrow} a^n \mathbf{b}^+ a^n$$
$$S \overset{*}{\Rightarrow} (a^n \mathbf{bb}^* a^n)(\mathbf{aa}^*)$$
$$= a^p b^q a^r, \text{ where } r > p$$

We can see that this language too is the product of context-free languages when we show that $\{a^n \mathbf{b}^+ a^n\}$ is context-free.

Let us also define the language

$$M_{qr} = \{a^p b^q a^r, \quad \text{where } p, q, r = 1 \quad 2 \quad 3 \dots, \quad \text{but } q > r \text{ while } p \text{ is arbitrary}\}$$
$$= \{abba \quad aabba \quad abbba \quad abbbaa \dots\}$$

One CFG for this language is

$$S \rightarrow ABX$$
$$X \rightarrow bXa \mid ba$$
$$B \rightarrow bB \mid b$$
$$A \rightarrow aA \mid a$$

which gives

$$(\mathbf{aa}^*)(\mathbf{bb}^*)(b^n a^n) = a^p b^q a^r, \quad \text{where } q > r$$
$$M_{qr} = (\mathbf{a}^+)(\mathbf{b}^+)(b^n a^n)$$

Let us also define

$$M_{rq} = \{a^p b^q a^r, \quad \text{where } p, q, r = 1 \quad 2 \quad 3 \ldots, \quad \text{but } r > q \text{ while } p \text{ is arbitrary}\}$$
$$= \{abaa \quad aabaa \quad abaaa \quad abbaaa \ldots\}$$

One CFG that generates this language is

$$S \rightarrow AXA$$
$$X \rightarrow bXa \mid ba$$
$$A \rightarrow aA \mid a$$

which gives

$$(\mathbf{aa*})(b^n a^n)(\mathbf{aa*}) = a^p b^q a^r, \quad \text{where } r > q$$
$$M_{rq} = (\mathbf{a^+})(b^n a^n)(\mathbf{a^+})$$

We need to define one last language.

$$M = \{\text{the complement of the language defined by } \mathbf{aa*bb*aa*}\}$$
$$= \{\text{all words } not \text{ of the form } a^p b^q a^r \quad \text{for } p, q, r = 1 \quad 2 \quad 3 \ldots\}$$
$$= \{a \quad b \quad aa \quad ab \quad ba \quad bb \quad aaa \quad aab \quad abb \quad baa \quad bab \ldots\}$$

M is the complement of a regular language and therefore is regular by Theorem 11 (p. 173); all regular languages are context-free by Theorem 21 (p. 259).

Let us finally assemble the language L, the union of these seven languages:

$$L = M_{pq} + M_{qp} + M_{pr} + M_{rp} + M_{qr} + M_{rq} + M$$

L is context-free because it is the union of context-free languages (Theorem 36, p. 376).

What is the complement of L? All words that are *not* of the form

$$a^p b^q a^r$$

are in M, which is in L, so they are not in L'. This means that L' contains only words of the form

$$a^p b^q a^r$$

But what are the possible values of p, q, and r? If $p > q$, then the word is in M_{pq}, so it is in L and not L'. Also, if $q > p$, then the word is in M_{qp}, so it is in L and not L'. Therefore, $p = q$ for all words in L'.

If $q > r$, then the word is in M_{qr} and hence in L and not L'. If $r > q$, the word is in M_{rq} and so in L and not L'. Therefore, $q = r$ for all words in L'.

Because $p = q$ and $q = r$, we know that $p = r$. Therefore, the words

$$a^n b^n a^n$$

are the only possible words in L'. All words of this form are in L' because none of them are any of the M's. Therefore,

$$L' = \{a^n b^n a^n \quad \text{for } n = 1 \quad 2 \quad 3 \ldots\}$$

But we know that this language is non-context-free from Chapter 16. Therefore, we have constructed a CFL, L, that has a non-context-free complement. ∎

We might observe that we did not need M_{pr} and M_{rp} in the formation of L. The union of the other five alone completely defines L. We included them only for the purpose of symmetry.

The fact that the complement of a CFL can be non-context-free is the reason that PDAs cannot be defined as deterministic if they are to correspond to all CFLs. Roughly speaking, we can operate on any deterministic machine and reverse its ACCEPT and REJECT conditions to convert it into a machine that accepts the complement of the language that was originally accepted. This halt-state reversal was illustrated in the **Example (May)** section of the preceding proof. Therefore, no **deterministic pushdown automaton (DPDA)** could accept the language $(a^n b^n a^n)'$ because *its* complement, $a^n b^n a^n$, would then be accepted by some other (derived) PDA, but this complement is non-context-free. Yet, because $(a^n b^n a^n)'$ can be generated by a CFG, we want it to be accepted by some PDA. This is why we were forced initially to define PDAs as nondeterministic machines.

The reason that we used the phrase "roughly speaking" in the previous paragraph is that the operation of converting even a deterministic PDA into a machine that accepts the complementary language is not as simple as merely reversing the symbols ACCEPT and REJECT in the picture of the machine. For one thing, all crash possibilities must first be eliminated and turned into edges leading peacefully to REJECT. But even then reversing halt states might not create a machine in which all strings not previously accepted become accepted. This is because there is the possibility that some input strings when fed into the original PDA were neither accepted nor rejected but looped forever. Reversing ACCEPT and REJECT will then leave a machine on which these inputs still loop forever. To prove the theorem rigorously that the complement of a language accepted by a DPDA can also be accepted by a DPDA, we would have to show how to eliminate the loop-forever possibilities and turn them into trips to REJECT. We could do this but it would be long.

MIXING CONTEXT-FREE AND REGULAR LANGUAGES

The union of a context-free language and a regular language must be context-free because the regular language is itself context-free and Theorem 36 (p. 376) applies. As to whether or not the union is also regular, the answer is that it sometimes is and sometimes is not. If one language contains the other, then the union is the larger of the two languages whether it be the regular or the nonregular context-free language.

EXAMPLE

PALINDROME is nonregular context-free and $(\mathbf{a} + \mathbf{b})^*$ is regular and contains it. The union is regular. On the other hand, PALINDROME contains the regular language $\mathbf{a}^*$ and so the union of these two is nonregular context-free. ■

We can provide a more interesting pair of examples where one language is not contained in the other.

EXAMPLE

The union of the nonregular context-free language $\{a^n b^n\}$ and the regular language $\mathbf{b}^* \mathbf{a}^*$ is nonregular as seen by the Myhill–Nerode theorem because each string $a^n b$ belongs in a different class (for each there is a unique element of $\mathbf{b}^*$ that completes a word in the union language).

The complement of $\mathbf{a}^*$ is regular and does not contain all of PALINDROME (because aaa is in PALINDROME, e.g.), nor does PALINDROME contain all of it (because ba is in the complement of **a***, e.g.). However, because PALINDROME does contain all of **a***, the union of the complement of **a*** and PALINDROME is all strings, which is a regular language.   ∎

On the other hand, we have no guarantee that the intersection of a context-free language and a regular language is even context-free, although it might even turn out to be regular. Certainly, if one is contained in the other, then the intersection will be the smaller language and have its property. But because we do not automatically know that the intersection of two context-free languages is context-free, the following theorem provides us with some nonobvious information.

THEOREM 41

The intersection of a context-free language and a regular language is always context-free.

PROOF

We will prove this theorem by constructive algorithm. We start with a PDA for the context-free language, called the PDAY, and an FA for the regular language, called the FAX, with states x_1, x_2, x_3, . . . and then we show how to construct a PDA for the intersection language, called INT. This construction will closely parallel the constructions given in the proof of Kleene's theorem that were later revealed to actually provide the basis of the intersection machine for two FAs (see p. 174).

Before we begin, let us assume that PDAY reads the entire input string before accepting the word. If it does not, then we use the algorithm of Theorem 29 (p. 311) to make it do so.

What we will do is label each of the states in PDAY with the name of the particular x-state in FAX that the input string would be in if it were being processed on FAX at the same time. The START state of PDAY we label with the START state of FAX, (x_1). If from the START state on PDAY we go to a PUSH state, then, because we have not yet read any input letters, the FAX simulation leaves us still in x_1. If we now go into a POP state in PDAY, we would still not have read any input letters and the string would remain in x_1 on FAX. Now if we do enter a READ state in PDAY, we still are in the FAX state we were formerly in, but as we leave the READ state by a- or b-edges, it will correspond to entering (possibly) new states in the FAX simulation. Remember that PDAY is a (possibly) nondeterministic machine and so there may be several a-edges leaving the READ state, but we label each of the states it takes us to with the x-state from FAX that an a-edge takes us to.

We could find another complication. In FAX, an a-edge takes us to x_3, whereas a b-edge takes us to x_8, but in PDAY both the a-edge and b-edge take us to the same PDAY state. This PDAY state must then be cloned; that is, two copies of it must be produced with identical sets of exiting edges but not entering edges. One of the clones will be the one the a-edge enters, and it will get the label x_3, whereas the other will be entered by the b-edge and get the label x_8. We continue to label the PDAY states with the corresponding FAX states. However, as we revisit a PDA state that is already labeled, it may have to be recloned again if it does not have the appropriate corresponding FAX state label. For example, if a POP state was already labeled with x_2 because of one way in which it was entered, it may happen to also be entered from a READ labeled x_9 by a b-edge and, unfortunately, a b-edge from x_9 on FAX takes us to x_9 again so we cannot happily enter this particular POP state. The answer is then that the POP state we enter must be labeled x_9 and be a clone of the POP-x_2 state.

To show that this algorithm is actually finite and does not create infinitely many new states, what we can do simply is name all the states in PDAY as $y_1, y_2, y_3, \ldots$ and simultaneously create all possible combinations of y_{this} and x_{that} and connect them by the rules of both PDAY and FAX appropriately. That is, if we are in y_p and x_q, and it is a READ state in PDAY (or else we do not change our x-status), and we read a b, then because PDAY says "if in y_p and reading a b, go to y_r," and FAX says "if in x_q and reading a b, go to x_s," we go to the new states y_r and x_s. This then, in a finite number of steps, almost completes the construction of our proposed intersection machine INT.

The construction is not yet complete because we did not explain that something special must happen to the ACCEPT states in order to be sure that the only words INT accepts are those accepted by both PDAY and FAX. If the processing of an input string terminates in an ACCEPT state that is labeled with an x_m that is not a final state in FAX, then the input would not be accepted on both machines. We must change all ACCEPT states that are labeled with nonfinal x-states into REJECTs. Now if a string is run on INT and reaches an ACCEPT state, we know it will be accepted by both component machines and is truly in the intersection language. ∎

EXAMPLE

Let C be the language EQUAL of words with the same total number of a's and b's. Let the PDA to accept this language be

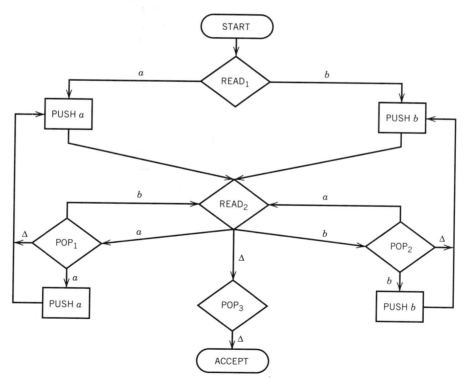

This is a new machine to us, so we should take a moment to dissect it. At every point in the processing of an input string, the STACK will contain whichever letter has been read more, a or b, and will contain as many of that letter as the number of extra times it has been read. If we have read from the TAPE six more b's than a's, then we shall find six b's in the

STACK. If the STACK is empty at any time, it means an equal number of a's and b's have been read.

The process begins in START and then goes to READ$_1$. Whatever we read in READ$_1$ is our first excess letter and is pushed onto the STACK. The rest of the input string is read in READ$_2$.

If during the processing we read an a, we go and consult the STACK. If the STACK contains excess b's, then one of them will be cancelled against the a we just read, POP$_1$–READ$_2$. If the STACK is empty, then the a just read is pushed onto the STACK as a new excess letter itself. If the STACK is found to contain a's already, then we must replace the one we popped out for testing as well as add the new one just read to the amount of total excess a's in the STACK. In all, two a's must be pushed onto the STACK.

When we are finally out of input letters in READ$_2$, we go to POP$_3$ to be sure there are no excess letters being stored in the STACK. Then we accept.

This machine reads the entire INPUT TAPE before accepting and never loops forever.

Let us intersect this with the FA below that accepts all words ending in the letter a:

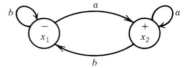

Now let us manufacture the joint intersection machine. We cannot move out of x_1 until after the first READ in the PDA.

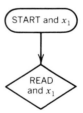

At this point in the PDA, we branch to separate PUSH states, each of which takes us to READ$_2$. However, depending on what is read in READ$_1$, we will either want to be in READ$_2$ and x_1, or READ$_2$ and x_2, so these must be two different states:

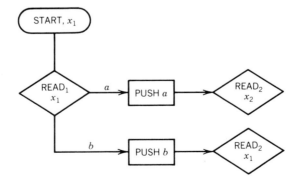

From READ$_2$ and x_2 if we read an a, we shall have to be in POP$_1$ and x_2, whereas if we read a b, we shall be in POP$_2$ and x_1. In this particular machine, there is no need for POP$_1$ and x_1 because POP$_1$ can only be entered by reading an a and x_1 can only be entered by reading a b. For analogous reasons, we do not need a state called POP$_2$ and x_2 either.

We shall theoretically need both POP$_3$ and x_1 and POP$_3$ and x_2 because we have to keep track of the last input letter. But even if POP$_3$ and x_1 should happen to pop a Δ, it cannot accept the input because x_1 is not a final state and so the word ending there is rejected by the FA. Therefore, we do not even bother drawing POP$_3$ and x_1. If a blank is read in READ$_2$, x_1, the machine peacefully crashes.

The whole machine looks like this:

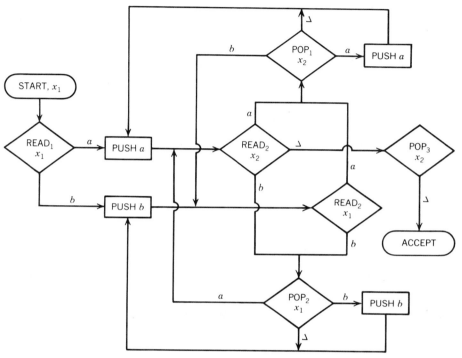

EXAMPLE

Let us reconsider the language DOUBLEWORD, which was shown in the previous chapter to be non-context-free. We can provide another proof of this fact by employing our last theorem. Let us assume for a moment that DOUBLEWORD were a CFL. Then when we intersect it with any regular language, we must get a context-free language.

Let us intersect DOUBLEWORD with the regular language defined by

aa*bb*aa*bb*

A word in the intersection must have both forms; this means it must be

$$ww \quad \text{where } w = a^n b^m \text{ for some } n \text{ and } m = 1 \quad 2 \quad 3 \ldots$$

This observation may be obvious, but we shall prove it anyway. If w contained the substring ba, then ww would have two of them, but all words in **aa*bb*aa*bb*** have exactly one such substring. Therefore, the substring ba must be the crack in between the two w's in the form ww. This means w begins with a and ends with b. Because it has no ba, it must be $a^n b^m$.

The intersection language is therefore

$$\{a^n b^m a^n b^m\}$$

But we showed in the last chapter that this language was non-context-free. Therefore, DOUBLEWORD cannot be context-free either. ∎

⚜ PROBLEMS

1. Find CFGs for these languages:
   (i) All words that start with an a or are of the form $a^n b^n$.
   (ii) All words that have an equal number of a's and b's or are of the form $a^n b^n$.
   (iii) All words in EVEN-EVEN*.
   (iv) All words of the form

$$a^n b^n a^m b^m, \quad \text{where } n, m = 1 \quad 2 \quad 3 \ldots, \quad \text{but } m \text{ need not} = n$$
$$= \{abab \quad aabbab \quad abaabb \quad aaaabbbbab \quad aaabbbaaaabbb \ldots\}$$

2. Find CFGs for these languages:
   (i) All words of the form

$$a^x b^y a^z, \quad \text{where } x, y, z = 1 \ 2 \ 3 \ldots \text{ and } x + z = y$$
$$= \{abba \quad aabbba \quad abbbaa \quad aabbbbaa \ldots\}$$

   Hint: Concatenate a word of the form $a^n b^n$ with a word of the form $b^m a^m$.

   (ii) All words of the form

$$a^x b^y a^z, \quad \text{where } x, y, z = 1 \quad 2 \quad 3 \ldots \text{ and } y = 2x + 2z$$
$$= \{abbbba \quad abbbbbbaa \quad aabbbbbba \ldots\}$$

   (iii) All words of the form

$$a^x b^y a^z, \quad \text{where } x, y, z = 1 \quad 2 \quad 3 \ldots \text{ and } y = 2x + 2z$$
$$= \{abbba \quad abbbbaa \quad aabbbbba \ldots\}$$

   (iv) All words of the form

$$a^x b^y a^z b^w, \quad \text{where } x, y, z, w = 1 \quad 2 \quad 3 \ldots$$
$$\text{and } y > x \quad \text{and} \quad z > w \text{ and}$$
$$x + z = y + w$$

   Hint: Think of these words as

$$(a^p b^p)(b^q a^q)(a^r b^r)$$

   (v) What happens if we throw away the restrictions $y > x$ and $z > w$?

3. (i) Find a CFG for the language of all words of the form

$$a^n b^n \quad \text{or} \quad b^n a^n, \quad \text{where } n = 1 \quad 2 \quad 3 \ldots$$

   (ii) Is the Kleene closure of the language in part (i) the language of all words with an equal number of a's and b's that we have called EQUAL?
   (iii) Using the algorithm from Theorem 38 (p. 384), find the CFG that generates the closure of the language in part (i).
   (iv) Compare this to the CFG for the language EQUAL given before (p. 239).
   (v) Write out all the words in

$$\text{(language of part (i))*}$$

   that have eight or fewer letters.

4. Use the results of Theorems 36, 37, and 38 and a little ingenuity and the recursive definition of regular languages to provide a new proof that all regular languages are context-free.

5. (i) Find a CFG for the language

$$L_1 = \mathbf{a(bb)}*$$

 (ii) Find a CFG for the language L_1*.
 (iii) Find a CFG for the language $L_2 = \mathbf{(bb)*a}$.
 (iv) Find a CFG for L_2*.
 (v) Find a CFG for

$$L_3 = \mathbf{bba*bb + bb}$$

 (vi) Find a CFG for L_3*.
 (vii) Find a CFG for

$$L_1* + L_2* + L_3*$$

 (viii) Compare the CFG in part (vii) to

$$S \rightarrow aS \mid bbS \mid \Lambda$$

 Show that they generate the same language.

6. A *substitution* is the action of taking a language L and two strings of terminals called s_a and s_b and changing every word of L by substituting the string s_a for each a and the string s_b for each b in the word. This turns L into a completely new language. Let us say, for example, that L was the language defined by the regular expression

$$\mathbf{a*(bab* + aa)*}$$

and say that

$$s_a = bb, \qquad s_b = a$$

Then L would become the language defined by the regular expression

$$\mathbf{(bb)*(abba* + bbbb)*}$$

 (i) Prove that after any substitution any regular language is still regular.
 (ii) Prove that after any substitution a CFL is still context-free.

7. Find PDAs that accept

 (i) $\{a^n b^m, \text{ where } n, m = 1 \quad 2 \quad 3 \ldots \text{ and } n \neq m\}$
 (ii) $\{a^x b^y a^z, \text{ where } x, y, z = 1 \quad 2 \quad 3 \ldots \text{ and } x + z = y\}$
 (iii) L_1, L_2 where

$$L_1 = \text{all words with a double } a$$
$$L_2 = \text{all words that end in } a$$

8. (i) Some may think that the machine argument that tried to prove Theorem 37 (p. 381) could be made into a real proof by using the algorithms of Theorem 29 (p. 311) to convert the first machine into one that empties its STACK and TAPE before accepting. If while emptying the TAPE, a nondeterministic leap is made to the START state of the second machine, it appears that we can accept exactly the language $L_1 L_2$. Demonstrate the folly of this belief.

(ii) Show that Theorem 37 can have a machine proof if the machines are those developed in Theorem 30 (p. 318).

(iii) Provide a machine proof for Theorem 38 (p. 384).

9. Which of the following are context-free?

(i) $(\mathbf{a})(\mathbf{a} + \mathbf{b})^* \cap$ ODDPALINDROME

(ii) EQUAL $\cap \{a^n b^n a^n\}$

(iii) $\{a^n b^n\} \cap$ PALINDROME$'$

(iv) EVEN-EVEN$'$ $\cap$ PALINDROME

(v) $\{a^n b^n\}'$ $\cap$ PALINDROME

(vi) PALINDROME $\cap \{a^n b^{n+m} a^m,$ where $n, m = 1 \quad 2 \quad 3 \ldots, \quad n = m$ or $n \neq m\}$

(vii) PALINDROME$'$ $\cap$ EQUAL

10. For the example on p. 389,

(i) Build a PDA for M_{qp} as defined earlier.

(ii) Show that $\{a^n \mathbf{b}^+ a^n\}$ is a CFL.

(iii) Build a PDA for M_{qr} as defined earlier.

(iv) Build a PDA for M_{rq} as defined earlier.

(v) Build a PDA for M as defined earlier.

11. (i) Show that

$$L_1 = \{a^p b^q a^r b^p, \quad \text{where } p, q, r \text{ are arbitrary whole numbers}\}$$

is context-free.

(ii) Show that

$$L_2 = \{a^p b^q a^p b^s\}$$

is context-free.

(iii) Show that

$$L_3 = \{a^p b^p a^r b^s\}$$

is context-free.

(iv) Show that

$$L_1 \cap L_2 \cap L_3$$

is non-context-free.

12. Recall the language VERYEQUAL over the alphabet $\Sigma = \{a \quad b \quad c\}$:

VERYEQUAL = {all strings of a's, b's, and c's that have the
same total number of a's as b's as c's}

Prove that VERYEQUAL is non-context-free by using a theorem in this chapter. (Compare with Chapter 20, Problem 19.)

13. (i) Prove that the complement of the language L

$$L = \{a^n b^m, \quad \text{where } n \neq m\}$$

is context-free, but that neither L nor L' is regular.

(ii) Show that

$$L_1 = \{a^n b^m, \quad \text{where } n \geq m\}$$

and

$$L_2 = \{a^n b^m, \quad \text{where } m \geq n\}$$

are both context-free and not regular.

(iii) Show that their intersection is context-free and nonregular.

(iv) Show that their union is regular.

14. (i) Prove that the language

$$L_1 = \{a^n b^m a^{n+m}\}$$

is context-free.

(ii) Prove that the language

$$L_2 = \{a^n b^n a^m, \quad \text{where either } n = m \text{ or } n \neq m\}$$

is context-free.

(iii) Is their intersection context-free?

15. In this chapter, we proved that the complement of $\{a^n b^n a^n\}$ is context-free. Prove this again by exhibiting one CFG that generates it.

16. Let L be a CFL. Let R be a regular language contained in L. Let $L - R$ represent the language of all words of L that are not words of R. Prove that $L - R$ is a CFL.

17. The algorithm given in the proof of Theorem 41 (p. 394) looks mighty inviting. We are tempted to use the same technique to build the intersection machine of two PDAs. However, we know that the intersection of two CFLs is not always a CFL. Explain why the algorithm fails when it attempts to intersect two PDAs.

18. (i) Take a PDA for PALINDROMEX and intersect it with an FA for **a*Xa***. (This means actually build the intersection machine.)

(ii) Analyze the resultant machine and show that the language it accepts is $\{a^n X a^n\}$.

19. (i) Intersect a PDA for $\{a^n b^n\}$ with an FA for **a(a + b)***. What language is accepted by the resultant machine?

(ii) Intersect a PDA for $\{a^n b^n\}$ with an FA for **b(a + b)***. What language is accepted by the resultant machine?

(iii) Intersect a PDA for $\{a^n b^n\}$ with an FA for **(a + b)*aa(a + b)***.

(iv) Intersect a PDA for $\{a^n b^n\}$ with an FA for EVEN-EVEN.

20. Intersect a PDA for PALINDROME with an FA that accepts the language of all words of odd length. Show, by examining the machine, that it accepts exactly the language ODDPALINDROME.

CHAPTER 18

Decidability

⚜ EMPTINESS AND USELESSNESS

In Part II, we have been laying the foundation of the theory of formal languages. Among the many avenues of investigation we have left open are some questions that seem very natural to ask, such as the following:

1. How can we tell whether or not two different CFGs define the same language?

2. Given a particular CFG, how can we tell whether or not it is ambiguous?

3. Given a CFG that is ambiguous, how can we tell whether or not there is a different CFG that generates the same language but is not ambiguous?

4. How can we tell whether or not the complement of a given context-free language is also context-free?

5. How can we tell whether or not the intersection of two context-free languages is also context-free?

6. Given two context-free grammars, how can we tell whether or not they have a word in common?

7. Given a CFG, how can we tell whether or not there are any words that it *does not* generate? (Is its language (**a** + **b**)* or not?)

These are very fine questions, yet, alas, they are all unanswerable. There are no algorithms to resolve any of these questions. This is not because computer theorists have been too lazy to find them. No algorithms have been found because no such algorithms exist— anywhere—ever.

We are using the word "exist" in a special philosophical sense. Things that have not yet been discovered but that can some day be discovered we still call existent, as in the sentence, "The planet Jupiter existed long before it was discovered by man." On the other hand, certain concepts lead to mathematical contradictions, so they cannot ever be encountered, as in, "The planet on which 2 + 2 = 5," "The smallest planet on which 2 + 2 = 5," or "The tallest married bachelor." In Part III, we shall show how to prove that some computer algorithms are just like married bachelors in that their very existence would lead to unacceptable contradictions. Suppose we have a question that requires a decision procedure. If we prove that no algorithm can exist to answer it, we say that the question is undecidable. Questions 1 through 7 are undecidable.

This is not a totally new concept to us; we have seen it before, but not with this terminology. In geometry, we have learned how to bisect an angle given a straightedge and compass. We cannot do this with a straightedge alone. No algorithm exists to bisect an angle using just a straightedge. We have also been told (although the actual proof is quite advanced) that even with a straightedge and compass we cannot trisect an angle. Not only is it true that no one has ever found a method for trisecting an angle, nobody ever will. And that is a theorem that has been proven.

We shall not present the proof that questions 1 through 7 are undecidable, but toward the end of the book we will prove something very similar.

What Exists	**What Does Not Exist**
1. What is known	1. Married bachelors
2. What will be known	2. Algorithms for questions 1 through 7 above
3. What might have been known but nobody will ever care enough to figure it out	3. A good 5¢ cigar
. . .	. . .

There are, however, some other fundamental questions about CFGs that we can answer:

1. Given a CFG, can we tell whether or not it generates any words at all? This is the question of **emptiness.**

2. Given a CFG, can we tell whether or not the language it generates is finite or infinite? This is the question of **finiteness.**

3. Given a CFG and a particular string of letters w, can we tell whether or not w can be generated by the CFG? This is the question of **membership.**

Now we have a completely different story. The answer to each of these three easier questions is "yes." Not only do algorithms to make these three decisions exist, but they are right here on these very pages.

THEOREM 42

Given any CFG, there is an algorithm to determine whether or not it can generate *any* words at all.

PROOF

The proof will be by constructive example. We show there exists such an algorithm by presenting one.

In Theorem 23 of Chapter 13, we showed that every CFG that does not generate Λ can be written without Λ-productions.

In that proof, we showed how to decide which nonterminals are nullable. The word Λ is a word generated by the CFG if and only if S is nullable. We already know how to decide whether the start symbol S is nullable:

$$S \overset{*}{\Rightarrow} \Lambda?$$

Therefore, the problem of determining whether Λ is a word in the language of any CFG has already been solved.

Let us assume now that Λ is not a word generated by the CFG. In that case, we can convert the CFG to CNF, preserving the entire language.

If there is a production of the form

$$S \rightarrow t$$

where t is a terminal, then t is a word in the language.

If there are no such productions, we then propose the following algorithm:

Step 1   For each nonterminal N that has some productions of the form

$$N \rightarrow t$$

where t is a terminal **or** string of terminals, we choose one of these productions and throw out all other productions for which N is on the left side. We then replace N by t in all the productions in which N is on the right side, thus eliminating the nonterminal N altogether. We may have changed the grammar so that it no longer accepts the same language. It may no longer be in CNF. That is fine with us. Every word that can be generated from the new grammar could have been generated by the old CFG. If the old CFG generated any words, then the new one does also.

Step 2   Repeat step 1 until either it eliminates S or it eliminates no new nonterminals. If S has been eliminated, then the CFG produces some words; if not, then it does not. (This we need to prove.)

The algorithm is clearly finite, because it cannot run step 1 more times than there are nonterminals in the original CNF version. The string of nonterminals that will eventually replace S is a word that could have been derived from S if we retraced in reverse the exact sequence of steps that lead from the terminals to S.

If step 2 makes us stop while we still have not replaced S, then we can show that no words are generated by this CFG. If there were any words in the language, we could retrace the tree from any word and follow the path back to S.

For example, if we have the derivation tree

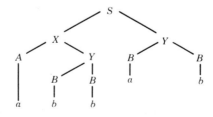

then we can trace backward as follows (the relevant productions can be read from the tree):

$$B \rightarrow b$$

must be a production, so replace all B's with b's.

$$Y \rightarrow BB$$

is a production, so replace Y with *bb*.

$$A \rightarrow a$$

is a production, so replace A with *a*.

$$X \rightarrow AY$$

is a production, so replace X with *abb*.

$$S \rightarrow XY$$

is a production, so replace S with *abbbb*.
Even if the grammar included some other production, such as,

$$B \rightarrow d \quad \text{(where } d \text{ is some other terminal)}$$

we could still retrace the derivation from *abbbb* to S, but we could just as well end up replacing S by *adddd*—if we chose to begin the backup by replacing all B's by *d* instead of *b*.

The important fact is that some sequence of backward replacements will reach back to S if there is any word in the language.

The proposed algorithm is therefore a decision procedure. ∎

EXAMPLE

Consider this CFG:

$$S \rightarrow XY$$
$$X \rightarrow AX$$
$$X \rightarrow AA$$
$$A \rightarrow a$$
$$Y \rightarrow BY$$
$$Y \rightarrow BB$$
$$B \rightarrow b$$

Step 1   Replace all A's by *a* and all B's by *b*. This gives

$$S \rightarrow XY$$
$$X \rightarrow aX$$
$$X \rightarrow aa$$
$$Y \rightarrow bY$$
$$Y \rightarrow bb$$

Step 1   Replace all X's by *aa* and all Y's by *bb*

$$S \rightarrow aabb$$

Step 1   Replace all S's by *aabb*.

Step 2   Terminate step 1 and discover that S has been eliminated. Therefore, the CFG produces at least one word. ∎

EXAMPLE

Consider this CFG:

$$S \rightarrow XY$$
$$X \rightarrow AX$$
$$A \rightarrow a$$
$$Y \rightarrow BY$$
$$Y \rightarrow BB$$
$$B \rightarrow b$$

Step 1   Replace all A's by a and all B's by b. This gives

$$S \rightarrow XY$$
$$X \rightarrow aX$$
$$Y \rightarrow bY$$
$$Y \rightarrow bb$$

Step 1   Replace all Y's by bb. This gives

$$S \rightarrow Xbb$$
$$X \rightarrow aX$$

Step 2   Terminate step 1 and discover that S is still there. This CFG generates no words.   ■

As a final word on this topic, we should note that this algorithm does not depend on the CFGs being in CNF, as we shall see in the problems at the end of this chapter.

We have not yet gotten all the mileage out of the algorithm in the previous theorem. We can use it again to prove the following.

THEOREM 43

There is an algorithm to decide whether or not a given nonterminal X in a given CFG is ever used in the generation of words.

PROOF

The first thing we want to decide is whether from X we can possibly derive a string of all terminals. Then we need also to decide whether, starting from S, we can derive a working string involving X that will lead to a word.

To see whether we can produce a string of all terminals from the nonterminal X, we can make use of the previous theorem and a clever trick.

Trick

Just for a moment, reverse S and X in all the production rules in the grammar. Now use the algorithm of the previous theorem to see whether this grammar produces any words from its start symbol. If it does, then X in the nontampered original grammar can produce a string of all terminals.

Let us call a nonterminal that *cannot* ever produce a string of terminals **unproductive.**

The algorithm that will answer whether X is ever used in the production of words from S will require blue paint.

Step 1   Find all unproductive nonterminals.

Step 2   Purify the grammar by eliminating all productions involving the unproductive nonterminals.

Step 3   Paint all X's blue.

Step 4   If any nonterminal is the left side of a production with anything blue on the right, paint it blue, and paint all occurrences of it throughout the grammar blue, too.

Step 5   The key to this approach is that all the remaining productions are guaranteed to terminate. This means that *any* blue on the right gives us blue on the left (not just *all* blue on the right. Repeat step 4 until nothing new is painted blue.

Step 6   If S is blue, X is a useful member of the CFG, because there are words with derivations that involve X-productions. If not, X is not useful.

Obviously, this algorithm is finite, because the only repeated part is step 4 and that can be repeated only as many times as there are nonterminals in the grammar.

It is also clear that if X is used in the production of some word, then S will be painted blue, because if we have

$$S \Rightarrow \cdots \Rightarrow (\text{blah})X(\text{blah}) \Rightarrow \cdots \Rightarrow \text{word}$$

then the nonterminal that put X into the derivation in the first place will be blue, and the nonterminal that put that one in will be blue, and the nonterminal from which that came will be blue . . . up to S.

Now let us say that S is blue. Let us say that it caught the blue through this sequence: X made A blue, A made B blue, and B made C blue . . . up to S. The production in which X made A blue looked like this:

$$A \rightarrow (\text{blah})X(\text{blah})$$

Now the two (blah)'s might not be strings of terminals, but it must be true that any nonterminals in the (blah)'s can be turned into strings of terminals because they survived step 2. So, we know that there is a derivation from A to a string made up of X with terminals

$$A \overset{*}{\Rightarrow} (\text{string of terminals})X(\text{string of terminals})$$

We also know that there is a production of the form

$$B \Rightarrow (\text{blah})A(\text{blah})$$

that can likewise be turned into

$$B \overset{*}{\Rightarrow} (\text{string of terminals})A(\text{string of terminals})$$
$$\overset{*}{\Rightarrow} (\text{string of terminals})X(\text{string of terminals})$$

We now back all the way up to S and realize that there is a derivation

$$S \overset{*}{\Rightarrow} (\text{string of terminals})X(\text{string of terminals})$$
$$\overset{*}{\Rightarrow} (\text{word})$$

Therefore, this algorithm is exactly the decision procedure we need to decide whether X is actually ever used in the production of a word in this CFG.   ■

A nonterminal that cannot be used in a production of a word is called **useless.** Theorem 43 says that uselessness is decidable.

EXAMPLE

Consider the CFG

$$S \rightarrow ABa \mid bAZ \mid b$$
$$A \rightarrow Xb \mid bZa$$
$$B \rightarrow bAA$$
$$X \rightarrow aZa \mid aaa$$
$$Z \rightarrow ZAbA$$

We quickly see that X terminates (goes to all terminals, whether or not it can be reached from S). Z is useless (because it appears in all of its own productions). A is blue. B is blue. S is blue. So, X must be involved in the production of words. To see one such word, we can write

$$A \rightarrow Xb$$
$$B \rightarrow bAA$$

Now because A is useful, it must produce some string of terminals. In fact,

$$A \overset{*}{\Rightarrow} aaab$$

So,

$$B \overset{*}{\Rightarrow} bAaaab$$
$$\Rightarrow bXbaaab$$

Now

$$S \Rightarrow ABa$$
$$\overset{*}{\Rightarrow} aaabBa$$
$$\overset{*}{\Rightarrow} aaabbXbaaaba$$

We know that X is productive, so this is a working string in the derivation of an actual word in the language of this grammar. ∎

⚜ FINITENESS

The last two theorems have been part of a project, designed by Bar-Hillel, Perles, and Shamir, to settle a more important question.

THEOREM 44

There is an algorithm to decide whether a given CFG generates an infinite language or a finite language.

PROOF

The proof will be by constructive algorithm. We shall show that there exists such a procedure by presenting one. If any word in the language is long enough to apply the pumping lemma (Theorem 34, p. 360) to, we can produce an infinite sequence of new words in the language.

If the language is infinite, then there must be some words long enough so that the pumping lemma applies to them. Therefore, the language of a CFG is infinite if and only if the pumping lemma can be applied.

The essence of the pumping lemma was to find a self-embedded nonterminal X. We shall show in a moment how to tell whether a particular nonterminal is self-embedded, but first we should also note that the pumping lemma will work only if the nonterminal that we pump is involved in the derivation of any words in the language. Without the algorithm of Theorem 43, we could be building larger and larger trees, none of which are truly derivation trees. For example, in the CFG

$$S \rightarrow aX \mid b$$
$$X \rightarrow XXb$$

the nonterminal X is certainly self-embedded, but the language is finite nonetheless.

So, the algorithm is as follows:

Step 1   Use the algorithm of Theorem 43 to determine which nonterminals are useless. Eliminate all productions involving them.

Step 2   Use the following algorithm to test each of the remaining nonterminals, in turn, to see whether they are self-embedded. When a self-embedded one is discovered, stop.
To test X:
   (i) Change all X's on the left side of productions into the Russian letter Ж, but leave all X's on the right side of productions alone.
   (ii) Paint all X's blue.
   (iii) If Y is any nonterminal that is the left side of any production with some blue on the right side, then paint all Y's blue.
   (iv) Repeat step 2(iii) until nothing new is painted blue.
   (v) If Ж is blue, then X is self-embedded; if not, it is not.

Step 3   If any nonterminal left in the grammar after step 1 is self-embedded, the language generated is infinite. If not, then the language is finite.

The explanation of why this procedure is finite and works is identical to the explanation in the proof of Theorem 43. ∎

EXAMPLE

Consider the grammar

$$S \rightarrow ABa \mid bAZ \mid b$$
$$A \rightarrow Xb \mid bZA$$
$$B \rightarrow bAA$$
$$X \rightarrow aZa \mid bA \mid aaa$$
$$Z \rightarrow ZAbA$$

This is the grammar of the previous example with the additional production $X \rightarrow bA$. As before, Z is useless, while all other nonterminals are used in the production of words. We now test to see whether X is self-embedded.

First, we trim away Z:

$$S \rightarrow ABa \mid b$$
$$A \rightarrow Xb$$
$$B \rightarrow bAA$$
$$X \rightarrow bA \mid aaa$$

Now we introduce Ж:

$$S \rightarrow ABa \mid b$$
$$A \rightarrow Xb$$
$$B \rightarrow bAA$$
$$Ж \rightarrow bA \mid aaa$$

Now the paint:

X is blue
$A \rightarrow Xb$, so A is blue
$Ж \rightarrow bA$, so $Ж$ is blue
$B \rightarrow A$, so B is blue
$S \rightarrow ABa$, so S is blue

Conclusion: Ж is blue, so the language generated by this CFG is infinite.   ■

⚜ MEMBERSHIP—THE CYK ALGORITHM

We now turn our attention to the last decision problem we can handle for CFGs.

THEOREM 45

Given a CFG and a string x in the same alphabet, we can decide whether or not x can be generated by the CFG.

PROOF

Our proof will be by constructive algorithm. Given a CFG in CNF and a particular string of letters, we will present an algorithm that decides whether or not the string is derivable from this grammar. This algorithm is called the CYK algorithm because it was invented by John Cocke and subsequently also published by Tadao Kasami (1965) and Daniel H. Younger (1967).

First, let us make a list of all the nonterminals in the grammar $S, N_1, N_2, N_3, \ldots$. And let the string we are examining for membership in the language be denoted by

$$x = x_1 x_2 x_3 \ldots x_n$$

In general, it may be that the letters are not all different, but what we are interested in here is the position of every possible substring of x. We shall be answering the question of which substrings of x are producible (by extended derivation) from which nonterminals. For example, if we already know that the substring $x_3 \ldots x_7$ can be derived from the nonterminal N_8, the substring $x_8 \ldots x_{11}$ can be derived from the nonterminal N_2, and we happen to have the CNF production $N_4 \rightarrow N_8 N_2$, then we can conclude that the total substring $x_3 \ldots x_{11}$ can be derived from the nonterminal N_4. Symbolically, from

$$N_8 \overset{*}{\Rightarrow} x_3 \ldots x_7 \quad \text{and} \quad N_2 \overset{*}{\Rightarrow} x_8 \ldots x_{11} \quad \text{and} \quad N_4 \rightarrow N_8 N_2$$

we can conclude that

$$N_4 \overset{*}{\Rightarrow} x_3 \ldots x_{11}$$

We wish to determine, in an organized fashion, a comprehensive list of which substrings of x are derivable from which nonterminals. If we had such a reliable list, we would know whether the nonterminal S produces the complete string x, which is what we want to know.

We start off our list with all the substrings of length 1 (the single letters) of x and for each we determine which nonterminals can produce them. This is easily done because all such derivations come immediately from the CNF productions nonterminal $\rightarrow$ terminal:

Substring	All Producing Nonterminals
x_1	$N_{this}, N_{that} \cdots$
x_2	$N_{such}, N_{so} \cdots$
$\cdots$	$\cdots$
x_n	$N_{something} \cdots$

Now we look at all substrings of length 2, such as $x_6 x_7$. This can only be produced from a nonterminal N_p if the first half can be produced by some nonterminal N_q and the second half by some nonterminal N_r, and there is a rule of production in the grammar that says $N_p \rightarrow N_q N_r$. We can systematically check all the rules of production and our list above to determine whether the length-2 substrings can be produced:

Substring	All Producing Nonterminals
$x_1 x_2$	$N \ldots$
$x_2 x_3$	$N \ldots$
$\cdots$	$\cdots$
$x_{n-1} x_n$	$N \ldots$

It may be the case that some of these substrings cannot be derived from any nonterminal, but it also may be the case that some can be derived in several ways.

We now move on to substrings of length 3—for example, $x_5 x_6 x_7$. This substring can also be derived from a production of the form $N \rightarrow NN$, where the first N produces the first half of the substring and the second N produces the second half of the substring, but now we have two different ways of breaking the substring into its two halves. The first half could be $x_5 x_6$ and the second half could be x_7, or the first half could be x_5 and the second half could be $x_6 x_7$. All nonterminals producing any of these four halves are already on our list, so a simple check of all the productions in the CFG will determine all the ways (if any) of producing this (and any other length-3) substring. Our list then grows:

Substring	All Producing Nonterminals
$x_1 x_2 x_3$	$N \ldots$
$x_2 x_3 x_4$	$N \ldots$
$\cdots$	$\cdots$
$x_{n-2} x_{n-1} x_n$	$N \ldots$

Our list keeps growing. Next, we examine all substrings of length 4. They can be broken into halves in three different ways: the first three letters and the last letter, the first two letters and the last two letters, the first letter and the last three letters. For all these possibilities, we check the list to see what nonterminals produce these halves and whether the two nonterminals can be merged into one by a rule of production: $N \rightarrow NN$.

Substring	All Producing Nonterminals
$x_1x_2x_3x_4$	N . . .
$x_2x_3x_4x_5$	N . . .
. . .	. . .

We continue this same process with substrings of length 5 (made into halves in four ways each), length 6, and so on. The whole process terminates when we have all of x as the length of the substring:

Substring	All Producing Nonterminals
x_1x_2 . . . x_n	N . . .

We now examine the set of producing nonterminals, and if S is among them, then x can be produced, and if S is not among them, then x simply cannot be produced by this CFG.

This algorithm is finite and decisive.   ■

EXAMPLE

Let us consider the CFG

$$S \rightarrow XY$$
$$X \rightarrow XA \mid a \mid b$$
$$Y \rightarrow AY \mid a$$
$$A \rightarrow a$$

and let us ask whether the string $x = babaa$ is a word in this language.

We begin our list with all the ways of producing the one-letter substrings of x:

Substring	All Producing Nonterminals
$x_1 = b$	X
$x_2 = a$	X,Y, A
$x_3 = b$	X
$x_4 = a$	X,Y, A
$x_5 = a$	X,Y, A

Now we look at the two-letter substrings. The substring $x_1x_2 = ba$ can only come from any production whose right side is XX, XY, or XA. Two of these are the right side of a production, and so x_1x_2 can be produced by S or X. The substring x_2x_3 can only come from any production whose right side is XX, YX, or AX. None of these is the right side of a production, and so this substring cannot be produced. The substring x_3x_4 can only come from productions whose right side is XX, XY, or XA, and so this substring can be produced by S or X. The substring x_4x_5 can only come from productions whose right side is XX, XY, XA, YX, YY, YA, AX, AY, or AA. Therefore, this substring can come from S, X, or Y. Our list now includes the following:

Substring	All Producing Nonterminals
x_1x_2	S, X
x_2x_3	—
x_3x_4	S, X
x_4x_5	S, X, Y

Now let us consider the substrings of length 3. The first is $x_1x_2x_3$. If we break this into the first half x_1 and the second half x_2x_3, we can see from the list that the second half cannot be produced at all. So, the correct way to break this is into x_1x_2 and x_3. As we see from the table, the first half can be produced from S or X and the second half can be produced only from X. This means that in order to form this substring, we would need a production whose right side is SX or XX. There are no such productions and so this substring cannot be generated.

Let us consider generating the substring $x_2x_3x_4$. We know it is unprofitable to consider the first half to be x_2x_3 so we break it into x_2 and x_3x_4. The list says that we can produce this combination from any production whose right side is XS, XX, YS, YX, AS, or AX. Unfortunately, none of these are right sides of any productions, so this substring cannot be produced either.

The last three-letter substring to consider is $x_3x_4x_5$. It can be factored into x_3 times x_4x_5, or x_3x_4 times x_5. The first of these give XS, XX, or XY; the second gives SX, SY, SA, XX, XY, or XA. Only XY and XA are on the right sides of a production and their left nonterminals are X and S.

Our list now includes the following:

Substring	All Producing Nonterminals
$x_1x_2x_3$	—
$x_2x_3x_4$	—
$x_3x_4x_5$	S, X

This may look fairly bleak, but it is conceivable that the string x still may be formed by multiplying x_1x_2 with the bottom row, so let us persevere.

The first four-letter substring is $x_1x_2x_3x_4$. From the list above, it is clear that the only hope of producing this substring is from the factoring x_1x_2 times x_3x_4. The list tells us that this can come from a production whose right side is SS, SX, XS, or XX. None of these are the right sides of productions, so this substring is unproducible.

The other four-letter substring is $x_2x_3x_4x_5$. The only hope here is to factor this as x_2 times $x_3x_4x_5$ because x_2x_3 and $x_2x_3x_4$ are both unproducible. This factorization gives us the possibilities XS, YS, AS, XX, YX, or AX. None of these are the right side of a production.

The list now includes the following:

Substring	All Producing Nonterminals
$x_1x_2x_3x_4$	—
$x_2x_3x_4x_5$	—

We finally come to the string x itself. We can see that it does not pay to factor it into a 1 times a 4, so the only other factorization possible is a 2 times a 3. Remember, because the grammar is in CNF, all factorizations must contain exactly two factors. Our last resort is therefore x_1x_2 times $x_3x_4x_5$. Each factor can be produced only by S or X, but no productions have the right side SS, XS, SX, or XX. Therefore, this word is unproducible from this grammar:

Substring	All Producing Nonterminals
$x_1x_2x_3x_4x_5$	—

We should note that for the grammar above, and for any other grammar without unit or Λ-productions, it is also possible to decide whether a proposed string is in the language generated by that grammar by drawing enough levels of the total language tree. If we draw the total language tree for the grammar above far enough to produce all five-letter words, we can then search the tree to see that *babaa* is not among them. This too could be developed into an effective decision procedure.

EXAMPLE

Let us consider the following CFG in CNF:

$$S \rightarrow AA$$
$$A \rightarrow AA$$
$$A \rightarrow a$$

Clearly, all the words in this grammar are of the form $\mathbf{a}*$, but are all the words in $\mathbf{a}*$ in the language of this grammar? We can see immediately that Λ and a are not, but *aa* is. Let us use the CYK algorithm to test to see whether $x = aaa$ is.

The list starts off easily enough:

Substring	All Producing Nonterminals
$x_1 = a$	A
$x_2 = a$	A
$x_3 = a$	A

We can see now that both substrings of length 2 are the same, *aa*, and are factorable into exactly AA. This is the right side of two productions whose left sides are S and A. Therefore, the list continues:

Substring	All Producing Nonterminals
x_1x_2	S, A
x_2x_3	S, A

There is only one length-3 substring, x itself, and it can be factored into x_1 times x_2x_3, or x_1x_2 times x_3. The first case gives the nonterminal possibilities AS or AA, and the second gives the possibilities SA or AA. Of these, only AA is the right side of a production (of two productions, actually). The left sides are S and A. Therefore, the list concludes with the following:

Substring	All Producing Nonterminals
$x = x_1x_2x_3$	S, A

From this list, we see that the word x can indeed be derived from the start symbol S and so it is in the language. It should also be clear that similarly any string of more than three a's can also be produced by this CFG from the nonterminals S and A. ∎

⚜ PARSING SIMPLE ARITHMETIC

The CYK algorithm of the previous section answered the question of *whether* a word was derivable from a certain grammar not *how* it was derived. This is also decidable, as we see in this section.

The grammars we presented earlier for AE (arithmetic expressions) were ambiguous. This is not acceptable for programming because we want the computer to know and execute exactly what we intend.

Two possible solutions were mentioned earlier:

1. Require the programmer to insert parentheses to avoid ambiguity. For example, instead of the ambiguous $3 + 4 * 5$, insist on

$$(3 + 4) * 5 \quad \text{or} \quad 3 + (4 * 5)$$

2. Find a new grammar for the same language that is unambiguous because the interpretation of "operator hierarchy" (i.e., $*$ before $+$) is built into the system.

Programmers find the first solution too cumbersome and unnatural. Fortunately, there are grammars (CFGs) that satisfy the second requirement.

We present one such grammar for the operations $+$ and $*$ alone, called PLUS-TIMES. The rules of production are

$$S \rightarrow E$$
$$E \rightarrow T + E \mid T$$
$$T \rightarrow F * T \mid F$$
$$F \rightarrow (E) \mid i$$

Loosely speaking, E stands for an expression, T for a term in a sum, F for a factor in a product, and i for any identifier by which we mean any number or storage location name (variable). The terminals clearly are

$$+ \quad * \quad ( ) \quad i$$

because these symbols occur on the right side of productions, but never on the left side.

To generate the word $i + i * i$ by leftmost derivation, we must proceed as follows:

$$S \Rightarrow E$$
$$\Rightarrow T + E$$
$$\Rightarrow F + E$$
$$\Rightarrow i + E$$
$$\Rightarrow i + T$$
$$\Rightarrow i + F * T$$
$$\Rightarrow i + i * T$$
$$\Rightarrow i + i * F$$
$$\Rightarrow i + i * i$$

The syntax tree for this is

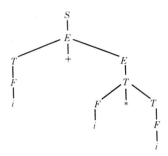

It is clear from this tree that the word represents the addition of an identifier with the product of two identifiers. In other words, the multiplication will be performed before the addition, just as we intended it to be in accordance with conventional operator hierarchy. Once the computer can discover a derivation for the formula, it can generate a machine-language program to accomplish the same task.

DEFINITION

Given a word generated by a particular grammar, the task of finding its derivation is called **parsing.**   ■

Until now we have been interested only in whether a string of symbols was a word in a certain language. We were worried only about the possibility of generation by grammar or acceptance by machine. Now we find that we want to know more. We want to know not just whether a string *can* be generated by a CFG but also *how*. We contend that if we know the (or one of the) derivation tree(s) of a given word in a particular language, then we know something about the *meaning* of the word. This section is different from the other sections in this book because here we are seeking to *understand* what a word says by determining how it can be generated.

There are many different approaches to the problem of CFG parsing. We shall consider three of them. The first two are general algorithms based on our study of derivation trees for CFGs. The third is specific to arithmetic expressions and makes use of the correspondence between CFGs and PDAs.

The first algorithm is called **top-down parsing.** We begin with a CFG and a **target word.** Starting with the symbol S, we try to find some sequence of productions that generates the target word. We do this by checking all possibilities for leftmost derivations. To organize this search, we build a tree of all possibilities, which is like the total language tree of Chapter 12. We grow each branch until it becomes clear that the branch can no longer present a viable possibility; that is, we discontinue growing a branch of the whole language tree as soon as it becomes clear that the target word will never appear on that branch, even generations later. This could happen, for example, if the branch includes in its working string a terminal that does not appear anywhere in the target word or does not appear in the target word in a corresponding position. It is time to see an illustration.

Let us consider the target word

$$i + i * i$$

in the language generated by the grammar PLUS-TIMES.

We begin with the start symbol S. At this point, there is only one production we can possibly apply, $S \rightarrow E$. From E, there are two possible productions:

$$E \rightarrow T + E, \qquad E \rightarrow T$$

In each case, the leftmost nonterminal is T and there are two productions possible for replacing this T.

The top-down leftmost parsing tree begins as shown below:

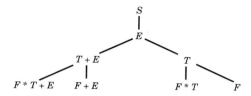

In each of the bottom four cases, the leftmost nonterminal is F, which is the left side of two possible productions:

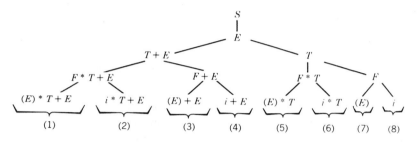

Of these, we can drop branch numbers 1, 3, 5, and 7 from further consideration because they have introduced the terminal character "(", which is not the first (or any) letter of our word. Once a terminal character appears in a working string, it never leaves. Productions change the nonterminals into other things, but the terminals stay forever. All four of those branches can produce only words with parentheses in them, not $i + i * i$. Branch 8 has ended its development naturally in a string of all terminals but it is not our target word, so we can discontinue the investigation of this branch, too. Our pruned tree looks like this:

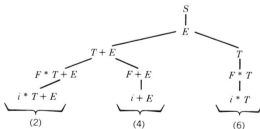

Because both branches 7 and 8 vanished, we dropped the line that produced them:

$$T \Rightarrow F$$

All three branches have actually derived the first two terminal letters of the words that they can produce. Each of the three branches left starts with two terminals that can never change. Branch 4 says the word starts with "$i +$", which is correct, but branches 2 and 6 can now produce only words that start "$i *$", which is not in agreement with our desired target word. The second letter of all words derived on branches 2 and 6 is $*$; the second letter of the target word is $+$. We must kill these branches before they multiply.

Deleting branch 6 prunes the tree up to the derivation $E \Rightarrow T$, which has proved fruitless as none of its offshoots can produce our target word. Deleting branch 2 tells us that we can eliminate the left branch out of $T + E$. With all the pruning we have now done, we can conclude that any branch leading to $i + i * i$ must begin

$$S \Rightarrow E \Rightarrow T + E \Rightarrow F + E \Rightarrow i + E$$

Let us continue this tree two more generations. We have drawn all derivation possibilities. Now it is time to examine the branches for pruning.

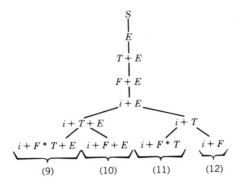

At this point, we are now going to pull a new rule out of our hat. Because no production in any CFG can decrease the length of the working string of terminals and nonterminals on which it operates (each production replaces one symbol by one or more), once the length of a working string has passed 5, it can never produce a final word of only 5 length. We can therefore delete branch 9 on this basis alone. No words that it generates can have as few as five letters.

Another observation we can make is that even though branch 10 is not too long and it begins with a correct string of terminals, it can still be eliminated because it has produced another $+$ in the working string. This is a terminal that all descendants on the branch will have to include. However, there is no second $+$ in the word we are trying to derive. Therefore, we can eliminate branch 10, too.

This leaves us with only branches 11 and 12 that continue to grow.

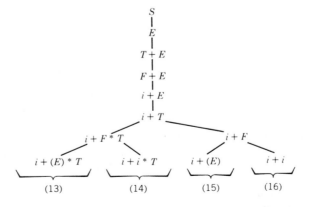

Now branches 13 and 15 have introduced the forbidden terminal "(", while branch 16 has terminated its growth at the wrong word. Only branch 14 deserves to live. At this point, we draw the top half of the tree horizontally:

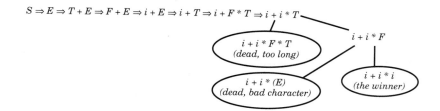

$$S \Rightarrow E \Rightarrow T + E \Rightarrow F + E \Rightarrow i + E \Rightarrow i + T \Rightarrow i + F * T \Rightarrow i + i * T$$

$i + i * F * T$
(dead, too long)

$i + i * F$

$i + i * (E)$
(dead, bad character)

$i + i * i$
(the winner)

In this way, we have discovered that the word $i + i * i$ can be generated by this CFG and we have found the unique leftmost derivation that generates it.

To recapitulate the algorithm: From every live node we branch for all productions applicable to the leftmost nonterminal. We kill a branch for having the wrong initial string of terminals, having a bad terminal anywhere in the string, simply growing too long, or turning into the wrong string of terminals.

With the method of tree search known as **backtracking,** it is not necessary to grow all the live branches at once. Instead, we can pursue one branch downward until either we reach the desired word, or else we terminate it because of a bad character or excessive length. At this point, we back up to a previous node to travel down the next road until we find the target word or another dead end, and so on. Backtracking algorithms are more properly the subject of a different course. As usual, we are more interested in showing what can be done, not in determining which method is best.

We have only given a beginner's list of reasons for terminating the development of a node in the tree. A more complete set of rules follows:

1. *Bad Substring:* If a substring of solid terminals (one or more) has been introduced into a working string in a branch of the total-language tree, all words derived from it must also include that substring unaltered. Therefore, any substring that does not appear in the target word is cause for eliminating the branch.

2. *Good Substrings but Too Many:* The working string has more occurrences of the particular substring than the target word does. In a sense, Rule 1 is a special case of this.

3. *Good Substrings but Wrong Order:* If the working string is *YabXYbaXX* but the target word is *bbbbaab,* then both substrings of terminals developed so far, *ab* and *ba,* are valid substrings of the target word, but they do not occur in the same order in the working string as in the word. So, the working string cannot develop into the target word.

4. *Improper Outer-terminal Substring:* Substrings of terminals developed at the beginning or end of the working string will always stay at the ends at which they first appear. They must be in perfect agreement with the target word or the branch must be eliminated.

5. *Excess Projected Length:* If the working string is *aXbbYYXa* and all the productions with a left side of *X* have right sides of six characters, then the shortest length of the ultimate words derived from this working string must have a length of at least $1 + 6 + 1 + 1 + 1 + 1 + 6 + 1 = 18$. If the target word has fewer than 18 letters, kill this branch. (We are assuming that all Λ-productions have been eliminated.)

6. *Wrong Target Word:* If we have only terminals left but the string is not the target word, forget it.

There may be even more rules depending on the exact nature of the grammar. These rules apply to more than just PLUS-TIMES, as we can see from the following example.

EXAMPLE

Let us recall the CFG for the language EQUAL:

$$S \rightarrow aB \mid bA$$
$$A \rightarrow a \mid aS \mid bAA$$
$$B \rightarrow b \mid bS \mid aBB$$

The word *bbabaa* is in EQUAL. Let us determine a leftmost derivation for this word by top-down parsing.

From the start symbol S, the derivation tree can take one of two tracks:

All words derived from branch 1 must begin with the letter a, but our target word does not. Therefore, by Rule 4, only branch 2 need be considered. The leftmost nonterminal is now A. There are three branches possible at this point:

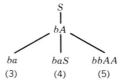

Branch 3 is a completed word but not our target word. Branch 4 will generate only words with an initial string of terminals *ba*, which is not the case with *bbabaa*. Only branch 5 remains a possibility. The leftmost nonterminal in the working string of branch 5 is the first A. Three productions apply to it:

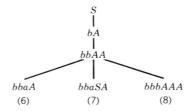

Branches 6 and 7 seem perfectly possible. Branch 8, however, has generated the terminal substring *bbb*, which all its descendants must bear. This substring does not appear in our target word, so we can eliminate this branch from further consideration.

In branch 6, the leftmost nonterminal is A; in branch 7, it is S.

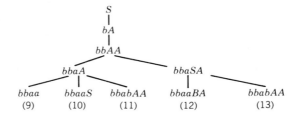

Branch 9 is a string of all terminals, but not the target word. Branch 10 has the initial substring *bbaa*; the target word does not. This detail also kills branch 12. Branch 11 and branch 13 are identical. If we wanted *all* the leftmost derivations of this target word, we would keep both branches growing. Because we need only one derivation, we may just as well keep branch 13 and drop branch 11 (or vice versa); whatever words can be produced on one branch can be produced on the other.

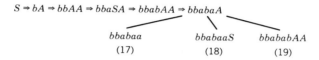

$$S \Rightarrow bA \Rightarrow bbAA \Rightarrow bbaSA \Rightarrow bbabAA$$

$$bbabaA \qquad bbabaSA \qquad bbabbAAA$$
$$(14) \qquad\qquad (15) \qquad\qquad (16)$$

Only the working string in branch 14 is not longer than the target word. Branches 15 and 16 can never generate a six-letter word.

$$S \Rightarrow bA \Rightarrow bbAA \Rightarrow bbaSA \Rightarrow bbabAA \Rightarrow bbabaA$$

$$bbabaa \qquad bbabaaS \qquad bbababAA$$
$$(17) \qquad\qquad (18) \qquad\qquad (19)$$

Branches 18 and 19 are too long, so it is a good thing that branch 17 is our word. This completes the derivation. ∎

The next parsing algorithm we shall illustrate is the **bottom-up parser.** This time we do not ask what were the first few productions used in deriving the word, but what were the last few. We work backward from the end to the front, the way sneaky people do when they try to solve a maze.

Let us again consider as our example the word $i + i * i$ generated by the CFG PLUS-TIMES.

If we are trying to reconstruct a leftmost derivation, we might think that the last terminal to be derived was the last letter of the word. However, this is not always the case. For example, in the grammar

$$S \rightarrow Abb$$
$$A \rightarrow a$$

the word *abb* is formed in two steps, but the final two *b*'s were introduced in the first step of the derivation, not the last. So instead of trying to reconstruct specifically a leftmost derivation, we have to search for any derivation of our target word. This makes the tree much larger. We begin at the bottom of the derivation tree, that is, with the target word itself, and step by step work our way back up the tree seeking to find when the working string was the one single S.

Let us reconsider the CFG PLUS-TIMES:

$$S \rightarrow E$$
$$E \rightarrow T + E \mid T$$
$$T \rightarrow F * T \mid F$$
$$F \rightarrow (E) \mid i$$

To perform a bottom-up search, we shall be reiterating the following step: Find all substrings of the present working string of terminals and nonterminals that are right halves of productions and substitute back to the nonterminal that could have produced them.

Three substrings of $i + i * i$ are right halves of productions, namely, the three i's, anyone of which could have been produced by an F. The tree of possibilities begins as follows:

Even though we are going from the bottom of the derivation tree to the top S, we will still draw the tree of possibilities, as all our trees, from the top of the page downward.

We can save ourselves some work in this particular example by realizing that all the i's come from the production $F \rightarrow i$ and the working string we should be trying to derive is $F + F * F$. Strictly speaking, this insight should not be allowed because it requires an idea that we did not include in the algorithm to begin with. But because it saves us a considerable amount of work, we succumb to the temptation and write in one step:

$$i + i * i$$
$$|$$
$$F + F * F$$

Not all the F's had to come from $T \rightarrow F$. Some could have come from $T \rightarrow F * T$, so we cannot use the same trick again.

The first two branches contain substrings that could be the right halves of $E \rightarrow T$ and $T \rightarrow F$. The third branch has the additional possibility of $T \rightarrow F * T$.

The tree continues:

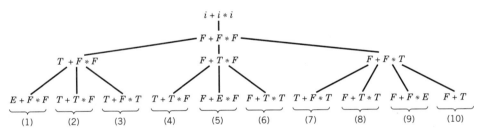

We never have to worry about the length of the intermediate strings in bottom-up parsing because they can never exceed the length of the target word. At each stage, they stay the same length or get shorter. Also, no bad terminals are ever introduced because no new terminals are ever introduced at all, only nonterminals. These are efficiencies that partially compensate for the inefficiency of not restricting ourselves to leftmost derivations.

There is the possibility that a nonterminal is bad in certain contexts. For example, branch 1 now has an E as its leftmost character. The only production that will ever absorb that E is $S \rightarrow E$. This would give us the nonterminal S, but S is not in the right half of any production. It is true that we want to end up with the S; that is the whole goal of the tree. However, we shall want the entire working string to be that single S, not a longer working string with S as its first letter. The rest of the expression in branch 1, "$+ F * F$", is not just going to disappear. So, branch 1 gets the ax. The E's in branch 5 and branch 9 are none too promising either, as we shall see in a moment.

When we go backward, we no longer have the guarantee that the "inverse" grammar is unambiguous even though the CFG itself might be. In fact, this backward tracing is probably not unique, because we are not restricting ourselves to finding a leftmost derivation. We should also find the trails of rightmost derivations and what-not. This is reflected in the occurrence of repeated expressions in the branches. In our example, branch 2 is now the same as branch 4, branch 3 is the same as branch 7, and branch 6 is the same as branch 8. Because we are interested here in finding any *one* derivation, not *all* derivations, we can safely kill branches 2, 3, and 6 and still find a derivation—if one exists.

The tree grows ferociously, like a bush, very wide but not very tall. It would grow too unwieldy unless we made the following observation.

Observation

No intermediate working string of terminals and nonterminals can have the substring "$E *$". This is because the only production that introduces the $*$ is

$$T \rightarrow F * T$$

so the symbol to the immediate left of an $*$ is originally F. From this F, we can only get the terminals ")" or i next to the star. Therefore, in a top-down derivation we could never create the substring "$E *$" in this CFG, so in bottom-up this can never occur in an intermediate working string leading back to S. Similarly, "$E +$" and "$* E$" are also forbidden in the sense that they cannot occur in any derivation. The idea of forbidden substrings is one that we played with in Chapter 3. We can now see the importance of the techniques we introduced there for showing certain substrings never occur [and everybody thought Theorems 2, 3, and 4 (see pp. 26–27) were completely frivolous]. With the aid of this observation, we can eliminate branches 5 and 9.

The tree now grows as follows (pruning away anything with a forbidden substring):

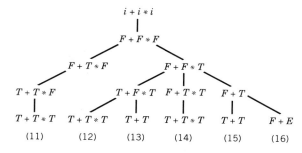

Branches 11, 12, and 13 are repeated in 14 and 15, so we drop the former. Branch 14 has nowhere to go, because none of the T's can become E's without creating forbidden substrings. So, branch 14 must be dropped. From branches 15 and 16, the only next destination is $T + E$, so we can drop branch 15 because 16 gets us there just as well by itself. The tree ends as follows:

$$i + i * i \Leftarrow F + F * F \Leftarrow F + F * T \Leftarrow F + T \Leftarrow F + E \Leftarrow T + E \Leftarrow E \Leftarrow S$$

which is the same as

$$S \Rightarrow E \Rightarrow T + E \Rightarrow F + E \Rightarrow F + T \Rightarrow F + F * T \Rightarrow F + F * F \overset{*}{\Rightarrow} i + i * i$$

(The symbol $\Leftarrow$ used above should be self-explanatory.)

Our last algorithm for "understanding" words in order to evaluate expressions is one based on the prefix notation mentioned in Chapter 12, called Łukasiewicz notation. This applies to not only arithmetic expressions, but also many other programming language instructions.

We shall assume that we are now using *postfix* notation, where the two operands immediately precede the operator:

$A + B$	becomes	$AB +$
$(A + B) * C$	becomes	$AB + C *$
$A * (B + C * D)$	becomes	$ABCD * + *$

An algorithm for converting standard infix notation into postfix notation was given in Chapter 12. Once an expression is in postfix, we can evaluate it without finding its derivation from a CFG, although we originally made use of its parsing tree to convert the infix into postfix in the first place. We are assuming here that our expressions involve only numerical values for the identifiers (i's) and only the operations $+$ and $*$, as in the language PLUS-TIMES.

We can evaluate these postfix expressions by a new machine similar to a PDA. Such a machine requires three new states:

1. $\boxed{\text{ADD}}$: This state pops the top two entries off the STACK, adds them, and pushes the result onto the top of the STACK.

2. $\boxed{\text{MPY}}$: This state pops the top two entries off the STACK, multiplies them, and pushes the result onto the top of the STACK.

3. $\overline{/\text{PRINT}/}$: The print state always follows a POP or READ. This prints the last character just popped or read.

The machine to evaluate postfix expressions can now be built as below, where the expression to be evaluated has been put on the INPUT TAPE in the usual fashion—one character per cell starting in the first cell.

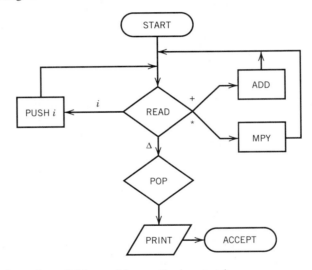

Let us trace the action of this machine on the input string:

$$7\ 5 + 2\ 4 + * 6 +$$

which is postfix for

$$(7 + 5) * (2 + 4) + 6 = 78$$

STATE	STACK	TAPE
START	Δ	7 5 + 2 4 + * 6 +
READ	Δ	5 + 2 4 + * 6 +
PUSH i	7	5 + 2 4 + * 6 +
READ	7	+ 2 4 + * 6 +
PUSH i	5 7	+ 2 4 + * 6 +
READ	5 7	2 4 + * 6 +

STATE	STACK	TAPE
ADD	12	2 4 + * 6 +
READ	12	4 + * 6 +
PUSH *i*	2 12	4 + * 6 +
READ	2 12	+ * 6 +
PUSH *i*	4 2 12	+ * 6 +
READ	4 2 12	* 6 +
ADD	6 12	* 6 +
READ	6 12	6 +
MPY	72	6 +
READ	72	+
PUSH *i*	6 72	+
READ	6 72	Δ
ADD	78	Δ
READ	78	Δ

We notice that just as we finished reading the entire input string, the STACK has only one element in it. We conclude processing by popping 78, printing 78, and accepting the input string.

What we have been using here is a PDA with arithmetic and output capabilities. Just as we expanded FAs to Mealy and Moore machines, we can expand PDAs to what are called **push-down transducers.** These are very important but belong to the study of the theory of compilers.

The task of converting infix arithmetic expressions (normal ones) into postfix can also be accomplished by a pushdown transducer as an alternative to depending on a dotted line circumnavigating a parsing tree. This time all we require is a PDA with an additional PRINT instruction. The input string will be read off of the TAPE character by character. If the character is a number (or, in our example, the letters *a*, *b*, *c*), it is immediately printed out, because the operands in postfix occur in the same order as in the infix equivalent. The operators, however, + and * in our example, must wait to be printed until after the second operand they govern has been printed. The place where the operators wait is, of course, the STACK. If we read *a* + *b*, we print *a*, push +, print *b*, pop +, print +. The output states we need are

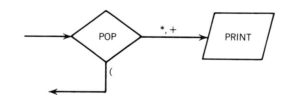

and

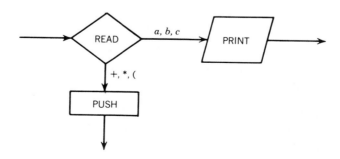

POP-PRINT prints whatever it has just popped, and READ-PRINT prints the character just read. READ-PUSH pushes whatever character "+" or "*" or "(" labels the edge leading into it. These are all the machine parts we need.

One more comment should be made about when an operator is ready to be popped. The second operand is recognized by encountering (1) a right parenthesis, (2) another operator having equal or lower precedence, or (3) the end of the input string.

When a right parenthesis is encountered, it means that the infix expression is complete back up to the last left parenthesis.

For example, consider the expression

$$a * (b + c) + b + c$$

The pushdown transducer will do the following:

1. Read a, print a.
2. Read *, push *.
3. Read (, push (.
4. Read b, print b.
5. Read +, push +.
6. Read c, print c.
7. Read), pop +, print +.
8. Pop (.
9. Read +, we cannot push + on top of * because of operator precedence, so pop *, print *, push +.
10. Read b, print b.
11. Read +, we cannot push + on top of +, so print +.
12. Read c, print c.
13. Read Δ, pop +, print +.

The resulting output sequence is

$$abc + * b + c +$$

which indeed is the correct postfix equivalent of the input. Notice that operator precedence is "built into" this machine. Generalizations of this machine can handle any arithmetic expressions including $-$, $/$, and $**$.

The diagram of the pushdown transducer to convert infix to postfix is given on the next page.

The table following it traces the processing of the input string

$$(a + b) * (b + c * a)$$

Notice that the printing takes place on the right end of the output sequence.

One trivial observation is that this machine will never print any parentheses. No parentheses are needed to understand postfix or prefix notation. Another is that every operator and operand in the original expression will be printed out. The major observation is that if the output of this transducer is then fed into the previous transducer, the original infix arithmetic expression will be evaluated correctly. In this way, we can give a PDA an expression in normal arithmetic notation, and the PDA will evaluate it.

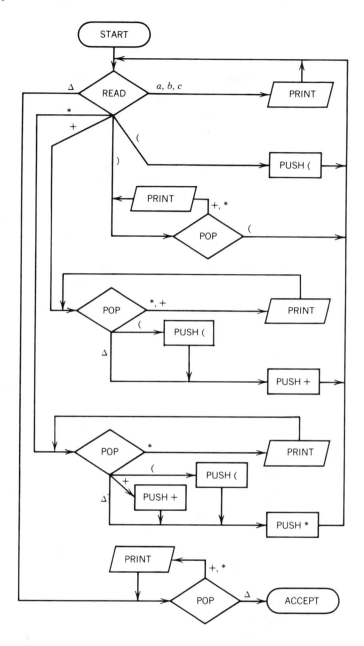

STATE	STACK	TAPE	OUTPUT
START	Δ	$(a + b) * (b + c * a)$	
READ	Δ	$a + b) * (b + c * a)$	
PUSH (	(	$a + b) * (b + c * a)$	
READ	(	$+ b) * (b + c * a)$	
PRINT	(	$+ b) * (b + c * a)$	a
READ	(	$b) * (b + c * a)$	a

STATE	STACK	TAPE	OUTPUT
POP	Δ	$b) * (b + c * a)$	a
PUSH (	(	$b) * (b + c * a)$	a
PUSH +	+ (	$b) * (b + c * a)$	a
READ	+ (	$) * (b + c * a)$	a
PRINT	+ (	$) * (b + c * a)$	ab
READ	+ (	$* (b + c * a)$	ab
POP	(	$* (b + c * a)$	ab
PRINT	(	$* (b + c * a)$	$ab +$
POP	Δ	$* (b + c * a)$	$ab +$
READ	Δ	$(b + c * a)$	$ab +$
POP	Δ	$(b + c * a)$	$ab +$
PUSH *	*	$(b + c * a)$	$ab +$
READ	*	$b + c * a)$	$ab +$
PUSH (	(*	$b + c * a)$	$ab +$
READ	(*	$+ c * a)$	$ab +$
PRINT	(*	$+ c * a)$	$ab + b$
READ	(*	$c * a)$	$ab + b$
POP	*	$c * a)$	$ab + b$
PUSH (	(*	$c * a)$	$ab + b$
PUSH +	+ (*	$c * a)$	$ab + b$
READ	+ (*	$* a)$	$ab + b$
PRINT	+ (*	$* a)$	$ab + bc$
READ	+ (*	$a)$	$ab + bc$
POP	(*	$a)$	$ab + bc$
PUSH +	+ (*	$a)$	$ab + bc$
PUSH *	* + (*	$a)$	$ab + bc$
READ	* + (*	$)$	$ab + bc$
PRINT	* + (*	$)$	$ab + bca$
READ	* + (*	Δ	$ab + bca$
POP	+ (*	Δ	$ab + bca$
PRINT	+ (*	Δ	$ab + bca *$
POP	(*	Δ	$ab + bca *$
PRINT	(*	Δ	$ab + bca * +$
POP	*	Δ	$ab + bca * +$

STATE	STACK	TAPE	OUTPUT
READ	*	Δ	$ab + bca * +$
POP	Δ	Δ	$ab + bca * +$
PRINT	Δ	Δ	$ab + bca * + *$
POP	Δ	Δ	$ab + bca * + *$
ACCEPT	Δ	Δ	$ab + bca * + *$

⚜ PROBLEMS

1. Decide whether or not the following grammars generate any words using the algorithm of Theorem 42 (p. 403):

   (i) $S \rightarrow aSa \mid bSb$

   (ii) $S \rightarrow XY$
   $X \rightarrow SY$
   $Y \rightarrow SX$
   $X \rightarrow a$
   $Y \rightarrow b$

   (iii) $S \rightarrow AB$
   $A \rightarrow BC$
   $C \rightarrow DA$
   $B \rightarrow CD$
   $D \rightarrow a$
   $A \rightarrow b$

   (iv) $S \rightarrow XS$
   $X \rightarrow YX$
   $Y \rightarrow YY$
   $Y \rightarrow XX$
   $X \rightarrow a$

   (v) $S \rightarrow AB$
   $A \rightarrow BSB$
   $B \rightarrow AAS$
   $A \rightarrow CC$
   $B \rightarrow CC$
   $C \rightarrow SS$
   $A \rightarrow a \mid b$
   $C \rightarrow b \mid bb$

2. Modify the proof of Theorem 42 so that it can be applied to any CFG, not just those in CNF.

3. For each of the following grammars, decide whether the language they generate is finite or infinite using the algorithm in Theorem 44 (p. 408):

   (i) $S \rightarrow XS \mid b$
   $X \rightarrow YZ$
   $Z \rightarrow XY$
   $Y \rightarrow ab$

   (ii) $S \rightarrow XS \mid b$
   $X \rightarrow YZ$
   $Z \rightarrow XY$
   $X \rightarrow ab$

   (iii) $S \rightarrow XY \mid bb$
   $X \rightarrow YX$
   $Y \rightarrow XY \mid SS$

   (iv) $S \rightarrow XY \mid bb$
   $X \rightarrow YY$
   $Y \rightarrow XY \mid SS$

   (v) $S \rightarrow XY$
   $X \rightarrow AA \mid YY \mid b$
   $A \rightarrow BC$
   $B \rightarrow AC$
   $C \rightarrow BA$
   $Y \rightarrow a$

   (vi) $S \rightarrow XY$
   $X \rightarrow AA \mid XY \mid b$
   $A \rightarrow BC$
   $B \rightarrow AC$
   $C \rightarrow BA$
   $Y \rightarrow a$

   (vii) $S \rightarrow SS \mid b$
   $X \rightarrow SS \mid SX \mid a$

   (viii) $S \rightarrow XX$
   $X \rightarrow SS \mid a$

4. Modify Theorem 44 so that the decision procedure works on all CFGs, not just those in CNF.

5. Prove that all CFGs with only the one nonterminal S and one or more live productions and one or more dead productions generate an infinite language.

For the following grammars and target strings, decide whether or not the word is generated by the grammar using the CYK algorithm:

6. $S \rightarrow SS$ $x = abba$
    $S \rightarrow a$
    $S \rightarrow bb$

7. $S \rightarrow XS$ $x = baab$
    $X \rightarrow XX$
    $X \rightarrow a$
    $S \rightarrow b$

8. $S \rightarrow XY$ $x = abbaa$
    $X \rightarrow SY$
    $Y \rightarrow SS$
    $X \rightarrow a \mid bb$
    $Y \rightarrow aa$

9. $S \rightarrow AB$ $x = bbaab$
    $A \rightarrow BB \mid a$
    $B \rightarrow AB \mid b$

10. $S \rightarrow AB \mid CD \mid a \mid b$ $x = bababab$
    $A \rightarrow a$
    $B \rightarrow SA$
    $C \rightarrow DS$
    $D \rightarrow b$

11. Modify the CYK algorithm so that it applies to any CFG, not just those in CNF.

12. The CYK algorithm can be described as bottom-up because it starts with the word and works up to the nonterminals. There is another method for deciding membership that is top-down in nature. Create a table with one column for each nonterminal that appears in the grammar and n rows, where n is the length of the subject word. The entries for cell (i, j) are those words of length i that can be derived from the nonterminal, N_j, at the head of the column. The first row is filled based on the dead productions $N \rightarrow t$. Subsequent rows are filled based on the productions $N \rightarrow N_1 N_2$. In the second row, cell $(2, z)$ is filled with all the words of length 2 that are the product of a letter from cell $(1, x)$ and a letter from cell $(1, y)$ for each rule $N_z \rightarrow N_x N_y$. In the third row, cell $(3, z)$ is filled with the words that are products of a word from row 2 and a word from row 1 in either order as long as the grammar includes a rule that generates that product. In the fourth row, the words can be made in three ways; the product of a letter and a 3-letter word, the product of two 2-letter words, the product of a 3-letter word and a single letter. When the table is complete, check cell (n, S) to see if w is among the words derived from S.

    For each of the following grammar–word pairs, construct such a table to determine whether the word can be generated by that grammar:

(i) $S \rightarrow XY$ (ii) $S \rightarrow AX \mid BY \mid a \mid b$ (iii) $S \rightarrow XY$
     $X \rightarrow XA \mid a \mid b$ $X \rightarrow SA$ $X \rightarrow SY \mid a \mid bb$
     $Y \rightarrow AY \mid a$ $Y \rightarrow SB$ $Y \rightarrow SS \mid aa$
     $A \rightarrow a$ $A \rightarrow a$
                        $B \rightarrow b$
     $w = babaa$ $w = ababa$ $w = abbaa$

13. Using top-down parsing, find the leftmost derivation in the grammar PLUS-TIMES for the following expressions:

(i) $i + i + i$

(ii) $i * i + i * i$

(iii) $i * (i + i) * i$

(iv) $((i) * (i + i)) + i$

(v) $(((i)) + ((i)))$

14. Using bottom-up parsing, find any derivation in the grammar PLUS-TIMES for the following expressions:

(i) $i * (i)$

(ii) $((i) + ((i)))$

(iii) $(i * i + i)$

(iv) $i * (i + i)$

(v) $(i * i) * i$

15. The following is a version of an unambiguous grammar for arithmetic expressions employing $-$ and $/$ as well as $+$ and $*$:

$$S \rightarrow E$$
$$E \rightarrow T \mid E + T \mid E - T \mid -T$$
$$T \rightarrow F \mid T * F \mid T/F$$
$$F \rightarrow (E) \mid i$$

Find a leftmost derivation in this grammar for the following expressions using the parsing algorithms specified:

(i) $((i + i) - i * i)/i - i$

(Do this by inspection; that means guesswork. Do we divide by zero here?)

(ii) $i/i + i$ (Top-down)

(iii) $i * i/i - i$ (Top-down)

(iv) $i/i/i$ (Top-down)

Note that this is not ambiguous in this particular grammar. Do we evaluate right to left or left to right?

(v) $i - i - i$ (Bottom-up)

16. Using the second pushdown transducer, convert the following arithmetic expressions to postfix notation and then evaluate them on the first pushdown transducer:

(i) $2 * (7 + 2)$

(ii) $3 * 4 + 7$

(iii) $(3 + 5) + 7 * 3$

(iv) $(3 * 4 + 5) * (2 + 3 * 4)$ *Hint:* The answer is 238.

17. Design a pushdown transducer to convert infix to prefix.

18. Design a pushdown transducer to evaluate prefix.

19. Create an algorithm to convert prefix to postfix.

20. The transducers we designed in this chapter to evaluate postfix notation and to convert infix to postfix have a funny quirk: They can accept some bad input strings and process them as if they were proper.

(i) For each machine, find an example of an accepted bad input.

(ii) Correct these machines so that they accept only proper inputs.

PART III

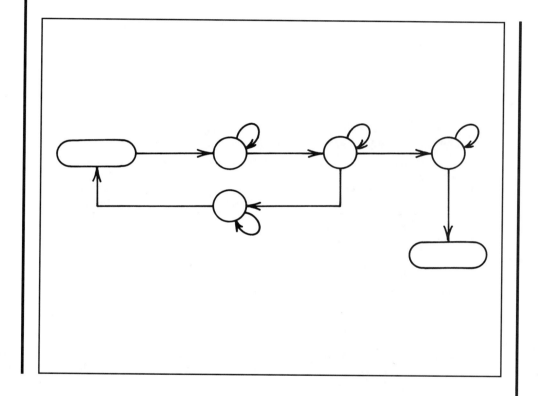

Turing Theory

CHAPTER 19

Turing Machines

⚜ THE TURING MACHINE

At this point it will help us to recapitulate the major themes of the previous two parts and outline all the material we have yet to present in the rest of the book in one large table:

Language Defined by	Corresponding Acceptor	Nondeterminism = Determinism?	Language Closed Under	What Can Be Decided	Example of Application
Regular expression	Finite automaton, transition graph	Yes	Union, product, Kleene star, intersection, complement	Equivalence, emptiness, finiteness, membership	Text editors, sequential circuits
Context-free grammar	Pushdown automaton	No	Union, product, Kleene star	Emptiness finiteness membership	Programming language statements, compilers
Type 0 grammar	Turing machine, Post machine, 2PDA, *n*PDA	Yes	Union, product, intersection, Kleene star	Not much	**Computers**

We see from the lower right entry in the table that we are about to fulfill the promise made in the introduction. We shall soon provide a mathematical model for the entire family of modern-day computers. This model will enable us not only to study some theoretical limitations on the tasks that computers can perform; it will also be a model that we can use to show that certain operations *can* be done by computer. This new model will turn out to be surprisingly like the models we have been studying so far.

Another interesting observation we can make about the bottom row of the table is that we take a very pessimistic view of our ability to decide the important questions about this mathematical model (which as we see is called a Turing machine).

We shall prove that we cannot even decide whether a given word is accepted by a given Turing machine. This situation is unthinkable for FAs or PDAs, but now it is one of the unanticipated facts of life—a fact with grave repercussions.

There is a definite progression in the rows of this table. All regular languages are context-free languages, and we shall see that all context-free languages are Turing machine languages. Historically, the order of invention of these ideas is as follows:

1. Regular languages and FAs were developed by Kleene, Mealy, Moore, Rabin, and Scott in the 1950s.

2. CFGs and PDAs were developed later, by Chomsky, Oettinger, Schützenberger, and Evey, mostly in the 1960s.

3. Turing machines and their theory were developed by Alan Mathison Turing and Emil Post in the 1930s and 1940s.

It is less surprising that these dates are out of order than that Turing's work predated the invention of the computer itself. Turing was not analyzing a specimen that sat on the table in front of him; he was engaged in inventing the beast. It was directly from the ideas in his work on mathematical models that the first computers (as we know them) were built. This is another demonstration that there is nothing more practical than a good abstract theory.

Because Turing machines will be our ultimate model for computers, they will necessarily have output capabilities. Output is very important, so important that a program with no output statements might seem totally useless because it would never convey to humans the result of its calculations. We may have heard it said that the one statement every program must have is an output statement. This is not exactly true. Consider the following program (written in no particular language):

1. READ X
2. If X = 1 THEN END
3. IF X = 2 THEN DIVIDE X BY 0
4. IF X > 2 THEN GOTO STATEMENT 4

Let us assume that the input is a positive integer. If the program terminates naturally, then we know X was 1. If it terminates by creating overflow or was interrupted by some error message warning of illegal calculation (crashes), then we know that X was 2. If we find that our program was terminated because it exceeded our allotted time on the computer, then we know X was greater than 2. We shall see in a moment that the same trichotomy applies to Turing machines.

DEFINITION

A **Turing machine,** denoted TM, is a collection of six things:

1. An alphabet Σ of input letters, which for clarity's sake does not contain the blank symbol Δ.

2. A TAPE divided into a sequence of numbered cells, each containing one character or a blank. The input word is presented to the machine one letter per cell beginning in the leftmost cell, called cell i. The rest of the TAPE is initially filled with blanks, Δ's.

cell i	cell ii	cell iii	cell iv	cell v	
					$\cdots$

TAPE HEAD

3. A TAPE HEAD that can in one step read the contents of a cell on the TAPE, replace it with some other character, and reposition itself to the next cell to the right or to the left of the one it has just read. At the start of the processing, the TAPE HEAD always begins by reading the input in cell i. The TAPE HEAD can never move left from cell i. If it is given orders to do so, the machine crashes. The location of the TAPE HEAD is indicated by ⬠.

4. An alphabet Γ of characters that can be printed on the TAPE by the TAPE HEAD. This can include Σ. Even though we allow the TAPE HEAD to print a Δ, we call this erasing and do not include the blank as a letter in the alphabet Γ.

5. A finite set of states including exactly one START state from which we begin execution (and which we may reenter during execution) and some (maybe none) HALT states that cause execution to terminate when we enter them. The other states have no function, only names:

$$q_1 \quad q_2 \quad q_3 \quad \cdots \qquad \text{or} \qquad 1 \quad 2 \quad 3 \quad \cdots$$

6. **A program,** which is a set of rules that tell us, on the basis of the state we are in and the letter the TAPE HEAD has just read, how to change states, what to print on the TAPE, and where to move the TAPE HEAD. We depict the program as a collection of directed edges connecting the states. Each edge is labeled with a triplet of information:

$$\text{(letter, letter, direction)}$$

The first letter (either Δ or from Σ or Γ) is the character the TAPE HEAD reads from the cell to which it is pointing. The second letter (also Δ or from Γ) is what the TAPE HEAD prints in the cell before it leaves. The third component, the direction, tells the TAPE HEAD whether to move one cell to the right, R, or one cell to the left, L.

No stipulation is made as to whether every state has an edge leading from it for every possible letter on the TAPE. If we are in a state and read a letter that offers no choice of path to another state, we *crash*; that means we terminate execution unsuccessfully. To terminate execution of a certain input successfully, we must be led to a HALT state. The word on the input TAPE is then said to be *accepted* by the TM.

A crash also occurs when we are in the first cell on the TAPE and try to move the TAPE HEAD left.

By definition, all Turing machines are **deterministic.** This means that there is no state q that has two or more edges leaving it labeled with the same first letter.

For example,

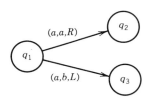

is not allowed. ∎

EXAMPLE

The following is the TAPE from a TM about to run on the input *aba*:

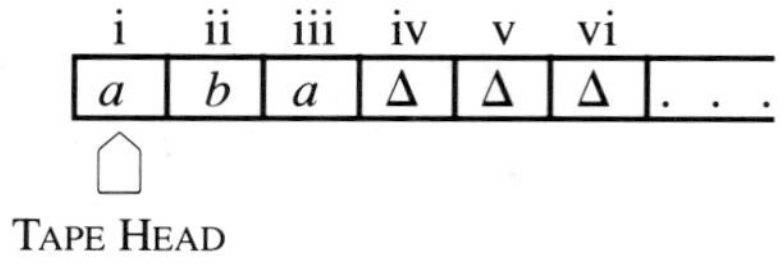

The program for this TM is given as a directed graph with labeled edges as shown below:

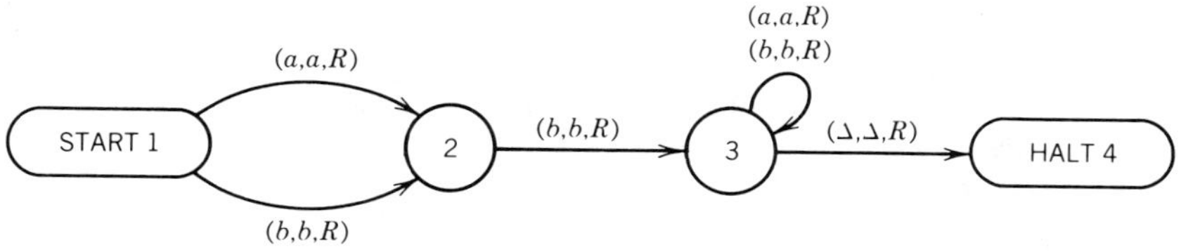

Notice that the loop at state 3 has two labels. The edges from state 1 to state 2 could have been drawn as one edge with two labels.

We start, as always, with the TAPE HEAD reading cell i and the program in the START state, which is here labeled state 1. We depict this as

$$\begin{matrix} 1 \\ \underline{a}ba \end{matrix}$$

The number on top is the number of the state we are in. Below that is the current meaningful contents of the string on the TAPE up to the beginning of the infinite run of blanks. It is possible that there may be a Δ inside this string. We underline the character in the cell that is *about to be read.*

At this point in our example, the TAPE HEAD reads the letter *a* and we follow the edge (*a*, *a*, *R*) to state 2. The instructions of this edge to the TAPE HEAD are "read an *a*, print an *a*, move right."

The TAPE now looks like this:

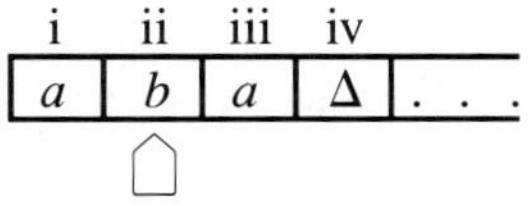

We can record the execution process by writing

$$\begin{matrix} 1 \\ \underline{a}ba \end{matrix} \rightarrow \begin{matrix} 2 \\ a\underline{b}a \end{matrix}$$

At this point, we are in state 2. Because we are reading the *b* in cell ii, we must take the ride to state 3 on the edge labeled (*b*, *b*, *R*). The TAPE HEAD replaces the *b* with a *b* and moves right one cell. The idea of replacing a letter with itself may seem silly, but it unifies the structure of TMs.

We are now up to

$$\begin{matrix} 1 \\ \underline{a}ba \end{matrix} \rightarrow \begin{matrix} 2 \\ a\underline{b}a \end{matrix} \rightarrow \begin{matrix} 3 \\ ab\underline{a} \end{matrix}$$

The TAPE now looks like this:

i	ii	iii	iv	
a	b	a	Δ	. . .

We are in state 3 reading an a, so we loop. That means we stay in state 3, but we move the TAPE HEAD to cell iv:

$$\underset{ab\underline{a}}{3} \rightarrow \underset{aba\underline{\Delta}}{3}$$

This is one of those times when we must indicate a Δ as part of the meaningful contents of the TAPE.

We are now in state 3 reading a Δ, so we move to state 4:

$$\underset{aba\underline{\Delta}}{3} \rightarrow \underset{aba\Delta\underline{\Delta}}{4}$$

The input string aba has been accepted by this TM. This particular machine did not change any of the letters on the TAPE, so at the end of the run the TAPE still reads $aba\Delta$ . . . . This is not a requirement for the acceptance of a string, just a phenomenon that happened this time.

In summary, the whole execution can be depicted by the following **execution chain**, also called a **process chain** or **trace of execution**, or simply a **trace:**

$$\underset{\underline{a}ba}{1} \rightarrow \underset{a\underline{b}a}{2} \rightarrow \underset{ab\underline{a}}{3} \rightarrow \underset{aba\underline{\Delta}}{3} \rightarrow \text{HALT}$$

This is a new use for the arrow. It is neither a production nor a derivation.

Let us consider which input strings are accepted by this TM. Any first letter, a or b, will lead us to state 2. From state 2 to state 3, we require that we read the letter b. Once in state 3, we stay there as the TAPE HEAD moves right and right again, moving perhaps many cells until it encounters a Δ. Then we get to the HALT state and accept the word. Any word that reaches state 3 will eventually be accepted. If the second letter is an a, then we crash at state 2. This is because there is no edge coming from state 2 with directions for what happens when the TAPE HEAD reads an a.

The language of words accepted by this machine is: All words over the alphabet {a b} in which the second letter is a b.

This is a regular language because it can also be defined by the regular expression

$$\textbf{(a + b)b(a + b)*}$$

This TM is also reminiscent of FAs, making only one pass over the input string, moving its TAPE HEAD always to the right, and never changing a letter it has read. TMs can do more tricks, as we shall soon see. ∎

EXAMPLE

Consider the following TM:

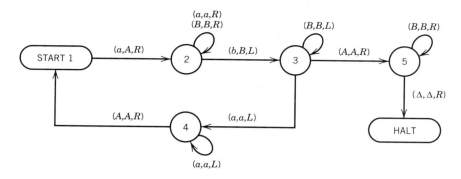

We have only drawn the program part of the TM, because initial appearance of the TAPE depends on the input word. This is a more complicated example of a TM. We analyze it by first explaining what it does and then recognizing how it does it.

The language this TM accepts is $\{a^n b^n\}$.

By examining the program, we can see that the TAPE HEAD may print any of the letters a, A, or B or a Δ, and it may read any of the letters a, b, A, or B or a blank. Technically, the input alphabet is $\Sigma = \{a \quad b\}$ and the output alphabet is $\Gamma = \{a \quad A \quad B\}$, because Δ is the symbol for a blank or empty cell and is not a legal character in an alphabet. Let us describe the algorithm, informally in English, before looking at the directed graph that is the program.

Let us assume that we start with a word of the language $\{a^n b^n\}$ on the TAPE. We begin by taking the a in the first cell and changing it to the character A. (If the first cell does not contain an a, the program should crash. We can arrange this by having only one edge leading from START and labeling it to read an a.) The conversion from a to A means that this a has been counted. We now want to find the b in the word that pairs off with this a. So, we keep moving the TAPE HEAD to the right, without changing anything it passes over, until it reaches the first b. When we reach this b, we change it into the character B, which again means that it too has been counted. Now we move the TAPE HEAD back down to the left until it reaches the first uncounted a. The first time we make our descent down the TAPE, this will be the a in cell ii.

How do we know when we get to the first uncounted a? We cannot tell the TAPE HEAD to "find cell ii." This instruction is not in its repertoire. We can, however, tell the TAPE HEAD to keep moving to the left until it gets to the character A. When it hits the A, we bounce one cell to the right and there we are. In doing this, the TAPE HEAD passed through cell ii on its way down the TAPE. However, when we were first there, we did not recognize it as our destination. Only when we bounce off of our marker, the first A encountered, do we realize where we are. Half the trick in programming TMs is to know where the TAPE HEAD is by bouncing off of landmarks.

When we have located this leftmost uncounted a, we convert it into an A and begin marching up the TAPE looking for the corresponding b. This means that we skip over some a's and over the symbol B, which we previously wrote, leaving them unchanged, until we get to the first uncounted b. Once we have located it, we have found our second pair of a and b. We count this second b by converting it into a B, and we march back down the TAPE looking for our next uncounted a. This will be in cell iii. Again, we cannot tell the TAPE HEAD to "find cell iii." We must program it to find the intended cell. The same instructions as given last time work again. Back down to the first A we meet and then up one cell. As we march down, we walk through a B and some a's until we first reach the character A. This will be the second A, the one in cell ii. We bounce off this to the right, into cell iii, and find an a. This we convert to A and move up the TAPE to find its corresponding b.

This time marching up the TAPE, we again skip over a's and B's until we find the first b. We convert this to B and march back down, looking for the first unconverted a. We repeat the pairing process over and over.

What happens when we have paired off all the a's and b's? After we have converted our last b into a B and we move left, looking for the next a, we find that after marching left back through the last of the B's, we encounter an A. We recognize that this means we are out of little a's in the initial field of a's at the beginning of the word.

We are about ready to accept the word, but we want to make sure that there are no more b's that have not been paired off with a's, or any extraneous a's at the end. Therefore, we move back up through the field of B's to be sure that they are followed by a blank; otherwise, the word initially may have been $aaabbbb$ or $aaabbba$.

When we know that we have only A's and B's on the TAPE, in equal number, we can accept the input string.

The following is a picture of the contents of the TAPE at each step in the processing of the string $aaabbb$. Remember, in a trace the TAPE HEAD is indicated by the underlining of the letter it is about to read:

$\underline{a}aabbb$
$A\underline{a}abbb$
$Aa\underline{a}bbb$
$Aaa\underline{b}bb$
$Aa\underline{a}Bbb$
$A\underline{a}aBbb$
$\underline{A}aaBbb$
$A\underline{a}aBbb$
$AA\underline{a}Bbb$
$AAa\underline{B}bb$
$AAaB\underline{b}b$
$AAa\underline{B}Bb$
$AA\underline{a}BBb$
$A\underline{A}aBBb$
$AA\underline{a}BBb$
$AAA\underline{B}Bb$
$AAAB\underline{B}b$
$AAABB\underline{b}$
$AAAB\underline{B}B$
$AAA\underline{B}BB$
$AA\underline{A}BBB$
$AAA\underline{B}BB$
$AAAB\underline{B}B$
$AAABB\underline{B}$
$AAABBB\underline{\Delta}$
HALT

Based on this algorithm, we can define a set of states that have the following meanings:

State 1   This is the START state, but it is also the state we are in whenever we are about to read the lowest unpaired a. In a PDA we can never return to the START state, but in a TM we can. The edges leaving from here must convert this a to the character A and move the TAPE HEAD right and enter state 2.

State 2   This is the state we are in when we have just converted an a to an A and we are looking for the matching b. We begin moving up the TAPE. If we read another a, we leave it alone and continue to march up the TAPE, moving the TAPE HEAD always to the right. If we read a B, we also leave it alone and continue to move the TAPE HEAD right. We cannot read an A while in this state. In this algorithm, all the A's remain to the left of the TAPE HEAD once they are printed. If we read Δ while we are searching for the b, we are in trouble because we have not paired off our a. So, we crash. The first b we read, if we are lucky enough to find one, is the end of the search in this state. We convert it to B, move the TAPE HEAD left, and enter state 3.

State 3   This is the state we are in when we have just converted a b to B. We should now march left down the TAPE, looking for the field of unpaired a's. If we read a B, we leave it alone and keep moving left. If and when we read an a, we have done our job. We must then go to state 4, which will try to find the leftmost unpaired a. If we encounter the character b while moving to the left, something has gone very wrong and we should crash. If, however, we encounter the character A before we hit an a, we know that we have used up the pool of unpaired a's at the beginning of the input string and we may be ready to terminate execution. Therefore, we leave the A alone and reverse directions to the right and move into state 5.

State 4   We get here when state 3 has located the rightmost end of the field of unpaired a's. The TAPE and TAPE HEAD situation looks like this:

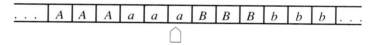

In this state, we must move left through a block of solid a's (we crash if we encounter a b, B, or Δ) until we find an A. When we do, we bounce off it to the right, which lands us at the leftmost uncounted a. This means that we should next be in state 1 again.

State 5   When we get here, it must be because state 3 found that there were no unpaired a's left and it bounced us off the rightmost A. We are now reading the leftmost B as in the picture below:

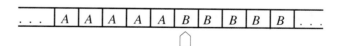

It is now our job to be sure that there are no more a's or b's left in this word. We want to scan through solid B's until we hit the first blank. Because the program never printed any blanks, this will indicate the end of the input string. If there are no more surprises before the Δ, we then accept the word by going to the state HALT. Otherwise, we crash. For example, $aabba$ would become $AABBa$ and then crash because, while searching for the Δ, we find an a.

This explains the TM program that we began with. It corresponds to the depiction above state for state and edge for edge.

Let us trace the processing of the input string $aabb$ by looking at its execution chain:

$$
\begin{array}{cccccc}
1 & 2 & 2 & 3 & 4 & 1 \\
\underline{a}abb & \to A\underline{a}bb & \to Aa\underline{b}b & \to A\underline{a}Bb & \to \underline{A}aBb & \to A\underline{a}Bb \\
2 & 2 & 3 & 3 & 5 & 5 \\
\to AA\underline{B}b & \to AAB\underline{b} & \to AA\underline{B}B & \to A\underline{A}BB & \to AA\underline{B}B & \to AAB\underline{B} \\
5 & & & & & \\
\to AABB\underline{\Delta} & \to \text{HALT} & & & &
\end{array}
$$

It is clear that any string of the form $a^n b^n$ will reach the HALT state. To show that any string that reaches the HALT state must be of the form $a^n b^n$, we trace backward. To reach HALT, we must get to state 5 and read a Δ. To be in state 5, we must have come from state 3 from which we read an A and some number of B's while moving to the right. So at the point we are in state 3 ready to terminate, the TAPE and TAPE HEAD situation is as shown below:

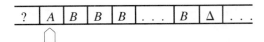

To be in state 3 means we have begun at START and circled around the loop some number of times:

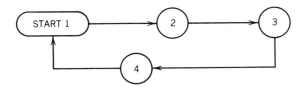

Every time we go from START to state 3, we have converted an a to an A and a b to a B. No other edge in the program of this TM changes the contents of any cell on the TAPE. However many B's there are, there are just as many A's. Examination of the movement of the TAPE HEAD shows that all the A's stretch in one connected sequence of cells starting at cell i. To go from state 3 to HALT shows that the whole TAPE has been converted to A's, then B's followed by blanks. If we put together all of this, to get to HALT, the input word must be $a^n b^n$ for some $n > 0$. ■

EXAMPLE

Consider the following TM:

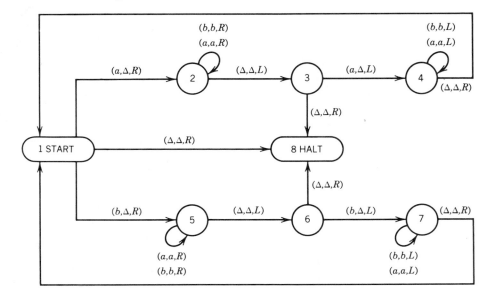

This looks like another monster, yet it accepts the familiar language PALINDROME and does so by a very simple deterministic algorithm.

We read the first letter of the input string and erase it, but we remember whether it was an *a* or a *b*. We go to the last letter and check to be sure it is the same as what used to be the first letter. If not, we crash, but if so, we erase it too. We then return to the front of what is left of the input string and repeat the process. If we do not crash while there are any letters left, then when we get to the condition where the whole TAPE is blank, we accept the input string. This means that we reach the HALT state. Notice that the input string itself is no longer on the TAPE.

The process, briefly, works like this:

$$abbabba$$
$$bbabba$$
$$bbabb$$
$$babb$$
$$bab$$
$$ab$$
$$a$$
$$\Delta$$

We mentioned above that when we erase the first letter, we remember what it was as we march up to the last letter. Turing machines have no auxiliary memory device, like a PUSHDOWN STACK, where we could store this information, but there are ways around this. One possible method is to use some of the blank space farther down the TAPE for making notes. In this case, we use a different trick. The memory of what letter was erased is stored in the path through the program the input takes. If the first letter is an *a*, we are off on the state 2 – state 3 – state 4 loop. If the first letter is a *b*, we are off on the state 5 – state 6 – state 7 loop.

All of this is clear from the descriptions of the meanings of the states below:

State 1   When we are in this state, we read the first letter of what is left of the input string. This could be because we are just starting and reading cell i or because we have been returned here from state 4 or 7. If we read an *a*, we change it to a Δ (erase it), move the TAPE HEAD to the right, and progress to state 2. If we read a *b*, we erase it and move the TAPE HEAD to the right and progress to state 5. If we read a Δ where we expect the string to begin, it is because we have erased everything, or perhaps we started with the input word Λ. In either case, we accept the word and we shall see that it is in EVENPALINDROME:

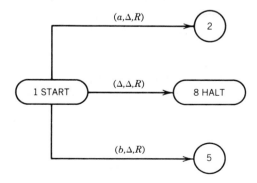

State 2   We get here because we have just erased an *a* from the front of the remaining input string and we want to get to the last letter of the remaining input string to

see whether it too is an a. So, we move to the right through all the a's and b's left in the input until we get to the end of the string at the first Δ. When that happens, we back up one cell (to the left) and move into state 3:

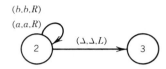

State 3   We get here only from state 2, which means that the letter we erased at the start of the string was an a and state 2 has requested us now to read the last letter of the string. We found the end of the string by moving to the right until we hit the first Δ. Then we bounced one cell back to the left. If this cell is also blank, then there are only blanks left on the TAPE. The letters have all been successfully erased and we can accept the word. Everything erased was in the form of an ODDPALINDROME, but it had a middle letter of a that was the last non-Δ on the TAPE. So, we go to HALT. If there is something left of the input string, but the last letter is a b, the input string was not a palindrome. Therefore, we crash by having no labeled edge to go on. If the last letter is an a, then we erase it, completing the pair, and begin moving the TAPE HEAD left, down to the beginning of the string again to pair off another set of letters:

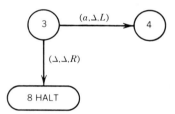

Notice that when we read the Δ and move to HALT, we still need to include in the edge's label instructions to write something and move the TAPE HEAD somewhere. The label (Δ, a, R) would work just as well, or (Δ, B, R). However, (Δ, a, L) might be a disaster. We might have started with a one-letter word, say, a. State 1 erases this a. Then state 2 reads the Δ in cell ii and returns us to cell i where we read the blank. If we try to move left from cell i, we crash on the very verge of accepting the input string.

State 4   Like state 2, this is a travel state searching for the beginning of what is left of the input string. We keep heading left fearlessly because we know that cell i contains a Δ, so we shall not fall off the edge of the earth and crash by going left from cell i. There may be a whole section of Δ's so the first Δ is not necessarily in cell i. When we hit the first Δ, we back up one position to the right, setting ourselves up in state 1 ready to read the first letter of what is left of the string:

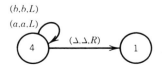

State 5   We get to state 5 only from state 1 when the letter it has just erased was a b. In

other words, state 5 corresponds exactly to state 2 but for strings whose remainder begins with a b. It too searches for the end of the string:

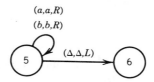

State 6   We get here when we have erased a b in state 1 and found the end of the string in state 5. We examine the letter at hand. If it is an a, then the string began with b and ended with a, so we crash since it is not in PALINDROME. If it is a b, we erase it and hunt for the beginning again. If it is a Δ, we know that the string was an ODDPALINDROME with middle letter b. This is the twin of state 3.

State 7   This state is exactly the same as state 4. We try to find the beginning of the string.

Putting together all these states, we get the picture we started with. Let us trace the running of this TM on the input string $ababa$:

$$
\begin{array}{ccccccccc}
1 & & 2 & & 2 & & 2 & & 2 \\
\underline{a}baba & \rightarrow & \Delta b\underline{a}ba & \rightarrow & \Delta ba\underline{b}a & \rightarrow & \Delta bab\underline{a} & \rightarrow & \Delta baba\underline{\;} \\
\end{array}
$$

$$
\begin{array}{ccccccccc}
 & & 2 & & 3 & & 4 & & 4 & & 4 \\
\rightarrow & \Delta baba\underline{\Delta} & \rightarrow & \Delta bab\underline{a} & \rightarrow & \Delta ba\underline{b}\Delta & \rightarrow & \Delta b\underline{a}b\Delta & \rightarrow & \Delta \underline{b}ab\Delta \\
\end{array}
$$

$$
\begin{array}{ccccccccc}
 & & 4 & & 1 & & 5 & & 5 & & 5 \\
\rightarrow & \Delta \underline{b}ab\Delta & \rightarrow & \Delta \underline{b}ab\Delta & \rightarrow & \Delta\Delta \underline{a}b\Delta & \rightarrow & \Delta\Delta a\underline{b}\Delta & \rightarrow & \Delta\Delta ab\underline{\Delta} \\
\end{array}
$$

$$
\begin{array}{ccccccccc}
 & & 6 & & 7 & & 7 & & 1 & & 2 \\
\rightarrow & \Delta\Delta a\underline{b}\Delta & \rightarrow & \Delta\Delta \underline{a}\Delta\Delta & \rightarrow & \Delta\Delta \underline{a}\Delta\Delta & \rightarrow & \Delta\Delta \underline{a}\Delta\Delta & \rightarrow & \Delta\Delta\Delta\underline{\Delta}\Delta \\
\end{array}
$$

$$
\begin{array}{ccccc}
 & & 3 & & 8 \\
\rightarrow & \Delta\Delta\underline{a}\Delta\Delta & \rightarrow & \Delta\Delta\underline{a}\Delta\Delta \\
\end{array}
$$

$$
\begin{array}{ccc}
 & & 8 \\
\rightarrow & \Delta\Delta\Delta\underline{\Delta}\Delta & \rightarrow & \text{HALT} \\
\end{array}
$$

Our first example was no more than a converted FA, and the language it accepted was regular. The second example accepted a language that was context-free and nonregular and the TM given employed separate alphabets for writing and reading. The third machine accepted a language that was also context-free but that could be accepted only by a nondeterministic PDA, whereas the TM that accepts it is deterministic.

We have seen that we can use the TAPE for more than a PUSHDOWN STACK. In the last two examples, we ran up and down the TAPE to make observations and changes in the string at both ends and in the middle. We shall see later that the TAPE can be used for even more tasks: It can be used as work space for calculation and output.

We shall eventually show that TMs are more powerful than PDAs because a TAPE can do more than a STACK. However, this intuitive notion is not sufficient proof because PDAs have the extra power of nondeterminism whereas TMs are limited to being deterministic. What we are ready to demonstrate is that TMs are more powerful than FAs.

THEOREM 46

Every regular language has a TM that accepts exactly it.

PROOF

Consider any regular language L. Take an FA that accepts L. Change the edge labels a and b to (a, a, R) and (b, b, R), respectively. Change the $-$ state to the word START. Erase the plus sign out of each final state and instead add to each of these an edge labeled (Δ, Δ, R) leading to a HALT state. Voilà, a TM.

We read the input string moving from state to state in the TM exactly as we would on the FA. When we come to the end of the input string, if we are not in a TM state corresponding to a final state in the FA, we crash when the TAPE HEAD reads the Δ in the next cell. If the TM state corresponds to an FA final state, we take the edge labeled (Δ, Δ, R) to HALT. The acceptable strings are the same for the TM and the FA.   ∎

EXAMPLE

Let us build a TM to accept the language EVEN-EVEN—the collection of all strings with an even number of a's and an even number of b's.

By the above algorithm, the machine is

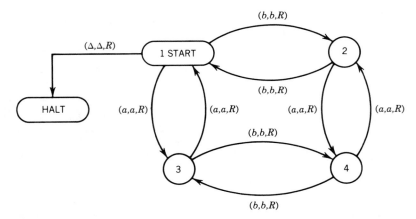

EXAMPLE   ∎

Now we shall consider a valid but problematic machine to accept the language of all strings that have a double a in them somewhere:

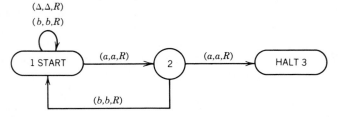

The problem is that we have labeled the loop at the START state with the extra option (Δ, Δ, R). This is still a perfectly valid TM because it fits all the clauses in the definition. Any string without a double a that ends in the letter a will get to state 2, where the TAPE HEAD will read a Δ and crash. What happens to strings without a double a that end in b? When the last letter of the input string has been read, we are in state 1. We read the first Δ

and return to state 1, moving the TAPE HEAD farther up the TAPE full of Δ's. In fact, we loop forever in state 1 on the edge labeled (Δ, Δ, R).

All the strings in $(\mathbf{a} + \mathbf{b})^*$ can be divided into three sets:

1. Those with a double a. They are accepted by the TM.
2. Those without aa that end in a. They crash.
3. Those without aa that end in b. They loop forever. ∎

Unlike on an FA, on a TM an input string cannot just run out of gas in some middle state. Because the input string is just the first part of an infinite TAPE, there are always infinitely many Δ's to read after the meaningful input has been exhausted.

These three possibilities exist for every TM, although for the examples we met previously the third set is empty. This last example is our first TM that can loop forever.

We have seen that certain PDAs also loop forever on some inputs. In Part II, this was a mild curiosity; in Part III, it will be a major headache.

DEFINITION

Every Turing machine T over the alphabet Σ divides the set of input strings into three classes:

1. **ACCEPT**(T) is the set of all strings leading to a HALT state. This is also called the *language accepted* by T.
2. **REJECT**(T) is the set of all strings that crash during execution by moving left from cell i or by being in a state that has no exit edge that wants to read the character the TAPE HEAD is reading.
3. **LOOP**(T) is the set of all other strings, that is, strings that loop forever while running on T. ∎

We shall consider this issue in more detail later. For now, we should simply bear in mind the resemblance of this definition to the output-less computer program at the beginning of this chapter.

While we have not yet shown that TMs can recognize all context-free languages, let us give some justification for introducing this new mathematical model of a machine by showing that there are some non-context-free languages that TMs can accept.

EXAMPLE

Let us consider the non-context-free language $\{a^n b^n a^n\}$. This language can be accepted by the following interesting procedure:

Step 1   We presume that we are reading the first letter of what remains on the input. Initially, this means we are reading the first letter of the input string, but as the algorithm progresses, we may find ourselves back in this step reading the first letter of a smaller remainder. If no letters are found (a blank is read), we go to HALT. If what we read is an a, we change it to a $*$ or some other marker, even Δ, and move the TAPE HEAD right. If we read anything else, we crash. This is all done in state 1.

Step 2 In state 2, we skip over the rest of the *a*'s in the initial clump of *a*'s, looking for the first *b*. This will put us in state 3. Here, we search for the *last b* in the clump of *b*'s: We read *b*'s continually until we encounter the first *a* (which takes us to state 4) and then bounce off that *a* to the left. If after the *b*'s we find a Δ instead of an *a*, we crash. Now that we have located the last *b* in the clump, we do something clever: We change it into an *a*, and we move on to state 5. The reason it took so many TM states to do this simple job is that if we allowed, say, state 2 to skip over *b*'s as well as *a*'s, it would merrily skip its way to the end of the input. We need a separate TM state to keep track of where we are in the data.

Step 3 The first thing we want to do here is find the end of the clump of *a*'s (this is the second clump of *a*'s in the input). We do this in state 5 by reading right until we get to a Δ. If we read a *b* after this second clump of *a*'s, we crash. If we get to the Δ, we know that the input is, in fact, of the form **a*b*a***. When we have located the end of this clump, we turn the last *two a*'s into Δ's. Because we changed the last *b* into an *a*, this is tantamount to killing off a *b* and an *a*. If we had turned that *b* into a Δ, it would have meant Δ's in the middle of the input string and we would have had trouble telling where the real ends of the string were. Instead, we turned a *b* into an *a* and then erased two *a*'s off the right end.

Step 4 We are now in state 8 and we want to return to state 1 and do this whole thing again. Nothing could be easier. We skip over *a*'s and *b*'s, moving the TAPE HEAD left until we encounter the rightmost of the *'s that fill the front end of the TAPE. Then we move one cell to the right and begin again in state 1.

The TM looks like this:

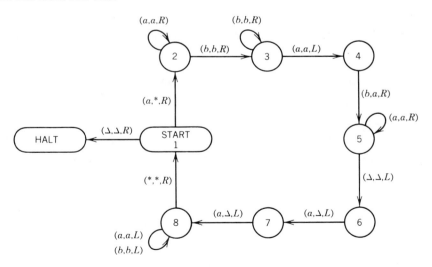

Let us trace the action of this machine on the input string *aaabbbaaa*:

$$
\begin{array}{ccccccccc}
\text{START} & & 2 & & 2 & & 2 & & 3 \\
\underline{a}aabbbaaa & \rightarrow & *\underline{a}abbbaaa & \rightarrow & *a\underline{a}bbbaaa & \rightarrow & *aa\underline{b}bbaaa & \rightarrow & *aab\underline{b}baaa \\
3 & & 3 & & 4 & & 5 & & 5 \\
\rightarrow \; *aabb\underline{b}aaa & \rightarrow & *aabbb\underline{a}aa & \rightarrow & *aabb\underline{b}aaa & \rightarrow & *aabba\underline{a}aa & \rightarrow & *aabbaa\underline{a}a \\
5 & & 5 & & 6 & & 7 & & 8 \\
\rightarrow \; *aabbaaa\underline{a} & \rightarrow & *aabbaaaa\underline{\Delta} & \rightarrow & *aabbaaa\underline{a} & \rightarrow & *aabbaa\underline{a} & \rightarrow & *aabba\underline{a}
\end{array}
$$

→ 8 / *aabba̲a → 8 / *aabba̲a → 8 / *aabba̲a → 8 / *aa̲bbaa → 8 / *a̲abbaa

→ 8 / *aabba̲a → 8 / *a̲abbaa → 2 / **a̲bbaa → 2 / **a̲bbaa → 3 / **a̲bbaa

→ 3 / **abba̲a → 4 / **a̲bbaa → 5 / **aba̲aa → 5 / **aba̲aa → 5 / **abaaa̲Δ

→ 6 / **abaa̲a → 7 / **aba̲a → 8 / **ab̲a → 8 / **ab̲a → 8 / **ab̲a

→ 8 / **ab̲a → 1 / **ab̲a → 2 / ***b̲a → 3 / ***b̲a → 4 / ***b̲a

→ 5 / ***a̲a → 5 / ***aa̲Δ → 6 / ***a̲a → 7 / ***a̲ → 8 / ***_

→ 1 / ***Δ̲ → HALT / ***ΔΔ

After designing the machine and following the trace, we should be aware of several things:

1. The only words accepted are of the form $a^n b^n a^n$ (here, $n = 0, 1, 2, 3, \ldots$)

2. When the machine halts, the TAPE will hold as many *'s as there were b's in the input.

3. If the input was $a^m b^m a^m$, the TAPE HEAD will be in cell $(m + 2)$ when the machine halts. ∎

THE SUBPROGRAM INSERT

Sometimes in the running of a Turing machine, we may wish to **insert** a character into the string on the TAPE exactly at the spot where the TAPE HEAD is pointing. This means that the newly inserted character will occupy this cell and every character on the TAPE to the right of it will be shifted one cell farther up the TAPE. The data on the TAPE to the left of the insertion point will be left alone. We allow for the possibility that the insertion point is cell i. After this insertion takes place, we shall want the TAPE HEAD to point to the cell to the right of the inserted character.

The part of the TM program that can affect such an insertion need not depend on whatever else the TM is doing. It is an independent subprogram, and once it is written, we can incorporate it into any other TM program by indicating that we are calling upon the insertion subprogram and specifying what character we wish to insert. We can insert an a by drawing the picture

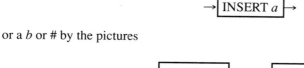

or a b or # by the pictures

→ INSERT b →   → INSERT # →

For example, we want INSERT b to act like this:

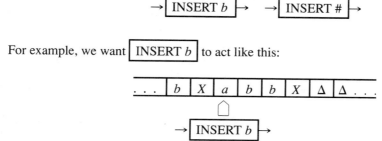

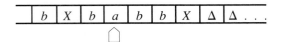

Now let us write a piece of TM program to insert a b into a TAPE on which the existing characters are all a's, b's, and X's followed, of course, by infinitely many blanks. The first thing we shall have the program do is insert a Q as a marker in the cell into which we are going to put the b. The reason we do not just write a b into this cell immediately is that the TAPE HEAD must move along up the TAPE and then return to the proper cell to the right of the insertion cell; it must be able to locate this spot.

Let us call the state in which our subprogram starts state 1. In this state, we read a character (either a, b, or X) and then we write a Q and move the TAPE HEAD to the right. In this next cell, we have to write exactly what it was that was displaced in the previous cell. This requires some memory. The memory we use will be in the form of keeping separate states that remember the displaced character. Let state 2 remember that what was just displaced was an a. Let state 3 remember that what was just displaced was a b. Let state 4 remember that what was just displaced was an X. In our example, the character set for the TAPE contained only three possibilities. This is a simplification that makes the diagram we shall produce more easily understood. But it will be clear that any finite character set can be shifted to the right by the same trick of creating a separate state for every character just erased.

If we are in state 2 and we now read a b, we remember that we must replace the a that was displaced, so we write an a, but now we realize that we have just displaced a b, which we owe to the TAPE in the next cell. This means that we belong in state 3, which serves as just such a memory device. Therefore, we draw an edge from state 2 to state 3 and label it (b, a, R). If we are in state 2 and we read an X, we go to state 4 on an edge labeled (X, a, R). In both cases, we have paid our debt of one a to the TAPE and created a new debt we will pay with the next instruction. If we are in state 2 and we read an a, we will return to state 2 on a loop labeled (a, a, R). We have paid the debt of one a but now owe another.

The situation for state 3 is similar. Whatever we read, we write the b that we owe and go to the state that remembers what character was sacrificed for the b. We have an edge to state 2 labeled (a, b, R), an edge to state 4 labeled (X, b, R), and a loop back to state 3 labeled (b, b, R). Also from state 4 we have an edge to state 2 labeled (a, X, R), an edge to state 3 labeled (b, X, R), and a loop labeled (X, X, R).

Eventually from state 2, 3, or 4, we will run out of characters and meet a Δ. When this happens, we go to a new state, state 5, from which we begin the rewinding process of returning the TAPE HEAD to the desired location. On our way to state 5, we must write the last character owed to the TAPE. This means that the edge from 2 to 5 is labeled (Δ, a, R). The edge from 3 to 5 is labeled (Δ, b, R). And the edge from 4 to 5 is labeled (Δ, X, R).

In state 5, we assume that we are reading another Δ because the character string has ended. This Δ we leave alone and move the TAPE HEAD down to the left and go to state 6. State 6 moves the TAPE HEAD over to the left in search of the Q, looping and not changing what it reads. When it does reach the inevitable Q (which we know exists because we put it there ourselves), we move to state 7, replacing the Q with the b that was the character we wished to insert in the first place, and move the TAPE HEAD to the right. It is clear that to insert any other character, all we would have to do is to change one component of the label on the edge from state 6 to state 7.

From state 7, we return to the rest of the TM program. The subroutine INSERT b looks like this:

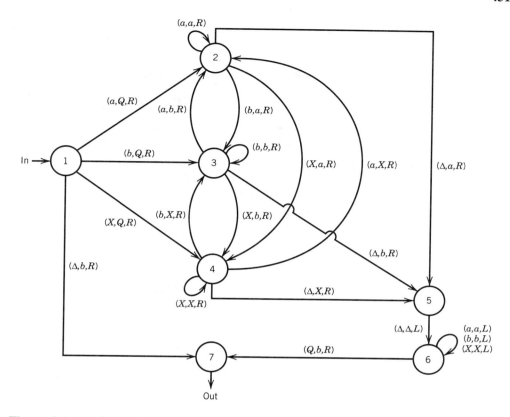

The usefulness of the subprogram INSERT can be seen immediately from the fact that when we begin processing an input string, we run the risk of moving the TAPE HEAD off the TAPE by inadvertently instructing it to move left when it is, in fact, in cell i, thereby causing an unanticipated crash. To prevent this, we can always begin all TM processing by inserting a brick wall, #, into cell i as the first step of the program. When moving the TAPE HEAD left down the TAPE, we can always be careful to bounce off of the brick wall if it is encountered. The entire input string is then bounded by # on the left and Δ on the right.

EXAMPLE

Let us consider a TM to accept the language EQUAL, of all strings with the same number of a's and b's. EQUAL is context-free but nonregular, and so the algorithm of Theorem 46 (p. 445) cannot be employed.

The algorithm we do propose (although it is by no means the best) is to run an alternating series of search and destroy missions. We will start by inserting a # into cell i. Then from cell ii on up we seek an a. When we find our first, we change it into an X and return the TAPE HEAD to cell ii. Then we search up the TAPE for a b. When we find the first, we change it into an X and return the TAPE HEAD to cell ii. We then go back and search for an a again, and so forth. The process will stop when we look for an a but do not find any by the time we reach Δ. We then scan down the TAPE to be sure that all the cells contain X's and there are no unmatched b's left. When we encounter # on this pass, we can accept the input.

The machine we built is on the next page.

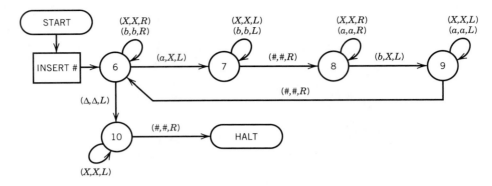

Let us follow the operation on *baab* starting in state 6. Starting in state 6 means that we have already inserted a # to the left of the input on the TAPE.

	6		6		7		7		8
	#*b̲aab*	→	#*ba̲ab*	→	#*b̲Xab*	→	#*b̲Xab*	→	#*b̲Xab*
	9		6		6		6		7
→	#*X̲Xab*	→	#*X̲Xab*	→	#*XX̲ab*	→	#*XXa̲b*	→	#*XXX̲b*
	7		7		8		8		8
→	#*X̲XXb*	→	#*XXX̲b*	→	#*XXX̲b*	→	#*XXX̲b*	→	#*XXX̲b*
	8		9		9		9		9
→	#*XXX̲b*	→	#*XXX̲X*	→	#*XX̲XX*	→	#*XX̲XX*	→	#*X̲XXX*
	6		6		6		6		6
→	#*X̲XXX*	→	#*XX̲XX*	→	#*XXX̲X*	→	#*XXXX̲*	→	#*XXXX̲Δ*
	10		10		10		10		10
→	#*XXXX̲Δ*	→	#*XXX̲X*	→	#*XX̲XX*	→	#*X̲XXX*	→	#*X̲XXX*	→	HALT

Notice that even after we have turned all *a*'s and *b*'s into *X*'s, we still have many steps left to check that there are no more non-*X* characters left.   ∎

⚜ THE SUBPROGRAM DELETE

For our last example, we shall build a TM subprogram that deletes; that is, it erases the contents of the cell the TAPE HEAD is initially pointing to, moving the contents of each of the nonempty cells to its right down one cell to the left to close up the gap and leaving the TAPE HEAD positioned one cell past where it was at the start. For example,

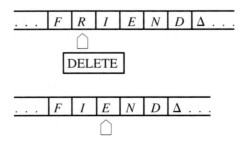

Just as with INSERT, the exact program of DELETE depends on the alphabet of letters found on the TAPE.

Let us suppose the characters on the TAPE are from the alphabet {*a   b   c*}. The subprogram to DELETE that is analogous to INSERT is

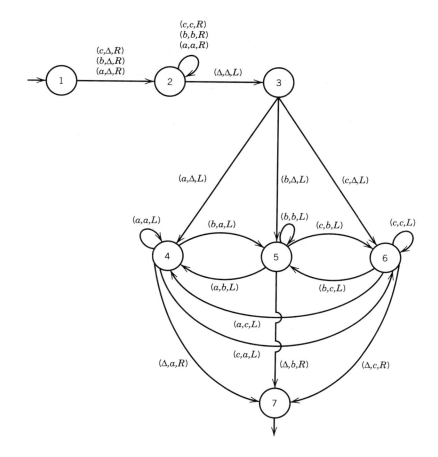

What we have done here is (1) erased the target cell, (2) moved to the right end of the non-Δ data, and (3) worked our way back down the TAPE, running the inverse of INSERT. We could just as easily have done the job on one pass up the TAPE, but then the TAPE HEAD would have been left at the end of the data and we would have lost our place; there would be no memory of where the deleted character used to be. The way we have written it, the TAPE HEAD is left in the cell immediately after the deletion cell.

Notice that although INSERT required us to specify what character is to be inserted, DELETE makes no such demand—it kills whatever it finds.

EXAMPLE

We can use the subprogram DELETE to accept the language EQUAL by the following (also wasteful) algorithm. First, INSERT # into cell i. As before, find the first a and delete it and return the TAPE HEAD to cell i. Now find the first b and delete it. Repeat this process until the hunt for the a is unsuccessful, that is, the TAPE HEAD does not catch an a here. It finds a Δ first. Now move one cell to the left, and if what is read is the #, the string is accepted; otherwise, what will be found are excess b's. If the input had excess a's, the program would crash in the hunt for the matching b. ∎

⚜ PROBLEMS

For Problems 1 and 2, consider the following TM:

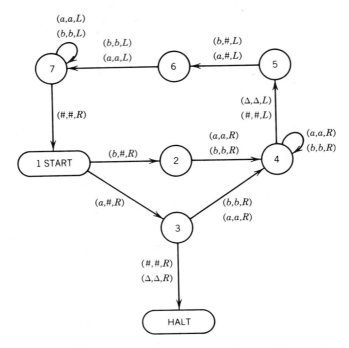

1. Trace the execution chains of the following input strings on this machine:

   (i) *aaa*

   (ii) *aba*

   (iii) *baaba*

   (iv) *ababb*

2. The language accepted by this TM is all words with an odd number of letters that have *a* as the middle letter. Show that this is true by explaining the algorithm the machine uses and the meaning of each state. Pay attention to the two necessary parts that must always be demonstrated:

   (i) Anything that has an *a* in the middle will get to HALT.

   (ii) Anything that gets to HALT has an *a* in the middle.

3. (i) Build a TM that accepts the language of all words that contain the substring *bbb*.

   (ii) Build a TM that accepts the language of all words that do not contain the substring *bbb*.

4. Build a TM that accepts the language ODDPALINDROME.

5. Build a TM that accepts all strings with more *a*'s than *b*'s, the language MOREA.

6. (i) Build a TM that accepts the language $\{a^n b^{n+1}\}$.

   (ii) Build a TM that accepts the language $\{a^n b^{2n}\}$.

7. (i) Show that the TM given in this chapter for the language PALINDROME has more states than it needs by coalescing states 4 and 7.

   (ii) Show that the TM given in this chapter for the language $\{a^n b^n\}$ can be drawn with one fewer state.

Problems 8 through 10 refer to the following TM. We assume that the input string is put on the TAPE with the symbol # inserted in front of it in cell i. For example, the input *ba* will be run with the TAPE initially in the form #*ba*Δ . . . . In this chapter, we saw how to do this using TM states. Here, consider it already done. The TM is then

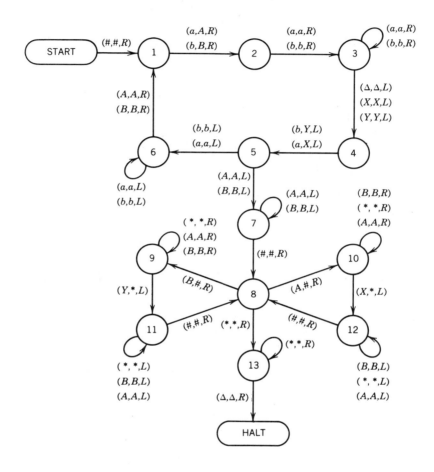

8. Trace the execution chains of the following input strings on this machine:

(i) *aa*
(ii) *aaa*
(iii) *aaaa*
(iv) *aabaab*
(v) *abab*

9. The language this TM accepts is DOUBLEWORD, the set of all words of the form *ss*, where *s* is a nonnull string in **(a + b)*** (see p. 200).

(i) Explain the meaning of each state and prove that all words in DOUBLEWORD are accepted by this TM.
(ii) Show that all words not in DOUBLEWORD are rejected by this machine.

10. (i) Show that states 11 and 12 can be combined without changing the language.
(ii) What other changes can be made?

11. An alternate TM to accept EVEN-EVEN can be based on the algorithm:

    1. Move up the string, changing a's to A's.

    2. Move down the string, changing b's to B's.

    We can modify this algorithm in the following way: To avoid the problem of crashing on the way down the TAPE, change the letter in the first cell to X if it is an a and to Y if it is a b. This way, while charging down the TAPE, we can recognize when we are in cell i.
        Draw this TM.

12. Follow the up–down method for a TM that recognizes EVEN-EVEN as explained in Problem 11 but use INSERT, not the X, Y trick, to build the TM.

13. Build a TM that accepts the language EVEN-EVEN based on the subroutine DELETE given in this chapter.

14. In the subroutine INSERT given in this chapter, is it necessary to separate states 6 and 7, or can they somehow be combined?

15. On the TM given in this chapter for the language $\{a^n b^n a^n\}$, trace the following words:

    (i) *aabbaa*
    (ii) *aabbaaa*
    (iii) *aabaa*
    (iv) *aabbaabb*
    (v) Characterize the nature of the different input strings that crash in each of the eight states.

16. Build a TM to accept the language $\{a^n b^n a^n\}$ based on the following algorithm:

    (i) Check that the input is in the form **a*b*a***.
    (ii) Use DELETE in an intelligent way.

17. Trace the subroutine DELETE in the following situations:

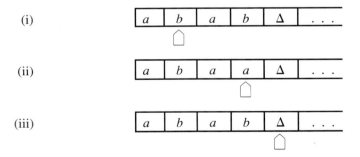

(i)

(ii)

(iii)

18. Draw a TM that does the same job as DELETE, but leaves the TAPE HEAD pointing to the first blank cell. One way to do this is by reading a letter, putting it into the cell behind it, and moving two cells up the TAPE.

19. (i) Draw a TM that loops forever on all words ending in a and crashes on all others.
    (ii) Draw a TM that loops forever on the input string *bab*, leaving the TAPE different each time through the loop.

20. Draw a TM that accepts the language PALINDROME', the complement of PALINDROME. This is, although we did not prove so, a non-context-free language.

CHAPTER 20

Post Machines

⚜ THE POST MACHINE

We have used the word "algorithm" many times in this book. We have tried to explain what an algorithm is by saying that it is a procedure with instructions so carefully detailed that no further information is necessary. The person/machine executing the algorithm should know how to handle any situation that may possibly arise. Without the need for applying any extra intelligence, it should be possible to complete the project. Not only that, but before even beginning we should be able, just by looking at the algorithm and the data, to predict an upper limit on the number of steps the entire process will take. This is the guarantee that the procedure is finite.

All this sounds fine, but it still does not really specify what an algorithm is. This is an unsatisfactory definition, because we have no precise idea of what a "procedure" is. Essentially, we have merely hidden one unknown word behind another. Intuitively, we know that arithmetic operations are perfectly acceptable steps in an algorithm, but what else is? In several algorithms, we have allowed ourselves the operation of painting things blue without specifying what shade or how many coats. An algorithm, it seems, can be made of almost anything.

The question of determining the appropriate components for mathematical algorithms was of great interest earlier in this century. People were discovering that surprisingly few basic operations were sufficient to perform many sophisticated tasks, just as shifting and adding are basic operations that can be used to replace hard-wired multiplication in a computer. The hope was to find a small set of basic operations and a machine that could perform them all, a kind of "universal algorithm machine," because it could then run any algorithm. The mathematical model itself would provide a precise definition of the concept of algorithm. We could use it to discuss in a meaningful way the possibility of finding algorithms for all mathematical problems. There may even be some way to make it program itself to find its own algorithms so that we need never work on mathematics again.

In 1936, the same fruitful year Turing introduced the Turing machine, Emil Leon Post (1897–1954) created the Post machine, which he hoped would prove to be the "universal algorithm machine" sought after. One condition that must be satisfied by such a "universal algorithm machine" (we retain the quotation marks around this phrase for now because we cannot understand it in a deeper sense until later) is that *any language* which can be precisely defined by humans (using English, pictures, or hand signals) should be accepted (or recognized) by some version of this machine. This would make it more powerful than an FA or a PDA. There are nonregular languages and non-context-free languages, but there should not be any non-Turing or non-Post languages. In this part of the book, we shall see to what extent Post and Turing succeeded in achieving their goals.

DEFINITION

A **Post machine,** denoted **PM,** is a collection of five things:

1. The alphabet Σ of input letters plus the special symbol #. We generally use $\Sigma = \{a \quad b\}$

2. A linear storage location (a place where a string of symbols is kept) called the **STORE,** or **QUEUE,** which initially contains the input string. This location can be read, by which we mean the *leftmost* character can be removed for inspection. The STORE can also be added to, which means a new character can be concatenated onto the *right* of whatever is there already. We allow for the possibility that characters not in Σ can be used in the STORE, characters from an alphabet Γ called the **store alphabet.**

3. READ states, for example,

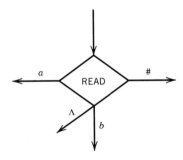

which remove the leftmost character from the STORE and branch accordingly. The only branching in the machine takes place at the READ states. There *may be* a branch for every character in Σ or Γ. Note the Λ branch that means that an empty STORE was read. PMs are deterministic, so no two edges from the READ have the same label.

4. ADD states:

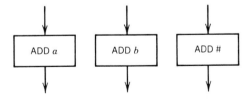

which concatenate a character onto the *right* end of the string in the STORE. This is different from PDA PUSH states, which concatenate characters onto the *left*. Post machines have no PUSH states. No branching can take place at an ADD state. It is possible to have an ADD state for every letter in Σ and Γ.

5. A START state (unenterable) and some halt states called ACCEPT and REJECT:

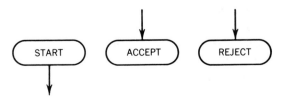

If we are in a READ state and there is no labeled edge for the character we have read, then we crash, which is equivalent to taking a labeled edge into a REJECT state. We can draw our PMs with or without REJECT states.   ■

The STORE is a first-in first-out (FIFO) stack in contradistinction to a PUSHDOWN or last-in first-out (LIFO) STACK. The contents of an originally empty STORE after the operations

is the string

$$abb$$

If we then read the STORE, we take the a branch and the STORE will be reduced to bb.

A Post machine does not have a separate INPUT TAPE unit. In processing a string, we assume that the string was initially loaded into the STORE and we begin executing the program from the START state on. If we wind up in an ACCEPT state, we accept the input string. If not, not. At the moment we accept the input string, the STORE could contain anything. It does not have to be empty, nor need it contain the original input string.

As usual, we shall say that the language defined (or accepted) by a Post machine is the set of strings that it accepts. A Post machine is yet another language-recognizer or-acceptor. As we have defined them, Post machines are deterministic, that is, for every input string there is only one path through the machine; we have no alternatives at any stage. We could also define a nondeterministic Post machine, NPM. This would allow for more than one edge with the same label to come from a READ state. It is a theorem that, in their strength as language-acceptors, NPM = PM. This we shall discuss in Chapter 22.

Let us study an example of a PM.

EXAMPLE

Consider the PM below:

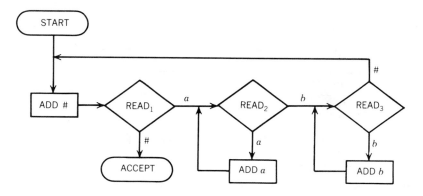

As required by our definition, this machine is deterministic. We have not drawn the edges that lead to REJECT states, but instead we allow the path to crash in the READ state if there is no place for it to go.

Let us trace the processing of the input $aaabbb$ on this PM:

STATE	STORE
START	*aaabbb*
ADD #	*aaabbb#* (Note this point.)
READ₁	*aabbb#*
READ₂	*abbb#*
ADD *a*	*abbb#a*
READ₂	*bbb#a*
ADD *a*	*bbb#aa*
READ₂	*bb#aa*
READ₃	*b#aa*
ADD *b*	*b#aab*
READ₃	*#aab*
ADD *b*	*#aabb*
READ₃	*aabb*
ADD #	*aabb#* (Note this point.)
READ₁	*abb#*
READ₂	*bb#*
ADD *a*	*bb#a*
READ₂	*b#a*
READ₃	*#a*
ADD *b*	*#ab*
READ₃	*ab*
ADD #	*ab#* (Note this point.)
READ₁	*b#*
READ₂	*#*
READ₃	Λ
ADD #	*#* (Note this point.)
READ₁	Λ
ACCEPT	

The trace makes clear to us what happens. The # is used as an end-of-input string signal (or flag). In $READ_1$, we check to see whether we are out of input; that is, are we reading the end-of-input signal #? If so, we accept the string. If we read a *b*, the string crashes. So, nothing starting with a *b* is accepted. If the string starts with an *a*, this letter is consumed by $READ_1$; that is, the trip from $READ_1$ to $READ_2$ costs one *a* that is not replaced. The loop at $READ_2$ puts the rest of the *a*'s from the front cluster of *a*'s behind the #. The first *b* read is consumed in the trip from $READ_2$ to $READ_3$. At $READ_3$, the rest of the first cluster of *b*'s is stripped off the front and appended onto the back, behind the *a*'s that are behind the #.

After the b's have been transported, we expect to read the character #. If we read an a, we crash. To survive the trip back from READ$_3$ to ADD #, the input string must have been originally of the form $\mathbf{a*b*}$.

In each pass through the large circuit READ$_1$–READ$_2$–READ$_3$–READ$_1$, the string loses an a and a b. Note the markers we have indicated along the side. To be accepted, both a's and b's must run out at the same time, since if there were more a's than b's, the input string would crash at READ$_2$ by reading a # instead of b, and if the input string had more b's than a's, it would crash in state READ$_1$ by reading a b.

Therefore, the language accepted by this PM is $\{a^n b^n\}$ (in this case, including Λ). ■

Post machines look considerably like PDAs, and, in fact, PDAs can accept the language $\{a^n b^n\}$ as the preceding PM (p. 459) does. However, we have seen that $\{a^n b^n a^n\}$ is non-context-free and cannot be accepted by a PDA. So, to show that PMs have some extra power beyond PDAs, we demonstrate one that accepts this language.

EXAMPLE

Consider the PM below:

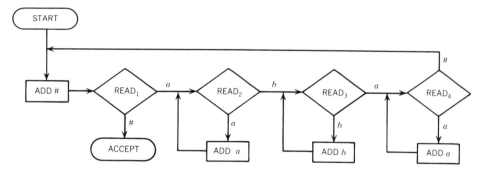

This machine is very much like the PM in the previous example. We start with a string in the STORE. We add a # to the back of it. We accept it in state READ$_1$ if the string was initially empty. If it starts with a b, we crash. If it starts with an a, we use up this letter getting to READ$_2$. Here, we put the entire initial clump of a's (all the way up to the first b) behind the #. We read the first b and use it getting to READ$_3$. Here, we put the rest of the clump of b's behind the a's behind the #. We had then better read another a to get to READ$_4$. In READ$_4$, a bunch of a's (minus the one it costs to get there) are placed in the store on the right, behind the b's that are behind the a's that are behind the #. After we exhaust these a's, we had better find a # or we crash. After reading the # off the front of the STORE, we replace it at the back of the STORE in the state ADD #. To make this return to ADD #, the input string must originally have been of the form $\mathbf{a*b*a*}$. Every time through this loop we use up one a from the first clump, one b from the b clump, and one a from the last clump.

The only way we ever get to ACCEPT is to finish some number of loops and find the STORE empty, because after ADD # we want to read # in state READ$_1$. This means that the three clumps are all depleted at the same time, which means that they must have had the same number of letters in them initially. This means that the only words accepted by this PM are those of the form $\{a^n b^n a^n\}$. ■

We should not think that we have *proven* that PMs accept a *larger* class of languages than PDAs. We have only demonstrated that PMs accept *some* context-free languages and *some* non-context-free languages. In Chapter 22, we shall show that PMs do, in fact, accept *all* CFLs. We shall then have to face the question, "Do they accept *all* none-CFLs?" This will be answered in Chapter 24.

Before we relate PMs to PDAs, we shall compare them to TMs, as Post himself did with the following three theorems.

⚜ SIMULATING A PM ON A TM

THEOREM 47

Any language that can be accepted by a PM can be accepted by some TM.

PROOF

As with many theorems before, we prove this one by constructive algorithm. In this case, we show how to convert any PM into a TM, so that if we have a PM to accept some language, we can see how to build a TM that will process all input strings exactly the same way as the PM, leading to HALT only when the PM would lead to ACCEPT.

We know that PMs are made up of certain components, and we shall show how to convert each of these components into corresponding TM components that function the same way. We could call this process **simulating** a PM on a TM.

The easiest conversion is for the START state, because we do not change it at all. TMs also begin all execution at the START state.

The second easiest conversion is for the ACCEPT state. We shall rename it HALT because that is what the accepting state is called for TMs.

The next easiest conversion is for the REJECT states. TMs have no reject states; they just crash if no path can be found for the letter read by the TAPE HEAD. So, we simply delete the REJECT states. (We often do this for PMs too.)

Now before we proceed any further, we should address the question of converting the PM's STORE into the TM's TAPE. The STORE contains a string of letters with the possibility of some occurrences of the symbol #.

Most often, there will be only one occurrence of the symbol # somewhere in the middle of the string, but even though this is usual in practice, it is not demanded by the definition.

We now describe how we can use the TM TAPE to keep track of the STORE. Suppose the contents of the STORE look like

$$x_1x_2x_3x_4x_5$$

where the x's are from the PM input alphabet Σ or the symbol # and none of them is Δ. We want the corresponding contents of the TM TAPE to be

Δ	. . . Δ	Δ	x_1	x_2	x_3	x_4	x_5	Δ	Δ	. . .

with the TAPE HEAD pointing to one of the x's. Notice that we keep some Δ's on the left of the STORE information, not just on the right, although there will only be finitely many Δ's on the left, because the TAPE ends in that direction.

We have drawn the TM TAPE picture broken because we do not know exactly where the x's will end up on the TAPE. The reason for this is that the PM eats up data from the left of the STORE and adds on data to the right. If at some point the STORE contains *abb* and we execute the instructions

READ–ADD *a*–READ–ADD *a*–ADD *b*–READ

the TM TAPE will change like this:

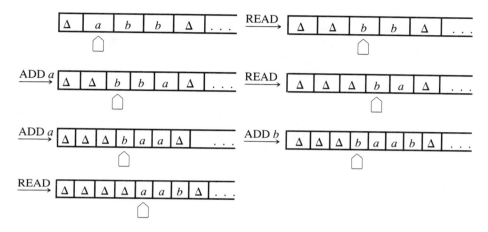

The non-Δ information wanders up to the right, while Δ's accumulate on the left.

Immediately after the START state on the TM, we shall employ the subprogram INSERT (from Chapter 19) to insert a Δ in cell i and to move the whole non-Δ initial input string one cell to the right up the TAPE.

We do this so that the first PM operation simulated is like all the others in that the non-Δ information on the TM TAPE has at least one Δ on each side of it, enabling us to locate the rightmost and leftmost ends of the input string by bouncing off Δ's.

There are two operations by which the PM changes the contents of the STORE: ADD and READ. Let us now consider how a TM can duplicate the corresponding actions on its TAPE.

If the PM at some point executes the state

the TM must change its TAPE from something like

$$\ldots \quad \Delta \quad \Delta \quad x_1 \quad x_2 \quad x_3 \quad x_4 \quad \Delta \quad \Delta \quad \ldots$$

to

$$\ldots \quad \Delta \quad \Delta \quad x_1 \quad x_2 \quad x_3 \quad x_4 \quad y \quad \Delta \quad \Delta \quad \ldots$$

To do this, the TAPE HEAD must move to the right end of the non-Δ characters, locate the first Δ, and change it to y. This can be done as follows:

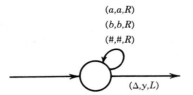

We have illustrated this in the case where $\Sigma = \{a \quad b\}$, but if Σ had more letters, it would only mean more labels on the loop. Notice also that we have left the TAPE HEAD again pointing to some non-Δ character. This is important. We do not want the TAPE HEAD wandering off into the infinitely many blanks on the right.

There is only one other PM state we have to simulate; that is the READ state. The READ states does two things. It removes the first character from the STORE, and it branches in accordance with what it has removed. The other states we have simulated did not involve branching.

For a TM to remove the leftmost non-Δ character, the TAPE HEAD must move leftward until the first blank it encounters. It should then back up one cell to the right and read the non-Δ character in that cell. This it must turn into a Δ and move itself right, never leaving the string of non-Δ's. This process will require two states in the TM:

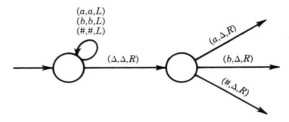

Notice that we leave the second state along different edges, depending on which character is being erased. This is equivalent to the PM instruction

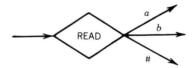

We should also note that because we were careful to insert a Δ in cell i in front of the input string, we do not have to worry about moving the TAPE HEAD left from cell i and crashing while searching for the Δ on the left side.

If while processing a given input the STORE ever becomes empty, then the TM TAPE will become all Δ's. It is possible that the PM may wish to READ an empty STORE and branch accordingly. If this alternative is listed in the PM, it should also be in the TM.

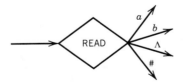

becomes

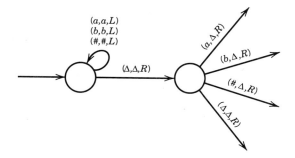

If the TAPE is all Δ's, the TAPE HEAD reads the cell it is pointing to, which contains a Δ, and moves to the right, "thinking" that it is now in the non-Δ section of the TAPE. It then reads this cell and finds another Δ, which it leaves as a Δ, and moves right again. The program branches along the appropriate edge. Just because the STORE is empty does not mean that the program is over. We might yet ADD something and continue. The TM simulation can do the same.

Thus, we can convert every PM state to a TM state or sequence of states that have the same function. The TM so constructed will HALT on all words that the PM sends to ACCEPT. It will crash on all words that the PM sends to REJECT (or on which the PM crashes), and it will loop forever on those same inputs on which the PM loops forever. ∎

EXAMPLE

Recall that our first PM of this chapter was

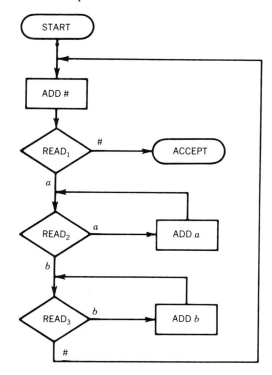

This PM accepts the language $\{a^n b^n\}$.

This time, we have drawn the machine vertically to facilitate its conversion into a TM. Following the algorithm in the proof, we produce the next machine, where, for the sake of simplicity, we have omitted the Δ-inserting preprocessor and assume that the input string is placed on the TM TAPE starting in cell ii with a Δ in cell i:

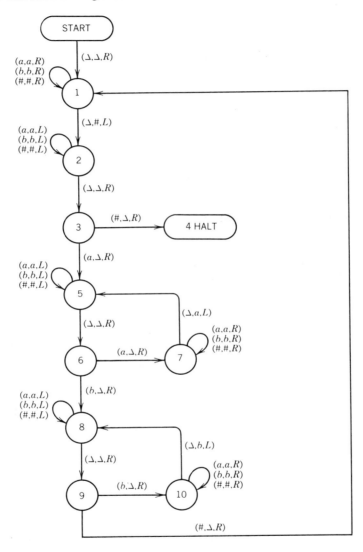

Notice that

TM State	Corresponds to	PM State
START		START
1		ADD #
2 and 3		READ $_1$
4		ACCEPT

5 and 6	READ $_2$
7	ADD a
8 and 9	READ $_3$
10	ADD b

We really should not have put the end-of-proof box on our discussion of Theorem 47 (see p. 465) as we did, because the proof is not over until we fully understand exactly how the separately simulated components fit together to form a coherent TM. In the preceding example, we see that edges between the independently simulated states always have TM labels determined from the PM. We can now claim to understand the algorithm of Theorem 47. We are not finished with this example until we have traced the execution of the TM on at least one input.

Let us trace the processing of the input string *aabb*:

	START		1		1		1
	$\Delta a a b b$	→	$\Delta \underline{a} a b b$	→	$\Delta a \underline{a} b b$	→	$\Delta a \underline{a} b b$
	1		1		2		2
→	$\Delta a a b \underline{b}$	→	$\Delta a a b b \underline{\Delta}$	→	$\Delta a a \underline{b} b \#$	→	$\Delta a a b \underline{b} \#$
	2		2		2		3
→	$\Delta a \underline{a} b b \#$	→	$\Delta \underline{a} a b b \#$	→	$\Delta \underline{a} a b b \#$	→	$\Delta a \underline{a} b b \#$
	5		5		6		7
→	$\Delta \Delta \underline{a} b b \#$	→	$\Delta \Delta \underline{a} b b \#$	→	$\Delta \Delta \underline{a} b b \#$	→	$\Delta \Delta \Delta \underline{b} b \#$
	7		7		7		5
→	$\Delta \Delta \Delta \underline{b} b \#$	→	$\Delta \Delta \Delta b b \underline{\#}$	→	$\Delta \Delta \Delta b b \# \underline{\Delta}$	→	$\Delta \Delta \Delta b b \# \underline{a}$
	5		5		5		6
→	$\Delta \Delta \Delta b \underline{b} \# a$	→	$\Delta \Delta \Delta b b \# a$	→	$\Delta \Delta \underline{\Delta} b b \# a$	→	$\Delta \Delta \Delta \underline{b} b \# a$
	8		8		9		10
→	$\Delta \Delta \Delta \Delta \underline{b} \# a$	→	$\Delta \Delta \Delta \Delta b \underline{\#} a$	→	$\Delta \Delta \Delta \Delta \underline{b} \# a$	→	$\Delta \Delta \Delta \Delta \Delta \underline{\#} a$
	10		10		8		8
→	$\Delta \Delta \Delta \Delta \Delta \# \underline{a}$	→	$\Delta \Delta \Delta \Delta \Delta \# a \underline{\Delta}$	→	$\Delta \Delta \Delta \Delta \Delta \# \underline{a} b$	→	$\Delta \Delta \Delta \Delta \Delta \# \underline{a} b$
	8		9		1		1
→	$\Delta \Delta \Delta \Delta \underline{\Delta} \# a b$	→	$\Delta \Delta \Delta \Delta \Delta \underline{\#} a b$	→	$\Delta \Delta \Delta \Delta \Delta \Delta \underline{a} b$	→	$\Delta \Delta \Delta \Delta \Delta \Delta a \underline{b}$
	1		2		2		2
→	$\Delta \Delta \Delta \Delta \Delta \Delta a b \underline{\Delta}$	→	$\Delta \Delta \Delta \Delta \Delta \Delta a \underline{b} \#$	→	$\Delta \Delta \Delta \Delta \Delta \Delta \underline{a} b \#$	→	$\Delta \Delta \Delta \Delta \Delta \Delta a \underline{b} \#$
	3		5		5		6
→	$\Delta \Delta \Delta \Delta \Delta \Delta \underline{a} b \#$	→	$\Delta \Delta \Delta \Delta \Delta \Delta \Delta \underline{b} \#$	→	$\Delta \Delta \Delta \Delta \Delta \Delta \Delta \underline{b} \#$	→	$\Delta \Delta \Delta \Delta \Delta \Delta \Delta \underline{b} \#$
	8		8		9		1
→	$\Delta \Delta \Delta \Delta \Delta \Delta \Delta \underline{\#}$	→	$\Delta \Delta \Delta \Delta \Delta \Delta \Delta \Delta \underline{\#}$	→	$\Delta \Delta \Delta \Delta \Delta \Delta \Delta \Delta \underline{\#}$	→	$\Delta \Delta \Delta \Delta \Delta \Delta \Delta \Delta \Delta \underline{\Delta}$
	2		3				
→	$\Delta \Delta \Delta \Delta \Delta \Delta \Delta \Delta \underline{\Delta} \#$	→	$\Delta \Delta \Delta \Delta \Delta \Delta \Delta \Delta \Delta \underline{\#}$	→	$\Delta \Delta \Delta \Delta \Delta \Delta \Delta \Delta \Delta \underline{\Delta}$		HALT

Here, we have decided that the initial Δ's from cell i up to the data are significant and have included them in the trace.

We can see from this execution chain that this is a TM that accepts $\{a^n b^n\}$. We already know that there are other (smaller) TMs that do the same job. The algorithm never guaranteed to find the best TM that accepts the same language, only to prove the existence of one such TM by constructive algorithm. ∎

We should note that the alphabet that appears on the TM TAPE produced by this algorithm is the same as the STORE alphabet of the PM.

In the TM we just constructed we have encountered a situation that plagues many TMs—piles of tedious multiple-edge labels that all say about the same thing:

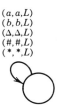

$$(a,a,L)$$
$$(b,b,L)$$
$$(\Delta,\Delta,L)$$
$$(\#,\#,L)$$
$$(*,*,L)$$

This is proper TM format for the instruction, "If we read an a, a b, a Δ, a #, or a *, leave it unchanged and move the TAPE HEAD left." Let us now introduce a shortened form of this sentence: $(a, b, \Delta, \#, *; = , L)$.

DEFINITION

If a, b, c, d, e are TM TAPE characters, then $(a, b, c, d, e; = , L)$ stands for the instructions

$$(a, a, L) \, (b, b, L) \, \ldots \, (e, e, L)$$

Similarly, we will employ $(a, b, c, d, e; = , R)$ for the set of labels

$$(a, a, R) \, (b, b, R) \, \ldots \, (e, e, R)$$ ∎

⚜ SIMULATING A TM ON A PM

Before we proceed, it will be useful for us to demonstrate that although a PM is provided with only two STORE instructions that seem to correspond to PDA STACK instructions, the PM READ and ADD are definitely more flexible.

THEOREM 48

There are subprograms that can enable a PM to add a character to the front (left end) of the string in the STORE and to read the character off of the back (right end) of the string.

PROOF

To add a character to the front of the STORE (which corresponds to a PDA PUSH instruction), we need to know the alphabet of characters already in the STORE and then employ a new character different from all of them. Let Γ be the character set in the STORE and $ be a character not in Γ.

Let us say that we wish to add the letter b to the front end of the store. What we will do is first ADD $ to the back of the STORE. Then we ADD b to the back of the STORE. And now we enter a loop in which we READ whatever is at the front of the STORE and, unless it is a $, we immediately ADD the very same character to the back of the STORE. This executes a shift-left cyclically operation. When we do eventually (or immediately) READ the $, we are done, for the next character is the b we meant to concatenate on the front of the STORE, and this b is followed by the entire string that used to be in the STORE before the operation began.

The PM subprogram that does this is

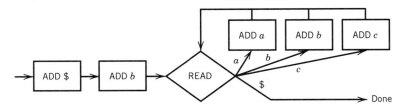

As an example, suppose the STORE originally contained *pqr*. Then the subprogram would produce this sequence of STORE changes:

$$pqr \rightarrow pqr\$ \rightarrow pqr\$b \rightarrow qr\$b \rightarrow qr\$bp \rightarrow r\$bp \rightarrow r\$bpq \rightarrow \$bpq \rightarrow \$bpqr \rightarrow bpqr$$

We will call this subprogram ADD FRONT *b*.

In order to write a subprogram that reads the back character from the STORE and branches according to whatever it reads, we will first write a program that takes the last character and puts it in the front of the STORE, leaving the rest of the string unaltered. We can then use the regular PM READ instruction to do the branching. So, what we will write is a program called SHIFT-RIGHT CYCLICALLY.

To do this, the basic strategy is to stick a marker (the $ will do again as long as it is not in the STORE character set Γ) onto the back of the STORE string. We then read two characters from the left of the store and, by being in an appropriate memory state, we ADD the first character to the back of the STORE, provided that the second character is not the $. We still have the second character that we have not yet added to the STORE, and we will not do so unless what we READ next (the third character) is not the $ either. We keep this third character in mind (in memory by virtue of a specialized state) until we have read the fourth and found it is not the $ yet. Eventually, we do encounter the $ and we know that the character we are holding in memory (the character before the $) was originally the last character in the STORE, and we add it on to the front of the STORE by the ADD FRONT subprogram we have just produced above:

This then is the subprogram for SHIFT-RIGHT CYCLICALLY:

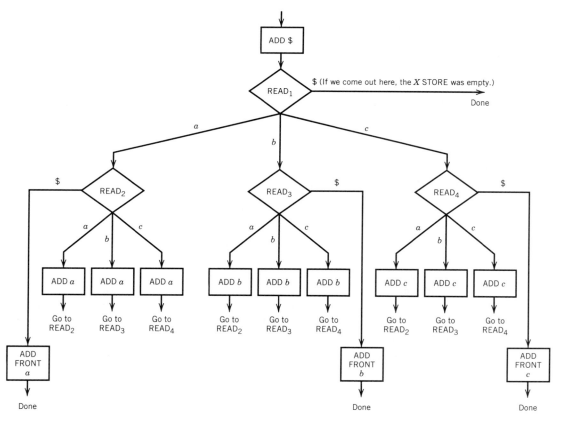

We have not drawn in the full spaghetti of edges but used the direction go to READ$_{\text{such}}$. We have used the old trick of the subprogram INSERT, of remembering what character has been read by being in a different READ state for each possibility. Thus, READ$_2$ remembers that the character we owe to the STORE is an a and it will be added to the back unless the next character is a $, in which case it will be added to the front. When we ascertain that the next character is a c, we ADD a and then go to READ$_4$ to determine which end of the STORE to add the c.

As we mentioned already, the full subprogram of reading the right end character of the STORE, which we call READ BACK, is

All told, we can read or add to either end of the STORE.

We are now in position to simulate a full TM on a PM.

We have shown that any language that can be accepted by a PM can also be accepted by some TM; however, that is only half the story.

THEOREM 49

Any language that can be accepted by a TM can be accepted by some PM.

PROOF

This proof will again be by constructive algorithm. We start by assuming that we have an appropriate TM for a certain language and from the TM we shall build a PM that operates on input strings in exactly the same way, step by step. Again, we shall be doing a simulation.

Before continuing with this proof, we should note that we intend to use a STORE alphabet that is larger than usual. Normally, we expect the STORE to contain the letters of the alphabet from the input-string language plus the symbol #. Here, we are going to put any character from the TM TAPE alphabet (which can be much larger, with many special symbols) into the STORE. In particular, the character Δ may have to be placed in the STORE as well as $A, B, C, \ldots$. If there are any who have philosophical qualms about adding Δ to the store as a character, let them not think of it as a blank but as the first letter of Dionysius. The simulation will work just as well. The language ultimately accepted by the PM will have initially only the letters of the input string on the TM, but other characters may be employed in the processing, just as with TMs.

We already have some feel for the correspondence between these two machines from Theorem 47 (p. 462). Still, one great problem stands out. In TMs we can read and change a character in the middle of the string, whereas with PMs we can only read and add onto the ends of the string. How can PMs simulate the action of TMs? A clever trick is needed here that makes use of the extra symbol # that PMs have, which we shall assume is not in either of the TM's alphabets, Γ or Σ. (If the TM did use this symbol in its TAPE alphabet Γ, then change it to boldface or italics or blue paint without changing the operation of the TM and freeing # as a symbol special to the PM.)

We shall make a correspondence between # and the position of the TAPE HEAD. The character string to the left of the TAPE HEAD on the TM TAPE will be placed to the right of the symbol # on the PM STORE and the character string to the right of (or at) the TAPE HEAD will be placed to the left of #.

By these confusing words, we mean to describe the correspondence of

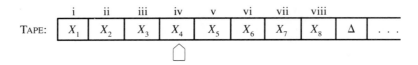

in the TM with

$$\text{STORE:} \quad X_4 \, X_5 \, X_6 \, X_7 \, X_8 \, \# \, X_1 \, X_2 \, X_3$$

in the PM.

Why do we do this? Because when the TAPE HEAD is reading cell iv as it is in the TM above, it reads the character X_4. Therefore, we must be set to read X_4 in the PM, which means it had better be the leftmost character in the STORE.

Here comes the beauty of this method of representation.

Suppose that while the TAPE HEAD is reading cell iv, as above, we execute the instruction (X_4, Y, R). This leaves us the TM situation:

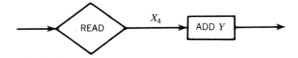

To maintain the correspondence, we must be able to convert the STORE in the PM to

$$\text{STORE:} \quad X_5 \, X_6 \, X_7 \, X_8 \, \# \, X_1 \, X_2 \, X_3 \, Y$$

This conversion can be accomplished by the PM instructions (states):

The X_4 is stripped off the front and a Y is stuck on the back, a very easy PM operation. Notice that both TM and PM are now set to read X_5.

Let us pause for a moment to see exactly how this conversion works. On the next page on the left is a TM that converts the input word "cat" into the word "dog" and crashes on all other inputs. This TM uses only right TAPE HEAD moves, so we can convert it easily to the PM on the left using the correspondence shown above:

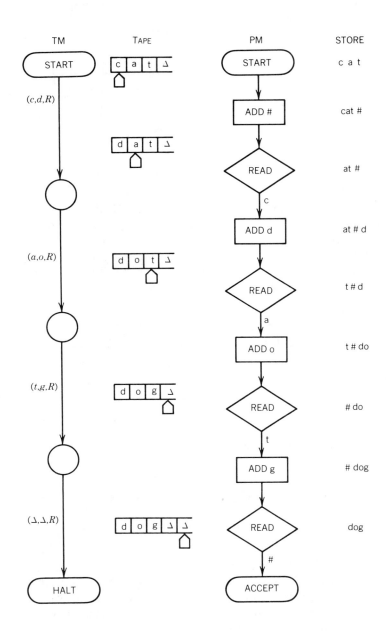

Notice how the correspondence between TAPE and STORE is preserved with every instruction. Let us return to the simulation.

Suppose instead that we had to simulate a left move; that is, we started with the original TAPE as earlier, with TAPE HEAD reading cell iv, and we were asked to execute the instruction (X_4, Y, L). This would leave the TAPE as

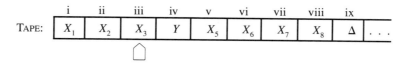

This TAPE status corresponds to the STORE contents

$$X_3 \, Y \, X_5 \, X_6 \, X_7 \, X_8 \, \# \, X_1 \, X_2$$

This is almost equivalent to the sequence

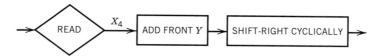

We say "almost" because we have the problem of what to do when the TM is instructed to move left when the TAPE HEAD is at cell i. Consider the TAPE situation below:

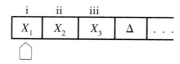

Here, (X_1, Y, L) causes a crash. Let us see what this instruction means when performed by the PM simulation.

In our PM version, we would start with the STORE contents

$$X_1 \, X_2 \, X_3 \, \#$$

We would then execute the sequence READ–ADD FRONT Y–SHIFT-RIGHT CYCLICALLY. The contents of the STORE changes as shown below:

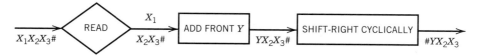

Because we have agreed in our simulation to keep the character that is in the TM cell being read by the TAPE HEAD to the left of the # in the PM store, the final STORE contents make no sense. It does somewhat "represent" a crash in that it shows that the TAPE HEAD is not reading anything, but it does not crash the PM. The PM could conceivably still continue processing the input and eventually reach ACCEPT. To be sure the PM stops processing, we must include in every PM simulation of a leftward TM move a test to see whether the first symbol in the STORE has become #.

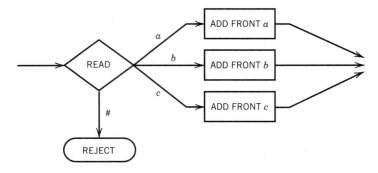

After we read a non-# character, we stick it back onto the front of the STORE.

Now we have a completely accurate treatment for (X, Y, L), but we realize that we have not fully covered the (X, Y, R) case yet. Another difficulty, similar to the problem we have just treated, arises when we want to move the TAPE HEAD right beyond the non-Δ's on the TAPE. If the TAPE status is like this:

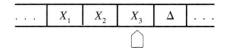

and the TM wants to execute the move

$$(X_3, Y, R)$$

we end up with

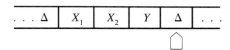

In the PM simulation of this, the STORE begins by containing

$$X_3 \# X_1 X_2$$

and after READ–ADD it contains

$$\# X_1 X_2 Y$$

which is again a meaningless formulation in our correspondence because the STORE starts with a #. When a move right causes the # to be the first character of the STORE, we should insert a Δ in front of # in the STORE to achieve

$$\Delta \# X_1 X_2 Y$$

which does correspond to the TM's TAPE status.

We can do this as before with a test after READ–ADD to see whether the STORE starts with a #. If it does, instead of crashing, we replace the # and ADD FRONT Δ.

The simulation is almost complete. All branching and TAPE modification that the TM requires can be performed by the PM we have designed. In any case, where the TM accepts the input string by branching to HALT, let the PM accept the string by branching to ACCEPT.

To start the PM, we must make it initially resemble the TM. The TM begins its processing by having the input string already on its TAPE:

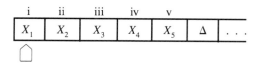

while a PM running on the same input according to the rules of PMs must start with the STORE containing exactly the same input string:

$$X_1 \, X_2 \, X_3 \, X_4 \, X_5$$

However, the STORE contents corresponding to the TM status would be

$$X_1 \, X_2 \, X_3 \, X_4 \, X_5 \, \#$$

To begin correspondence, we have to add a # to the right. Therefore, our initial sequence in the PM must always be

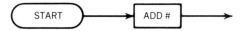

In converting a TM into a PM we have the quandry of what to do about a TM START state that is reentered. In the PM the in-edges will go into this ADD # instead. Now the correspondence is complete; all words accepted by the TM will be accepted by the PM. All input strings that crash on one will crash on the other, and all input strings that loop forever on the TM will do the same on the PM.   ■

This is a very inefficient conversion algorithm, so we shall illustrate it on a very small TM.

EXAMPLE

Consider this TM:

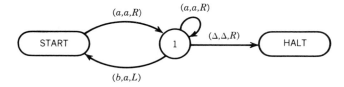

This machine accepts all words starting with an a and, in so doing, it turns the input into a string of solid a's. When converted into a PM by the algorithm above, the resultant machine is

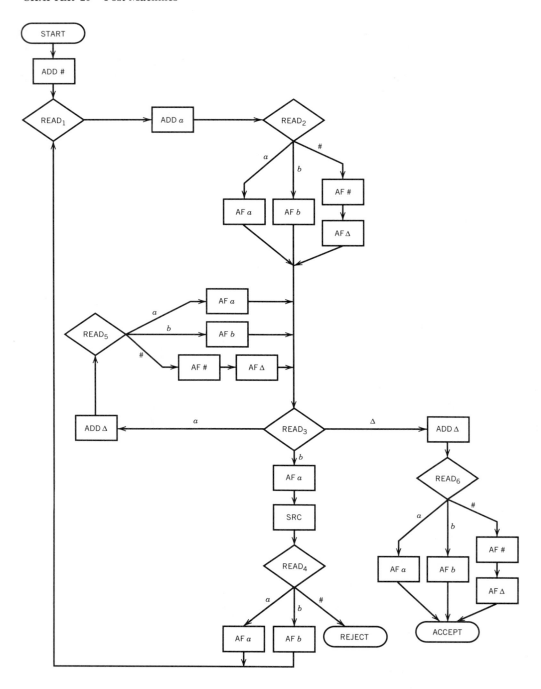

Here, we have used the abbreviations AF for ADD FRONT and SRC for SHIFT-RIGHT CYCLICALLY. To understand the equivalence, let us explain the meaning of the READ states:

READ$_1$ acts like the reenterable TM START state.

READ$_2$ is a TAPE-HEAD-reading-Δ checker, as are READ$_5$ and READ$_6$.

READ$_3$ corresponds to TM state 1.

READ$_4$ is a crash-while-moving-left checker. ∎

Taken together, Theorems 47 and 49 tell us that PMs and TMs have the same power. We may write

$$PM = TM$$

PROBLEMS

Problems 1 through 4 refer to the following PM:

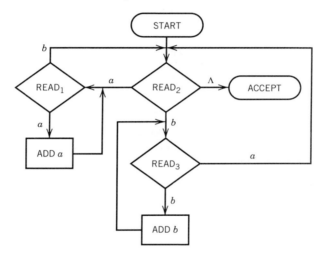

1. Trace the paths of the following input strings on this PM. At every step, name the current state and the contents of the STORE.
    (i) *abab*
    (ii) *baabba*
    (iii) *aaabbb*
    (iv) *aabbbb*
    (v) *bbabaaa*

2. (i) Show that if an input has exactly one more *a* than *b*, it will crash on this PM in state READ$_1$.
    (ii) Show that if an input string has exactly one more *b* than *a*, it will crash on this PM in state READ$_3$.
    (iii) Show that if an input string has more than one more *a* than *b* or more than one more *b* than *a*, then it will loop forever on this PM.

3. Show that the language accepted by this PM is EQUAL, all words with the same number of *a*'s and *b*'s.

4. Draw a PM that accepts the language UNEQUAL, the complement of EQUAL.

5. Draw a PM that accepts the language $\{a^n b^{3n}\}$. (*Hint:* Use the subroutine SHIFT-RIGHT CYCLICALLY.)

6. Draw a PM that accepts the language EVENPALINDROME.

7. (i) Draw a PM that accepts the language ODDPALINDROME.
   (ii) Draw a PM that accepts the language PALINDROME.

8. Draw a PM that accepts the language EVENPALINDROME' (the complement of EVENPALINDROME).

9. (i) Explain why, even though a PM is deterministic, the complement of a language accepted by a PM might not be accepted by any PM.
   (ii) Find an example of a PM that does not accept the complementary language by reversing ACCEPT and REJECT states.
   (iii) Find a PM that accepts exactly the same language if its ACCEPT and REJECT states are reversed.

10. Prove that all regular languages can be accepted by some PM. (This is not hard. Simply follow the line of argument in the proof of Theorem 28, p. 310.)

11. (i) Convert the following TM into a PM using the algorithm of Theorem 49 (p. 470) (make use of the subroutine SHIFT-RIGHT CYCLICALLY):

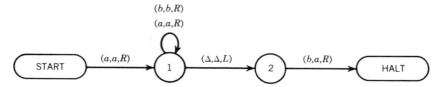

Run the following input strings on both the TM and PM:
   (ii) *a*
   (iii) *ab*
   (iv) *abb*
   (v) What is the language accepted by the two machines?
   (vi) Build a smaller PM that accepts the same language.

12. (i) Build a PM that takes in any string of *a*'s and *b*'s and leaves in its STORE the complement string that has the *a*'s and *b*'s switched.
   (ii) Build a PM that takes in any string of *a*'s and *b*'s and exchanges the first and last letters and then accepts.

13. (i) Build a PM that accepts the language MIDDLEA of all words that have an *a* as the middle letter. (These words obviously must have odd length.)
   (ii) Prove that this language is nonregular.
   (iii) Prove that this language is context-free.

14. Convert the PM built in Problem 13 into a TM by the algorithm in this chapter.

15. Build a PM that accepts the language MOREA (all words with more *a*'s than *b*'s) by using the following algorithm:

   Step 1 On one pass through the data, look for a pair of consecutive letters that are unequal and cancel them both.
   Step 2 Repeat the operation above until there are no letters to cancel.
   Step 3 If there is an *a* left, accept the word.

   Run this machine on the following input strings:

     (i) *aabb*

    (ii) *aaabb*

   (iii) *ababa*

   (iv) *ababab*

16. Build a PM that takes any input from the language defined by $(\mathbf{a} + \mathbf{b})^*$ and deletes all substrings of the form *aaa*, leaving all else in the word intact.

17. Build a PM that sorts the letters of a string. That is, if *aba* is fed in, the machine leaves *aab* in its STORE and accepts. Also, *bbbaba* becomes *aabbbb*.

18. Build a PM that starts with any string *s* from $(\mathbf{a} + \mathbf{b})^*$ and leaves

$$sb^{\text{length}(s)}$$

This is the language TRAILING-COUNT we have seen before (p. 204).

19. (i) Outline a TM that takes any input string of *a*'s and *b*'s and runs to HALT, leaving on its TAPE the same string reversed.

    (ii) Outline a PM that does the same thing.

20. Let *L* be a language accepted by the PM *P*. Let the reverse of *L* be the language of all the words in *L* spelled backward. Prove that there is some *PM*, *G*, that accepts transpose (*L*).

CHAPTER 21

Minsky's Theorem

⚜ THE TWO-STACK PDA

We shall soon see that Turing machines are fascinating and worthy of extensive study, but they do not seem at first glance like a natural development from the machines that we had been studying before. There was a natural extension from FAs to PDAs that made it easy to prove that all regular languages could also be accepted by PDAs. There is no such natural connection between PDAs and TMs; that is, a TM is not a souped-up PDA with extra gizmos.

We found that the addition of a PUSHDOWN STACK made a considerable improvement in the power of an FA. What would happen if we added two PUSHDOWN STACKs, or three, or seventy?

DEFINITION

A **two-pushdown stack machine,** a **2PDA,** is like a PDA except that it has two PUSH-DOWN STACKs, STACK$_1$ and STACK$_2$. When we wish to push a character x into a STACK, we have to specify which stack, either PUSH$_1$ x or PUSH$_2$ x. When we pop a STACK for the purpose of branching, we must specify which STACK, either POP$_1$ or POP$_2$. The function of the START, READ, ACCEPT, and REJECT states remains the same. The input string is placed on the same read-only INPUT TAPE. One important difference is that we shall insist that a 2PDA be deterministic, that is, branching will only occur at the READ and POP states and there will be at most one edge from any state for any given character. ■

Because we have made 2PDAs deterministic, we cannot be certain whether they are even as powerful as PDAs; that is, we cannot be certain that they can accept every CFL because the deterministic PDAs cannot.

We shall soon see that 2PDAs are actually stronger than PDAs. They can accept all CFLs and some languages that are non-context-free.

EXAMPLE

Consider the 2PDA on the next page:

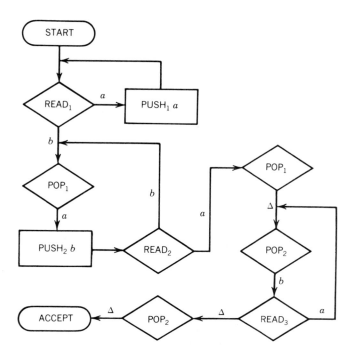

There are many REJECT states that we have not drawn in. As far as we are concerned, it is fine for the machine to crash when it reads or pops a character for which there is no path. This does not make the machine nondeterministic.

We have numbered the READ states but not the POPs because they already have numeric labels designating which STACK is to be popped and extra numbers would be confusing.

The first thing that happens to an input string is that the initial clump of a's is stripped away and put into $STACK_1$ in a circuit involving $READ_1$. Then a b takes us into a circuit involving $READ_2$, where we pop an a from $STACK_1$ for every b we read from the INPUT TAPE. Every time we pass through this circuit, we push a b into $STACK_2$. When we are done, we check to make sure that $STACK_1$ is now empty. If we pass this test, we know that there were as many b's in the b-clump as a's in the a-clump. We now enter a circuit involving $READ_3$ that reads through another clump of a's from the input and matches them against the number of b's we have put into $STACK_2$ in the previous circuit. If both the INPUT TAPE and $STACK_2$ become empty at the same time, then there were as many a's at the end of the TAPE as b's in $STACK_2$. This would mean that the whole initial input string was of the form $a^n b^n a^n$.

We can check this by processing $aabbaa$ as follows:

TAPE	STATE	STACK$_1$	STACK$_2$
$aabbaa$	START	Δ	Δ
$abbaa$	$READ_1$	Δ	Δ
$abbaa$	$PUSH_1\ a$	a	Δ
$bbaa$	$READ_1$	a	Δ
$bbaa$	$PUSH_1\ a$	aa	Δ

TAPE	STATE	STACK$_1$	STACK$_2$
baa	READ$_1$	*aa*	Δ
baa	POP$_1$	*a*	Δ
baa	PUSH$_2$ *b*	*a*	*b*
aa	READ$_2$	*a*	*b*
aa	POP$_1$	Δ	*b*
aa	PUSH$_2$ *b*	Δ	*bb*
a	READ$_2$	Δ	*bb*
a	POP$_1$	Δ	*bb*
a	POP$_2$	Δ	*b*
Δ	READ$_3$	Δ	*b*
Δ	POP$_2$	Δ	Δ
Δ	READ$_3$	Δ	Δ
Δ	POP$_2$	Δ	Δ
Δ	ACCEPT	Δ	Δ

■

So, we see that a 2PDA can accept one language that a PDA cannot. Are there languages that a 2PDA cannot accept? Is a 3PDA stronger? Is a nondeterministic 2PDA stronger? Which is stronger, a 2PDA or a PM? The subject could, at this point, become very confusing. However, many of these questions are settled by a theorem of Marvin Minsky (1961).

⚜ JUST ANOTHER TM

THEOREM 50

$$2\text{PDA} = \text{TM}$$

In other words, any language accepted by a 2PDA can be accepted by some TM and any language accepted by a TM can be accepted by some 2PDA.

PROOF

In the first part of this proof, we shall show that if the language L can be accepted by some 2PDA, then we can construct a TM that will also accept it. There may be several 2PDAs that accept L, so we fix our attention on one of them, call it P.

This demonstration will, of course, be by constructive algorithm. We shall show how to construct a TM that parallels the actions of the 2PDA. (We have also used the words "corresponds," "simulates," "duplicates," and "emulates" and the phrase or "processes exactly the same way." These words are not technically different.)

The 2PDA has three locations where it stores information: the INPUT TAPE, STACK$_1$, and STACK$_2$. The TM we build has only one information storage location, the TAPE. Therefore, we must put on the TAPE the information found in all three 2PDA locations. There is other information that is carried in the knowledge of what state we are in, but that will correspond easily between the 2PDA and the TM.

Suppose at some stage in the process the 2PDA has this status:

$$\begin{array}{ll} \text{TAPE} & X_1 \, X_2 \, X_3 \, X_4 \\ \text{STACK}_1 & Y_1 \, Y_2 \, Y_3 \, Y_4 \, Y_5 \\ \text{STACK}_2 & Z_1 \, Z_2 \end{array}$$

where the X's, Y's, and Z's are letters from the input and stack alphabets of the 2PDA. Our definition of 2PDAs was sketchy and did not mention whether each STACK had its own alphabet or whether there was some other rule. Because a STACK does not *have* to use all of the characters in its STACK alphabet, there is no real difference, so let us assume that the X's are from Σ and the Y's and Z's from Γ.

In our setup, we encode these three strings on the TM TAPE as follows:

Step 1 Assume the characters # and $ are not used by the 2PDA (if they are, find other special symbols).

Step 2 In the first section of the TM TAPE, we store the input string. Initially, we insert a Δ into cell i, moving the data unchanged up the TAPE and later, as the letters of input are read by the 2PDA, we change them one by one into Δ's on the TM TAPE. The status of the TM TAPE corresponding to the current status of the 2PDA TAPE as described above after two input letters are read is

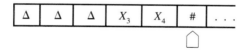

In what we have pictured above, two letters from the input string, those that were in cell ii and cell iii, have been read by the 2PDA and thus converted into Δ's on the TM. Because the number of letters in the input string cannot be increased (a 2PDA can read its TAPE but not write on it), we can put a permanent marker "#" on the TM TAPE at the end of the input string before we begin running. Throughout our processing, the marker will stay exactly where it is. This # will be the home base for the TAPE HEAD. After simulating any action of the 2PDA, the TM TAPE HEAD will return to the # before beginning its next operation.

In our model, the TM instructions that simulate the operation of the 2PDA state:

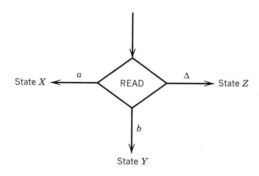

must accomplish the following chores:

1. Move the TAPE HEAD to the left to find the rightmost of the front Δ's.

2. Bounce back to the right to find the next input letter to be read; in other words, scan right for the first non-Δ.

3. If this character is #, the input has been exhausted and we go to state Z otherwise.

4. Change this letter into a Δ and back up one space to the left (so that we do not accidentally step on the # without knowing it).

5. Branch according to what was read; if it was an a, take an edge to the simulation of state X, if a b, take an edge to state Y.

6. Before continuing the processing, return to the TAPE HEAD to # by moving right until it is encountered.

In TM notation, this looks like this:

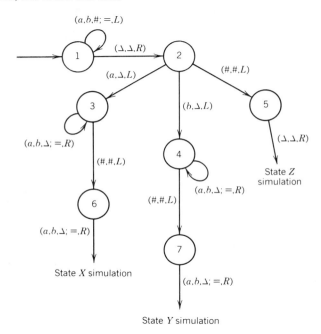

Notice that we are making use of the multiple instruction notation defined in Chapter 20 on p. 468.

$$(p, q, r, s; =, R) \text{ stands for } (p, p, R), (q, q, R), (r, r, R), (s, s, R)$$

In state 1, we are looking for the Δ's at the beginning of the TAPE. We get to state 2 when we have found one and bounced off to the right, either onto the first letter of the remainder of the string or else back onto #. If the string was empty when we got to read it, we follow the edge from state 2 to state 5. The edge from state 5 bounces us off the Δ that is to the left of # and leaves the TAPE HEAD reading the # as we want.

The reason we make such a fuss about knowing where we leave the TAPE HEAD is not because it matters in the simulation of any particular step, but because it helps us glue together the simulated steps. This is somewhat like building a house and returning the hammer to the tool shed after driving in each nail. It is not efficient, but we never lose the hammer.

Step 3 The contents of the two PUSHDOWN STACKS will appear to the right of the #
on the TM TAPE. We place the contents of STACK$_1$ on the TAPE, then the $
marker, and then the contents of STACK$_2$. The TAPE would then look like this:

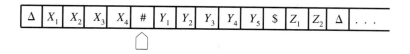

To simulate a POP$_1$ instruction, we move the TAPE HEAD from the # one cell to the right,
branch on what we read, and return the TAPE HEAD to the same cell it just read, and along
each branch we run the TM subprogram DELETE. If we deleted first, we would not remember what the character used to be. After simulating the POP$_1$, we return the TAPE HEAD safely
to point to the # again. The PM state:

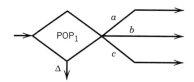

becomes

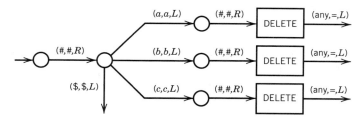

Here, we have used the label (any, $=$, L) to mean "whatever is read, write the same thing,"
and move the TAPE HEAD to the left. We should also note that popping an empty STACK$_1$ is
the same as reading the $ right after the #.

To simulate a PUSH$_1$ X, we move the TAPE HEAD one cell to the right and run the TM
subprogram INSERT X. We then return the TAPE HEAD to point to # by moving two cells to
the left:

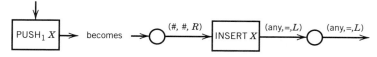

To simulate a POP$_2$, we advance the TAPE HEAD up the TAPE to the cell one past the $.
This we read and branch and return to and delete, as with POP$_1$. Again, we return the TAPE
HEAD to the #-cell.

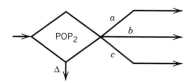

becomes

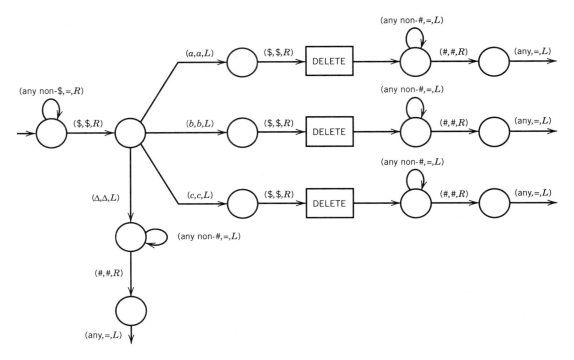

The label (any non-$, =, R) means that we move the TAPE HEAD right without changing the contents of the TAPE, and we stay in the same state until we read the $. The label (any non-#, =, L) has an analogous meaning. It takes half the subprogram to return the TAPE HEAD.

To simulate a PUSH₂ X, we advance the TAPE HEAD one cell past the $ and run the TM subprogram INSERT X. We then return the TAPE HEAD to its usual position.

becomes

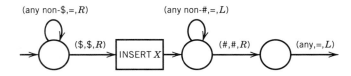

When the 2PDA branches to an ACCEPT state, we enter the TM HALT state and accept the input string.

The individual parts fit together perfectly because each component finds the TAPE HEAD pointing to # and leaves it in the same place.

End of steps.

So far, we have proven only half of Minsky's theorem. We have shown that TMs can do everything 2PDAs can do. We still have to show that any language accepted by a TM can be accepted by some 2PDA.

To make the proof of this section easier, we shall prove that any language accepted by a

PM can be accepted by some 2PDA. By Theorem 49 (p. 470), this implies that 2PDAs can do anything TMs can do and so it is enough to prove our result.

These two machines are already considerably closer to each other than TMs and 2PDAs, because both 2PDAs and PMs operate on the ends of storage locations with instructions inside states. In TMs, the instructions are on the edges; a TAPE is much more complex to access, because we can read and write in its middle. We shall show how STACK$_1$ (on the 2PDA) can act in as versatile a manner as the STORE (on the PM) with the help of her brother STACK$_2$.

The PM starts with the input string already in the STORE, so we must transfer the input string from the TAPE of the 2PDA into STACK$_1$. We do this as follows:

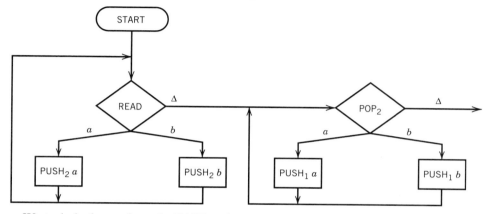

We took the letters from the TAPE and put them first in STACK$_2$. But because of the nature of a PUSHDOWN STACK, the string was reversed. If the input was initially *aabb*, what can be read from STACK$_2$ is *bbaa*. When it is transferred again to STACK$_1$, the input string is reversed once more to become *aabb* as it was on the TAPE so that POP$_1$ now has an *a* as the first letter. The TAPE is now empty, and so we never refer to it again.

The two states with which a PM operates on its STORE are READ and ADD. The READ is a branch instruction and completely corresponds to the 2PDA instruction POP$_1$ by eliminating the leftmost character and branching accordingly.

The ADD instruction is not so directly correspondent to any 2PDA instruction, because PUSH$_1$ introduces a new character on the left of the string in STACK$_1$, whereas ADD introduces a new character on the right of the string in the PM's STORE.

We can, however, simulate the action of ADD X with the following set of 2PDA instructions:

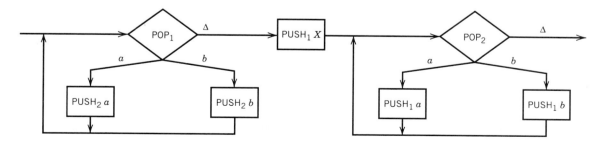

Here, we first empty STACK$_1$ into STACK$_2$ (in STACK$_2$ the contents appear backward), then we insert the character X in STACK$_1$, and then we read back the string from STACK$_2$ into STACK$_1$ (it is back in correct order now). The net result is that we have an additional X on the right of the string in STACK$_1$, which means at the bottom of the stack.

a	Δ		Δ	b		X	b		a	Δ
b		$\rightarrow$		b	$\rightarrow$		b	$\rightarrow$	b	
b				a			a		b	
									X	

STACK₁ STACK₂   STACK₁ STACK₂   STACK₁ STACK₂   STACK₁ STACK₂

STACK$_2$ is used only to initialize STACK$_1$ and to simulate the ADD instruction and for no other purpose.

The only other states a PM has are REJECT and ACCEPT, and those stay completely the same in the 2PDA. Therefore, we have finished describing this conversion process. We can completely simulate a PM on a 2PDA. Because we can simulate a TM on a PM, we can conclude that we can simulate a TM on a 2PDA.

This completes the proof of Minsky's theorem.   ■

To illustrate the action of the algorithms in the proof, we shall now present the mandatory examples of a 2PDA converted into a TM and a PM converted into a 2PDA. In both cases, the conversion does not change the language accepted by the machine.

EXAMPLE

No higher purpose would be served by constructing a 3000-state TM corresponding to a complicated 2PDA, so we choose a very simple 2PDA and claim that it is pedagogically sufficient.

One of the simplest 2PDAs is shown below:

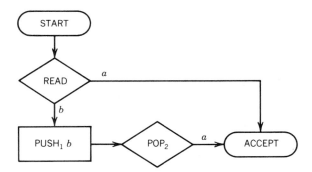

This machine accepts all words beginning with a and crashes on all words beginning with b because POP$_2$ cannot produce an a.

Many simple TMs can accept this language, but to know this, we must *understand* the language. If we automatically follow the algorithm described in the proof of Theorem 50, we then produce a TM that must accept the same language as this 2PDA whether we know how to characterize the language by some simple English sentence or not. That is the whole point of "proof by constructive algorithm."

The TM we must build is shown below:

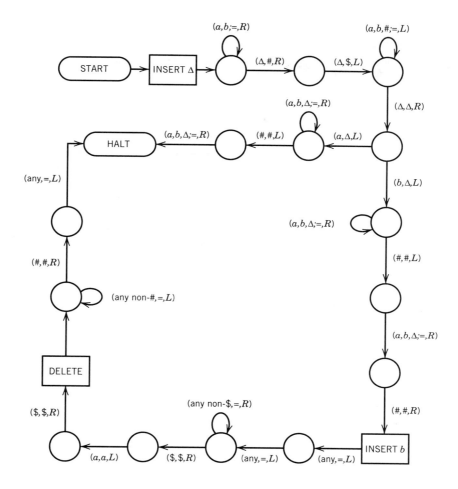

The pleasure of running strings on this machine is reserved for Problem 16. ∎

EXAMPLE

Consider the following PM:

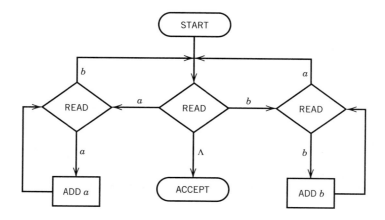

In the problem section of the last chapter, this was seen to accept the language EQUAL, of all strings with the same total number of a's and b's (cf. p. 477).

When we convert this into a 2PDA by the algorithm described in the proof of Minsky's theorem, we obtain the following:

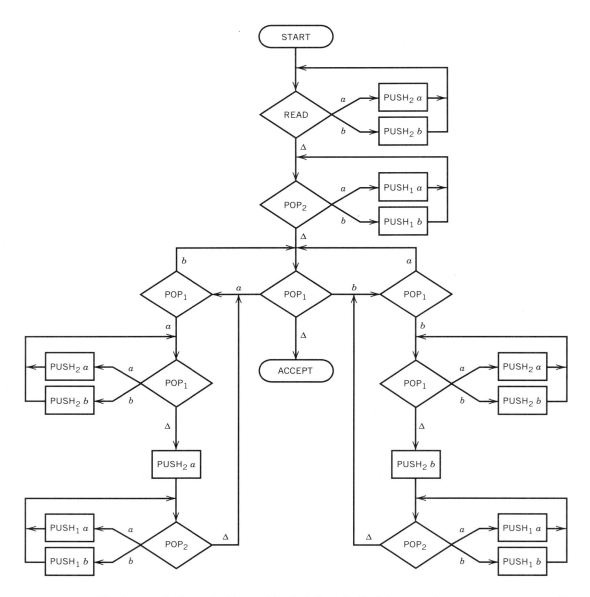

Tracing words through this machine is left to the Problems section.   ∎

If a pushdown automaton with two STACKs is already as powerful as a TM, it stands to reason that a PDA with three STACKs will be even more powerful than a TM and a PDA with four STACKs even more powerful yet, and so on. This chain of reasoning is certainly true for ocean liners, but it runs aground for PDAs. None of these is any more powerful than a TM.

THEOREM 51

Any language accepted by a PDA with n STACKs (where n is 2 or more), called an **nPDA,** can also be accepted by some TM. In power we have

$$n\text{PDA} = \text{TM} \qquad \text{if } n \geq 2$$

PROOF

We shall sketch very quickly how the action of a 3PDA can be simulated by a TM as an illustration of the general idea.

Suppose that we have a 3PDA that is running on a certain input string. In the middle of the process, we have some information on the INPUT TAPE and in the STACKs. Suppose the status is

$$
\begin{array}{ll}
\text{TAPE} & w_1\, w_2\, w_3\, w_4 \\
\text{STACK}_1 & x_1\, x_2 \\
\text{STACK}_2 & y_1\, y_2\, y_3\, y_4\, y_5 \\
\text{STACK}_3 & z_1\, z_2\, z_3
\end{array}
$$

We want to represent all of this on the TAPE of the TM as

Δ ... Δ	$w_1 w_2 w_3 w_4$	$\#_1$	$x_1 x_2$	$\#_2$	$y_1 y_2 y_3 y_4 y_5$	$\#_3$	$z_1 z_2 z_3$	Δ ...

Instead of inventing new characters, we let the kth STACK be marked by the starting symbol $\#_k$. The operation of the conversion is so obvious that anyone who requires a further explanation will not understand it when it is presented.

So, a TM can accept anything that an nPDA can. Obviously, an nPDA can accept anything a 2PDA can ,which is anything a TM can.

Therefore, in power

$$n\text{PDA} = \text{TM} \qquad \text{for } n \geq 2 \qquad \blacksquare$$

Once we reach the level of a TM, it is *hard* to go farther. There is good reason to believe that it is *impossible* to go farther, but that is a discussion for Chapter 25.

Symbolically, we can represent the power comparison of our various mathematical models of machines as follows:

$$\text{FA} = \text{TG} = \text{NFA} < \text{DPDA} < \text{PDA} < 2\text{PDA} = n\text{PDA} = \text{PM} = \text{TM}$$

(Note that, as of this point, we have not yet proven that 2PDA is definitely stronger than PDA because a PDA is nondeterministic, but we shall do so soon.)

The underlying structure of this book is now finally revealed:

PART I	FA	0	PDA
PART II	PDA	1	PDA
PART III	TM	2	PDA

The machines in our highest class are all deterministic. Perhaps a nondeterministic nPDA

(*Nn*PDA), a nondeterministic Post machine (NPM), or a nondeterministic Turing machine (NTM) would be even stronger. In the next chapter, we shall see that this is not the case. All these nondeterministic machines are only equivalent in power to the TM, not stronger. We have gone about as far as we can go.

⚜ PROBLEMS

Consider the following 2PDA:

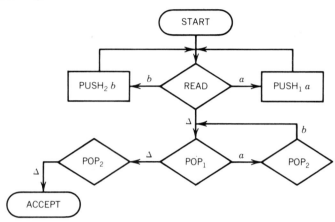

1. Trace the execution of these input strings on this machine.
    (i) *aabb*
    (ii) *babab*

2. Prove that the language accepted by this 2PDA is the language EQUAL.

3. Draw a 3PDA that accepts the language $\{a^n b^n a^n b^n\}$.

4. Draw a PM that accepts the language $\{a^n b^n a^n b^n\}$.

5. Draw a 2PDA that accepts the language $\{a^n b^n a^n b^n\}$.

6. Let us use the alphabet $\Sigma = \{a \quad b \quad c \quad d\}$. Build a 3PDA that accepts the language $\{a^n b^n c^n d^n\}$.

7. Outline a 2PDA that accepts the language defined in the previous problem.

Let us define the language VERYEQUAL over the alphabet $\Sigma = \{a \quad b \quad c\}$ as all strings that have as many total a's as total b's as total c's (see p. 375):

$$\text{VERYEQUAL} = \{abc \quad acb \quad bac \quad bca \quad cab \quad cba \quad aabbcc \quad aabcbc \ldots\}$$

8. Draw a TM that accepts VERYEQUAL.

9. Draw a PM that accepts VERYEQUAL.

10. (i) Draw a 3PDA that accepts VERYEQUAL.
     (ii) Draw a 2PDA that accepts VERYEQUAL.

11. Draw a 2PDA that accepts the language EVEN-EVEN and keeps at most two letters in its STACKs.

12. Draw a 2PDA that accepts MIDDLEA (see p. 478).

13. Outline a 2PDA that accepts PALINDROME.

14. Draw a 2PDA that accepts TRAILING-COUNT. (p. 204)

15. Draw a 2PDA that accepts MOREA. (p. 205)

16. On the TM that was formed from the 2PDA in the example on p. 489, trace the execution of the following input strings:
    (i) *abb*
    (ii) *baa*

17. On the 2PDA that was formed from the PM in the example on p. 490, trace the execution of the following input strings:
    (i) *abba*
    (ii) *babab*

18. (i) Draw a 3PDA to accept the language $\{a^n b^{2n} c^n\}$ over the alphabet $\Sigma = \{a \quad b \quad c\}$.
    (ii) Draw a 2PDA to accept this language.
    (iii) Draw a deterministic PDA that accepts that language.

19. If L is a language accepted by a 2PDA, prove that TRANSPOSE(L) (p. 91) is also a language accepted by 2PDA.

20. (i) Without referring to the material in any other chapter, show that any language that can be accepted by a 3PDA can be accepted by a 2PDA.
    (ii) Generalize.

CHAPTER 22

Variations on the TM

⚜ THE MOVE-IN-STATE MACHINE

Turing machines can be drawn using different pictorial representations. Let us consider the diagram below, which looks like a cross between a Mealy and a Moore machine:

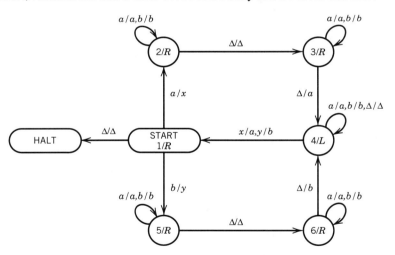

This is a new way of writing the program part of a TM; we still use the same old TAPE and TAPE HEAD. In this picture the edges are labeled as in a Mealy machine with input-slash-output instructions. An edge labeled p/q says, "If the TAPE HEAD is reading a p, change it to a q and follow this arrow to the next state." The edge itself does not indicate in which direction the TAPE HEAD is to be moved. The instructions for moving the TAPE HEAD are found once we enter the next state. Inside the circles denoting states, we have labels that are name-slash-move indicators. For example, $4/L$ says, "You have entered state 4; please move the TAPE HEAD one cell to the left." When we commence running the machine in the START state, we do not execute its move instruction. If we reenter the start state, then we follow its move instruction.

Let us call machines drawn in this fashion **move-in-state machines.** After analyzing the preceding machine, we shall prove that move-in-state machines have the same power as TMs as we originally defined them.

The action of the preceding move-in-state machine drawn is to start with any word on its TAPE, leave a space, and make an exact copy of the word on the TAPE. If we start with the word w, we end up with the string $w\Delta w$:

baab	becomes	*baabΔbaab*
a	becomes	*aΔa*
Δ . . .	becomes	Δ . . .

The algorithm is as follows: We start in state 1. If we read an a, we take the high road: state 2 – state 3 – state 4 – state 1. If we read a b, we take the low road: state 5 – state 6 – state 4 – state 1. Suppose that we read an a. This is changed into an x as we travel along the edge labeled a/x to state 2, where the TAPE HEAD is moved right. In state 2, we now skip over all the a's and b's remaining in w, each time returning to state 2 and moving the TAPE HEAD right. When we reach the first Δ after the end of w, we take the edge labeled Δ/Δ to state 3. This edge leaves the Δ undisturbed. The TAPE HEAD is moved by state 3 to the right again. In state 3, we read through all the letters we have already copied into the second version of w until we read the first Δ. We then take the Δ/a edge to state 4. Along the edge, we change the Δ into an a (this is the letter we read in state 1). State 4 moves the TAPE HEAD left, reading through all the a's and b's of the second copy of w, then through the Δ, and then through the a's and b's of the part of the original w that has not already been copied.

Finally, we reach the x with which we marked the letter a that we were copying. This we change back to an a on the edge labeled x/a, y/b going to state 1. State 1 tells us to move the TAPE HEAD to the right, so we are ready to copy the next letter of w. If this letter is an a, we take the high road again. If it is a b, we change it to a y and take the route state 5 – state 6 to find the blank that we must change to a b in the second copy. Then in state 4, we move the TAPE HEAD back down to the y and change it back to a b and return to state 1. When we have finished copying all of w, state 1 reads a Δ and we halt.

The following is the trace of the operation of this machine on the input string *baa*:

$$\frac{1}{b\underline{a}a} \rightarrow \frac{5}{y\underline{a}a} \rightarrow \frac{5}{ya\underline{a}} \rightarrow \frac{5}{yaa\underline{\Delta}} \rightarrow \frac{6}{yaa\Delta\underline{\Delta}} \rightarrow \frac{4}{yaa\underline{\Delta}b} \rightarrow \frac{4}{ya\underline{a}\Delta b}$$

$$\rightarrow \frac{4}{y\underline{a}a\Delta b} \rightarrow \frac{4}{\underline{y}aa\Delta b} \rightarrow \frac{1}{b\underline{a}a\Delta b} \rightarrow \frac{2}{bx\underline{a}\Delta b} \rightarrow \frac{2}{bxa\underline{\Delta}b} \rightarrow \frac{3}{bxa\Delta\underline{b}}$$

$$\rightarrow \frac{3}{bxa\Delta b\underline{\Delta}} \rightarrow \frac{4}{bxa\Delta b\underline{a}} \rightarrow \frac{4}{bxa\Delta\underline{b}a} \rightarrow \frac{4}{bx\underline{a}\Delta ba} \rightarrow \frac{4}{b\underline{x}a\Delta ba} \rightarrow \frac{1}{ba\underline{a}\Delta ba}$$

$$\rightarrow \frac{2}{ba\underline{x}\Delta ba} \rightarrow \frac{3}{bax\Delta ba} \rightarrow \frac{3}{bax\Delta b\underline{a}} \rightarrow \frac{3}{bax\Delta ba\underline{\Delta}} \rightarrow \frac{4}{bax\Delta b\underline{a}a} \rightarrow \frac{4}{bax\Delta\underline{b}aa}$$

$$\rightarrow \frac{4}{ba\underline{x}\Delta baa} \rightarrow \frac{4}{ba\underline{x}\Delta baa} \rightarrow \frac{1}{baa\underline{\Delta}baa} \rightarrow \text{HALT}$$

It is not obvious that move-in-state machines have the same power as TMs. Why is that? Because move-in-state machines are limited to always making the *same* TAPE HEAD move every time we enter a particular state, whereas with TMs we can enter a certain state, having moved the TAPE HEAD left or right. For example, the TM situations:

and

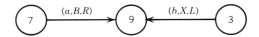

cannot simply be converted into move-in-state TMs by adding TAPE HEAD moving instructions into state 9. However, we can get around this difficulty in a way analogous to the method we used for converting Mealy into Moore machines. The next two theorems prove

$$\text{Move-in-state} = \text{TM}$$

THEOREM 52

For every move-in-state machine M, there is a TM, T, which accepts the same language. That is, if M crashes on the input w, T crashes on the input w. If M loops on the input w, T loops on the input w. If M accepts the input w, then T does too. We require even more. After halting the two machines, leave exactly the same scattered symbols on the TAPE.

PROOF

The proof will be by constructive algorithm.

This conversion algorithm is simple. One by one, in any order, let us take every edge in M and change its labels. If the edge leads to a state that tells the TAPE HEAD to move right, change its labels from X/Y to (X, Y, R). If the edge leads to a state that tells the TAPE HEAD to move left, change its labels from X/Y to (X, Y, L). To make this description complete, we should say that any edge going into the HALT state should be given the TAPE HEAD move instruction, R.

When all edge labels have been changed, erase the move instructions from inside the states. For example,

becomes

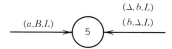

The resulting diagram is a TM in normal form that operates exactly as the move-in-state machine did. The trace of a given input on the move-in-state machine is the same as the trace of the same input on the converted TM. ■

EXAMPLE

The move-in-state machine above that copies input words will be converted by the algorithm given in this proof into the following TM:

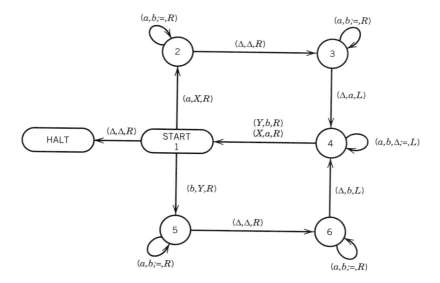

THEOREM 53

For every TM T, there is a move-in-state machine M that operates in exactly the same way on all inputs—crashing, looping, or accepting. Furthermore, the move-in-state machine will always leave the same remnants on the TAPE that the TM does.

PROOF

The proof will be by constructive algorithm.

We cannot simply "do the reverse" of the algorithm in the last proof. If we try to move the TAPE HEAD instructions from the edges into the states themselves, we sometimes succeed and sometimes fail, depending on whether all the edges entering a given state have the same TAPE HEAD direction or not. This is a case of déjà vu. We faced the same difficulty when converting Mealy machines into Moore machines—and the solution is the same. If edges with different TAPE HEAD movement directions feed into the same state, we must make two copies of that state, one labeled move R and one labeled move L, each with a complete set of the same exit edges the original state had. The incoming edges will then be directed into whichever state contains the appropriate move instruction.

For example,

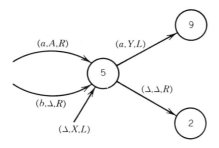

becomes

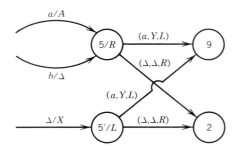

Some states become twins; some remain single. State by state we make this conversion until the TM is changed into a move-in-state machine that acts on inputs identically to the way the old TM used to.

If the START state has to split, only one of its clones can still be called START—it does not matter which, because the edges coming out of both are the same.

If a state that gets split loops back to itself, we must be careful to which of its clones the loops go. It all depends on what was printed on the loop edge. A loop labeled with an R will become a loop on the R twin and an edge from the L twin. The symmetric thing happens to a TM edge with an L move instruction.

This process will always convert a TM into an equivalent move-in-state machine, equivalent both in the sense of language-acceptor and in the sense of TAPE-manipulator. ■

EXAMPLE

Let us consider the following purely random TM:

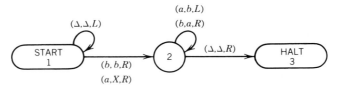

When the algorithm of the preceding theorem is applied to the states of this TM in order, we obtain the following conversion:

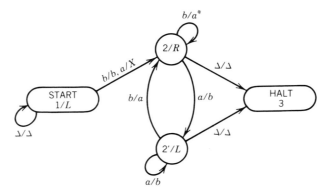

Notice that HALT 3 is the same as writing HALT $3/R$, but if the edge entering HALT moved left, we would need a different state because input might then crash while going into the HALT state. ■

We have been careful to note that when we combine the last two theorems into one statement

$$TM = \text{move-in-state machine}$$

we are not merely talking about their power as language-recognizers, but as transducers as well. Not only do the same words run to HALT on the corresponding machines, but also they leave identical outputs on the input TAPE. The importance of this point will be made clear later.

⚜ THE STAY-OPTION MACHINE

Another variation on the definition of the TM that is sometimes encountered is the "stay-option" machine. This is a machine exactly like a TM except that along any edge we have the option of not moving the TAPE HEAD at all—the stay option. Instead of writing L or R as directions to the TAPE HEAD, we can also write S for "stay put."

On the surface, this seems like a ridiculous thing to do, because it causes us to read next the character that we have just this instant printed. However, the correct use of the stay option is to let us change states without disturbing the TAPE or TAPE HEAD, as in the example below:

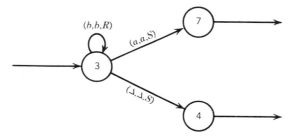

We stay in state 3 skipping over b's until we reach an a or a Δ. If we reach an a, we jump to state 7 and there decide what to do. If we reach a Δ, we go to state 4, where more processing will continue. In either case, we are reading the first of the new characters.

The question arises, "Does this stay option give us any extra real power, or is it merely a method of alternate notation?" Naturally, we shall once again prove that the stay option adds nothing to the power of the already omnipotent TM.

EXAMPLE

We have had some awkward moments in programming TMs, especially when we wanted to leave the TAPE HEAD pointing to a special symbol such as a * in cell i or a # in between words. We used to have to write something like

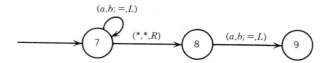

State 7 backs down the TAPE looking for the *. State 8 finds it, but the TAPE HEAD bounces off to the right. We then have to proceed to state 9 to leave the TAPE HEAD pointing to the *.

With the stay option this becomes easier:

■

DEFINITION

Let us call a TM with a stay option a **stay-option machine.**

■

We now show that the stay option, although it may be useful in shortening programs, adds no new power to the TM.

THEOREM 54

$$\text{stay-option machine} = \text{TM}$$

In other words, for any stay-option machine there is some TM that acts the same way on all inputs, looping, crashing, or accepting while leaving the same data on the TAPE; and vice versa.

PROOF

Because a TM is only a stay-option machine in which we have not bothered to use the stay option, it is clear that for any TM there is a stay-option machine that does the same thing—the TM itself. What remains for us to show is that if the stay option is ever used, we can replace it with other TM programming and so convert a stay-option machine into an equivalent TM.

To do this, we simply follow this replacement rule. Change any edge

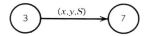

into

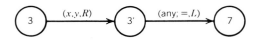

introducing a new state 3′. It is *pat*ently obvious that this does not change the processing of any input string at any stage.

When all stay-option edges have been eliminated (even loops), what remains is the desired regular TM.

■

Now that we have shown that the stay-option is harmless, we shall feel free to use it in the future when it is convenient.

EXAMPLE

Here, we shall build a simple machine to do some subtraction. It will start with a string of the form **#(0 + 1)*** on its TAPE. This is a # in cell i followed by some binary number. The job of this stay-option machine is to subtract 1 from this number and leave the answer on the TAPE. This is a *binary decrementer.*

The basic algorithm is to change all the rightmost 0's to 1's and the rightmost 1 to 0. The only problem with this is that if the input is zero, that is, of the form **#0***, then the algorithm gives the wrong answer because we have no representation for negative numbers.

The machine below illustrates one way of handling this situation:

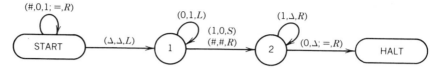

What happens with this machine is

START	#101001000
Becomes state 1	#101001000Δ
Becomes state 1	#101001111
Becomes state 2	#101000111

If we are in state 2 and we are reading a 0, we must have arrived there by the edge $(1, 0, S)$, so in these cases we proceed directly to $(0, 0, R)$ HALT.

If, on the other hand, we arrive in state 2 from the edge $(\#, \#, R)$, it means we started with zero, **#0***, on the TAPE:

START	#0000
Becomes state 1	#0000Δ
Becomes state 1	#1111
Becomes state 2	#1111
Becomes state 2	#ΔΔΔΔΔ

In state 2, we erase all these mistaken 1's. If the input was zero, this machine leaves an error message in the form of the single character #.

In this machine, there is only one stay-option edge. Employing the algorithm from the preceding theorem, we leave the state 1–state 2 edge $(\#, \#, R)$ alone, but change the state 1–state 2 edge $(1, 0, S)$ as follows:

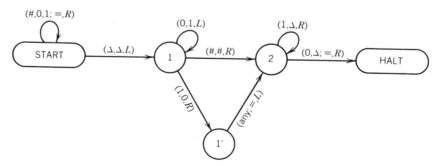

There are some other minor variations of TMs that we could investigate. One is to allow the TAPE HEAD to move more than one cell at a time such as

$$(X, Y, 3R) = (\text{read } X, \text{write } Y, \text{move 3 cells to the right})$$

This is equivalent to

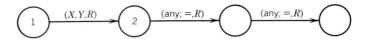

Some other instructions of this ilk are

$$(X, Y, 2L) \quad \text{or} \quad (X, Y, 33R)$$

It is clear that these variations do not change the power of a TM as acceptor or transducer; that is, the same input strings are accepted and the stuff they leave on the TAPE is the same. This is, in fact, so obvious that we shall not waste a theorem on it.

THE k-TRACK TM

In addition to variations involving the move instructions, it is also possible to have variations on the TAPE structure. The first of these we shall consider is the possibility of having more than one TAPE.

The picture below shows the possibility of having four TAPES stacked one on top of the other and one TAPE HEAD reading them all at once:

TAPE 1	a	b	b	a	a	. . .
TAPE 2	Δ	Δ	Δ	Δ	Δ	. . .
TAPE 3	b	Δ	Δ	a	Δ	. . .
TAPE 4	b	b	a	b	b	. . .

In this illustration, the TAPE HEAD is reading cell iii of TAPE 1, cell iii of TAPE 2, cell iii of TAPE 3, and cell iii of TAPE 4 at once. The TAPE HEAD can write something new in each of these cells and then move to the left to read the four cell ii's or to the right to read the four cell iv's.

DEFINITION

A k-**track TM**, or k**TM**, has k normal TM TAPES and one TAPE HEAD that reads corresponding cells on all TAPES simultaneously and can write on all TAPES at once. There is also an alphabet of input letters Σ and an alphabet of TAPE characters Γ. The input strings are taken from Σ, while the TAPE HEAD can write any character from Γ.

There is a program of instructions for the TAPE HEAD consisting of a START state, HALT states, other states, and edges between states labeled

$$\begin{pmatrix} p, t \\ q, u \\ r, v \\ s, w \\ \bullet \bullet \bullet \end{pmatrix} M$$

where $p, q, r, s, t, u, v, w, \ldots$ are all in Γ and M is R or L, meaning that if what is read from TAPE 1 is p, from TAPE 2 is q, from TAPE 3 is r, from TAPE 4 is s, and so on, then what will be written on TAPE 1 is *t*, on TAPE 2 is *u*, on TAPE 3 is *v*, on TAPE 4 is *w*, and so on. The TAPE HEAD will be moved in the direction indicated by *M*.

To operate a *k*TM, we start with an input string from Σ* on TAPE 1 starting in cell i, and if we reach HALT, we say that the string is in the language of the *k*TM. We also say that the content of *all* the TAPES is the output produced by this input string.   ■

This is a very useful modification of a TM. In many applications, it allows a natural correspondence between the machine algorithm and traditional hand calculation, as we can see from the examples below. Notice that we use the words track and TAPE interchangeably for a *k*TM.

EXAMPLE

When a human adds a pair of numbers in base 10, the algorithm followed is usually to line them up in two rows right-adjusted, find the right-hand column, and perform the addition column by column moving left, remembering whether there are carries and stopping when the last column has been added.

The following 3TM performs this algorithm exactly as we were taught in third grade except that it uses a column of $'s to mark the left edge. Track 1 and track 2 contain the numbers to be added and track 3 is all blanks. The total will be found on track 3 when we reach HALT.

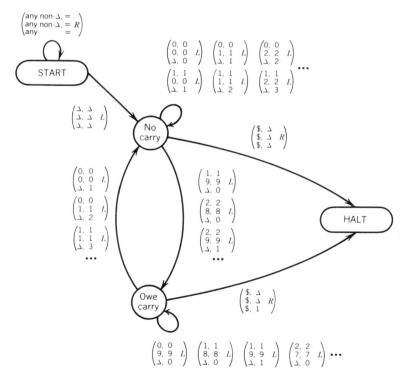

The loop from no-carry back to itself takes care of all combinations:

$$\begin{pmatrix} u & u & \\ v & v & L \\ \Delta & u+v & \end{pmatrix}$$

where $u + v$ is less than 10.

The edges from no-carry to owe-carry are labeled

$$\begin{pmatrix} u & & u & \\ v & & v & L \\ \Delta & u + v - 10 & & \end{pmatrix}$$

where $u + v \geq 10$.

The loop from owe-carry back to itself is

$$\begin{pmatrix} u & & u & \\ v & & v & L \\ \Delta & u + v - 9 & & \end{pmatrix}$$

where $u + v \geq 9$.

The edge from owe-carry to no-carry is

$$\begin{pmatrix} u & & u & \\ v & & v & L \\ \Delta & u + v + 1 & & \end{pmatrix}$$

where $u + v \leq 8$.

We trace this input on this 3TM:

START	START	START	START	START	
$ 4 2 9	$ 4 2 9	$ 4 2 9	$ 4 2 9	$ 4 2 9 Δ	
$ 9 3 3 →	$ 9 3 3 →	$ 9 3 3 →	$ 9 3 3 →	$ 9 3 3 Δ	
$̲ Δ Δ Δ	$ Δ̲ Δ Δ	$ Δ Δ̲ Δ	$ Δ Δ Δ̲	$ Δ Δ Δ Δ̲	

	No-carry	Owe-carry	No-carry	Owe-carry	HALT
	$ 4 2 9	$ 4 2 9	$ 4 2 9	$ 4 2 9	Δ 4 2 9
→	$ 9 3 3 →	$ 9 3 3 →	$ 9 3 3 →	$ 9 3 3 →	Δ 9 3 3
	$ Δ Δ Δ̲	$ Δ Δ̲ 2	$ Δ̲ 6 2	$̲ 3 6 2	1 3̲ 6 2

The correct total, 1362, is found on TAPE 3 only. The data left on the other TAPES is not part of the answer. We could have been erasing TAPE 1 and TAPE 2 along the way, but this way is closer to what humans do.

We could have started with both input numbers on TAPE 1 and let the machine transfer the second number to TAPE 2 and put the $'s in the cell i's. These chores are not difficult. ■

Considering TMs as transducers has not seemed very important to us before. In a PDA, we never considered the possibility that what was left in the STACK when the input was accepted had any deep significance. Usually, it was nothing. In our early TM examples, the TAPE often ended up containing random garbage. But, as the example above shows, the importance of the machine might not be simply that the input was accepted, but what **output** was generated in the process. This is a theme that will become increasingly important to us as we approach the back cover.

We should now have a theorem that says that kTMs have no greater power than TMs do as either acceptors or transducers. This is true, but before we prove it, we must discuss what it means. As we have defined it, a kTM starts with a single line of input just as a TM does. However, the output from a kTM is presumed to be the entire status of all k TAPES. How can a TM possibly hope to have output of this form? We shall adapt a convention of correspondence that employs the interlacing cells on one TAPE to simulate the multiplicity of kTM tracks.

We say that the 3TM TAPE status

a	d	g	. . .
b	e	h	. . .
c	f	i	. . .

corresponds to the one-TAPE TM status

a	b	c	d	e	f	g	h	i	. . .

This is an illustration for three tracks, but the principle of correspondence we are using applies equally well to *k*-tracks.

We can now prove our equality theorem.

THEOREM 55

Part 1   Given any TM and any *k*, there is a *k*TM that acts on all inputs exactly as the TM does (that means either loops, crashes, or leaves a corresponding output).

Part 2   Given any *k*TM for any *k*, there is a TM that acts on all inputs exactly as the *k*TM does (that means loops, crashes, or leaves a corresponding output).

In other words, as an acceptor or transducer,

$$\text{TM} = k\text{TM}$$

PROOF

Proof of Part 1

One might think that Part 1 of this proof is trivial. All we have to do is leave TAPE 2, TAPE 3, . . . , TAPE *k* always blank and change every TM edge label from (X, Y, Z) in the original TM into

$$\begin{pmatrix} X & Y & \\ \Delta & \Delta & Z \\ \Delta & \Delta & \end{pmatrix}$$

The end result on TAPE 1 will be exactly the same as on the original TM. This would be fine except that under our definition of correspondence

a	b	c	d	. . .
Δ	Δ	Δ	Δ	. . .
Δ	Δ	Δ	Δ	. . .

does not correspond to the TM TAPE status

a	b	c	d		. . .

but rather to the TM Tape status

a	Δ	Δ	b	Δ	Δ	c	Δ	Δ	d	Δ	Δ	. . .

To have a kTM properly correspond to a TM once we have adopted our definition of correspondence, we must convert the answer Tape on the kTM from

a	b	c	d	. . .
Δ	Δ	Δ	Δ	. . .
Δ	Δ	Δ	Δ	. . .

into this form

a	d . . .
b	. . .
c	. . .

The subroutine to do this begins as follows:

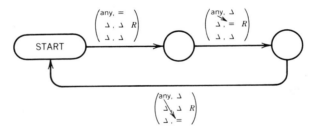

This notation should be transparent. The arrow from "any" to " = " means that into the location of the " = " we shall put whatever symbol occupied the location of the "any."

We now arrive at

a	Δ	Δ	d	. . .
Δ	b	Δ	Δ	. . .
Δ	Δ	c	Δ	. . .

We need to write a variation of the DELETE subroutine that will delete a character from one row without changing the other two rows.

To do this, we start with the subprogram DELETE exactly as we already constructed it in Chapter 19 and we make k (in this case, 3) offshoots of it. In the first, we replace every edge label as follows:

$$(X, Y, Z)$$

becomes

$$\begin{pmatrix} X,\ Y & \\ \text{any,} = & Z \\ \text{any,} = & \end{pmatrix}$$

This then will be the subroutine that deletes a character from the first row, leaving the other two rows the same; call it DELETE-FROM-ROW-1. If on the TAPE

1	4	7	10	13 . . .
2	5	8	11	. . .
3	6	9	12	. . .

we run DELETE-FROM-ROW-1 while the TAPE HEAD is pointing to column 3, the result is

1	4	10	13	. . .
2	5	8	11	. . .
3	6	9	12	. . .

We build DELETE-FROM-ROW-2 and DELETE-FROM-ROW-3 similarly.

Now we rewind the TAPE HEAD to column 1 and do as follows:

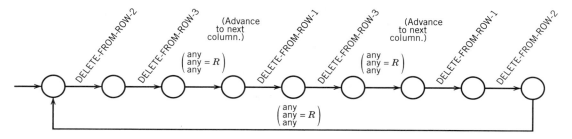

Thus, we convert the TAPE

a	Δ	Δ	d	Δ . . .
Δ	b	Δ	Δ	Δ . . .
Δ	Δ	c	Δ	Δ . . .

into

a	d	Δ . . .
b	Δ	Δ . . .
c	Δ	Δ . . .

To get out of this endless loop, all we need is an end-of-data marker and a test to tell us when we have finished converting the answer on track 1 into the k-track form of the answer. We already know how to insert these things, so we call this the conclusion of the proof of Part 1.

Proof of Part 2

We shall now show that the work of a kTM can be performed by a simple TM. Surprisingly, this is not so hard to prove.

Let us assume that the kTM we have in mind has $k = 3$ and uses the TAPE alphabet $\Gamma = \{a \quad b \quad \$\}$. (Remember, Δ appears on the TAPE but is not an alphabet letter.) There are only $4 \times 4 \times 4 = 64$ different possibilities for columns of TAPE cells. They are

$$
\begin{pmatrix} \Delta \\ \Delta \\ \Delta \end{pmatrix} \begin{pmatrix} \Delta \\ \Delta \\ a \end{pmatrix} \begin{pmatrix} \Delta \\ \Delta \\ b \end{pmatrix} \begin{pmatrix} \Delta \\ \Delta \\ \$ \end{pmatrix} \ldots \begin{pmatrix} a \\ \$ \\ b \end{pmatrix} \ldots \begin{pmatrix} \$ \\ \$ \\ \$ \end{pmatrix}
$$

The TM we shall use to simulate the 3TM will have a TAPE alphabet of $64 + 3$ characters:

$$
\Gamma = \left\{ a \quad b \quad \$ \quad \begin{pmatrix} \Delta \\ \Delta \\ \Delta \end{pmatrix} \begin{pmatrix} \Delta \\ \Delta \\ a \end{pmatrix} \quad \ldots, \quad \begin{pmatrix} \$ \\ \$ \\ \$ \end{pmatrix} \right\}
$$

We are calling symbols such as

$$
\begin{pmatrix} a \\ a \\ \Delta \end{pmatrix}
$$

a *single* TAPE character, meaning that it can fit into *one* cell of the TM and can be used in the labels of the edges in the program. For example,

will be a legal simple instruction on our simple TM.

These letters are admittedly very strange, but so are some others soon to appear.

We are now ready to simulate the 3TM in three steps:

Step 1   The input string $X_1 X_2 X_3 \ldots$ will be fed to the 3TM on TAPE 1 looking like this:

X_1	X_2	X_3	. . .
Δ	Δ	Δ	. . .
Δ	Δ	Δ	. . .

Because our TM is to operate on the same input string, it will begin like this:

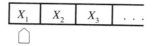

To begin the simulation, we must convert the whole string to triple-decker characters corresponding to the 3TM. We could use something like these instructions:

$$\left(a, \begin{pmatrix} a \\ \Delta \\ \Delta \end{pmatrix}, R\right) \quad \left(\$, \begin{pmatrix} \$ \\ \Delta \\ \Delta \end{pmatrix}, R\right) \quad \left(b, \begin{pmatrix} b \\ \Delta \\ \Delta \end{pmatrix}, R\right) \quad \left(\Delta, \begin{pmatrix} \Delta \\ \Delta \\ \Delta \end{pmatrix}, R\right) \dots$$

We must have some way of telling when the string of X's is done. Let us say that if the X's are a simple input word, they contain no Δ's and therefore we are done when we reach the first blank. The program should be

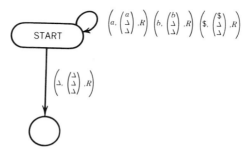

We shall now want to rewind the TAPE HEAD to cell i so we should, as usual, have marked cell i when we left it so that we could back up without crashing. (This is left as a problem below.) If the 3TM ever needs to read cells beyond the initial ones used for the input string, the simulating TM will have to remember to treat the new Δ's encountered as though they were

$$\begin{pmatrix} \Delta \\ \Delta \\ \Delta \end{pmatrix}$$

Step 2 Copy the 3TM program exactly for use by the simulating TM. Every 3TM instruction

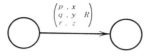

becomes

$$\left(\begin{pmatrix} p \\ q \\ r \end{pmatrix}, \begin{pmatrix} x \\ y \\ z \end{pmatrix}, R\right)$$

which is a simple TM instruction.

Step 3   If the 3TM crashes on a given input, so will the TM. If the 3TM loops forever
on a given input, so will the simple TM. If the 3TM reaches a HALT state, we
need to decode the answer on the TM. This is because the 3TM final result

d	g	j	m	Δ	$\ldots$
e	h	k	Δ	Δ	$\ldots$
f	i	l	Δ	Δ	$\ldots$

will sit on the TM as:

$\begin{pmatrix} d \\ e \\ f \end{pmatrix}$	$\begin{pmatrix} g \\ h \\ i \end{pmatrix}$	$\begin{pmatrix} j \\ k \\ l \end{pmatrix}$	$\begin{pmatrix} m \\ \Delta \\ \Delta \end{pmatrix}$	Δ	$\ldots$

but the TM TAPE status corresponding to the 3TM answer is actually

d	e	f	g	h	i	j	k	l	m	Δ	Δ	$\ldots$

We must therefore convert the TM TAPE from triple-decker characters to simple
single-letter strings.

This requires a state with 64 loops like the one below:

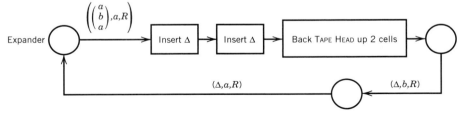

Once the answer has been converted into a simple string, we can halt. To know
when to halt is not always easy because we may not always recognize when the
3TM has no more non-Δ data. Reading 10:

$$\begin{pmatrix} \Delta \\ \Delta \\ \Delta \end{pmatrix}$$

does not necessarily mean that we have transcribed all the useful information
from the 3TM. However, we can tell when the simple TM is finished expanding triples. When the expander state reads a single Δ, it knows that it has hit
that part of the original TM TAPE not needed in the simulation of the 3TM. So,
we add the branch

Expander $\bigcirc$ $\xrightarrow{(\Delta,\Delta,R)}$ (HALT)

This completes the conversion of the 3TM to a TM. The algorithm for k other than 3 is entirely analogous. ∎

We shall save the task of providing concrete illustrations of the algorithms in this theorem for the Problems section.

⚜ THE TWO-WAY INFINITE TAPE MODEL

The next variation of a TM we shall consider is actually Turing's own original model. He did not use the concept of a "half-infinite" TAPE. His TAPE was infinite in both directions, which we call **doubly infinite,** or **two-way infinite**. (The TAPES as we defined originally are sometimes called **one-way infinite** TAPES.)

The input string is placed on the TAPE in consecutive cells somewhere and the rest of the TAPE is filled with blanks. There are infinitely many blanks to the left of the input string as well as to the right of it. This seems to give us two advantages:

1. We do not have to worry about crashing by moving left from cell i, because we can always move left into some ready cell.

2. We have two work areas not just one in which to do calculation, because we can use the cells to the left of the input as well as those farther out to the right.

By convention, the TAPE HEAD starts off pointing to the leftmost cell containing non-blank data.

The input string *abba* would be depicted as

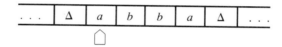

We shall number the cells once an input string has been placed on the TAPE by calling the cell the TAPE HEAD points to cell i. The cells to the right are numbered as usual with increasing lowercase Roman numerals. The cells to the left are numbered with zero and negative lowercase Roman numerals. (Let us not quibble about whether the ancient Romans knew of zero and negative numbers.)

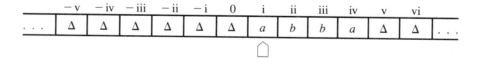

THEOREM 56

TMs with two-way TAPES are exactly as powerful as TMs with one-way TAPES as both language-acceptors and -transducers.

PROOF

The proof will be by constructive algorithm.

First, we must show that every one-way TM can be simulated by a two-way TM. We cannot get away with saying, "Run the same program on the two-way TM and it will give the same answer" because in the original TM if the TAPE HEAD is moved left from cell i, the input crashes, whereas on the two-way TM it will not crash. To be sure that the two-way TM does crash every time its TAPE HEAD enters cell 0, we must proceed in a special way.

Let 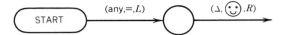 be a symbol not used in the alphabet Γ for the one-way TM. Insert ☺ in cell 0 on the two-way TM and return the TAPE HEAD to cell i:

From here, let the two-way TM follow the exact same program as the one-way TM.

Now if, by accident, while simulating the one-way TM, the two-way TM ever moves left from cell i, it will not crash immediately as the one-way TM would, *but* when it tries to carry out the *next* instruction, it will read the ☺ in cell 0 and find that there is no edge for that character anywhere in the program of the one-way machine. This will cause a crash, and the input word will be rejected.

One further refinement is enough to finish the proof. (This is one of the subtlest of subtleties in anything we have yet seen.) The one-way TM may end on the instruction

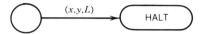

where this left move could conceivably cause a crash, preventing successful termination at HALT without actually *reading* the contents on cell 0, merely moving in. To be sure that the one-way TM also crashes in its simulation, it must read the last cell it moves to. We must change the one-way TM program to

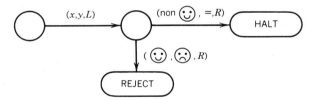

We have yet to prove that anything a two-way TM can do can also be done by a one-way TM. And we will not. What we shall prove is that anything that can be done by a two-way TM can be done by some 3TM. Then by the previous theorem there is a one-way TM, which can do anything this 3TM can do.

Let us start with some particular two-way TM. Let us wrap the doubly infinite TAPE around to make the figure below:

cell i	cell ii	cell iii	cell iv	cell v	. . .
cell 0	cell −i	cell −ii	cell −iii	cell −iv	. . .

Furthermore, let us require every cell in the middle row to contain one of the following five symbols: Δ, ↑, ↓, ↑↑, ↓↓.

The single arrows will tell us which of the two cells in the column we are actually reading. The double arrows, for the tricky case of going around the bend, will appear only in the first column. The middle track will always contain one double arrow, at most one single arrow and Δ's for all the rest.

If we are in a positively numbered cell and we wish to simulate on the 3TM the two-way TM instruction

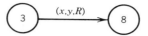

we can simply write this as

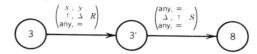

where S is the stay option for the TAPE HEAD. The second step is necessary to move the arrow on track 2 to the correct column. We do not actually need S. We could always move one more left and then back.

For example,

	0	i	ii	iii	iv		
. . .	Δ	a	b	b	a	Δ	. . .

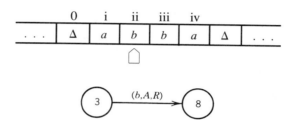

causes

	i	ii	iii	iv	
. . .	a	A	b	a	. . .

Analogously,

a	b	b	a	Δ	. . .
$\uparrow\uparrow$	$\uparrow$	Δ	Δ	Δ	. . .
Δ	Δ	Δ	Δ	Δ	. . .

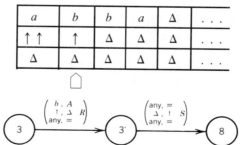

causes

a	A	b	a	Δ	. . .
$\uparrow\uparrow$	Δ	$\uparrow$	Δ	Δ	. . .
Δ	Δ	Δ	Δ	Δ	. . .

If we were in a negatively numbered cell on the two-way TM and asked to move *R*, we would need to move left in the 3TM.

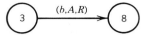

could become

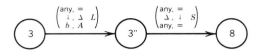

This is because in the two-way TM moving right from cell − iii takes us to cell − ii, which in the 3TM is to the left of cell − iii.

In the two-way TM, the TAPE status

	−iii	−ii	−i	0	i	ii	
. . .	Δ	b	a	a	b	Δ	Δ	. . .

and the instruction

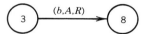

causes

	−iii	−ii	−i	0	i	ii	
. . .	Δ	A	a	a	b	Δ	Δ	. . .

Analogously, in the 3TM the TAPE status

i	ii	iii	iv	v	
Δ	Δ	Δ	Δ	Δ	. . .
↓ ↓	Δ	Δ	↓	Δ	. . .
b	a	a	b	Δ	. . .
0	−i	−ii		−iv	

and the instructions

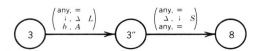

will cause the result

i	ii	iii	iv	v	
Δ	Δ	Δ	Δ	Δ	. . .
↓ ↓	Δ	↓	Δ	Δ	. . .
b	a	a	A	Δ	. . .

0   −i   ⌂   −iii   −iv

The tricky part comes when we want to move right from cell 0. That we are in cell 0 can be recognized by the double down arrows on the middle TAPE.

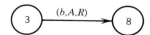

can also be

$$\left(\begin{matrix} any, = \\ \downarrow\downarrow, \uparrow\uparrow \; S \\ b, A \end{matrix} \right)$$

This means that we are now reading cell i, having left an A in cell 0.

There is one case yet to mention. When we move from cell $-$ i to the right to cell 0, we do not want to lose the double arrows there. So instead of just

$$\left(\begin{matrix} any, = \\ \Delta, \downarrow \; S \\ any, = \end{matrix} \right)$$

we also need

$$\left(\begin{matrix} any, = \\ \downarrow\downarrow, = \; S \\ any, = \end{matrix} \right)$$

The full 3TM equivalent to the two-way TM instruction

$$ 3 \quad \xrightarrow{(X,Y,R)} \quad 8 $$

is therefore

$$\left(\begin{matrix} X, Y \\ \uparrow, \Delta, R \\ any, = \end{matrix} \right) \quad \left(\begin{matrix} any, = \\ \Delta, \uparrow, S \\ any, = \end{matrix} \right)$$

$$\left(\begin{matrix} any, = \\ \downarrow, \Delta, L \\ X, Y \end{matrix} \right) \quad 3" \quad \left(\begin{matrix} any, = \\ \Delta, \downarrow, S \\ any, = \end{matrix} \right) \left(\begin{matrix} any, = \\ \downarrow\downarrow, = S \\ any, = \end{matrix} \right)$$

$$\left(\begin{matrix} any, = \\ \downarrow\downarrow, \uparrow\uparrow, S \\ X, Y \end{matrix} \right)$$

By analogous reasoning, the equivalent of the left move

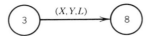

is therefore

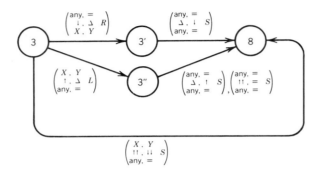

where 3′ is used when moving left from a negative cell, 3″ for moving left from a positive cell, the second label on 3″ to 8 for moving left from cell ii into cell i, and the bottom edge for moving left from cell i into cell 0.

We can now change the program of the two-way TM instruction by instruction (edge by edge) until it becomes the analogous program for the 3TM.

Any input that loops/crashes on the two-way TM will loop/crash on the 3TM. If an input halts, the output found on the two-way TM corresponds to the output found on the 3TM as we have defined correspondence. This means it is the same string, wrapped around. With a little more effort, we could show that any string found on track 1 and track 3 of a 3TM can be put together on a regular half-infinite TAPE TM.

Because we went into this theorem to prove that the output would be the same for the one-way and two-way TMs, but we did not make it explicit where on the one-way TM TAPE the output has to be, we can leave the matter right where it is and call this theorem proven. ■

EXAMPLE

The following two-way TM takes an input string and leaves as output the *a-b* complement of the string; that is, if *abaaa* is the input, we want the output to be *babbb*.

The algorithm we follow is this:

1. In cell 0, place a *.

2. Find the last nonblank letter on the right and erase it. If it is a *, halt; if it is an *a*, go to step 3; if it is a *b*, go to step 4.

3. Find the first blank on the left, change it to a *b*, and go to step 2.

4. Find the first blank on the left, change it to an *a*, and go to step 2.

The action of this algorithm on *abaaa* is

$$abaaa \rightarrow *abaaa \rightarrow *abaa \rightarrow b*abaa \rightarrow b*aba \rightarrow bb*aba \rightarrow bb*ab$$
$$\rightarrow bbb*ab \rightarrow bbb*a \rightarrow abbb*a \rightarrow abbb* \rightarrow babbb* \rightarrow babbb$$

If we follow this method, the output is always going to be left in the negatively numbered cells. However, on a two-way TAPE this does not have to be shifted over to start in cell i since there is no way to distinguish cell i. The output is

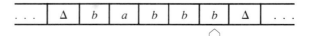

which can be considered as centered on the TAPE (infinitely many Δ's to the right, infinitely many Δ's to the left).

The program for this algorithm is

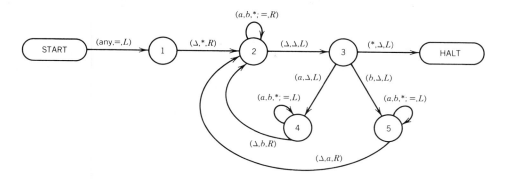

Let us trace the working of this two-way TM on the input ab:

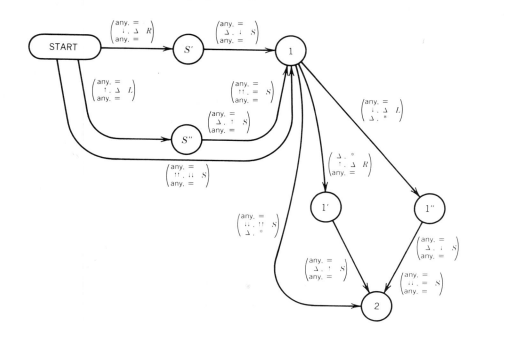

When converted to a 3TM, this program begins as follows:

The task of completing this picture is left for obsessive compulsives.   ■

There are other variations possible for TMs. We recapitulate the old ones and list some new ones below:

Variation 1   Move-in-state machines
Variation 2   Stay-option machines
Variation 3   Multiple-track machines
Variation 4   Two-way infinite TAPE machines
Variation 5   One TAPE, but multiple TAPE HEADS
Variation 6   Many TAPES with independently moving TAPE HEADS
Variation 7   Two-dimensional TAPE (a whole plane of cells, like infinitely many tracks)
Variation 8   Two-dimensional TAPE with many independent TAPE HEADS
Variation 9   Make any of the above nondeterministic

At this point, we are ready to address the most important variation: nondeterminism.

⚜ THE NONDETERMINISTIC TM

DEFINITION

A **nondeterministic TM,** or **NTM,** is defined like a TM, but allows more than one edge leaving any state with the same first entry (the character to be read) in the label; that is, in state Q if we read a Y, we may have several choices of paths to pursue:

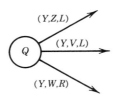

An input string is accepted by an NTM if there is *some* path through the program that leads to HALT, even if there are some choices of paths that loop or crash.   ■

We do not consider an NTM as a transducer because a given input may leave many possible outputs. There is even the possibility of infinitely many different outputs for one particular input as below:

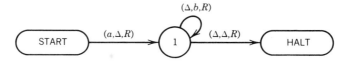

This NTM accepts only the input word a, but it may leave on its TAPE any of the infinitely many choices in the language defined by the regular expression **b***, depending on how many times it chooses to loop in state 1 before proceeding to HALT.

For a nondeterministic TM, T, we do not bother to separate the two types of nonacceptance states, reject(T) and loop(T). A word can possibly take many paths through T. If some loop, some crash, and some accept, we say that the word is accepted. What should we do about a word that has some paths that loop and some that crash but none that accept? Rather than distinguish crash from loop, we lump them together as not in the language Accept(T).

Two NTMs are considered equivalent as language-acceptors if

$$\text{Accept}(T_1) = \text{Accept}(T_2)$$

no matter what happens to the other input strings.

THEOREM 57

$$\text{NTM} = \text{TM}$$

PROOF

First, we show that any language accepted by an NTM can be accepted by a (deterministic) TM. The proof will be by constructive algorithm. We shall start with any NTM and construct a deterministic 3TM that accepts the same language. Because we know that 3TM = TM, this will complete the proof. ■

Let us start by numbering each edge in the entire NTM machine by adding a number label next to each edge instruction. These extra labels do not influence the running of the machine, they simply make description of paths through the machine easier. For example, the NTM below:

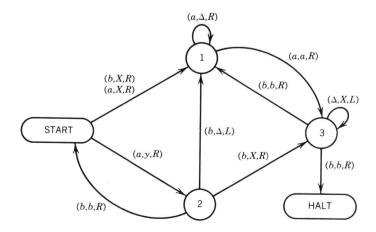

(which does nothing interesting in particular) can be edge-instruction-numbered to look like:

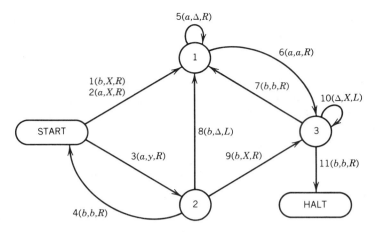

There is no special order for numbering the edge instructions. The only requirement is that each instruction receive a different number.

In an NTM, every string of numbers determines at most one path through the machine (which also may or may not crash). The string of numbers

$$1-5-6-10-10-11$$

represents the path

$$\text{START}-\text{state }1-\text{state }1-\text{state }3-\text{state }3-\text{state }3-\text{HALT}$$

This path may or may not correspond to a possible processing of an input string—but it is a path through the graph of the program nonetheless.

Some possible sequences of numbers are obviously not paths—for example,

$$9-9-9-2-11$$
$$2-5-6$$
$$1-4-7-4-11$$

The first does not begin at START, the second does not end in HALT, and the third asks edge 7 to come after edge 4, but these do not connect.

To have a path traceable by an input string, we have to be careful about the TAPE contents as well as the edge sequence. To do this, we propose a three-track TM on which the first track has material we shall discuss later, the second track has a finite sequence of numbers (one per cell) in the range of 1 to 11, and the bottom track has the input sequence to be simulated—for example,

						. . .
11	4	6	6	Δ	Δ	. . .
a	b	a	Δ	Δ	Δ	. . .

In trying to run an NTM, we shall sometimes be able to proceed in a deterministic way (only one possibility at a state), but sometimes we may be at a state from which there are several choices. At this point, we would like to telephone our mother and ask her advice about which path to take. Mother might say to take edge 11 at this juncture and she might be right; branch 11 does move the processing along a path that will lead to HALT. On the other hand, she might be way off base. Branch 11? Why, branch 11 is not even a choice at our current crossroads. (Some days mothers give better advice than other days.)

One thing is true. *If* a particular input can be accepted by a particular NTM, *then there is* some finite sequence of numbers (each less than the total number of instructions, 11 in the NTM above) that label a path through the machine for that word. If mother gives us all possible sequences of advice, one at a time, eventually one sequence of numbers will constitute the guidance that will help us follow a path to HALT. If the input string cannot be accepted, nothing mother can tell us will help. For simplicity, we presume that we ask mother's advice even at deterministic states.

So, our 3TM will work as follows:

On this track we run the input using mother's advice.
On this track we generate mother's advice.
On this track we keep a copy of the original input string.

If we are lucky and the string of numbers on track 2 is good advice, then track 1 will lead us to HALT.

If the numbers on track 2 are not perfect for nondeterministic branching, then track 1 will lead us to a crash. Track 1 cannot loop forever, because it has to ask mother's advice at every state and mother's advice is always a finite string of numbers.

If mother's advice does not lead to HALT, it will cause a crash or simply run out and we shall be left with no guidance. If we are to crash or be without mother's advice, what we do instead of crashing is start all over again with a new sequence of numbers for track 2. We do the following:

1. Erase track 1.

2. Generate the *next sequence* of mother's advice.

3. Recopy the input from where it is stored on track 3 to track 1.

4. Begin again to process track 1, making the branching shown on track 2.

What does this mean: Generate the *next sequence* of mother's advice? If the NTM we are going to simulate has 11 edge labels, then mother's advice is a *word* in the regular language defined by

$$(1 + 2 + 3 + \cdots + 11)*$$

We have a natural ordering for these words (the words are written with hyphens between the letters):

One-letter words	1 2 3 . . . 9 10 11
Two-letter words	1-1 1-2 . . . 1-11 2-1 2-2 2-3 . . . 11-11
Three-letter words	1-1-1 1-1-2 1-1-3 . . . 11-11-10 11-11-11
Four-letter words	1-1-1-1 . . .

If a given input can be accepted by the NTM, then at least one of these words is good advice. Our 3TM works as follows:

1. Start with Δ's on track 1 and track 2 and the input string in storage on track 3.

2. Generate the next sequence of mother's advice and put it on track 2. (When we start up, the "next sequence" is just the number 1 in cell i.)

3. Copy track 3 onto track 1.

4. Run track 1, always referring to mother's advice at each state.

5. If we get to HALT, then halt.

6. If mother's advice is imperfect and we almost crash, then erase track 1 and go to step 2.

Mother's advice could be imperfect in the following ways:

i. The edge she advises us to take is unavailable at the state we are in.

ii. The edge she advises is available, but its label requires that a different letter be read by the TAPE HEAD than the letter our TAPE HEAD is now reading from track 1.

iii. Mother is fresh out of advice; for example, her advice on this round was a sequence of five numbers, but after five edges we are not yet in HALT.

Let us give a few more details of how this system works in practice. We are at a certain state reading the three tracks. Let us say they read

The bottom track does not matter when it comes to the operation of a run, only when it comes time to start over with new advice.

We are in some state reading a and 6. If mother's advice is good, there is an edge from the state we are in that branches on the input a. But let us not be misled; mother's advice is not necessarily to take edge 6 at this juncture.

To find the current piece of mother's advice, we need to move the TAPE HEAD to the first unused number in the middle track. *That* is the correct piece of mother's advice. After 30 edges, we are ready to read the thirty-first piece of mother's advice. The TAPE HEAD will probably be off reading some different column of data for track 1, but when we need mother's advice, we have to look for it.

Our problem is that we have only one TAPE HEAD but we want to keep track of where we are on two different TAPE tracks, and it would only be coincidence if the two active cells were in the same column. What is worse is that we wish to alternate reading what is on track 1 and what is on track 2. After each TAPE HEAD move on track 1, we want to go back to track 2 to get our directions, and then we want to return to track 1 to carry them out. Essentially, what we must do is mark our spot on track 1 so we know how to return to it. We do this by one of our favorite uses of artistic expression—blue paint. Let us assume that we have two copies of the alphabet of TAPE characters for track 1: one in black ink and one in blue. When we have to leave track 1 to dig up our new instructions from track 2, we turn the character to which the TAPE HEAD was pointing into its blue version. When we wish to return to where we were on track 1, we run the TAPE HEAD up from cell i until we reach the blue letter. There we turn it back into black and resume execution of mother's instruction.

Similarly, when we drop back to track 2 to get mother's next instruction, we have to be able to find out where we were in executing her advice so far. If we erase her advice as we read it, it will be impossible to generate the lexicographically next string of mother's advice if we fail to accept the input through this set of instructions. We need to keep mother's advice intact but mark just how far along we are. The answer is blue paint, of course. The piece of mother's advice we are trying to follow will be painted blue as we leave. If following that piece of advice does not cause a crash or lead to HALT, then we shall return for more advice. We rewind the TAPE HEAD to cell i and scan track 2 until we get to the blue instruction number. This one we turn back to black and read the next one, turning it blue.

If we are out of mother's advice, which we notice when the next cell on track 2 contains a Δ, it is time to erase track 1, increment track 2, copy track 3 to track 1, rewind the TAPE HEAD to cell i, and read mother's first instruction.

How can we actually implement these ideas in practice? The first thing we must do is to insert end markers in cell i on all tracks. That is easy using the subprogram INSERT $. The second thing we have to do is copy track 3 (which always keeps a pristine version of the input to be simulated) onto track 1. This we do basically with the simple 3TM program segment

We know that on our first iteration mother's advice starts out simply as the number 1, but exactly how we can increment it when the time comes is another question. We have already seen incrementation done in binary in this chapter (p. 500), and incrementation in base 11 (or however many edge instructions the NTM has) is quite similar. We wind the TAPE HEAD up the TAPE to the first Δ and bounce off to the left. If it is not yet an 11, increase it by 1. If it is an 11, set it equal to 1 and move the TAPE HEAD left to increase the next digit. If this is not an 11, we are done. If it is, set it equal to 1 and repeat. If we get to $ having found only 11's, then we know that the string of 1's we have created is too short (like going from 999 to 1000, only easier). So, we run up the TAPE and add another 1 to the end of the non-Δ string.

Suppose someone asks us how we know to use base 11 and not some other number? Then we know that he has lost the point of what we are doing. We are initially presented with an NTM, and given it specifically, we are going to make a particular 3TM that will run on all inputs, not the same as the NTM does, but with the same result—acceptance only when the NTM accepts. We are allowed to examine the NTM before building our 3TM (it would be quite advisable to do so). This is when we discover how many edge instructions the NTM has and, therefore, when we learn how to design the mother's advice-incrementing subprogram.

Now suppose we have retrieved a piece of mother's advice and it says to take edge instruction 6. How do we actually do this on our 3TM? Some of the states in our 3TM must have the meaning "in the simulation of the input we are in state x on the NTM and we must now go seek mother's advice," and some of the states have the meaning, "in the simulation of the input on the NTM we are in state x and mother has just advised us to take edge y." We leave a state of the second type and find mother's advice and then we arrive at a state of the second type. While there, we make a detour to have the TAPE HEAD find and read the next letter of the simulation on track 1. Now we are all set. We are in a state that knows where we are on the NTM, which edge we wish to follow, and what character is being read by the TAPE HEAD. Then if possible, we execute that instruction; that is, we change the TAPE cell contents, move the TAPE HEAD, and go to a 3TM state that represents the next NTM state the instruction would have us enter. All this 3TM programming we can build from looking at the NTM alone, without reference to any particular input string. There are only a finite number of total possibilities for being in NTM state x and trying to follow instruction y, and they are connected by 3TM edges in an obvious way.

Most likely, we cannot follow mother's capricious advice (even though she has told us a thousand times) in any particular situation. Her randomly chosen edge instruction has a low probability of starting from the state we are in, and less considering we might not be reading the proper character from track 1. Even then, the instruction we are asked to follow might move the TAPE HEAD inadvertently into cell i (which contains the cushion $, but it does mean the NTM would have crashed). In any of these events, mother's advice turns out to have been infelicitous. And we must wipe the slate clean and start again with the next advice.

However, we must always remember that if there actually is a path for this particular input from START to HALT on the NTM, then there is some sequence of edge instructions comprising that path, and sooner or later that very path will be mother's advice. So every word accepted by the NTM is accepted by the 3TM. If a given input has no path to acceptance on the NTM, then the 3TM will run forever, testing one sequence of mother's advice after another ad infinitum. Nothing ever crashes on the 3TM; it just optimistically loops forever.

We have shown a TM can do what an NTM can do. Obviously, an NTM can do anything that a TM can do, simply by not using the option of nondeterminism. ∎

The next theorem may come as a surprise, not that the result is so amazing but that it is strange that we have not proven this already.

THEOREM 58

Every CFL can be accepted by some TM.

PROOF

We know that every CFL can be accepted by some PDA (Theorem 30, p. 318) and that every PDA PUSH can be written as a sequence of the PM instructions ADD and SHIFT-RIGHT CYCLICALLY (p. 469). What we were not able to conclude before is that a PM could do everything a PDA could do because PDAs could be nondeterministic, whereas PMs could not. If we convert a nondeterministic PDA into PM form we get a nondeterministic PM.

If we further apply the conversion algorithm of Theorem 47 (p. 462) to this nondeterministic PM, we convert the nondeterministic PM into a nondeterministic TM.

Using our last theorem, we know that every NTM has an equivalent TM.

Putting all of this together, we conclude that any language accepted by a PDA can be accepted by some TM. ∎

⚜ THE READ-ONLY TM

So far, we have considered only variations of the basic mathematical model of the TM that do not affect the power of the machine to recognize languages. We shall now consider a variation that does substantially *hamper* the capacity of the TM: the restriction that the TAPE HEAD can write nothing new on the TAPE.

DEFINITION

A **read-only TM** is a TM with the property that for every edge label in the program the READ and WRITE fields are the same. This means that if the TAPE HEAD reads an x, it must write an x, no matter what x is. All edge labels, therefore, are of the form (x, x, y), where y is either L or R. Because the TAPE HEAD cannot change the contents of the TAPE, the input alphabet equals the output alphabet. The TAPE HEAD can move back and forward over the input string as much as it wants, but the contents of the TAPE remain unchanged. ∎

As a transducer, a read-only TM is very easy to describe: output = input. The interesting question is, "What types of languages can a read-only TM recognize as an acceptor?"

It is conceivable that some advantage can be gained by reading some of the blank cells to the right of the input string on the TAPE before the machine decides to halt, loop, or crash, but because nothing can be written in these cells, they cannot be used to store information. Also, after the first Δ all the rest are known to be blank and nothing about the particular input string on the TAPE can be learned from them. For these reasons, it is customary to require a read-only TM to accept or reject a string by the time it has read its first Δ, if not sooner.

A read-only TM is sometimes called a two-way FA, because it acts like an FA in the sense that the transitions from state to state take place by reading without writing. The modifier "two-way" is intended to explain how letters can be reread once they have already been scanned. Our original model of the FA did not involve a TAPE or TAPE HEAD, and the letters were deemed to have been consumed by the machine once ingested. However, we could have begun our discussion of mathematical models of computing with the TM (which was historically first) and then defined the FA as a read-only one-way TM. One justification for calling a read-only TM an FA is that, unlike our other variations of the Turing model, the read-only machine does not have the same power as a TM but only the power of a standard FA, as we shall now prove.

An FA and a PDA can read each letter of their input string only once, but the PDA has a note pad on which it can record some facts about what it has read. We have seen that this extra ability substantially increases its capacity to recognize languages. Although a read-only TM does not have a note pad, if a question does arise at some point in the processing where the machine must make a branching decision in the program based on some previously available but forgotten information, the TAPE HEAD can move back down the TAPE to the left to recheck what it had once read. The difficulty is that once it has done this, how is it ever going to return to the exact spot on the TAPE where the question first arose? The read-only TAPE HEAD is unable to leave a marker. When it scans back up the TAPE to where the branch point was encountered, it may well be going through a different sequence of states than it traversed in its first trip up the TAPE. We have seen situations in which the choice of the series of states itself carried the required information. However, it is possible that, even with the information in hand, the TAPE HEAD can still not relocate the TAPE cell from which it started backtracking. The additional freedom of motion of the TAPE HEAD might not actually increase the power of the machine as much as we may wish.

All of this very informal speculation suffers from excessive anthropomorphism and the following pathetic fallacy. As we have noted before, a programmer's inability to figure out how to do something is not a proof that it cannot be done. It is not the machine that is unable to return to the correct spot, but the human who constructed the program who might not be able to figure out how to relocate the position or to employ special powers to make the relocation unnecessary. Perhaps a more clever program can employ the back-and-forth ability of read-only TMs to recognize all CFLs or some other more interesting set of languages. What we need here is a mathematical proof.

Because we intend to show that a read-only TM can accept only regular languages, perhaps a good way to do this is to show how to convert the whole machine into one regular expression as we did in the proof of Kleene's theorem in Chapter 7, by developing an elaborate constructive algorithm. In order to turn FAs into expressions, we introduced the notion of a generalized transition graph, which is an FA in which the edges are labeled with regular expressions instead of single alphabet letters. With a little effort we shall show that this strategy can be made to work in our present case as well.

To accomplish the conversion of the TM into a regular expression, we shall now define a **transition edge** in a read-only TM to be an edge whose label has the form (r, D), where r is a regular expression and D a TAPE HEAD direction: L, R, or S. The meaning of the edge

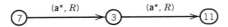

is that *if* the machine is ever in state 7 and the cell being read on the TAPE, possibly when joined to the next few cells to the right of it, form any string belonging to the language defined by the regular expression **ab*aa**, *then* the TAPE HEAD may move to the right across all of those cells and the program will progress to state 3.

This is necessarily a nondeterministic option because a string of a's could leave the program below in two different states, depending on how many were read to get to state 3:

We must be careful to define what we mean by reading a string of letters to the *left*. Suppose, moving leftward, we read the letter r followed by the letter a followed by the letter t. It is logical to say that the string read is *rat*, but it is also logical, and more useful, to note that the string traversed was *tar*, which sits on the TAPE in that very order when read by our usual convention of left to right. We shall adopt this second view. For example, starting with this situation

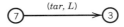

if we traverse the edge below going from state 7 to state 3,

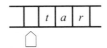

we will end up with the TAPE HEAD as indicated:

We can now define a **transition Turing machine** (TTM) to be a nondeterministic read-only TM, which allows transition edges.

Let us clear up one possible point of confusion. It makes no sense in the definition of transition edge to allow the regular expression to be the empty expression $\emptyset$, because this would mean that the TAPE HEAD would move without passing over any letters in the cells, which is obviously impossible.

Let us recall the main operation in the analogous part of the proof of Kleene's theorem (p. 96): the process of bypassing a state in the transition graph by hooking up all the edges that lead into the state with all the edges that lead out of the state in all possible ways so as to make that state unnecessary to the operation of the machine. By reiterating this procedure, we were able to eliminate, one by one, all the states except for the start state and one final state. From the label of the edge between these two, we could then read off the regular expression equivalent to the language accepted by the machine. Our question is whether, by employing the model of the TTMs, we are able to imitate the steps in the proof of Kleene's theorem and produce a regular expression equivalent to the language accepted by any given read-only TM.

If we wish to connect an incoming right-moving edge with an outgoing right-moving edge, the situation is completely analogous to the case of Kleene's theorem.

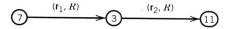

is equivalent to

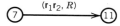

in exactly the same sense that we were able to make this substitution for TGs. Any word from the language of $r_1 r_2$ *could* take us from state 7 to state 3 to state 11 if we parsed it correctly. This then represents a nondeterministic option. If there is a different way of parsing the expression that causes the input to crash, so be it. Acceptance by nondeterministic machines means that there is *some* way to reach HALT, not that all paths do.

We can even handle the case of a right-moving loop at the middle state without any worry.

Clearly,

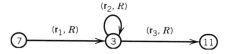

is equivalent to

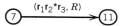

The amalgamation of left-moving edges is similar but with a slight twist. The path below:

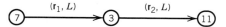

is equivalent to

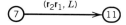

The reason for the reversal in the concatenation is that the read field in the edge label indicates the combined string as it appears from left to right on the TAPE. In going from state 7 to state 3, we might traverse a section of the TAPE containing the letters *ward* (first the d, then the r, then the a, then the w), and then, while going from state 3 to state 11, we might traverse the letters *back* (first the k . . .). Altogether, we have then traversed the string *backward*.

The case of a left-moving loop at the middle state can be handled exactly as the loop in the right-moving case; that is, it introduces a starred regular expression in the concatenation.

The real problem comes in figuring out what the net effect might be of combining two edges that move the TAPE HEAD in opposite directions. Let us consider what can we do with

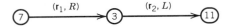

First, the TAPE HEAD moves up the TAPE to the right, scanning over a string from the language of r_1; then it moves leftward down the TAPE, covering a string from the language of r_2. Considering the freedom possible between these two regular expressions, we have no way of telling whether the TAPE HEAD ends up to the right or left of where it started. It is even possible that after all this travel it is back where it started, reading the same cell in state 11 that it was reading in state 7.

If we are to replace this sequence of two edges with one edge running from state 7 to state 11, that one edge must have three labels allowing for the three possibilities of motion of the TAPE HEAD. The new edge must have the form

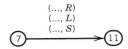

Note that we must allow for the possibility of the stay option discussed earlier in this chapter. The question now is what regular expressions are we going to fill in where the dots are?

Let us first consider the situation where the TAPE HEAD ends up to the right of where it started. The string that appears to have been the one traversed is not all the letters that were covered going up the TAPE to the right and then partially back down to the left, but only those letters that were not read twice. For example, if the TAPE situation is

and the two edges executed are

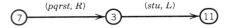

then by state 3 the situation is

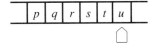

and by state 11 it is

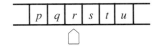

which is equivalent to the execution of the single instruction

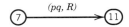

This situation is a little more subtle than we might have imagined. We would like to have been able to invoke Theorem 16 (p. 202), the division theorem for regular languages, to say that if we follow a word from r_1 going up to the right, and then come back down to the left over a word in r_2, the result is the same as covering a word from the language $\text{Pref}(r_2 \text{ in } r_1)$, which, as we recall, is the language of prefixes that, when added to some words in r_2, make them into some words in r_1. However, as we can see from the preceding example, after the TAPE HEAD has moved over the string $pqrst$, it is pointing to the cell *after* the last of these letters. If the TAPE HEAD moves to the right over a word from r_1, the next letter it reads is no longer part of the word from r_1 but a new arbitrary letter unanticipated by the language r_1. In the preceding example, this is the letter u.

It is also true that when the TAPE HEAD moves down the TAPE to the left, covering a word from the language of r_2, the cell it ends up pointing to contains a letter (the letter r in the preceding example) that is neither part of the r_2 string nor part of the short-form agglomerated instruction (pq, R). An end letter (u) is added and a middle letter (r) is wasted. Therefore, if we want to write

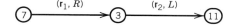

equals

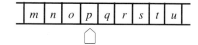

it is inaccurate to claim that

$$r_3 = \text{Pref}(r_2 \text{ in } r_1)$$

without some substantial modification.

The total string of cells read by the TAPE HEAD is not just the word from r_1 but one cell *more* than that. If this cell contains a blank, then the processing is over. The only other possibility is that this cell contains an a or b, if we assume that is the total alphabet to be found on the TAPE, in which case the total string of letters involved is a word in the language defined by the regular expression

$$r_1(a + b)$$

It is also clear that the string of letters read only once (the pq in the earlier example) is not the prefix of the word from r_2 but one letter *more* than that. In fact, it is the prefix left over when a string from the language defined by the regular expression

$$(a + b)r_2$$

has been removed. The accurate definition of r_3 is then

$$r_3 = \text{Pref}((a + b)r_2 \text{ in } r_1(a + b))$$

By Theorem 16, we know that this prefix language is regular and must therefore be definable by some regular expression that we can call r_3.

This accounts for the situations in which the TAPE HEAD ends up to the right of where it started, but it is also possible that after reading up the TAPE over a word in r_1 and then down over a word in r_2, it ends up to the left of where it started. As an example of this, let us consider the following situation. Start with

m	n	o	p	q	r	s	t	u

(In this diagram, as in all diagrams in this section, all the letters must be either a's or b's because the only thing ever found on the TAPE in a read-only TM is the untouched initial input.)

If we execute the two instructions

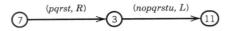

the net result is to leave the situation

m	n	o	p	q	r	s	t	u

which is equivalent to having executed the one instruction

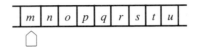

As before, we wish to replace the two instructions

$$(\mathbf{r}_1, R)\ (\mathbf{r}_2, L)$$

with one instruction of the form

$$(\mathbf{r}_3, L)$$

where $\mathbf{r}_3$ is a regular expression defining the appropriate language. It is almost true that $\mathbf{r}_3$ is the language of prefixes that, when added to the front of words in $\mathbf{r}_1$, give us words in $\mathbf{r}_2$. However, as before, we must add an extra letter onto the end of the string in $\mathbf{r}_1$ to account for the fact that $\mathbf{r}_2$ will include the cell immediately to the right of the $\mathbf{r}_1$ string. But this alone is not enough of an adjustment.

We can see from the example above that the letter p is read going up the TAPE to the right and read going down the TAPE to the left, and yet it is still the first letter in the resultant $\mathbf{r}_3$ move. The string nop is, in fact, the prefix of the string $qrstu$ in the word $nopqrstu$. Instead of subtracting exactly the words in $\mathbf{r}_1$ from the string in $\mathbf{r}_2$, what we need to do is subtract all but the first letter of the $\mathbf{r}_1$ word, so that this letter will still be there for $\mathbf{r}_3$ to read.

If we wish to define $\mathbf{r}_3$ as the prefix of something in the language of $\mathbf{r}_2(\mathbf{a} + \mathbf{b})$, that something is the language formed by taking each word in $\mathbf{r}_1$ and chopping off its first letter and adding a new last letter. Let us call this language $\text{Chop}(\mathbf{r}_1)(\mathbf{a} + \mathbf{b})$. The correct definition of $\mathbf{r}_3$ is then

$$\mathbf{r}_3 = \text{Pref}(\text{Chop}(\mathbf{r}_1)(\mathbf{a} + \mathbf{b})\ \text{in}\ \mathbf{r}_2)$$

We may be tempted to ask the question whether $\text{Chop}(\mathbf{r}_1)$ is a regular language. It so happens that it is, as anyone who does the exercises at the end of this chapter will discover. But we can apply Theorem 16 without knowing this fact. The language $\text{Pref}(Q\ \text{in}\ R)$ was shown to be regular whenever R is regular, no matter what flavor Q comes in. Q is certainly some language, and that is all we need to know.

Therefore, we have shown that there is some regular expression $\mathbf{r}_3$ that we can use in the edge label to make

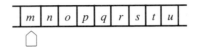

the equivalent of

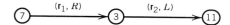

whenever the TAPE HEAD ends up to the left of the cell from which it started. Let us note clearly here that we have presented a proof of the existence of such a regular expression without providing a constructive algorithm for producing it from r_1 and r_2.

The last case we have to consider is the one where the TAPE HEAD ends up in state 11 back at the same cell from which it started. It reads some word from r_1 going up the TAPE to the right on its way to state 3 and then reads some word from $Chop(r_1(a + b))$ on its way to state 11. The net result is that what was read was Λ. This is described by the edge

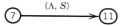

which need only be included as an option when $Chop(r_1(a + b))$ and r_2 have a word in common. Therefore, the full description of the results of

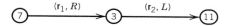

when summarized as one edge from state 7 to state 11 is

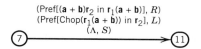

the last option existing only if there is a word in common between $Chop(r_1(a + b))$ and r_2.

This completely handles the situation in which we wish to replace a right-moving edge followed by a left-moving edge by one single edge, albeit with multiple labels. The only detail is showing how to replace a left-moving edge followed by a right-moving edge by one single edge—we do this with mirrors. Abracadabra, we are done (cf. p. 534).

We have therefore proven the following.

THEOREM 59

A read-only TM, also known as a two-way FA, accepts exclusively regular languages. ■

This result was proven by Rabin and independently by J. C. Shepherdson. Because the proof depends heavily on the nonconstructive step of finding the regular expressions for the prefix languages, we are spared the trouble of illustrating the technique with a concrete example.

⚜ PROBLEMS

1. Convert these TMs to move-in-state machines:

(i)

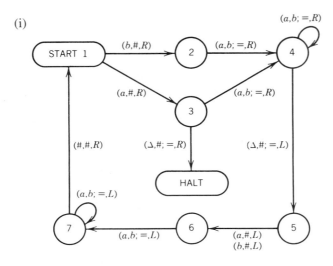

(ii)

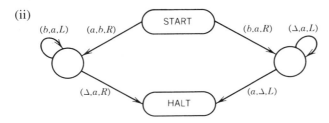

2. (i) Draw a move-in-state machine for the language ODDPALINDROME.
   (ii) Draw a move-in-state machine for the language $\{a^n b^n\}$.
   (iii) Draw a move-in-state machine for the language EQUAL.
   (iv) Draw a move-in-state machine for the language: all words of odd length with a as the middle letter, MIDDLEA.

3. Discuss briefly how to prove that multiple-cell-move instructions, such as $(x, y, 5R)$ and $(x, y, 17L)$ mentioned on p. 502, do not increase the power of a TM.

4. In the description of the algorithm for the 3TM that does decimal addition "the way humans do," we skimmed too quickly over the conversion of data section. The input is presumed to be placed on track 1 as two numbers separated by delimiters—for example,

$	8	9	$	2	6	$	Δ	
$	Δ							
$	Δ							

The question of putting the second number onto the second track is a problem that we ignored in the discussion in the chapter. Write a 3TM subprogram to do it.

5. In the proof of Theorem 55 (p. 506), where kTM = TM, we used two different methods for storing the k-tracks on the one TM tape. One was interlacing the tracks, and the other was using a vector alphabet. There is a third more simplistic method: Store the

working section of each of the k-tracks sequentially separated by markers. Show that this model can simulate a kTM for some arbitrary k. What other markers will be needed?

6. (i) Outline a 5TM that does decimal addition for three numbers simultaneously, the numbers being on tracks 2, 3, and 4. The sum should be left on track 5, and track 1 is reserved for carries.

(ii) Outline a 4TM that does the same task without the need for carries.

7. Outline a 5TM that multiplies two binary numbers initially on tracks 1 and 2. The product should be placed on track 3, using tracks 4 and 5 as a working area.

8. Design a 2TM that accepts DOUBLEWORD in the following two steps:

(i) Draw a 2TM that finds the middle letter of an input string of even length. Track 1 consists of just the input string. The program should place two markers on track 2, y below the first letter in the string and z below the last letter. Next, the program should bring the two markers toward each other one cell at a time. Let the program crash on odd-length strings. Finally, erase the y marker.

(ii) Using the above 2TM as a preprocessor, complete the machine to recognize DOUBLEWORD. Reinsert the y marker at the front of the string, and, moving the markers to the right one cell at a time, compare the letters.

9. (i) Outline two procedures for a 3TM, to INSERT or DELETE a character from track 2 only, leaving the other tracks unchanged.

(ii) Draw a 3TM that accepts the language EQUAL$'$ by splitting the a's and b's of the input on track 1 onto tracks 2 and 3 separately and then comparing them.

10. Design a pattern that matches 2TM. The input is a long string on track 1 and a short string on track 2. The program halts only if the string on track 2 is a substring of the string on track 1.

11. On a 2TM track 1 contains a string of the form $(\mathbf{a} + \mathbf{b})^+$ which is to be interpreted as a unary representation of numbers as strings of a's, separated by single b's.

(i) Using a 2TM, find the largest of the numbers on track 1 and copy it to track 2.

(ii) Using a 3TM, sort the list in descending order.

12. Outline a 2TM that takes as input on track 1 a^n and leaves on track 2 the binary representation of n.

13. (i) Outline a 6TM that determines whether its binary input on track 1 is a perfect square by generating squares and comparing them to the input number. The program terminates when the square is found or the length of the track 1 square is greater than the length of the input number.

(ii) Outline a 7TM that accepts the language

$$\text{SQUARE} = \{a^n \mid n \text{ is a square}\} = \{a \quad aaaa \quad aaaaaaaaa \ \ldots\}$$

(See p. 204.)

14. Draw a kTM that accepts MOREA (p. 205).

15. Outline an argument that shows how a two-way TM could be simulated on a TM using the trick of interlacing cells on the TAPE. That is, the TAPE starts with a $ in cell i, and then cell ii represents cell 0 on the two-way TM, cell iii on the TM represents cell i on the two-way TM, cell iv on the TM represents cell $-$ i on the two-way TM, cell v represents cell ii, and so on. Show how to simulate the two-way TM instructions on this arrangement for a TM.

16. On a certain two-way TM, the input is the single letter a surrounded by all Δ's. Unfortunately, the TAPE HEAD is somewhere else on the TAPE and we do not know where. Our job is to arrange for the TAPE HEAD to find the a.

   (i) Show that if the two-way TM is nondeterministic, the problem is easy.
   (ii) Show that if the two-way TM has two tracks, the problem can be solved.
   (iii) Outline a solution for the one-track deterministic two-way TM.

17. (i) Outline a proof that a nondeterministic PM has the same power as a regular PM.
   (ii) Outline a proof that a nondeterministic 2PDA has the same power as a regular 2PDA.

18. (i) If we had introduced the proof that kTMs were the same as TMs earlier, would it have made the proof that PM = TM, or that 2PDA = TM, any easier?
   (ii) If we had introduced the proof that NTM = TM earlier, would it have made the proof that PM = TM, or that 2PDA = TM, any easier?

19. Prove that if **r** is a regular language, Chop(**r**), defined as the language of all non-Λ words in **r** with their first letter removed, is also regular.

20. Complete the proof of Theorem 59 (p. 531).

   (i) Show the details of how to replace a left-moving edge followed by a right-moving edge with a single edge.
   (ii) Explain what can be done about loops.

CHAPTER 23

TM Languages

RECURSIVELY ENUMERABLE LANGUAGES

We have an independent name and an independent description for the languages accepted by FAs: The languages are called **regular,** and they can be defined by regular expressions. We have an independent name and an independent description for the languages accepted by PDAs: The languages are called **context-free,** and they can be generated by context-free grammars. We are now ready to discuss the characteristics of the languages accepted by TMs. They will be given an independent name and an independent description. The name now; the description later.

DEFINITION

A language L over the alphabet Σ is called **recursively enumerable** if there is a TM T that accepts every word in L and either rejects (crashes) or loops forever for every word in the language L', the complement of L.

$$\text{accept}(T) = L$$
$$\text{reject}(T) + \text{loop}(T) = L'$$

∎

EXAMPLE

The TM drawn on p. 446 divided all inputs into three classes:

$$\text{accept}(T) = \text{all words with } aa$$
$$\text{reject}(T) = \text{strings all without } aa \text{ ending in } a$$
$$\text{loop}(T) = \text{strings all without } aa \text{ ending in } b, \text{ or } \Lambda$$

Therefore, the language $(\mathbf{a} + \mathbf{b})^*\mathbf{aa}(\mathbf{a} + \mathbf{b})^*$ is recursively enumerable.

∎

A more stringent requirement for a TM to recognize a language is given by the following.

535

DEFINITION

A language L over the alphabet Σ is called **recursive** if there is a TM T that accepts every word in L and rejects every word in L'; that is,

$$\text{accept}(T) = L$$
$$\text{reject}(T) = L'$$
$$\text{loop}(T) = \phi$$

■

EXAMPLE

The following TM accepts the language of all words over $\{a \quad b\}$ that start with a and crashes on (rejects) all words that do not.

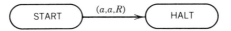

Therefore, this language is recursive.   ■

This term "recursively enumerable" is often abbreviated "r.e.," which is why we never gave an abbreviation for the term "regular expression." The term "recursive" is not usually abbreviated. It is obvious that every recursive language is also recursively enumerable, because the TM for the recursive language can be used to satisfy both definitions. However, we shall soon see that there are some languages that are r.e. but not recursive. This means that *every* TM that accepts these languages must have some words on which it loops forever.

We should also note that we could have defined r.e. and recursive in terms of PMs or 2PDAs as well as in terms of TMs, because the languages that they accept are the same. It is a point that we did not dwell on previously, but because our conversion algorithms make the operations of the machines identical section by section, any word that loops on one will also loop on the corresponding others. If a TM, T, is converted by our methods into a PM, P, and a 2PDA, A, then not only does

$$\text{accept}(T) = \text{accept}(P) = \text{accept}(A)$$

but also

$$\text{loop}(T) = \text{loop}(P) = \text{loop}(A)$$

and

$$\text{reject}(T) = \text{reject}(P) = \text{reject}(A)$$

Therefore, languages that are recursive on TMs are recursive on PMs and 2PDAs as well. Also, languages that are r.e. on TMs are r.e. on PMs and 2PDAs, too.

Turing used the term "recursive" because he believed, for reasons we discuss later, that any set defined by a recursive definition could be accepted by a TM. We shall also see that he believed that any calculation that could be defined recursively by algorithm could be performed by TMs. That was the basis for his belief that TMs are a universal algorithm device. The term "enumerable" comes from the association between accepting a language and listing or generating the language by machine. To enumerate a set (say, the squares) is to generate the elements in that set one at a time (1, 4, 9, 16, . . .). We take up this concept again later.

There is a profound difference between the meanings of recursive and recursively enumerable. If a language is regular and we have an FA that accepts it, then if we are presented a string w and we want to know whether w is in this language, we can simply run it on the machine. Because every state transition eats up a letter from w, in exactly length(w) steps we have our answer. This we have called an effective decision procedure. However, if a language is r.e. and we have a TM that accepts it, then if we are presented a string w and we would like to know whether w is in the language, we have a harder time. If we run w on the machine, it may lead to a HALT right away. On the other hand, we may have to wait. We may have to extend the execution chain seven billion steps. Even then, if w has not been accepted or rejected, it still eventually might be. Worse yet, w might be in the loop set for this machine, and we shall never get an answer. A recursive language has the advantage that we shall at least someday get the answer, even though we may not know how long it will take.

We have seen some examples of TMs that do their jobs in very efficient ways. There are some TMs, on the other hand, that take much longer to do simple tasks. We have seen a TM with a few states that can accept the language PALINDROME. It compares the first and last letter on the INPUT TAPE, and, if they match, it erases them both. It repeats this process until the TAPE is empty and then accepts the word.

Now let us outline a worse machine for the same language:

1. Replace all a's on the TAPE with the substring bab.
2. Translate the non-Δ data up the TAPE so that it starts in what was formerly the cell of the last letter.
3. Repeat step 2 one time for every letter in the input string.
4. Replace all b's on the TAPE with the substring $aabaa$.
5. Run the usual algorithm to determine whether or not what is left on the TAPE is in PALINDROME.

The TM that follows this algorithm also accepts the language PALINDROME. It has more states than the first machine, but it is not fantastically large. However, it takes many, many steps for this TM to determine whether aba is or is not a palindrome. While we are waiting for the answer, we may lose patience and mistakenly think that the machine is going to loop forever. If we knew that the language was recursive and the TM had no loop set, then we would have the faith to wait for the answer.

Not all TMs that accept a recursive language have no loop set. A language is recursive if *at least one* TM accepts it and rejects its complement. Some other TMs that accept the same language might loop on some inputs.

Let us make some observations about the connection between recursive languages and r.e. languages.

THEOREM 60

If the language L is recursive, then its complement L' is also recursive. In other words, the recursive languages are closed under complementation.

PROOF

It is easier to prove this theorem using PMs than TMs. Let us take a language L that is recursive. There is then some PM, call it P, for which all the words in L lead to ACCEPT and all the words in L' crash or lead to REJECT. No word in Σ^* loops forever on this machine.

Let us draw in all the REJECT states so that no word crashes but, instead, is rejected by landing in a REJECT. To do this for each READ, we must specify an edge for each possible character read. If any new edges are needed, we draw

Now if we reverse the REJECT and ACCEPT states, we have a new machine that takes all the words of L' to ACCEPT and all the words of L to REJECT and still never loops.

Therefore, L' is shown to be recursive on this new PM. We used the same trick to show that the complement of a regular language is regular (Theorem 11), but it did not work for CFLs because PDAs are nondeterministic (Theorem 40, p. 387).   ∎

We cannot use the same argument to show that the complement of a recursively enumerable set is recursively enumerable, since some input string might make the PM loop forever. Interchanging the status of the ACCEPT and REJECT states of a PM keeps the same set of input strings looping forever, so they will be undecided.

Observation

The reason it is easier to prove this theorem for a PM than for a TM is that not all TM rejections are caused by being in a state and having no exit edge labeled for the TAPE character being read. Some crashes are caused by moving the TAPE HEAD left while in cell i. Crashes of this sort can be converted into the more standard type of crash by inserting a marker in cell i that would then stand for crashing by going left of cell i; this would be a special marker to the left of any other end-of-TAPE marker that the program would want to insert. If that marker is ever read, we would be transferred to a TM state with no outgoing edges whatsoever. In this state, we would crash in the usual TM way, by being unable to exit from a non-HALT state. This method of unifying TM crashes will be useful for us later.

Just because the TM we know for a particular language has a loop set does not mean that there is not one that does not. Nor does it mean that we actually have to find the one that does not loop in order to establish that the language is recursive.

THEOREM 61

If L is r.e. and L' is also r.e., then L is recursive.

PROOF

From the hypotheses, we know that there is some TM, say, T_1, that accepts L and some TM, say, T_2, that accepts L'. From these two machines we want, by constructive algorithm, to build a TM, call it T_3, that accepts L and rejects L' because then T_3 would be the machine that proves L is recursive.

The first thing we want to do is change T_2 so that it rejects L' and only L'. It is not enough to turn the HALT state into a reject state; we must also be sure that it never crashes on any of the words it used to crash on. The words it formerly looped on are fine because they are not in L' and they can still loop forever. The new machine we want, call it T_2', has the following characteristics:

$$L' = \text{accept}(T_2) = \text{reject}(T_2')$$
$$\text{loop}(T_2) \subset \text{loop}(T_2')$$
$$\text{reject}(T_2) \subset \text{loop}(T_2')$$

To do this we must eliminate all the crashes. The crash that occurs from moving the Tape Head left from cell i can be made into a typical TM crash, that is, being in a non-HALT state but being unable to exit. This can be accomplished by the trick mentioned in the preceding observation. But this is not enough for our purposes here because we must eliminate *all the crashes* in total and change them to loop-forevers. This we do by going state by state and finding every character that has no existing exit edge and drawing a new one going to a new state called NOWHERESVILLE on an edge labeled (it, $=$, R). For example, if a state had no b exit edge, we would draw one to NOWHERESVILLE labeled (b, b, R). Once we get to NOWHERESVILLE, of course, we are stuck there, because it has only one exit edge that is a loop labeled (any, $=$, R). So once in NOWHERESVILLE, we spend an eternity slowly inching our way up the Tape. The machine now has the same accept set, but the reject set has been merged into the loop set.

Now we want to make the accept set a reject set. This is easy. We accept an input by arriving at a HALT state. If we erase the edges that lead into the HALT states, then when the program is in the states that would naturally have fed into the HALTs, given what the Tape Head is reading, a crash would occur instead, and the input will be rejected. This then is our T_2'. It accepts nothing, rejects exactly L'_1 and loops often.

We also want to modify T_1 in a similar way so that its accept set remains the same, that is, L, but its reject set is merged into its loop set so that it too never crashes. This we accomplish by adding its own NOWHERESVILLE. Call this modified TM T_1'.

What we now have can be summarized as

$$\text{accept}(T_1') = L = \text{loop}(T_2')$$
$$\text{loop}(T_1') = L' = \text{reject}(T_2')$$

Very simply, what we would like T_3 to do is to run the input string simultaneously on T_1' and T_2'. If the input string is in the language L, sooner or later it will be accepted by T_1'; if it is in the language L', it will, sooner or later, be rejected by T_2'. And while we are waiting for one of these two events to occur, the nondeciding machine will not interrupt us by crashing. Now, because we cannot actually run the same input string on the two TMs simultaneously (they might want to change the Tape into incompatible things), the next best thing we can do is simulate running the input on the two machines alternately. That is, we take the first edge on T_1', then the first edge on T_2', then the second edge on T_1', then the second edge on T_2', then the third edge on T_1', and so on, until either T_1' takes us to HALT or T_2' crashes. A machine like this is actually possible to build, and we will do it now.

Let us for convenience call the states in T_1' START $= x_1, x_2, x_3, \ldots$ and the states in T_2' START $= y_1, y_2, y_3, \ldots$. The Tape in T_3 will always look like this:

#	a	b	b	x_5	b	A	a	*	b	Δ	a	a	a	y_8	b	a	a	Δ	Δ	Δ	Δ	Δ	. . .

where the meaning of this is as follows. Cell i always contains a #. Between this # and the one and only * is the Tape status at the moment of the simulation of T_1', with the exception that in front of the cell that the T_1' Tape Head will next be reading is the name of the state that T_1' has just arrived in. Then comes the symbol * that separates the simulation of T_1' and the simulation of T_2'. Then the rest of the Tape is exactly what the current status of the Tape on T_2' would be at this moment, with the exception that in front of the cell that the T_2' Tape Head will next be reading is the name of the state that T_2' has just entered. We assume that the # and the * as well as the names of the states are all unused by T_1' and T_2' as TAPE characters. This is a safe assumption because in our simulation they are both painted a very rare shade of blue.

When we start with a simple input of T_3, we have to use a subprogram to set up the simulation. It inserts # in cell i and x_1 in cell ii, runs to the end of the input and inserts * and y_1, and then runs up and down the TAPE, copying the input string into the blank cells after the y_1. And then the TAPE HEAD is returned to point to x_1.

For example, the input *abb* goes from

a	b	b	Δ	Δ	. . .

to

#	x_1	a	b	b	*	y_1	a	b	b	Δ	Δ	. . .

(The subprogram to do this is generously provided by the reader.)

Before we proceed with the simulation, we should say a word about what happens when T_1' wants to read more cells of the TAPE than the few we have allotted it between the # and *. Whenever T_1' moves its TAPE HEAD right, we immediately ask whether or not it is reading a *. If it is, we leave it alone, back up one cell, insert a Δ, and (because INSERT leaves the TAPE HEAD to the right of the insertion) read the *, leave it alone, and back up again to read the Δ.

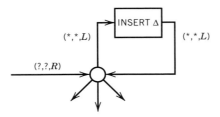

In this way, we can insert as many blanks as the simulation of T_1' needs. These blanks can be changed into other things, or other things can be made into blanks. So, blanks can occur in the middle of the data and at the end of the data in the simulation of either TM. The T_2' simulation will never try to move left and read the * because that would correspond to a crash on T_2' of moving left from cell i, but that is not how T_2' crashes, as we have guaranteed.

If the T_1' simulation ever enters HALT, then T_3 halts and accepts the input. If the T_2' simulation ever crashes, then T_3 crashes and the input is rejected.

We still have to make explicit how T_3 can "make a move on the T_1' side and then make a move on the T_2' side alternately." To understand this, let us first see what happens immediately after the setup subprogram is done. The TAPE HEAD is reading x_1, which in turn is sitting in front of an *a*. T_3 is in a state called SIMULATE-T_1'. This is the first important T_3 state.

For every state x_k in T_1', this state has an outgoing edge labeled $(x_k, =, R)$ going to a different T_3 destination subprogram called SIM-x_k. The first thing we do in this subprogram is back up one cell and run subprogram DELETE, thereby removing the symbol x_k from the TAPE. Then we read the letter that is in the next cell on the TAPE. This is the letter that the T_1' TAPE HEAD would be reading if the input were running on T_1' alone. The program for T_1' tells us what to change this letter to and then where to move the TAPE HEAD and then which T_1' state to go to next. The simulation has all this information built into it. It changes the T_3 TAPE and simulates moving the T_1' TAPE HEAD by inserting the name of the next T_1' state to be executed on the running of T_1' to the left of the appropriate TAPE cell. For example, if the T_3 TAPE status is

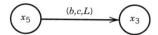

and state x_5 on T_1' has the (unique) outgoing b-edge

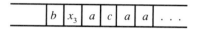

then the simulation would change the T_3 TAPE into

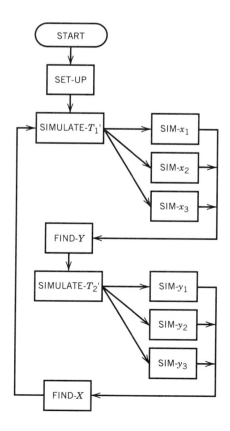

The state SIM-x_5 treats each edge coming out of x_5 individually. Here, it correctly corresponds to being in state x_3 about to read an a.

After doing this, SIM-x_k then returns to the main T_3 program to the state FIND-Y. In this state, the T_3 TAPE HEAD is pushed right until it hits any y symbol. When it does, it enters another important state called SIMULATE-T_2'. This state reads the y_k and branches to the appropriate subprogram SIM-y_k, where it does its T_2' act. Once that has been completed, it returns to the main T_3 program to a state called FIND-X. This runs the TAPE HEAD left down the TAPE until it finds the (one and only) x_k. From here it goes into the state SIMULATE-T_1' and the process repeats itself.

The outline of the whole T_3 is

The halting or crashing of T_3 takes place entirely within the simulations and we are certain that, for every input, one or the other will take place. The language that will be accepted will be L and all of L' will be rejected.   ■

Again, the machines produced by the algorithm in this proof are very large (many, many states), and it is hard to illustrate this method in any but the simplest examples.

EXAMPLE

Consider the language $L = \mathbf{b(a + b)}^*$. L can be accepted by the following TM, T_1:

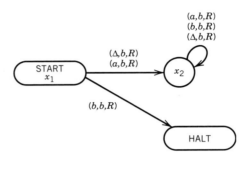

$$\text{accept}(T_1) = L$$
$$\text{loop}(T_1) = L'$$
$$\text{reject}(T_1) = \phi$$

The machine T_1 proves that L is r.e., but not that L is recursive. The TM below, T_2,

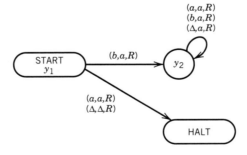

accepts the language L' and loops on L.

The first machine is already in T_1' format and the only adjustment necessary in the second to make it into T_2' is to eliminate the HALT state and its incoming edges. We can combine them per the algorithm in the proof to produce T_3, which accepts L and rejects L', thereby proving that L is recursive:

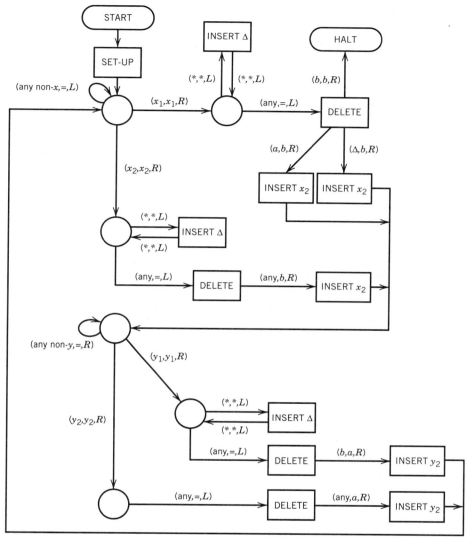

The first question that comes to most minds now is, "So what? Is the result of Theorem 61 so wonderful that it was worth a multipage proof?" The answer to this is not so much to defend Theorem 61 itself, but to examine the proof.

We have taken two different TMs (they could have been completely unrelated) and combined them into one TM that processes an input as though it were running simultaneously on both machines. This is such an important possibility that it deserves its own theorem.

THEOREM 62

If T_1 and T_2 are TMs, then there exists a TM, T_3, such that

$$\text{accept}(T_3) = \text{accept}(T_1) + \text{accept}(T_2)$$

In other words, the union of two recursively enumerable languages is recursively enumerable; the set of recursively enumerable languages is closed under union.

PROOF

The algorithm in the proof of Theorem 61 is all that is required. First, we must alter T_1 and T_2 so that they both loop instead of crash on those words that they do not accept.

Now nothing stops the two machines from running in alternation, accepting any words and only those words accepted by either. The algorithm for producing T_3 can be followed just as given in the proof of Theorem 61.

On the new machine

$$\text{accept}(T_3) = \text{accept}(T_1) + \text{accept}(T_2)$$
$$\text{loop}(T_3) = \text{all else}$$
$$\text{reject}(T_3) = \phi$$ ∎

We have proven that the class of recursively enumerable languages is closed under union by amalgamating two TMs. We are now interested in the question of the intersection of two recursively enumerable languages. For regular languages, we found that the answer to the question of closure under intersection was yes but for context-free languages the answer was no. We could deduce that the closure of two regular languages is regular based on the facts that the union and complement of regular languages are also regular. Then by DeMorgan's Law, the intersection, which is the complement of the union of the complements, must also be regular. Because the complement of a context-free language is not necessarily context-free, this proof strategy does not carry over and, indeed, we saw that the intersection of context-free languages need not be context-free. With recursively enumerable languages, we have a third situation. They are closed under union and intersection but (we shall see) not under complement.

THEOREM 63

The intersection of two recursively enumerable languages is also recursively enumerable.

PROOF

Let one of the languages be accepted by TM_1 and the other be accepted by TM_2. We shall now construct a third TM by the following set of modifications:

Step 1   Build a TM preprocessor that takes a two-track TAPE and copies the input from track 1 onto track 2 and returns the TAPE HEAD to cell column i and begins processing at the START state of TM_1.

Step 2   Convert TM_1 into a machine that uses a two-track TAPE doing all of its processing exactly as before but referring only to the top track. Also change the HALT state of TM_1 into a state that rewinds the TAPE HEAD to cell column i and then branches to the START state of TM_2.

Step 3   Convert TM_2 into a machine that uses a two-track TAPE, doing all of its processing exactly as before but referring only to the bottom track. Leave the HALT state untouched.

We can now build a new TM that first runs the input string on TM_1 and then, if and only if the string is accepted, it runs the same input on TM_2. The HALT state of this combined machine is analogous to the HALT state of TM_2, but it is reached only when the input has halted on both TMs. This machine then accepts those words, and only those words, that are accepted by both initial machines. It is, therefore, a TM acceptor of the intersection language. ■

THE ENCODING OF TURING MACHINES

It is now time to ask our usual questions about the class of r.e. languages. We have answered the question about the union and intersection of r.e. languages, but that still leaves open product, Kleene closure, complement, the existence of non-r.e. languages, and the decidability of emptiness, finiteness and membership. We shall attack these in a slightly different order than we did for the other language classes we analyzed.

TMs do seem to have immense power as language-acceptors or language-recognizers, yet there are some languages that are not accepted by any TM, as we shall now prove by "constructing" one.

Before we can describe such a language, we need to develop the idea of encoding TMs.

Just as with FAs and PDAs, we do not have to rely on pictorial representations for TMs. We can make a TM into a summary table and run words on the table as we did with PDAs in Chapter 15. The algorithm to do this is not difficult. First, we number the states 1, 2, 3, . . . and so on. By convention, we always number the START state 1 and the HALT state 2. Then we convert every instruction in the TM into a row of the table as shown below:

From	To	Read	Write	Move
1	3	a	a	L
3	1	Δ	b	R
8	2	b	a	R

. . .

where the column labeled "Move" indicates in which direction the TAPE HEAD is to move.

EXAMPLE

The TM shown below:

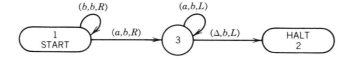

can be summarized by the following table:

From	To	Read	Write	Move
1	1	b	b	R
1	3	a	b	R
3	3	a	b	L
3	2	Δ	b	L

Because we know that state 1 is START and state 2 is HALT, we have all the information in the table necessary to operate the TM. ■

We now introduce a coding whereby we can turn any row of the TM into a string of a's and b's.

Consider the general row

From	To	Read	Write	Move
X_1	X_2	X_3	X_4	X_5

where X_1 and X_2 are numbers, X_3 and X_4 are characters from $\{a \quad b \quad \#\}$ or Δ, and X_5 is a direction (either L or R).

We start by encoding the information X_1 and X_2 as

$$a^{x_1}ba^{x_2}b$$

which means a string of a's of length X_1 concatenated to a b concatenated to a string of a's X_2 long concatenated to a b. This is a word in the language defined by $\mathbf{a^+ba^+b}$.

Next, X_3 and X_4 are encoded by this table:

X_3, X_4	Code
a	aa
b	ab
Δ	ba
$\#$	bb

Next, we encode X_5 as follows:

X_5	Code
L	a
R	b

Finally, we assemble the pieces by concatenating them into one string. For example, the row

From	To	Read	Write	Move
6	2	b	a	L

becomes

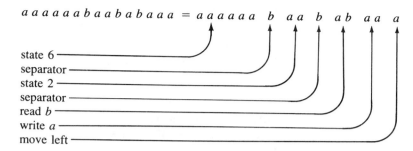

Every string of a's and b's that is a row is of the form definable by the regular expression

$$\mathbf{a^+ba^+b(a + b)^5}$$
$$= (\text{at least one } a)b(\text{at least one } a)b(\text{five letters})$$

It is also true that every word defined by this regular expression can be interpreted as a row of a TM summary table with one exception: We cannot leave a HALT state. This means that $\mathbf{aaba^+b(a + b)^5}$ defines a forbidden sublanguage.

Not only can we make any row of the table into a string, but we can also make the whole summary table into one long string by concatenating the strings that represent the rows.

EXAMPLE

The preceding summary table can be made into a string of a's and b's as follows:

From	To	Read	Write	Move	Code for Each Row
1	1	b	b	R	*ababababb*
1	3	a	b	R	*abaaabaaabb*
3	3	a	b	L	*aaabaaabaaaba*
3	2	Δ	b	L	*aaabaabbaaba*

One one-word code for the whole machine is

abababababbabaaabaaabbaaabaaabaaabaaaabaabbaaba

This is not the only one-word code for this machine because the order of the rows in the table is not rigid. We can standardize the code word by insisting that the row codes be amalgamated in their lexicographic order.   ■

It is also important to observe that we can look at such a long string and decode the TM from it, provided that the string is in the proper form, that is, as long as the string is a word in the **code word language (CWL)**.

(For the moment, we shall not worry about the forbidden HALT-leaving strings. We consider them later.)

$$\text{CWL} = \text{the language defined by } (\mathbf{a^+ba^+b(a + b)^5})*$$

ALGORITHM

The way we decode a string in CWL is as follows:

Step 1   Count the initial clump of *a*'s and fill in that number in the first entry of the first empty row of the table.

Step 2   Forget the next letter; it must be a *b*.

Step 3   Count the next clump of *a*'s and fill in that number in the second column of this row.

Step 4   Skip the next letter; it is a *b*.

Step 5   Read the next two letters. If they are *aa*, write an *a* in the Read box of the table. If they are *ab*, write a *b* in the table. If they are *ba*, write a Δ in the table. If they are *bb*, write a # in the table.

Step 6   Repeat step 5 for the table Write entry.

Step 7   If the next letter is an *a*, write an *L* in the fifth column of the table; otherwise, write an *R*. This fills in the Move box and completes the row.

Step 8   Starting with a new line of the table, go back to step 1, operating on what remains of the string. If the string has been exhausted, stop. The summary table is complete.   ∎

EXAMPLE

Consider the string

abaaabaaaabaaabaaabaaaabaaabaababababa

The first clump of *a*'s is one *a*. Write 1 in the first line of the table. Drop the *b*. The next part of the string is a clump of three *a*'s. Write 3 in row 1, column 2. Drop the *b*. Now *aa* stands for *a*. Write *a* in column 3. Again, *aa* stands for *a*. Write *a* in column 4. Then *b* stands for *R*. Write this in column 5, ending row 1. Starting again, we have a clump of three *a*'s so start row 2 by writing a 3 in column 1. Drop the *b*. Three more *a*'s, write a 3. Drop the *b*. Now *aa* stands for *a*; write it. Again, *aa* stands for *a*; write it. Then *b* stands for *R*. Finish row 2 with this *R*. What is left is three *a*'s, drop the *b*, two *a*'s, drop the *b*, then *ab*, and *ab*, and *a*, meaning *b*, and *b*, and *L*. This becomes row 3 of the table. We have now exhausted the CWL word and have therefore finished a table.

The table and machine are

From	To	Read	Write	Move
1	3	*a*	*a*	*R*
3	3	*a*	*a*	*R*
3	2	*b*	*b*	*L*

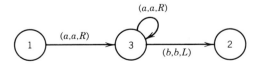

∎

The result of this encoding process is that every TM corresponds to a word in CWL. However, not all words in CWL correspond to a TM. There is a little problem here because when we decode a CWL string, we might get an improper TM such as one that is nondeterministic or repetitive (two rows the same) or violates the HALT state, but this should not dull our enthusiasm for the code words. These problems will take care of themselves, as we shall see.

⚜ A NON-RECURSIVELY ENUMERABLE LANGUAGE

The code word for a TM contains all the information of the TM, yet it can be considered as merely a name—or worse yet, input. Because the code for every TM is a string of a's and b's, we might ask what happens if this string is run as input on the very TM it stands for. We shall feed each TM its own code word as input data. Sometimes it will crash, sometimes loop, sometimes accept.

Let us define the language ALAN as follows.

DEFINITION

> ALAN = {all the words in CWL that are *not* accepted by the TMs they
> represent or that do not represent any TM} ∎

EXAMPLE

Consider the TM

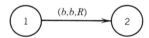

The table for this machine is simply

From	To	Read	Write	Move
1	2	b	b	R

The code word for this TM is

> *abaabababb*

But if we try to run this word on the TM as input, it will crash in state 1 because there is no edge for the letter a leaving state 1.

Therefore, the word

> *abaabababb*

is in the language ALAN. ∎

EXAMPLE

The words

$$aababaaaaa \quad \text{and} \quad aaabaabaaaaa$$

are in CWL but do not represent any TM, the first because it has an edge leaving HALT and the second because it has no START state. Both words are in ALAN.   ∎

EXAMPLE

In one earlier example, we found the TM corresponding to the CWL word

$$abaaabaaaabaaabaaabaaaabaaabaababababa$$

When this word is run on the TM it represents, it is accepted. This word is *not* in ALAN.   ∎

EXAMPLE

If a TM accepts all inputs, then its code word is not in ALAN. If a TM rejects all inputs, then its code word is in ALAN. Any TM that accepts the language of all strings with a double *a* will have a code word with a double *a* and so will accept its own code word. The code words for these TMs are not in ALAN. The TM we built in Chapter 19 to accept the language PALINDROME has a code word that is not a palindrome. Therefore, it does not accept its code word and its code word is in ALAN.   ∎

We shall now prove that the language ALAN is not recursively enumerable. We prove this by contradiction. Let us begin with the supposition that ALAN is r.e. In that case, there would be some TM that would accept all the words in ALAN. Let us call one such TM T. Let us denote the code word for T as code(T). Now we ask the question:

$$\text{Is code}(T) \text{ a word in the language ALAN or not?}$$

There are clearly only two possibilities: yes or no. Let us work them out with the precision of Euclidean geometry.

CASE 1: code(T) is in ALAN

CLAIM	REASON
1. T accepts ALAN.	1. Definition of T.
2. ALAN contains no code word that is accepted by the machine it represents.	2. Definition of ALAN.
3. code(T) is in ALAN.	3. Hypothesis.
4. T accepts the word code(T).	4. From 1 and 3.
5. code(T) is not in ALAN.	5. From 2 and 4.
6. Contradiction.	6. From 3 and 5.
7. code(T) is not in ALAN.	7. The hypothesis (3) must be wrong because it led to a contradiction.

Again, let us use complete logical rigor.

CASE 2: code(T) is not in ALAN

CLAIM	REASON
1. T accepts ALAN.	1. Definition of T.
2. If a word is not accepted by the machine it represents, it is in ALAN.	2. Definition of ALAN.
3. code(T) is not in ALAN.	3. Hypothesis.
4. code(T) is not accepted by T.	4. From 1 and 3.
5. code(T) is in ALAN.	5. From 2 and 4.
6. Contradiction.	6. From 3 and 5.
7. code(T) is in ALAN.	7. The hypothesis (3) must be wrong because it led to a contradiction.

Both cases are impossible; therefore, the assumption that ALAN is accepted by some TM is untenable. ALAN is not recursively enumerable.

THEOREM 64

Not all languages are recursively enumerable.   ∎

This argument usually makes people's heads spin. It is very much like the old "liar paradox," which dates back to the Megarians (attributed sometimes to Eubulides and sometimes to the Cretan Epimenides) and runs like this. A man says, "Right now, I am telling a lie." If it is a lie, then he is telling the truth by confessing. If it is the truth, he must be lying because he claims he is. Again, both alternatives lead to contradictions.

If someone comes up to us and says, "Right now, I am telling a lie," we can walk away and pretend we did not hear anything. If someone says to us, "If God can do anything, he can make a stone so heavy that He cannot lift it," we can burn him as a blaspheming heretic. If someone asks us, "In a certain city the barber shaves all those who do not shave themselves and only those. Who shaves the barber?", we can answer, "The barber is a woman." However, here we have used this same old riddle not to annoy Uncle Charlie, but to provide a mathematically rigorous proof that there are languages that TMs cannot recognize.

The liar paradox and other logical paradoxes are very important in computer theory, as we can see by the example of the language ALAN. In fact, the whole development of the computer came from the same kind of intellectual concern as was awakened by consideration of these paradoxes.

The study of logic began with the Greeks (in particular, Aristotle and Zeno of Elea) but then lay dormant for millennia. The possibility of making logic a branch of mathematics began in 1666 with a book by Gottfried Wilhelm von Leibniz, who was also the coinventor of calculus and an early computer man (see Chapter 1). His ideas were continued by George Boole in the nineteenth century.

About a hundred years ago, Georg Cantor invented set theory and immediately a connection was found between set theory and logic. This allowed the paradoxes from logic, previously a branch of philosophy, to creep into mathematics. That mathematics could contain paradoxes had formerly been an unthinkable situation. When logic was philosophical and rhetorical, the paradoxes were tolerated as indications of depth and subtlety. In mathematics, paradoxes are an anathema. After the invention of set theory, there was a flood of paradoxes from Cesare Burali-Forti, Cantor himself, Bertrand Russell, Jules Richard, Julius König, and many other mathematical logicians. This made it necessary to be much more precise about which sentences do and which sentences do not describe meaningful mathematical operations. This led to Hilbert's question of the decidability of mathematics and then to the development of the theory of algorithms and to the work of Gödel, Turing, Post, Church (whom we shall meet shortly), Kleene, and von Neumann, which in turn led to the computers we all know (and love). In the meantime, mathematical logic, from Gottlob Frege, Russell, and Alfred North Whitehead on, has been strongly directed toward questions of decidability.

The fact that the language ALAN is not recursively enumerable is not its only unusual feature. The language ALAN is defined in terms of TMs. It cannot be described to people who do not know what TMs are. It is quite possible that all the languages that can be thought of by people who do not know what TMs are are recursively enumerable. (This sounds like its own small paradox.) This is an important point because, since computers are (approximate) TMs, and since our original goal was to build a universal algorithm machine, we want TMs to accept practically everything. Theorem 64 is definitely bad news. If we are hoping for an even more powerful machine to be defined in Part IV of this book that will accept all possible languages, we shall be disappointed for reasons soon to be discussed.

⚜ THE UNIVERSAL TURING MACHINE

The idea of encoding a TM program into a string of a's and b's to be fed into itself is potentially more profitable than we have yet appreciated. When a TM program is made into an input string, it may be fed into other TMs for other purposes. What we shall now design is a TM that can accept as input two strings separated by a marker, where the first string is the encoding of some TM program and the second string is data that our machine will operate on as if it were the TM described by the first input string. In other words, our new TM will simulate the running of the encoded TM on the data string. This is not a simulation in the sense of the proof of Theorem 61 (p. 538), where we designed a special TM to act as if it were two particular TMs operating simultaneously. There we built a very different T_3 for each pair of starting machines T_1 and T_2. What we shall construct here is one and only one, good for all time, TM that can imitate the action of *any* TM described to it on *any* arbitrary data string we choose. The states and edges of our TM will not vary, but it will, by referring to the half of the input that is the encoded TM program, mimic those operations on the other half of the input, the intended data string fed into the encoded machine.

We might ask, "What is the advantage of such a thing?" If we want to see how TM T_1 acts on a particular input string, why not just feed T_1 the input in person? Why bother to feed an encryption of T_1 and the data into a second TM to run a simulation? There are many reasons for designing such a machine, and they will become evident shortly, but a computer science major should be ashamed of asking such a question when the answer is obvious. What we are building is a *programmable* TM. Instead of building a different **computer** for each possible program, we are building a computer that accepts a set of instructions (a program) and input data and acts on the data according to the instructions.

Let us recapitulate the impetus for the invention of the computer. Hilbert asked for an algorithm that would generate a solution for any mathematical problem posed to it. The solution could be either a simple numerical answer, a mathematical proof, or an algorithm for resolving special classes of questions. In order to begin working on such an ambitious project, logicians began to design small instruction sets in which all mathematical problems could be stated, and from which all mathematical solutions could be composed. Gödel constructed a mathematical statement that, if it were provable, would be false, but if it were not provable, would be true. This meant that Hilbert's abstract goal could not be reached in total, because the truth or provability of Gödel's statement would always remain unanswered. But it was possible that the trouble caused by Gödel's statement could be contained, and that the bulk of Hilbert's ambition could somehow still be fulfilled.

That was until the work of Turing. He introduced the universal algorithm machine that could execute any mathematical algorithm that could theoretically ever be designed. He used it to show that it had irreparable severe limitations; that is, there were mathematical problems that simply could not be solved by any algorithm. This universal algorithm machine is the TM we have been describing (and will build) in this section, and the limitations just mentioned will be elucidated soon in terms of the TM language questions that arise naturally in their analogy to regular and context-free languages.

Even though Turing's universal machine was limited in theory, still it could execute all known algorithms and all algorithms discoverable in the future. Although not enough to satisfy Hilbert's dream, this is still quite a feat. By fortunate accident, Turing's model of a programmable machine was so simple that soon after his theoretical paper was published, people began to build real physical models of what was originally intended as an abstract mathematical construct to settle (or scuttle) a project in pure mathematics. Electrical engineers had already been working on producing more and more sophisticated calculating devices, performing sequences of arithmetic operations, boosted by the speedy revolution in electronic technology that was simultaneously being developed with no apparent connection to the crisis in mathematical logic.

Instead of having to build a different electronic device for each algorithm, Turing's mathematical work showed how one universal machine would suffice to simulate all algorithms with a very restricted working set of instructions and memory capabilities. The mathematical project was not completed until von Neumann (a star mathematician, logician, and engineer) showed how to actualize a programmable computer in which the instructions, because they are fed in as data, could not only operate on the separate data field, but also could modify their own program as it was running. This allowed the writing of programs that could change their conditional branching instructions, evolve by writing new instructions for themselves, and potentially learn from their experience on one data set to change what they do to another. This then was the final step in the theoretical foundation of what is a computer. In this text, we emphasize Turing's contribution but pay little to von Neumann's extension of it. That is only because we have to draw the line somewhere.

DEFINITION

A **universal TM,** a **UTM,** is a TM that can be fed as input a string composed of two parts: The first is the encoded program of any TM T followed by a marker, the second part is a string that will be called data. The operation of the UTM is that, no matter what machine T is, and no matter what the data string is, the UTM will operate on the data as if it were T. If T would have crashed on this input, it will crash; if T would loop forever, it will loop forever; and if T would accept the input, the UTM does so too. Not only that but the UTM will leave on its TAPE the encoded T, the marker, and the contents of what T would leave on its TAPE when it accepts this very input string.   ■

We have been careful to imply that there does not exist only one unique UTM but perhaps many, depending on the choice of encoding algorithm for the machine T and the algorithm chosen for simulation. In the previous section, we encoded TMs into strings of a's and b's. It will be easier for us to describe the working of a UTM employing a different encoding algorithm, one that is slightly less universal as it makes restrictions on the number of states the TM to be simulated can have and on the size of that TM's TAPE character set. Let us assume, for the time being, that the TM to be encoded has at most 1 million states q_1 = START, q_2 = HALT, q_3, q_4, ... Let us also assume that there are at most 1 million different characters that the TM T can ever employ on its TAPE (including its input alphabet): $c_1, c_2, \ldots$.

We can now reduce every row of the tabular description of the TM T to a series of syllables of the form $q_x c_y c_z M q_w$, where M is either L or R. In order to be sure that no confusion arises, let us assume that none of the characters c is the same as any of the characters q and that neither of them is the same as L or R. Let us also assume that this character set does not contain our particular set of markers # and $.

This is truly a limitation because UTMs are supposed to be able to handle the simulation of any T, not just one with under a million states and under a million characters. However, these assumptions will have the advantage of simplifying the description of the UTM because the name of each state and each character is one symbol long, as opposed to the encoding given in the previous section where there could be arbitrarily many states and characters and their corresponding designations could increase in length enormously (unboundedly). After we are finished designing our limited model, we will describe how it could be modified to run on the unrestricted encoding in the previous section.

With this encoding scheme, every TM can be fully encoded into a word formed from the concatenation of finitely many syllables of the type described above. Every substring of two consecutive q's necessarily denotes the break between two edge instructions in the TM T. Every substring of two consecutive c's necessarily denotes a read and write section of an edge instruction and is necessarily followed by an L or R. To distinguish this encoding strategy from the one presented before, we call this encryption TM coding, TMC, and we designate the TMC code word for the machine T as TMC T.

THEOREM 65

UTMs exist.

PROOF

Initially, the UTM TAPE will contain the following: the cell i marker #, the TMC code for some TM T, the separator $, and the data field d_1, d_2, d_3, . . . made up of a finite string of characters from the alphabet $\{c_1 \quad c_2 \quad \ldots\}$.

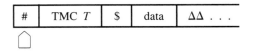

This is the correct form of the input string into the UTM. We are not responsible for what may happen to an input string that is not in this precise form. The first state of the UTM is, of course, START. From there we go to a state searching for the first character of the data string.

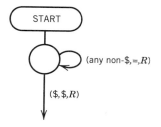

We are now in a UTM state reading the first character of the data string. Instead, we insert the state we know the simulated machine T to be in at this moment, that is, its START state q_1.

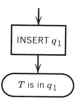

This marks the fact that T is in the state to the left of the UTM Tape Head and its own Tape Head is reading a cell whose contents are those the UTM Tape Head is now reading. Except for the q_x, which we shall continue to employ as a T Tape Head indicator throughout the simulation, the data field of the UTM Tape will always be kept exactly the same as the whole TM T Tape.

We are now ready to do our main iteration. Based on the state we know we are in on the simulation and the character we know we are reading in the simulation, we head for the appropriate one of the million squared possible combination states q_x & c_y.

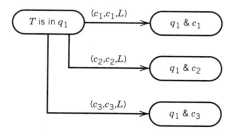

We shall now proceed as if we are farther along into our simulation and we have reached the situation of being in state q_x on T and reading character c_y on the T Tape. On the UTM we are in state q_x & c_y. Once we know that we are in such a situation, we wind the UTM Tape Head left until we cross the \$, entering the TMC code for T, and we search there for the substring $q_x c_y$ because this represents being in state q_x on TM T and reading the character c_y. At most, one such substring exists because T is deterministic. The following UTM code will accomplish this:

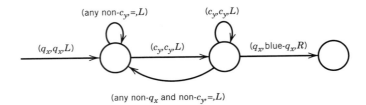

When we get to this state, we have found the correct TM T edge to take to simulate the running of the T machine. We have marked its state by turning it blue. So we need a blue set of q's as characters too. We mark it so that we can run up the T TAPE simulation to the right of the $, do the writing, and still later return to this instruction. What would happen if we ran down the whole UTM TAPE to cell i and read the # without finding the substring we were looking for? The answer is that T would have no c_y-edge coming out of state q_x and we would have to simulate a crash. We have our choice of ways for doing this so we leave the selection of this option up to the UTM purchaser.

We must now simulate the operation of being in q_x reading a c_y on TM T. We must find what character T wants to convert the c_y into. Then we must go to a state that remembers what that character is (there are a million of them, one for each possible character), run the TAPE HEAD up the UTM TAPE until it crosses the $ barrier, enters the T TAPE simulation, finds the unique q-symbol on this side of the $, and change the next cell from c_y to this new character.

We are not yet done with the simulation. We must now run back down the UTM TAPE looking for the blue-q to the left of the $ and find out how T wants its TAPE HEAD moved and what T-state it wants to enter next. Here, the UTM program is as follows. Un-blue the q-state, skip the read field of the TMC T-edge, skip the write field, and branch on the TAPE HEAD move field, and then branch again on the new state until we reach the appropriate one of the 2 million states, "L & q_z" or "R & q_z."

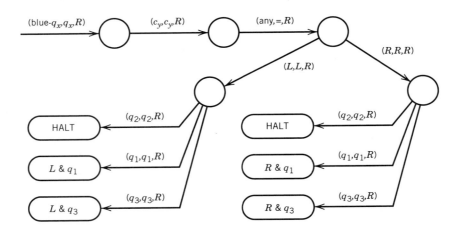

When we are in this M- and q- state, we race back up the UTM TAPE, past the $ marker, and up to where we read q_x again. This time we DELETE it and INSERT the new q_z either two cells before or one cell after the cell we are in, depending on whether the simulation of T wanted the T TAPE HEAD moved left or right.

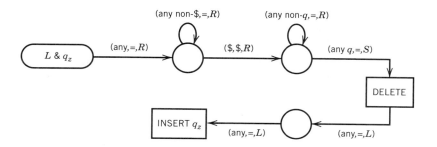

After inserting q_z, we branch on the character c_w that we encounter in the cell after it to an appropriate q_z & c_w state. Then we move left down the TAPE, searching for the substring $q_z c_w$ and the whole process reiterates.

The only way the UTM terminates execution is when the TMC T instruction is to move to state $q_z = q_2$, which is the T HALT state. The UTM cannot quite halt yet itself because it still has a q-marker on the data side of the $. This marker is the only q-symbol on this half of the TAPE. We run the TAPE HEAD up, search, and destroy. Then we go to the UTM HALT.

This UTM has a large TAPE alphabet. A million c's, a million black q's, a million blue q's, an L, an R, a #, and a $. It also has more than a trillion states. But it does exactly what we want it to do. Without knowing what T is and what the data are (only knowing that the state names of T have been changed to q's, the character names on the T TAPE have been changed to c's, and that there are at most a million of each), it correctly simulates the operation of the machine T on this data.

We promised an explanation about what we should do to build a real UTM that accepted all CWL words of TMs with an unbounded number of states and an unbounded number of characters. In this case, instead of simply having a state q & c, we need to mark the whole q and c field on the right side of the $ by making it blue and then crossing the $, moving left, and searching for an identical substring corresponding to the encoding of the same state and data. To mark an arbitrarily large substring of TAPE cells and then search a specified range (between # and $) for the identical substring is not hard TM programming, and we could have proven this theorem that way. But the approach we took is slicker and more intuitive than a mess of non-mnemonic a's and b's. But once we have understood our machine, it is clear that UTMs do exist, not just that there are rumors of them having been sighted circling the skies in remote places.   ∎

By the way, aren't there a great many similarities between a UTM and a computer? We could have made the analogy even closer. We could have numbered (i.e., addressed) the cells in memory and the cells in the program section by inserting fixed-length bit codes in front of them. We could have set aside some register space, especially including an instruction counter instead of blue paint to remember where we are in the program. Then we could have used an address bus and a data bus to turn the TM's linear memory into random access memory. But all these are relatively minor variations. The basic work of simulating a varying set of instructions on arbitrary data by employing a fixed procedure was all worked out in the UTM by Turing.

⚜ NOT ALL r.e. LANGUAGES ARE RECURSIVE

Now that we have designed the UTM, we may use it to settle some questions about recursively enumerable languages, which is what Turing did initially.

We have already defined the language ALAN as all CWL words that are not accepted by the TMs they might represent. Let us now consider the other side of the coin.

DEFINITION

Let MATHISON be the language of all CWL words that *do* represent TMs and *are* accepted by the very machines they represent. (Mathison was Turing's middle name, so do not seek any further mathematical interpretation.) ∎

THEOREM 66

MATHISON is recursively enumerable.

PROOF

The TM that accepts MATHISON is very much like our UTM, but it has an initializing subprogram. We start with an input string and then convert the TAPE to

#	original input string	$	second copy of original input string	ΔΔ . . .

We now run the UTM program exactly as written above. If it ends in a HALT, then we know that the original input was accepted when run on the TM it represents.

It is conceivable that some arbitrary input string that did not really represent a TM could somehow trick a UTM into accepting itself. In fact, it is easy to see how this might happen. The input might be the encoding of a nondeterministic TM and the UTM found a path to HALT without realizing the input was bogus. Alternately, the input might have some semblance of a TM code word but include a garbage subsequence that luckily did not get in the way of the UTM search for states and edges on its way to HALT. In order to avoid these cases, we need a prescreening subprogram to check the input string to be sure that it is in the correct form of a deterministic TM. Because CWL is a regular language, we know there is a TM that accepts it (Theorem 46, p. 445) and then all that need be checked further is the existence of moves out of the HALT state and the possibility of nondeterministic branching—all of which is elementary TM programming and, hence, so trivial for us that we need not bother making a further issue of it.

Once we know that the input is, in fact, a code word for a TM, the procedure above will halt when and only when the input is a word in MATHISON. ∎

THEOREM 67

The complement of a recursively enumerable language might not be recursively enumerable.

PROOF

Because CWL is a regular language, its complement CWL′ is also regular. Because CWL′ is regular, it is also recursively enumerable. The union of CWL′ and MATHISON is therefore the union of two r.e. languages and so is r.e. itself. Call this language *L*. *L* = CWL′ + MATHISON. *L* is r.e., but its complement is ALAN that is not r.e.:

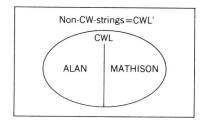

THEOREM 68

There are recursively enumerable languages that are not recursive.

PROOF

The language L just defined is not recursive because that would mean ALAN $= L'$ would be r.e., which by p. 551 it is not.

⚜ DECIDABILITY

We have answered some of the usual questions about languages for the class of r.e. languages, and some others will be answered in the next chapter. What we face now is the question of membership for a language defined by a TM.

Suppose we are given an input string w and a TM T. Can we tell whether or not T halts on w? This is called **the halting problem** for TMs. If the answer were "yes," this question probably would not have a name, merely a theorem number. We shall indeed prove that there is no such decision procedure in our idiosyncratic sense of that term.

To the suggestion, "Why don't we just run w on T and see what happens?", the answer is that this proposal might work, T might halt or crash while we are watching, or it might keep on running for a long time. It may run so long that we begin to suspect that w is in loop(T), but suspecting so does not make it so. T might run for seven years and then decide to accept w.

Because we have been claiming that TMs can execute any mathematical algorithm, what we would expect to find as a halting problem decision procedure is a special TM. Into this special machine we place w and T (encoded, of course) and out comes the answer of whether T accepts w. The UTM is not our solution because all that will do is simulate T; we need something better. The hope of converting T itself into a machine that never loops is doomed because if we could always do that for any TM, all recursively enumerable languages would be recursive, which we know they are not. So, what then is the answer?

THEOREM 69

There is no TM that can accept any string w and any coded TM T and always decide correctly whether T halts on w. In other words, the halting problem cannot be decided by a TM.

PROOF

Suppose for a moment that there was a TM that answers the halting problem. Let us call this machine HP. If we feed HP the CWL code for any TM T and then a # followed by any input string w, HP will, in finite time, halt itself and print out "yes" somewhere on its TAPE if T halts on w and "no" if it does not.

   Let us modify HP as follows. Let us make it loop forever if it were about to print "yes" and halt. We could do this by taking whatever section of the program was about to print the final s and make it loop instead. For those pairs of inputs for which it was going to print "no," we make no modification.

   Now we stick a subprogram, acting as a preprocessor, onto the front of the HP program. This preprocessor takes the left-of-# part of the input string and decides whether it is a word in CWL. If the input is not, the preprocessor crashes. If it is, then the preprocessor deletes the w part of the original input and puts two copies of the same string onto the TAPE, separated by a #, and feeds into the main HP program. This means that the HP is going to analyze whether the code word that gets past the preprocessor is an encoded TM that accepts its own code word as an input. If the answer is "yes", then the modified machine loops forever. If the answer is "no," then it prints "no" and halts. In other words, regardless of what slanders are printed on the TAPE, this modified HP halts *only* on those inputs that are code words of TMs which do not accept their own code word as input. Therefore, this modified HP accepts exactly the language ALAN. But ALAN is not r.e. This contradiction disproves the assumption that there exists a TM to decide the halting problem. ∎

   As if this situation were not bad enough, even more is true.

THEOREM 70

There is no TM that can decide, for every TM T, fed into it in encoded form, whether or not T accepts the word Λ.

PROOF

Suppose, for a moment, there was such a machine called LAMBDA. That is, for all TMs T, when we feed the code for T into LAMBDA, it prints out "yes" if Λ is accepted by T and "no" if Λ is not. We shall now prove that such a machine cannot exist by demonstrating how, by employing it, we could answer the halting problem by building a successful machine HP.

   We can build HP in this fashion. HP, remember, is fed an encoded TM program for T and a word w and is asked to decide whether T halts on w. The first thing that HP will do is create a new TM, in encoded form, out of T and w. Basically, what it will do is modify T by attaching a subprogram preprocessor that writes w on an empty TAPE. This new TM (preprocessor + T) will be called T^*. HP does not write the word w anywhere, nor does it run the machine T. What it does is take the letters of $w = w_1 w_2 w_3 \ldots$ and automatically construct a set of new TM states, connected in a line with edges labeled (Δ, w_1, R), (Δ, w_2, R), (Δ, w_3, R), $\ldots$. This then is the preprocessor subprogram. HP now encodes the preprocessor and concatenates it with the code it was given for T to obtain the code word for T^*.

   With T^* constructed like this, it is clear that the only word T^* can possibly accept is Λ, because all other inputs would crash in the preprocessor stage. Not only that, but T^* can only accept Λ if after w is put on the TAPE and the machine runs like T, then T accepts w. In fact, T^* accepts Λ if and only if T accepts w.

   Now this clever old HP has, by modifying the code of T into the code for T^*, reduced the question it was supposed to answer into a question the machine LAMBDA can answer. So, the next section of the HP program is to act like LAMBDA on the code for T^*. This will print out "yes" or "no," whichever is the truth about Λ for T^*, which will also be the answer for w and T. Therefore, if LAMBDA exists, then HP exists. But HP does not exist. ∎

So, not only can we not determine whether T accepts a given arbitrary word w, we cannot even tell whether when started on an empty TAPE (i.e., the input Λ), it will halt. This is sometimes called the **blank tape problem,** and it too is unsolvable by TM.

Given how little success we are having deciding things about TMs by TM, the next result should be no surprise.

THEOREM 71

There is no TM that, when fed the code word for an arbitrary TM, can always decide whether the encoded TM accepts *any* words. In other words, the emptiness question for r.e. languages cannot be decided by TM.

PROOF

We shall prove this by a method analogous to that used in the last proof. We shall assume that there is such a TM, call it NOTEMPTY, that can decide whether the language for any TM, T^*, fed into it can accept any words and prints out "yes" or "no" accordingly, and from this TM NOTEMPTY, we shall be able to construct a working model of LAMBDA. Because LAMBDA cannot exist, we can conclude that NOTEMPTY cannot exist either.

We can build LAMBDA in the following way. Let us say that LAMBDA is fed the encoded TM T and asked whether it halts on a blank TAPE. What LAMBDA does is attach to T a preprocessor subprogram that erases any input that happens to be on the TAPE. This preprocessor is essentially the loop (any non-Δ, Δ, R). It is important that it only erase the input (the non-Δ part of the TAPE) and not loop forever. It now leaves the TAPE HEAD in cell i. Now when it has finished attaching this preprocessor to T, it determines the new code word for the joint machine called T^* and feeds this into NOTEMPTY. If the language of T^* is not empty, this means that T^* accepts some words. In the operation of T^*, these words would first be erased and then T run on the blank TAPE that remains. In other words, if T^* accepts anything, then T accepts Λ. And if T accepts Λ, then T^* accepts everything. So, the LAMBDA machine can be built from the NOTEMPTY machine, if the latter existed. ∎

The construction in the proof of the last machine actually said that LAMBDA exists if there is a TM that can determine whether the language accepted by a given TM is infinite, because the language of T^* is empty or infinite depending on whether T accepts Λ. Because LAMBDA does not exist, the machine to decide finiteness also cannot exist. Thus, we have actually proven this result.

THEOREM 72

There does not exist a TM that can decide, for any encoded TM T fed into it, whether or not the language of T is finite or infinite. ∎

We have been careful in the last three theorems to say that membership, Λ, and emptiness are all not decidable by a TM. We did not have the nerve yet to claim that these questions could not be decided by *any* means. That time, however, is approaching.

⚜ PROBLEMS

1. Show that each of the following languages is recursive by finding a TM that accepts them and crashes on all strings in their complement:
   - (i) EVEN-EVEN
   - (ii) EQUAL
   - (iii) ODDPALINDROME
   - (iv) TRAILINGCOUNT
   - (v) MOREA

   Consider the following TMs for Problems 2 through 4:

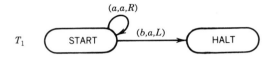

2. What are $\text{accept}(T_1)$, $\text{loop}(T_1)$, and $\text{reject}(T_1)$? Be careful about the word b.

3. What are $\text{accept}(T_2)$, $\text{loop}(T_2)$, and $\text{reject}(T_2)$?

4. Draw the TM that accepts the language

$$\text{accept}(T_1) + \text{accept}(T_2)$$

5. Trace the execution of these input strings on the machine of Problem 4:
   - (i) Λ
   - (ii) b
   - (iii) aab
   - (iv) ab

6. Prove that all regular languages are recursive.

7. Prove that all CFLs are recursive.

8. Prove that if L, M, and N are three r.e. languages such that no two have a word in common yet their union is all possible strings, then they are all recursive.

9. Let L be a language and L' its complement. Prove that one of the following cases must be true:
   - (i) Both L and L' are recursive.
   - (ii) Neither L nor L' is r.e.
   - (iii) One is r.e. but not recursive while the other is not r.e.

10. (i) Prove that the union of two recursive languages is recursive.
    (ii) Prove that the intersection of recursive languages is recursive.

11. Suppose that L is r.e. but not recursive and that T accepts L. Prove that $\text{loop}(T)$ is infinite.

12. Using nondeterministic TMs, show that the product and Kleene closure of r.e. languages are r.e.

13. Convert the following TMs first into summary tables and then into their code words in CWL. What are the six languages accepted by these TMs?

(i)

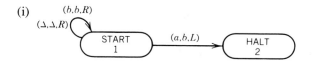

(ii)

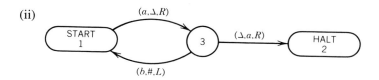

(iii)

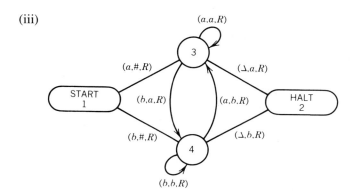

(iv)

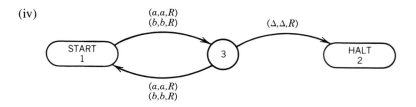

(v)

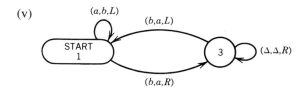

(vi)

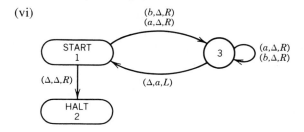

Run each of the six encoded words on their respective machines to see which are in the language ALAN.

14. Can the code word for any TM be a palindrome? Prove your answer.

15. Decode the following words from CWL into their corresponding TMs and run them on their corresponding TMs to see which are in ALAN and which are in MATHISON:

(i) *abaabbbbab*
(ii) *abaabaabba*
(iii) *abaabaabbb*
(iv) *abaaabaaabbaaabaababbbb*
(v) *abaaabaaabaaaabaababbbab*
(vi) *abababab*

16. Outline a TM that accepts only CWL words that actually *are* encoded TMs.

17. In Chapter 11 (just before Theorem 17), the blue paint method was presented to determine whether an FA accepts any words at all. Using the TM depicted below, show that this method fails to decide whether a TM accepts any words:

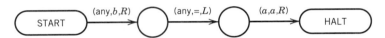

18. Given a TM, T_1, and any string w, there is clearly a TM, T_2, that first screens its input to see whether it is the particular string w; if it is not the input is accepted, if it is w, then T_1 is run on the input w. Pictorially,

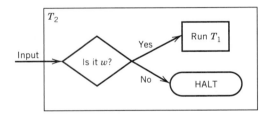

Show that there is no decision procedure to determine whether any given TM (say T_2) accepts *all* strings or not.

19. Show that there is no TM that can decide, given code(T_1) and code(T_2), whether accept(T_1) = accept(T_2). *Hint*: Choose a T_2 such that this problem reduces to the ACCEPTALL machine of the previous problem.

20. (Oddly enough, this problem has nothing to do with computer theory, yet it has everything to do with the contents of this chapter.)

In the English language, we can observe that some adjectives apply to themselves. For example, the word "short" is a fairly short word. We might say, "short" is short. Also, the adjective "polysyllabic" is indeed polysyllabic. Some other possible adjectives of this type are "unfrequent," "melodious," "arcane," "unhyphenated," "English," "non-palindromic," and "harmless." Let us call all these adjectives that describe themselves *homothetic*. Let us call all other adjectives (those that do not describe themselves) *heterothetic*. For example, the words "gymnastic," "myopic," and "recursive" are all heterothetic adjectives. The word "heterothetic" is an adjective and therefore like all adjectives it is either homothetic or heterothetic. Which is it?

CHAPTER 24

The Chomsky
Hierarchy

⚜ PHRASE-STRUCTURE GRAMMARS

We have not yet developed all the information presented in the table at the beginning of Chapter 19. For one thing, we have not discovered the language structures that define recursively enumerable sets independent of the concept of TMs. This we shall do now.

Why are context-free languages called "context-free"? The answer is that if there is a production $N \rightarrow t$, where N is a nonterminal and t is a terminal, then the replacement of t for N can be made in *any* situation in any working string. This gave us the uncomfortable problem of the itchy itchy itchy bear in Chapter 12. It could give us even worse problems.

As an example, we could say that in English the word "base" can mean cowardly, whereas "ball" can mean a dance. If we employ the CFG model, we could introduce the productions

$$\text{Base} \rightarrow \text{cowardly}$$
$$\text{Ball} \rightarrow \text{dance}$$

and we could modify some working string as follows:

$$\text{Baseball} \Rightarrow \text{cowardly dance}$$

What is wrong here is that although base *can* sometimes mean cowardly, it does not always have that option. In general, we have many synonyms for any English word; each is a possibility for substitution:

$$\text{Base} \rightarrow \text{foundation} \mid \text{alkali} \mid \text{headquarters} \mid \text{safety station} \mid \text{cowardly} \mid \text{mean}$$

However, it is not true in English that base can be replaced by any one of these words in each of the sentences in which it occurs. What matters is the **context** of the phrase in which the word appears. English is therefore not an example of a CFL. This is true even though, as we saw in Chapter 12, the model for context-free languages was originally abstracted from human language grammars. Still, in English we need more information before proceeding with a substitution. This information can be in the form of the knowledge of the adjoining words.

> Base line $\rightarrow$ starting point
> Base metal $\rightarrow$ nonprecious metal
> Way off base $\rightarrow$ very mistaken | far from home

Here, we are making use of some of the context in which the word sits to know which substitutions are allowed, where by *context* we mean the immediately adjoining words in the sentence. The term context could mean other things, such as the general topic of the paragraph in which the phrase sits; however, for us context means some number of the surrounding words.

Instead of replacing one character by a string of characters as in CFGs, we are now considering replacing one whole string of characters (terminals and nonterminals) by another. This is a new kind of production and it gives us a new kind of grammar. We carry over all the terminology from CFGs such as "working string" and "the language generated." The only change is in the form of the productions. We are developing a new mathematical model that more accurately describes the possible substitutions occurring in English and other human languages. There is also a useful connection to computer theory, as we shall see.

DEFINITION

A **phrase-structure grammar** is a collection of three things:

1. A finite alphabet Σ of letters called **terminals.**
2. A finite set of symbols called **nonterminals** that includes the **start symbol** S.
3. A finite list of productions of the form

$$\text{String 1} \rightarrow \text{string 2}$$

where string 1 can be any string of terminals and nonterminals that contains at least one nonterminal and where string 2 is any string of terminals and nonterminals whatsoever.

A **derivation** in a phrase-structure grammar is a series of working strings beginning with the start symbol S, which, by making substitutions according to the productions, arrives at a string of all terminals, at which point generation must stop.

The **language generated** by a phrase-structure grammar is the set of all strings of terminals that can be derived starting at S. ∎

EXAMPLE

The following is a phrase-structure grammar over $\Sigma = \{a \quad b\}$ with nonterminals X and S:

$$\begin{array}{ll} \text{PROD 1} & S \rightarrow XS \mid \Lambda \\ \text{PROD 2} & X \rightarrow aX \mid a \\ \text{PROD 3} & aaaX \rightarrow ba \end{array}$$

This is an odd set of rules. The first production says that we can start with S and derive any number of symbols of type X—for example,

$$\begin{align} S &\Rightarrow XS \\ &\Rightarrow XXS \\ &\Rightarrow XXXS \\ &\Rightarrow XXXXS \\ &\Rightarrow XXXX \end{align}$$

The second production shows us that each X can be any string of a's (with at least one a):

$$X \Rightarrow aX$$
$$\Rightarrow aaX$$
$$\Rightarrow aaaX$$
$$\Rightarrow aaaaX$$
$$\Rightarrow aaaaa$$

The third production says that any time we find three a's and an X, we can replace these four symbols with the two-terminal string ba.

The following is a summary of one possible derivation in this grammar:

$$S \overset{*}{\Rightarrow} XXXXX$$
$$\overset{*}{\Rightarrow} aaaaaXXXX \quad \text{(after } X \overset{*}{\Rightarrow} aaaaa\text{)}$$
$$\Rightarrow aabaXXXX \quad \text{(by PROD 3)}$$

$$\Rightarrow aabaaaXXX \quad \text{(after } X \overset{*}{\Rightarrow} aa\text{)}$$
$$\Rightarrow aabbaXX \quad \text{(PROD 3)}$$

$$\Rightarrow aabbaaaX \quad \text{(after } X \overset{*}{\Rightarrow} aa\text{)}$$
$$\Rightarrow aabbba \quad \text{(after PROD 3)} \quad \blacksquare$$

This is certainly a horse of a different color. The algorithms that we used for CFGs must now be thrown out the window. Chomsky Normal Form is out. Sometimes, applying a production that is not a Λ-production still makes a working string get shorter. Terminals that used to be in a working string can disappear. Leftmost derivations do not always exist. The CYK algorithm does not apply. It is no longer possible just to read the list of nonterminals off of the left sides of productions. We cannot tell the terminals from the nonterminals without a scorecard.

All CFGs are phrase-structure grammars in which we restrict ourselves as to what we put on the left side of productions. So, all CFLs can be generated by phrase-structure grammars. Can any other languages be generated by them?

THEOREM 73

At least one language that cannot be generated by a CFG can be generated by a phrase-structure grammar.

PROOF

To prove this assertion by constructive methods, we need only demonstrate one actual language with this property. A nonconstructive proof might be to show that the assumption

$$\text{Phrase-structure grammar} = \text{CFG}$$

leads to some devious contradiction but, as usual, we shall employ the preferred constructive approach here. (Theorem 64 on p. 551 was proved by devious contradiction and see what became of that.)

Consider the following phrase-structure grammar over the alphabet $\Sigma = \{a \quad b\}$:

$$\text{PROD 1} \quad S \rightarrow aSBA$$
$$\text{PROD 2} \quad S \rightarrow abA$$

$$\text{P\small{ROD}} \; 3 \quad AB \rightarrow BA$$
$$\text{P\small{ROD}} \; 4 \quad bB \rightarrow bb$$
$$\text{P\small{ROD}} \; 5 \quad bA \rightarrow ba$$
$$\text{P\small{ROD}} \; 6 \quad aA \rightarrow aa$$

We shall show that the language generated by this grammar is $\{a^n b^n a^n\}$, which we have shown in Chapter 16 is non-context-free.

First, let us see one example of a derivation in this grammar:

$$
\begin{array}{lll}
S & \Rightarrow aSBA & \text{P\small{ROD}} \; 1 \\
& \Rightarrow aaSBABA & \text{P\small{ROD}} \; 1 \\
& \Rightarrow aaaSBABABA & \text{P\small{ROD}} \; 1 \\
& \Rightarrow aaaabABABABA & \text{P\small{ROD}} \; 2 \\
& \Rightarrow aaaabBAABABA & \text{P\small{ROD}} \; 3 \\
& \Rightarrow aaaabBABAABA & \text{P\small{ROD}} \; 3 \\
& \Rightarrow aaaabBBAAABA & \text{P\small{ROD}} \; 3 \\
& \Rightarrow aaaabBBAABAA & \text{P\small{ROD}} \; 3 \\
& \Rightarrow aaaabBBABAAA & \text{P\small{ROD}} \; 3 \\
& \Rightarrow aaaabBBBAAAA & \text{P\small{ROD}} \; 3 \\
& \Rightarrow aaaabbBBAAAA & \text{P\small{ROD}} \; 4 \\
& \Rightarrow aaaabbbBAAAA & \text{P\small{ROD}} \; 4 \\
& \Rightarrow aaaabbbbAAAA & \text{P\small{ROD}} \; 4 \\
& \Rightarrow aaaabbbbaAAA & \text{P\small{ROD}} \; 5 \\
& \Rightarrow aaaabbbbaaAA & \text{P\small{ROD}} \; 6 \\
& \Rightarrow aaaabbbbaaaA & \text{P\small{ROD}} \; 6 \\
& \Rightarrow aaaabbbbaaaa & \text{P\small{ROD}} \; 6 \\
& = a^4 b^4 a^4
\end{array}
$$

To generate the word $a^m b^m a^m$ for some fixed number m (we have used n to mean any power in the defining symbol for this language), we could proceed as follows.

First, we use P\small{ROD} 1 exactly $(m-1)$ times. This gives us the working string

$$\underbrace{aa \ldots a}_{m-1} \quad S \quad \underbrace{BABA \ldots BA}_{\substack{(m-1) \; B\text{'s alternating} \\ \text{with} \\ (m-1) \; A\text{'s}}}$$

Next, we apply P\small{ROD} 2 once. This gives us the working string

$$\underbrace{aa \ldots a}_{m} \quad b \quad \underbrace{ABAB \ldots BA}_{\substack{m \; A\text{'s} \\ m-1 \; B\text{'s}}}$$

Now we apply P\small{ROD} 3 enough times to move the B's in front of the A's. Note that we should not let our mathematical background fool us into thinking that $AB \rightarrow BA$ means that the A's and B's commute. No. We cannot replace BA with AB — only the other way around. The A's can move to the right through the B's. The B's can move to the left through the A's. We can only separate them into the arrangement B's, then A's. We then obtain the working string

$$\underbrace{aa \ldots a}_{m} \quad b \quad \underbrace{BB \ldots B}_{m-1} \quad \underbrace{AA \ldots A}_{m}$$

Now using PRODS 4, 5, and 6, we can move left through the working string, converting B's to b's and then A's to a's.

We will finally obtain

$$\underbrace{aa \ldots a}_{m} \quad \underbrace{bb \ldots b}_{m} \quad \underbrace{aa \ldots a}_{m} = a^m b^m a^m$$

We have not yet proven that $\{a^n b^n a^n\}$ is the language generated by the original grammar, only that all such words can be derived. To finish the proof, we must show that no word not in $\{a^n b^n a^n\}$ can be generated. We must show that every word that is generated *is* of the form $a^n b^n a^n$ for some n.

Let us consider some unknown derivation in this phrase-structure grammar. We begin with the start symbol S and we *must* immediately apply either PROD 1 or PROD 2. If we start with PROD 2, the only word we can generate is aba, which is of the approved form.

If we begin with PROD 1, we get the working string

$$a \, SBA$$

which is of the form

$$\underbrace{\llcorner \quad \quad \lrcorner}_{\text{some } a\text{'s}} \; S \; \underbrace{\llcorner \quad \quad \quad \quad \lrcorner}_{\text{equal } A\text{'s and } B\text{'s}}$$

The only productions we can apply are PRODS 1, 2, and 3, because we do not yet have any substrings of the form bB, bA, or aA. PRODS 1 and 3 leave the form just as above, whereas once we use PROD 2, we immediately obtain a working string of the form

$$\underbrace{\llcorner \quad \quad \lrcorner}_{a\text{'s}} \; abA \; \underbrace{\llcorner \quad \quad \quad \quad \lrcorner}_{\text{equal } A\text{'s and } B\text{'s}}$$

If we never apply PROD 2, we never remove the character S from the working string and therefore we never obtain a word. PROD 2 can be applied only one time, because there is never more than one S in the working string.

Therefore, in every derivation before we have applied PROD 2, we have applied some (maybe none) PROD 1's and PROD 3's. Let the number of PROD 1's we have applied be m. We shall now demonstrate that the final word generated must be

$$a^{m+1} b^{m+1} a^{m+1}$$

Right after PROD 2 is applied, the working string looks like this:

$$\underbrace{\llcorner \quad \quad \quad \lrcorner}_{\text{exactly } m \ a\text{'s}} \; abA \; \underbrace{\llcorner \quad \quad \quad \lrcorner}_{\substack{\text{exactly } m \ A\text{'s} \\ \text{and } m \ B\text{'s} \\ \text{in some order}}}$$

The only productions we can apply now are PRODS 3, 4, 5, and 6. Let us look at the working string this way:

$$a^{m+1} \qquad b \qquad \substack{\text{Nonterminals} \\ (m+1) \ A\text{'s} \\ m \ B\text{'s}}$$

Any time we apply PROD 3, we are just scrambling the right half of the string, the sequence of nonterminals. When we apply PROD 4, 5, or 6, we are converting a nonterminal into a terminal, but it must be the nonterminal on the border between the left-side terminal string and the right-side nonterminal string. We always keep the shape

terminals   Nonterminals

(just as with leftmost Chomsky derivations), until we have all terminals. The A's eventually become a's and the B's eventually become b's. However, none of the rules for PRODS 4, 5, or 6 can create the substring ab. We can create bb, ba, or aa, but never ab. From this point on, the pool of A's and B's will be converted into a's and b's without the substring ab. That means it must eventually assume the form **b*a***.

$a^{m+1}b$ $\underline{\text{Nonterminals}}$
             $(m + 1) A\text{'s}$
             $m B\text{'s}$

must become

$$a^{m+1} \quad b \quad b^m \quad a^{m+1}$$

which is what we wanted to prove.   ∎

As with CFGs, it is possible to define and construct a *total language tree* for a phrase-structure grammar. To every node, we apply as many productions as we can along different branches. Some branches lead to words; some may not. The total language tree for a phrase-structure language may have very short words way out on very long branches (which is not the case with CFLs). This is because productions can sometimes shorten the working string, as in the example

$$S \rightarrow aX$$
$$X \rightarrow aX$$
$$aaaaaaX \rightarrow b$$

The derivation for the word ab is

$$S \Rightarrow aX$$
$$\Rightarrow aaX$$
$$\Rightarrow aaaX$$
$$\Rightarrow aaaaX$$
$$\Rightarrow aaaaaX$$
$$\Rightarrow aaaaaaX$$
$$\Rightarrow aaaaaaaX$$
$$\Rightarrow ab$$

EXAMPLE

The total language tree for the phrase-structure grammar for $\{a^n b^n a^n\}$ on p. 567 begins

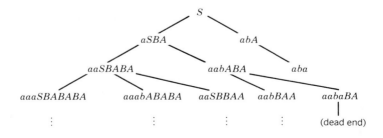

Notice one interesting thing that can happen in a phrase-structure grammar. A working string may contain nonterminals and yet no production can be applied to it. Such a working string is not a word in the language of the grammar; it is a dead end.   ∎

The **phrase-structure languages** (those languages generated by phrase-structure grammars) are a larger class of languages than the CFLs. This is fine with us, because CFGs are inadequate to describe all the languages accepted by TMs.

We found that the languages accepted by FAs are also those definable by regular expressions and that the languages accepted by PDAs are also those definable by CFGs. What we need now is some method of defining the languages accepted by TMs that does not make reference to the machines themselves (simply *calling* them recursively enumerable contributes nothing to our understanding). Perhaps phrase-structure languages are what we need. (Good guess.) Also, because we already know that some languages cannot be accepted by TMs, perhaps we can find a method of defining *all possible* languages, not just the r.e. languages. Although we have placed very minimal restrictions on the shape of their productions, phrase-structure grammars do not have to be totally unstructured, as we see from the following result.

THEOREM 74

If we have a phrase-structure grammar that generates the language L, then there is another grammar that also generates L which has the same alphabet of terminals and in which each production is of the form

string of nonterminals $\rightarrow$ string of terminals and nonterminals

(where the left side cannot be Λ, but the right side can).

PROOF

This proof will be by constructive algorithm using the same trick as in the proof of Theorem 25.

Step 1   For each terminal a, b, . . . introduce a *new* nonterminal (one not used before): A, B, . . . and change every string of terminals and nonterminals into a string of nonterminals above by using the new symbols. For example,

$$aSbXb \rightarrow bbXYX$$

becomes

$$ASBXB \rightarrow BBXYX$$

Step 2   Add the new productions

$$A \rightarrow a$$
$$B \rightarrow b$$

These replacements and additions obviously generate the same language and fit the desired description. In fact, the new grammar fits a stronger requirement. Every production is either

string of nonterminals $\rightarrow$ string of nonterminals

or

one nonterminal $\rightarrow$ one terminal

(where the right side can be Λ, but not the left side).   ∎

EXAMPLE

The phrase-structure grammar over the alphabet $\{a \quad b\}$, which generates $\{a^n b^n a^n\}$, which we saw above,

$$S \rightarrow aSBA$$
$$S \rightarrow abA$$
$$AB \rightarrow BA$$
$$bB \rightarrow bb$$
$$bA \rightarrow ba$$
$$aA \rightarrow aa$$

turns into the following, when the algorithm of Theorem 74 is applied to it:

$$S \rightarrow XSBA$$
$$S \rightarrow XYA$$
$$AB \rightarrow BA$$
$$YB \rightarrow YY$$
$$YA \rightarrow YX$$
$$XA \rightarrow XX$$
$$X \rightarrow a$$
$$Y \rightarrow b$$

Notice that we had to choose new symbols, X and Y, because A and B were already being employed as nonterminals.

■

DEFINITION

A phrase-structure grammar is called **type 0** if each production is of the form

nonempty string of nonterminals $\rightarrow$ any string of terminals and nonterminals   ■

The second grammar above is type 0. Actually, what we have shown by Theorem 74 is that all phrase-structure grammars are equivalent to type 0 grammars in the sense that they generate the same languages.

Some authors *define* type 0 grammars by exactly the same definition as we gave for phrase-structure grammars. Now that we have proven Theorem 74, we may join the others and use the two terms interchangeably, forgetting our original definition of type 0 as distinct from phrase-structure. As usual, the literature on this subject contains even more terms for the same grammars, such as **unrestricted grammars** and **semi-Thue grammars.**

Beware of the sloppy definition that says type 0 includes all productions of the form

any string $\rightarrow$ any string

because that would allow one string of terminals (on the left) to be replaced by some other string (on the right). This goes against the philosophy of what a *terminal* is, and we do not allow it. Nor do we allow frightening productions of the form $\Lambda \rightarrow something$, which could cause letters to pop into words indiscriminately (see *Gen,* I:3 for "$\Lambda \rightarrow$ light").

Names such as *nonterminal-rewriting grammars* and *context-sensitive-with-erasing grammars* also turn out to generate the same languages as type 0. These names reflect other nuances of formal language theory into which we do not delve.

One last remark about the name type 0. It is not pronounced like the universal blood donor but rather as "type zero." The 0 is a number, and there are other numbered types.

Type 0 is one of the four classes of grammars that Chomsky, in 1959, cataloged in a hierarchy of grammars according to the structure of their productions.

The Chomsky Hierarchy of Grammars

Type	Name of Languages Generated	Production Restrictions $X \rightarrow Y$	Acceptor
0	Phrase-structure = recursively enumerable	X = any string with nonterminals Y = any string	TM
1	Context-sensitive	X = any string with nonterminals Y = any string as long as or longer than X	TMs with bounded (not infinite) TAPE, called linear-bounded automata LBAs*
2	Context-free	X = one nonterminal Y = any string	PDA
3	Regular	X = one nonterminal $Y = t N$ or $Y = t$, where t is terminal and N is nonterminal	FA

*The size of the tape is a linear function of the length of the input, cf. problem 20.

We have not yet proven all the claims on this table, nor shall we. We have completely covered the cases of type 2 and type 3 grammars. Type 1 grammars are called context-sensitive because they use some information about the context of a nonterminal before allowing a substitution. However, they require that no production shorten the length of the working string, which enables us to use the top-down parsing techniques discussed in Chapter 18. Because they are very specialized, we treat them only briefly (cf. p. 588). In this chapter, we prove the theorem that type 0 grammars generate all recursively enumerable languages.

Two interesting languages are not on this chart. The set of all languages that can be accepted by deterministic PDAs, called simply the **deterministic context-free languages.** We have seen that they are closed under complementation, which makes more questions decidable. They are generated by what are called **LR(k) grammars,** which are grammars generating words that can be parsed by being read from left to right, taking k symbols at a time. This is a topic of special interest to compiler designers. This book is only an introduction and does not begin to exhaust the range of what a computer scientist needs to know about theory to be a competent practitioner.

The other interesting class of languages that is missing is the collection of recursive languages. No algorithm can, by looking only at the structure of the grammar, tell whether the language it generates is recursive—not counting the symbols, not describing the production strings, nothing.

These six classes of languages form a nested set as shown in this Venn diagram:

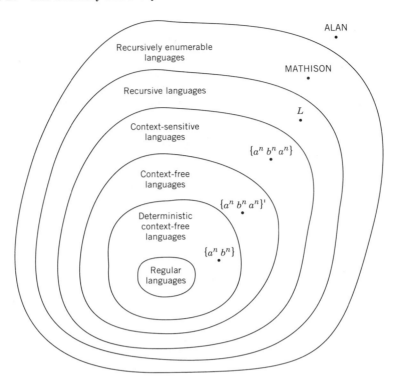

We have discussed most of the examples that show no two of these categories are really the same. This is important—just because a condition *looks* more restrictive does not mean it actually *is* in the sense that different languages fulfill it. Remember that FA = NFA.

$\{a^n b^n\}$ is deterministic context-free but not regular.

The complement of $\{a^n b^n a^n\}$ is a CFL, but it cannot be accepted by a DPDA.

$\{a^n b^n a^n\}$ is context-sensitive but not context-free. (The grammar we just examined above that generates this language meets the conditions for context sensitivity.)

L stands for a language that is recursive but not context-sensitive. We shall present one of these on p. 590.

MATHISON is recursively enumerable but not recursive.

ALAN comes from outerspace.

Counting "outerspace," we actually have seven classes of languages. The language of all computer program instructions is context-free; however, the language of all computer programs themselves is r.e. English is *probably* context-sensitive except for poetry, which (as e.e. cummings proved in 1923) is from outerspace.

 TYPE 0 = TM

We shall now prove that r.e. = type 0. This was first demonstrated by Chomsky in 1959. The proof will be given in two parts, Theorem 75 and Theorem 76.

THEOREM 75

If L is generated by a type 0 grammar G, then there is a TM that accepts L.

PROOF

The proof will be by constructive algorithm. We shall describe how to build such a TM. This TM will be nondeterministic, and we shall have to appeal to Theorem 57 (p. 519) to demonstrate that there is therefore also some deterministic TM that accepts L.

The TAPE alphabet will be all the terminals and nonterminals of G and the symbol $\$$ (which we presume is not used in G). When we begin processing, the TAPE contains a string of terminals. It will be accepted if it is generated by G but not be accepted otherwise.

Step 1   We insert a $\$$ in cell i, moving the input to the right, and insert another $\$$ in the cell after the input string and an S after that. We leave the TAPE HEAD pointing to the second $\$$:

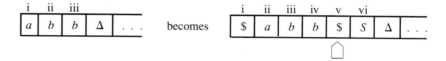

Step 2   We now enter a great central state that will serve the same purpose as the central POP in the PDA simulation of a CFG in Chapter 15. The field of the TAPE beginning with the second $\$$ is where we will keep track of the working string. The basic strategy is to simulate the derivation of the input word in the working string field.

We shall construct a branch from this central state that simulates the application of each production to a working string as follows. Consider any production

$$x_1 x_2 x_3 \ \cdots \ \rightarrow \ y_1 y_2 y_3 \ \cdots$$

where the x's are any left side of a production in the grammar G and the y's are the corresponding right side. Move the TAPE HEAD nondeterministically up and down the working string until it stops at some cell containing x_1. We now scan the TAPE to be sure that the immediate next subsequence is $x_1 x_2 x_3 \ldots$. When we are confident that we have found this string, we roll the TAPE HEAD back to point to x_1 (which we have conveniently marked) and proceed with a sequence of deletes:

$$\rightarrow \boxed{\text{DELETE}} \rightarrow \boxed{\text{DELETE}} \rightarrow \boxed{\text{DELETE}} \rightarrow \ \cdots$$

just enough to delete the exact string of x's. Then we insert the specified string of y's by this sequence:

$$\rightarrow \boxed{\text{INSERT } y_1} \rightarrow \boxed{\text{INSERT } y_2} \rightarrow \ \cdots$$

just as many as y's on the right side. This accurately converts the working string into another working string that is derivable from it in the grammar G by application of this production.

We add a loop like this for each production in the grammar G:

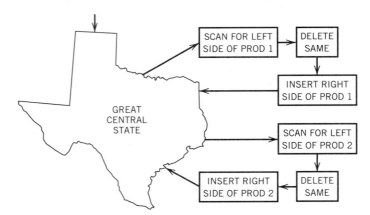

Step 3   If we were lucky enough to apply just the right productions, at just the right points in the working string, and in just the right sequence to arrive at a string of all terminals, we nondeterministically branch to a subprogram that compares the working string to the input string. If they match exactly, then the TM halts. If the input was in fact derivable, then some choice of path through this NTM will lead to HALT. If not, then either we will come to a working string from which there are no applicable productions and crash, or else we loop forever, producing longer and longer working strings, none of which will ever be equal to the input.

This NTM accepts any word in the language generated by G and only these words.   ■

THEOREM 76

If a language is r.e., it can be generated by a type 0 grammar.

PROOF

The proof will be by constructive algorithm. We must show how to create a type 0 grammar that generates exactly the same words as are accepted by a given TM. From now on, we fix in our minds a particular TM.

Our general goal is to construct a set of productions that "simulate" the working of this TM. But here we run into a problem: Unlike the simulations of TMs by PMs or 2PDAs, a grammar does not start with an input and run it to halt. A grammar must start with S and end up with the word. To overcome this discrepancy, our grammar must first generate all possible strings of a's and b's (not as final words but as working strings with nonterminals in them) and then test them by simulating the action of the TM upon them.

As we know, a TM can badly mutilate an input string on its way to the HALT state, so our grammar must preserve a second copy of the input as a backup. We keep the backup copy intact while we act on the other as if it were running on the input TAPE of our TM. If this TM ever gets to a HALT state, we erase what is left of the mutilated copy and are left with the pristine copy as the word generated by the grammar. If the second copy does not run successfully on the TM (it crashes or loops forever), then we never get to the stage of erasing the working copy. Because the working copy contains nonterminals, this means that we never produce a string of all terminals. This will prevent us from ever successfully generating a word not in the language accepted by the TM. A derivation that never ends corresponds to an input that loops forever. A derivation that gets stuck at a working string with nonterminals still in it corresponds to an input that crashes. A derivation that produces a real word corresponds to an input that runs successfully to HALT.

That is a rough description of the method we shall follow. The hard part is this: Where can we put the two different copies of the string so that the productions can act on only one copy, never on the other? In a derivation in a grammar, there is only one working string generated at any time. Even in phrase-structure grammars, any production can be applied to any part of the working string at any time. How do we keep the two copies separate? How do we keep the first copy intact (immune from distortion by production) while we work on the second copy?

The surprising answer to this question is that we keep the copies separate by interlacing them. We store them in alternate locations on the working string.

We also use parentheses as nonterminals to keep straight which letters are in which copy. All letters following a "(" are in the first (intact) copy. All symbols before a ")" are in the second (TM TAPE simulation) copy. We say "symbol" here because we may find any character from the TM TAPE sitting to the left of a ")".

When we are finally ready to derive the final word because the second TAPE-simulating copy has been accepted by the TM, we must erase not only the remnants of the second copy, but also the parentheses and any other nonterminals used as TM-simulation tools.

First, let us outline the procedure in even more detail, then formalize it, and then finally illustrate it.

Step 1   In our approach, a string such as *abba* will be represented initially by the working string

$$(aa)(bb)(bb)(aa)$$

We need to be able to generate all such working strings. The following productions will suffice:

$$S \rightarrow (aa)S \mid (bb)S \mid \Lambda$$

Later we shall see that we actually need something slightly different because of other requirements of the processing.

Remember that "(" and ")" are nonterminal characters in our type 0 grammar that must be erased at the final step.

Remember too that the first letter in each parenthesized pair will stay immutable while we simulate the TM processing on the second letter of each pair as *if* the string of second letters were the contents of the TM TAPE during the course of the simulation:

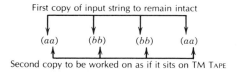

First copy of input string to remain intact

(aa) (bb) (bb) (aa)

Second copy to be worked on as if it sits on TM TAPE

Step 2   Because a TM can use more TAPE cells than just those that the input letters initially take up, we need to add some blank cells to the working string. We must give the TM enough TAPE to do its processing job. We do know that a TM has a TAPE with infinitely many cells available, *but* in the processing of any particular word it accepts, it employs only finitely many of those cells—a finite block of cells starting at cell i. If it tried to read infinitely many cells in one running, it would never finish and reach HALT. If the TM needs four extra cells of its TAPE to accept the word *abba*, we add four units of $(\Delta\Delta)$ to the end of the working string:

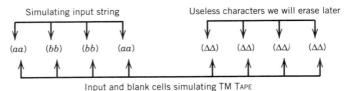

Notice that we have made the symbol Δ a nonterminal in the grammar we are constructing.

Step 3   To simulate the action of a TM, we need to include in the working string an indication of *which* state we are in and *where* the TAPE HEAD is reading. As with many of the TM simulations we have done before, we can handle both problems with the same device.

We shall do this as follows. Let the names of the states in the TM be q_0 (the start state), q_1, q_2, ... We insert a q in front of the parentheses of the symbol now being read by the TAPE HEAD. To do this, we have to make all the q's nonterminals in our grammar.

Initially, the working string looks like this:

$$q_0(aa)(bb)(bb)(aa)(\Delta\Delta)(\Delta\Delta)(\Delta\Delta)(\Delta\Delta)$$

It may sometime later look like this:

$$(aA)(b\Delta)(bX)q_6(aA)(\Delta b)(\Delta M)(\Delta\Delta)(\Delta\Delta)$$

This will mean that the TAPE contents being simulated are $A\Delta XAbM\Delta\Delta$ and the TAPE HEAD is reading the fourth cell, while the TM program is in state q_6.

To summarize, at every stage, the working string must:

1. Remember the original input.

2. Represent the TAPE status, including TAPE HEAD position.

3. Reflect the state the TM is in.

Step 4   We also need to include as nonterminals in the grammar all the symbols that the TM might wish to write on its TAPE, the alphabet Γ. The use of these symbols was illustrated above.

Step 5   Now in the process of simulating the operation of the TM, the working string could look like this:

$$(aa)q_3(bB)(b\Delta)(aA)(\Delta A)(\Delta A)(\Delta\Delta)(\Delta M)$$

The original string we are interested in is *abba*, and it is still intact in the positions just after "("s.

The current status of the simulated TM TAPE can be read from the characters in front of the close parentheses. It is

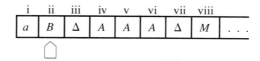

The TM is in state q_3, and the TAPE HEAD is reading cell ii as we can tell from the positioning of the q_3 in the working string.

To continue the simulation, we need to be able to change the working string to reflect the specific instructions in the particular TM; that is, we need to be able to simulate all possible changes in TAPE status that the specific TM program might produce.

Let us take an example of one possible TM instruction and see what productions we must include in our grammar to simulate its operation. If the TM is,

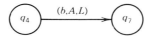

then our productions are from state q_4 while reading a b, print an A, go to state q_7, and move the TAPE HEAD left.

We need a production that causes our representation of the prior status of the TM to change into a working string that represents the outcome status of the TM. We need a production like

$$(\text{Symbol}_1\text{Symbol}_2)q_4(\text{Symbol}_3 b) \rightarrow q_7(\text{Symbol}_1\text{Symbol}_2)(\text{Symbol}_3 A)$$

where Symbol_1 and Symbol_3 are any letters in the input string (a or b) or the Δ's in the extra ($\Delta\Delta$) factors, and Symbol_2 is what is in the TAPE in the cell to the left of the b being read. Symbol_2 will be read next by the simulated TAPE HEAD:

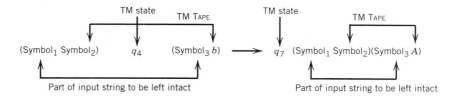

This is not just one production, but a whole family of possibilities covering all considerations of what Symbol_1, Symbol_2, and Symbol_3 are:

$$(aa)q_4(ab) \rightarrow q_7(aa)(aA)$$
$$(aa)q_4(bb) \rightarrow q_7(aa)(bA)$$
$$(aa)q_4(\Delta b) \rightarrow q_7(aa)(\Delta A)$$
$$(ab)q_4(ab) \rightarrow q_7(ab)(aA)$$
$$(ab)q_4(bb) \rightarrow q_7(ab)(bA)$$
$$\cdots$$
$$(bX)q_4(\Delta b) \rightarrow q_7(bX)(\Delta A)$$

Notice that the way this simulation is set up there is no corresponding grammatical production for moving left from cell i because there would be no $(\text{Symbol}_1\ \text{Symbol}_2)$ in front of q_1 for such a move.

The simulation of a TM instruction that moves the TAPE HEAD to the right can be handled the same way:

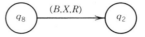

"If in a state q_8 reading a B, write an X, move the TAPE HEAD right, and go to state q_2" translates into the following family of productions:

$$q_8(\text{Symbol}_1 B) \rightarrow (\text{Symbol}_1 X)q_2$$

where Symbol_1 is part of the immutable first copy of the input string, or one of the extra Δ's on the right end. Happily, the move-right simulations do not involve as many unknown symbols of the working string.

We need to include productions in our grammar for all possible values for Symbol_1.

Let us be clear here that we do not include in our grammar productions for all possible TM instructions, only for those instructions that do label the edges in the specific TM we are trying to simulate.

Step 6   Finally, let us suppose that after generating the doubled form of the word and simulating the operation of the TM on its TAPE, we eventually are led into a HALT state. This means that the input we started with is accepted by this TM. We then want to let the type 0 grammar finish the derivation of that word—in our example, the word *abba*—by letting it mop up all the garbage left in the working string. The garbage is of several kinds: There are Δ's, the characters in Γ, the q-symbol for the HALT state itself, and, let us not forget, the extra *a*'s and *b*'s that are lying around on what we think are TAPE-simulating locations, but which just as easily could be mistaken for parts of the final word, and then, of course, the parentheses.

We also want to be very careful not to trigger this mop-up operation unless we have actually reached a HALT state.

We cannot simply add the productions

$$\text{Unwanted symbols} \rightarrow \Lambda$$

because this would allow us to accept any input string at any time. Remember in a grammar (phrase-structure or other) we are at all times free to execute any production that can apply. To force the sequencing of productions, we must have some productions that introduce symbols that certain other productions need before they can be applied. What we need is something like

If there is a HALT state in the working string, then unwanted symbols $\rightarrow \Lambda$.

We can actually accomplish this conditional wipe-out in type 0 grammars in the following way: Suppose q_{11} is a HALT state. We first add productions that allow us to put a copy of q_{11} in front of each set of parentheses. This requires all possible productions of these two forms:

$$(\text{Symbol}_1 \text{Symbol}_2)q_{11} \rightarrow q_{11}(\text{Symbol}_1 \text{Symbol}_2)q_{11}$$

where Symbol$_1$ and Symbol$_2$ are any possible parenthesized pair. This allows q_{11} to propagate to the left. We do this for HALT states and only HALT states.
We also need

$$q_{11}(\text{Symbol}_1\text{Symbol}_2) \rightarrow q_{11}(\text{Symbol}_1\text{Symbol}_2)q_{11}$$

allowing q_{11} to propagate to the right.

This will let us spread the q_{11} to the front of each factor as soon as it makes its appearance in the working string. It is like a cold: Every factor catches it. In this example, we start with q_{11} in front of only one parenthesized pair and let it spread until it sits in front of every parenthesized pair:

$$(aA)(bB)q_{11}(bB)(aX)(\Delta X)(\Delta M)$$
$$\Rightarrow (aA)q_{11}(bB)q_{11}(bB)(aX)(\Delta X)(\Delta M)$$
$$\Rightarrow q_{11}(aA)q_{11}(bB)q_{11}(bB)(aX)(\Delta X)(\Delta M)$$
$$\Rightarrow q_{11}(aA)q_{11}(bB)q_{11}(bB)q_{11}(aX)(\Delta X)(\Delta M)$$
$$\Rightarrow q_{11}(aA)q_{11}(bB)q_{11}(bB)q_{11}(aX)q_{11}(\Delta X)(\Delta M)$$
$$\Rightarrow q_{11}(aA)q_{11}(bB)q_{11}(bB)q_{11}(aX)q_{11}(\Delta X)q_{11}(\Delta M)$$

The q's that are not HALT states cannot be spread because we do not include such productions in our grammar to spread them.

Now we can include the garbage-removal productions

$$q_{11}(a \text{ Symbol}_1) \rightarrow a$$
$$q_{11}(b \text{ Symbol}_1) \rightarrow b$$
$$q_{11}(\Delta \text{ Symbol}_1) \rightarrow \Lambda$$

for any choice of Symbol$_1$. This will rid us of all the TAPE simulation characters, the extra Δ's, and the parentheses, leaving only the first copy of the original input string we were testing. Only the immutable copy remains; the scaffolding is completely removed. ∎

ALGORITHM

Here are the formal rules describing the grammar we have in mind. In general, the productions for the desired type 0 grammar are the following, where we presume that S, X, Y are not letters in Σ or Γ:

PROD 1 $S \rightarrow q_0 X$

PROD 2 $X \rightarrow (aa)X$

PROD 3 $X \rightarrow (bb)X$

PROD 4 $X \rightarrow Y$ ·

PROD 5 $Y \rightarrow (\Delta\Delta)Y$

PROD 6 $Y \rightarrow \Lambda$

PROD 7   For all TM edges of the form

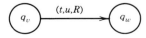

create the productions

$$q_v(at) \rightarrow (au)q_w$$
$$q_v(bt) \rightarrow (bu)q_w$$
$$q_v(\Delta t) \rightarrow (\Delta u)q_w$$

PROD 8   For all TM edges of the form

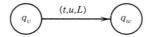

create the productions

$$(\text{Symbol}_1 \text{Symbol}_2) q_v (\text{Symbol}_3 t) \rightarrow q_w (\text{Symbol}_1 \text{Symbol}_2)(\text{Symbol}_3 u)$$

where Symbol_1 and Symbol_3 can each be a, b, or Δ and Symbol_2 can be any character appearing on the TM TAPE, that is, any character in Γ.

PROD 9   If q_x is a HALT state in the TM, create these productions:

$$q_x(\text{Symbol}_1 \text{Symbol}_2) \rightarrow q_x(\text{Symbol}_1 \text{Symbol}_2) q_x$$
$$(\text{Symbol}_1 \text{Symbol}_2) q_x \rightarrow q_x(\text{Symbol}_1 \text{Symbol}_2) q_x$$

$$q_x(a\ \text{Symbol}_2) \rightarrow a$$
$$q_x(b\ \text{Symbol}_2) \rightarrow b$$
$$q_x(\Delta\ \text{Symbol}_2) \rightarrow \Lambda$$

where $\text{Symbol}_1 = a$, b, or Δ and Symbol_2 is any character in Γ.

These are all the productions we need or want in the grammar.   ■

Notice that PRODS 1 through 7 are the same for all TMs. Production sets 7, 8, and 9 depend on the particular TM being simulated.

Now come the remarks that convince us that this is the right grammar (or at least one of them). Because we must start with S, we begin with PROD 1. We can then apply any sequence of PROD 2's and PROD 3's so that, for any string such as *baa*, we can produce

$$S \overset{*}{\Rightarrow} q_0(bb)(aa)(aa)X$$

We can do this for any string whether it can be accepted by the TM or not. We have not yet formed a word, just a working string. If *baa* can be accepted by the TM, there is a certain amount of additional space it needs on the TAPE to do so, say, two more cells. We can create this work space by using PRODS 4, 5, and 6 as follows:

$$\Rightarrow q_0(bb)(aa)(aa)Y$$
$$\Rightarrow q_0(bb)(aa)(aa)(\Delta\Delta)Y$$
$$\Rightarrow q_0(bb)(aa)(aa)(\Delta\Delta)(\Delta\Delta)Y$$
$$\Rightarrow q_0(bb)(aa)(aa)(\Delta\Delta)(\Delta\Delta)$$

Other than the minor variation of leaving the Y lying around until the end and eventually erasing it, this is exactly how all derivations from this grammar must begin. The other productions cannot be applied yet because their left sides include nonterminals that have not yet been incorporated into the working string.

Now suppose that q_4 is the only HALT state in the TM. In order ever to remove the parentheses from the working string, we must eventually reach exactly this situation:

$$\overset{*}{\Rightarrow} q_4(b?)q_4(a?)q_4(a?)q_4(\Delta?)q_4(\Delta?)$$

where the five ?'s show some contents of the first five cells of the TM TAPE at the time it accepts the string *baa*. Notice that no rule of production can ever let us change the first entry inside a parenthesized pair. This is our intact copy of the input to our simulated TM.

We could only arrive at a working string of this form if, while simulating the processing of the TM, we entered the HALT state q_4 at some stage:

$$\overset{*}{\Rightarrow} (b?)(a?)q_4(a?)(\Delta?)(\Delta?)$$

When this happened, we then applied PROD 9 to spread the q_4's.

Once we have q_4 in front of every open parenthesis, we use PROD 9 again to reduce the whole working string to a string of all terminals:

$$\overset{*}{\Rightarrow} baa$$

All strings such as *ba* or *abba* . . . can be set up in the form

$$q_0(aa)(bb)(bb)(aa) \ . \ . \ . \ (\Delta\Delta)(\Delta\Delta) \ . \ . \ . \ (\Delta\Delta)$$

but only those that can then be TM-processed to get to the HALT state can ever be reduced to a string of all terminals by PROD 9.

Notice that we can use PROD 9 to put a HALT state q_x behind the last parenthesis at the end of the working string. However, if we do, it will never be removed by PROD 9 rules, and so it is self-destructive to do so.

In short, all words accepted by the TM can be generated by this grammar and all words generated by this grammar can be accepted by the TM. ∎

EXAMPLE

Let us consider a simple TM that accepts all words ending in *a*:

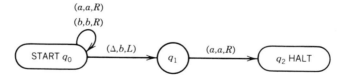

Note that the label on the edge from q_0 to q_1 could just as well have been (Δ, Δ, L), but this works too.

Any word accepted by this TM uses exactly one more cell of TAPE than the space the input is written on. Therefore, we can begin with the productions

$$\begin{aligned}
&\text{PROD } 1 \quad S \rightarrow q_0 X \\
&\text{PROD } 2 \quad X \rightarrow (aa)X \\
&\text{PROD } 3 \quad X \rightarrow (bb)X \\
&\text{PROD } 4 \quad X \rightarrow (\Delta\Delta)
\end{aligned}$$

This is a minor variation, omitting the need for the nonterminal Y and PRODS 4, 5, and 6.

Now there are four labeled edges in the TM; three move the TAPE HEAD right, one left. These cause the formation of the following productions. From

we get

PROD 7(i) $q_0(aa) \rightarrow (aa)q_0$
PROD 7(ii) $q_0(ba) \rightarrow (ba)q_0$
PROD 7(iii) $q_0(\Delta a) \rightarrow (\Delta a)q_0$

From

we get

PROD 7(iv) $q_0(ab) \rightarrow (ab)q_0$
PROD 7(v) $q_0(bb) \rightarrow (bb)q_0$
PROD 7(vi) $q_0(\Delta b) \rightarrow (\Delta b)q_0$

From

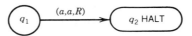

we get

PROD 7(vii) $q_1(aa) \rightarrow (aa)q_2$
PROD 7(viii) $q_1(ba) \rightarrow (ba)q_2$
PROD 7(ix) $q_1(\Delta a) \rightarrow (\Delta a)q_2$

From

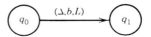

we get

PROD 8 $(uv)q_0(w\Delta) \rightarrow q_1(uv)(wb)$

where u, v, and w can each be a, b, or Δ. (Because there are really 27 of these, let us pretend we have written them all out.)

Because q_2 is the HALT state, we have

PROD 9(i) $q_2(uv) \rightarrow q_2(uv)q_2$ where $u, v = a, b, \Delta$
PROD 9(ii) $(uv)q_2 \rightarrow q_2(uv)q_2$ where $u, v = a, b, \Delta$
PROD 9(iii) $q_2(au) \rightarrow a$ where $u = a, b, \Delta$
PROD 9(iv) $q_2(bu) \rightarrow b$ where $u = a, b, \Delta$
PROD 9(v) $q_2(\Delta u) \rightarrow \Lambda$ where $u = a, b, \Delta$

These are all the productions of the type 0 grammar suggested by the algorithm in the proof of Theorem 76 (p. 575).

Let us examine the total derivation of the word *baa*:

TM Simulation

State	Tape	Derivation	Production No.
		$S \Rightarrow q_0 X$	1
		$\Rightarrow q_0(bb)X$	3
		$\Rightarrow q_0(bb)(aa)X$	2
		$\Rightarrow q_0(bb)(aa)(aa)X$	2
q_0	$b\;a\;a\;\Delta\;\cdots$	$\Rightarrow q_0(bb)(aa)(aa)(\Delta\Delta)$	4
q_0	$b\;a\;a\;\Delta\;\cdots$	$\Rightarrow (bb)q_0(aa)(aa)(\Delta\Delta)$	7v
q_0	$b\;a\;a\;\Delta\;\cdots$	$\Rightarrow (bb)(aa)q_0(aa)(\Delta\Delta)$	7i
q_0	$b\;a\;a\;\Delta\;\cdots$	$\Rightarrow (bb)(aa)(aa)q_0(\Delta\Delta)$	7i
q_1	$b\;a\;a\;b\;\cdots$	$\Rightarrow (bb)(aa)q_1(aa)(\Delta b)$	8 $u = a$, $v = a, w = \Delta$
q_2	$b\;a\;a\;b$	$\Rightarrow (bb)(aa)(aa)q_2(\Delta b)$	7vii

= HALT

		Derivation	Production No.
		$\Rightarrow (bb)(aa)q_2(aa)q_2(\Delta b)$	9ii, $u = a, v = a$
		$\Rightarrow (bb)q_2(aa)q_2(aa)q_2(\Delta b)$	9ii, $u = a, v = a$
		$\Rightarrow q_2(bb)q_2(aa)q_2(aa)q_2(\Delta b)$	9ii, $u = b, v = b$
		$\Rightarrow bq_2(aa)q_2(aa)q_2(\Delta b)$	9iv
		$\Rightarrow baq_2(aa)q_2(\Delta b)$	9iii
		$\Rightarrow baaq_2(\Delta b)$	9iii
		$\Rightarrow baa$	9v

Notice that the first several steps are a setting-up operation and the last several steps are cleanup.

In the setting-up stages, we could have set up any string of a's and b's. In this respect, grammars are nondeterministic. We can apply these productions in several ways. If we set up a word that the TM would not accept, then we could never complete its derivation because cleanup can occur only once the HALT state symbol has been inserted into the working string, as this can only be when the TM being simulated has reached HALT. Once we have actually begun the TM simulation, the productions are determined, reflecting the fact that TMs are deterministic.

Once we have reached the cleanup stage, we again develop choices. We could follow something like the sequence shown. Although there are other successful ways of propagating the q_2 (first to the left, then to the right, then to the left again . . .), they all lead to the same completely saturated working string with a q_2 in front of everything. If they do not, the cleanup stage will not work and an all-terminal string will not be produced. ∎

Now that we have the tool of type 0 grammars, we can approach some other results about recursively enumerable languages that were too difficult to handle in Chapter 23 when we could only use TMs for the proofs, or can we?

⚜ THE PRODUCT AND KLEENE CLOSURE OF r.e. LANGUAGES

THEOREM 77

If L_1 and L_2 are recursively enumerable languages, then so is L_1L_2. The recursively enumerable languages are closed under product.

PROOF

The proof will be by the same constructive algorithm we used to prove Theorem 37 (p. 380).

Let L_1 and L_2 be generated by type 0 grammars. Add the subscript 1 to all the nonterminals in the grammar for L_1 (even the start symbol, which becomes S_1). Add the subscript 2 to all the nonterminals in the grammar for L_2.

Form a new type 0 grammar that has all the productions from the grammars for L_1 and L_2 plus the new start symbol S and the new production

$$S \rightarrow S_1 S_2$$

This grammar generates all the words in L_1L_2 and only the words in L_1L_2. The grammar is type 0, so the language L_1L_2 is r.e. No? No.

Surprisingly, this proof is bogus. Consider the type 0 grammar

$$S \rightarrow a$$
$$aS \rightarrow b$$

The language L generated by this grammar is the single word a, but the grammar for the language LL that we have described in this alleged proof is

$$S \rightarrow S_1 S_2$$
$$S_1 \rightarrow a \qquad S_2 \rightarrow a$$
$$aS_1 \rightarrow b \qquad aS_2 \rightarrow b$$

which allows the derivation

$$S \Rightarrow S_1 S_2$$
$$\Rightarrow aS_2$$
$$\Rightarrow b$$

while, clearly, LL contains only the word aa.

What goes wrong here is that in the proof for CFGs the possible substitutions represented by the productions of the two languages could not interact because the right side of each production was a single nonterminal indexed by its grammar of origin. However, in this situation substrings could occur in the working string spanning the break between that which comes from S_1 and that which comes from S_2. These substrings might conceivably be the left side of some production lying entirely with one of these languages, but a production that could not arise within S_1 or S_2 alone.

In order to prevent this, we use the following trick. We index even the terminals in each grammar with the subscript of its grammar. In this way, we turn the terminals into nonterminals for the purpose of keeping the left sides of the rules of production distinct. What we suggest is that a production in L_1 like

$$abXSbS \rightarrow bXX$$

becomes

$$a_1 b_1 X_1 S_1 b_1 S_1 \rightarrow b_1 X_1 X_1$$

We also have to add the productions

$$a_1 \rightarrow a \qquad b_1 \rightarrow b \qquad a_2 \rightarrow a \qquad b_2 \rightarrow b$$

so that we can finally reach a string of a's and b's as a final word in the product language.

We do not have to worry that a derivation will de-subscript the a's and b's prematurely and recreate the problem that we had before, because no substring of the working string, spanning the break in languages, can be the left side of any production in S_2 because all such left sides have every factor subscripted with a 2.

This then completes the proof of the theorem by constructive algorithm. ∎

THEOREM 78

If L is recursively enumerable, then $L*$ is also. The r.e. languages are closed under Keene star.

PROOF

If we try to prove this theorem by a constructive algorithm similar to that for Theorem 38 (p. 384) for CFGs, we would start with

$$S \rightarrow SS \mid \Lambda$$

and allow each S to produce an arbitrarily long sequence of S's, each turning into a word of L. However, we may encounter the same problem that we saw in the last theorem. Some of the S's would produce strings of terminals that can conceivably attach themselves onto part of the derivation from the next S and make an otherwise unreachable production possible. The idea that we could index each copy of the productions from S with a separate index runs into a separate problem. Because the number of words from L that we wish to concatenate to form a word in $L*$ is potentially unbounded, the number of copies of S we need to make initially is also unbounded. This means that, because each S is to become a different nonterminal, the total number of nonterminals in the grammar is potentially unbounded. This violates the definition of a grammar — even a type 0 grammar.

In order to keep the nonterminals in neighboring syllables from interacting, all we need is two copies of the grammar for L, one indexed with 1's (even the a's and b's) and one indexed with 2's. We must then be sure that from the initial S we derive only alternating types of S's. The following productions will do the trick:

$$S \rightarrow S_1 S_2 S \mid S_1 \mid \Lambda$$

From this S we can produce only the strings Λ, S_1, $S_1 S_2$, $S_1 S_2 S_1$, $S_1 S_2 S_1 S_2$, ... Again, we can have no cross-pollination of the derivations from neighboring S's. This and the indexing of the entire grammar for L and the productions de-subscripting the terminals constitute the complete grammar for $L*$. ∎

EXAMPLE

If L is the language generated by the type 0 grammar

$$S \rightarrow a \qquad aS \rightarrow b$$

then $L*$ is generated by the grammar

$$S \rightarrow S_1 S_2 S \mid S_1 \mid \Lambda$$
$$S_1 \rightarrow a_1$$
$$a_1 S_1 \rightarrow b_1$$
$$S_2 \rightarrow a_2$$
$$a_2 S_2 \rightarrow b_2$$
$$a_1 \rightarrow a \qquad b_1 \rightarrow b \qquad a_2 \rightarrow a \qquad b_2 \rightarrow b$$ ■

⚜ CONTEXT-SENSITIVE GRAMMARS

DEFINITION

A generative grammar in which the left side of each production is not longer than the right side is called a **context-sensitive grammar,** denoted CSG, or type 1 by the table on p. 573. ■

Context-sensitive languages are actually what we presume to be the model for all human languages, but because we do not have a mathematical definition for the class of "human languages," we cannot expect to have a mathematical proof of this fact. One thing that we do know about context-sensitive languages is that they are recursive.

THEOREM 79

For every context-sensitive grammar G, there is some special TM that accepts all the words generated by G and crashes for all other inputs.

PROOF

Let us assume the input string we are going to test is w, and we shall describe how T works on w.

All the rules of production in a type 1 grammar do not shorten the working string. They may lengthen it or leave it the same length. So, the derivation for w is a sequence of working strings, each as long as or longer than the one before it.

In the shortest derivation for w, there is no looping, by which we mean that each working string is different. It may be possible in the grammar G to replace XY with ZW and then ZW with XY to get the same working string a second time, but it cannot be necessary to do so, and it cannot be part of the shortest derivation.

A derivation is a path in the total language tree of G, which is just like the total language trees for CFGs. We start at S and derive a second row by applying all the productions applicable to produce new nodes of the tree. We can then reiterate the procedure and apply all productions possible to each existing node in a given row to produce the next row of the tree. Every time we produce a new node, we check to be sure that it is different from all the other previously derived nodes.

Our particular TM will not generate the entire language derivable from G. It will terminate any branch of the tree whose end node exceeds w in length. This will then be a finite tree because there are only finitely many strings of characters from G of length w or less. Therefore, in a finite number of steps, it will either find a derivation for w, determine that there is none, or crash.

Can a TM do all this? Of course. We start with w and insert markers around it. Then we write S. Next we put a row marker to indicate that we are starting a new row of the tree. Subsequently we enter a state that scans all the nodes on the previous row to see which have substrings that are left sides of some rule of production in G. This TM is a specialized machine and has all the information about the productions in G programmed into it, so this scanning procedure is part of the TM program. The machine then copies the old node and makes the substitution (using the appropriate sequence of DELETES and INSERTS) and then checks to see if the new node it just made is worth keeping. This means that the string is not a duplicate of another node and not longer than w. Then we check to see whether the new node is w. If it is, we go to HALT. If it is not, we put a node marker on the TAPE and return to the next node of the previous row not yet fully exploited (having left an indication of where we already have been). Once we have explored all the nodes on the previous row, we have finished creating the new row of the tree, and we place a row marker on the TAPE and reiterate.

This TM will terminate if it does generate w, or if it finds that while operating on a certain row, it was able to contribute no new nodes to the next row. This is recognized by seeing whether it prints two consecutive row markers. If it does this, it crashes. By the discussion above, it must eventually do one of these two things. Therefore, this TM proves the language of G is recursive. ∎

Why does this construction work for all type 1 grammar*s and y*et not carry over to show that all type 0 grammars are also recursive? The answer is that because type 0 grammars can have productions that decrease the length of the working string, we cannot use the simple length analysis to be sure that w does not lie somewhere farther down any particular branch of the tree. No branches can be terminated and the tree may grow indefinitely.

Knowing that a language is recursive translates into being able to decide membership for it.

THEOREM 80

Given G, a context-sensitive grammar, and w, an input string, it is decidable by a TM whether G generates w.

PROOF

We have not been very specific about how one inputs a grammar into a TM, but we can imagine some string of delimiters separating the productions, possibly allowing the production arrow to be a TAPE character as well. What the TM we have in mind does is create the CWL code word for the TM based on G described in the previous theorem. Then it feeds both the coded TM and w into the universal TM. Because w either halts or crashes on the coded TM, this procedure will, indeed, lead to a decision about w's membership in the language generated by G. ∎

THEOREM 81

There is at least one language L that is recursive but not context-sensitive.

PROOF

This we shall prove by constructing one.

In the previous theorem, we indicated that there was some method for encoding an entire context-sensitive grammar into a single string of symbols. Listing the productions in any order with their arrows and some special symbol as a separator is fine, because then a TM can decide whether, given an input string, it is the code word for some CSG. It would have to see that between any two separators there was one and only one arrow and that the string on the right of the arrow was not shorter than the string on the left. It would also have to ensure that the left side of each production has some nonterminals. All these are elementary TM tasks.

Let us define the language L (we ran out of Turing's names) as follows:

$L = \{$all the code words for context-sensitive grammars that cannot be generated by the very grammars they encode$\}$

Observation

L is recursive. We can feed any string over the code word alphabet first into the TM that checks to be sure it represents a CSG and then into the membership testing machine both as gram*mar a*nd input. This will definitely decide whether the input is a code word for a grammar that accepts it; only it returns the exact opposite answer to the one we want for L. We can either modify the machine to reverse HALT and crash (as we have done before) or use this TM the way it is now to show that the complement of L is recursive, and conclude that L is recursive that way.

Observation

L is not a context-sensitive language. If it were, then all its words would be generated by some CSG G. Let us consider the code word for G. If this code word is in L, then (as with words in L) it cannot be generated by the grammar it represents. But that would mean that some word in L cannot be generated by G, which is a contradiction. On the other hand, if the code word for G is not in L, that means the code word for G cannot be generated by the grammar it represents, and as such, by the definition of L, must be in L. Another contradiction. The solution is that there is no such grammar G.

Taking the two observations together proves L is our counter-example.   ∎

⚜ PROBLEMS

For problems 1, 2, and 3 consider the grammar

$$\begin{array}{ll} \text{PROD 1} & S \rightarrow ABS \mid \Lambda \\ \text{PROD 2} & AB \rightarrow BA \\ \text{PROD 3} & BA \rightarrow AB \\ \text{PROD 4} & A \rightarrow a \\ \text{PROD 5} & B \rightarrow b \end{array}$$

1. Derive the following words from this grammar:
   (i) *abba*
   (ii) *babaabbbaa*

2. Prove that every word generated by this grammar has an equal number of a's and b's.

3. Prove that all words with an equal number of a's and b's can be generated by this grammar.

4. (i) Find a grammar that generates all words with more a's than b's, MOREA p. 205.
   (ii) Find a grammar that generates all the words not in EQUAL.
      (iii) Is EQUAL recursive?

For Problems 5 through 7, consider the following grammar over the alphabet $\Sigma = \{a \quad b \quad c\}$:

$$\begin{array}{ll} \text{PROD 1} & S \rightarrow ABCS \mid \Lambda \\ \text{PROD 2} & AB \rightarrow BA \\ \text{PROD 3} & BC \rightarrow CB \\ \text{PROD 4} & AC \rightarrow CA \\ \text{PROD 5} & BA \rightarrow AB \end{array}$$

$$\text{Prod 6} \quad CB \rightarrow BC$$
$$\text{Prod 7} \quad CA \rightarrow AC$$
$$\text{Prod 8} \quad A \rightarrow a$$
$$\text{Prod 9} \quad B \rightarrow b$$
$$\text{Prod 10} \quad C \rightarrow c$$

5. Derive the following words:

   (i) *ababcc*

  (ii) *cbaabccba*

6. Prove that all words generated by this grammar have equal numbers of a's, b's, and c's.

7. Prove that all words with an equal number of a's, b's, and c's can be generated by this grammar, the language VERYEQUAL, p. 375.

Problems 8 through 10 consider the following type 0 grammar over the alphabet $\Sigma = \{a \quad b\}$:

$$\text{Prod 1} \quad S \rightarrow UVX$$
$$\text{Prod 2} \quad UV \rightarrow aUY$$
$$\text{Prod 3} \quad UV \rightarrow bUZ$$
$$\text{Prod 4} \quad YX \rightarrow VaX$$
$$\text{Prod 5} \quad ZX \rightarrow VbX$$
$$\text{Prod 6} \quad Ya \rightarrow aY$$
$$\text{Prod 7} \quad Yb \rightarrow bY$$
$$\text{Prod 8} \quad Za \rightarrow aZ$$
$$\text{Prod 9} \quad Zb \rightarrow bZ$$
$$\text{Prod 10} \quad UV \rightarrow \Lambda$$
$$\text{Prod 11} \quad X \rightarrow \Lambda$$
$$\text{Prod 12} \quad aV \rightarrow Va$$
$$\text{Prod 13} \quad bV \rightarrow Vb$$

8. Derive the following words from this grammar:

    (i) Λ

   (ii) *aa*

  (iii) *bb*

  (iv) *abab*

9. Show that if w is any string of a's and b's, then the word

$$ww$$

can be generated by this grammar.

10. Suppose that in a certain generation from S we arrive at the working string

$$wUVwX$$

where w is some string of a's and b's.

   (i) Show that if we now apply Prod 10, we will end up with the word ww.

  (ii) Show that if instead we apply Prod 11, first we cannot derive any other words.

  (iii) Show that if instead we apply Prod 2, we must derive the working string

$$waUVwaX$$

  (iv) Show that if instead we apply Prod 3, we must derive the working string

$$wbUVwbX$$

(v) Use the fact that UVX is of the form $wUVwX$ with $w = \Lambda$ to prove that all words generated by this grammar are in the language DOUBLEWORD (p. 200).

11. Consider the following type 0 grammar over the alphabet $\Sigma = \{a\}$. *Note:* There is no b.

$$
\begin{array}{lll}
\text{PROD 1} & S & \rightarrow a \\
\text{PROD 2} & S & \rightarrow CD \\
\text{PROD 3} & C & \rightarrow ACB \\
\text{PROD 4} & C & \rightarrow AB \\
\text{PROD 5} & AB & \rightarrow aBA \\
\text{PROD 6} & Aa & \rightarrow aA \\
\text{PROD 7} & Ba & \rightarrow aB \\
\text{PROD 8} & AD & \rightarrow Da \\
\text{PROD 9} & BD & \rightarrow Ea \\
\text{PROD 10} & BE & \rightarrow Ea \\
\text{PROD 11} & E & \rightarrow a
\end{array}
$$

(i) Draw the total language tree of this language to find all words of five or fewer letters generated by this grammar.

(ii) Generate the word $a^9 = aaaaaaaaa$.

(iii) Show that for any $n = 1, 2, \ldots$, we can derive the working string

$$A^n B^n D$$

(iv) From $A^n B^n D$, show that we can derive the working string

$$a^{n^2} B^n A^n D$$

(v) Show that the working string in part (iv) generates the word

$$a^{(n+1)^2}$$

(vi) Show that the language of this grammar is

$$
\begin{aligned}
\text{SQUARE} &= \{a^{n^2} \quad \text{where } n = 1 \quad 2 \quad 3 \ldots\} \\
&= \{a \quad\quad aaaa \quad a^9 \quad a^{16} \ldots\}
\end{aligned}
$$

12. What language is generated by the grammar

$$
\begin{array}{lll}
\text{PROD 1} & S & \rightarrow aXYba \\
\text{PROD 2} & XY & \rightarrow XYbZ \mid \Lambda \\
\text{PROD 3} & Zb & \rightarrow bZ \\
\text{PROD 4} & Za & \rightarrow aa
\end{array}
$$

Prove any claim.

13. Analyze the following type 0 grammar:

$$
\begin{array}{lll}
\text{PROD 1} & S & \rightarrow A \\
\text{PROD 2} & A & \rightarrow aABC \\
\text{PROD 3} & A & \rightarrow abC \\
\text{PROD 4} & CB & \rightarrow BC \\
\text{PROD 5} & bB & \rightarrow bb \\
\text{PROD 6} & bC & \rightarrow b
\end{array}
$$

(i) What are the four smallest words produced by this grammar?

(ii) What is the language of this grammar?

14. Show that the class of context-sensitive language is closed under union.

15. Show that the class of context-sensitive languages is closed under product.

16. Show that the class of context-sensitive languages is closed under intersection.

17. Show that the class of context-sensitive languages is closed under Kleene closure.

18. Show that if L is a CSL, then so is transpose(L).

19. A context-sensitive language is said to be in Kuroda normal form (after S. Y. Kuroda) if every production is of one of the following four forms:

$$A \rightarrow a$$
$$A \rightarrow B$$
$$A \rightarrow BC$$
$$AB \rightarrow CD$$

(i) Show that for every CSL there is a CSG in Kuroda normal form that generates it.
(ii) Can this KNF be useful as a tool in parsing, that is, in deciding membership?

20. In the proof that every type 1 grammar can be accepted by some TM, we simulated the productions of the grammar by a series of DELETEs followed by a series of INSERTs.

(i) Show that if the grammar being simulated were context-sensitive, the working string simulation field would never be larger than the input itself.
(ii) Show that this means that the total length of the section of the TM TAPE being used in the simulation reaches a maximum of $2n + 2$ cells, where n is the length of the input string. This is a simple linear function of the size of the input. This is what is meant by the terminology "linear bounded automaton."

CHAPTER 25

Computers

⚜ DEFINING THE COMPUTER

The finite automata, as defined in Chapter 5, are only language-acceptors. When we gave them output capabilities, as with Mealy and Moore machines in Chapter 8, we called them *transducers*. The pushdown automata of Chapter 14 similarly do not produce output and are only language-acceptors. However, we recognized their potential as transducers for doing parsing in Chapter 18, by considering what is put into, left in, or popped from the STACK as output.

TMs present a completely different situation. They always have a natural output. When the processing of any given TM terminates, whatever is left on its TAPE can be considered to be the intended, meaningful output. Sometimes, the TAPE is only a scratch pad where the machine has performed some calculations needed to determine whether the input string should be accepted. In this case, what is left on the TAPE is meaningless. For example, one TM that accepts the language EVENPALINDROME works by cancelling a letter each from the front and the back of the input string until there is nothing left. When the machine reaches HALT, the TAPE is empty.

However, we may use TMs for a different purpose. We may start by loading the TAPE with some data that we want to process. Then we run the machine until it reaches the HALT state. At that time, the contents of the TAPE will have been converted into the desired output, which we can interpret as the result of a calculation, the answer to a question, a manipulated file—whatever.

So far, we have been considering only TMs that receive input from the language defined by $(\mathbf{a} + \mathbf{b})^*$. To be a useful calculator for mathematics, we must encode sets of numbers as words in this language. We begin with the encoding of the natural numbers as strings of a's alone:

$$\text{The code for } 0 = \Lambda$$
$$\text{The code for } 1 = a$$
$$\text{The code for } 2 = aa$$
$$\text{The code for } 3 = aaa$$

$$\cdots$$

This is called **unary encoding** because it uses one digit (as opposed to binary, which uses two digits, or decimal with ten).

Every word in $(\mathbf{a} + \mathbf{b})^*$ can then be interpreted as a sequence of numbers (strings of a's) separated internally by b's. For example, the decoding of ($abaa$) is 1, 2 and

$$bbabbaa = (\text{no } a\text{'s})b(\text{no } a\text{'s})b(\text{one } a)b(\text{no } a\text{'s})b(\text{two } a\text{'s})$$

represents 0, 0, 1, 0, 2.

Notice that we are assuming that there is a group of a's at the beginning of the string and at the end even though these may be groups of no a's. For example,

$$abaabb = (\text{one } a)b(\text{two } a\text{'s})b(\text{no } a\text{'s})b(\text{no } a\text{'s})$$

which represents 1, 2, 0, 0.

When we interpret strings of a's and b's in this way, a TM that starts with an input string of a's and b's on its TAPE and leaves an output string of a's and b's on its TAPE can be considered to take in a sequence of specific input numbers and, after performing certain calculations, leaves as a final result another sequence of numbers—output numbers.

We are considering here only TMs that leave a's and b's on their TAPES; no special symbols or extraneous spaces are allowed among the letters, unless they too are given special output meanings.

We have already seen TMs that fit this description that had no idea they were actually performing data processing, because the interpretation of strings of letters as strings of numbers never occurred to them. "Calculation" is one of those words that we never really had a good definition for. Perhaps we are at last in a position to correct this.

EXAMPLE

Consider the following TM called ADDER:

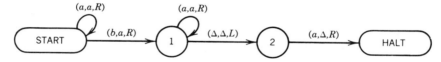

In START, we skip over some initial clump of a's, leaving them unchanged. When we read a b, we change it to an a and move to state 1. In state 1, a second b would make us crash. We skip over a second clump of a's until we run out of input string and find a Δ. At this point, we go to state 2, but we move the TAPE HEAD *left*. We have now backed up into the a's. There must be at least one a here because we changed a b into an a to get to state 1. Therefore, when we first arrive at state 2, we erase an a and move the TAPE HEAD right to HALT and terminate execution.

For an input string to be accepted (lead to HALT), it has to be of the form **a*ba***. If we start with the input string $a^n b a^m$, we end up with a^{n+m} on the TAPE.

When we decode strings as sequences of numbers as above, we identify $a^n b a^m$ with the two numbers n and m. The output of the TM is decoded as $(n + m)$.

Under this interpretation, ADDER takes two numbers as input and leaves their sum on the TAPE as output.

This is our most primitive example of a TM intentionally working as a calculator. ∎

If we used an input string not in the form **a*ba***, the machine would crash. This is analogous to our computer programs crashing if the input data are not in the correct format.

Our choice of unary notation is not essential; we could build an "adding machine" for any other base as well.

EXAMPLE

Let us build a TM that adds two numbers presented in binary notation and leaves the answer on the TAPE in binary notation.

We shall construct this TM out of two parts. First, we consider the TM T_1 shown below:

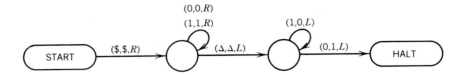

This TM presumes that the input is of the form

$$\$(0 + 1)*$$

It finds the last bit of the binary number and reverses it; that is, 0 becomes 1, 1 becomes 0. If the last bit was a 1, it backs up to the left and changes the whole clump of 1's to 0's, and the first 0 to the left of these 1's turns into a 1. All in all, this TM adds 1 to the binary number after the $. If the input was of the form $\$1*$, the machine finds no 0 and crashes.

In general, T_1 increments by 1.

Now let us consider the TM T_2. This machine will accept a nonzero number in binary and subtract 1 from it. The input is presumed to be of the form $\$(0 + 1)*\$$ but not $\$0*\$$.

The subtraction will be done in a three-step process:

Step 1   Reverse the 0's and 1's between the $'s. This is called taking the 1's complement.

Step 2   Use T_1 to add 1 to the number now between the $'s. Notice that if the original number was not 0, the 1's complement is not a forbidden input to T_1 (i.e., not all 1's).

Step 3   Reverse the 0's and 1's again.

The total result is that what was x will become $x - 1$.

The mathematical justification for this is that the 1's complement of x (if it is n bits long) is the binary representation of the number

$$(2^n - 1) - x$$

Because when x is added to it, it becomes n solid 1's $= 2^n - 1$.

x becomes $(2^n - 1) - x$ (Step 1)

Which becomes $(2^n - 1) - x + 1 = (2^n - 1) - (x - 1)$, the 1's complement of $x - 1$ (Step 2)

Which becomes $(2^n - 1) - [(2^n - 1) - (x - 1)] = (x - 1)$ (Step 3)

For example,

$$\$1010\$ = \text{binary for } 10$$

Becomes $\$0101\$ = $ binary for 5
Becomes $\$0110\$ = $ binary for 6
Becomes $\$1001\$ = $ binary for 9

T_2 is next shown.

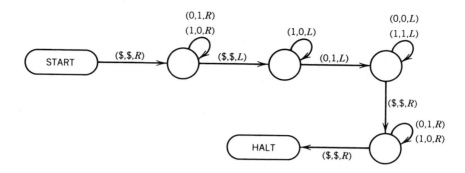

We generally say T_2 decrements by 1.

The binary adder we shall now build works as follows: The input strings will be of the form

$$\$(0 + 1)*\$(0 + 1)*$$

which we call

$$\$\ x\text{-part}\quad\$\ y\text{-part}$$

We shall interpret the x-part and y-part as numbers in binary that are to be added. Furthermore, we make the assumption that the total $x + y$ has no more bits than y itself. This is analogous to the addition of numbers in the arithmetic registers of a computer where we presume that there will be no overflow.

If y is the larger number and starts with the bit 0, the condition is guaranteed. If not, we can INSERT 0 in front of y.

The algorithm to calculate $x + y$ in binary will be this:

Step 1 Check the x-part to see whether it is 0. If yes, halt. If no, proceed.
Step 2 Subtract 1 from the x-part using T_2 above.
Step 3 Add 1 to the y-part using T_1 above.
Step 4 Go to step 1.

The final result will be

$$\$\ 0\ *\$\quad (x + y \text{ in binary})$$

Let us roughly illustrate the algorithm using analogous decimal numbers:

	$4$7
Becomes	$3$8
Becomes	$2$9
Becomes	$1$10
Becomes	$0$11

The full TM is

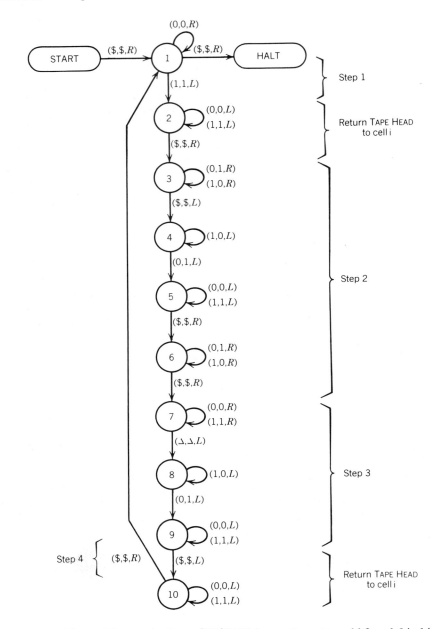

Let us run this machine on the input $10$0110 in an attempt to add 2 and 6 in binary.

	START		1			2		3		3
	$1̲0$0110	→	$10̲$0110		(x ≠ 0)	→	$1̲0$0110	→	$1̲0$0110	→	$0̲0$0110
	3		4			4		5		6		6
→	$0̲1$0110	→	$01̲$0110	→	$0̲0$0110	→	$1̲0$0110	→	$1̲0$0110	→	$0̲0$0110
	6		7			7		7		7
→	$01$0̲110	(x ← x − 1)	→	$01$0̲110	→	$01$01̲10	→	$01$011̲0	→	$01$0110̲
	7		8			9		9		9
→	$01$0110Δ	→	$01$011̲0	→	$01$01̲11	→	$01$0̲111	→	$01$0̲111	→	$01$0̲111
			10			10		10		1		1
(y ← y + 1)	→	$01$0111	→	$0̲1$0111	→	$0̲1$0111	→	$0̲1$0111	→	$01̲$0111

			2		2		3		3	3
	$(\mathbf{x} \neq \mathbf{0})$	→	$\$\underline{0}1\$0111$	→	$\underline{\$}01\$0111$	→	$\$\underline{0}1\$0111$	→	$\$1\underline{1}\$0111$	→ $\$10\underline{\$}0111$
	4		5		5		6		6	6
→	$\$1\underline{0}\$0111$	→	$\$\underline{1}1\$0111$	→	$\underline{\$}11\$0111$	→	$\$\underline{1}1\$0111$	→	$\$0\underline{1}\$0111$	→ $\$00\underline{\$}0111$
			7		7		7		7	7
	$(\mathbf{x} \leftarrow \mathbf{x} - \mathbf{1})$	→	$\$00\$\underline{0}111$	→	$\$00\$0\underline{1}11$	→	$\$00\$01\underline{1}1$	→	$\$00\$011\underline{1}$	→ $\$00\$0111\underline{\Delta}$
	8		8		8		8		9	
→	$\$00\$011\underline{1}$	→	$\$00\$01\underline{1}0$	→	$\$00\$0\underline{1}00$	→	$\$00\$\underline{0}000$	→	$\$00\underline{\$}1000$	$(\mathbf{y} \leftarrow \mathbf{y} + \mathbf{1})$
	10		10		10		1		1	1
→	$\$0\underline{0}\$1000$	→	$\$\underline{0}0\$1000$	→	$\underline{\$}00\$1000$	→	$\$\underline{0}0\$1000$	→	$\$0\underline{0}\$1000$	→ $\$00\underline{\$}1000$
			HALT							
	$(\mathbf{x} = \mathbf{0})$	→	$\$00\$\underline{1}000$							

The correct binary total is 1000, which is on the TAPE when the TM halts. ■

DEFINITION

If a TM has the property that for every word it accepts, at the time it halts, it leaves one solid string of *a*'s and *b*'s on its TAPE starting in cell i, we call it a **computer.** The input string we call the **input** (or **string of input numbers**), and we identify it as a sequence of nonnegative integers. The string left on the TAPE we call the **output** and identify it also as a sequence of nonnegative integers. ■

In the definition above, we use the semiambiguous word "identify" because we do not wish to restrict ourselves to unary encoding or binary encoding or any other particular system.

COMPUTABLE FUNCTIONS

Now we finally know what a computer is. Those expensive boxes of electronics sold as computers are only approximations to the real McCoy. For one thing, they almost never come with an infinite memory like a true TM. At this stage in our consideration, we are dealing only with zero and the positive integers. Negative numbers and numbers with decimal points can be encoded into nonnegative integers for TMs as they are for electronic digital computers. We do not worry about this generality here. Let us define the new symbol "$\dot{-}$" to use instead of the regular minus sign.

DEFINITION

If m and n are nonnegative integers, then their **simple subtraction** is defined as

$$m \dot{-} n = \begin{cases} m - n & \text{if } m \geqslant n \\ 0 & \text{if } m \leqslant n \end{cases}$$

Essentially what $\dot{-}$ does is perform regular subtraction and then rounds all negative answers back up to 0. ■

Simple subtraction is often called **proper subtraction** or even **monus.**

EXAMPLE

Consider the TM below called MINUS:

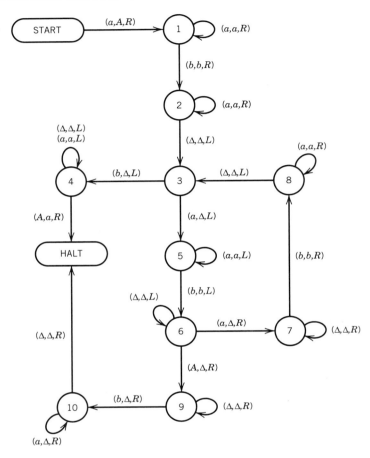

This machine works as follows. To get from START to state 3, the input on the TAPE must have been of the form a^+ba^*, or else the machine would crash. This can be interpreted as starting with two numbers, the first of which is not 0.

Along the way to state 3, we have changed the first a into A—the usual expedient to guarantee that we do not accidentally move left from cell i while backing up.

Notice that the TAPE HEAD is reading the last nonblank character when we enter state 3. If what is being read in state 3 is a b, it signifies that our task (which we have not yet explained) is done. We erase the b and move to state 4. This state leaves all a's and Δ's as it finds them and seeks the A in cell i. When this is found, it is changed back into an a and the process halts.

If the character read in state 3 is an a, a different path is followed. The a is erased while moving to state 5. Here, we move left, seeking the center b. When we find it, we reach state 6 and continue left in search of the last a of the initial group of a's. We find this, erase it, and move to state 7. State 7 moves right, seeking the center b. We cross this going to state 8 where we seek the last a of the second group of a's. When this is located, we return to state 3. The circuit

state 3 — state 5 — state 6 — state 7 — state 8 — state 3

cancels the last a of the second group against the last a of the first group.

For example, what starts as *Aaaaabaa* becomes *Aaaa△ba△*, which then becomes *Aaa△△b△△*. Now from state 3, we follow the path state 3-state 4-HALT, leaving *aaa* on the TAPE alone. This is the correct result of the subtraction $5 \div 2$.

The only possible deviation from this routine is to find that the *a* that is to be cancelled from the first group is the *A* in cell i. This could happen if the two groups of *a*'s are initially the same size, or if the second group is larger:

$$\underline{a}abaa \rightarrow Aab\underline{a}\underline{a} \rightarrow A\underline{a}ba \, \triangle \rightarrow A\triangle b\underline{a} \rightarrow \underline{A}\triangle b \triangle \rightarrow \triangle \underline{\triangle} b \triangle \rightarrow \triangle \, . \, . \, .$$

or

$$\underline{a}abaaa \rightarrow Aab\underline{a}\underline{a}\underline{a} \rightarrow A\underline{a}baa \, \triangle \rightarrow A\triangle baa \rightarrow \underline{A}\triangle ba\triangle \rightarrow \triangle \underline{\triangle} ba\triangle \rightarrow \triangle \, . \, . \, .$$

If this happens, states 9 and 10 erase everything on the TAPE and leave the answer zero (an all-blank TAPE). It is not recorded whether this zero is the exact answer or a rounded-up answer.

If we start with $a^m b a^n$ on the TAPE, we will be left with a^{m-n} unless $m \le n$, in which case we will be left with only blanks.

This machine then performs the operation of simple subtraction as defined by the symbol "$\div$". ∎

Notice that although this TM starts with a string in $(\mathbf{a} + \mathbf{b})^*$ and ends with a string in $(\mathbf{a} + \mathbf{b})^*$, it does use some other symbols in its processing (in this case, *A*).

DEFINITION

If a TM takes a sequence of numbers as input and leaves only one number as output, we say that the computer has acted like a mathematical **function.** Any operation that is defined on all sequences of *K* numbers (for some number $K \ge 1$) and that can be performed by a TM is called **Turing-computable** or just **computable.** ∎

The TMs in the last two examples, ADDER and MINUS, provide a proof of the following theorem.

THEOREM 82

Addition and simple subtraction are computable. ∎

In both of these examples, $K = 2$ (addition and subtraction are both defined on a sequence of two numbers). Both of these are functions (they leave a one-number answer).

THEOREM 83

The function MAX (x, y), which is equal to the larger of the two nonnegative integers *x* and *y*, is computable.

PROOF

We shall prove this by describing a TM that does the job of MAX.

Let us use the old trick of building on previous results, in this case the machine MINUS.

MINUS does make the decision as to which of the two numbers m or n is larger. If m is larger, $m \dot- n$ leaves an a in cell i. If n is larger than (or equal to) m, cell i will contain a Δ. However, after the program is completed, it is too late to leave m or n on the TAPE, because all that remains is $m \dot- n$.

Instead of erasing the a's from the two groups as we do in MINUS, let us make this modification. In the first section, let us turn the a's that we want to erase into x's and let us turn the a's of the second section that we want to erase into y's. For example, what starts as $aaaaabaa$ and on MINUS ends as aaa now should end as $Aaaxxbyy$.

Notice that we have left the middle b instead of erasing it, and we leave the contents of cell i A if it should have been a or, as we shall see, leave it a (if it should have been Δ).

The TM program that performs this algorithm is only a slight modification of MINUS.

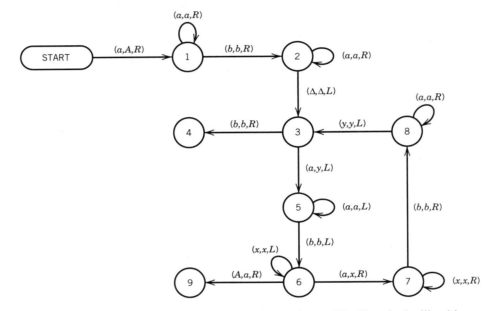

If we arrive at state 4, the first input group of a's is larger. The TAPE looks like this:

$$Aa \ldots aaxx \ldots xxb\underset{.}{y}y \ldots yy$$

with the TAPE HEAD reading the y to the right of the b. To finish the job of MAX, we must go right to the first Δ, then sweep down leftward, erasing all the y's and the b as we go and changing x's into a's, and finally stopping after changing A into a:

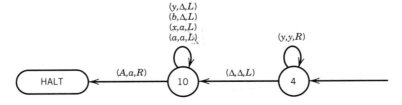

If we arrive at state 9, the second group is larger than or equal to the first. Then TAPE now looks like this:

$$a\underset{.}{x}x \ldots xxbaa \ldots aayy \ldots yy$$

with the TAPE HEAD reading cell ii. Here, what we have to do is leave a number of a's equal to the former constitution of the second group of *a*'s (the current *a*'s and *y*'s together). Now since there are as many symbols before the *b* as *y*'s, all we really need to do is erase the *b* and the *y*'s, change the *x*'s to *a*'s, and shift the other *a*'s one cell to the left (into the hole left by *b*). For example, *axxxbaayyyy* becomes *aaaaΔaaΔΔΔΔ* and then *aaaaaa*.

This TM program does all this:

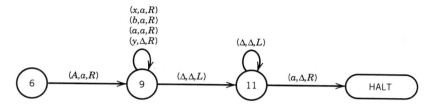

What we actually did was change the *b* into an *a* instead of Δ. That gives us one too many *a*'s, so in state 11 we back up and erase one.

This machine is one of many TMs that does the job of MAX. ∎

EXAMPLE

Let us trace the execution of the input *aaabaa* on this TM:

	1	1	1	2	2	2
aaabaa →	*Aaabaa* →	*Aaabaa* →	*Aaabaa* →	*Aaabaa* →	*Aaabaa* →	*AaabaaΔ*
3	5	5	6	7	8	8
→ *Aaabaa* →	*Aaabay* →	*Aaabay* →	*Aaabay* →	*Aaxbay* →	*Aaxbay* →	*Aaxbay*
3	5	6	6	7	7	8
→ *Aaxbay* →	*Aaxbyy* →	*Aaxbyy* →	*Aaxbyy* →	*Axxbyy* →	*Axxbyy* →	*Axxbyy*
3	4	4	4	10	10	10
→ *Axxbyy* →	*Axxbyy* →	*Axxbyy* →	*AxxbyyΔ* →	*Axxbyy* →	*AxxbyΔ* →	*AxxbΔΔ*
10	10	10	HALT			
→ *AxxΔΔ* →	*AxaΔΔ* →	*AaaΔΔ* →	*aaaΔΔ*			

This is the correct answer because

$$\text{MAX}(3, 2) = 3$$

∎

EXAMPLE

To give equal time to the state 9–state 11–HALT branch, we trace the execution of the input *aabaaa*:

	1	1	2	2	2	2
aabaaa →	*Aabaaa* →	*Aabaaa* →	*Aabaaa* →	*Aabaaa* →	*Aabaaa* →	*AabaaaΔ*
3	5	5	5	6	7	8
→ *Aabaaa* →	*Aabaay* →	*Aabaay* →	*Aabaay* →	*Aabaay* →	*Axbaay* →	*Axbaay*
8	8	3	5	5	6	6
→ *Axbaay* →	*Axbaay* →	*Axbaay* →	*Axbayy* →	*Axbayy* →	*Axbayy* →	*Axbayy*
9	9	9	9	9	9	11
→ *axbayy* →	*aabayy* →	*aaaayy* →	*aaaayy* →	*aaaaΔy* →	*aaaaΔΔ* →	*aaaaΔΔ*
11	11	HALT				
→ *aaaΔ* →	*aaaa* →	*aaaΔ*				

∎

THEOREM 84

The IDENTITY function

$$\text{IDENTITY}(n) = n \qquad \text{for all } n \geqslant 0$$

and the SUCCESSOR function

$$\text{SUCCESSOR}(n) = n + 1 \qquad \text{for all } n \geqslant 0$$

are computable.

Note: These functions are defined on only one number ($K = 1$), so we expect input only of the form **a***.

PROOF

The only trick in the IDENTITY function is to crash on all input strings in bad format, that is, not of the form **a***:

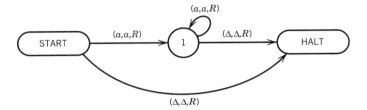

Similarly, SUCCESSOR is no problem:

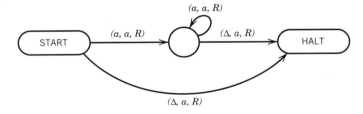

DEFINITION

The **ith of n selector function** is the function that starts with a sequence of n nonnegative numbers and erases most of them, leaving only the ith one (whether that one is the largest or not). It is written

$$\text{SELECT}/i/n(\,,\,,\,)$$

where there is space for exactly n numbers inside the parentheses. For example,

$$\text{SELECT}/2/4(8, 7, 1, 5) = 7$$
$$\text{SELECT}/4/9(2, 0, 4, 1, 5, 9, 2, 2, 3) = 1$$
∎

THEOREM 85

The ith of n selector function is computable for every value of i and n (where we assume i is less than or equal to n).

PROOF

We shall build a TM that shows that the "third of five" selector function is computable. The other SELECT/i/n functions can be constructed similarly.

The TM that operates as

$$\text{SELECT}/3/5(r, s, t, u, v)$$

begins with input of the form

$$a^r b a^s b a^t b a^u b a^v$$

It marks the first cell with a *; erases the first clump of a's and the first b, the next a's, and the next b; saves the next a's; and erases the next b, the next a's, the next b, and the last a's, all the time moving the TAPE HEAD to the right.

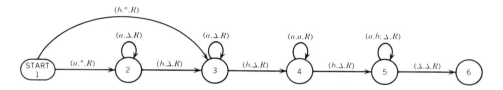

$$aaababaabaaaaba$$

becomes

$$*\Delta\Delta\Delta\Delta\Delta\Delta aa\Delta\Delta\Delta\Delta\Delta\Delta$$

We now choose to shift the remaining a's down to the left to begin in cell i, which we marked with a *. We can use the TM subroutine DELETE Δ. We keep deleting the Δ in cell i until the contents of cell i becomes an a. Then we stop. ∎

THEOREM 86

Multiplication is computable.

PROOF

The proof will be by constructive algorithm. This machine, called MPY, takes strings of the form $a^m b a^n$ and leaves on the TAPE a^{mn}. To make things easier on ourselves, we shall build a machine that rejects the input if n or m is zero; however, if we wanted to, we could build the machine differently to allow multiplication by zero (see the Problems section).

The algorithm this machine will follow is to insert a b in the first cell and place the symbol # after the entire input string. Then to the right of the #, it will write one copy of the string a^n for each a in the string a^m, one by one erasing the a's in the first string. For example, the multiplication of 3 times 2 proceeds in these stages:

$$baaabaa\#$$
$$b\Delta aabaa\#aa$$
$$b\Delta\Delta abaa\#aaaa$$
$$b\Delta\Delta\Delta baa\#aaaaaa$$

The machine will then erase everything between and including the second b and the #. The TAPE now looks like this:

$$b\Delta\Delta\Delta\Delta\Delta\Delta\Delta aaaaaa$$

For this machine, we shall spell out a simplified version of DELETE to shift the string of a's leftward to begin in cell ii. We do this because we want to make a complete trace of the runnings of the full TM.

MPY begins like this:

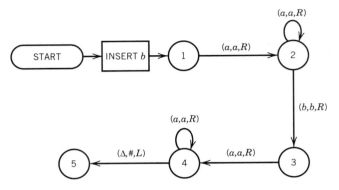

So far, we have checked the form of the input (so we can crash on improper inputs) and placed the initial b and the # where we want them.

Now we go back and find the first a in a^m and convert it into a Δ:

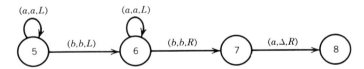

Now we find the beginning of the second factor a^n:

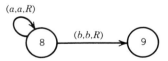

Now one by one, we turn these a's in the second factor into A's and copy them on the other side of the #:

$$b\Delta aaabaa\#$$
$$b\Delta aaabAa\#a$$
$$b\Delta aaabAA\#aa$$

In state 9, we convert the first a into an A. In state 10, we move the TAPE HEAD to the right going through a's and the # and perhaps other a's until we find the Δ. To get to state 11, we change the first Δ to an a and start the trip back down the TAPE leftward. In state 11, we skip over a's and the # and more a's until we find the last copied A. In state 12, we look to the right of this A. If there is a #, then there are no more a's to copy and we go to state 13. If there is another a, it must be copied so we change it to A and go back to state 10.

In state 13, we must change the A's back to a's so we can repeat the process. Then we look for the next a in the first factor:

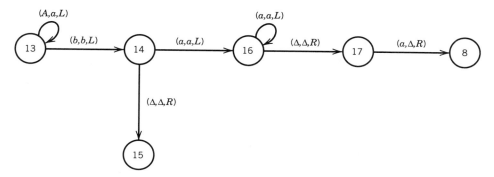

After changing the A's back to a's, we move left, through the middle b, into whatever is left of the first factor a^m. If the cell to the immediate left of b is blank, then the multiplication is finished and we move to state 15. If the cell to the left of b has an a in it, we go to state 16. Here, we move leftward through the a's until we find the first Δ, then right one cell to the next a to be erased. Changing this a to a Δ, we repeat the process of copying the second factor into the Δ's after the # and a's by returning to state 8.

When we get to state 15, we have the simple job left of erasing the now useless second factor:

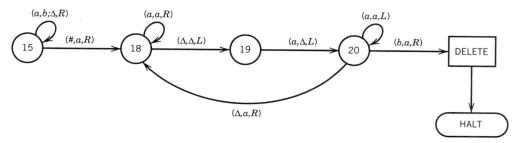

Going to state 18, we change the # into an a so we must later erase the end a. Using states 18 and 19, we find the end a and erase it. In state 20, we go back down the TAPE to the left to see if there are more Δ's in front of the answer. If so, we make one an a and go back to state 18. If not, we encounter the b in cell i, delete it, and halt. This completes the machine MPY. ■

EXAMPLE

Let us write out the full trace of MPY on the input *baabaa*:

START	INSERT b	1	2	2
$\underline{a}abaa$ $\rightarrow$	$\underline{b}aabaa$ $\rightarrow$	$b\underline{a}abaa$ $\rightarrow$	$ba\underline{a}baa$ $\rightarrow$	$baa\underline{b}aa$

3 → baab<u>a</u>a	4 → baaba<u>a</u>	4 → baabaa<u>△</u>	5 → baabaa<u>#</u>
5 → baabaa<u>#</u>	5 → baabaa<u>#</u>	6 → ba<u>a</u>baa#	6 → b<u>a</u>abaa#
6 → <u>b</u>aabaa#	7 → b<u>a</u>abaa#	8 → b△<u>a</u>baa#	8 → b△<u>a</u>baa#
9 → b△ab<u>a</u>a#	10 → b△abA<u>a</u>#	10 → b△abAa<u>#</u>	10 → b△abAa#<u>△</u>
11 → b△abAa<u>#</u>a	11 → b△abA<u>a</u>#a	11 → b△abA<u>a</u>#a	12 → b△abA<u>a</u>#a
10 → b△abAA<u>#</u>a	10 → b△abAA#<u>a</u>	12 → b△abAA#a<u>△</u>	13 → b△abAA#<u>a</u>a
11 → b△abAA<u>#</u>aa	11 → b△abA<u>A</u>#aa	14 → b△abAA<u>#</u>aa	16 → b△abA<u>A</u>#aa
13 → b△ab<u>A</u>a#aa	13 → b△ab<u>a</u>a#aa	14 → b△<u>a</u>baa#aa	16 → b△<u>a</u>baa#aa
17 → b△<u>a</u>baa#aa	8 → b△△<u>b</u>aa#aa	9 → b△△b<u>a</u>a#aa	10 → b△△bA<u>a</u>#aa
10 → b△△bAa<u>#</u>aa	10 → b△△bAa#<u>a</u>a	10 → b△△bAa#a<u>a</u>	10 → b△△bAa#aa<u>△</u>
11 → b△△bAa#a<u>a</u>a	11 → b△△bAa#<u>a</u>aa	11 → b△△bAa<u>#</u>aaa	11 → b△△bA<u>a</u>#aaa
11 → b△△<u>A</u>a#aaa	12 → b△△bA<u>a</u>#aaa	10 → b△△bAA<u>#</u>aaa	10 → b△△bAA#<u>a</u>aa
11 → b△△bAA#a<u>a</u>a	11 → b△△bAA#aa<u>a</u>	11 → b△△bAA#aaa<u>△</u>	11 → b△△bAA#aa<u>a</u>
12 → b△△bAA#<u>a</u>aaa	13 → b△△bA<u>A</u>#aaaa	13 → b△△bA<u>a</u>#aaaa	13 → b△△b<u>a</u>a#aaaa
14 → b△△<u>b</u>aa#aaaa	15 → b△△<u>b</u>aa#aaaa	15 → b△△△<u>a</u>a#aaaa	15 → b△△△<u>a</u>#aaaa
15 → b△△△△△<u>#</u>aaaa	18 → b△△△△△a<u>a</u>aaa	18 → b△△△△△aa<u>a</u>aa	18 → b△△△△△aaa<u>a</u>a
18 → b△△△△△aaaa<u>a</u>	18 → b△△△△△aaaaa<u>△</u>	19 → b△△△△△aaaa<u>a</u>	20 → b△△△△△aaa<u>a</u>
20 → b△△△△△aa<u>a</u>a	20 → b△△△△△a<u>a</u>aa	20 → b△△△△△<u>a</u>aaa	20 → b△△△△△<u>a</u>aaa
18 → b△△△△a<u>a</u>aaa	18 → b△△△△aa<u>a</u>aa	18 → b△△△△aaa<u>a</u>a	18 → b△△△△aaaa<u>a</u>
18 → b△△△△aaaaa<u>△</u>	19 → b△△△△aaaa<u>a</u>	20 → b△△△△aaa<u>a</u>	20 → b△△△△aa<u>a</u>a
20 → b△△△△a<u>a</u>aa	18 → b△△△△<u>a</u>aaa	18 → b△△△<u>a</u>aaaa	18 → b△△△a<u>a</u>aaa
18 → b△△△aa<u>a</u>aa	19 → b△△△aaa<u>a</u>a	20 → b△△△aaaa<u>a</u>	20 → b△△△aaaaa<u>△</u>
20 → b△△△aaaa<u>a</u>	20 → b△△△aaa<u>a</u>	18 → b△△△aa<u>a</u>a	18 → b△△△a<u>a</u>aa
18 → b△△△<u>a</u>aaa	18 → b△△<u>a</u>aaaa	18 → b△△a<u>a</u>aaa	19 → b△△aa<u>a</u>aa
20 → b△△aaa<u>a</u>a	20 → b△△aaaa<u>a</u>	20 → b△△aaaaa<u>△</u>	20 → b△△aaaa<u>a</u>
20 → b△△aaa<u>a</u>	20 → b△△aa<u>a</u>a	18 → b△△a<u>a</u>aa	18 → b△△<u>a</u>aaa

	20		18		18		18
→	bΔΔaaaa	→	bΔaaaaa	→	bΔaaaaa	→	bΔaaaaa
	18		18		19		20
→	bΔaaaaa	→	bΔaaaaaΔ	→	bΔaaaaa	→	bΔaaaa
	20		20		20		20
→	bΔaaaa	→	bΔaaaa	→	bΔaaaa	→	bΔaaaa
	18		18		18		18
→	baaaaa	→	baaaaa	→	baaaaa	→	baaaaa
	18		19		20		20
→	baaaaaΔ	→	baaaaa	→	baaaa	→	baaaa
	20		20		20		DELETE HALT
→	baaaa	→	baaaa	→	baaaa	→	aaaaa → aaaa ∎

This is how one TM calculates that 2 times 2 is 4. No claim was ever made that this is a *good* way to calculate that $2 \times 2 = 4$, only that the existence of MPY proves that multiplication *can* be calculated, that is, is computable.

We are dealing here with the realm of possibility (what is and what is not possible), not optimality (how best to do it); that is why this subject is called computer *theory,* not "a practical guide to computation."

Remember that electricity flows at (nearly) the speed of light, so there is hope that an electrical TM could calculate 6×7 before next April.

TMs are not only powerful language-recognizers, but they are also powerful calculators.

EXAMPLE

A TM can be built to calculate square roots, or at least to find the integer part of the square root. The machine SQRT accepts an input of the form ba^n and tests all integers one at a time from 1 on up until it finds one whose square is bigger than n.

Very loosely, we draw this diagram (in the diagram, we have abbreviated SUCCESSOR "Suc," which is commonly used in this field:

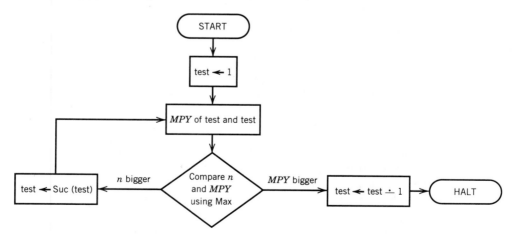

Therefore, we can build SQRT out of the previous TMs we have made. ∎

⚜ CHURCH'S THESIS

What functions cannot be computed by a TM? The answer is surprising: "It is believed that there are *no* functions that can be defined by humans, whose calculation can be described by *any* well-defined mathematical algorithm that people can be taught to perform, that *cannot* be computed by TMs. The TM is believed to be the ultimate calculating mechanism."

This statement is called **Church's thesis** because Alonzo Church (1936 again) gave many sophisticated reasons for believing it. Church's original statement was a little different because his thesis was presented slightly before Turing invented his machines. Church actually said that any machine that can do a certain list of operations will be able to perform all conceivable algorithms. He tied together what logicians had called recursive functions (after the work of Gödel) and computable functions (after the goal of Hilbert). TMs can do all that Church asked, so they are one possible model of the universal algorithm machines Church described.

Unfortunately, Church's thesis cannot be a theorem in mathematics because ideas such as "can ever be defined by humans" and "algorithm that people can be taught to perform" are not part of any branch of known mathematics. There are no axioms that deal with "people." If there were no axioms that dealt with triangles, we could not prove any theorems about triangles. There is no known definition for "algorithm" either, as used in the most general sense by practicing mathematicians, except that, if we believe Church's thesis, we can define algorithms as what TMs can do. This is the way we have (up to today) resolved the old problem of, "Of what steps are all algorithms composed? What instructions are legal to put in an algorithm and what are not?"

Not all mathematicians are satisfied with this. Mathematicians like to include in their proofs such nebulous phrases as "case two can be done similarly," "by symmetry we also know," or "the case of $n = 1$ is obvious." Many mathematicians cannot figure out what other mathematicians have written, so it is often hopeless to try to teach a TM to do so. However, our *best* definition today of an algorithm is that it is a TM.

Turing had the same idea in mind when he introduced his machines. He argued as follows.

If we look at what steps a human goes through in performing a calculation, what do we see? (Imagine a woman doing long division, e.g.) She writes some marks on a paper. Then by looking at the marks she has written, she can make new marks or, perhaps, change the old marks. If the human is performing an algorithm, the rules for putting down the new marks are finite. The new marks are entirely determined by what the old marks were and where they were on the page. The rules must be obeyed automatically (without outside knowledge or original thinking of any kind). A TM can be programmed to scan the old marks and write new ones following exactly the same rules. The TAPE HEAD can scan back and forth over the whole page, row by row, and recognize the old marks and replace them with new ones. The TM can draw the same conclusions a human would as long as the human was forced to follow the rigid rules of an algorithm instead of using imagination.

Someday, someone might find a task that humans agree is an algorithm but that cannot be executed by a TM, but this has not yet happened. Nor is it likely to. People seem very happy with the Turing–Post–Church idea of what components are legal parts of algorithms.

There are faulty "algorithms" that do not work in every case that they are supposed to handle. Such an algorithm leads the human up to a certain point and then has no instruction on how to take the next step. This would foil a TM, but it would also foil many humans. Most mathematics textbooks adopt the policy of allowing questions in the Problems section that cannot be completely solved by the algorithms in the chapter. Some "original thinking" is required. No algorithm for providing proofs for all the theorems in the Problems section is ever given. In fact, no algorithm for providing proofs for all theorems in general is known. Better or worse than that, it can be *proved* that no such algorithm exists.

We have made this type of claim at several places throughout this book; now we can make it specific. We can say (assuming as everyone does that Church's thesis is correct) that anything that can be done by algorithm can be done by TM. Yet we have shown in the previous chapter that there are some languages that are not recursively enumerable. This means that the problem of deciding whether a given word is in one such particular language cannot be solved *by any algorithm*.

When we proved that the language PALINDROME is not accepted by any FA, that did not mean that there is no algorithm in the whole wide world to determine whether or not a given string is a palindrome. There are such algorithms. However, when we proved that ALAN is not r.e., we proved that there is no possible decision procedure (algorithm) to determine whether or not a given string is in the language ALAN.

Let us recall from Chapter 1 the project proposed by David Hilbert. When he saw problems arising in set theory, he asked that the following statements be proven:

1. Mathematics is consistent. Roughly, this means that we cannot prove both a statement and its opposite, nor can we prove something horrible like $1 = 2$.

2. Mathematics is complete. Roughly, this means that every true mathematical assertion can be proven. Because we might not know what "true" means, we can state this as: Every mathematical assertion can either be proven or disproven.

3. Mathematics is decidable. This, as we know, means that for every type of mathematical problem there is an algorithm that, in theory at least, can be mechanically followed to give a solution. We say "in theory" because following the algorithm might take more than a million years and still be finite.

Many thought that this was a good program for mathematical research, and most believed that all three points were true and could be proved so. One exception was the mathematician G. H. Hardy, who hoped that point 3 could never be proven, because if there were a mechanical set of rules for the solution of all mathematical problems, mathematics would come to an end as a subject for human research.

Hardy did not have to worry. In 1930 Kurt Gödel shocked the world by *proving* that points 1 and 2 are not both *true* (much less provable). Most people today hope that this means that point 2 is false, because otherwise point 1 has to be. Then in 1936, Church, Kleene, Post, and Turing showed that point 3 is false. After Gödel's theorem, all that was left of point 3 was, "Is there an algorithm to decide whether a mathematical statement has a proof or a disproof, or whether it is one of the unsolvables." In other words, can one invent an algorithm that can determine whether some other algorithm (possibly undiscovered) does exist that could solve the given problem? Here, we are not looking for the answer but merely good advice as to whether there even *is* an answer. Even this cannot be done. Turing's proof of the undecidability of the halting problem meant, in light of Church's thesis, that there is no possible algorithm to decide whether a proposed algorithm really works (terminates). Church showed that the first-order predicate calculus (an elementary part of mathematics) is undecidable. All hope for Hilbert's program was gone.

We have seen Post's and Turing's conception of what an algorithm is. Church's model of computation, called the **lambda calculus,** is also elegant but less directly related to computer theory on an elementary level, so we have not included it here. The same is true of the work of Gödel and Kleene on μ-recursive functions. Two other interesting models of computation can be used to define "computability by algorithm." A. A. Markov (1951) defined a system today called **Markov algorithms,** or **MA,** which are similar to type 0 grammars, and J. C. Shepherdson and H. E. Sturgis (1963) proposed a **register machine,** or **RM,** which is similar to a TM. Just as we might have suspected from Church's thesis, these methods turned out to have exactly the same power as TMs. Of the mathematical logicians mentioned, only Turing and von Neumann carried their theoretical ideas over to the practical construction of electronic machinery and precipitated the invention of the computer.

⚜ TMs AS LANGUAGE GENERATORS

So far, we have seen TMs in two of their roles as transducer and as acceptor:

$$X_1, X_2, X_3 \dots \xrightarrow{\text{inputs}} \boxed{\text{TRANSDUCER}} \xrightarrow{Y_1, Y_2, Y_3 \ \text{outputs}}$$

$$X_1, X_2, X_3 \dots \xrightarrow{\text{inputs}} \boxed{\text{ACCEPTOR}} \begin{array}{l} \text{YES} \\ \text{NO} \end{array}$$

As a transducer, it is a computer, and as an acceptor, it is a decision procedure. There is another purpose a TM can serve. It can be a generator:

$$\boxed{\text{GENERATOR}} \xrightarrow{X_1, X_2, X_3 \dots}$$

DEFINITION

A TM is said to **generate** the language

$$L = \{w_1 \quad w_2 \quad w_3 \dots\}$$

if it starts with a blank TAPE and after some calculation prints a # followed by some word from L. Then there is some more calculation and the machine prints another # followed by another word from L. Again, there is more calculation and another # and another word from L appears on the TAPE. And so on. Each word from L must eventually appear on the TAPE inside of #'s. The order in which they occur does not matter and any word may be repeated indefinitely. ■

This definition of generating a language is also called **enumerating** it. With our next two theorems, we shall show that any language that can be generated by a TM can be accepted by some TM and that any language that can be accepted by a TM can be generated by some TM. This finally explains why the languages accepted by TMs were called **recursively enumerable.**

THEOREM 87

If the infinite language L can be generated by the TM T_g, then there is another TM, T_a, that accepts L.

PROOF

The proof will be by constructive algorithm. We shall show how to convert T_g into T_a.

To be a language-acceptor, T_a must begin with an input string on its TAPE and end up in HALT when and only when the input string is in L.

The first thing that T_a does is put a $ in front of the input string and a $ after it. In this way, it can always recognize where the input string is no matter what else is put on the TAPE. Now T_a begins to act like T_g in the sense that T_a imitates the program of T_g and begins to generate all the words in L on the TAPE to the right of the second $. The only modification is that every time T_g finishes printing a word of L and ends with a #, T_a leaves its copy of the program of T_g for a moment to do something else. T_a instead compares the most recently generated word of L against the input string inside the $'s. If they are the same, T_a halts and accepts the input string as legitimately being in L. If they are not the same, the result is inconclusive. The word may yet show up on the TAPE. T_a therefore returns to its simulation of T_g.

If the input is in L, it will eventually be accepted. If it is not, T_a will never terminate execution. It will wait forever for this word to appear on the TAPE.

$$\text{accept } (T_a) = L$$
$$\text{loop } (T_a) = L'$$
$$\text{reject } (T_a) = \phi$$

Although the description above of this machine is fairly sketchy, we have already seen TM programs that do the various tasks required: inserting $, comparing strings to see if they are equal, and jumping in and out of the simulation of another TM. This then completes the proof. ∎

THEOREM 88

If the language L can be accepted by the TM T_a, then there is another TM, T_g, that generates it.

PROOF

The proof will be by constructive algorithm. What we would like to do is to start with a subroutine that generates all strings of a's and b's one by one in size and alphabetical order:

$$\Lambda \ a \ b \ aa \ ab \ ba \ bb \ aaa \ aab \dots$$

We have seen how to do this by TM before in the form of the binary incrementor appropriatley modified. After each new string is generated, we run a simulation of it on the machine T_a. If T_a halts, we print out the word on the TAPE inside #'s. If T_a does not halt, we skip it and go on to the next possibility from the string generator, because this string is not in the language.

Unfortunately, if the T_a simulation does not halt or crash, we are stuck waiting forever and we cannot go on to test the next possible input string. What we must do is not invest an indefinite amount of time investigating the acceptability of every word on T_a. Now, of course, we cannot simply abandon a calculation that has been running a long time and say, "well, it's probably hopeless" since we know by the very fact that the halting problem is undecidable, that *some* input strings which look like they are going to run forever are, surprisingly, eventually accepted. So, we cannot wait for every string to be decided, nor can we abandon any string that is running too long. What can we do?

The answer is that we run some number of steps of the simulation of the T_a on a given input and then, assuming that no conclusive answer has been reached, we abruptly abandon this calculation and simulate the running of the next string on T_a with the intention of returning to the simulation of the previous string at some later time and carrying it further. If we do this is an organized fashion, it will all work out.

Let us number the possible input strings $st(1)$, $st(2)$, $st(3)$, in the usual lexicographic order. Let us, for the moment, assume that our simulation machine T_g has four tracks. On the second track it generates, in order, all the integers (in a who-cares-which representation). Let us assume that at some point in the operation of T_g, track 2 has the number N on it.

Now on track 3 we generate, one by one, *all* possible input strings from $st(1)$ up to $st(N)$. Each time we generate another input string, we copy the string from track 3 to track 4 and simulate the running of T_a on it. But we only run the simulation for exactly N steps (this means N edges of the T_a program), that is, unless T_a crashes or halts before then. If N steps have not been enough to draw a T_a-membership conclusion on the input suggested by track 3, tough luck. We waste no more effort on this input string at this iteration. We erase track 4 and we go back down to track 3 and generate the next input string to be tested. If, however, the input string has been accepted within the N steps of the T_a simulation we are prepared to expend, then we print the input string on track 1 between appropriate #'s. We still erase track 4 and go back to track 3 for the next input string to be tested, but we have successfully found and printed a word in the language L.

When we go back down to track 3 to get the next string, we have to be sure that we have not already tried all the strings up to $st(N)$. In order to be sure of this, we must keep a counter on track 2 telling us how many strings we have indeed produced. If we have not gone up to N yet, then we do produce the next string and repeat the process. If, however, we find that we have already gone up to our limit $st(N)$, then what we must do is erase this track and increment track 2. Track 2 now has the contents $N + 1$ on it. We begin again to generate strings on track 3. We start once more with $st(1)$ and test them to see if they are words accepted by T_a. We generate *all* the strings on track 3 from $st(1)$ to $st(N + 1)$ and one by one simulate on track 4 the running of them on T_a—for exactly $N + 1$ steps, this time. Again, if they are neither accepted nor rejected, they are abandoned temporarily. If they are accepted, they are printed on track 1, *even if they have been printed on track 1 already*. The simulation of T_a on a particular input string begins at the very beginning START state of T_a, even though we have once before already simulated the first N steps of the processing. Maybe N steps were not enough, but $N + 1$ steps will do the trick. If no decision is made in $N + 1$ steps, then we erase track 4 and get the next input test case from track 3, unless we have already generated up to $st(N + 1)$, in which case we erase track 3 and increment track 2 to $N + 2$.

Clearly, the only strings that appear on track 1 are the words that have been discovered to already be in L by having been accepted by T_a. It is also true that every word in L will eventually appear on track 1. This is because every word in L is accepted by T_a in some finite number of steps, say, M steps. Eventually, track 2 will reach M; this does not yet mean that the word will appear on this round of the iteration. Suppose that the word itself is string $st(K)$ and K is bigger than M. Then when track 2 has reached M, track 4 will test all the strings from $st(1)$ to $st(M)$ for acceptance by T_a but $st(K)$ will not yet be tested. Once, however, track 2 reaches K, track 3 will generate $st(K)$ and track 4 will realize that it is accepted by T_a within K steps and it will be printed on track 1. So, track 1 will eventually contain each of the words in L and only the words in L.

We can write this TM program in pseudocode as follows:

1. Initialize track 2 to 0 and clear all other tracks.

2. Increment N on track 2 (i.e., $N \leftarrow N + 1$), $J \leftarrow 1$, clear tracks 3 and 4.

3. Do while $J \leq N$ generate $st(J)$ on track 3, copy to track 4, simulate a maximum of N steps of T_a on track 4, print $st(J)$ on track 1 if appropriate, clear track 4, $J \leftarrow J + 1$.

4. Goto 2.

There are some issues that need to be addressed. The first is that once a word is accepted by N being large enough to generate it on track 3 and accept it on track 4, it will then also be generated on every subsequent iteration of step 3 in the algorithm. It will be generated as a test string, accepted by T_a, and printed on track 1 over and over. This is true but it is not a damning complaint because the definition of a language-generator allowed for repeated appearances of words in L on the TAPE. But this is excessive. Without running the risk of looping forever, we could add a step to our procedure that checks to see whether $st(J)$ is actually a new word before printing it on track 1.

Another quibble that needs to be thought through is that, although it is true that we have shown a multitrack TM can be simulated on a one-track TM, the simulation allowed the information from the other tracks to appear on the one-track TM TAPE. That happened because this issue arose when we were still considering TMs solely as language-acceptors, and all that was important was whether we got to HALT or not on a given input. All that is different now. If we are to simulate a four-track TM on a one-track TM, how are we going to avoid putting garbage on the TAPE that gets confused with the mission of L-language-word-generation? The answer is that we can simulate the different tracks on the TM separated by dividers other than the word demarkers used by T_g to indicate words generated in L. We could let track 1 be the first field with its numerous #'s and L words. Then we could put a special symbol on the TAPE to indicate the beginning of track 2—let us say a "Ψ". We could use another Ψ to separate the track 2 simulating field from the track 3 simulating field, and another to mark off track 4. These fields, even if bounded between Ψ's, are arbitrarily expandable and contractible using the subroutines INSERT and DELETE. The TM TAPE is thus

# word # word # . . . #	Ψ	track 2 number	Ψ	track 3 test string	Ψ	track 4 T_a simulation
. . . field 1 . . .		. . . field 2 . . .		. . . field 3 . . .		. . . field 4 . . .

Slowly but surely, the TAPE will include every particular word of L between #'s in field 1 and only the words of L between the #'s. As field 1 grows, it will never erase that which it has calculated. The other fields will change and recede into oblivion. ∎

One thing we have to be careful about here is to realize that even if we have cleared up the repetition problem, the words that appear on the T_g TAPE are not necessarily going to be the words in L in their usual lexicographic order. This means that the word bbb may appear first and the word ab, also in the language L, may only appear many, many cells later. The reason for this is that the T_a path to accept the word ab may be much longer (in steps) than the path to accept bbb, and so our T_g simulating machine will discover that bbb is an acceptable word first.

One might suggest, at this point in the discussion, that this problem may be easily cleared up by a simple expediency analogous to that which avoided duplications from appearing in field 1; namely, right before we go to write a word on track 1, why not just sort the words already there and insert the new word into its proper position? This is a fine suggestion but it does not solve the problem. Remember that T_g is an infinitely running machine. As we have defined it, it will even run forever to generate a *finite* language L. Step 4 in the algorithm *always* reverts back to step 2. This means that the occasion on which ab will be recognized as being a word in L and then be inserted on track 1 in front of bbb will be an unpredictable occurrence in the indefinite future.

Now one might suggest that this is all true of the inferior machine we have designed for T_g in the proof above, but a much smarter model language-generator for L might exist that *does* turn out the words of L in size order. The answer to this is that that is quite true, but only for some languages L, and not others as the next theorem indicates.

THEOREM 89

The words in a language L can be generated by a TM in size order if and only if L is recursive.

PROOF

First, we shall show that if the language L is recursive, then it can be generated by some T_g in size order. This is easy. We take the machine we designed earlier to generate all strings in size order, but instead of running each of them only a limited amount in order to avoid entering an infinite loop, we start with a T_a for L that never loops at all. Such exist for all L's that are recursive. Now we can test the strings in size order, simulate them finitely on T_a, and print them out on track 1 if and only if they reach HALT.

We shall now prove that if L is a language that can be generated by some T_g in size order, then L must be recursive. Out of the assumed order-generating T_g, we shall make a T_a that accepts L and rejects all of L'. This is also easy. Into T_a we input the string to be tested, and call it w. We then simulate the running of T_g until its output of words of L has progressed to the extent the words being generated are larger than w. This will only take a finite amount of time. When we know the whole language L out as far as w, we simply check to see whether w is among the words generated thus far by T_g. If it *is*, we accept it; if *not*, we reject it. This is a complete decision procedure. ■

Because not all languages are recursive, we know that, oddly enough, there are TMs that can generate certain languages L but never in size order. Actually, and subtly, this is not quite true. What we do know is that we cannot *depend* on these language-generating TMs to produce L in size order, but they just might do it anyway. It might just be the case that the associated T_a happens always to accept shorter words by shorter paths. We would, however, never know that this was going to happen reliably. We could never be sure that no word out of order is ever going to appear on the TAPE. If we could be sure, then by the proof above, L would have to be recursive. This emphasizes the distinction between what is knowable and decidable and what may just happen adventitiously.

Another example of this distinction is the suggestion that instead of working so hard in the construction of T_g to avoid looping forever on inputs in $\text{loop}(T_a)$, we could simply let this decision be made by nondeterminism. The nondeterministic TM to generate L simply (fortuitously) skips over all the troublesome words in $\text{loop}(T_a)$ and simulates the acceptance of the good ones. If there is a nondeterministic TM to generate L, then we can turn it into a deterministic one, no? In light of the previous theorem, we know there must be something (or some things) wrong with this proposal. What they are, we leave for the Problems section.

As we can see, we have just begun to appreciate TMs; many interesting and important facts have not been covered (or even discovered). This is also true of PDAs and FAs.

For a branch of knowledge so new, this subject has already reached some profound depth. Results in computer theory cannot avoid being of practical importance, but at the same time we have seen how clever and elegant they may be. This is a subject with twenty-first century impact that yet retains its old world charm.

⚜ PROBLEMS

1. Trace these inputs on ADDER and explain what happens:

   (i) *aaba*
   (ii) *aab*
   (iii) *baaa*
   (iv) *b*

2. (i) Build a TM that takes an input of three numbers in unary encoding separated by b's and leaves their sum on the TAPE.

(ii) Build a TM that takes in any number of numbers in unary encoding separated by b's and leaves their sum on the TAPE.

3. Describe how to build a binary adder that takes three numbers in at once in the form

$$\$(0 + 1)^*\$(0 + 1)^*\$(0 + 1)^*$$

and leaves their binary total on the TAPE.

4. Outline a TM that acts as a binary-to-unary converter, that is, it starts with a number in binary on the TAPE

$$\$(0 + 1)^*\$$$

and leaves the equivalent number encoded in unary notation.

5. Trace these inputs on MINUS and explain what happens:

(i) *aaabaa*

(ii) *abaaa*

(iii) *baa*

(iv) *aaab*

6. Modify the TM MINUS so that it rejects all inputs not in the form

ba*ba*

and converts $ba^n ba^m$ into $ba^{n \div m}$.

7. MINUS does proper subtraction on unary encoded numbers. Build a TM that does proper subtraction in binary encoded inputs.

8. Run the following input strings on the machine MAX built in the proof of Theorem 83 (p. 601):

(i) *aaaba*

(ii) *baaa*   (Interpret this.)

(iii) *aabaa*

(iv) In the TM MAX above, where does the TAPE HEAD end up if the second number is larger than the first?

(v) Where does it end if they are equal?

(vi) Where does it finish if the first is larger?

9. MAX is a unary machine; that is, it presumes its input numbers are fed into it in unary encoding. Build a machine (TM) that does the job of MAX on binary encoded input.

10. Build a TM that takes in three numbers in unary encoding and leaves only the largest of them on the TAPE.

11. Trace the following strings on IDENTITY and SUCCESSOR:

(i) *aa*

(ii) *aaaba*

12. Build machines that perform the same function as IDENTITY and SUCCESSOR but on binary encoded input.

13. Trace the input string

bbaaababaaba

on SELECT/3/5, stopping where the program given in the proof of Theorem 85 ends, that is, without the use of DELETE Δ.

14. In the text, we showed that there was a different TM for SELECT/*i*/*n* for each different set of *i* and *n*. However, it is possible to design a TM that takes in a string form

$$(a*b)*$$

and interprets the initial clump of *a*'s as the unary encoding of the number *i*. It then considers the word remaining as the encoding of the string of numbers from which we must select the *i*th.
   (i) Design such a TM.
   (ii) Run this machine on the input

$$aabaaabaabaaba$$

15. On the TM MPY, from the proof of Theorem 86 (p. 605), trace the following inputs:
   (i) *babaa*
   (ii) *baaaba*

16. Modify MPY so that it allows us to multiply by 0.

17. Sketch roughly a TM that performs multiplication on binary inputs.

18. Prove that division is computable by building a TM that accepts the input string ba^mba^n and leaves the string ba^qba^r on the TAPE, where *q* is the quotient of *m* divided by *n* and *r* is the remainder.

19. Show that a TM can decide whether or not the number *n* is prime. This means that a TM exists called PRIME that, when given the input a^n, will run and halt, leaving a 1 in cell i if *n* is a prime and a 0 in cell i if *n* is not prime.

20. What is wrong with the nondeterministic approach to building an ordered language generator as described on p. 616.

BIBLIOGRAPHY

The formal mathematical model of finite automata was introduced in

McCulloch, W. S., and W. Pitts, "A Logical Calculus of the Ideas Imminent in Nervous Activity," 5 *Bulletin of Mathematical Biophysics,* 115–33 (1943).

Regular expressions were invented and proven equivalent to FAs in

Kleene, S. C., "Representation of Events in Nerve Nets and Finite Automata," in Shannon, C. E., and McCarthy, J. (eds.), *Automata Studies,* Princeton Univ. Press, Princeton, NJ (1956), pp. 3–42.

Transition graphs come from

Myhill, J., "Finite Automata and the Representation of Events," Wright Air Development Center Technical Report 57-642, Wright Patterson Air Force Base, OH (1957), pp. 112–37.

Nondeterminism was introduced and the fact that NFA = DFA was first proven in

Rabin, M. O., and D. Scott, "Finite Automata and Their Decision Problems," 3 *IBM Journal of Research and Development,* 114–25 (1959).

Mealy machines come from

Mealy, G. H., "A Method for Synthesizing Sequential Circuits," 34 *Bell System Technical Journal,* 1045–79 (1955).

Moore machines come from

Moore, E. F., "Gedanken Experiments on Sequential Machines," in Shannon, C. E., and McCarthy, J. (eds.), *Automata Studies,* Princeton Univ. Press, Princeton, NJ (1956), pp. 129–53.

Both pumping lemmas come from

Bar-Hillel, Y., M. Perles, and E. Shamir, "On Formal Properties of Simple Phrase Structure Grammars," in Y. Bar-Hillel (ed.), *Language and Information,* Addison-Wesley, Reading, MA (1964), pp. 116–50.

The Myhill–Nerode theorem, while similar to Myhill above, is in

Nerode, A., "Linear Automaton Transformations," 9 *Proceedings of the American Mathematical Society,* 541–44 (1958).

The fact that 2DFA = 1DFA comes from

Shepherdson, J. C., "The Reduction of Two-way Automata to One-way Automata," 3 *IBM Journal of Research and Development,* 198–200 (1959).

Context-free grammars and the whole Chomsky hierarchy were first formalized in

Chomsky, N., "On Certain Formal Properties of Grammars," 2 *Information and Control,* 137–67 (1959).

PDAs and their connection to CFGs were discovered in

Oettinger, A. G., "Automatic Syntactic Analysis and the Pushdown Store," in *Proceedings of the Symposia in Applied Mathematics,* Vol. 12, American Mathematical Society, Providence, RI (1961), pp. 104–29.

Chomsky, N., "Context-free Grammars and Pushdown Storage," 65 *MIT Research Laboratory Electronics Quarterly Progress Report,* 187–94 (1962).

Schutzenberger, M. P., "Finite Counting Automata," 5 *Information and Control,* 91–107 (1962) and "On Context-free Languages and Pushdown Automata," 6 *Information and Control,* 246–64 (1967).

Evey, J., "The Theory and Application of Pushdown Store Machines: Mathematical Linguistics and Machine Translation," Harvard Computation Laboratory Report NSF-10, Cambridge, MA (1963).

TMs were first defined and used to describe the halting problem in

Turing, A. M., "On Computable Numbers with an Application to the Entscheidungs-Problem," 2 *Proceedings of the London Mathematical Society*, 230–265 (1936). See also a correction in the same journal, 43, 544–46.

What we call Post machines were introduced as the "Post normal system" as a set of rewriting rules in

Post, E., "Finite Combinatory Processes: Formulation I," 1 *Journal of Symbolic Logic*, 103–5 (1936).

2PDA = TM comes from

Minsky, M. L., "Recursive Unsolvability of Post's Problem of 'Tag' and Other Topics in Theory of Turing Machines," 74 *Annals of Mathematics*, 437–55 (1961).

Church's thesis and theory of computation are contained in

Church, A. "An Unsolvable Problem in Elementary Number Theory," 58 *American Journal of Mathematics*, 345–63 (1936).

The equivalence of linear-bounded automata and CSLs is in

Kuroda, S. Y. "Classes of languages and linear-bounded automata," 7 *Information and Control*, 207–33 (1964).

THEOREM INDEX

INDEX